French Iı
and Pioneers in the Making
of America

French Immigrants and Pioneers in the Making of America

MARIE-PIERRE LE HIR

McFarland & Company, Inc., Publishers
Jefferson, North Carolina

ISBN (print) 978-1-4766-8442-0
ISBN (ebook) 978-1-4766-4485-1

LIBRARY OF CONGRESS AND BRITISH LIBRARY
CATALOGUING DATA ARE AVAILABLE

Library of Congress Control Number 2022009111

Aquatint print of New Orleans by J. L. Bouqueto de Woiseri
celebrating the Louisiana Purchase, 1803

Printed in the United States of America

*McFarland & Company, Inc., Publishers
Box 611, Jefferson, North Carolina 28640
www.mcfarlandpub.com*

To family and friends,
both sides of the Atlantic Ocean,
to students and colleagues,
past, present, and future

Table of Contents

Preface

A contribution to Francophone historical studies, *French Immigrants and Pioneers in the Making of America* is the book I wished I had been able to use in class when I first taught a large general education course on the French-speaking world. It is primarily written for an audience of specialists, teachers and students of French interested in discovering the long and fascinating saga of the French in North America. This past is seldom taught at American colleges and universities, and when it is, it is usually not done in French departments, where the term "Francophonie" normally means something else. From personal experience teaching a course on North American Francophonie for many years, however, I know that students react with surprise and a great deal of interest when they discover this material. And yet, paradoxically, most American students who graduate in French know nothing about it.

My own path of discovery of the French roots of the United States was strewn with chance encounters, just hints at first, really: a historical plaque explaining the name of a river, the "Cache la Poudre" in Northern Colorado; a fellow graduate student writing his PhD dissertation on the French who had come to Iowa centuries before us; a personal exploration of Cleveland's Francophile past[1]; and last but not least, a conversation with an elderly Tucsonan named Elgin, who was researching his family history. Elgin had in his possession the copy of an old letter written in French that he wanted to understand because it dealt with people his great-grand uncle had done business with. The author of Elgin's letter, Charles Gratiot (1786–1855), had written it in "Saint-Louis, le 23 avril 1800." It was a business letter between two fur traders, Gratiot's partner being the (future) German American mogul John Jacob Astor (1763–1848).[2] Elgin's great-grand uncle, William Morrison,[3] a Canadian at the time, was also engaged in the fur business.[4] A light bulb went on in my head when I looked at this document: the language chosen by the letter writer and spoken in Saint-Louis in 1800 was not English, but French! From Colorado to Iowa, from Ohio to Arizona, my personal map of the United States featured isolated French dots. I decided to connect them.

In the process, I have found, I believe, answers to a few perplexing questions: Why is French still the second most-commonly taught foreign language in the United States after Spanish? Why are Americans so interested in things French? Once it is understood that our French roots predate the United States' creation and continue to reach into the present, these questions find an easy answer. The names of rivers (Cache la Poudre, Platte), cities (Saint-Louis, Baton Rouge, Louisville, Lafayette) and people (Bonneville, Crapo, Ducey, Duval, Québedeaux), several thousands of them, all evoke this French heritage. Most of the stories behind those names are forgotten but they deserve to be told. The purpose of my book is to do just that.

Introduction

All America is riddled like Swiss cheese, with pockets of French.
—Clark Blaise, *Tribal Justice*, 1975[1]

Within the discipline of French, very few scholars based in the United States work on American Francophonie. In fact, the study of the literatures and cultures of former French colonies of Africa and the Caribbean has almost completely absorbed the meaning of the term "Francophonie." It is as if there had never been any French presence in the United States apart from a few places once inhabited by French Canadians. As Susan Pinette points out, the Franco-American heritage is practically invisible in the United States[2] and this although "[f]rom 1534 to 1803, the French dominated the interior of the New World along the inland water routes" (Charron, 818). Here is a typical example: the only French people who appear in my son's textbook on colonial America, *Everyday Life in Early America*, are Huguenots who settled on the East Coast and a traveler, Chastellux, who described the brand-new United States. Similarly, the book edited by Daisy Martin in 2013 titled *Exploration & Colonial America*, a compilation of original documents ranging from 1492 to 1755, devotes 30 out of 700 pages to documents of French provenance. André Prévos has a point when he claims that "a majority of Americans would probably be embarrassed if asked to name half a dozen famous Frenchmen who lived in nineteenth century America, even though it was estimated that, in 1930, about one entry in ten in the *Dictionary of American Biography* had some French connection" (1).[3] The French North American heritage fares no better in France. To take a recent example, the article devoted to the year 1763 in the 2017 *Histoire Mondiale de la France* centers on the expulsion of the Jesuits from France, not on the fall of New France. The Louisiana Purchase is not deemed important enough to warrant an entry. Similarly, Régis Debray mentions Irish, German, and Scandinavian immigrants to the United States, but he leaves out the French in his discussion of the (supposed) American primacy of space over time.[4]

"France formerly possessed in North America a vast empire, extending from Labrador to the Floridas, and from the shores of the Atlantic to the most distant lakes of Upper Canada," Chateaubriand wrote in the prologue of *Atala*. France lost New France in 1763 but neither the French language nor the French people disappeared from the Midwest, the West, and the South once those areas became U.S. territory. They stayed and their past is our past, even when they no longer speak French or carry, or not, a vestige of their heritage in their names. As Christopher Hodson and Brett Rushforth put it:

Even for those who favor a more traditional definition of "colonial America" as a kind of pre-United States history comprising only Britain's mainland North American colonies, keeping the French out of the story is as difficult as it is distorting [because] their presence shaped

British and Spanish colonial histories in profound ways: economically, culturally, and geographically [23].

A map of the United States is a puzzle inviting the reader to decipher this French North American past. Cities have French names: Peoria, New Rochelle, Louisville, Versailles, Frenchtown, Chicago, Detroit, New Orleans, Brest in Michigan, three named "Montpelier" and fifty named "Paris." Some names have been misspelled or transformed, hiding their French origin: "Ogeese Creek" in Kansas was originally "La Crique d'Auguste"; "Bois brûlé" in Missouri became "Bob Ruly"; "Purgatoire" in Arizona became "Picket Wire"; "Duclos has become Decloe and Declue; Desgagne is Degonia; Grenier is Greenia; Page is Pashia; Trottier is Trokey, and Richard is Ricaw" (Belting, 77). Some mountains in the United States have French names: "Grand Teton" retained its French name as a hidden wink to the Rabelaisian sauciness of the French explorers who discovered it[5] but "les Montagnes des Roches" simply became "the Rocky Mountains."[6] Many U.S. towns pay homage to French historical figures, Charlevoix, Michigan, named for the famous French Jesuit priest[7]; several to the Marquis de Lafayette, to Napoleon in Indiana and Alabama where there was a county of Marengo before the state of Alabama even existed, or to Victor Hugo, "Hugoton" in Kansas.

I propose therefore to expand the current definition of "Francophonie," a term that normally means the literatures and cultures of African countries once colonized by France (1830–1962), to include the French of North America, past and present. This proposal owes much to colleagues in 19th-century French studies who organized the 2004 annual colloquium around the theme of French legacies and invited historians Carl Ekberg and Margaret Kimball-Brown to present their work on French Upper Louisiana. Following this enlightening introduction to the North American francophone world, my knowledge in this area has greatly benefited from the outstanding scholarship of a newer generation of historians, Gilles Havard, Cécile Vidal, François Furstenberg, and many others mentioned here.

The emergence of American Francophonie is certainly a welcome new development. But so far, the small minority of Francophone studies scholars who do focus on North America in French departments in the United States seem to embrace a synchronic approach, with research focusing on linguistic issues or contemporary traces of French presence in the United States.[8] Not surprisingly, *la jeune francophonie américaine* also tends to limit itself to areas of the United States that are still linguistically partly Francophone, the American Northeast and Louisiana, and in the process to adopt an identity-based approach that encourages descendants of Franco-Americans, and seemingly those only, to reclaim their heritage.[9] This is not to say that historical literature on the French in America is lacking, on the contrary. Even if traditionally only a small percentage of historians have specialized in French colonial studies of North America, there is by now a wealth of historical writings on the topic. Unfortunately, this scholarship comes with two drawbacks if its intended audience consists of students and professors of French: being written by historians for historians it tends to be very specialized; being written by historians of different nationalities, it also tends to be fragmented along national lines, with Québécois working on Québec, for instance, and Americans on Maine and Louisiana.[10] Typically, a huge swath of the first French colonial empire is left out, places that French people born in France or North America were the first to settle in today's states of Arkansas, Oklahoma, Missouri, Kansas, Nebraska, Iowa, Minnesota,

North Dakota, South Dakota, Wyoming, Montana, Colorado, and Wisconsin.[11] *French Immigrants and Pioneers in the Making of America* favors the historical over the contemporary and the global over the local, in other words, the outlook privileged by the contemporary historians of colonial North America who have indeed "made New France new again" (Havard and Vidal).[12]

By talking about French roots I do not mean to frame the early stories told here in a national context of the kind we know today, first because European states were still in the process of formation when our story begin; second because being the subject of a king residing an ocean away did not inspire the same kind of loyalty that citizens of modern nation-states are typically expected to display[13]; and third because French North America is best understood "on its own, deeply transnational terms" (Hodson and Rushforth, 20). Elizabeth Avery, who studied "the influence of French immigration on the political history of the United States," correctly observed that this influence is two-fold:

> At the outset we are confronted by the fact that, in the main, the settlers fall into two groups: the French Protestants, mostly refugees from persecution at home, who came to the Atlantic colonies; and the French Catholics, who, coming for purpose of traffic or sent by a paternal government, founded settlements in the "old Northwest" and the Mississippi Valley [10].

While French Protestants assimilated rather well to the Anglo population of the East Coast, the Franco-Americans of New France kept their own language, ways, and traditions, or mixed with the Native Americans. As long as France was a monarchy governed by "a paternal government," the wide distance between the metropole's capital and the colonial centers, as well as the delays in communication occasioned by infrequent exchanges, were circumstances that created a sense of autonomy among the habitants of New France unknown in metropolitan France. In both cases, Maldwyn A. Jones' observation applies: "the fact that they had been uprooted from their old surroundings meant that they faced the necessity of coming to terms with an unfamiliar environment and a new status" (5). For Jones, however, "American foundations"—the title of the first chapter of her book, *American Immigration*—start in 1607 with the arrival of the pilgrims. And yet, not only did the French settlers share the spirit of independence characteristic of their Anglo counterparts, but they were also the very first European pioneers of North America thanks to their alliances with Native American nations. For as Creagh points out, the French could not have done it without the First Nations' assistance because "the colonial economy depended on the Indians who were both the pillars of trade and the purveyors of foodstuff" (*Nos Cousins*, 25).[14]

Hodson and Rushforth convincingly argue that the French colonial experience can serve "as a bridge between many 'continental divides' that fragment early American history," on the one hand a European history that reduces the Atlantic world to the British and Spanish empires,[15] and on the other, a history of North America divided between Atlantic and continental approaches. By recalling the history of the French North American empire I hope to help open these "new vistas for framing the larger history of North America both before and after the establishment of the United States" they envision,[16] to create a historical narrative that takes into account not only the French and the Franco-Americans, but also the Native Americans and the Africans with whom they interacted and mixed.[17] All together they wove the country's early multilingual and multicultural fabric prior to the American conquest of the West, although, as David MacDonald points out, "[e]vidence for the lives of individual women, Indians, Africans, and

African Creoles is scarce and rarely consists of more than a few facts and perhaps an anecdote or two" (xi).[18]

Chapter I, "Voyages of Discovery During the Renaissance," investigates the reasons that moved Europeans in general, and the French in particular, to sail the oceans far away from home. Although land had served as the economy's engine for centuries, it became scarce as the population increased, forcing farmers to move to villages and learn trades. In the process, a new type of economy emerged, based on money instead of land. The Renaissance also ushered in new ideas and technologies—such as firearms and the printing press—that were to transform society radically. By the end of the 16th century, the European kingdoms had become stable entities ruled by monarchs who were able to control their realms through taxation and military power. They could also engage in new ventures such as the exploration of new worlds, as did Francis I of France when he sent Verrazano and Cartier in search of a new route to China. The Renaissance spirit also led to a desire for religious reformation that found its expression in a split within the Catholic Church and the creation of Protestant denominations. In the European kingdoms that remained loyal to Rome such as France, Protestants no longer felt welcome and some of them sought to relocate to the New World. None of these early French settlements lasted longer than a few years, however.

Chapter II, "The Rise of the French Colonial Empire, 1600–1660," centers on the first permanent French settlements on the north American continent, in Acadia and Canada along the St. Lawrence River, as well as in the Caribbean. The founding of New France dates back to the first decade of the 17th century when Champlain and his men built the hamlet that was to become Quebec City. During the reign of Louis XIII, Prime Minister Richelieu encouraged the formation of private companies that played a key role in developing the fur trade. Explorers like Etienne Brûlé and Jean Nicollet and missionaries like Jean de Quen and Jean de Brébeuf, who spent a great deal of time living among Native Americans, served as interpreters and cultural intermediaries. The early French colonization of Caribbean islands took on a more violent turn due to conflicts with rival European nations. Privateers and buccaneers, the famous pirates of the Caribbean, were at the forefront of the French settlements on the islands of St. Kitts, Tortuga, Saint-Domingue (the future Haiti), Martinique and Guadeloupe.

Following an introduction to Louis XIV's conception of power, Chapter III, "French America, 1661–1683," examines the impact of the King's absolutist policies on his colonial empire. Colbert, with some success, encouraged the formation of trading companies that would rival those of the Dutch and the British all over the world. After New France became a French province in 1663, it served as ideal ground to implement royal policies without interference from intermediary assemblies. The new institutions that were created in Canada and Acadia in those days, like the Sovereign Council, were designed in France and the highest-ranking officials who served in the colony, the Governor General and the Intendant, were appointed by the King. But while New France can therefore be seen as the embodiment of absolutism on paper, in practice the size of the province and the scarcity of police and army on the ground made it impossible to monitor and control the population as was done in France. As a result, the pioneer spirit of adventure and the freedom enjoyed by the *coureurs des bois*, or white Indians, lived on. It can be argued that Louis XIV exerted more influence on the destiny of the Caribbean colonies, by actively encouraging the development of sugar plantations and the slave trade, than on New France.

Chapter IV, "The Sun King's Colonial Empire, 1684–1715," is about royal policies and decisions that affected the French colonial empire during the second half of Louis XIV's reign. As the royal administration provided military aid to New France, expelled Huguenots, and introduced slavery in the French Caribbean, it extended its grip on the colonies, thereby also shaping their identity. With the string of wars that periodically tore it apart, 17th-century Europe looked a lot like its medieval incarnation, except that the existence and the size of three colonial empires, England, France, and Spain, was now the main stake of these bloody struggles. Shortly before the turn of the century, Louis XIV therefore embarked on an ambitious strategy of land occupation and military defense in North America that was meant to block England's access to the West. Settlements and forts sprung up in the both the Illinois Country and Louisiana, often next to the villages of friendly Native Americans, who fought hostile First Nations and England alongside the French. The colonies had little say in their own fate. Rather it was determined by treaties signed in Europe. Acadia, the first colony to be settled by the French, for instance, became the property of England at the end of the War of the Spanish Succession in 1713, although the vast majority of the inhabitants were French, Abenaki, or Franco-Abenaki.

Despite setbacks in the East, France continued to consolidate its hold on North America during four decades of peace, as laid out in Chapter V, "France's American Colonies, 1715–1755." Two private and a royal trading companies made huge investments in Louisiana in terms of financial and human capital, expecting proportionate returns. Natchez and Natchitoches were founded in 1716; New Orleans, two years later. Although sparely populated, the new colony of Louisiana stretched all the way to the Illinois country, an area that became the most typically French region of North America and the provider of foodstuff for the colony down river. Conflicts between the French and the Native Americans arose over navigation rights on the Mississippi River and, as plantations multiplied, over ownership of the best lands. The War of the Austrian Succession gave France an opportunity to try and reconquer Acadia, but that hope was soon dashed.

Chapter VI, "North America Won and Lost, 1756–1783," recalls how war between England and France broke out again less than a decade later, as the struggle for colonial worldwide supremacy intensified. In France, where an intellectual elite critical of absolutism undermined the monarchy from within, little support remained for oversea wars that cost a lot of lives and money, as explained in section 1, "Decline of the Absolute Monarchy." Section 2, "The Seven Years' War," shows that, with much less support from the metropole than the adversary, the Franco-Americans and their Native Americans fought bravely and won early battles, but France ended up losing North America nonetheless. Section 3 examines the fate of Franco-Americans in Louisiana, Illinois, Canada, and Acadia immediately after 1763. Section 4 recalls the role played by France in securing the United States' independence from Great Britain.

Chapter VII, "Franco-American Relations in the Age of Revolutions," centers on the friendship between France and the United States in the 1770s and 1780s as well as the deterioration of the bonds linking the two nations in the last decade of the 18th century. More specifically, section 1 recalls the positive American reaction to the French Revolution in its initial phase. Following a brief overview of the subsequent unfolding of the French Revolution, section 2 explains why the friendship to France became such a hot-button issue in the United States at that time. Section 3 deals with enemies of the French Republic who found refuge in the United States during the French Revolution and with the different roles they played during their stay. Section 4 focuses on a series of diplomatic incidents that led France and the United States to the brink of war.

Most of Chapter VIII explores the fate of the French, French Canadians, and Franco-Amerindians once their lands became part of United States territory. Section 1 takes a necessary detour to the Caribbean to explain why France decided to sell Louisiana to the United States, section 2, how the sale proceeded and what it meant concretely. Section 3, "French Guides to the Wild West," recalls that the Franco-American residents of what had been Spanish Louisiana, and then again French Louisiana again for a very short time, showed the way to the famous explorers who are remembered today as the discoverers of the Western part of the United States. Section 4 brings back from oblivion those Franco-Americans who were actually recognized as great explorers in the antebellum era but were mostly forgotten later on.

France continued to send immigrants to the United States during the first part of the 19th century, and as showed in Chapter IX, numerous reasons led them to leave Old Europe behind. The first part of the chapter, "French Political Refugees in Antebellum America," describes the waves of immigration from France unleashed by virtually every change of political regime—and there were many. In France, a number of people disillusioned with their political and social circumstances listened to reformers who promised to create a better world. As recalled in section 2, many of them migrated to the New World where they founded Utopian communities that are described here. Immediately prior to the Civil War, the discovery of gold in California sent thousands and thousands of people from all over the world to the West Coast. The French took part in the Gold Rush as well, as indicated in section 3. Finally, the last section concentrates on the role played by prominent Franco-Americans on both sides of the Civil war, advocates of the abolition of slavery like John Frémont, as well as proponents of the status quo, such as rich plantation owners of Lower Louisiana like Pierre Soulé.

The last chapter examines domestic and foreign Franco-American relations in the context of nation formation in the late 19th century. Beginning with an account of the influx of Franco-Canadians to the Northeast and the emergence of new Francophone minorities in that area and the Midwest, the first section traces the progressive assimilation of the old Francophone population into the national fold. Turning to the international scene, section 2 presents the Western, a fictional account of the Conquest of the West and of the birth of the American nation, as a literary and cinematic genre that foregrounds individualism and appeals to a male public in the formative stage of any democracy. As a gift to France, the Western is also emblematic of the friendship between France and the United States, as was the Statue of Liberty in the context a Francophilia pervasive among American elites at the end of the 19th century. Centering on key moments in Franco-American relations in the 20th century the last section analyzes the expression of anti- and pro-sentiment for the other nation in an effort to deflate national stereotypes. Each chapter concludes with suggestions for further readings and activities.

Chapter I

Voyages of Exploration During the Renaissance

Recounting his 1534 voyage to the New World, Captain Jacques Cartier (1491–1557) thus described his second chance meeting with a group of Native Americans near Chaleur Bay, a gulf he thus named, by the Gaspé Peninsula:

> [W]e saw a large number of savages, who were mackerel fishing, which are very plentiful; there were about forty canoes of them, and more than two hundred men, women and children, who after meeting us on shore, came familiarly (freely) to our ships with their canoes. We gave them knives, glass chaplets (beads), combs and other articles of little value, which greatly pleased them; they lifted their hands to heaven as they sang and danced in their canoes. They can with truth be called savages, as there are no people poorer than these in the world, and I believe they do not possess anything to the value of five pennies, apart from their canoes and nets [Cartier, 29–30].

Cartier's initial picture of the Indians is one of peace and togetherness: men, women, and children are fishing together on top a school of mackerel, feeling relatively secure in the presence of newcomers—perhaps, in this case, due to their numeric superiority. They are also curious about the foreigners, grateful for their gifts and demonstrative in their appreciation. The French captain judges them according to his own values: these Native Americans are "savages," not because of their "savage" customs but because of their material poverty: apart from their boats and their nets, they own nothing.[1] At the same time, Cartier clearly derives a sense of superiority from the fact that unlike the poor Indians, he possesses "things," a superiority conveyed by the pity he feels for them.

In this original scene, then, the French and the aborigines get along but at the same time, the French willy-nilly introduce their materialism to a people that was doing just fine without it.[2] In that regard, Cartier's description sets the stage for future Franco-Amerindian intercultural encounters that were to be peaceful and form "the basis of New France's existence" and at the same time profoundly disruptive due to the "exposure to diseases carried by newcomers" that were to lead to "the catastrophic collapse of the Native populations" (Havard, *The Great Peace*, 4).[3] The Breton captain's narrative also begs the question as to what the French were doing in North America at the time. A chapter on voyages of discovery must begin by examining why Western Europeans suddenly felt the need to leave home in the 16th century.[4]

1. The Primacy of Land in the Economy of Western Europe

In the Middle Ages the vast majority of Western Europeans were confined to a skimpy world. What Thomas Hobbes characterized as their "nasty, brutish, and short" lives in *Leviathan* (1651), thirty years if they were lucky, revolved around some small parcel of land from which they drew subsistence.[5] All social life revolved around the lord's castle standing in the middle of the fields. For the lords, land was a source of wealth. Land acquired through inheritance, marriage, purchase, or conquest was the main source of economic and legal power at a time when money was rare. As the saying "No land without lord, no lord without title" (*Nulle terre sans seigneur, nul seigneur sans titre*) reminds us, land was a sign of social power. For that reason, it was also at stake in all the power struggles, in all the wars that tore Western Europe apart from the fall of the Roman Empire to the Renaissance.

The quest for new land was not a direct cause of the Crusades, the wars of religion that sent a steady flow of European pilgrims and armies to the Middle East from 1095 to 1291.[6] But they led nonetheless to the formation of "Crusader states" such as the kingdom of Jerusalem (today's Israel), the county of Tripoli (the Western part of Lebanon), or the principality of Antioch (the border between today's Turkey and Syria). These conquests did little to alleviate the problem of land scarcity. In France it became an issue as the population grew from six million in 850 to 16 million by 1226. As farms could not expand to feed growing families, useless mouths had to go away and they gathered in towns. This momentous process of migration from castle to village had numerous advantages, however. It gave more autonomy to the inhabitants of the *bourg*, or village, the *bourgeois* who protected their rights through guilds (Elias 208–214). Increased use of money in commercial transaction also radically transformed the economy.[7]

As Norbert Elias has showed in the *Civilizing Process*, land became scarcer for kings as well. Medieval monarchs were accustomed to reward knights for their loyal services through land grants so that, as a result, kingdoms tended to shrink in size. By the end of the first millennium, the kingdom of France had become so tiny that many vassals, the dukes of Anjou, Aquitaine, Brittany, Burgundy, Gascony, for instance, owned more land than the king. The duke of Normandy is the best example of this tendency. Although a vassal of Philip I, King of France, history knows him better as William the Conqueror (1027–1087), King of England in 1066.[8] The constant wars fought during this period had as their stake the formation of powerful states.[9] In the 11th century, the military balance of power was even when similarly powerful lords fought each other (Labrune and Toutain, 32–33). In the 12th century, a process of elimination of the weakest slowly took place. By the 13th and 14th centuries, competition was restricted to the winners of the contest, the two most powerful lords, the kings of England and France (Elias, 257–261, 277–289). But the contest over land and power was not over yet. The kings of France and England fought from 1187 to 1214 over Aquitaine, Anjou, and Maine, and for the Crown of France (Labrune and Toutain, 34–37). They went at it again during the Hundred Years' War, from 1337 to 1447, as both the house of Plantagenet (England) and the house of the Valois (France) claimed the throne of France as legitimate heirs to the Capetian dynasty. These wars were horrendous, savage. They caused devastation, famines and they spread diseases, most notoriously, the Black Plague (1347–1352). Within a half century, the population of France declined from 20 million in 1345 to 12 million in 1400 (Haine, 44).

France lost to England for most of the interminable war and almost disappeared when the 1420 Treaty of Troyes even recognized Henry V of England (1386–1422) as King of France. The turning point in France's favor was the war Joan of Arc waged to free the city of Orleans in 1429 and to reclaim the throne for Charles VII (1403–1461). Following the king's coronation in Reims, the French retook Paris and eventually recovered all of France. After the Battle of Castillon in 1453, the French Crown was able to assert control over its lands. The kingdom of France started to resemble the France we know today when Charles VII's successor, Louis XI (1423–1483), enlarged the royal realm by adding Anjou, Maine, and Provence through inheritance in 1481 and Burgundy through war in 1482 (Haine, 45–46). Charles VIII's marriage to Ann of Brittany won her duchy for the French Crown in 1491 (Labrune and Toutain, 44–45).

At the same time as the kingdom grew in size, the expanding money-based economy gave kings an advantage over lords. Both could issue money, but unlike feudal money, money coined in royal mints had universal validity.[10] Money thus gave the royal authority another boost.[11] Louis IX already understood this point well when, in 1262, he introduced a gold currency used in commercial transactions throughout the kingdom, the *écu*. The power money conferred to kings in the process of state consolidation is thus another factor—next to the depletion of state treasuries occasioned by never-ending wars—that explains the royal thirst for precious metal during the Renaissance.[12]

Once a state was mature enough, Elias explains, once its borders were not constantly threatened, a king no longer needed combats to prove his valor, or a clergy to vouch for his legitimacy. The monarch was able to spend less time on military affairs and more on retaining power through other means, administrative and legal.[13] The measures taken by Philip IV the Fair (1268–1314) illustrate how the French state grew stronger at the beginning of the 14th century. King Philip IV set in motion the process that took France away from complete submission to the Church's authority by kidnapping Pope Boniface and moving the Papacy to Avignon. He scored double by having his successor, French Pope Clement V, suppress the Knights Templars, a wealthy Catholic military order that played an important role in banking and to whom the kingdom was heavily indebted. He also expulsed the Jews, who were owed money as well, and got his hands on their gold and silver (Labrune and Toutain, 36–37).

It is not surprising that the heydays of state formation in Western Europe correspond to the end of the chivalry. As the invention of firearms transformed military warfare, the chivalry gradually lost its role, power, and its prestige. As land was the knights' source of wealth, they found themselves not only at a disadvantage in the money economy but also competing with a new social elite for the king's favor, as "rising bourgeois elements, with the help of the monarchy, gradually displaced knights and clergy directly from their positions: within the governmental apparatus, as officials" (Elias, 331). The bourgeois had an edge on them for two reasons: their business experience was handy when it came to administering the kingdom efficiently and they were less likely than knights to resort to physical force to challenge royal authority. In time, they proved invaluable in the elaboration and enforcement of laws applicable to the entire kingdom. They too, in other words, significantly contributed to the consolidation of the state.[14]

The rise of the bourgeoisie points to another characteristic of the Renaissance, the emergence of a new form of capital: cultural capital. On the one hand, the monopoly on knowledge previously held by religious orders was challenged by the increased importance played by bourgeois expertise in law and administration. On the other hand, peace allowed for the development of the artistic activities like music and poetry that were from then on to share the feudal lords' and knights' time with war and war games. With its emphasis on love as a theme, the courtly literature that blossomed during the late Middle Ages has been seen rightly as an implicit critique of the social violence of earlier times and as the expression of more peaceful aspirations (Elias, 45–182). The troubadours, minstrels, magicians, jugglers who visited and stayed at the courts of great dukes and princes offered forms of entertainment that sparked the imagination and rewarded talent and skill rather than brute force.[15] Cultural capital was all the more interesting that it too could be used as both a sign and an instrument of power by those who hired artists. As life became sweeter for the top social tier, the need for the luxuries of life also became stronger. Kings needed gold, the wealthy, refined goods unavailable under European climes. But unfortunately, the spice, fine teas, silk clothes, and porcelain ware, could no longer travel the Silk Road Marco Polo had rediscovered in 1275. With the fall of Constantinople that marked the end of Byzantium and its replacement by the Ottoman Empire in 1453, Europe lost its land route to the Far East.

2. The Renaissance Spirit of Adventure

The word "renaissance" means "rebirth" in French and the 16th century is so called because it was an era of renewal in the arts and sciences.[16] The Renaissance began in Italy in the 14th century and spread throughout Europe in the 15th and 16th centuries (Labrune and Toutain, 46–47). Of particular importance for the period is Gutenberg's invention of the printing press in 1439 (Weber, 97–100). The Renaissance heralded the dawn of a new era in Western Europe at a time when state formation was complete and three very powerful kings reigned in Europe: Henri VIII, who became King of England in 1509; Francis I (François I), who ascended to the French throne in 1515; and Charles V of Spain who became King of the Spanish Empire and of the Holy Roman Empire in 1519.[17] Henri VIII ruled over England from 1509 till 1547, Francis I France from 1515 to 1547. As a warrior he fought in several wars. But he was also a humanist and a patron of the Arts. In Italy, he befriended Leonardo da Vinci and brought him back to France (Haine, 49). Charles V became King of Spain and the Spanish American Empire in 1516 (as Charles I). He ruled the Holy Roman Empire (Spain, Germany, Italy, the Two Sicilies, and Brabant [Netherland-Belgium]) from 1519 to 1556 (Weber, 266–267). Compared to Charles V's Empire, the French kingdom was very small. Moreover, it consisted of a patchwork of provinces each with their own customs and language. In 1539, French became the kingdom's official language, but for legal matters only. French was therefore the language of the elite only.

The three most powerful European kings in the 16th century brought a great deal of innovation to their countries. When it came to conquest, however, they were also fierce competitors. The challenges they faced came from two areas, religion, following the Reformation,[18] and war, in the form of the old, ongoing struggle for dominance in Europe and abroad. During this period, France and Spain fought each other on the continent and abroad over Italy: The houses of Valois (France) and Habsburg (Spain) were embroiled in dynastic disputes and fought six wars over Milan and Naples. France lost big in 1525 when the Spaniards captured Francis I and kept him prisoner for a year, but these wars ended in 1559 a few years after Charles V's abdication.[19]

Religious strife started in Germany with the Reformation advocated by Martin Luther in 1517 (Weber, 171). In England, the Reformation led to a complete break with the Holy See in 1533 and to Henry VIII's ascent to the spiritual leadership of the Anglican Church a year later (Weber, 133). This event marks the birth of Anglicanism, a national religion.[20] The French kings of the Renaissance belonged to the

Valois-Angoulême dynasty and were Catholics. But the Reformation took roots in France as well. French Protestants, or Huguenots, took their inspiration from the teachings of Jean Calvin (1509–1564) who preached a reformed religion based on predestination. But by questioning Catholic orthodoxy, the Huguenots did more than promote reform in the Church. They attacked France's very identity as "the eldest daughter" of the Roman Catholic Church. The French hailed King Clovis baptism in 496 as the founding moment of both the French monarchy and of its alliance with the Roman Catholic Church. To attack the Church was therefore to attack the monarchy. The civil war between Catholics and Protestants that thus began was to divide France and the royal family for forty years.

The Renaissance is associated with the spirit of adventure that led to the "discovery" of new lands. In 1402, Jean de Béthencourt, Lord of Grainville, explored and conquered the Canary Islands and offered them to the King of Castile.[21] Sea voyages of exploration started for good after the fall of Byzantine Empire in 1453, once the land road to India and China closed and with it, the flow of rare goods Western European elites had grown accustomed to. King Francis I, who wanted to revive commerce with Asia via land, opened diplomatic channels with the Ottoman Empire and, in 1536, signed an alliance treaty with Suleiman the Magnificent that was to last over 250 years. But commerce with Asia by land had become all but impossible due to internal conflicts within the Ottoman Empire. Traveling by sea to "China" seemed a safer bet. The rich European nations of Spain and Portugal financed expeditions to obtain rare goods through new maritime routes and "discovered" new lands in the process.[22]

In 1420, Portugal rediscovered and started settling on Madeira, an archipelago off the coast of Morocco.[23] In 1427, another sea voyage during the reign of Henry the Navigator led to the discovery in mid–Atlantic of the Azores islands.[24] As they provided fresh water, these islands became welcome ports of call for Portuguese sailors exploring the coast of Africa or for Spanish navigators en route to the new world. At the end of the 15th century, Christopher Columbus was sailing for the Spanish Crown in search of a new route to Asia when he landed in America in 1492. Within a period of ten years, he explored most of the Caribbean islands, part of the coast of Mexico, Belize, and Honduras (Favier, 470–536).[25]

Early on, Spain and Portugal outdistanced all other European nations in the race to discover new lands. As a result, the Pope found it appropriate to divide all newly discovered lands between the two kingdoms through the 1494 Treaty of Tordesillas (Eccles, *The French*, 1). Portugal also sought to reach India by sea and, in 1497–1498, Vasco de Gama successfully sailed the dangerous route around the horn of Africa. In 1500 Pedro Alvares Cabral (1467–1520) reached the coast of Brazil (Favier, 537–552). Another sailor from Portugal, Ferdinand Magellan (1480–1521) was the first to sail around the world. Sponsored by Charles V of Spain, the voyage lasted from 1519 to 1521 and Magellan died before it ended, killed by aborigines he was trying to convert to Christianity (Favier, 552–567).

Why were the voyages of discovery so important? As Magellan's story makes clear, converting pagans to the "true religion" was part of the operation. But they also enriched the great sovereigns of Europe as they brought new resources, riches, control over commercial routes,[26] and lands, thereby increasing their power. They clearly expanded human knowledge of the world: sailing around the world, for instance, brought proof that the earth is round. Last but not least, through the development of trade and commerce, they increased the well-being of European elites, and theirs only: for as Robert Mandrou

reminds us, material and social insecurity were the lot of the vast majority of French, and all European people, in the 16th and 17th century (Mandrou, I, 250–264).

The colonization of America started from Northern Europe in the late 10th and early 11th century when the Vikings tried and failed to settle in Canada.[27] By the early 16th century, France and England were clearly lagging behind in terms of explorations but they were eager to catch up. In 1497, Henri VII, King of England, commissioned John Cabot (1450–1498) to search for a new route to Asia.[28] Landing in North America, he discovered that other Europeans were already there. Norman, Breton, and Basque sailors knew the coast of Labrador and Newfoundland as excellent cod fishing grounds prior to Cabot's voyage.[29] Dickinson states that by the middle of the 16th century fifty French ports sent ships to Newfoundland waters every year, Saint-Malo alone 24 in 1541, and Bordeaux 22 in 1546 (Dickinson, 26). Hodson and Rushforth believe that "the French dwarfed their rivals' efforts" in that area (20) but Havard and Vidal take a more moderate view, stating that "around 1580 […] as many as 500 ships, half of them French—the others from Spain, Portugual, and England—were fishing in these 'newfound lands'" (*Histoire*, 57). All these sea-faring captains were highly trained, having learned their trade in "the unforgiving maritime school of the North Atlantic" (McGrath, 110). Between 1530 and 1600, whaling and the capture of seals, elephant seals, and walruses, also became a major commercial activity for fishermen from France and Spain as grease and oil were used in candle making and skins in tailoring.[30] Moreover, as fishermen had to go to land to salt their cod in order to preserve it, or to extract oil from sea mammals and skin them, they inevitably met Native Americans eager to barter. These encounters probably gave rise to the fur trade that started in the late 16th century and developed fully in the next.

3. Verrazano, Cartier: First Steps in North America for the French

Some time after Cabot's voyage, in 1508, Jean Ango, a shipowner from Dieppe tried to establish a settlement in Newfoundland.[31] At his death, his son, also named Jean Ango, inherited the seventy ships in his fleet and his lucrative spice business. A friend of the King, the wealthy merchant, together with a consortium of bankers from Rouen and Dieppe, financed the first French expedition to the New World in the hope of finding the Northwest Passage to Asia.[32] Sea captain Jean de Verrazane, better known as Giovanni de Verrazano (1485–1528) was selected to lead the expedition. A member of one of the Dieppe banking families, he had grown up and learned navigation in this seaport.[33] Once in royal employ, Verrazano's mission was to explore the unknown coast of North America between Florida and Newfoundland.[34] In 1524, he was the first European to set foot in that part of the world. He named this land "Francesca" in honor of King Francis I (*François*, in French) and the name apparently stuck since "[b]y mid-century, the labels 'Terra Francesca' or 'Tierra Francisca' […] began to appear on maps made by not only the French[35] but also those of Italian, Portuguese, and even Spanish cartographers" (McGrath, 47). For Marcel Trudel, therefore, "New France was born in 1524" (*Histoire*, 33).

Opposite, facing: **Sixteenth-century map indicating cod rich areas near Labrador and New-foundland [*Carte du XVIème siècle siècle montrant des secteurs riches en morue*] (courtesy Library and Archives Canada).**

At Pamlico Sound, Verrazano thought that he had found the Northwest Passage. He wrote: "From our ship, we could see the oriental sea in the Northwest. This sea is probably the one that borders the Southern region of India and Cathay [China]" (quoted in Trudel, *Histoire*, 42). According to Paule Hoffman, this "discovery" gave rise to the "legend" that "an arm of the Pacific Ocean existed," reaching far East into the North American continent (105). Verrazano was enchanted by the coast of Virginia, near Chesapeake Bay, and called it *l'Arcadie*, Arcadia, like the beautiful region of Greek mythology. He was the first to describe the site that would become New York: "A very pleasant place, located between two hills, with a very large and deep river flowing into the sea" (Trudel, *Histoire*, 43). He called it "Angoulême" in honor of his patron Francis I, who was also Count of Angoulême. During his voyage, Verrazano encountered several Native American tribes. He liked those of Massachusetts, calling them "the most beautiful and most civilized nation" encountered on his journey. He disliked those of Rhode Island, labeling them "a mean race, as nasty and cruel as the former were polite" (quoted in Trudel, *Histoire*, 45).

Francis I did not keep *Terra Francesca* very long. Charles V of Spain ordered new explorations of the North American coast and a year after Verrazano, the Portuguese explorer Estêvão Gomes (Esteban Gomez, 1483–1538) also explored the Bay of New York. Then Vasquez de Ayllon explored the coast of North and South Carolina and Panfilo de Narvaez the coast of Florida. Verrazano, "the gifted discoverer who failed" (Weinmann, 40), was disappointed by the outcome of his exploratory journeys. Pamlico Sound was not the Northwest Passage, so there would be no commerce with Asia. He was, however, enthusiastic about the East Coast: beautiful land, great climate, magnificent forests, excellent soil, plenty of excellent water, lots of wildlife. He hoped that later explorations might uncover gold mines there. Verrazano completed two more voyages of discovery. But in 1527, his ship ended up in Brazil instead of North America. On a third voyage, he explored Florida, the Bahamas, and the Lesser Antilles. But when he went ashore alone on the island of Guadeloupe, he was killed and eaten by the aborigines. Popular U.S. history long ignored Verrazano's discovery of the Bay of New York. Henry Hudson and his 1609 voyage totally eclipsed the French navigator's earlier achievement. Only in the 1950s did the city of New York finally acknowledge Verrazano's exploit by naming a new bridge after him, the Verrazano-Narrows Bridge.

Despite early failures, Francis I did not give up on his dream of exploring the New World. In 1532, he commissioned a new voyage of discovery. A Breton sailor from Saint-Malo, Jacques Cartier, who had sailed to Newfoundland earlier on and may even have taken part in one of Verrazano's voyages, was charged with "traveling from the kingdom to the New Lands and exploring isles where large quantities of gold and other riches are rumored to be hidden" (quoted in Trudel, *Histoire*, 69).[36] The sailing ships used by sea faring nations in those days were carracks, like Columbus' 60 tons *Niña* or caravels, like his 200 tons *Santa Maria*. Cartier, an unknown navigator who was well-connected socially,[37] sailed with three of these ships.[38] In 1534, he was the first European to sail and map the Gulf of the Saint-Lawrence.[39] On Prince Edward Island, he encountered Native Americans, Mi'kmaq, and traded goods with them. According to Jean-Marc Soyez, the population of Canada numbered over 100,000 Native Americans when the French arrived in North America.[40] With over 30,000 members, the Hurons (or Wyandot people) formed the largest nation, followed by the Algonkins/Crees, the Iroquois (Mohawks, Oneida, Cayuga, Onondaga, and Seneca) and the Petun, each with around 15,000 each. There were also 10,000 Attawandaron (Neutres); 6,000 Innus (Montagnais-Naspkaps,

Oumaniocks, Papinachois); 5,500 Abenaki (Mi'kmaq, Attikamègues); 5,000 Mohicans; and 1,000 Inuits.[41]

As Cartier recalled in the account of his first voyage, he had a cross erected in Gaspé as a way of taking possession of the region on behalf of the King of France.[42] It bore the inscription "Long live the King of France." Cartier encountered a group of Iroquoian fishermen in Gaspé Bay and met with their Chief, Donnacona. He first kidnapped, then convinced Donnacona, to let him take two of his sons to France. As a result, Domagaya and Taignoagny spent eight months in Saint-Malo where they learned to speak French. By the end of his first voyage, Cartier was sure that he had reached Asia. He had found no gold but he had mapped the region, which he called "Canada." He had gained some knowledge of the Iroquoian culture: they came from further inland, south of the St. Lawrence River. He had made an alliance with them through his promise to bring back the Chief's sons as well as European goods.

Cartier returned to Canada in 1535. With Domagaya and Taignoagny now able to translate, communication flowed easier when he met with Donnacona in Stadaconé (Stadacona, Quebec City today). A conflict over the Frenchman's plans soon arose, however. Donnacona who drew prestige and power from being the only Native American in contact with the French, objected to Cartier's desire to continue exploring the continent. Cartier carried on regardless. Sailing down the St. Lawrence, he arrived in Hochelaga, which he renamed *Mont Réal* (Mount Royal), and met with a larger Iroquoian tribe. Rapids, which he called "La Chine" (China Rapids), prevented him for going any further.[43] When Cartier returned to Stadaconé in October, Donnacona did not hide his displeasure. Cartier found it wise to have a fort built in preparation for the French's first Canadian winter. It turned out to be particularly harsh. A scurvy epidemic broke out, killing over 50 Iroquoians and 25 of the 110 Frenchmen. A remedy the Indians taught the French saved the rest of them: a tea made of anedda bark and leaves (Soyez, 35–26). Having learned from Donnacona that gold was to be found in the Saguenay kingdom, Cartier decided to take the Iroquoian chief back to France so he could confirm the gold rumor to the King. That was also a way to get this former ally out of his way as Agona had now become Cartier's best friend. Donnacona was well-treated in France but he died there in 1539 (Soyez, 38).

In France, the 1534 *Affaire des Placards*, the posting of anti–Catholic pamphlets in various cities and on the King's bedroom door, was interpreted as a challenge to Francis I's authority and dealt with accordingly: the 1540 edict of Fontainebleau condemned the "Protestant heresy" as treason (Labrune and Toutain, 48). But this condemnation did not prevent the King from appointing Jean-François de La Rocque de Roberval (1500–1560), a Huguenot friend of his, Lieutenant General of Canada in 1540. For Roberval, the goal of the voyage was no longer to find the Northwest Passage but to establish a colony in Canada.[44]

Cartier, for whom it was now a third voyage to the New World, was part of the expedition. In May 1541, he left for Canada ahead of Roberval, setting sail from Saint-Malo with five ships and 400 people, many of them convicts and prisoners. They landed near the location of present-day Quebec City and established what they thought would be the first permanent European settlement in North America, Charlesbourg-Royal, close by Agona's settlement of Stadacona, but without asking the Iroquoian's chief for permission. Cartier resumed his explorations in September, returning to Hochelaga with long boats, in search of the Saguenay gold. When he returned to Charlesbourg-Royal, relations with the Native Americans had deteriorated. Cartier and his men collected loads of what they thought were diamonds and gold, and then, in September 1542, sailed home with two ships and the mineral collection. They passed Roberval's ships off the coast of Newfoundland but disregarded the Lieutenant General's orders to turn around. In France, however, Cartier learned that his diamonds were simply quartz crystals and iron ore (Soyez, 38–45).

Lack of resources had delayed Roberval's departure. As the Lieutenant General needed more money to fund the colony, he left for a pirating expedition that yielded a few British ships. In April 1542, he was finally ready to sail for Canada with 200 colonists aboard three ships. During the Atlantic crossing, a love affair developed between Roberval's cousin, young Marguerite de la Rocque, and a young man. Out of displeasure, greed, or both, Roberval abandoned the young couple and a maid on the "Isle of Demons" in the Gulf of Saint-Lawrence. All died except for Marguerite who was rescued by fishermen and returned to France to tell her story. Another Marguerite, the queen of Navarre and the King of France's sister, published it in her *Heptameron* (1558). Roberval's settlement, which he had renamed *France-Roy*, lasted less than two years. The long, harsh winter months, disease, and raids by the former Iroquoian allies, forced the French to abandon the colony and to sail back home in 1543. It would take another 50 years for the idea of settling in Canada to be revived. As Havard and Vidal point out, however, "envisioning colonization just from the vantage point of official explorations would be considering the visible part of the iceberg only" (Havard and Vidal, *Histoire* 55).[45] The Bretons, Normans, and Basques did not stop coming to North America after Roberval's departure. In fact, as we will see in the next chapter, the fur trade had already started in the last two decades of the 16th century.

4. Escaping the Wars of Religion: Brazil, Florida, Carolina

During the second half of the 16th century, foreign and civil wars both slowed down and created incentives for settling in the New World.[46] They slowed the process of colonization because the government's attention primarily focused on domestic matters. They created new incentives for colonial expansion for the French Protestant minority as it searched for places that would be safer than France. Under Francis I, the French monarchy's prestige and power increased considerably but royal power was challenged nonetheless, particularly under Henri II who ruled the French kingdom from 1547 to 1559. The challenges were the same, religion strife between Protestants and Catholics, and the struggle for supremacy in Europe and abroad. The War of Italy that had resumed between 1542 and 1546 started again in 1551 and lasted until 1559. The wars of religion were not unique to France. In England, Parliament recognized Elizabeth I as the legitimate heir to the throne in 1558 but Catholics saw her as an imposter. They sought to replace her Mary Stuart, who was Queen of Scotland, and, for less than a year, Queen of France, as wife of 15-year-old King Francis II. When he died of a bad infection in December 1559, his mother Catherine of Medici became the kingdom's Regent because the next in the line of succession, her ten-year-old son, Charles IX, was too young to rule. Chancellor Michel de l'Hôpital preached religious tolerance in vain in the early 1560s. Eight wars of religion were to ravage France between 1562 and 1598 with support from England for the Protestants and Spain for the Catholics.[47]

Protestants who wanted to settle in the New World had a strong ally in Gaspard de Coligny (1519–1572).[48] This Marshal had served with distinction in the Wars of Italy[49] and converted to Protestantism in 1559. But even before his conversion, he worked to establish colonies in the New World where Protestants could find refuge from persecution. A friend of Coligny, Admiral Nicolas Durand de Villegaignon (1510–1571), commanded the 1555 expedition that was meant to create a refuge for 600 colonists and soldiers, Huguenots and Catholics. Villegaignon, a Knight of the Order of Saint-John of Jerusalem (Knight of Malta), was not a Huguenot himself,[50] but an advocate of religious tolerance.[51] The French took possession of the small island of Serigipe[52] in the Rio de Janeiro Bay, where they built a fort, Fort Coligny, and a village. The colony was to be known as *France Antarctique*. French sailors were already familiar with the coast where they cut and loaded the *bois-brésil* (brazilwood), a wood that produced a natural red dye that was very sought after at the time. Villegaignon's goal may have been in part to take control of this lucrative business.

The colony's chaplain, André Thévet (1502–1590) soon fell ill and returned to France but not empty-handed: he was bringing tobacco (*l'herbe pétun*) back to France. In 1557, Thévet also published an account of his observations in Brazil, *Singularités de la France antarctique*, a work that is now considered as one of the founding texts of American ethnography.[53] Thévet devoted forty chapters of his work to the Tupinamba Indians he had interviewed with help of a French interpreter who had spent ten years with them. The chapters on cannibalism are famous because Michel de Montaigne (1553–1592) commented on this practice in his *Essays* (1580),[54] but Thévet dealt with many other topics, the Tupinambas' rituals (marriage, funerals), diseases and cures, and the plants they grew for food (cassava, sweet potato). From them he learned about tobacco's property as an appetite and thirst suppressant, hence the future practice of giving tobacco to soldiers.[55] He also described the Brazilian fauna and flora, and commenting on the Natives' friendliness with strangers, reported that they went as far as to fell, trim, and carry brazilwood several miles for their European visitors.

Portugal had started colonizing Brazil in 1534 but was reducing the Tupinambas to slavery.[56] Villegaignon made friends with those who were rebelling against the Portuguese. In 1557, a second group of 300 colonists arrived in the colony. It included Jean de Léry (1536–1613), a reformed pastor who wrote the colony's history.[57] With Villegaignon in charge, life in the colony was austere and strictly regulated. But religious strife between Catholics and Protestants led to the expulsion of the Huguenots from the island. Some went to live with the Tupinambas and some returned to France in 1558, as did Villegaignon. Indignant about this Protestant colony on Catholic soil, the Portuguese destroyed Fort Coligny in 1560. The remaining French escaped to the mainland and went to live with the Tupinambas. In 1565, the Portuguese fought them anew in a war that lasted two years. In the end, they expelled the French from Brazil.

By the 1560s the persecution of Protestants had become a frequent and bloody occurrence in France. In fact, Roberval himself was murdered in Paris as he left a Calvinist gathering in 1560. Coligny therefore thought it would be a good thing to establish a French colony as a refuge for Protestants in Florida despite the peninsula's proximity to the Spanish Colonial Empire.[58] The Spaniards had explored and claimed the area but decided against settling there. So why not? Coligny chose Jean Ribault (1520–1565) to lead the expedition.[59] Two French royal ships left Le Havre in February 1562 with 150 men, took the same route as Verrazano, and reached the mouth a river near today's

Jacksonville, Florida. They set up a cross to mark French possession and built a wooden fort they called Charlesfort in honor of King Charles IX.[60] Ribault then sailed back to France for supplies, leaving behind an officer, Captain Albert de la Pierra, and a few dozen men to take care of the fort. War forced him to change his plans, however, as he had to assist Huguenots in Dieppe and seek refuge in London for a while. The British arrested and jailed him as a spy but he spent his time wisely, writing his memoirs.

Once peace returned in the spring of 1573, Coligny decided to send a new expedition to Charlesfort under the command of René Goulaine de Laudonnière (c. 1529–1574). Just before it left, however, they learned that the settlement had been abandoned. The men had rebelled against Captain Albert and killed him. After fourteen months of infighting and hunger, they had decided to leave and tried to make it back to France on a makeshift boat. Some of them had perished on route and others had resorted to cannibalism to survive until an English ship finally rescued those who were still alive. In April 1564, de La Laudonnière arrived in Florida and moved the settlement further up the St. Johns River (Nowell, 83). They called it Fort Caroline, again in honor of the king, Charles IX, *Carolus* in Latin.[61] Supplies lasted for over a year, but conflicts erupted between de la Laudonnière and the men, and between the French and the Utina, a tribe of the Timucua First Nation. Some sailors also defied orders and went on piracy expeditions against the Spaniards, a decision they would come to regret.

A year later, in late summer 1565, Ribault left for Fort Caroline with a flotilla of six

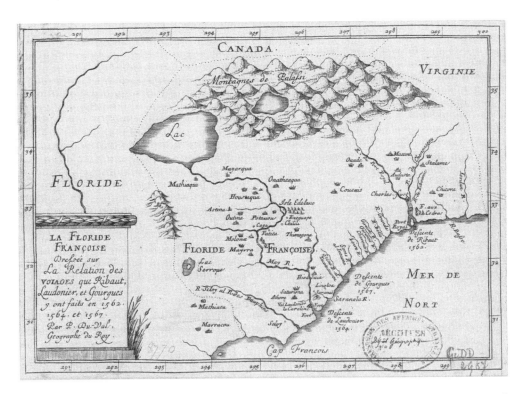

French Florida Based on Travel Accounts by Ribaut, Laudonier and Gourges in 1562, 1564 and 1567 [*La Floride Françoise dressée sur la relation des voiages que Ribaut, Laudonier, et Gourgues y ont faits en 1562, 1564 et 1567*]. Map by P. Du-Val, 1677 (courtesy Bibliothèque nationale de France/Gallica).

war ships carrying 600 settlers. The Spaniards were growing really unhappy with this settlement, however. They had claimed Florida for Spain and they did not want any Huguenot neighbors, particularly sailors who would attack their ships. Pedro Menéndez de Avilés (1519–1574) received the order to kill the French, whom King Philip II of Spain regarded as Lutheran corsairs, and to destroy their fort.[62] Menéndez, whose armada suffered great losses during the Atlantic crossing, unloaded his remaining ships south of the mouth of the Saint John's River, establishing St. Augustine in the process. Although informed that Ribault was bringing reinforcement to Fort Caroline, the Spanish commander did not know his exact whereabouts. But he was willing to bet that he could make it to the French colony before Ribault and capture the fort by surprise. Menéndez's strategy worked: despite a raging hurricane, he sent his men on the 30-mile foot journey from St. Augustine to Fort Caroline. Four days later, these 400 men attacked Fort Caroline by land, slaughtering most men. A few dozen settlers were able to escape, including Laudonnière, carpenter Nicolas Le Challeux, and painter Jacques Le Moyne de Morgues (1533–1588).[63] They lived to write accounts of this event.[64] Two of the three French ships at anchor were able to escape Spanish fire and later returned to pick up survivors.

Meanwhile Ribault, whose strategy was to attack St. Augustine by sea, was sailing north into the eye of the hurricane. When three French ships wrecked south of St. Augustine, Menéndez soon tracked down the 140 survivors. Famished after being stranded on a sandbar for a week, they offered no resistance and surrendered. Except for 16 men who self-identified as Catholics, however, all were murdered.[65] Ribault, meanwhile, and with him presumably several hundred Frenchmen, were still at large. In early October, however, Menéndez found out that Ribault's ship, *La Trinité*, had sunk as well. A new Spanish expedition marched off, not to rescue survivors, but again to kill them all, Ribault included this time. The Spaniards then took over Fort Caroline and renamed it San Mateo.

Legend has it that the dead bodies of the French Protestants were hung from trees in the Matanzas inlet together with a sign from Menéndez bearing the following inscription: "I did not do this to Frenchmen but to Lutherans."[66] It is a fact that in 1568, a French privateer named Dominique de Gorgues (also spelled Gourgues) went on a revenge expedition, and that together with native Taquatacourou and 200 French sailors, he burned San Mateo to the ground and slaughtered the Spanish colonists. Again, legend has it that he too left a sign that read: "I did not do this to Spaniards or converts but to traitors, thieves, and murderers." Beyond the religious fanaticism that impelled these men to murder each other, the Florida story raises the question of the inevitability of French defeat. In response to this question, John McGrath concludes that "the Spaniards were simply more determined to protect their silver fleets than the French were to establish a colony in Florida" (170). But as this account shows, luck also had a lot to do with the outcome. Besides, although the French expeditions to Florida and Carolina did not reach the status of permanent settlement they had initially sought, the accounts of sea captains and explorers like Thévet, Léry, Laudonnière, and Ribault stand out as important documents about the Timucua, their ways of life and customs, as well as the Florida fauna and flora. Painter, Le Moyne de Morgues, who survived the Fort Caroline massacre, left significant artistic renderings of nature and of people as well.[67]

The Franco-Spanish conflicts of Florida served as a prelude to the hardening of the French wars of religion in the 1570s. King Charles IX and Catherine of Medici reacted erratically towards Protestants, moving from tolerance at first, to repression. In 1570, they agreed to a truce with the Protestants, the Peace of St. Germain, because they were losing the civil war and preferred to grant them four "places of safety," i.e., military strongholds, to outright capitulation. In a gesture of conciliation, they also reinstated Coligny to the King's Council in 1571 and arranged for the marriage of the King's sister, Marguerite ("Queen Margot"), to a Protestant, King Henry III of Navarre (future King Henri IV of France). Conservative Catholics and the Church of Rome strongly objected to this marriage, which took place nonetheless on August 18, 1572. But four days later, Catholics tried to murder Coligny, the most prominent Huguenot, in a group of aristocrats who had gathered in Paris for the wedding.

Fearing reprisals on the part of the Huguenots for this assassination attempt, King Charles IX, went on the offensive and ordered the elimination of all Protestant leaders, an unfortunate decision that unleashed the infamous St. Bartholomew's Day Massacre. By the time Catholic mob violence had spread from Paris to the rest of France an estimated 5,000 to 30,000 Protestants had been killed, a slaughter that considerably weakened the Huguenot movement.[68] The assassinations continued over the next decades. When Charles IX died of tuberculosis in 1574, his brother Henri III became king, only to be challenged on his right by the Catholic League, and in particular by his cousin, Henri de Guise, who was very popular in Paris. Henri de Guise succeeded in chasing the King out of Paris in 1588 and nearly dethroned him. Henri III avenged himself by having his cousin murdered the same year. A year later, a fanatic Catholic monk avenged Henri de Guise's death by murdering the King. Ironically, Henri III's murder led to the scenario the League had feared the most: the accession of a Protestant, Henri of Navarre, to the throne. Facing huge opposition from Catholics, Henri IV converted to Catholicism in 1593, after famously declaring that *"Paris vaut bien une messe"* ("Paris is worth a mass") (Haine, 49–51). It took him five years to be accepted as king but today "good King Henri" is remembered for the Edict of Toleration (1598) and the country's prosperity during his reign. However, he too was murdered by a fanatic monk in 1610.[69]

As we saw in this chapter, the thirst for rare goods and precious metals and the competition with other sovereigns for control over trade routes sent European explorers to the four corners of the world from the Renaissance onward. Despite the struggles for land that tore Europe apart for most of its first millennium and a half, colonization as a land grab operation came as an afterthought in the case of North America. The world explorers and colonizers came from was torn between the civilizing influence of scientific and artistic progress in an age of renewal and the brevity and unpredictability of daily life in a world riddled with violence, constant wars, religious fanaticism, diseases, and insecurity for all: in short, a world hardly less "savage" than the new world Jacques Cartier and his men encountered when they landed in Canada. But despite repeated attempts to settle in North America so as to better search for gold, find the route to China, or escape religious persecution, the French failed to establish permanent settlements in North America in the 16th century. However, it would be wrong to conclude that these failures were uniquely French: after all, so did English attempts to settle in North Carolina and Virginia at the time.[70] Besides, much knowledge was gained from these explorations in terms of navigation and cartography. Learning from the mistakes of these early pioneers, the next generation would soon be able to create permanent settlements in North America.

Sometimes the borderline between history and legend is tenuous. We know that the French were familiar with the coast of Brazil in Coligny's days but could it be that they were there earlier? More precisely: did a Frenchman discover the New World? Did another Frenchman go to Brazil before the Portuguese? The two following stories were thought to be true until very recently. According to one of them, Jean Cousin, a sailor from Normandy, reached the mouth of the Amazon River in 1488 and thus discovered the New World before Columbus (Nowell, 82). As the story goes, a member of Cousin's expedition, Alonzo Pinzon, would have advised Columbus on this 1492 voyage. The famous anthropologist Claude Levi-Strauss did not outright discount the possibility that a Frenchman may have discovered America but as he pointed out, Cousin's claim could no longer be supported by any kind of evidence "since the archives in Dieppe, with Cousin's narrative among them, were lost in the fire started by an English bombardment in the seventeenth century" (86). Today, historians no longer believe it ever happened.

According to the second story, a captain named Gonneville would have visited an unknown land, thought later on to be Terra Australis, in 1504.[71] As the story goes, he brought a Native American back to France, and being unable to take him back, married him to his daughter. According to Margaret Sankey, Gonneville's discovery seemed so credible for centuries to French authorities that "the impetus for discovery by the French during the 18th century was inflected by [that] belief" (42). By the late 20th century, however, historians no longer believed that the voyage ever took place, and even questioned Gonneville's existence.

5. Tips for Further Investigations

Interesting People to Look Up

Giovanni da Verrazzano (or Jean de Verrazane) (c. 1485–1528)
Jacques Cartier (1491–1557)
Jean-François de La Rocque de *Roberval* (c. 1500–1560)
Nicolas Durand de Villegaignon (1510–1572)
Gaspard II de Coligny (1519–1572)
Jean *Ribault* (or Ribaut) (1520–1565)
René Goulaine de Laudonnière (1529–1574)
Jacques Le Moyne de Morgues (1533–1588)

Related Primary Texts

Cartier, Jacques. *Jacques Cartier and his Four Voyages to Canada* (1540).
Gourgues, Dominique. *Histoire mémorable de la reprinse de l'isle de la Floride* (1568).
Laudonnière, René de. *Three Voyages* (1565).
Léry, Jean de. *History of a Voyage to the Land of Brazil, otherwise called America* (1578).
Montaigne, Michel de. "Of Cannibals," in Montaigne's *Essays* (ca. 1588).
Navarre, Marguerite de. Story of Marguerite de Roberval. Tale 67, Day 7 in *The Heptameron* (1558).
Ribault, Jean, *Voyage to Florida* (1562).
Thévet, André. *Les singularitéz de la France Antarctique* (1557).

Related Films and Works of Fiction

Canadian Diamonds (1960), documentary by René Bonnière and Pierre Perrault, 29 minutes.
Les Grandes découvertes. Daily Motion, Educathèmes TV, 23 minutes.
The Land of Jacques Cartier (1960) documentary, 29 minutes.

CHAPTER II

The Rise of the French Colonial Empire, 1600–1660

Seafaring European nations made numerous attempts to settle in North America in the 16th century. The Portuguese captain João Vaz Corte-Real (1420–1496) probably reached Newfoundland as early as 1473 and Portugal claimed that part of the world as a result of the Treaty of Tordesillas anyway.[1] Hardly had Verrazano raised the "Lilies of France" over Francesca when Lucas Vázquez de Ayllon established a colony in that area in 1526. Like the French settlements of the 16th century, it too failed, as did the Spanish settlement on Chesapeake Bay in 1570 and the first French settlement in the Caribbean. In 1538, Jesuit refugees founded the small colony of Dieppe on the island of Saint-Christophe [Saint Kitts] but the Spaniards plundered the little town and chased its inhabitants a few months later.[2]

It took almost a century for the French to return to North America and the Caribbean. In the absence of settlers, colonization remained an empty word. Sir Francis Drake (c. 1540–1596), for instance, claimed New Albion on the Pacific Coast for Queen Elizabeth I of England in 1579, a decade before he defeated the Spanish Armada (Nowell, 119), but short of a British presence in the area, the claim remained just that.[3] Up to the end of the 16th century, the exception, the only North American settlement that had a continuous European presence from the time it was established to the present, was St. Augustine, founded in 1565 by Pedro Menéndez de Avilés as he was destroying the French Huguenot colonies of Florida and Carolina.[4]

In the early 17th century, however, Europeans started establishing permanent settlements in North America.[5] Religious persecution under James I (1566–1625), king of Great Britain from 1603 to 1625, led to the exodus of dissidents who founded Jamestown, Virginia, in 1607 and to the arrival of Pilgrims who settled in Plymouth, Massachusetts, in 1620.[6] As opposed to James I, Henri IV (1553–1610), who had abjured the Protestant faith and converted to Catholicism to become King of France in 1589, practiced tolerance towards Huguenots. He is best known for having signed the 1598 edict of toleration, the famous *Edit de Nantes*, which marked the end of the first wave of religious persecution in France.[7] Prior to the proclamation of the edict, however, many French Huguenots had already left France for Protestant countries, mostly England, Holland, some German states, and Switzerland. Some of these Huguenots joined the British and Dutch pilgrims who founded the colonies of Plymouth and Jamestown.[8]

1. The Founding of New France, 1600–1617

Wishing to benefit from colonial expansion but unwilling to carry the financial burden, the French Crown initially outsourced colonization to merchants and trading companies.[9] In 1578, King Henri IV appointed a Breton nobleman, the marquis de la Roche-Mesgoüez (1536–1606), Lieutenant General of New France.[10] As the wars of religion were raging, nothing happened until 1598 when peace returned and the commission was renewed.[11] La Roche then took off for North America and established a colony on Sand Island, off the coast of Nova Scotia. Forty former beggars and inmates lived on the island for three years, relying on supplies brought from France once a year. When the supply ship failed to appear in 1602, however, a mutiny took place during which the men killed the colony's leaders. Only eleven people were still alive when the supply ship finally arrived in 1603. Acknowledging the colony's failure all sailed back to France.[12]

Merchants from Saint-Malo, including Jacques Cartier's nephew Jacques Noël and the latter's sons, regularly visited the St. Lawrence valley to trade with Native Americans in the last quarter of the 16th century. If the fur trade took on such an important economic role during the next centuries, it is not only because it became fashionable to wear fur in France and in Europe, but also because the world had become colder. The boom in the fur trade corresponds to the Little Ice Age that lasted roughly from the Renaissance to the 19th century (Havard and Vidal, *Histoire*, 58). John B. Brebner writes that fur replaced fish as the favored exchange commodity "about 1581, when a group of merchants of Saint-Malo began to send their vessels up the river either to tap virgin sources of fur or to intercept the flow of them from the interior" (121). From then on, he notes, Europeans were the ones seeking Native Americans instead of the other way around.[13] Another factor that accounts for increased European demand for fur was the closure of the habitual supply channels, Sweden, and Russia, due to war. Canada had plenty of beaver pelt to offer (Allaire, 50).

As Marcel Trudel points out, early French fur traders like Noël and his associate Chaton de La Jeannaye were interested in commercial ventures, not in colonization—and this in spite of the royal charter enjoining them to found a Catholic colony in Canada (*Histoire*, 226). Networks for the fur trade soon developed in North America with annual fairs taking place in Tadoussac,[14] where the Montagnais[15] stayed during summer. There was so much trade going on that special ships were built to transport the fur. Due to this rush, however, competition became fierce, particularly after the Native Americans learned how to take advantage of the situation and prices increased (Dickinson, 29). Free trade had led to a glut, to blows, and even ship burning (Havard and Vidal, *Histoire*, 60). The market was ripe for a correction.

In 1599, Pierre de Chauvin de Tonnetuit (1550–1603), a navy captain and merchant from Honfleur, requested and obtained from the King a fur trading monopoly for Canada for a period of ten years in exchange for his promise to establish a Catholic colony.[16] His friend, Pierre Du Gua, Sieur de Monts (1558–1628), a wealthy merchant from Saintonge, agreed to partner with him and to finance the expedition. François Gravé du Pont (1560–1629), the expedition's captain, was a sailor from Saint-Malo with previous experience in the St. Lawrence valley fur business. He was to play "a central role at a time when French colonial designs were taking shape, at the juncture of the 16th and 17th centuries" (Havard and Vidal, *Histoire*, 72). The first expedition took place in 1600. The new partners established a trading post in Tadoussac, which is the oldest surviving French settlement in North America. When they returned to France, they took two Montagnais, native speakers of Innu, a language that is part of the Cree language group, to learn French and serve as interpreters for the next expedition.[17]

When Chauvin died in 1603, de Monts obtained his fur trade monopoly for a period of seven years (1603–1610). Chauvin's title of Viceroy of Canada had gone to Aymar de Clermont-Chaste (1514–1603), a French admiral, who, as governor of the seaport of Dieppe, had welcomed Henri IV in 1589 during the Wars of Religion and loaned the King a great deal of money.[18] The admiral, who had privileged access at court,[19] was the organizer of the famous 1603 voyage that brought Champlain to the New World for the first time. The expedition's three ships left Honfleur, Normandy, in early March with Pont Gravé as navigator. Also traveling back to Canada were the two Montagnais.[20]

Samuel Champlain was born between 1567 and 1574 in Jacopolis sur Brouage, a seaport north of Bordeaux surrounded by salt marshes that the "white gold" trade had enriched.[21] Salt gave it also a special connection to North America as many fishing boats bound to the coast of Labrador and Newfoundland loaded up in Brouage prior to leaving France. Close to the Huguenot stronghold of La Rochelle, the village of 4,000 souls was a strategic stake in the wars of religion. In 1578, Henri III made it a *ville royale* (in order to confiscate its riches), shortened its name to Brouage and appointed Richelieu as its governor. Educated by the local parish priest, Champlain learned how to navigate and to draw maps early on. He volunteered and fought during the last three years of the wars of religion in the royal army (1595–1598) against Bretons who rejected the "heretical king" and, with support from Spain, were threatening secession. At the end of the war, he helped his uncle, Guillaume Allène, a famous and wealthy privateer, transport Spanish troops from Brittany to Cadix in southern Spain. He then joined a Spanish expedition to the Caribbean and to Mexico and had the brilliant idea of consigning his observations, maps, and drawings to a manuscript entitled *Bref Discours*.[22]

Upon his return to France in the summer of 1601, Champlain received an inheritance from his uncle Allène who had passed away. In Brouage he reconnected with a friend with whom he had served in the army, René Rivery de Potonville. He showed him his manuscript, Rivery showed it to a well-connected acquaintance, De Chaste, who showed to

SIEUR DE MONTS.

Pierre Dugua, Sieur De Monts (1560–1620), first governor of Acadia (courtesy Library and Archives Canada).

the King in late 1601. His Majesty was apparently impressed since he invited young Champlain to court, awarded him a stipend, and granted him royal protection. Although he had no official title during the 1603 expedition, Champlain's job was to document the voyage as he had done before. Most of what we know of the voyages of discovery to New France in the early 17th century comes from Champlain's *Voyages*.[23]

The French arrived at Tadoussac on March 15, 1603. According to Champlain's account of the expedition, there was a feast at Tadoussac where tobacco was smoked (hence the French expression "*tabagie de Tadoussac*") to celebrate the alliance between the French, Algonquins, and Montagnais.[24] The returning Native Americans, who had been treated well and introduced to the King of France, had apparently only good things to say about the French. After watching Algonquin women perform the scalp dance, Pont Gravé and Champlain continued to explore the St. Lawrence valley, to map it, all the while engaging in the fur trade.[25] Relations with the Native Americans were so good that they invited the French to stay and that a young Montagnais and a woman, an Iroquois captive, traveled back to France with them when they left. De Chaste did not make it: he died in Canada prior to departure. Back in France in September, Champlain reported to the King and, in hope of raising funds for the next expedition, published the account of his first voyage: "*Des Sauvages, ou Voyage de Samuel Champlain de Brouage, fait en la France nouvelle, l'an mil six cens trois*" [*Of Savages, or Voyage by Samuel Champlain of Brouage Made to New France in 1603*].[26] The term *savage*, derived from the Latin word for *forest*, was frequently used to designate Amerindians but, as Champlain's title illustrates, not necessarily in a pejorative sense.[27]

In 1603, the King tasked Pierre Du Gua de Monts[28] with the establishment of a French colony in Acadia where sixty new colonists would arrive every year.[29] In April 1604, two ships, including the *Don de Dieu* [*Gift of God*] featured on Quebec City's flag today, cast off from Le Havre with a crew of nearly eighty and again, Pont Gravé as navigator.[30] Also part of the expedition were Jean de Biencourt, Baron of Poutrincourt and Saint-Just (1557–1615), as second in command, and Samuel Champlain, whose role was to provide detailed maps and a faithful account of the expedition—which he did.[31] The explorers sailed along *Baie française* (Bay of Fundy, Fundy being a deformation of the French adjective *fendu*, a reference to its shape). Having established a temporary settlement on Sainte Croix Island (now in Maine), they spent summer and fall exploring, sailing along the coast of Maine, down the rivers Penobscot and Kennebeg in Maine and as far along the Atlantic coast as *Cap Blanc* (Cape Cod).[32] They spent the harsh winter on Sainte Croix Island, losing nearly half their men to disease. Pont Gravé, who had sailed back to France before winter to get more supplies, returned in June 1605 with an additional 40 men. They spent the summer of 1605 searching for a better place to settle and selected a cove they named *Port Royal* (the future Annapolis Royal, Nova Scotia) on the Bay of Fundy. The men simply took apart the Sainte Croix settlement and rebuilt it in Port Royal. Only twelve men died that winter. Created in 1605, Port Royal is the second settlement in North America after St. Augustine that Europeans have continuously occupied since its foundation.[33]

De Monts, as de facto governor of the area, granted the *seigneurie* of Port-Royal with adjoining fishing rights and fur privileges to Poutrincourt.[34] In that system, the *seigneurs* were subjects of the King of France who awarded them plots of land in return for their promise to clear land, bring settlers, and provide military assistance in times of need.[35] The same kind of relation existed between the *seigneur* and his tenants, the habitants:

they paid rent and gave part of their harvest in exchange for the construction and main-tenance of a mill. The *seigneur* was also a judge.[36] In July 1606, a new group of colonists arrived. It included a Parisian apothecary, Louis Hébert (1575–1627)[37] and a lawyer, Marc Lescarbot (1570–1641).[38] A friend of Poutrincourt, Lescarbot staged the first play of the colony, which was published a *History of New France* in 1609, and gave Champlain the unofficial title of "royal cartographer."[39] Exploration continued in summer and fall. In an inlet of the Bay of Fundy, Champlain spotted seams of copper ore, and while no effort was made to mine it, the name stuck, "Les Mines," which gives its English name to the place, "Minas Basin." Winter passed more pleasantly than the previous year thanks to Cham-plain's establishment of *l'ordre de bon temps* [the Order of Good Cheer], a kind of social club focused on good food and drink.[40] But when de Monts lost his trading monopoly in spring 1607, as a result of other traders' complaints to the King, the entire colony was ordered back to France.

Du Gua de Monts left the settlement in the good care of a friend, Mi'kmaq chief Merbertou.[41] Although he continued to invest in colonization projects, de Monts never went back to New France. Poutrincourt returned to Port Royal in 1610 with three of his sons and Charles Saint-Etienne de La Tour (1593–1666) but British colonists from Vir-ginia destroyed the settlement in 1613. The Frenchmen left again except for one of the young Poutrincourts who remained with de La Tour to rebuild the settlement in a more secure location down river and to continue trading in fur. In 1613, de La Tour established a small trading post, Fort Pentagouet, to do business with the Penobscot Indians in what is now Castine, Maine. Samuel Argall immediately raided that settlement as well, but de la Tour rebuilt it. This was the first in long series of skirmishes for control over the border between New England and New France. Upon his death in 1623, Poutrincourt made de La Tour his heir. Charles de La Tour, who later served as governor of Acadia twice, lived the rest of his life and died in New France.[42]

Du Gua de Monts returned to France in September 1607 only to find out a few months later that the King had agreed to extend his trade monopoly for one more year. Pont Gravé and Champlain, each in command of a ship, were put in charge of the expedi-tion and weighed anchor in April 1608. In June, they reached Tadoussac where a skirmish ensued with a Basque captain who, in spite of the royal privilege for the fur trade held by de Monts, did not want to give up his business in the area. Pont Gravé was wounded but Champlain managed to calm things down, at least temporarily. His men loaded the equipment needed for the construction of shelters on two longboats and rowed down the St. Lawrence River to the Point of Quebec, a place Champlain had noticed earlier on and identified as propitious for a settlement. They immediately built a small stockade sur-rounded by a moat and three buildings and they planted a vegetable garden. These events mark the foundation of Quebec City.[43]

As Heinz Weinman points out, Quebec City, like Rome, has its foundational myth: in July 1608 Champlain was the target of an assassination attempt by Basques fishermen who were also after his possessions.[44] After one of the conspirators blew the whistle, how-ever, the main culprit was tried, found guilty, and put to death. The other three were sent to France for trial.[45] The winter of 1608–09 devastated the small colony: five of the 28 col-onists died of dysentery and ten more from scurvy. Unlike Cartier, Champlain did not know of the Indian remedy against scurvy, the anedda tea. But in the spring of 1609, he made friends with his Montagnais and Algonquins neighbors, and pledged to assist in their wars against the Iroquois (Mohawks) who lived south of the river. In mid–June,

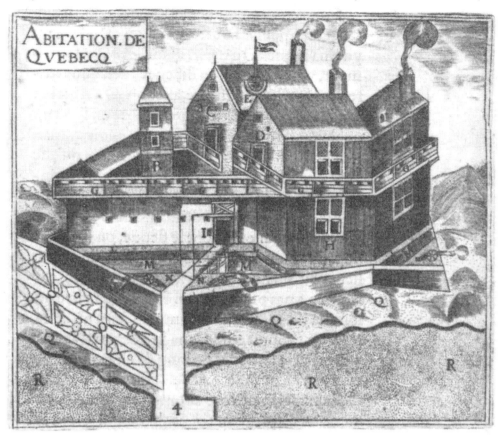

The settlement at Québec [*L'habitation de Québec*]. 1608 foundation of Quebec by Samuel Champlain (courtesy Library and Archives Canada).

therefore, he set off with nine men and over three hundred Native Americans, Algonquins, Montagnais, and Hurons,[46] who had also become the French's allies.[47] According to Champlain's own account, the goal of the expedition was the capture of an Iroquois fort but when rapids blocked the way, seven of the Frenchmen and a large number of native warriors turned around. Champlain continued on foot with two of his men and 60 Algonquins, taking advantage of this peaceful military campaign to map out the region. He was the first European to explore the shores of the lake that now bears his name, Lake Champlain, and to give French names to several rivers. He also learned native languages and consigned his observations on his allies' customs to his notebooks. Finally, at the end of July, the enemy was in sight. The Iroquois outnumbered the assailing party, but the French had (primitive) firearms, arquebuses, and won the battle easily against bows and arrows.

Champlain spent several weeks in Quebec City, handed over command of the settlement to a trusted settler, and then left for France with Pont Gravé. In October 1609, he dutifully reported to de Monts and to the King who turned down their request for a renewal of the royal privilege. The Duke of Sully (1560–1641), a French prime minister renowned for his economic savvy, thought that competition was more beneficial to trade than monopolies. De Monts and Champlain persisted in their endeavors nonetheless, forming a trading company with Rouen merchants.[48] Champlain then left Honfleur with Pont Gravé and a dozen craftsmen, arriving in Canada at the end of April 1610.

Once again, Champlain went to war against the Iroquois with his Native American allies in June and once again, in spite of an arrow wound, they won the battle.[49] In celebration of their victory, Champlain and the Algonquin Chief Iroket exchanged two young men: Marsolet went to live with the Algonquins and Savignon, Iroquet's son, with the French.[50] But bad news awaited Champlain upon his return to Quebec: the fur business was disastrous and the King of France, Henri IV, had been assassinated in May. His nine-year-old son, Louis XIII (1601–1643), was now officially king of France, which left the Queen Mother, Marie of Medici, in charge of the kingdom (Weber, 298–299). She would rule from 1610 to 1617, a period Yves-Marie Bercé, in *The Birth of Absolutism,* has characterized as "the most prosperous and brilliant of the early modern age" (43). Unfortunately, Marie of Medici seems to have had little interest in New France.

Champlain wasted no time. Leaving a crew of 16 men in Quebec, he sailed back to France in September so as to re-establish connections at court and garner support for the colony. He made friends with a wealthy commoner, Nicolas Boullé, a Secretary to the King's Chamber, who was interested in arranging a marriage for his daughter with a promising young man. Thus, forty-year-old Samuel and twelve-year-old Hélène (1598–1645) were married in December 1610. Having received her substantial dowry, Champlain then returned to Québec, per marriage contract without his wife—as he had agreed to wait two years to consummate the marriage.[51] In May 1611, following a harrowing crossing, Champlain was back at the Quebec settlement. He soon set out for the agreed upon gathering with the Algonquins, Montagnais, and Hurons. As he arrived early, he looked for a suitable place to establish another settlement and found one near Mont Royal, which he called Place Royale. He built a wall and planted a garden. A month later, he reconnected with Marsolet, who was traveling with the Algonquins. He now dressed like a Native and mastered their language. After exchanging gifts and collecting fur, the French agreed to come back the following year. One Frenchman left with the Hurons, another with the Algonquins. Champlain spent a few weeks in the settlement of Quebec before sailing back to France, leaving less than two dozen men to watch over the settlement.

As Du Gua de Monts's efforts to obtain a trade monopoly for New France remained fruitless, he had to dissolve the Rouen Company. Champlain then turned to his connections at court to try and get support for the colony. His ally this time was Charles de Bourbon, Count of Soissons (1566–1612), a cousin of Henri IV, who convinced young Louis XIII to grant him the fur trade monopoly for the St. Lawrence valley. In October 1612, the King appointed de Bourbon Lieutenant General of New France and granted him a privilege of twelve years for the fur trade. De Bourbon would never set foot in North America, nor would his successor, the Prince of Condé. So once appointed *lieutenant,* Champlain was the *de facto* governor of the colony. Before returning to the New World, he published an account of his voyages from 1604 to 1612.

In New France, Champlain was still expected to find the passage to India or China, which is why he set out to explore the Ottawa River valley upon his return to North America. Hoping to find the sea of the North (Hudson Bay), he trusted his Native American guide and interpreter who had assured him that he knew how to get there when in fact he did not. Disappointed, Champlain returned to Quebec City and soon left for

France again. Business kept him there until March 1615. During the months spent in France, he created the Company of Saint-Malo and Rouen Merchants and wrote about his latest explorations (Chaillet-Bert, 133). When he returned to Quebec the four Franciscan missionaries he had asked the King to provide were part of the journey and the first Catholic services were soon celebrated in New France.

In July 1615, Champlain tried again to reach the Hudson Bay but ended up by Lake Huron instead. He was wounded during a battle against Iroquois warriors but it was the last time he went to war for the First Nations. Forced to spend the winter in a Huron village, he gathered a wealth of information on Native American customs.[52] An incident Champlain described in his account of this trip, his getting lost in the woods for three days during a deer hunt, illustrates how dangerous and terrifying life in the New World could be in those days.[53] In late spring, the brave explorer returned to Quebec, made some improvement to the settlement, and sailed back to France where political strife divided the kingdom once again.

2. New France Under Louis XIII and Richelieu, 1617–1643

Led by the Queen Mother and a very young king, the monarchy's future was uncertain during the Regency.[54] On the one hand, some signs pointed to stabilization. The Parliament of Paris lent some support to the King by censoring a book on regicide in 1610, in effect condemning tyrannicide, a theory that had offered a convenient ethical justification in some quarters for Henri IV's assassination (Bercé, 32–34). Gallicanism also strengthened the monarchy by the weakening the ties between Rome and France, as this religious and political doctrine granted French bishops more autonomy from the Papacy in their dioceses (Bercé, 57). On the other hand, royal princes challenged Marie of Medici, which is why she sought the people's support and summoned the Estates General in 1614 (the last time prior to 1788) (Bercé, 43–63). In April 1617, Louis XIII staged a coup against in his mother. The young king disagreed with her pro–Spain policies—particularly after she made him marry a Habsburg princess, Ann of Austria, against his will in 1615. He had her main adviser, Concino Concini (1569–1617), murdered. Marie of Medici was put under house arrest at her castle at Blois, and unpopular ministers in the King's Council as well as prominent princes were arrested (Bercé, 70–79). Among them was Champlain's benefactor, the Prince of Condé, who had to spend two years in jail.

Champlain's position in 1617 was shaky at best. In fact, it corresponds to the description Yves-Marie Bercé provides of "the minister of the early modern period," a man whose "position depended entirely on the fragile and all too human friendship of the prince" (80). Champlain lost his title of lieutenant in 1617. Whether or not he went back to Quebec in 1617 is subject to debate. Louis Hébert, on the other hand, who had already stayed twice in Acadia, moved to the Quebec settlement with wife and children in 1617, making them the first French family to live off the land in Canada. As he obtained his land grant as early as 1623, he was also the first *seigneur* of the St. Lawrence valley and the first farmer (Havard and Vidal, *Histoire*, 415).[55] Champlain spent most of his time in France until May 1618, writing a memoir to the King and another to the Chamber of Commerce to try to garner support for the colony. Caught between associates who wanted to reap commercial profits but had little interest in supporting the colony and erratic royal policies that flip-flopped between monopoly and free trade, he spent a few difficult years.

In May 1620, however, Champlain's appointment as lieutenant of New France was confirmed and he left for his tenth voyage to the New World, taking along his young wife this time. He spent most of the next four years making administrative improvements and maintaining good relations with the First Nations. However, as Hélène had a hard time adjusting to the rough colonial life, the Champlains returned to France in August 1624. That same year, Armand Jean du Plessis de Richelieu, better known as Cardinal de Richelieu (1585–1642), became head of the King's Council,[56] and the close working relationship that existed between them strengthened the French monarchy (Bercé, 81–88). Royal power and authority also increased because the King relied on a small Assembly of *notables* instead of the Parliament of Paris, a move that considerably weakened that body.[57] Louis XIII's greatest accomplishment in those years was to bring peace to France by putting an end to the last French war of religion, to quash, in 1628, the armed Huguenot rebellion that had started in 1620 in La Rochelle (Bercé, 91–102).

As in previous religious conflicts, the war led some Huguenots to leave France and immigrate to Holland, Switzerland, and above all England. A case in point is Nicolas Martiau (1591–1657), a Huguenot from the Ile de Ré, near La Rochelle, who became a British subject in 1619 and married in England. A year later, the Martiau family lived in Jamestown, Virginia. Martiau is particularly well-suited to illustrate both the reality and the invisibility of the French element in American society. For who could recognize a French ancestry in American household names of actors and entertainers like Earl W. Bascom, Elizabeth Taylor, Elvis Presley, and Tom Cruise? Writers Harper Lee and Tennessee Williams? Generals like Thomas Nelson and Robert E. Lee? And yet, all are descendants of Nicolas Martiau, who is also George Washington's earliest immigrant forefather.[58]

While the defeated Huguenots were going over to the enemy, Richelieu made it his goal to establish France as a power broker in Europe. He decided to challenge Spain's aspiration towards universal dominion and to assert his nation's presence in the world. To that effect, he founded the first corps of French marines in 1622 (Balvay, *L'Epée*, 38) and did his best to improve France's position in the world of commerce. The Portuguese had started trading in India in 1498, when Vasco de Gama landed in Calicut, and established a colony on the western coast of India in the 16th century. The Dutch had done the same on the eastern coast. French explorers and pirates tried to follow suit but with little success: the Dutch destroyed their ships. In 1624, France and the United Provinces (Netherlands) signed a free-trade agreement for West and East India. As the British and the Dutch East India Companies already traded in Persia, Richelieu thought France should do the same. In 1628, he sent Pacifique de Provins (1588–1648), a Capuchin Father, to Persia to restart diplomatic relations between the two countries and establish a mission in Isfahan. But the land route to Asia remained dangerous in the 17th century because of rebellions in the Ottoman Empire. Between 1630 and 1642, therefore, the sea route was favored. These are the years when the French took possession of land and ports in Madagascar (Port-Dauphin) and the Mascarene Islands: Port-Louis on the Île de France (Mauritius); Saint-Denis, on the Île de Bourbon (Réunion). The *Company of the Orient* was created in 1642 to trade with the East Indies, that is Southern and Southeast Asia. It had a fifteen-year exclusive trading monopoly for Madagascar and the Mascarene islands (Howell, 93).

In 1629, Louis XIII signed a royal decree, *Code Michau*, that was the government's response to the people's complaints that had been recorded during the 1614 General Estates (Kadlec, 4). Written by a prominent jurist, Michel de Marillac (1553–1632), and a team of lawyers, *Code Michau* was "the monarchy's first attempt to achieve so many reforms in a single document" (Kadlec, 2): with its 561 articles touching upon as many topics, it was rightly perceived as an effort to "unify the kingdom's legislation" (Kadlec, 24)—and thus also to curtail local institutions' power. Article 383, which placed the entire kingdom under the direct, universal jurisdiction of the king, sought to replace the feudal adage "no land without lord, no lord without title." The other interesting articles of the Michau Code had to do with ways and means of encouraging trade. On the one hand, the Code allowed noblemen to engage in commercial activities *sans déroger* (without ceasing to belong to the nobility).[59] On the other hand, it rewarded commoners who had built a large ship and used it to trade for at least five years with titles of nobility. In effect, it made it easier to create trading companies like the English and the Dutch East India Companies. In theory at least.[60]

Two years earlier, in 1627, Richelieu had appointed Champlain governor of New France and created a new trading company, the *Compagnie des Cent-Associés*, which had a trading monopoly for New France.[61] According to its statutes, the company had broad jurisdiction over an immense territory. Its monopoly was granted in perpetuity for the fur trade and for fifteen years for other merchandise. In exchange of this generous package, the Company was to bring thousand Catholic settlers to New France. Its charter contained an interesting clause concerning France's early policies of cultural assimilation. It reads:

> Descendants of the French who will reside in the said country, *as well as the savages who will gain knowledge of the faith and adopt it as best they can,* will be considered French. If they come to France, they will enjoy the same privileges as those who were born there [quoted in Soyez, 119].

Converting natives was therefore a priority if they were to adopt the French way of life. In 1625, the first Jesuit missionaries arrived in New France.[62] The "annual reports" that they wrote from 1632 to 1673, *The Jesuit Relations*, remain up to this day one of the most important sources of knowledge about Native American languages and cultures. For as Havard and Vidal point out, it was most of the time the colonizers' job to learn the languages of the colonized because, initially at least, the Native Americans seldom felt inclined to learn French (*Histoire*, 321).

From the start, the *Compagnie des Cent-Associés* fared poorly (Havard et Vidal, *Histoire*, 86–88). As would happen again, and again, the Franco-British conflict in Europe carried over to the New World. Construction of the Quebec City ramparts began in 1620 but in July 1629, the Kirke brothers, French Huguenots working for the British,[63] laid siege and then attacked the city. They captured the French fleet and Richelieu's new trading company. Champlain had to surrender and the French to leave the colony—although some chose to go live with their Indian allies rather than surrender or go back to France. Champlain then spent several years as a prisoner in England writing new memoirs.

Once the 1632 Treaty of Saint-Germain-en-Laye put an end to the Franco-English war and New France was returned to the Crown, Champlain embarked on his 12th and last voyage to Canada, taking with him over two hundred colonists. He had a new stockade built in Trois-Rivières and the settlement at Quebec rebuilt. But his health was declining, and he died on Christmas day 1635. This was a momentous year: the year Richelieu created the French Academy, *l'Académie Française*, to rule on all matters pertaining to the French language; the year Richelieu convinced the king of France of the necessity to intervene in the Thirty Years' War, notwithstanding the facts that the wars of religion were over in France, that the queen of France, Ann of Austria, was a sister of the King of Spain; and that the queen of Spain, Elizabeth of France, a sister of the French King.[64]

The Royal government financed this war through huge tax increases (a 50 percent tax hike between 1626 and 1632) and a threefold increase again between 1632 and 1635. Royal civil servants, named *intendants*, were dispatched to the provinces to ensure control over the population.[65] They administered tax collection and justice and worked in collaboration with governors appointed by the King.[66] As a result, a centralized fiscal administration started to replace the old local collection agencies. From 1636 onward, peasants revolted frequently in light of the scale of fiscal demands and the brutal methods of recovery, such as armed taxed collectors (Bercé, 145–150). Another sure indication of the monarchy's slow move towards absolutism was the extraordinary military build-up that occurred during those years. The size of the royal armies went from 30,000 men in the 1620s to 100,000 men by 1634, and 200,000 men by 1640. They had reached 250,000 in 1643, the year Louis XIII died (Bercé, 140).[67]

Friendly relations with the First Nations (Mi'kmaq, Montagnais, Algonquins, and Hurons) had made the establishment of the French in the St. Lawrence valley and Acadia possible. Champlain never underestimated the importance of retaining their trust and friendship if colonization was to succeed. The Hurons, as the largest allied native confederacy and as the main providers of the furs that were sent to France, played a key role in the colony's economy: they did the bulk of the work. As a result, few French workers were needed which explains, in part, why the pace of French colonization was slow (Havard and Vidal, 80–86).[68]

Isaac de Razilly (1587–1635), whom Richelieu had charged with the task of colonizing Acadia, set out in 1632 for Canada with a group of 300 colonists, six missionaries, and lots of supplies.[69] Also part of the voyage were Charles de Menou d'Aulnay (1604–1650) and the Denys brothers, Simon and Nicolas (1598–1688), who wrote a history of Acadia. They chose to settle on the Atlantic coast where they built the village of La Hève, a fort, and a trading post. A farming community soon developed around the settlement and La Hève became a welcome port of call for European fishermen. Nicolas Denys engaged in the wood and fish business several miles away from the settlement.[70] Following Razilly's accidental death in 1635, d'Aulnay, who was married to the wealthy Jeanne Motin, ran the trading company they had founded. He also led the colony on behalf of the governor, another relative, who had remained in France. D'Aulnay relocated the Acadian capital from La Hève to Port Royal, where he built a new fort and brought more settlers. Under his leadership, land was reclaimed from the sea thanks to a system of dikes and drainage sluices (called *aboiteaux*) used in Western France in the *marais poitevin* to dry up tidal marshlands (Gregory Kennedy). According to some sources, the fact that farms were settled on new land may have sent a signal to the Mi'kmaq that the French were not there to steal their land and may therefore also explain why relations between the two nations were good.[71]

However, quarrels among the French leaders soon marred the early history of Acadia. When d'Aulnay forbade Nicolas Denys to export his goods, the latter left Acadia and returned to La Rochelle. While in France, he obtained a *seigneury* in Acadia in 1636 and got married in 1642. In 1641, he tried to have de La Tour arrested because his fur business cut into his own. In 1643, de La Tour retaliated by sending a group of English mercenaries to attack d'Aulnay's trading post and steal his goods, upon which, in 1645, d'Aulnay succeeded in taking over de La Tour's fort while the latter was away. Now in control of the entire Acadian area, D'Aulnay obtained the title of Lieutenant-General for Acadia as a reward for his development of the colony. In 1647, he took over a fishing and trading post Denys had established on Miscou Island. After his death in 1650, however, de La Tour was able to prove that d'Aulnay had wronged him and not only to reclaim his possessions but also to take over his enemy's governorship and even to marry his widow. Economic interest, however, had prompted this marriage as both husband and wife were the target of another player, Emmanuel Le Borgne, a wealthy merchant who had loaned d'Aulnay vast sums of money and was trying to recuperate his assets (Havard and Vidal, 90–91).

3. French Pioneers of Champlain's Period: Brûlé, Nicollet, De Quen, and Brébeuf

When the pace of immigration started to pick up, "a majority [of the French immigrants] came from the maritime provinces of Normandy, Britany, Anjou, Poitou, and Charente" (Royot, 18).[72] This was not the case for Etienne Brûlé, born in 1591 or 1592 near Paris.[73] He was 18 years old when he accompanied Champlain on one of his voyages and showed interest in living with Native Americans so as to learn their language and culture. After spending a year with the Montagnais, Brûlé often served as Champlain's guide and interpreter. He became a rugged frontiersman who loved adventure and freedom and adopted the native lifestyle. In fact, he spent most of his time in New France living with Native American tribes. He was the first European to venture on the Ottawa and Rideau Rivers and to see Chaudière Falls in 1610, the first to set foot in Ontario, Michigan, and Pennsylvania. He is the prototype of the *coureur des bois*, the "White Indian."[74] He thereby also exemplifies the French approach to early colonization identified by Ronald Creagh: "The beginnings of colonization offered a stark contrast between the Franco-Canadians, adventurous and dynamic, and the Anglo-Americans, rooted on the Atlantic Coast, from New England to Virginia, who look, on the whole, like sedentary farmers" (Creagh, *Nos Cousins d'Amérique*, 46).

Brûlé left no recollections of his own life, so everything we know about him comes from Champlain who, in his writings, accused him of disloyal competition for working with other fur traders than those he sanctioned. Like the Jesuits, he disapproved of Brûlé's adoption of Huron customs: "Brûlé is licentious and otherwise depraved, thus setting a bad example to the savages, for which he should be severely punished," he wrote. In the 1620s, Brûlé was ordered to spend a year in Québec where he taught native languages to the Jesuits. He was then sent back to Europe and prohibited from coming back to New France. In 1629, Brûlé took his revenge by going to England and offering his services to British. He served as a guide for the English expedition that took Quebec City in 1629. He returned to his previous life, was captured by the Iroquois, but escaped. The Hurons refused to believe his story: they stabbed him to death and ate him, sometime between 1630 and 1633 (See Edwards and Jurgens).

Jean Nicollet—also spelled Nicolet—(c. 1598–1642), Sieur de Belleborne, was a friend of Etienne Brûlé and Samuel Champlain.[75] A native of Cherbourg, Nicollet arrived in 1618 in Quebec City to train as an interpreter. As was customary, he underwent linguistic immersion, first among the Algonquins on Allumette Island on the Ottawa River, then with the Ottawa and Algonquin in the region of Lake Nipissing where he stayed for nine years. Thus began the long relationship between the French and the Anishinaabe nations of the Great Lakes, which included "the Ottawa, Potawatomi, Chippewa,[76] Algonquin, Nipissiing, and Mississauga" (McDonnell, 5).[77] He built and ran a trading post and lived with a Nipissing woman with whom he had a daughter, Madeleine. When his linguistic services were requested, he moved with his daughter to Quebec City and lived there until the 1629 capture of the city by the Kirke brothers. He was among the French who chose to live with the Hurons rather than go to France following the city's capture. Later, after the French reclaimed Quebec City, he explored Lake Michigan, Mackinac Island, and—although this is subject to more controversy—the *Baie des Puants* (Green Bay).[78] It is believed that he was the first European to set foot in what is now the state of Wisconsin.

The first missionaries arrived in New France during Champlains' tenure as governor and shortly thereafter. Among them was Jean de Quen (1603–1659) who came to New France as a Jesuit missionary in 1635. De Quen taught French and Native American boys in Quebec City, established a mission at Trois-Rivières, and moved to Tadoussac in 1642 to convert Montagnais. Although Europeans had been in the area for a long time, no one had explored the Saguenay River because of the Native Americans' reluctance to guide them. De Quen, however, was able to travel upriver with Indian guides, not as an explorer, but as priest seeking to help sick members of the nation of the Porcupine. In 1647, he was the first European to paddle across Lake Piékouagami which he renamed Lake Saint-Jean. He returned a few times to the land of the Porcupine and founded the mission of Métabetchouan on its bank in 1652.[79]

In the context of colonization, the significance of the grievances expressed by the French population at the time of the 1614 Estates General lie in the snapshot they provide of their fears and aspirations. They tell us, among other things, which kind of French people were attracted to the New World, namely the poor who could no longer deal with the tax burden, would-be farmers without land, and people with particularly strong religious convictions. The Catholic Counter-Reformation of the early 17th century reignited religious fervor in France.[80] St. Vincent de Paul (1581–1661) chose to dedicate his life to the poor. New religious orders, such as the Sulpicians (1641) appeared and existing congregations such as the Society of Jesus (founded in 1534 by Ignatius of Loyola) or the Discalced Carmelites (founded in 1562) experienced a wave of new vocations.[81]

Several such individuals with personal journeys steeped in mysticism came to the St. Lawrence valley where they endeavored to spread the Catholic faith among the aborigines.[82] Noël Brûlard de Sillery (1577–1640), a knight of Malta turned Catholic priest, established a settlement for Native American converts in 1637.[83] A nun, Marie Guyart (1599–1672) established the Ursuline order in 1636 in Quebec City and founded the first school for girls.[84] Then Jean-Jacques Olier de Verneuil and Jérôme le Royer de la Dauversière, two priests of the *Compagnie du Saint-Sacrement*, to which Molière's character Tartuffe supposedly belonged, created the Society of Our Lady of Montreal for the "conversion of the savages" in 1639 after experiencing the same mystic vision. Once they were granted a *seigneurie* on the Isle of Montreal, Paul de Chomedey, sieur de Maisonneuve, led the expedition that founded Ville-Marie (Montreal) in 1642.[85] Forty men, three of them with wives and children, accompanied him and together they built a compound large enough to house fifty people. However, as Iroquois trappers and their Dutch partners were already trading fur in the area, the missionaries' presence may have been a factor in the start of the Iroquois wars.[86]

These religious settlers were in many ways similar to the Native Americans they set out to convert. As Leslie Choquette has pointed out, some believed in sea monsters and all went to the New World to reclaim it from the claws of the devil. In France, witches and werewolves peopled the popular imagination. Beggars suspected of kidnapping children, women said to cast spells on neighbors, all of them filled villagers with fear at a time when such accusations still led to trials that could end up deadly.[87] For the deeply religious, the challenge of converting pagans and the risks incurred in the process only heightened the glory of the task. They were ready to sacrifice their lives for a divine cause.

Jean de Brébeuf was one of those people. Born in Normandy in 1593, he was ordained as a Jesuit priest in 1617.[88] Although he suffered from tuberculosis, he asked to go to New France on a mission and his wish was granted. He arrived in Quebec in 1625 with the first group of Jesuit missionaries. Brébeuf wrote most of what we know about him. After traveling 800 miles from Quebec City via the Ottawa River, he spent four years (1625–1629) with the Hurons, learning their ways and language. When Quebec City fell to the British, Brébeuf returned to France where he spent the next five years but he returned to New France in 1634, determined to pick up where he had left. After an initial resistance on the part of the Hurons, he was invited back. Initially, he was not successful as a missionary: his first conversions took place in 1635. His job was not an easy one as he was blamed for bad harvests, defeats in battle, and epidemics. Father Jérôme Lalemant took over his mission in 1638. In 1640, Brébeuf and another missionary, Chomonot, tried to evangelize the *Neutres* (Neutral People or Attawandaron) of the shores of Lake Erie. They failed. Brébeuf went back to Quebec City where he lived from 1641 to 1644. He spent three more years with the Hurons (1644–1647) and finally met with success when thousands converted. And so it came to pass that the Hurons became a nation divided between a traditionalist majority and a Christian minority. In 1648 and 1649, the Iroquois attacked the Hurons villages and the mission. Brébeuf was tortured and put to death. He was canonized in 1930 with seven other missionaries, known as the North American Martyrs.[89]

4. Settling in the West Indies

Much of what we know about the early French settlements in the Caribbean come from the history of the French Indies written by Jean-Baptiste du Tertre (1610–1687) in the 1660s.[90] In spite of repeated failures in the 16th century, South America continued to exert a strong attraction on explorers. So full of promise seemed this land, that the Spaniards, the Dutch, the French, and the British fought over the region for a century. A few French sailors settled around Cayenne as early as 1503 but the first real French colony in Guyana appeared a century later. In 1604, Daniel de la Touche de La Revardière, a captain in the French navy of Huguenot persuasion left from Saint-Malo, Brittany, to explore the northern coast of Brazil.[91] Accompanying him on this journey was Jean Mocquet, a world traveler and king's apothecary, whose role on the expedition was to gather "rarities" for the royal collections. Two ship owners, Jacques Ruffault et Charles des Vaux, established a colony they called Equinoctial France. The settlement did not last due to hostility on the part of the Natives and to tropical diseases. Upon their return to France, they introduced two Tupinamba Indians to King Henri IV who appointed de la Touche "Lieutenant General of all lands situated between the Amazon and the Orinoco Rivers."[92] The third attempt, in the 1620s, finally succeeded and ships of colonists were sent to Guyana, 300 men in 1643 and 1200 in 1664 once the equatorial colony came under control of the Company of the West Indies (Devèze, 122–127).

Success came a bit faster for French settlers of the Caribbean islands. In 1625, Pierre Belain d'Esnambuc (1585–1636), a French privateer from Normandy, took possession of Saint-Christophe (Saint-Kitts) in spite of the presence of a two-year-old British colony.[93] He also founded the Saint-Kitts Isles Company (*la compagnie des îles de Saint-Christophe*). The French and the British would fight over the island and split its possession for over a century. With Richelieu's blessings, the colonial project became more ambitious in 1626.[94] Belain d'Esnambuc was appointed governor of St. Kitts and received permission to colonize all Caribbean islands that were not already occupied by Christians. According to Blackburn, "[t]he success of the St. Christopher Company prompted incorporation into a wider entity, the Company of the Isles of America, which initiated the settlement of the neighboring islands" (281). Within a period of ten years, d'Esnambuc and his second in command, Charles Liénard, sieur de L'Olive (c. 1601–1643), had established new colonies on Tortuga, Martinique, and Guadeloupe.[95]

French *boucaniers* (buccaneers)[96] started using the *île de la tortue* (Tortuga) as their base of operations in the Caribbean around 1625. The Spaniards repeatedly tried to chase them and to destroy their settlements but to no avail. In 1629, d'Esnambuc established a small colony on the island: it later became the springboard for the colonization of Saint-Domingue (Santo Domingo/ Hispaniola). In 1640, a navy officer, François Levasseur, took official possession of the island on behalf of the King of France. Appointed governor following his successful campaign, he made it his mission to rule as he saw fit. A Huguenot himself, he forbade the celebration of Catholic services and had a prison nicknamed "Purgatory" to mock Catholic "superstitions." He also tried to root out *matelotage* (homosexuality)[97] among the pirates and buccaneers by bringing hundreds of French women to the island. He died in 1652, murdered by two of his officers. In 1655, the British claimed Tortuga but they appointed a Frenchman, Jérémie Deschamps, as the colony's governor in 1660. Deschamps promptly claimed Tortuga for France.

Martinique was discovered by Christopher Colombus during his fourth voyage (1502). The island was already occupied by the Carib people who did not welcome Europeans. Over the course of the 16th century, Martinique was visited by French, Dutch, and British sailors in search of fresh water. A few of them also traded with the Caribs. In 1635, d'Esnambuc landed in the bay of Saint-Pierre with a hundred men after being chased from St. Kitts. He built Fort Saint-Pierre and established the first colony on behalf of the French Crown and the Company of the Isles of America. When he died in 1636, his nephew Jacques Dyel du Parquet (1606–1658) took over as governor of the island and director of the trading company. Du Parquet was governor of Martinique for ten years.[98] As in New France, there was a distinction between the honorific title of Lieutenant General of the French Isles, in effect a Vice-Roy, and the various governors of specific islands. Philippe de Longvilliers, Seigneur de Poincy (1584–1660) was Lieutenant General from 1639 to 1660 and lived on St. Kitts (Butel, *Histoire des Antilles*, 39–50).

Christopher Columbus discovered the island of Guadeloupe and gave it its name: Santa Maria de Guadalupe[99] (Heuman, 1–3). The Spaniards found no gold and the population being hostile, they left. They abandoned the Lesser Antilles[100] to the French, British, and to the buccaneers. The first French colony on Guadeloupe was founded in Sainte Rose by Jean du Plessis d'Ossonville, a distant relative of Richelieu, a few months before his death in 1635. Charles Liénard de l'Olive, who worked for the Company of the Isles of America, became governor of the colony and held the title for five years.[101] As the French stole land, food, and women from the Carib people, they met with resistance. War raged between 1636 and 1639: there were few French casualties, but the Caribs were crushed (Devèze, 148–149).[102] The few who escaped massacre fled to the south of the island and signed a peace treaty with the French in 1641. In 1643, the French founded the city of Basse-Terre in the southern part of the island. In 1648, the Company of the Isles of America went bankrupt.[103] Charles Houël du Petit Pré (1616–1682), the governor of Guadeloupe from 1643 to 1664, obtained a trade monopoly for the surrounding islands, Desirade, Marie-Galante and Les Saintes, as well.

It is interesting to note that several French colonizers of America, Villegaignon, de Chaste, de Montmagny,[104] and de Poincy, belonged a Roman Catholic military order, the Order of Knights of the Hospital of Saint John of Jerusalem (*l'Ordre de Saint-Jean de Jérusalem*) that dated back to the Crusades. Like the Chivalry in general, the order had fallen on hard times and survived in the 15th and 16th centuries by fighting the Muslim Barbary Pirates in the Mediterranean from strongholds of Rhodes and Malta. Increasingly, however, they had given up some of their autonomy and agreed to serve in foreign navies, the French navy in particular. As governors or lieutenant generals, they were the representatives of the King of France, not of their order. But they tended to act increasingly on their own behalf in the West Indies.

De Poincy is a case in point. Not only did he treat St. Kitts as his own property, he also took important decisions without consulting the Company of the Isles of America or the King of France (Butel, *Histoire*, 47). When he was fired in 1645, he prevented the new governor, Thoisy, from taking over. Instead, he had him arrested and sent back to France in 1647 (Butel, *Histoire*, 45). He had to pay a fine for his bad deeds but he remained on St. Kitts and continued to establish colonies on the Caribbean islands of St. Barts, St. Martin (1648) and St. Croix, one of the Virgin Islands (1650). When the Company of the Isles of America went bankrupt, de Poincy convinced the Grand Master of the Order of Saint John of Jerusalem to purchase these islands from the King of France. As a result, the Order of the Knights of Jerusalem managed these colonies for the following 14 years.

The French used their Caribbean colonies to grow manioc, potatoes, tobacco, indigo during the first decades of their existence and later cocoa and cotton.[105] Tobacco, which was gaining in popularity in Europe, soon became such a favorite crop that Richelieu introduced a tax on tobacco sales in 1629.[106] Indentured servants, some of them Huguenots, provided the labor force and "were required to do the most demanding tasks on plantations" (Heuman, 10). Young, unskilled laborers [*les engagés*] worked for three to seven years in exchange for passage, food, lodging during their indenture. In the 1630s, the indentured servants were primarily Irish on Barbados, but the first group of 550 indentured servants who grew tobacco in Guadeloupe came from France (Butel, *Histoire*, 35). Soon so much tobacco was being produced that by the end of the 1630s the market flooded. The price of tobacco fell so low that the British and French governors of St. Kitts ordered existing stocks destroyed (Heuman, 10). They also placed an 18-month long moratorium on tobacco cultivation.[107] Meanwhile, the Pope forbade its consumption under penalty of excommunication in 1642 and sugar hit all-time highs.

In the 17th century, most plantation owners thought that slaves were a more reliable labor force than indentured servants and that they were better suited for the labor-intensive cultivation and production of sugar (Blackburn, 286). French merchants considered themselves at a competitive disadvantage in that regard because France prohibited the slave trade since the 1630s. A French captain who requested authorization to transport slaves to Martinique in 1638, for instance, saw his request denied. The Dutch, by contrast, practiced the slave trade between Angola and Brazil and relied on slaves for their labor force. Slavery was nothing new.[108] The Portuguese practiced the slave trade as early as 1441. The Spaniards introduced slaves from the kingdom of Dahomey on Hispaniola in 1507 and Cuba in 1513.[109] The Dutch had been growing sugar cane successfully in plantations of Northeast Brazil since the 1620s. The British started growing sugar cane on Barbados in 1640. The French wanted to do the same on Martinique but in the absence of slaves on the island, French agricultural products were more expensive and could not compete with Dutch and British goods.

How profitable were the French isles in those days? In Martinique, the first sugar mill appeared in 1640 and the first slaves a year later. The French had gone through the Dutch, who held the monopoly on the trade during the first half of the 17th century, to purchase them (Blackburn, 282). Charles Houël, the governor of Guadeloupe, also went through the Dutch in order to bend the law, i.e., to import slaves and to export sugar. He even went further when, in 1654, he invited the Dutch, who had just lost their Brazil colony to the Portuguese, to settle on Guadeloupe. At that time, 80 percent of the population of Guadeloupe was of European origin and two thirds were indentured servants. But thanks to the Dutch, Houël gained direct access to the slave trade, and as a result, there were already 3,000 slaves in Guadeloupe two years later. However, French sugar production did not take off until the second half of the 17th century when another drop in the price of tobacco, due to overproduction, made sugar cane a more attractive crop again.[110]

In this chapter, we traced the rise of the first French colonial empire[111] that is the first phase of colonization in the early 17th century in Acadia, down the St. Lawrence River Valley, on Native American lands further West, and finally in the Caribbean. Louise P. Kellogg rightly credits Champlain for his achievements as an explorer: "What earlier explorers had not succeeded in doing, Samuel de Champlain accomplished—the discovery of the sources of the St. Lawrence and the exploration of the Great Lakes of North America" (43). "With Champlain," she adds, "the period of conjecture ends, and that of careful, scientific exploration begins" (43). Particularly in these early days, French settlement depended on the good-will of the First Nations who already lived in those areas, as Champlain and explorers like Brûlé, Nicollet, or missionaries like De Quen and Brébeuf recognized.[112] But with the consolidation of the French monarchy during the first half of the 17th century, colonization became a more ambitious and systematic endeavor as both Louis XIII and Richelieu sought to challenge the dominance of Spain in Europe and beyond. Therefore, from the 1620s onward, they also encouraged, and partly subsidized, colonization efforts in the Caribbean islands as well as in North America.[113]

Richelieu died in 1642 and Louis XIII a year later. Since his son, Louis XIV, was only five years old at that point, the Queen of France, Ann of Austria, ruled as a regent for almost ten years. With the assistance of another Cardinal as Prime Minister, Jules Mazarin (1602–1661), she was able to bring "the overweening nobles and ambitious magistrates to heel" by 1653 (Weber, 276).[114] Moreover, Mazarin scored a significant diplomatic coup when he succeeded in ending the war between France and Spain that had gone on since 1635. The 1659 Treaty of the Pyrenees that concluded hostilities and the 1660 marriage of Louis XIV and Maria Teresa, daughter of the King of Spain Philip IV, sealed the peace between the two nations, temporarily at least.[115] It also effectively ended the Spanish Golden Age. Until then, the house of Habsburg that ruled Spain and Austria had been the European powerhouse. France was to replace it in the following decades.

5. *Tips for Further Investigations*

Interesting People to Look up

Henri Membertou (1507–1611)
Aymar de Clermont-Chaste (1514–1603)
Troïlus de La Roche-Mesgouez (1536–1606)
Pierre de Chauvin de Tonnetuit (1550–1603)
Jean de Biencourt de Poutrincourt et de Saint-Just (1557–1615)
Pierre du Gua de Monts (or de Mons) (1558–1628)
François Gravé du Pont (or Pontgravé) (1560–1629)
Samuel de Champlain (1567–1635)
Marc Lescarbot (c. 1570–1641)

Related Primary Texts

Champlain, Samuel. *Voyages of Sieur de Champlain to New France, Made in the Year 1615.*
Denys, Nicolas. *Description and Natural History of the Coasts of North America* (1632–1670).
Raynal, Abbé. "Involvement of the French in the wars of the Indians. Lack of success of the colony," in *A History of the Two Indies*, ed. P. Jimack, 212–216.
Raynal, Abbé. "Misguided French plans for the settling Guiana and their disastrous execution," in *A History of the Two Indies*, ed. P. Jimack, 173–176.
Related Films or Works of Fiction
Black Robe (Bruce Beresford, 1991). Based on a 1984 historical novel by Brian Moore and set in 1634 New France.
Québec 1603–Samuel de Champlain (Denys Arcand, 1964).

French America, 1661–1683

At no time in the history of the first French colonial empire did a king exert as much control over the colonies as Louis XIV did during his reign.[1] One may divide his personal reign, which started at Mazarin's death in 1661, into two phases: a period during which the King still listened to a few advisers (1661–1683) and a period when, following the move of the government to the renovated palace of Versailles in 1682, he ruled as an absolute monarch.[2] Chapter III centers on the former, chapter IV on the latter. In 1661, France was already a powerful European nation in terms of population size, wealth, and military strength. The two first decades of Louis XIV's reign, however, correspond to a period of "French hegemony," when "France dominated Europe more completely than any single power since Rome" (Weber, 276). Eugen Weber, who is not a great fan of the French king,[3] characterizes the kingdom of France Louis XIV inherited in 1661 the following way:

> [a]n extensive kingdom, committed by long historical evolution to a strong crown, proud and contentious nobles, an enterprising, legalistic middle class; a power which expanded on lines its predecessors had laid down, whose wealth came largely from the land, whose force rested on her armies, not her fleets [294].

In this chapter, we briefly examine the Sun King's government and his policies during the first part of his reign in section 1, "Absolutism in the Making." Section 2, "Colonial Policies Under Louis XIV," deals with mercantilism, the organization of oversea trade and with France's colonial policies. Section 3, "New France Under Colbert," assesses the impact of these policies on New France. In section 4, "Exploring North America," the focus is on further expeditions that took place between 1661 and 1683, and, in particular, on the discovery, for the French at least since Native Americans lived on its shores, of the mighty Mississippi River.

1. Absolutism in the Making

From the start of his reign, Louis XIV decided to do without a prime minister, he "resolved to be his own prime minister, alone to know all the secrets and hold all the strings of power" (Weber, 237). Equipped with the necessary self-discipline and work habits to do the job, this "energetic and industrious man" (Weber, 300) ruled with a small Council of ministers, each selected for their knowledge and abilities in their area of expertise. Chancellor Michel Le Tellier (1603–1685) was in charge of war and military matters from 1643 to his death.[4] Jean-Baptiste Colbert (1619–1683) became Secretary of State for the Navy in 1663, a position that covered the French overseas colonies.[5] He added two portfolios in 1665, economy and finances, and kept all three until death in 1683. In order to retain absolute control, the King did not hesitate to create rivalries among his ministers or to have opponents arrested without any due process through *lettres de cachet*.[6] Whether he truly declared that he was the state or not (*L'état, c'est moi*), he certainly acted in that way. "State power under Louis would achieve a hitherto unknown amount of control over three critical administrative functions: use of armed force, formulation and execution of laws, and collection and expenditure of revenue" (Haine, 56).[7]

Old traditional institutions like the *Estates General* or the Parliaments stopped being consulted and lost their relevance. Several new "law and order" institutions were created. In addition to the General Hospital (*l'hôpital général*) that had opened in Paris to house the homeless, beggars, and prostitutes in 1656,[8] another new institution, the police, now had the task of rounding up all these vagrants, many of them soon bound for New France. The new Parisian police force was responsible for public order, including orderly conduct. In the capital, the chief of police also had wide attributions related to public safety[9]: the cleaning and lighting of the streets as well as the capital's food supply, all in the interest of preventing unrest and riots. In the provinces, a mounted police force, the *maréchaussée*, was ready to intervene at the slightest sign of peasant rebellion (Haine, 57). In an effort to ensure that his decisions would be enforced, Louis XIV created an administration composed of appointed personnel, commissioners and intendants, who did not purchase their office, as had been done in the past, but were appointed instead by the King and served at his pleasure. The duty of these civil servants was to apply economic and fiscal policies and to carry out justice.[10]

Louis XIV was ambitious: his goal was to make France a superpower in Europe and the world. To that effect, he waged war six times during his reign and fought on the battlefield himself in the Netherlands (1672–1678) and Prussia (1684–1697).[11] As commander-in-chief of the Armed Forces, the King presided over the formation of a permanent, "increasingly efficient army, created, maintained, improved according to Louis's will by the men who served him, no longer drawn from the rebellion-prone older nobility but from the bourgeoisie, their fortune focused wholly on the king's command" (Weber, 237). Barracks and hospitals were built for the soldiers, including the *Hôtel des Invalides* in Paris, conceived as a hospital and retirement home for the wounded.[12] Like his father, the King worried about France's porous borders, encircled as the kingdom was by the Habsburgs. To mitigate border security issues, military engineer Sébastien Le Prestre de Vauban (1633–1707) designed and built the star-shaped fortifications he is famous for all along France's borders (Weber, 338). Although France still lagged behind in terms of fleet, she made significant investments in its naval forces, with the development of royal arsenals in strategic harbors such as Dunkirk, Le Havre, Brest, Lorient, Rochefort, Marseille, Toulon, and the construction of war ships (Acerra and Meyer, 44–48).

If one aspect of Louis XIV's approach to power was the importance he granted to control and repression, the other side of the coin was his politics of charm and representation. Despite his martial frame of mind, Louis XIV believed in diplomacy when it came to international relations. His reign marks the birth of the French diplomatic corps, and the era when French became the language of diplomacy.[13] Staging the glory of France through the arts, having his court serve as the avant-garde of European taste and fashion were some of the strategic weapons the King used to underscore France's prominence in Western Europe. He built on Richelieu's and his father's legacy in the area of linguistic and cultural policies, continuing to view the French language and literature as national resources and creating institutions for their preservation.[14] Already before Versailles, "[a]t Louis XIV's estate of Marly, [...] the whole design reminded the beholder of the role the monarch was supposed to play. [...] Louis XIV dwelt in the center, in a pavilion decorated with solar symbols and dedicated to Jupiter, king of the gods" (Weber, 239).

Wars and the politics of prestige cost money and, as usual, the state coffers were not as full as they needed to be. It was Colbert's role, as finance minister, to find new sources of revenue. During the first part of Louis XIV's personal reign, Colbert oversaw efforts that aimed at unifying the kingdom, in terms of fiscal legislation.[15] As he understood the importance of possessing accurate information, he made an inventory of national resources that touched upon demography, defense, economy, society, religion and revenue. Thus, for instance:

> Colbert discovered on taking office that only 25 percent of the tax money actually reached the royal treasury; the other 75 percent disappeared into the pockets of tax farmers and corrupt officials or were swallowed up in interest payments on the royal debt. Colbert clamped down on the tax farmers and repudiated part of the debt. At the time of his death in 1683, the crown was collecting 80 percent of the tax revenue raised [Haine, 60].

The fiscal reforms Colbert introduced included a 15 percent decrease of the direct tax (the *taille*), the imposition of new sales taxes, as well as the search for fake noblemen who had to pay high fees for pretending to be what they were not. As a result, "the royal revenues increased throughout the 1660s" (Weber, 300). And yet, according to Weber, the tools available to run the French state smoothly were still insufficient to overcome "interference and local control" (Weber, 233).[16]

2. Colonial Policies Under Louis XIV

The dominant economic theory in Europe in the 17th and 18th centuries was mercantilism, a system, or rather, according to Eugen Weber, "a weapon," that originated in the need of each state to "develop and marshal its resources, attempting to become self-sufficient, especially in the sinews of war" (Weber, 145). Wealth, in other words, was understood as limited and national strength as residing in manufacturing and commercial independence from other nations. Mercantilism, which can therefore be defined as an "economic nationalism" (Weber, 146), calls for state intervention in manufacturing and trade and for protectionism, i.e., high duties on foreign goods or even their outright banning. From a mercantilist point of view, a nation's trade balance serves as the main indicator of its prosperity. Not surprisingly, this economic approach fitted perfectly with colonial expansion.[17] For advocates of mercantilism, the importance of oversea colonies was obvious: they were supposed to provide what the home country lacked in terms of raw materials and agricultural products.[18] In the perfect mercantilist world envisioned by economists at the time trade was to take place exclusively between the home country and its colonies.

All great projects Colbert undertook reveal the state's firm grip on the kingdom's affairs. "It was in France that state intervention went furthest, in a policy often connected with Colbert who said, 'Commercial companies are the armies of the king, manufactures his reserves'" (quoted in Weber, 337). Colbert, who fought laziness, unemployment, and French merchants' "lack of enterprise" (Weber 337), encouraged manufacturing, from the French word *manufactures* (state-owned factories), for the large-scale production of luxury goods (mirrors, tapestries, silk stockings, soap, linen, among others) as well as weapons. In order to improve transport and communications and to boost domestic trade, he had new roads and waterways built across France (Haine, 61–62).[19]

By the 17th century, the riches uncovered by exploration and produced by colonization were the object of intense commercial competition among European nations.[20] By mid-century, the Dutch had replaced the Spaniards as the dominant world power and the Dutch East and West India Companies (1602) served as models for many other national companies. The United Provinces of the Netherlands were enjoying their "Golden Century." They formed the wealthiest European nation thanks to their formidable fleet, their presence in all corners of the world, and their dominant commercial position. England and France were envious and determined to carve out their own piece of the pie. During the second half of the 17th century alone, England went to war against the Netherlands three times, starting in 1652 under Oliver Cromwell (1599–1658). Uncharacteristically, France would even side with England for two years during the third Anglo-Dutch (1672–74) war.[21]

In order to compete with the Dutch, Colbert created two state-owned trading companies in 1664, both with broad powers and similar charters, the *Compagnie française des Indes occidentales* (the French West Indies, or West India, Company) and the *Compagnie française des Indes orientales* (the French East Indies, or East India, Company).[22] According to its charter, the East India Company's mission was to "navigate and transact from the Cape of Good Hope to all the seas of the Orient and India." Its statutes as a company were that of a Royal Manufacture. It was endowed with a capital of 8.8 million pound and a fifty-year trade monopoly. It was tax exempt and backed by the Royal Treasury. Naming ambassadors, declaring war, and signing treaties were some of its powerful attributions.[23] Its headquarters were in Lorient, Brittany, a port, shipyard, and city created *ex nihilo* as a base for the company.[24] The French had a lot of catching up to do: "In 1664, Colbert estimated that out of the total of 20,000 ships that made out the European merchant fleet, 16,000 belonged to the Dutch, and 500 to 600 only to the French" (Devèze, 195).[25]

The French East India Company created settlements in India: Surat in 1668; Chandernagore (Chandannagar) in 1673; and Pondichéry (Puducherry) in 1674 (Nowell, 93–94). In the 17th century, Siam, the most powerful kingdom between India and China, fascinated Westerners with its refined culture and its religious tolerance. In 1680, as France was establishing diplomatic relations with King Phra Naraï (1633–1688), it sent a magnificent ship, the *Soleil de l'Orient* (*Sun of the Orient*) to Siam loaded with royal presents. Built in Lorient in 1671 and designed for long-distance trade with the far east, the ship, one of the largest galleons ever built at the time, was equipped with 60 cannons, and had a crew of 300. The King of Siam reciprocated, sending a team of ambassadors and a real treasure onboard The *Sun of the Orient* when it departed Bantam, Java, in 1681. Unfortunately, it was last seen off the coast of Madagascar and never made it back to port. Neither the ship nor the Siamese treasure were ever found. Already hurt by the Franco-Dutch war of 1672–78, the East India Company suffered from the loss of its most precious ship.[26] Then, in 1682, its trade monopoly was revoked and pirates in the Indian Ocean (the "Pirate Round") added to its distress at the turn of the century. Nonetheless, Siamese ambassadors visited France in 1684 and 1686 and Louis XIV did his best to impress his visitors with receptions and feasts organized at Versailles during their visit. Unfortunately, King Phra Naraï was overthrown in 1688.

Sailing the Atlantic Ocean was the fleet of the West Indies Company, the trading company that absorbed both the Company of the One Hundred Associates and the Company of the Inhabitants that had replaced it in 1648. To bring the West Indies Company into existence, Colbert also revoked the trade privilege granted to Houël du Petit Pré for Guadeloupe and to Jacques Dyel du Parquet in Martinique.[27] Governor Jérémie Deschamps sold the island of Tortuga to the West Indies Company. As for the other isles, those de Poincy had purchased on behalf of the Order of the Knights of Jerusalem, their mortgage was yet not paid in full when de Poincy passed away in 1660. Colbert seized the opportunity and in 1665 gave control of these islands to the West Indies Company, which also took over the western portion of Hispaniola, French Saint-Domingue (Haiti). In the end, the West Indies Company controlled all of France's American possessions and held a monopoly on trade with New France, the Caribbean Islands, and Guyana that was supposed to last for decades. Headquartered in Le Havre, it was so wealthy that it was able to equip 45 ships in a few months. In return for these tremendous privileges, it had to use its profits from the tobacco and sugar trade to populate New France.[28]

Louis XIV and Colbert did not see eye to eye on trade policies. The Company of the West Indies focused on tobacco; Louis XIV thought that France ought to produce more sugar.[29] Colbert believed in mercantilism, the King favored free trade. In 1666, two years only after the creation of the West Indies Company, the King decreed freedom of trade for French merchants and gave them access to all Caribbean islands (1670). As a result, the French West Indies Company started to lose ground and Colbert himself, according to Stewart Mims, "realized that the instrument he had chosen in 1664 to carry out his plan for establishing commerce with the West Indies was no longer suited to that end in 1671" (164). The Franco-Dutch war that started in 1672 added to the Company of the West Indies' woes so that by 1674, it was insolvent.[30] Louis XIV then revoked its trading privilege and replaced it with two new tax farms.[31]

"Tax farming" was an ancient method of tax collection that consisted in having the king sell the right to collect tax revenue to a "farmer" (tax collector) for a fixed, agreed-upon sum.[32] As the revenue collected always exceeded payment to the royal authority, tax-farmers could become immensely rich. Historically, there were three major tax farms in France, the *gabelle* (tax on salt); *l'octroi de Paris*, an excise duty on certain goods, such as oil, sugar, wine, upon entry in Paris; and customs duties between provinces. One of the two new farms added in 1674, the tobacco farm (*ferme du tabac*), granted exclusive rights on tobacco sales; the other, the Domain of the West (*domaine d'occident*), granted exclusive rights to collect a 3 percent tax on all goods of American origin, both New France and the Caribbean, as well as duties on seigneurial royalties and on some estates.[33] In 1675, the latter, which also included the fur trade around Tadoussac, went to Jean Oudiette,[34] as representative of an association of wealthy merchants for the yearly amount of 350,000 *livres* a year (about half a million dollars). From then on, it became illegal for the inhabitants of New France to engage in the fur trade without a license in order to let the tax-farmer enjoy the fruits of his privilege. In this case, the person to whom the farmer had sub-leased its fur trade monopoly was Charles Aubert de La Chesnaye (1632–1702), the wealthiest man in New France.[35]

In 1674, Louis XIV briefly awarded the *ferme du tabac* to the governess of his children, his mistress, and future wife, Françoise d'Aubigné (1635–1719), who had spent part of her youth in Martinique. She cashed in her privilege and used the proceeds to purchase the castle and title of de Maintenon. The buyer was also Jean Oudiette. By that time, Saint-Domingue had become a major producer of tobacco. In the 1660s, the governor of Tortuga, Bertrand d'Ogeron de La Bouëre (1613–1673), had encouraged buccaneers to settle and grow tobacco on Saint-Domingue.[36] Colonization began in earnest when d'Ogeron brought over hundreds of indentured servants, usually with three-year contracts, from France. Plantations of tobacco, indigo, cotton, and cacao multiplied and new settlements were established along the northern coast of Saint-Domingue in the 1670s. Founded in 1665, Port-de Paix became Saint-Domingue's colonial capital in 1676.[37] The island's population grew rapidly: 1,500 inhabitants in 1669, mostly indentured servants; 4,500 in 1677, due in part to the influx of small tobacco planters chased from Martinique and Guadeloupe.[38] At that point the island still served as a base for buccaneers but most of them would be chased away in the 1680s.[39]

The merchants focused on the short term: they purchased tobacco from the Saint-Domingue growers at a very low price, ruining many buccaneers in the process, and sold it at such a prohibitive price in France that within a few years tobacco consumption was halved. This short-sightedness led to competition and contraband and as a result most of the tobacco sold in France in the last quarter of the 17th century came from Virginia instead of the French West Indies.[40] But the most lucrative crop was sugar and its cultivation was encouraged in all French Caribbean islands.[41] To really make money in the sugar trade, however, plantation owners needed cheaper labor than indentured servants, and so they asked the Company of the West Indies to bring more slaves to the French Caribbean islands.[42] But this was easier said than done as the Dutch alone were entitled to purchase slaves on the coast of Africa, on behalf of Spain (Devèze, 155–156).

Colbert did not want any open confrontation with the Dutch economic powerhouse, so France initially limited itself to establishing diplomatic relations with a few African rulers. But already as the Franco-Dutch war was brewing in 1670–71, the plan was to take over Dutch settlements, albeit a bit later. As France had a hard time defending its Caribbean colonies during the war with the Netherlands,[43] Louis XIV took a drastic measure to ensure success: he placed Guadeloupe and Martinique under his direct control. The King was not opposed to slavery.[44] In 1672, his cousin James, Duke of York,[45] set up the Royal African Company for the purpose of trading in gold, silver, and slaves. In 1673, Louis XIV established the *Compagnie du Sénégal* for the same purpose. The Company of Senegal had no trading monopoly. French merchants were thus encouraged to participate in the triangular trade especially after the Truce of Ratisbon with Spain (1684) considerably reduced piracy in the Caribbean. A "new colonial age" (Butel, 51) thus began for the French Caribbean.

3. New France Under Colbert[46]

Louis XIV's personal reign inaugurated a period of direct state intervention in New France. In 1663, the colony became a French province, a decision that had important consequences in terms of demography, financial support, and defense.[47] "From 1669 onward, the French colonies were placed under the authority of the *ministère de la marine* (Secretary of the Navy), created by Colbert" (Havard and Vidal, 70). By 1665, when construction on the ramparts was complete, Quebec City became the only fortified city in North America.[48] The social organization of New France echoed this symbolic reminder of medieval times.[49] In New France as in France, 17th-century society was based, in theory if not always in practice, on a hierarchical structure crowned at the top by the Church, its first rank reflecting the importance granted to spiritual and religious life since those days. The second order was the nobility, which consisted of the nobility of sword, the descendants of the medieval knights, as well as the nobility of robe, bourgeois ennobled for administrative and financial services rendered to the Crown. The largest part of the population, over 90 percent of the French people belonged to the third order, the Third Estate. This social structure was by and large well-accepted as it was believed to be the world order laid down by Providence itself. It also provided a measure of stability against pervasive forces of violence and destruction. The price to pay for that "protection" was a social inequality inscribed in law.[50]

In daily life in France, for instance, commoners were mindful of rules of precedence and customs that dictated who could walk on the sidewalk and who could not; who was entitled to cross a threshold or to speak first; who had to keep his hat on; who was allowed to wear which clothes or to marry whom. In general, therefore, the aspirations of those eager to climb up the social ladder were the object of mockery, as the success of Molière's 1670 play *Le Bourgeois gentilhomme* (*The would-be Gentleman*) illustrates. A reminder of the reality of strong social barriers, this message was particularly well received at a court where the nobility was under tight control and had little else left to distinguish itself from wealthy merchants than its monopoly on good taste and fashion as well as a refined use of the French language evidence in the art of conversation. In New France, however, those rules did not apply, or at least not to such an extent.[51] Social mobility was possible. Wealthy commoners like Jacques Cartier and Samuel Champlain, although they belonged to the Third Estate, were in many ways *honnêtes hommes* or *gentilhommes* (gentlemen, members of the gentry), and were treated as such, even at court.[52]

And yet, after Champlain, the leadership of New France was granted to governors who were all noblemen, as the particle *de* in their name indicates: Charles de Montmagny (1635–1648); Louis de Coulonge (1648–51); Jean de Lauson (1651–1657); Pierre d'Argenson (1657–1661); Pierre d'Avaugour (1661–1663), etc.[53] In Colbert's days, the title was no longer Governor but Governor General. The Governor General was a vice-Roy in charge of military affairs and of diplomacy.[54] The office of Governor General required moving from Quebec City to Montreal in the summer in order to renew contacts with Native American allies and discuss matters of common interest with the chiefs. A new administrator, the Intendant, took care of the administration of justice, public order, as well as finance.

Conflicts were frequent between the representative of the nobility of sword, the Governor General who had official preeminence in the colony, and that of the nobility of robe, the intendant (or *commissaire ordonnateur* in Louisiana) who held the power of the purse. Under Colbert, the French government remunerated these officials well and therefore forbade them to take part in the fur business but most of them disregarded the prohibition. The other important institution in New France was the Sovereign Council (*Conseil Souverain*). It had existed informally since the 1640s but received official recognition in 1663, at which time the number of its members increased from three to nine. In addition to the governor and the intendant, members of the Sovereign Council included the bishop, captain of the militia, and five councilors, who formed the court of appeal.[55]

The Council had wide-ranging authority over the political, economic, and social life of the colony, since its attributions included public spending, the regulation of the fur trade, and the relations between colonists and merchants. It was within its purview to create lower courts and to appoint magistrates, although only one member of the

Council, the Attorney General, was required to have studied law. Whereas the law still varied in metropolitan France from province to province, much to the King's chagrin, New France was subject to a single set of laws, the Custom of Paris, from 1664 onward. New reforms came into play later on: in 1667, the "Code Louis" for civil and criminal procedures; in 1673, the Code Savary for trade regulations, and in 1685, the *Code Noir* for slavery. That year, Louis XIV made it illegal to publish anything in New France as well.[56]

With regard to the fur business, the strengthening of royal authority took the form of top-down measures emanating from the Sovereign Council, the implementation of a permit system for fur traders in the *Pays d'en Haut in* 1681 for instance, and later, in 1696, the arbitrary closing of all trading posts of the *Pays d'en Haut*. On occasion, the Council responded to commoners' complaints. In 1680, it made a small percentage of uncleared land available to farmers. In 1686, it declared it illegal to seize cattle, the farmers' source of livelihood, as a means of settling debts. In 1701, it intervened again to stop grain hoarding, seized the hidden merchandise, and sold it at low price to the poor. The Council's authority could also reach into the private lives of the settlers, so for instance when it distinguished between deserving and undeserving poor or demanded certificates of good character from potential innkeepers. The Sovereign Council was also at liberty to amend verdicts.[57]

The other Very Important Person in New France was the man in charge of religious matters for the entire colony, the Bishop of Quebec. In 1658, the Vatican appointed François de Montmorency-Laval (1623–1708) as the first bishop of New France. He arrived the following year and worked ceaselessly to advance the Catholic agenda for three decades. It should be pointed out, however, that he was not as successful as the stereotypical image of the pious Quebecois would imply.[58] Complaints about the immorality of the *coureurs des bois* sufficiently indicate that in the very least that segment of the population was able to escape the grip of Church and of the law[59]:

> The violent pleasures, the debauchery, missionaries were complaining about, were often spectacular: the coureurs slept with as many Indian women as they wanted, they went hunting and got drunk with Indians, they engaged in brawls, shot their guns haphazardly. "Good food, women, gambling, and drinking, all was par for the course," Baron La Hontan wrote as someone who had witnessed the *coureurs des bois* up close... [quoted in Creagh, *Nos Cousins*, 54].

But it can also be argued, as Havard and Vidal have done convincingly,[60] that the harsh judgment passed on the white Indians' conduct was just a reflection of the rigid sexual code French Catholics, and in particular missionaries, adhered to. Young Frenchmen delighted in the sexual freedom women enjoyed in most First Nations. In the colony along the St. Lawrence, Colbert and the French authorities encouraged Franco-Indian marriages as long as the Native Americans were willing to convert.[61] For the French minister, "the French and the Indians were to form 'the same people and the same blood'" (quoted in Creagh, *Nos Cousins*, 27).[62] But the mixed-race nation Colbert envisioned emerged mostly out of the gaze of the authorities, in the margins of the empire. If miscegenation remained relatively rare in Canada when French women were available, it was a "generalized" phenomenon in Acadia where the French had settled first, and a very common one in the Illinois country between 1680 and 1720 (Havard and Vidal, *Histoire*, 378–379).

The most common crimes prosecuted in the province of New France, violent assault and forgery (counterfeit money, fake playing cards) also point to a risk-taking mentality hardly compatible with the teachings of the Church.[63] Even the habitants dared to take their chances, an opportunity that French peasants did not have. The pressure of government and religious institutions was far more intense in the Old World, and so was the culture of fear that some tried to export. In 1661, Laval-Montmorency, a bishop who believed in Marie de l'Incarnation's visions, in witches, and in bad omens, found settler Daniel Vuil guilty of casting an evil spell on sixteen-year-old Barbe Halay. Pierre de Voyer d'Argenson, vicomte de Mouzay (1625–1709) and Governor general of New France voided the verdict shortly before his return to France but his successor, Pierre Dubois d'Avaugour had Vuil put to death for sorcery. Even if Vuil's was the only witchcraft trial that ended deadly in New France, it is still revealing of a mentality that seems utterly foreign to 21st-century readers.[64]

Relations between representatives of the Church and the Government were not always smooth, and not only on the issue of the sale of alcohol and firearms to Native Americans.[65] Bishop Laval was asked and agreed and to serve as interim governor twice, in 1663 and 1682 but the royal edict of 1682 that made witchcraft non-actionable in a court of law points to the waning influence of the Church and to its further removal from state matters. More significantly, Bishop Laval met with resistance unfamiliar to him on the part of the habitants when he tried to enforce payment of the tithe in the province (Choquette, "From Sea Monsters…," 51). To add insult to injury, the Superior Council sided with the people.[66]

The most famous governor of New France at the end of the 17th century was Louis de Buade, Count of Frontenac, who served two terms (1672–1682 and 1689–1698).[67] Frontenac belonged to the King's inner circle. Born in the royal castle of Saint-Germain-en-Laye, he had King Louis XIII as his godfather. He served as an army officer in the Thirty Years' War from 1635 to 1648, became a colonel at age twenty-one, and distinguished himself as a commanding officer of an expedition against the Turks in Crete in 1669. Unhappy in marriage, he separated from his wife, led an extravagant life on his country estate, went hopelessly into debt, and then lived at court. The King named Frontenac Governor of New France at a time when bad blood between the Governor General and the intendant had negative effects on the colony's administration. During his first term, Frontenac acted independently and not always in accordance with his superiors in France. His disagreement with the Bishop over the sale of alcohol to Native Americans got him fired in 1682.[68]

The first intendant, Jean Talon, Count of Orsainville (1626–1694), was a man of experience who resided in New France most of the time between 1665 and 1672.[69] Talon, whom Louise Kellogg describes as "the most energetic of the early rulers of New France" (131), believed that diversification was key to creating a sound economic basis for the colony. He developed the lumber industry, shipbuilding, and encouraged mining. He introduced new crops, flax and hops, for instance, and even started the first brewery of New France, the *Brasserie du Roy*. As a means of expanding cultivated land, he also granted more *seigneuries* than anyone before him.[70] Talon had many projects in store for New France but he needed more hands to complete them than were available.

Canada depended on numerous offspring and low mortality for its population growth (Havard and Vidal, 204).[71] Immigration to New France was small compared to New England.[72] Fear of competition explains, in part, the slow pace of colonization in French North America. Trading companies and the group of established colonists that had a say locally, often paid newcomers, *engagés*, to return to France after three years.

These skilled workers, farm hands, and servants arrived mostly prior to the 1660s when they made up 20 percent of the New France population. Disagreement within the government over the right way to colonize New France, particularly from the 1660s to the 1680s, may also account for Canada's small population size: the authorities in France encouraged settlement along the St. Lawrence River but experts on the ground like intendant Talon and Governor Frontenac envisioned a province stretching "from the St. Lawrence to Mexico" (quoted in Havard and Vidal, 103).

The prescribed method for establishing settlements in New France was the Canadian *rang*, or "longlot," a narrow, elongated, strip of land along the St. Lawrence River.[73] Because *habitations* were grouped together, this mode of settlement had the advantage of allowing for better control and more efficient protection of the people while at the same time ensuring that the population of New France would remain predominantly French. However, it had the disadvantage of slowing down the colony's geographic expansion due to a rhythm set by the creation of new parishes along the St. Lawrence River. Settlers would ask the Bishop for a new parish once their current church was too far away and once there were enough families in the same situation to support a priest and pay for the construction and the maintenance of a church. However, while the church played an important role in the community because it served as its social hub, it would be wrong to conclude that the Catholic faith was more solidly implanted in New France than in France in the 17th century. On the contrary, it seems that the opposite was the case.[74]

Another reason often evoked to explain the French Crown's relative lack of investment in its American colonies, apart from the disappointment of not finding gold or a profitable trade route to China, is the fear of seeing metropolitan France lose its rank as the most populated country of Western Europe.[75] French efforts to prevent an exodus to the colonies partially account for New France's slow development relative to New England. As Jones correctly observed, "[t]o the [British] colonies, immigrants represented the solution of a chronic labor shortage, the means of promoting land settlement and of developing resources" (41). To the French Crown, by contrast, immigration meant depopulation. Margret K. Brown suggests that the publication of the *Jesuits' Relations* (1632–1673) may also have been a deterrent to immigration because these accounts "told wondrous tales of conversion," but at the same time "horrible stories of torture and death at the hands of the natives" (*History*, 8).

The census taken under Jean Talon's administration as soon as he arrived in 1665 put the population of New France at 3,215, a figure that was considerably smaller than that of New England, over 100,000 by then, or even much lower than the French Caribbean islands: 15,000. To solve the demographic conundrum—how to populate New France without depopulating the kingdom—a highly original solution was devised: to raise and educate orphan girls at the King's expense for the sole purpose of marrying colonists. The result was that 770 "King's daughters" (*les filles du roy*) arrived in New France between 1662 and 1673.[76] Incentives for jumpstarting families and growing the population included rewards for early marriages and financial stipends for large families: 300 pounds for families with ten children and 400 pounds for families with 12 children. There was also a strong disincentive to reject marriage: a tax on singles! To avoid paying it, you had to be married by age 20 for a man, 16 for a woman (Soyez, 147). These measures worked miracles: the population of New France doubled in ten years.

What did New France society look like in the second half of the 17th century?

The *seigneurs* (lords) formed a small oligarchy that tended to be wealthy, but more and more opportunities arose for the common folk as the colony expanded. Whether they were born in France or in North America, commoners were the lifeline of the colony. By the 1660s, all trades and professions were represented in the province.[77] The stonecutters, masons, carpenters, joiners, cartwrights, coopers, lock-, gun-, and blacksmiths who came to the New World built it from scratch and gave it its physical appearance and its solidity. Those craftsmen used construction materials that were available, wood and stone mostly, to raise barns and houses. They assembled sawmills, cut planks, and built wood frame houses—or log cabins in places too far away from a sawmill. The first churches or chapels were no different from these houses and often lacked a bell. Normandy-style houses, with their distinct mixture of half-timbering and stucco, appeared a bit later, mostly in Acadia, brought perhaps by gunsmith Abraham Dugas (1616–1698) who settled in Port Royal in 1640, married Marguerite Doucet in 1647, and spent the rest of his life with her there.

The Governor granted *seigneuries* to noblemen and clerics, although by the 1660s over two-thirds of them were held by the former.[78] The size of the *seigneuries* also varied greatly, with a small group of families holding the largest ones.[79] The lords typically lived in Quebec or Montreal and had a steward run their estate. But the gap between rich and poor was not as wide in New France as it was in France, even if its institutions were an Old-World export. In the cities, most merchants and traders owned their house and lived fairly well.[80] Writing in the 1680s about his own experiences in the colony, Louis-Armand d'Arce, baron of Lahontan (1666–1716), observed that the New France peasants were better off than many noblemen living on their country estates in France. For one thing, there were enough forests and streams to hunt and fish at will without incurring a penalty for poaching. As Leslie Choquette observed, in France peasants complained because the price of bread was too high, in New France because it was too low and a low price for them meant a small profit. A.L. Burt similarly writes that "the competition of the Old World was turned upside down in the New World. Here it was between seignors for tenants, and not between peasants for the land of the seignors" (94). He further notes that the habitants paid no taxes in New France and that the *corvée* of building a road or a mill was as much a benefit to them as it was to the *seigneur*. Besides, life on the frontier made the external signs of social distinction that were so visible in France disappear in New France, since, with a few exceptions, both *seigneurs* and habitants alike had to furnish the manual labor necessary for their upkeep. Once in the New World, in short, the French acquired the spirit of independence that characterized, much later, the American pioneers. They were free to leave the colony's boundaries, go explore the continent, and set up camp in the wilderness with, or near, Native American villages.

.   From Champlain onward, governors had sought to meet the First Nations halfway culturally. Although the French espoused their Native American allies' enmities, they made a greater effort to understand friendly nations' cultures. Moreover, "[d]uring the seventeenth century, the authorities in New France and the Catholic Church encouraged unions between French people and Amerindians, in an attempt to reestablish a gender balance in the colonial population" (L-P Rousseau, 797–798).[81] The native way of life may not have seemed too foreign to 17th-century settlers from the French countryside. After all, Honoré de Balzac still compared the people of Brittany to the Mohicans much later, in his 1799 novel *The Chouans*.

4. Exploring North America

From the very start, French explorers relied on Native American allies and guides to explore the North American continent and since Champlain's days, being allies meant providing mutual support in all circumstances, including war. It was this "Franco-Amerindian alliance that gave New France its strength" (Havard and Vidal, *Histoire*, 384). The French had had conflictual relations with the Iroquois since Cartier's days.[82] In spite of efforts to improve them and long periods of peace, European competition over the fur trade exacerbated these conflicts.[83] In the 1640s, war broke out between the Iroquois, traditional allies of the Dutch who gave them firearms, and the Hurons, who only received firearms from the French if they converted to Christianity (Labelle, 5).[84] Since only a minority had done so, the Hurons were clearly at a disadvantage when war with the Iroquois broke out, especially since the many diseases brought by the French had already reduced their numbers. Between 1648 and 1650 the Iroquois attacked the twenty Huron villages spread out around the Georgian Bay of Lake Huron, decimating Native inhabitants and French missionaries. Quebec and even Tadoussac were also the target of Iroquois raids from 1650 to 1653. Survivors fled down the St. Lawrence towards Quebec, down the Ohio Valley, and towards Michigan.

As Havard notes, "the destruction of Huronia by the Five Nations in 1649–50 created a new situation. The surviving Hurons from the Great Lakes came back together and joined with the Petun, forming the Huron-Petun (or Tionontati) group while the French ventured further into the west to rebuild the fur-trading network" (*The Great Peace*, 31).[85] From the vantage point of the Great Lake nations who were traditional enemies of the Iroquois, the destruction of Huronia was certainly threatening and reinforced the need for a strong alliance with the French. But it also created new opportunities as they suddenly found themselves in a good position to fill the void left by the loss of the Huron-French trade. Indeed, as soon as the Franco-Iroquois Wars officially ended in 1653,[86] "[t]he first reported fur convoy from the *Pays d'en haut* arrived in Montreal in 1654" (McDonnell, 36). Havard points out similarly that "[t]he Great Lakes nations (Odawas, Potawatomis, Sauks, Miamis, Huron-Petuns, etc.) that were most often at war with the Iroquois at the end of the seventeenth century could appreciate both the material advantages of alliance with the French and Onontio's[87] military aid, although they sometimes found this aid insufficient" (Havard, *The Great Peace of Montreal of 1701*, 41). In 1683, the French erected Fort de Buade at the straights of Mackinac in the Michigan Upper Peninsula, next to the mission of St. Ignace Marquette had created in 1671 and the Great Lakes native village of Michilimackinac, center of the fur trade.

As war with the First nations, and indirectly with the Dutch continued in the early 1660s, Versailles started to help. Prior to New France's incorporation as a province the metropole had provided scant support to protect settlers, but once it became responsible for the colony's military defense, it sent the 1,200 soldiers of the Carignan-Salières regiment in 1665.[88] Their mission was to put an end to the Franco-Iroquois wars. As traditional allies of the Dutch until then, the Iroquois were already on weak ground after the Dutch lost their colony to the British in 1664.[89] The Peace of Quebec, the treaty signed in 1667 between on the one hand the French and their Native American allies and on the other hand the Five Nations, temporarily secured peace with the Iroquois and the regiment left.[90] As one of the habitants' duties under the seigneurial system was to lodge these soldiers, their replacement by a colonial militia was probably a relief to the population.

However, troops from the *Compagnies franches de la Marine* (another name for the Troupes de la Marine) would continue to arrive regularly during the last wave of Franco-Iroquois wars.[91]

Peace made it possible again to expand up north towards *les Pays d'en Haut* and, in disregard of the official settlement policy, to establish new trading posts near Native American villages. It also became customary to build forts to protected troops stationed there on an ongoing basis.[92] Thus Fort Saint-Louis, later called Fort Chambly after the commander who had it built, was part of a line of five forts between Montreal and Lake Champlain that protected the area from Mohawk attacks. But blood alliances between the French and the Native Americans were more effective than the soldiers' weapons in allowing the explorers' further progress westward. Moreover, if the French were keenly interested in Franco-Indian marriages at the time, the reverse was also true, as McDonnell points out:

> French traders along the St. Lawrence who wanted furs quickly came to realize that they needed the patronage of their Anishinaabe counterparts to survive in the turbulent world of the *pays d'en haut*. Fortunately for them, well-connected Odawa women such as Charles de Langlade's mother, Domitilde, actively sought out fur trade husbands who would be of benefit to their kin relations. And in marrying French traders, Anishinaabe women created expansive kinship networks that stretched east as well as west and eventually came to encompass peoples and communities that ranged from the Mississippi River to Montreal [*Masters of Empire*, 16].[93]

In fact, it was the Ottawa who first sought out the French at Trois-Rivières.[94] Médard Chouart des Groseilliers (1618–1698) started trading with them at that point and in 1659–60 left home and his brother-in-law, Pierre-Esprit Radisson (1636–1710), to explore the Northern forests between the Hudson Bay and Lake Superior, where the Cree had told them they would find the best fur.[95] In 1659, they established a trading post in Chagouamigon, on the Southwestern tip of Lake Superior, the future site of a mission (1665). They were among the first to meet with members of the Sioux and Cree nations. In 1660, after Groseilliers and Radisson returned to Quebec City with lots of beaver pelts, they suggested to Governor d'Agenson that it would be cheaper to open a trading post on the Hudson Bay and to move the fur by sea from there. But d'Argenson was unhappy with them as their private ventures undermined the colony's business. He therefore denied them permission for further exploration of that region, nixed their idea of establishing a trading company up north, confiscated their fur, and even jailed Groseilliers for trading without a license. Whereupon Groseilliers and Radisson decided to find out if the British would be more receptive to their ideas than the French.[96] They were. Although Dutch privateers captured them on their way to England in 1665, the two Frenchmen managed to reach London, pitch their idea, and return to Canada to implement it. They built a fort on the Rupert River, gathered a rich cargo of furs, went back to London and found backers for a new trading Company: the famous the Hudson's Bay Company was born (1670). Groseilliers and Radisson then worked for five years for the Hudson's Bay Company.[97] The French authorities soon recognized their error and exploration of the *Pays d'en haut* resumed often under pressure of a clergy in search of new souls to save. In fact, it was a priest, Charles Albanel (1616–1696),[98] who convinced Groseilliers to stop working for the British and to return to French employ. Groseilliers subsequently joined the *Compagnie de la Baie d'Hudson,* the French company created to compete with the Hudson's Bay Company. Radisson created another trading post.

The Native American allies of the French "did not look kindly on the increasingly distant expeditions of the French *coureurs de bois*, who were going far beyond Michili-mackinac and Green Bay to trade with the Assiniboines and the Sioux in order to obtain pelts at the source and thus at lower cost" (Havard, *The Great Peace*, 41). Ronald Creagh gives us an idea of how widespread the phenomenon was by the second half of the 17th century: "[o]f the five hundred officers and soldiers who landed in Canada in 1665, about 100 became *coureurs de bois* when their commission ended" (*Nos Cousins*, 53). McDonnell's figures are even higher: "Intendant Talon estimated that there were some three or four hundred *coureurs de bois*—literally runners of the woods, referring to illegal fur traders—active in the west, mostly on private fur-trading missions. By 1680, his successor guessed there might be as many as eight hundred" (45). Apart from the military, the *coureurs des bois* were also recruited among servants who had completed their indenture and small farmers with no land. Most of the time, Creagh adds, they made more money for the merchants than they did for themselves (53).[99]

Intendant Jean Talon, who was interested in expanding the colony, designed a two-pronged strategy to boost France's position as a colonial power: to claim possession of the *Pays d'en Haut* on the one hand, and to pursue the exploration of the vast North American continent westward and southward.[100] In 1670, Talon instructed Simon Daumont de Saint-Lusson to explore the land of the Ottawa,[101] Nipissing, Illinois, and other nations, in search of the Northwest Passage, and, in the process, to find and take possession of a famed copper mine (Creagh, *Nos Cousins*, 60). In June 1671, Saint-Lusson left Quebec City for a gathering of fourteen Native American nations at Sault-Sainte-Marie, where the Jesuits had established a mission a few years earlier.[102] The pageant was organized by Nicolas Perrot (1644–1717),[103] a man deemed "France's best representative among the Indians of the west," according to the *Dictionary of Canadian Biography*. His knowledge of native languages and his character had earned him the "esteem, confidence, and even affection of the Potawatomis, Menominees, Foxes, Miamis, Mascoutens, and Sioux." A commoner, Perrot succeeded in convincing chiefs of these First Nations that the French were their friends, which led them to attend the elaborate ceremony that took place at Sault Sainte Marie in June 1671 when Saint-Lusson claimed possession of the *Pays d'en haut* on behalf of the French Crown. The point of this pageant was to proclaim the unity of "Onontio's family," Onontio being the French King represented here by his vice-roy, the governor, and to obtain the hospitality of all these First Nations, in other words "the freedom for the French to come and go on their lands as they pleased" (Havard and Vidal, *Histoire*, 110).[104]

Many other men explored the continent during the second half of the 17th century, among them Daniel Greysolon Dulhut (1639–1710),[105] Louis Jolliet (1645–1700),[106] and Jacques Marquette (1637–1775).[107] Daniel Greysolon Dulhut was born near Lyon, France, in 1639.[108] An army officer, he arrived in New France in 1674, spent four years in Montreal, then left to explore the region beyond Lake Superior. Dulhut made friends with the Saulteaux (*Saulteurs* or Chippewa) who helped him get in touch with Sioux. In 1679 he helped the Ojibwa become middlemen between the French and the Dakota in the fur trade. He also established a prosperous trading post in the place that still bears his name: Duluth, Minnesota. Dulhut had heard of a great salted sea in the far West. He took off in that direction, descending the Sainte Croix River to the Mississippi. There he learned from traders that some people were slandering him and accusing him of treason in Quebec. Honor demanded that he go back to Montreal and even France to clear his name, which he did. When he returned to New France in 1682, he established more trading posts north of Lake Superior. He helped build Fort de Buade and Fort Kaministiquia north of Lake Superior, near Thunder Bay.[109]

In 1673, Jolliet and Marquette became the first Europeans to explore and map the valley of the "great river" that Ojibwe Indians called "Messipi,"[110] and the French the "Colbert River"[111] at the time. Their mission was to add territory to New France and to find out where the great river ended. Born in France, Jacques Marquette became a Jesuit priest and a teacher. He arrived in New France in 1666, learned the Huron language, and established several missions (Sault-Sainte-Marie, La Pointe).[112] He heard of the Mississippi from Illinois Indians and requested a leave of absence to explore the river. A few years younger than Marquette, Louis Jolliet is the first explorer of North America to be born in New France. He came from a family of well-establish settlers who owned land and, as a child, learned several Native American languages. He then studied in a Jesuit seminary in Quebec City to become a priest but changed his mind and did not take his vows.

In 1673, Marquette, Jolliet and five Franco-Indians left Fort St. Ignace in Upper Michigan with only two canoes. They paddled to Green Bay, then took the Fox River to Prairie du Chien, where they entered the Mississippi, and went as far as south the mouth of the Arkansas River. According to Willard H. Rollings, Marquette "was not greeted by six thousand threatening warriors like those who had challenged de Soto; instead, he was met by friendly Quapaw living in four moderate-sized villages" (41).[113] On the way back, the explorers took a shortcut, the Illinois River, and stopped at the Old Kaskaskia Village, home to around a thousand members of the Illinois Confederacy (Brown, *History*, 2–3). The party spent the winter in Illinois territory, the first Europeans to stop in "Eschikagou, Algonquian for 'a foul smelling place,'" the future city of Chicago (Fisher, "Chicago," 252). M.J. Morgan elaborates:

> One of the tragic mysteries of the French discovery of the Mississippi occurred when the canoe of Louis Joliet capsized on his return trip to Quebec in 1674. Joliet was likely the "the most expert map maker" in New France at that time; he had visited France and may have spent time in cartographic workshops learning the use of the astrolabe. With his training and careful documentation, he and Father Marquette charted one thousand miles of the Mississippi, and Joliet may well have noted in detail the area that would become the heart of the French settlement in southern Illinois. The loss of all of Joliet's notes, journals, sketches, and maps in the Ottawa River capsizing may well be one of the accidents of history that changed history [*Land of Big Rivers*, 69–70].

In 1675, Marquette returned to Old Kaskaskia, also called *La Vantum*, where he founded the mission of the Immaculate Conception, the first mission in the Illinois country (Brown, *History*, 3). He died of dysentery shortly after returning to St. Ignace mission. Cities in Michigan, Wisconsin, Iowa, and Illinois are named after Marquette and there is also Marquette University in Milwaukee.

In 1675, Jolliet married a Canadian woman, daughter of a fur trader, and they had seven children. Louis received a land grant, first in the area of Sept-Isles, then on Anticosti Island. In 1679, he travelled to the Hudson Bay to establish contacts with Native Americans on behalf of the New France authorities (Bouchard, 124–127). In 1694, he explored the coast of Labrador and brought back the first accounts on the Innuits. Late in life, he taught cartography and hydrography in Quebec City. He was also a musician and played organ in church. He died in 1700 but his body was never found. Several cities in the United States are named after him: Joliet in Illinois, Montana, Indiana, Pennsylvania, and there is also one in Quebec, Joliette.

On April 7, 1682, Cavelier de la Salle completed the exploration of the Mississippi valley started by Jolliet and Marquette.[114] Earlier on, in 1669, La Salle had explored Lower Michigan and built Fort Miami (St. Joseph, Michigan).[115] He had also accompanied Frontenac to a meeting with First Nations on Lake Ontario and they had built Fort Cataraqui as a fur trading post and a base for explorations in 1673. Thanks to Frontenac's protection, La Salle had served as Fort Cataraqui's first administrator and renamed the place Fort Frontenac in honor of his patron. In 1679, he had a full-sized ship built on a small island above Niagara Falls, *Le Griffon*—"so called in honor of Frontenac's coat of arms"— that allowed him, Father Hennepin,[116] "and 32 sailors, to explore Lake Erie, Lake Huron, and Lake Michigan" (Dupré). It was the largest ship to sail the Great Lakes up to then, but it disappeared in a storm on its way back to Niagara, together with its crew. During those years, La Salle formed alliances with the Illinois and the Miami and gave them firearms, a gift that was one of the causes of the re-awakening of the Franco-Iroquois wars after 1684.[117] Over the course of his many journeys, La Salle built two other forts, the earlier versions of present-day cities: Fort Conti (Niagara Falls, New York) in 1679 and Fort Crèvecoeur (Peoria, Illinois) in 1680.[118]

La Salle's 1682 voyage down the Mississippi River started at Fort Crèvecoeur. The party of 41 men, half French, half Native American stopped near Old Kaskaskia, the Grand Village of the Illinois, which according to their reports, was now home to 6,000 Native Americans. There, but on the other side of the Illinois River, they founded Fort

Building the Griffon [*Construction du Griffon*], 1679. La Salle's ship was the largest to sail on the Great Lakes at the time. Woodcut by Father Louis Hennepin, 1687 (courtesy Library and Archives Canada).

Saint-Louis, Illinois, near a bluff called Starved Rock. Further down river, as they were hunting for food one day, one of the men, a blacksmith named Prudhomme, disappeared. Thinking that he had been captured by the Chickasaw Indians, they prepared to stay for a while and built Fort Prudhomme—perhaps, Memphis, Tennessee, although the fort's exact location is subject to controversy. But Prudhomme had just lost his way in nature and he returned unharmed after ten days. They pursued their exploration of the Mississippi Valley and reached the river's mouth in April 1682.[119] La Salle claimed the entire Mississippi River basin for France and called it *Louisiana* in honor of King Louis XIV. In 1683, after returning to Quebec, he left for France to request permission from the King to start a new colony in Louisiana.

While La Salle was away, Governor Lefebvre de la Barre (1622–1688) entered into a partnership with two powerful merchants, Le Ber and La Chesnaye, with the goal of taking over La Salle's profitable trading post at Fort Frontenac.[120] Lahontan, who served as commander at Fort St. Joseph (Port Huron, Michigan) during the events he recalled, asserted in his writings that the governor was greedy and corrupt. Troops showed up at Fort Frontenac in 1683, officially in the context of a peace settlement with the Iroquois Confederacy, but more truthfully as part of a fur trade operation organized for the governor's benefit. Sometime later, La Barre sent the Chevalier de Baugy to seize Fort Saint-Louis from Tonty, perhaps at the Iroquois's request (Creagh, *Nos Cousins*, 71). He also gave permission to capture goods from unlicensed traders to the Iroquois, who, unfortunately for him, also seized his own shipments. According to several accounts, La Barre's revenge was the real reason for the resurgence of the Franco-Iroquois war in 1684. The conflict ended badly for the governor who was forced to sign a peace treaty deemed shameful in Versailles and lost his governorship to Jacques-René de Brisay, Marquis de Denonville, in 1685 (Lyons). Meanwhile La Salle had obtained permission to start a colony in Louisiana and left France with four ships and 300 colonists. Due to an unfortunate chain of events that included piracy, shipwrecks, and poor navigation, the expedition failed, however. With only one ship left, La Salle and the remaining 36 passengers landed in Texas instead of the mouth of the Mississippi![121] Sadly, the Texas settlement lasted only a year. In 1687, La Salle faced a mutiny and his own men killed him.

The strengthening of the royal authority so keenly felt in France during the first part of Louis XIV's personal reign manifested itself in New France as well through the creation of new institutions and the appointment of high officials, the Governor General, the intendant, devoted to the King. Nonetheless, the royal grip on the colony was never as strong as it was on the mother country. Colonization proceeded at a low pace in the St. Lawrence Valley due to the difficulty of recruiting settlers and differences of opinion among officials over the right way to colonize the province. Nonetheless, serious efforts were made to support the colony both in terms of demography, with the "filles du roy" program, and military support, with the dispatch of a regiment. In the context of commercial competition and war with the Dutch and the English, alliances with Native Americans, often sealed at the personal level by marriage, were key to New France's survival in the 1660s and later to its expansion westward. French knowledge of the North American continent increased tremendously during the third quarter of the 17th century, with the explorations of the Upper Country, the *Pays d'en haut*, by Groseilliers and Radisson, who mapped the area up to Hudson Bay, and by Dulhut, who explored the Lake Superior area. Marquette and Joliet discovered the Mississippi Valley that Cavelier de la Salle finished exploring all the way to Gulf of Mexico ten years later, in 1682. By the end of the 17th century, the French were going further and further west. They already knew *la rivière Des Moines* (the Des Moines River), which goes through the current capital of Iowa and bears the same name.[122] And yet in many ways, the French colonization of North American had barely begun.

5. Tips for Further Investigations

Interesting People to Look Up

Charles Le Moyne de Longueuil et de Châteauguay (1626–1685)
Charles Aubert de La Chesnaye (1632–1702)
René-Robert Cavelier de la Salle (1643–1687)
Nicolas Perrot (1644–1717)
Henri de Tonty (1649–1704)
Louis Armand de Lahontan (1666–1716)
Domitilde de Langlade (1699–1782)

Related Primary Texts

Lahontan, Armand de. *Mémoires de l'Amérique Septentrionale.*
Lahontan, Armand de. *Nouveaux Voyages dans l'Amérique Septentrionale.*
Lahontan, Armand de. *Supplément aux Voyages ou Dialogues avec le sauvage Adario.*
Leclerq, Chrestien. "A Micmac Responds to the French, ca 1677."
Perrot, Nicolas. *Mémoire sur les mœurs, coustumes et relligion des sauvages de l'Amérique septentrionale.*
Radisson, Pierre-Esprit. *Voyages of Peter Esprit Radisson.*
Raynal, Abbé. "The Development of French Canada," in *A History of the Two Indies*, ed. P. Jimack, 228–229.
Raynal, Abbé. "Difficulties France had to overcome in Canada," in *A History of the Two Indies*, ed. P. Jimack, 230–231.
Raynal, Abbé. "The French are finally roused to action," in *A History of the Two Indies*, ed. P. Jimack, 216–218.
Raynal, Abbé. "The fur trade," in *A History of the Two Indies*, ed. P. Jimack, 218–220.
Raynal, Abbé. "Voyages, settlements, wars and commerce of the French in the East Indies," in *A History of the Two Indies*, ed. P. Jimack, 47–61.
Raynal, Abbé. "The Way of life of the French Canadians," in *A History of the Two Indies*, ed. P. Jimack, 220.
Tonty, Henri de. "Voyages et établissements des Français sur les lacs et le Mississippi."
Tonty, Henri de, and Cavelier de La Salle. *On the discovery of the Mississippi.*
Related Films, Exhibits, and Fiction
La Belle, the Ship that Changed History. Exhibition at the Bullock Museum, Austin, TX.
The Other Side of the Ledger [*La face cachée des transactions*] *An Indian View of the Hudson's Bay Company* (1972).
Simiot, Bernard. "1. Mathieu Carbec." *Ces Messieurs de Saint-Malo*. Paris: Albin Michel, 1983. The first part of the novel covers the years 1660 to 1684.
Versailles, Season 1. 2015 Canal+ TV series, available on Netflix.

Chapter IV

The Sun King's Colonial Empire, 1684–1715

This chapter describes how New France fared during the second half of Louis XIV's reign, from 1684, shortly after Colbert's death and the court's move to the palace of Versailles[1] a year earlier, to 1715 when the King passed away.[2] As in the preceding chapter, our examination must start in Versailles, where Louis XIV now ruled as an absolute monarch. In his desire to transform France into the most powerful kingdom in Europe, the King followed two guiding principles that are covered in section 1, "Louis XIV's Politics of Prestige and War": the carrot and the stick, or more precisely, how to impress other nations by the magnificence of his kingdom and his court; and how to continue to gain respect by winning on the battlefield. Out of the wealth of legislative documents that were produced in those years by the monarch's efficient administration two had a profound impact on New France. They are the topic of Section 2, "Royal Edicts on Religion and Slavery."

The last two sections trace the impact the two European wars fought between 1688 and 1713 had on New France. Sometimes referred to as the first and second French and Indian Wars, they were actually struggles between the French and the British empires, to which Native Americans of enemy tribes provided support. As Havard and Vidal point out, "[c]olonials, in many regards, participated as much in the wars of their allies as the latter turned into mercenaries at the service of the French Empire" (*Histoire de l'Amérique française*, 294). From the capture of trading posts and forts the British had established on the Hudson Bay to attacks on New England settlements aimed at cutting supply routes, the fur trade was the main stake in the struggle between France and England, as is showed in section 3, "New France during the War of the Grand Alliance, 1688–1697." While war caused misery for the many, particularly in Acadia, and greatly disturbed trade, some found ways to benefit, and to do so legally: might often makes right in an absolutist regime. The War of the Grand Alliance made the two colonial powers realize that, ultimately, their goal was the elimination of the weakest of them. Speeding up efforts at the end of the war, the French took pre-emptive measures and sought to create a defensive line around the territory they claimed as part of New France. A chain of forts appeared linking Quebec to Louisiana, an area they settled at the time. Would this huge investment in military and financial resources deliver the expected results?

1. Louis XIV's Politics of Prestige and War

By the 1680s, France was at the apogee of her power. Louis XIV sought to enhance his country's prestige not only by winning on the battlefield but also by impressing

The Four Corners of the World. America [*Les Quatre parties du monde. L'Amérique*]. Seventeenth-century engraving by Guilliaume de Geyn (courtesy Bibliothèque nationale de France/Gallica).

visitors and subjects with monuments conveying her majesty through their size and beauty: new bridges, mansions and palaces, and arches of triumph. His reign marked a period of intense construction activity culminating in the appearance of specialized monuments such as the Observatory, the royal theater, the *Comédie française* (1680), and the new seat of government, the Palace at Versailles (Haine, 58–59).

With its striking combination of all art forms—architecture, sculpture, painting, decoration, and landscaping—Versailles remains the most distinct manifestation of Louis XIV's grandiose ambitions. The King was a statesman concerned with his reputation and glory and a great communicator who understood the importance of propaganda. Early on, he had chosen the sun, a symbol of life, order, and regularity, as his emblem.[3] In order to prevent aristocratic rebellions away from court, he now demanded that powerful aristocrats live at court. From 1682 onward, therefore, 10,000 men and women of noble birth resided at Versailles, the royal residence. Louis XIV's court was a vivid testimony to the royal politics of control and prestige:

> [H]e (Louis XIV) domesticated the proud nobility, turning their pretensions from politics towards his glittering court, persuading them that there alone amid the artificial pomp of its stage effects lay beauty, profit, and real life. The courtesans were shut in a gilded cage of ceremonies and pensions, of gifts and dowries, benefits and places; the public was awed by power, dazzled by the scale of buildings and displays, charmed by the royal style, affected by official propaganda [Weber, 299].

Versailles featured the best French culture had to offer at the time: the work of great painters (Lebrun, Mignard, Rigaud); musicians (Lully, Couperin); architects and landscape architects (Le Vau, Le Nôtre); and intellectuals: Jean de La Fontaine (1621–95); Blaise Pascal (1623–62); Madame de Sévigné (1626–96); and the Duke of Saint-Simon (1675–1755). Aristocrats were eager to participate in daily rituals codified in a court etiquette that included orbiting the King from morning to evening dressed in magnificent attire and extravagant hairdos.[4] Whereas "[a]t the court of Louis XIII, the manners, perfumes, women's make-up, gloves and fashion were for the most part Spanish" (Weber, 265), at the court of his son, they were French. The King forbade behaviors and habits he found offensive, such as smoking, swearing, and dueling. Not only did he micro-manage everyday life at court he also imposed restrictions on the type of administrative and military positions nobles who were deemed inoffensive enough to be allowed to live on their estate could occupy in the provinces. Stripped of any real political power, court aristocrats had the duty of setting the socio-cultural tone for the nation and beyond, and of cultivating the arts of pleasant conversation and refined living. French culture seduced the nobility of other European nations in those years. It became fashionable to speak French and to adopt the French way of life in high society circles everywhere in Europe (Fumaroli).

By the last quarter of the 17th century, New France had become a real colony, with vibrant towns like Quebec City, Montreal, and Trois-Rivières. Impressive buildings adorned the city of Quebec, many of them built by congregations: Notre-Dame Basilica in 1633; the Ursuline Monastery in 1642; the Quebec Seminary in 1663; the Church of *Notre-Dame des Victoires* starting in 1687.[5] New official buildings and private residences rose from the ground in the first two decades of the 18th century, making the colony start looking more and more like metropolitan France. The governor's official residence in Quebec City, Château Saint Louis, was rebuilt during the last decade of the 17th century and enlarged in the 1720s. Montreal added Château Ramezay[6] in 1705 and Château Vaudreuil, Governor Vaudreuil's private mansion, in the 1720s. Both were every bit as fancy as any Parisian *hôtel particulier* at the time. Montreal became "an important center of diplomacy[7] and trade for the Amerindians of the Great Lakes":

> Each year, from June to September, Montreal received Native ambassadors from the west and sometimes from Iroquoia. It was in a sense the summer capital of Canada; during that season, the governor and the intendant, like a travelling court, would leave the town of Quebec to set up in Montreal, essentially, as an administrator noted, to deal with matters "in relation to the affairs of the savages" [*The Great Peace*, 5].

The colony was also self-sufficient by then, training its own craftsmen and artists, for instance,[8] and self-centered: "[T]he mass of the Canadians—habitants, artisans, labourers, and small shopkeepers—[...] had few direct ties with France. Their economic existence, their peculiar mores, virtually everything in their lives was firmly rooted in Canada" (Eccles, *The French*, 125). Although social mobility was still far greater in New France than in France, "a privileged class" emerged when *seigneurs* started opting for military careers. As a result "the ethos of the nobility rather than the bourgeoisie gained a much stronger hold on the upper strata of colonial society [...] and [s]ocial life among the military fur-trading elite was [...] rendered urbane and agreeable" (Eccles, *The French*, 125, 126).

If the last decades of Louis XIV's reign (1685–1715) undoubtedly marked the height of his influence, European kingdoms resented the bellicose spirit and military aggressiveness of their neighboring country, especially after France nearly "devoured" the Low

Countries in the 1670s (Weber, 278).[9] From 1688 to 1697, the kingdom was embroiled in the War of the Grand Alliance—also known as the War of the League of Augsburg, the Nine Years' War, and King William's War—following Louis XIV's intervention in England's Glorious Revolution.[10] In 1688, William III, the Dutch Prince of Orange, invaded England and toppled his father-in-law, King James II.[11] A Catholic convert, James had become King of England in 1685 at his brother's death and had been friendly to France. The Treaty of Whitehall signed by the two nations in 1686, for instance, prohibited each of them from encroaching into the other's territory in the Americas and from aiding Indian tribes at war. Seeking to restore James II to the throne of England, Louis XIV supported his followers, the Catholic Jacobites, against the Protestant Williamites. But he did not succeed. Instead, the throne of England went to James II's daughter, Mary, and to her Dutch husband, William. With James II back in French exile, the treaty of Whitehall had little effect and the wars in Europe continued to carry over to North America for decades to come.

As France was moving towards a more centralized and absolutist regime, England was shifting in the opposite direction. In exchange for military support in the Netherlands' war against France, William and Mary agreed to rule as constitutional monarchs. The 1689 Bill of Rights reaffirmed the rights and duties of Parliament expressed in the 1628 Petition of Rights—regular sessions, free elections, and freedom of speech in chambers. It also prohibited tax levying without representation; arbitrary arrests and "cruel and unusual punishments." Some rights reversed measures that had been taken by James II, so for instance the Protestants' right to bear arms to defend themselves, a practice the previous king had forbidden it (Weber, 311).

In such a bellicose environment, it is hardly surprising that militarization became a salient characteristic of the last decades of Louis XIV's reign. In New France, it took the form of a deployment of companies of Royal Navy troops (*les troupes de la marine*), an entity created by Colbert, whose function was to defend New France against Iroquois and English incursions. As opposed to the army regiments that answered to the Secretary of War and were "privately purchased and owned by their colonel, [...] commissions in the Troupes de la Marine were not purchased and promotion was based on merit" (Eccles, *The French*, 123). Eccles notes that while their numbers were not particularly high in absolute terms, the 1,600 soldiers stationed in New France by 1685 transformed New France into a military society.[12] Most of the Marine officers were Canadians, a more suitable outlet for their energies, the authorities thought, than running wild in the woods or clearing land on their *seigneurie*. Besides, these young men, who formed the Canadian upper class, knew the land and were used to guerrilla warfare. The contrast between England and France in matters of government, the tension between French centralization and English decentralization, is also reflected in two distinct ways of appointing and promoting officers in the North America. In New England, these appointments were the purview of the governor and local authorities, but in New France they came directly from the King, through the Secretary of Navy, upon the recommendation of the Governor General and the intendant (Eccles, *The French*, 124–125).

Although the French were often victorious on the battlefield and at sea, the War of the Grand Alliance did not cause a major change in the balance of power in Europe. Peace did not last long either. War broke out again in 1701 when Charles II of Spain, dying childless in 1700, named one of Louis XIV's grandsons, Philip, Duke of Anjou, as his successor to the throne of Spain. Austria, England, and Holland were worried that France would become too powerful if Philip became not only King of Spain but also King of France. They banded together again as the Grand Alliance and, from 1701 to 1713, fought the War of the Spanish Succession, also known as Queen Ann's War in North America.

2. Royal Edicts on Religion and Slavery

In addition to measures related to war, Louis XIV signed two laws that had a significant impact on France's colonies in 1685. The first, the Edict of Fontainebleau, dealt with religion, the other, the *Code Noir*, with slavery. In matters of religion, Louis XIV's policy, is best summed up in the motto "One Kingdom, One Faith." French Protestants made up only 5 percent of the population by the middle of the 17th century but they were constantly harassed.[13] Already when Mazarin was Prime Minister, the French monarchy "embarked on a campaign of tearing down Protestant houses of worship, eventually destroying almost 700 of them" (Haine, 60). Then in 1685, Louis XIV went further: he signed the Edict of Fontainebleau that revoked Henri IV's edict of religious toleration (the *édit de Nantes*), in effect expelling Protestants from the kingdom of France unless they converted.[14] Legally, Huguenots could no longer reside in the metropole or in the colonies. Butler states that a total of 161,300 Protestants left France between 1660 and 1690 (23).

Among them was Gabriel Gustave de Crocketagne the ancestor of folk hero Davy Crockett (1786–1836).[15] Daniel Perrin (1642–1719), another Huguenot refugee from this period, arrived in New York via the Isle of Jersey in 1665 and settled with his French wife on Staten Island in an area that now bears the nickname "Huguenot." A few years later, in 1678, another group of French Huguenots emigrating via Germany purchased a tract of land from the Lenape Nation and founded the town of New Paltz. Ten years later, in 1688, 33 French Huguenot families from La Rochelle founded the city of *Nouvelle Rochelle* (New Rochelle, New York), north of New York City. Elias Boudinot (1740–1821), who served as President of the Confederation Congress in 1782–1783, and as Director of the U.S. Mint from 1795 to 1805, was a descendant of a family from Aunis, France, who settled in New York City at that time. The French-speaking city attracted immigrants from France and new Huguenot refugees for nearly a century. A few, like Isaac Lenoir, who arrived in 1696 in New York,[16] and Pierre Dieppe (1697–1714),[17] who settled in Virginia in 1714, preferred the South to New England.[18]

The exodus of Huguenots who left France to settle in England, Holland, Switzerland, and German principalities before sailing to British North America, created a brain drain and would fan Francophobe flames in the host countries for generations to come. Life in the thirteen colonies, however, was not always easy for those French immigrants. Maldwyn Jones writes that "[c]olonial immigration restrictions [...] took no account of the nationality of newcomers, [...] immigrants of practically every non–English stock incurred the open hostility of earlier comers" (44). She points out that "[a]mong the first sufferers were the French Huguenots who came at the end of the seventeenth century," that in their case, the nationality bias overrode the common religious affiliation with Protestantism. She also mentions that "in 1691 a small Huguenot settlement at French-town in Rhode Island was attacked and dispersed by a mob" (44).[19]

Despite the danger attached to disregarding royal edicts, a minority of Huguenots chose to stay in France and some, about a thousand according to historians, even settled in New France. Pierre Meyzonnat, a privateer known as capitaine Baptiste who distinguished himself in Acadia during the War of the Spanish Succession, falls in that category.[20] The edict of Fontainebleau also targeted Jansenists because of their belief in predestination. The Pope condemned these "aristocrats of Christianity" because Jansenist doctrine went against the Church's tenets.[21] Their abbey of Port-Royal, where the philosopher Blaise Pascal (1623–1662) and the playwright Jean Racine (1639–1699) had received their education, was razed in 1709 (Haine, 61). By the end of the 17th century, the Crown had succeeded in repressing all forms of dissent, religious, with the Edict of Nantes now revoked, and political, with the nobility kept busy at Versailles. Louis XIV could rule France as an absolute monarch, both head of state and head of government.

The other law Louis XIV promulgated in 1685 was the *Code Noir* (Black Code), a set of policies regulating the slave trade and the treatment of slaves.[22] The Code granted no rights to slaves, except the obligation to receive baptism and to be married in the Roman Catholic faith. It also spelled out the masters' responsibilities ("to feed, to clothe, and provide for the well-being of their slaves"). If it authorized corporal punishment and discouraged interracial unions, it also allowed slaves to marry and prohibited the separation of couples and families as well as torture. Masters also had the right to free their slaves. Overall, however, the Code's main effect was to make slavery official and legal in the French Caribbean, and later in Louisiana.[23]

By 1680, a hundred French Caribbean plantations had more than 20 slaves. In order to encourage sugar cultivation, Louis XIV decided to grant titles of nobility to owners of large sugar plantations, that is plantations with more than 100 slaves.[24] Jean-Baptiste Palouet, Antoine Cornette, Nicolas de Gabaret, Charles François d'Angennes, all four in Martinique, qualified. As a result, large plantations owned by aristocrats, the *grands blancs*, became the norm. Conversely, this development led to land speculation and forced the poorest, the small landowners, off their property.

> With the rise of sugar, white society changed dramatically. Most small planters could not afford the large capital investments which sugar required. Instead a different class of planter emerged in the Caribbean, prepared to invest heavily in slave, land, and equipment. By the end of the seventeenth century, a far more elaborate social structure had replaced the simple division between masters and indentured servants. The model for white society which was to characterize the Caribbean for the next 200 years had become established [Heuman, 45].

In those days, Saint-Pierre was the commercial capital not only of Martinique but also of the entire French Caribbean.[25] Fort-Louis, also named Fort Royal, was the other main city on the island, its administrative center.

During Louis XIV's reign, Martinique's nobility had strong connections to court. The life of Charles François d'Angennes (1648–1691) is a good illustration of this phenomenon. As a 25-year-old, d'Angennes had sold his castle and title to the King's mistress who thus became Madame de Maintenon (1674). He then fought the buccaneers in the Caribbean (1676–78) and served as governor of a small West Indies island, Marie Galante (1679–86). Royal favors and protection allowed d'Angennes to accumulate a huge fortune in the sugar business. Within less than two decades (1674–1692), the number of sugar mills doubled in Martinique.[26] Unlike d'Angennes, who died in Martinique, many plantation owners were absentee landlords who returned to France and delegated the work to "planting attorneys" and overseers (Heuman, 45). The *petits blancs*, the economic insecure sector of white society, was also the most racist (Heuman, 48). The slaves were at the bottom of the pyramid, and the former slaves, the free blacks, in-between. Notwithstanding the *Black Code*'s good intentions, mortality rates were high for slaves due to disease, hard labor, unhealthy living conditions, and harsh treatments. The slave population of the isles grew through the constant arrival of new slaves instead of natural reproduction. It also increased considerably after 1674. There were 6,323 slaves in Guadeloupe in 1664 and 9,706 in 1710. "It has been estimated that some 157,000 slaves were imported into the French American colonies prior to 1700, supplied by the Dutch and English, as well as French merchants" (Blackburn, 295).[27]

In early modern France, the slave trade was the quickest road to wealth and social promotion not only for French merchants of the Atlantic seaports and aristocrats like d'Angennes but also for Huguenot middle class families like the Ducasse and the Faneuil. In 1685, after the Edict of Fontainebleau revoked the French Protestants' rights, they too had to choose between conversion to Catholicism, persecution, or exile.[28] Jean-Baptiste Ducasse (1646–1715) and Peter (Pierre) Faneuil (1700–1743) took different roads at that point. As a Huguenot, Ducasse already faced discrimination prior to the Edict of Fontainebleau: he could not become as an officer of the Royal Navy as he wished. Instead, he became an officer in the merchant marine, working for Company of the West Indies and the Company of Senegal.[29] As Director of the Company of Senegal, he became the first major French participant in the slave trade. In 1677, Ducasse took possession of the island of Gorée near Dakar, Senegal. It soon became infamous for its House of Slaves, the place where slaves stayed prior to their departure for the New World. Between 1677 and 1685, Ducasse bought 2,000 slaves a year and sold most of them to d'Angennes. But in 1685, he had to choose between conversion and exile. He chose the former. In 1686, Ducasse and his bride abjured their faith prior to their marriage in Dieppe, France. An appointment as officer in the Royal Navy rewarded Ducasse for his conversion. For ten years, when his country was at war, Ducasse fought along French pirates in the Caribbean. Once the fighting was over, he encouraged the buccaneers to settle down and develop plantations. Paul Butel writes that he played a major role in the "'integration of pirates' in Caribbean society" and helped "speed up the agricultural colonization" (85).[30] His services as a privateer earned him the position of governor of Saint Domingue (1691–1700) where he became even wealthier (Butel, *Histoire des Antilles*, 84–87).

The Faneuils, a wealthy Huguenot family of merchants from La Rochelle chose to immigrate to a Protestant country instead of converting to Catholicism. They were part of the group of settlers who founded New Rochelle. Benjamin and Ann Faneuil had two sons and three daughters, all born in in New Rochelle, including Pierre (Peter) who was born in 1700. When Benjamin died in 1709, the Faneuil children moved to Boston to live with their uncle, Andrew, one of the richest men in New England. Andrew Faneuil had made his fortune in Boston real estate and in the triangular trade. Peter Faneuil went to work for him and soon made a fortune of his own trading with the British Caribbean colonies, Spain, and England. Peter Faneuil owned ships that transported slaves to the West Indies and sugar, rum, and fish to the New England colonies.[31] When Andrew died in 1735, Peter inherited his fortune. One of America's wealthiest men, Peter never married, preferring the life of the Jolly Bachelor—which was the name of one of his ships. According to a contemporary, Lucius M. Sargent, Peter Faneuil "lived as magnificently as a nobleman, as hospitably as a bishop, and as charitably as an apostle." In 1740, Peter financed the construction of a covered market in Boston. Faneuil Hall was completed shortly before his death. Damaged in a fire in 1761, it served as an assembly hall during the American Revolution.

3. New France During the War of the Grand Alliance, 1688–1697

Conflicts between New France and New England continued during King William's War. They were nothing new—the Kirke brothers had occupied Quebec City as early as 1629—but skirmishes along the border between the two colonies occurred more frequently and they intensified in the 1680s and 1690s. The fur trade was big business and its control, in the Hudson Bay and elsewhere, a central stake in the war.[32] The French fur traders had lost ground since the founding of the Hudson's Bay Co. in 1670 despite the establishment of de la Barre's *Compagnie du Nord* in 1682.[33] In addition, when the ships from France did not arrive as scheduled in 1685, the intendant had no supplies to distribute and no money to pay soldiers. Two ingenious innovations came out of this dilemma, however: paper money "made from packs of playing cards" was used to pay the troops and "rankers in the Troupes de la Marine to augment the colony's meagre supply of labor" (Eccles, *The French*, 127–128). But if allowing soldiers to make money on the side was a smart temporary fix, it created serious problems down the road: at times they were not ready for action fast enough when needed. Fortunately, the Canadian militia was more responsive and better trained.

In 1686, Governor Denonville decided to drive the British away from Hudson Bay. In order to complete this task, he selected Pierre de Troyes, the captain of a company of marines he had met on the ship that had brought him to New France in 1685. In March 1686, De Troyes led a group of 100 soldiers and militiamen, 30 percent French, 70 percent Canadian up north to the *Pays d'en haut*. Three of the Le Moyne brothers of Montreal, each in charge a group of 30 men, joined them. In June, they attacked Fort Monsoni and were able to recover a French ship and British cannons. After destroying Fort Rupert and capturing another ship, they used the ships to lay siege on Fort Sainte Anne. A few days later, the fort commander surrendered.[34]

Denonville was not as successful fighting the Five Nations. One of his assignments when he was appointed Governor General of New France in 1685, was to make peace with the Iroquois once and for all. Although he "prevented the Iroquois and the British from breaking the French hold on the fur trade," he was unable to reach a peace agreement with the Iroquois (Eccles, *Frontenac*, 185). With his health declining, he resigned, and Frontenac was appointed to replace him as Governor General in April 1689 (Eccles, *Frontenac*, 199). Once King William's War broke out, 1,500 Iroquois encouraged by New England settlers attacked the French village of Lachine near Montreal and slaughtered its inhabitants on August 4, 1689.[35] The French forces were close-by but failed to intervene and protect the settlers.[36] The Lachine massacre, which led to the death of 200 men, the destruction of 56 farms, and the capture of 120 prisoners, could not go unpunished.

As settlers in New York were supplying the Iroquois with weapons, and the British and their Iroquois allies raiding French villages,[37] Denonville asked for authorization to attack New York City. The Anglo-Iroquois alliance, he contended, would not hold if New York was taken by the French and the Iroquois' supply line to British goods disappeared. It was imperative to act and to act quickly: "By the end of 1689, the people

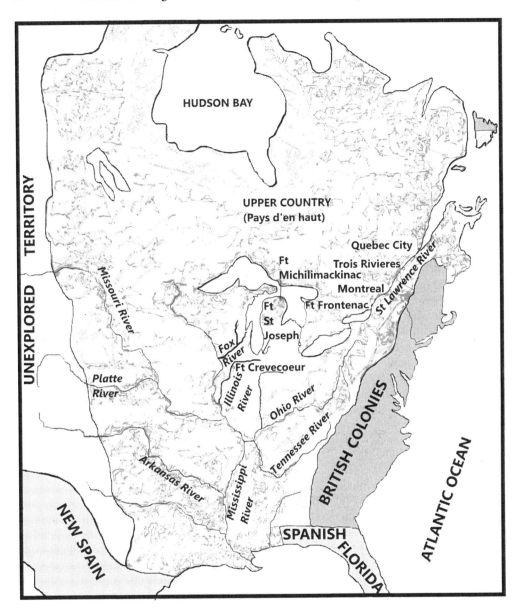

New France in the 1680s (author's map).

of New France considered their plight to be desperate. There seemed to be no way of curbing the continual Iroquois attacks" (Eccles, *Frontenac*, 223). As Denonville was retiring, his replacement was to carry out this mission. But when Frontenac arrived in New France to serve his second term as Governor General (1689–1698), in October 1689, it was already too late into the season to follow up on this plan. Instead, the new Governor General attacked British settlements in Albany, New York, "the main Iroquois supply base" (Eccles, *The French*, 106), as well as in Massachusetts and Maine in 1690. The Abenaki, led by Jean-Vincent d'Abbadie, Baron of Saint-Castin (1652–1707), were fighting in Acadia. Saint Castin had long lived among the Abenaki, married into the tribe, and become one of their chiefs.[38] The French Canadians, who were used to the Native

American style of war, the *petite guerre*, or *guerrilla*, had adopted it, and could fight better than the regular French soldiers and their English counterparts (Eccles, *The French*, 108).[39] Their numbers were small in comparison, however.

Antoine Laumet de La Mothe, sieur de Cadillac (1658–1730), a colorful figure who left his mark on New France, makes his appearance in north American historical records during the War of the Grand Alliance.[40] Cadillac had arrived in New France in 1663, married the daughter of a business partner, with whom he had 13 children, and obtained the *seigneurie* of Les Douacques (Bar Harbor, Maine) in 1688. Although viewed as a troublemaker by the French authorities, Frontenac considered him as a valuable asset: his knowledge of the New England coast, acquired while in service of privateer François Guyon, would come in handy if the French took New York. Louis Phélypeaux, Count of Pontchartrain (1643–1727)[41] and Secretary of State for the Navy in charge of the colonies, therefore appointed Cadillac as an officer in the Troupes de la Marine for the duration of the War of the Grand Alliance (Eccles, *The French*, 114).[42] Cadillac subsequently participated in several information gathering missions along the coast of New England in preparation of French attacks.

The British response to the French raids was a military campaign that led to the English re-conquest of Acadia and the partial destruction of Port Royal, home to several hundred Frenchmen by then, including the Cadillacs. The governor of Massachusetts, Williams Phips, had decided to retaliate against Frontenac's attacks by invading Canada in the hope of getting rid of the French in North America once and for all. Taking Quebec City was part of Phips's plan, so when his fleet reached its walls, he demanded its surrender. Frontenac's response has become legendary: "I have no reply to make to your general other than from the mouths of my cannons and muskets." The 1690 Battle of Quebec ended with a French victory and made Frontenac even more popular in the colony than he already was. The French had also held their ground in the Hudson Bay: between 1686 and 1697, Pierre Le Moyne d'Iberville (1661–1706),[43] the Navy officer the Chevalier de Troyes had left in charge of operations at Fort Monsoni, had taken over most English positions in that area.[44] South of the St. Lawrence valley, the Canadians had achieved excellent results as well.[45] But the British had warned they would come back and take Quebec City, so the war was far from over.

To the extent that it created a supply glut, the war paralyzed the lifeline of the French colony, the fur trade: "By 1695, the supply had risen to four times the annual demand of the French market, and the Company of the Farm, which had to accept all beaver at fixed prices, found itself with a surplus of 3.5 million livres' weight, with more flooding in" (Eccles, *The French*, 109). Pontchartrain suspected that Frontenac who, like all the officers in command of western forts, "reaped rich harvest of beaver pelts" (Eccles, 109), was dragging his feet to add to the glut and benefit from it later instead of engaging the Iroquois.[46] An advocate of western expansion, Frontenac had found an eager ally in Cadillac whom he appointed Commander at Fort de Buade (Michillimakinak) in the *Pays d'En-Haut* in 1694.[47] During his two-year tenure, Cadillac enriched himself considerably "by selling unlimited quantities of brandy to the Indians" and as a fur trader "by fleecing the coureurs des bois"—who dared not complain because he was known as Frontenac protégé (Zoltvany). In 1695, while exploring the Great Lakes, Cadillac made an important discovery, the strait (*détroit* in French) connecting Lake Huron and Lake Erie.

In 1696, Frontenac went to war against the Oneida and Onondaga, thereby weakening the Iroquois nations who ended up suing for peace. The Treaty of Ryswick that ended to the War of the Grand Alliance in 1697 officially suspended Franco-British hos-tilities in North America. France agreed to recognize King William as the legitimate King of England and to return to England the Hudson Bay d'Iberville had fought so hard to win for the French. The treaty was nonetheless beneficial to France in the form of territo-rial expansion in Europe.[48] In New France, settlers and merchants faced a dire economic situation due to the fur glut. Pontchartrain sought to solve it by ordering the immedi-ate closure of the military posts in the *Pays d'en haut*. But the objections of New France administrators, who feared that abandoning the west would encourage the Iroquois and the English to move in, made him change his mind.[49]

The last years of the century witnessed changes in administrative personnel. Pontchartrain was promoted to Chancellor of France in 1699 and succeeded by his son, Jérôme Phélypeaux de Pontchartrain (1674–1747), as Secretary of the Navy. Frontenac died towards the end of 1698 and Louis Hector de Callière (1648–1703) was appointed Governor General of New France.[50] Callière, who inherited the task of ending war with the Iroquois, was successful. His signature achievement is the signing of the Treaty of Montreal,[51] an event that took months to prepare and brought representatives from 39 allied First Nations to Montreal in 1701.[52] That same year, Cadillac established *Fort Pontchartrain du Détroit*, now the city of Detroit, before sailing to France to try and sell his new pet project to Pontchartrain: to make Detroit the center of the French fur trade. With its ideal location further south than Machilimakinac (Fort de Buade), on the trad-ing route between the Missouri, the Mississippi, and the Great Lakes, he argued, the straight "would serve as a barrier to English penetration of the west and restrain the Iro-quois" (Eccles, *The French*, 114).[53] Despite reasonable objections on the part of the New France establishment, Cadillac gained support in Versailles for his plan. By then, Louis XIV's colonial emphasis had already shifted from north to south, away from Canada towards Louisiana.

4. New France during the War of the Spanish Succession, 1701–1714

No sooner had war ended in New France than it was looming again in Europe due to uncertainties associated with the Spanish succession. If a Habsburg became King of Spain, France would have two frontiers to defend in North America but if Louis XIV's grand-son was chosen, Spain and France would become allies. In both cases, it became impera-tive to assert French presence in North America. Many ideas were considered on how best to proceed. Vauban, the military engineer famous for the star-shaped design of his forts, penned a memoir on the means of strengthening and expanding France's North American colonies in 1699. As a remedy to the "small size of population, the proliferation of priests, and the self-serving policies of the trade companies," he suggested providing enough men, mostly soldiers and craftsmen, and sufficient equipment to develop agriculture on a large scale.[54] But the Secretary of the Navy did not follow up on his recommendations.[55]

Instead, Louis XIV decided to assert French presence in Louisiana, to fend off attacks either from Mexico, if Spain remained an enemy of France, or from New Eng-land, if Spain became an ally (Eccles, *The French*, 113). Much to the chagrin of the authori-ties of New France, who had a lot to lose in terms of support and authority, and over their objections,[56] the instructions from Versailles were to maintain existing trading posts and missions in the Great Lakes and the Illinois Country and to strengthen their defense by building new forts. The idea was to build a continuous chain of forts (*chaîne de postes*) from Acadia, through the St. Lawrence River Valley, the Great Lakes, and the Mississippi Valley, all the way down to Louisiana.[57]

The plan to settle Louisiana was executed immediately. Pierre Le Moyne d'Iberville left Brest with four ships in 1698 and succeeded where La Salle had failed: he landed in Louisiana.[58] The French immediately built Fort de la Boulaye and put Louis Antoine Juchereau de St. Denis (1676–1744), d'Iberville's cousin, in charge.[59] Then the Marine troops added Fort Maurepas (Biloxi, by Gulfport) and Fort Louis de la Mobile (Mobile, Alabama). While exploring the left bank of the Mississippi River, d'Iberville and his men inquired about a red pole they had seen planted in the ground. It turned out to be a Native American marker for hunting grounds. The French name stuck: "Baton Rouge" appeared on maps in 1698. Upon leaving Louisiana, d'Iberville appointed Enseign Sauvole (1671–1701) as commander at Fort Maurepas in 1699 and then as the first governor of Louisiana in 1700.[60] After Sauvole's sudden death in 1701, d'Iberville's younger brother, the 21-year-old Jean-Baptiste Le Moyne de Bienville (1680–1767), assumed command of the colony.[61] The Louisiana forts were meant to mark the end of the "cordon drawn at the rear of the English colonies to hem them in between the Atlantic and the Appalachia" (Eccles, *The French*, 114). The Governor General of New France who replaced Callière in 1702, Louis Rigaud de Vaudreuil (1643–1725), had no authority in the new southern colony.

The Illinois settlements were recent but so were the New England settlements at the time. When the village of Kaskaskia was founded by "Kaskaskias and French traders who had married into the tribe, New York had passed seventy-seven years; the city of Philadelphia only a score. Quebec lacked but five years of ending its first century" (Belting, 10). In the Mississippi valley, French Canadians continued to settle and to create new villages, mostly in the "Country of the Illinois," thereby opening a new chapter in the history of New France.[62] The French settlements were few and far between, however. In 1682, La Salle had left Henri de Tonty in charge of Fort Saint Louis on the Illinois River,[63] prior to returning to France.[64] By 1685, De Tonty had learned of his friend's ill-fated expedition to Texas but since rumor had it that La Salle was alive, de Tonty had left to meet him. He had sailed down the Mississippi River as far as the Gulf of Mexico, but he had not found him. On his way back in 1686, de Tonty had established a trading post at the confluence of the Arkansas and Mississippi Rivers, near a Quapaw village. It became the Arkansas Post, the first French settlement in Louisiana (Rollings, 49).

Morris Arnold sees Tonty as the prototype of the "governing entrepreneur," the type of French official already encountered in the Great Lake area that was to become prevalent in Louisiana as well: commandants that were not "government officials who were coincidentally in business, but […] businessmen who were coincidentally in government" (132).[65] Yet between its foundation and the 1720s, the Illinois Country was known for giving "shelter mostly to hunters and vagabond of small means and less cultivation" (Arnold, 131).[66] But what traders and subsistence farmers enjoyed, was independence, or at least far more freedom than they would ever have possibly enjoyed in metropolitan France at the time. One could put this freedom to good or bad uses, to enslave friendly Native Americans out of greed, or to live peacefully near them, to discover new people and cultures, or to destroy them. The French certainly did both.[67]

The Illinois Indians[68] abandoned the original village of Kaskaskia in 1692 and the mission moved to the same new location as the Illinois village (Brown, *History*, 3–4).[69] In 1696, a priest founded the mission of the Holy family, a log cabin in the Native American village of Cahokia, and he was joined a few years later by a group of "French priests from the Seminary of Quebec" (Rollings, 49).[70] At that time, Ekberg explains, "early French explorers used it [the term 'Illinois country'] to designate the region associated with the Illinois Indian nation, roughly the northern two-thirds of the present state of Illinois, plus adjacent areas in Missouri, Iowa, and Wisconsin" (*French Roots*, 32). In that area, however, New England was not the enemy, hostile Native American Nations like the Sioux and the Fox were. In 1703, the Kaskaskia village "was threatened with attacks by the Sioux from the west and the Kaskaskia moved again down to a peninsula between the Mississippi and what was known then as the Metchigamia River" (Brown, *History*, 5). Game and fish were abundant and "beaver so plentiful that the skins were used for money" (Belting, 12). Moreover, "[t]he bottom land between the two rivers was one of the most fertile strips in the whole of the Mississippi Valley" (Belting, 11).

Kaskaskia soon prospered not only because of the material advantages it enjoyed thanks to a generous natural environment but also to spirit of its founders:

> Half a century or more separated life in the Illinois country from life in the villages of old France. In a sense, it was half a century ahead with the Revolution already in the past. The traders who founded Kaskaskia had been born in Canada; they were pioneers, the sons of pioneers, independent and self-sufficient. And if the government that ruled them seemed autocratic in comparison with the government of their English neighbors, that autocracy was more apparent than real. In the wilderness, they acknowledged no lord; in the village they made their own law [Belting, 41].

Among the challenges early habitants of the Illinois country encountered were the Mississippi floods, which forced the relocation of several villages,[71] and the rowdy behavior of the part-time residents, the voyageurs and *coureurs des bois*, who caused trouble "by inciting Indian forays in order to obtain slaves to sell to the English" (Belting, 12). As the priests were complaining about their debauchery, the French authorities dispatched a few soldiers to keep the peace, a first time in 1708 and also in 1711 (Brown, *History*, 5).[72] One of those soldiers, Pénicaut [also spelled "Pénicault"], was stationed in Kaskaskia for four months and wrote about life in a village that "was still an Indian village with a few resident Canadian traders" at the time (Brown, 6).[73]

The implementation of the fortification project decided in Versailles depended once again on the good-will of the Native Americans of the Illinois Country and Louisiana:

> Not one canoe would have survived the trip up to the *pays d'en haut* without the help of Indian guides and translators. Not one fur would have made it to Europe without the interventions of Native trappers and the consensual trade of Indians. Little westward expansion would have taken place without the consent of the people of the straits, and almost certainly no posts would have been built in the heart of Indian country that could provision or protect unwelcome travelers. The French were there because the Anishinaabeg wanted them there [McDonnell, *Masters of Empire*, 17].

McDonnell's comments pertain to the Great Lakes nations and the *Pays d'en haut*, but they apply to all Native American nations the French encountered and sought to befriend. As a result, the forts were often built near Indian villages, and as such, had a crucial military and economic function.[74] They were places where French soldiers, settlers, and merchants constantly interacted with Native Americans (Balvay, *L'Epée*, 77).

From Champlain's days onward, the governors of New France had sought to meet the First Nations halfway[75] and new forms of sociability had developed in the zones of cross-cultural interaction that the forts and their surroundings represented.[76] As France sought to assert its sovereignty over this vast country, the French and the Natives continued to adhere to old rituals, the calumet, or pipe-smoking, ceremony,[77] the tattooing of the French and the baptism of Native Americans. New ones made their appearance such as the adoption of French officers in Native American tribes and vice-versa.[78] Soldiers who decided to settle down once their service commitment ended often married Native American women. For the French, the fort represented a zone of intercultural contact. For the British, by contrast, it was the point where savagery and civilization met,[79] a stronghold devoted to the protection of settlers from Native Americans incursions. Since the English conceived of the frontier as a moving line, the fort was also the opening door to further colonization.[80]

In times of war, however, the French had to make extra efforts to maintain good relations with their Native American allies. After the creation of Detroit, for instance, "it required all the considerable diplomatic skill of the governor general, Philippe Rigaud de Vaudreuil, to prevent a wholesale defection of the western allies" (Eccles, *The French*, 115). Shortly thereafter, even before the Duke of Anjou had been crowned King of Spain, war had started again and the governor had all the more reasons to hope that the Peace of Montreal would hold and that the Iroquois would not renew their traditional alliance with New England. The War of the Spanish Succession was to last from 1701 to 1713 in Europe, its twin in North America, Queen Ann's War, from 1702 to 1713. As the hostilities started, Vaudreuil signaled to his English counterpart that the French would not attack New York.[81] New York was spared, but the war was fought on numerous other theaters of operations, along the New England border, in the Illinois country, in Louisiana, but mostly in Acadia.

On the Acadian peninsula, where settlers were mostly cattle farmers with small herds of cows, sheep, and goats, the French relied on their long alliance with the Abenaki for their economic welfare as well as for war (Eccles, *The French*, 117). Despite regular British attacks, the villages were flourishing particularly in the Minas Basin (Grand-Pré, Les Mines, Quobequid). Parishioners had even paid for the construction of their church, Saint-Charles des Mines, in 1690 during King William's war. A few years later, in 1704, the Recollects brothers, who were very active in New France, had built the first brick house in Port Royal, by then home to nearly 400 inhabitants, in spite of a 17-day-long British blockade that year.[82] The French and their Abenaki allies had the upper hand in guerrilla warfare, but the British had command of the sea. After the former attacked Deerfield, east of Albany, in 1704, the British organized the invasion of Acadia, laying siege to Port-Royal in 1709. As Quebec City was being threatened as well at the time, no reinforcement could be sent and Port Royal, soon to be renamed Annapolis-Royal, had to surrender. Nothing came out of the attempt to take Quebec but the French lost Acadia.

Developing Louisiana while fighting the War of the Spanish Succession was not an easy task as it stretched financial and military resources.[83] When the French arrived in Louisiana, the Mississippi delta was home to the Native Americans tribes of "the Natchez, Houmas,[84] Biloxis, Choctaws, and Chickasaws" (Lappas, "Mississippi," 816). There are no precise figures on the Native American population of Louisiana at the turn of the 18th century but estimates range from 100,000 to 200,000 for Lower Louisiana alone (Havard and Vidal, *Histoire*, 201).[85] As in other areas of cross-cultural contact, the native population suffered from diseases brought by the French. The Chitimacha, who lived in the Mississippi delta, were nonetheless friendly until 1706 when a few planters started to reduce them to slavery.[86]

When Fort Louis (Mobile) obtained Louisiana's first Roman Catholic parish in 1703, life in the capital of Louisiana was tough and void of religiosity and morality. The presence of priests and missionaries would do little over the rest of the century to alter the prevailing unorthodox character of this rough frontier town. The population of Fort Louis was predominantly male and understandably small: 279 inhabitants in 1708; 178 in 1710, and 400 in 1712. According to Jesuit accounts, it was composed primarily of bachelors, soldiers and visiting *coureurs des bois* whose favorite pastimes were "drinking, gambling and lechery." Some trappers engaged in human trafficking and sold *sauvagesses*, Native American women they captured, in the capital. Efforts to bring gentler mores to the colony failed. Neither the 22 women dispatched from France to Louisiana in 1704 to marry male residents of the colony nor the dozen young ladies brought in 1712 by Governor Cadillac's wife made any dent in predominantly male frontier values.

Cadillac, who was appointed as Governor of Louisiana in 1710, sailed to France instead of taking office. He wanted financial backing and convinced Pontchartrain to let Antoine Crozat (1655–1738), a wealthy financier who had made a fortune in the slave trade, lease the colony:

> Like the minister of Marine twelve years before, the millionaire entrepreneur could not keep himself from falling under the amazing Gascon's spell. In September, 1712 a company was formed for the development of Louisiana to which Crozat contributed 600,000 to 700,000 *livres* and Cadillac his administrative talents [Zoltvany, "Laumet"].

The land grant for Louisiana Crozat obtained included not only Lower, but also Upper Louisiana (Illinois Country), as well as an exclusive trade monopoly (Rollings, 49).[87] The Cadillac family settled in Fort Louis and Cadillac took office. But Crozat and Cadillac soon disagreed on how best to expand the colony. Cadillac would have liked to expand westwards towards Spanish Texas and Mexico, but Crozat opted for the north so as to strengthen communications between Lower Louisiana—in today's terms roughly Alabama, Louisiana, Arkansas, and Mississippi—and Upper Louisiana, which covered Missouri, Illinois, and Indiana.[88] A new administrative structure was set up in Lower Louisiana, with an extension in Illinois Country where a "Provincial Council" had jurisdiction "from the Kansas River in the West to the Wabash in the east, and from Fort d'Orleans in the south to the small post of Peoria in the north" (Brown, 8).[89]

During his term as governor of Louisiana, Cadillac continued to put his interests first and "true to his old self, was quarrelling furiously with his colleagues in government" (Zoltvany, "Laumet"). He made enemies with the Company of the Mississippi's financial officer, Jean-Baptiste Du Bois Duclos, and with Bienville, now the King's Commandant—allegedly after the latter refused to marry one of his daughters! By 1716, Crozat had had enough of Cadillac's antics and relieved him his functions. The Cadillacs returned to France and the former governor of Louisiana died there, in the small town of Castelsarrasin, in 1730. In light of this less than brilliant career, Zoltvany rightly wonders how one of the "worst scoundrels ever to set foot in New France" could have become one of "its great early heroes," in honor of whom, for instance, a U.S. luxury car brand is named.[90]

While Bienville was appeasing the Native American nations of Lower Louisiana despite the obstacles Cadillac put in his way, the New France authorities were trying to put out another fire lit by the Governor of Louisiana in the Great Lakes area. Cadillac's plan for Detroit had been approved in Versailles and a great number of Native American tribes had answered his call and moved to the area. In this multicultural environment, tempers flared up easily and conflicts between members of rival Native American Nations often degenerated. The Fox Wars, in fact, grew out of a conflict over women. It arose when the Mascouten, who were allied with the Fox (Meskwaki), came to Detroit in 1712 to claim their wives, mothers, and sisters, who had been taken prisoners by Ottawa and Illinois warriors and used as slaves.

Slavery was a Native American practice that had existed long before the French's arrival in North America. After a brutal initiation into a tribe, captured enemies became slaves. Their function was often to "replace" a member of the tribe who has passed away. The French word for "slave" in the Native American context was "panis," a deformation of the word "Pawnee"—because many slaves came from that tribe.[91] In the context of the Fox wars, slaves were often sent to work in the St. Lawrence valley for French settlers who thought that they would be able to use them as bargaining chips in case of Fox attacks. Like their Native American allies, the French of the Great Lakes area started taking prisoners of war as slaves. They did not introduce slavery, but they became willing participants in this ugly business during the War of the Spanish Succession.[92]

Instead of mediating between the rival fractions, the French commandant of Detroit became embroiled in a battle that lasted over two weeks (Havard and Vidal, *The French*, 294–295). In the end, the Fox fled, only to be pursued, killed, or taken prisoners. It was the start of a war that would last three decades and greatly perturb the fur trade. The Fox controlled the Fox River, a communication link that was vital for the fur trade in the Great Lakes-Mississippi water system.[93] The river also provided access to western tribes the French were interested in trading with, particularly the Sioux, but the Fox, who were enemies of the Sioux, would not allow the French to pass. After they seized French merchandise on the river and laid siege to Fort Pontchartrain (Detroit) in 1712, the French attacked, causing a war that ended four years later when Louis de la Porte de Louvigny and his 800 French soldiers defeated the Fox in Wisconsin at *Little Butte des Morts*. By 1716, 2000 of the 3500 Fox people were dead and many enslaved.

The 1713 treaty of Utrecht that ended the War of the Spanish Succession greatly benefited England (Hiller). France had to recognize British sovereignty over Rupert's Land (Hudson's Bay Co.), Newfoundland, Acadia, and half of Saint Kitts. In Acadia, France only retained Ile Royale (Cape Breton Island) and *Ile Saint-Jean* (Prince Edward Island). The relocation of 3,000 colonists from Acadia in 1716 caused a lot of headaches to the governor of Ile Royale, Philippe Pastour de Costebelle (1661–1717) and to his successor in 1717, Joseph de Monbeton de Brouillan, nicknamed Saint-Ovide (1676–1755), who would remain in office until 1739. Peace was restored but at great cost for France. In fact, the Treaty of Utrecht, inaugurated a period of decline for the country on the European as well as the North American scene.

By the end of the 17th century, New France was part of a vast French colonial empire.

The West Indies, the French islands of the Caribbean, and the East Indies, the French islands of the Indian Ocean, occupied a special place in this empire because of their strategic location as military outposts in overseas territories and of a climate propitious to the production of rare agricultural goods such as sugar and coffee:

> The splendor of the French court helped to advertise and promote French luxury products, setting a standard for the aristocracy and the haute bourgeoisie throughout the continent. At Versailles, without intending it, Louis XIV had built a showcase for the exotic produce of the plantations: chocolate served from gleaming silver pots; snuff taken from elegant little boxes, banqueting tables with elaborate sugar confections [Blackburn, 301].

Just before the end of the War of the Spanish succession, New France was at its apex. In 1713 the colony covered an immense territory extending from Newfoundland, through Acadia, Canada, and Illinois country to Louisiana and the Gulf of Mexico. The treaty of Utrecht had just made a small dent in it. Nonetheless, France and England had already fought two European wars with ramifications in North America. France won the first of these two French and Indian Wars, but the power balance tilted in favor of England after the second. The Acadians bore the brunt of this defeat: although French by language and culture, they were now British subjects.

The Abenaki of Acadia, who were not party to the treaty of Utrecht, resented the British take-over of Acadia, now renamed Nova Scotia, so war resumed. It was called Father Rale's War after one of the leaders, who together with Chief Gray Lock and Chief Paugus of the Wabanaki Confederacy[94] waged war on New England. The conflict lasted from 1722 to 1725 and took place along the Kennebec River in Maine, a river that the French regarded as the border between the two colonies. French priests had established four missions and three forts in the area to protect the colony from enemy incursions. The Wabanaki lost that war. Father Rale was killed in 1724, Chief Paugus in 1725. Chief Grey Lock took the Abenaki to New Brunswick and to the St. Lawrence Valley. The Drummer's Treaty restored peace in 1725 and the French left Maine. They continued to live in Acadia, however, except in Annapolis Royal and Canso that were now English settlements. The Abenaki's refusal to become British subjects sowed the seeds for the next war, Father Le Loutre's War in the late 1740s.

Given how many wars had been fought by the French against the Iroquois and would be fought in the 18th century against other Native American nations during the French regime, Francis Parkman's observation that "Spanish civilization crushed the Indian; English civilization scorned and neglected him; [and] French civilization embraced and cherished him" (quoted in Balvay, 14), is clearly an exaggeration, even if, like all cultural stereotypes, it contains a grain of truth. The cliché of the "French as friend of the aborigine" on which Parkman elaborated went as far back as the Renaissance—it is found in Montaigne's writings, for instance—but it received a new impulse in the 18th century through the work of the Baron de Lahontan. This poor nobleman had lived in New France, first as a settler in Acadia in the 1680s, and then as the commanding officer at St. Joseph on the St. Clair River in the early 1690s—before Fort Pontchartrain of the Detroit was established.[95] Although he had himself fought against the Iroquois, Lahontan left a very positive image of the Native Americans in his writings. Published in 1703, his *New Voyages to North America* are said to have contributed to the eighteenth-century myth of the "noble savage"[96] and inspired Jean-Jacques Rousseau, the Enlightenment philosopher.

5. Tips for Further Investigations

Interesting People to Look Up

Guillaume Couture (1618–1701)
Louis-Hector de Callière (1648–1703)
Pierre Meyzonnat (1663–1714)
Claude-Charles Le Roy, dit Bacqueveille de la Potherie (1663–1736)
Pierre Le Blond de La Tour (1673–1723)
Raudot, Antoine-Denis (1679–1737)
Bernard-Anselme de Saint-Castin (1689–1720)

Related Primary Texts

Durand, du Dauphiné. *Un Français en Virginie* [1686].
Durand, of Dauphiné. *A Frenchman in Virginia* [1686].
Raynal, Abbé. "The Europeans go into Africa to buy men to cultivate the plantations of the West Indies. Conduct of this trade," in *A History of the Two Indies*, ed. P. Jimack, 147–162.

Related Films and Work of Fiction

D'Iberville, TV series in 39 episodes, Quebec 1967–1968.
Simiot, Bernard. "2. Mathieu Carbec." *Ces Messieurs de Saint-Malo*. Paris Albin Michel, 1983. The second part of the novel corresponds to the years covered in this chapter, from 1684 to the Treaty of Utrecht in 1713.
Versailles, Seasons 2 and 3, 2015 Canal+ TV series, available on Netflix.

CHAPTER V

France's American Colonies, 1715–1755

The chapter describes New France at its apogee, when it stretched from Canada to the Upper Country, the *Pays d'en haut* up north, and from the Illinois Country to Louisiana. it also discusses the challenges posed by the gigantic size of the colony. As Havard and Vidal explain, the province of New France had grown so considerably by that time as to become unmanageable:

> In theory, this huge territory constituted one single colony under the authority of the governor of New France; in practice, it worked as three different colonies (Acadia; Canada, which included the St. Lawrence Valley and the Upper Countries; and Louisiana), each with its own links to the home country. Less a single colony governed by the general-governor at Quebec, New France functioned more like a loosely structured confederacy, unified by a collection of administrative, military, demographic, economic, and cultural links [Havard and Vidal, "Making New France New Again"].

Louisiana itself was divided into Lower and Upper Louisiana since 1718, when the Illinois Country (Upper Louisiana) became part of Louisiana instead of Canada.[1] Although this area of the French colony played a considerable role in the development of the United States after the Louisiana Purchase, when it became the Gateway to the West, its history is often overlooked. Section 3, "Upper Louisiana: the Illinois Country," therefore draws from the work of historians who have devoted their research to this topic to present the French Illinois Country.[2]

Developing New France was a challenging undertaking as conflicts and wars multiplied in the 18th century as the result of tribal and colonial rivalries. Both colonial powers, England and France, relied on Native American allies to advance their agenda but these alliances often shifted.[3] Section 2, "Settling Louisiana: the 1720s, 1730s, and 1740s," examines several of the conflicts that occurred in those years between the French and the Native American nations who opposed them. As we will see in section 4, "Trouble in Acadia, 1744–1748," the conflict for colonial supremacy in North America intensified with France's entry, in 1744, in the War of the Austrian Succession (1740–1748). Known as King George's War, it was particularly devastating in Acadia. But first, the focus is on Louisiana during its initial phase of development, when it was run by John Law's Company of the West.

1. Banking on Louisiana: John Law and the Company of the West (1717–1720)

Political and financial uncertainty characterized the four decades of the 18th century on which this chapter centers. When King Louis XIV died in 1715, one of his great-grand

78

sons, five-year-old Louis, became King Louis XV.[4] During his minority, Philip of Orleans (1674–1723), a nephew of Louis XIV, served as Regent and ruled with a Council. Louis XIV had succeeded in making France the most powerful nation in Europe, militarily and culturally, but his love of war and glory had come at a heavy price. France had long had recourse to public borrowing to cover deficits and this practice had reached catastrophic proportions during the Sun King's reign. At the King's death, the state treasury was empty due to the regime's politics of glory and prestige and the extravagant way of life at Versailles. France was also weak because it lacked banking institutions and hence a solid financial foundation.

Philip of Orleans hired a Scottish economist, John Law (1671–1729), to address the financial crisis. John Law proposed two remedies to fix the problem, banking and investments. In 1716, he founded the *Banque Générale Privée* (General Private Bank), which became the Royal Bank two years later, and he introduced paper notes in order to facilitate the circulation of money. The bank's function was to serve as a central institution for tax collection but it was also an investment bank. John Law then proceeded to create a similar central institution for trade, a joint stock trading company, by merging existing companies into one. Banking on the development of Louisiana, Law first targeted Crozat's company, the Mississippi Company,[5] which he renamed the Company of the West (*la Compagnie d'Occident*) in 1717.[6] The Company of the West promised huge benefits to shareholders.[7] In order to boost confidence in Louisiana, they were told of its unlimited agricultural potential—thanks to all the "exotic" crops like rice, indigo, tobacco, and sugar cane that grew there due to an abundance of sun and water—and of the attractiveness of the region. Law's plan worked well at first. So many investors were attracted by the company's royal status and by the Louisiana dream that the Royal Bank was able to settle the State's debts.

One of the objectives of the trading company created by John Law was "to establish company plantations along the Mississippi Valley to raise foodstuff for the French Caribbean islands" (Rollings), so that the islands could focus on growing exotic crops. Following the cession of the western part of Hispaniola to the French in 1698, Saint-Domingue had started to produce sugar on a big scale. There were already over fifty sugar refineries on the French part of the island in 1701, and by 1720, Saint Domingue had become the world's number one producer of sugar (Devèze, 256). It owed this performance to the labor of slaves whom the French were able to purchase directly from Africa after 1719. The white population grew as well, leading to the island's early urban development. Founded in 1711, the city of Cap Français (now Cap Haitien) replaced Port de Paix as Saint Domingue's capital.[8]

Good communications between the Caribbean and Louisiana were deemed essential to the Company of the West's mission. New Orleans, founded in 1718 by Le Moyne de Bienville, was meant to be a city-port, a trade center that would serve as the link to Upper Louisiana and New France, via the Mississippi, and to the Caribbean, France, and Africa, by sea. The city was located on land previously occupied by the Chitimachas, who had been subdued or exiled by then. In accordance with the Company of the West's instructions, Bienville selected this site for three reasons: first, because it seemed well protected from Mississippi floods; second, because the soil seemed suitable for cultivating wheat; and third because it was close enough to the fort at Mobile.[9] Further down river, Fort La Balize also provided military protection after 1721. But New Orleans could only become the trade center the Company envisioned if it had a good harbor. One of the administrators' initial preoccupations therefore, was to overcome the navigation problem created by the sandbars and debris blocking access to the city from the sea.[10] New Orleans, *La Nouvelle Orléans,* was named in honor of the city of Orleans, France, and of Philip, Duke of Orleans and Regent of France at the time. It became the third capital of Louisiana and the governor's place of residence in 1723, after Biloxi (1720–23) and prior to that Mobile, which became a military and commercial center.[11] Adrien de Pauger (?–1726) designed New Orleans's *Vieux Carré,* today's French quarter, and engineer Pierre Le Blond de La Tour (1673–1724) used slave labor to raise its first buildings.[12]

The thirst for silver and gold was still strong in France and the Company of the West was willing to work hard to get its hands on it. It was imperative "to open trade routes to the Spanish colonies and exchange French goods for Mexican silver" (Rollings). Such was Louis Juchereau de St. Denis's mission when he pushed the exploration of Louisiana up north to the Red River and founded Fort Saint Jean Baptiste as a trading outpost with Spanish Texas and Mexico in 1716. The fort later became the site of the future city of Natchitoches, Louisiana (Rollings, 50).[13] In 1719, similarly, Jean-Baptise Bénard de La Harpe (1683–1765) visited the First Nation of the Caddo and established a trading post on the Red River, Fort Malouin,[14] near what is now Texarkana, Texas.[15] The same year, Claude Charles Du Tisné (1681–1730) led the first expedition to Osage and Wichita Country in present-day Kansas (Rollings, 51).[16]

One of the Company's dearest hope was to find and mine precious metals. At the turn of the century, French explorers had found lead in the Illinois country, a metal used to produce ammunition, and they had mined it on a small scale. Cadillac also prospected for silver and gold with his son in the Illinois during his ill-fated journey up north in 1715, without finding what he wanted.[17] By 1717, rumors about precious metals had reached France. The Company of the West therefore wanted to find the deposits allegedly located in the Illinois Country. It was ready to spend "enormous sums of money to explore and exploit the natural resources of Louisiana" and it did (Rollings, 50). No mine opened in the early years of the Company of the West's regime, but the importance granted to the Illinois Country is sufficiently reflected in its insistence on having it be part of Louisiana instead of Canada (Havard and Vidal, *Histoire,* 231).

For decades, the only French fort in the Illinois Country had been Fort St. Louis, created by La Salle in 1682 and commanded by Pierre de Liette (1672–1729) from 1714[18] to 1718.[19] When the Illinois Country became Upper Louisiana, part of Louisiana instead of Canada,[20] it soon obtained its own Provincial Council[21] and its own military district.[22] In 1718 therefore, the Company of the West sent Lieutenant Pierre Dugué de Boisbriand[23] (1675–1736), a cousin of Pierre Le Moyne d'Iberville, to the Illinois Country, to prepare a settlement (Ekberg, *French Roots,* 33–42). Boisbriand had another fort built, Fort de Chartres,[24] at the time "the most comfortable and the most solid fort in North America" (Creagh, *Nos Cousins,* 83). This wooden fort was meant to protect French interests and French lives. For if the local Native Americans, the Illinois, were loyal to the French, "groups associated with them, the Miami and the Pianksshaw, for example, tended to favor the British," and other tribes, "the Fox and Sioux, raided into the area frequently, causing difficulties in the trade activities" (Brown, *History,* 57). But in addition to serving as a military outpost and housing "two companies of infantry at the garrison" (Brown, *History,* 60),[25] Fort de Chartres was also the seat of the government and administration for Upper Louisiana (Brown, *History,* 61–62). The Mississippi floods were not kind to the fort, which was destroyed and rebuilt several times. After Boisbriand returned to New

Orleans to serve as Governor of Louisiana in 1724, new commandants were appointed on a regular basis at Fort de Chartres.[26]

Spain had explored and claimed the Great Plains in the 16th century, but the actual occupants of the land were Pawnees and Otoe-Missouria who controlled access to the Missouri and Platte Rivers.[27] In the first decades of the 18th century, as French explorers were pushing further west, Etienne Véniard de Bourgmont (1679–1734) reached the mouth of *la rivière platte*, the French translation of the Otoe name for the Platte River.[28] By canoeing up river, the French were entering Nebraska, Spanish territory, at a time when war was looming again in Europe. The French were not yet at war with Spain when the Governor of New Mexico sent Lieutenant-General Pedro de Villasur and a party of Spanish, Pueblo, and Apache guides to the Great Plains to capture French traders and settlers who were encroaching on what they regarded as their territory. Using a Pawnee slave as an interpreter, Villasur tried in vain to talk the Pawnees into handing over the few French traders who lived among them. Instead, the interpreter escaped and the Pawnees, Otoes, and the French attacked the Villarsur expedition in August 1720, killing nearly 50. The Spaniards gave up on the Great Plains at that time and the French trade expanded in this area.

The War of the Quadruple Alliance had broken out in 1718 in Europe and was once again a war of succession caused by King Philip V of Spain's ambitions.[29] France only joined the alliance in 1719 and faced Spain along the Florida border in North America. Le Moyne de Bienville, who was starting his third term as governor of Louisiana when war broke out, led a military expedition to Pensacola, Florida, in May 1719. The French were victorious and Pensacola was briefly French, from August 1719 until the peace treaty was signed. It was returned it to Spain after the war in 1722.

Officially, the Company of the West was opposed to Indian slavery.[30] Native Americans were viewed as potential partners in the pelt trade instead, and appreciated for their talents as farmers (Rollings, 50). The Natchez, one of the three largest of the First Nations of Lower Louisiana, were a sedentary people of around 3,000 souls in 1700 spread out over several villages. In French eyes, they were the most civilized Native Americans around because of their skills in agriculture, their high standard of living, and a class society not unlike their own, divided as it was between nobles and commoners, called "stinkers." Moreover, the Natchez chief not only used the sun as his emblem, as Louis XIV did, but he also was the "Grand Soleil," the Great Sun (Balvay, *L'Epée*, 54–55). As the first Canadian governors of Louisiana had experience in Franco-Amerindian diplomacy, Franco-Natchez relations were initially based on mutual respect and were generally good (Balvay, *L'Epée*, 137). But Governor Cadillac, who had a "reputation for arrogance, pomposity, self-righteousness, and generally unpleasant disposition" (Woods, 418), gave the Natchez a first cause for resentment in 1715.

Cadillac went through Natchez territory without stopping to smoke the calumet, the peace pipe, which meant that he failed to renew the Franco-Natchez alliance. Feeling slighted, the Natchez retaliated by killing four French traders. Cadillac then ordered his military commander to avenge them. It was Jean-Baptiste Le Moyne de Bienville, a man who had served as governor for 11 years and would serve in that capacity 17 more years after Cadillac's recall and return to France. Bienville, who understood that peaceful relations with the Native Americans were key to the success of France's colonial project, managed to end the first war with the Natchez to French advantage by enlisting the defeated enemy's assistance in the building of a fort near the Grand Village of the Natchez, Fort

Rosalie.[31] The fort was located on the site of a trading post created by the La Loire brothers several years earlier, the site of the future Natchez, Louisiana. Thus in 1716, the two oldest towns of Louisiana were born, Natchitoches and Natchez.

Compared to Saint-Domingue, Lower Louisiana was still a work in progress at that time. Like Canada,[32] the colony attracted fewer settlers than the West Indies, although, like Louisiana, the latter endured not only hurricanes and yellow fever but also earthquakes. On a positive note, there were twice as many French people in Louisiana in 1718 than in 1712, but Native Americans greatly outnumbered the 800 white residents and more hands were needed to get the plantations going. John Law's agents increased Louisiana's population by transporting whoever they could put their hands on, a motley crew of adventurers, foreigners, indentured servants, convicts, and women of ill-repute. Criminals convicted of such offenses as deserting and salt smuggling, a crime punished by three years of forced labor on the royal galleys, saw their sentence frequently "commuted to life in Louisiana."[33] People from Alsace, a French province since just 1648, were encouraged to leave for the oversea colony. Most of those who did settled in an area later known as the "German Coast," although they too spoke French, but a few moved up to Illinois Country (Brown, *History*, 27–31). Although "the company was never able to meet its quota of settlers as specified in its charter,"[34] it tried, and "it did send many shiploads of immigrants to Louisiana" (Ekberg, 87).

Another scheme to augment the population was reminiscent of the strategy used in Canada half a century earlier. Between 1717 and 1721, the Company of the West and the Company of the Indies sent 120 young women of childbearing age to the colony.[35] The *filles de la cassette*—called "casket girls" in English by phonetic permutation—were orphans who had been educated by nuns and received a small trunk containing a trousseau as well as a 50 pound dowry in exchange for their promise to marry a settler.[36] At the same time, the Paris Chief of Police provided 256 women jailed at the *Salpêtrière* prison. They had been arrested for living on the streets, begging, or prostitution and were sentenced to banishment to Louisiana. They were known there as the "Baleine Brides" because "*La Baleine*" (the Whale) was the name of the ship that transported a first group of 90 of them.[37] They made up nearly a quarter of the female population of the colony when they arrived. A small percentage of them settled down and became part of the Louisiana bourgeoisie but most reverted to their former way of life. Several hundred men also came to Louisiana after being given the choice between prison in France or freedom in the colony. This involuntary, mostly urban, labor force was unsuitable for manual labor, so the bulk of the hard work was done by slaves.

By 1719, French settlers had already enslaved Native Americans in Illinois country and the Mississippi delta[38]—in addition to the slaves they had stolen from the Spaniards. But as planters found Indian slave labor less productive than African slave labor, they brought a first shipment of African slaves to Mobile in 1719,[39] a year that marks the beginning of the slave trade between Louisiana and Africa. By 1720, there were already 2,000 African slaves working on Louisiana plantations. African women slaves started replacing Native American concubines at that point as well.[40]

John Laws' policies of colonial expansion worked relatively well but Louisiana fell short on the promises made to investors. Returns on investments in the Company of the West turned out to be much lower than expected, which led to a drastic drop in share value. But the "Law's system" collapsed primarily because the Royal bank had issued more paper money that its coin reserves were worth. Investors lost confidence when John

Law made it illegal for households to own more than 500 pounds in metal currency. At the end of 1720, shareholders demonstrated in front the Company's headquarters in Paris, demanding their money back, and payment in gold. Investor panic led to the Company's bankruptcy, undermining French investors' confidence in paper money for a long time to come. Dismissed from all his positions, John Law fled France in public disgrace.[41]All hope for Louisiana was not lost: out of the ruins of the Company of the West a new one emerged: the Company of the Indies.

2. Settling Louisiana: The 1720s, 1730s, and 1740s

Margret Kimball Brown has argued that "[t]he effect [of the 'Mississippi Bubble'] on Louisiana actually was not severe, because the Company of the West, reorganized again as the Company of the Indies, continued to function" (*History*, 7).[42] In France, by contrast, there were a few changes in government at the time. Louis XV's official reign started on February 15, 1723, when he turned 13. Philip of Orleans died a few months later, and as the King was still a teenager, the Duke of Bourbon-Condé (1692–1740) became his prime minister. The Duke of Bourbon was unpopular from the start because the 1720 Mississippi Bubble that had ruined so many people had made him wealthy. As he had been among the first to demand his money back, public opinion held him partly responsible for the financial crisis and the Company of the West's downfall. But the Duke's main concern was not solving France's financial problems, it was finding a suitable bride for Louis XV, a task to which he devoted most of his time. Indeed, his main accomplishment was to arrange the King's 1725 marriage to Marie Leszczynska, the daughter of the deposed King of Poland, Stanislas I. She was 22 and the King 15 but they were happily married for many years.[43]

Louis XV dismissed the Duke of Bourbon over his rivalry with his beloved tutor, Cardinal de Fleury, whom he chose as his new Prime Minister in 1726. Fleury faced numerous problems when he came to power: the national debt, inflation, price increases on grain, and thus also on bread. But he managed to stabilize the currency and not just to balance the budget but to have the state treasury show a surplus of 15,000,000 *livres* by 1739. He also jumpstarted the industrial sector (canals, roads) and continued to develop trade. His ministry marks the most prosperous part of Louis XV's reign. Fleury, who worried about Great Britain's increasing assertiveness at sea, also doubled the French navy's budget (Haines, 63–64).[44]

Jean-Frédéric Phélypeaux, Count of Maurepas (1701–1781), became Secretary of State for the Navy in 1723 and, an ocean away from Versailles, Charles de la Boische, marquis of Beauharnois (1661–1749), became Governor General of New France, in 1726, the year Fleury became Prime Minister.[45] New France was something of a family affair for Beauharnois: his brother François, another relative of Pontchartrain, owned land in Acadia and had served as intendant of New France from 1702 to 1705. His brother Claude was a Navy Commander who sailed numerous times between France and New France to transport troops and supplies. The new governor's mission was to consolidate France's interests in North America, to oversee westward expansion, and to strengthen links with Louisiana. The last assignment was a tall order at a time when, as Havard and Vidal pointed out, it took nine months to travel from New Orleans to Quebec. Nonetheless, New France continued to take shape along the St. Lawrence River and to expand westward during Beauharnois's tenure. A Canadian officer of the colonial troops, René Boucher de La Perrière, and several missionaries constructed Fort Beauharnois on the Upper Mississippi River in 1727.[46] It was meant to provide a base from which to trade with the Sioux and to continue searching for the *mer de l'Ouest*, the Western sea.[47]

One of Governor Beauharnois's first actions upon taking office in 1726 was to sign a peace treaty with the Fox—as war was bad for (the fur) business. But peace did not last, first because the practice of raiding Fox villages and enslaving men, women, and children continued and second because the French ignored Fox demands for their relatives' return. A second wave of wars thus took place between the Fox and the French assisted by the Illinois, Ottawa, Ojibwe, and Huron, their allies. Sadly, the French strategy was to get rid of the Fox problem for good that time around. The outcome of this genocidal policy was truly tragic since only a few hundred Fox remained alive by 1733. The survivors found refuge with the Sauk and understandably later allied with the British to take on the French.[48]

After the Fox wars ended, New France re-established its presence in the *Pays d'en haut* and continued to spread out up north.[49] In the Upper countries, Pierre Gaultier de Varennes de la Vérendrye (1685–1749) explored the area between Lake Superior and the source of the Saskatchewan River (today's border between Alberta and British Columbia) between 1731 and 1739.[50] Born in 1685 in Trois-Rivières in a family of landowners, he went to a Jesuit school and served a cadet in the colonial army. He married and had four sons, but as a fur trader, was still interested in exploring new routes. Like many Canadian explorers, De la Vérendrye conducted his fur business and his explorations at the same time.[51] He was the first to mention the *Gens du Serpent*, the Snake Indians, a term applied to the Paiute, Bannock and Shoshone Nations. Thanks to him, the fur trade expanded further west, for as Kellogg notes, it "was the main reason for the presence of the French in the West" (364).[52] In the process, it led to the creation of new forts and trading posts. La Vérendrye would have liked to find the route to the "Western Ocean" but he failed in his quest. In the 1740s two of his sons went further than he had, crossing the prairie as far as Wyoming. They were the first Europeans to see the Rocky Mountains.

Explorations continued in the south as well. Further journeys took La Harpe to Galveston in 1721, an area he mapped accurately, and up the Arkansas River in 1722, where he made contact with the Quapaw Indians, and set up base near one of their villages (Rollings, 51–53). In 1723, Bourgmont explored the Missouri River with a group of fellow soldiers and built a fort, Fort d'Orléans, near present-day Brunswick, Missouri, in 1723. This accomplishment earned him the title of "Commandant of the Missouri River" (Havard and Vidal, *Histoire*, 138). Bourgmont, who was married to a Missouria princess, established peaceful relations with the Padouca (the Apache) and the Kaw (Kansa). In 1725, he brought a delegation of Native American chiefs to France. His guests visited the palaces of Versailles, Marly, and Fontainebleau, and even hunted with the King. Bourgmont also brought his American wife but listed her as a servant on the guest list: he already had a wife in France.[53]

In 1739, Pierre and Paul Mallet left Canada at the head of a small expedition. They tracked along the Missouri River, the Loup, Platte, South Platte, and Arkansas Rivers, and after hiring a Native American guide, found their way to Santa Fe where they stayed for nine months.[54] The Spaniards rejected their offer to create commercial ties between the two colonies, but one of the Frenchmen married and stayed in New Spain.[55] On the way back, the Canadians followed the river that now bears their name. They traded with the Comanche and encountered Apache as well as Canadian trappers once they reached the Arkansas River. Finishing their journey by boat on the Mississippi, they arrived in New Orleans at the end of a nearly two-year-long voyage. Pierre Mallet later completed two more trips to New Mexico but neither yielded the desired outcome, which was to establish trade relations with the Spanish colony.

Conflicts with Native American Nations were ongoing in Louisiana. In 1721, when the creation of new plantations led to further conflicts over land and resources, the French established a military post at Baton Rouge.[56] War with the Natchez resumed in 1722, 1723, and then again during Etienne de Périer's tenure as Governor of Louisiana (1727–1733) for want of both diplomacy and gifts.[57] An officer of the French Navy, Périer had come to Louisiana with the Indies Company and made himself known by having the first dyke built along the Mississippi. He had also encouraged settlement and the cultivation of tobacco on Natchez lands, which were better suited for farming than the marshes around New Orleans. Antoine Le Page du Pratz (1695–1775), who wrote one of the first histories of Louisiana, was among these settlers.[58] While du Pratz apparently had good relations with the Natchez,[59] the commander stationed at Fort Rosalie in 1729 did not. Périer had appointed Captain Détchéparre[60] (also known as the Sieur de Chépart) a year earlier and the French officer had quickly made himself unpopular with the settlers and the Natchez alike.

Détchéparre decided that the best place for his own plantation was right in the middle of the Natchez Grand Village, which was the site of the temple of the Sun and thus, sacred ground. Not only that, but he also demanded that the Natchez clear the village immediately, an unfair ultimatum that prompted a revolt. The Natchez suddenly realized that the French were not planning to share the land with them, but rather intended to squeeze them out. Around 300 French, and 1,200 Natchez people lived around Fort Rosalie, which served as the local military base and trading post. At the end of a day-long battle in November 1729, Fort Rosalie, had been burnt to the ground and 235 French men, women, and children were dead. The Natchez spared 54 women and children and 100 slaves whom they released to the Sieur de Louboey, commander at Mobile, when he arrived the following January (Havard and Vidal, *Histoire*, 297–305).

Fearing a general uprising, Governor Périer overreacted: he first had the small, peaceful tribe of the Chaoucha, slaughtered, and then relentlessly pursued the Natchez. After defeating them near Natchitoches, he captured the Great Sun and his entourage, including *Bras Piqué* (Tattooed Arm), the Female Sun, who had been particularly friendly with the French. He sent the prisoners to Saint-Domingue and had them sold at auction as slaves (Creagh, *Nos Cousins*, 30). A few survivors escaped and went on to live with the Chickasaw and the Cherokee. If life was more peaceful in Lower Louisiana afterwards, it is no doubt because the Natchez had stopped to exist as a nation.

Faced with all these troubles, the Company of the Indies gave up on Louisiana. It returned the colony to the direct control of the Crown in 1731 (Belting, 17). Louisiana's retrocession to France did not immediately bring a change in leadership since Etienne Périer kept his position as Louisiana governor. However, a new office reporting directly to the Secretary of State for the Navy was created, the post of *Commissaire Ordonnateur,* a civil officer in charge of justice, police, and public finance—including armed forces and navy, much like the intendant in Quebec. Edmé Gatien Salmon was the first officer to occupy that office from 1731 to 1744. Louisiana's retrocession to the crown also marked the end of the slave trade between Africa and Louisiana (1731). But as inter-colonial trade was encouraged, the slaves kept coming, albeit from the Caribbean islands instead of Africa.[61]

The triangular trade played a key-role in France's economic expansion in the 1700s. For over a century, shipowners of Nantes, Bordeaux, and many others French Atlantic seaports, became wealthy through a kind of commerce that rested on the exchange of "goods" instead of money. Africa provided slaves for the Caribbean colonies, the colonies provided colonial goods and raw material for Europe, and Europe provided manufactured goods to both Africa and the colonies. Sugar consumption in France went up from virtually nothing in the 16th century to 4 kg a year per capita at the end of the 18th century. Consumption of coffee, tea, and tobacco shot up as well. Saint-Domingue continued to expand—Les Cayes was founded in 1726 on the island's southern coast—and the slave population to increase.[62] The slave population in Martinique grew from 2,400 in in 1671 to 22,590 in 1701, to 55,683 in 1736, to 65,905 in 1751, to 90,000 in 1774 (Devèze, 161).

England holds the record for the number of slave ships that took part in the triangular trade between 1500 and 1815, with three ports, Liverpool (4,894 ships), London (2,704 ships) and Bristol (2,064 ships) at the top. With the exception of Nantes (1,714 ships), the slave ships leaving the French Atlantic seaports of La Rochelle (448 ships), Bordeaux (419 ships), Saint-Malo (218 ships), and Lorient (137 ships), numbered in the hundreds instead of the thousands, as they did in Portugal, Holland, and Denmark. Of a total of 3,300 French ships involved in the slave trade between 1680 and 1815, 84 percent left in the 18th century and their number increased over the century from an average of 34 ships in the 1740s, 50 in the 1760–70s, and over 100 in the 1780s. Only 5 percent of the slaves transported from Africa came to North America. Ninety-five percent ended up in the Caribbean sugar colonies, the British colonies of Jamaica and Barbados and the French colonies of Guadeloupe, Martinique, and Saint-Domingue.[63]

Guillaume Aubert estimates that the Company of the West and the Company of the Indies transported a total of "7,000 settlers [...] and more than 5,500 African slaves" between 1717 and 1731 alone ("Louisiana," 739).[64] Although slaves could be found everywhere in New France, the master-slave relations varied greatly from one part of the colonial empire to the next: "In Montreal—a city overwhelmingly white—a black slave living in a white household composed of masters and indentured servants, lived a very different kind of life as a black slave on a Mississippi plantation among several dozen other black slaves" (Havard and Vidal, Histoire, 477). From 1724 onward, the Code Noir, Louis XIV's manual on how to treat slaves, was used not only in the island colonies but in Louisiana as well, making New Orleans part of "a greater Caribbean world marked by racial slavery" (Vidal, 499).[65] In Louisiana, every person of means had slaves, "Indians, Cajuns, even the Catholic Church" (Creagh, Nos Cousins, 131).[66]

Although it seldom happened, slaves could earn their freedom, more commonly from owners who were former soldiers or women. Freed slaves tended to live in small, separate communities.[67] They contributed to the creolization of Louisiana society—the emergence of a culture based in both French and African cultures.[68] Slaves from hundreds of different African tribes speaking different languages introduced Voodoo first to the Caribbean islands and then to Louisiana.[69] As slaves were required to receive baptism, Animist spiritual beliefs characteristic of Voodoo sometimes mixed with Catholic rituals to create new syncretic forms of religious practice. Creole French also developed as the result of these intercultural contacts.[70]

Life in New Orleans was unlike any Canadian city in the first decades of the 18th century. Although the noblemen of Canada and the large plantation owners of Louisiana were attached to the French way of life and wore fashionable wigs and clothing imported from Paris,[71] the French gentry still breathed the air of freedom in Louisiana.[72] In New Orleans' cosmopolitan environment, a nobleman like the Chevalier de Louboey did not care about the scandal caused by his relationship with a married woman. The social and religious constraints that kept people in their place or forced them to hide secrets elsewhere were simply missing. Mother Tranchepain, the first superior of the Ursuline Convent of New Orleans, noted rather bitterly in 1728 that "religion [was] little known and practiced even less" in Louisiana.[73] One of Bienville's assignments when he became governor of Louisiana for the fourth time in 1733 was to change this state of affairs, to civilize the local population. With the assistance of intendant Salmon, he tried to do just that by prohibiting gambling and drinking during church services and by issuing De Louboey an official, public reprimand. Along the same lines, the policy regarding interracial marriages changed to the extent that such unions, although encouraged in the past, required prior approval from the authorities after 1735.[74] Yet, in spite of these concerted efforts to make Louisiana adopt the same moral and social standards as France, frontier life just went on, albeit a little more discreetly perhaps.

During his new term as governor, Bienville's task was also to end the war with the Chickasaw who had accepted Natchez refugees and refused to hand them over to the French.[75] In 1720, the former had killed a French officer who was living with them and acting as a spy. When the Choctaw retaliated on behalf of their French allies, the Chickasaw systematically attacked French shipments on the Mississippi, in effect blocking French commerce.[76] Control of the Mississippi waterway was a central stake in the struggle for colonial expansion between the two imperial nations of France and Great Britain and their respective Native American allies.[77] By the end of the 17th century, the Allegheny Mountains were no longer an invincible barrier for the British settlers who were advancing fast towards the French Mississippi corridor (Creagh, *Nos Cousins*, 86).[78]

In 1726, around 500 French soldiers were stationed in Lower Louisiana.[79] The Choctaw fought on their side, the Chickasaw were allies of the British, and the Natchez split their allegiance between them. As these alliances were fragile, the Europeans had to apply diplomacy and be generous with gifts.[80] Which kinds of goods and gifts? Michaël Augeron provides the inventory of a French trading post in Spanish Texas that the Spanish authorities compiled in 1754 following their arrest of the post's owner, a Frenchman named Blancpain. What he had to sell were guns, pistols, gunpowder, flint and gunsmith tools, knives and blades of all sizes and purpose, cooking pots and caldrons, metal tools (axes, hoes, sickles), hooks, fishing lines, and harpoons, sewing needles, for cloth and leather, shirts for men, women, and children, textile in bulk, blankets, mirrors, hats, combs, decorative crosses, pendants, small bells, buttons, metal rings, tobacco, sugar, and brandy (Augeron, 139–140).

Bienville offered a bounty of gunpowder and bullets to the Choctaw for Chickasaw prisoners and scalps. This operation was largely successful, enabling commerce on the Mississippi to resume for a while. But in the end, neither two years of guerrilla warfare between enemy First Nations (1734–36) nor the massive display of French military power in 1736 (nearly 1,000 men) achieved the desired effects (Brown, *History*, 132–133). Put simply, Bienville's two campaigns against the Chickasaw did not go well for the French. During the first campaign, commander Pierre d'Artaguiette's attack on a Chickasaw fort failed and cost him his life.[81] The second campaign was perhaps even more vexing given the extreme cost of the operation. In 1739, nearly 3,000 French and Choctaw warriors took off for battle against the Chickasaw. Pierre-Joseph Céloron de Blainville (1693–1759)[82] and his men left Fort Michilimackinac for Fort de l'Assomption (Memphis, Tennessee), a nearly 800 miles journey, to assist Bienville in his military campaign.[83] But poor logistics and unfavorable weather conditions led to its termination and peace negotiations barely saved the French from outright defeat. Nonetheless, the resumption of war between the Choctaw and the Chickasaw gave Bienville a vague sense of security: as long as the Amerindians were fighting each other, they left the French alone and in control the colony.[84]

3. Upper Louisiana: The Illinois Country

The area of Illinois country south of today's St. Louis, the towns of Cahokia,[85] Kaskaskia[86] and the network of villages that included Prairie du Rocher, St. Philippe, and Fort de Chartres expanded fast compared to Canada and Louisiana. Philippe François Renault opened and directed an industrial lead mine, La Motte mine, in Missouri in 1721.[87] He had received authorization to bring 500 slaves to work in the mine, near what is now Fredericktown, Missouri, but according to Brown, the number of slaves working in the mine was much smaller.[88] A few miles away from Fort de Chartres, Renault created another village on the East bank of the Mississippi, St. Philippe, which grew as a prosperous farming community. Apart from its strategic location as link between Canada and Louisiana, and its potential as a mining district, the Illinois country mattered to the French greatly because of its rich soil. On the one hand, it was better suited for European-style agriculture than either Canada or Louisiana, particularly for growing wheat, the cereal needed for bread, a staple of French diet.[89]

The early habitants of the Illinois country were French Canadians who settled there because of the rich bottom lands and "the availability of Christian Indian women" (Brown, *History*, 6). They "took up land wherever they liked, cleared it for farming, and built homes within fenced lots" (Brown, *History*, 68). But once a civil government was established, they were viewed as squatters as they had no legally valid claims to their lands. During his tenure, Boisbriand started to legalize their claims, to recognize them "as grants from the king" after the fact (Brown, *History*, 68).[90] He also made new land grants "in areas that were or were to become the villages of Kaskaskia, Fort de Chartres, Prairie du Rocher, and St Philippe" (Brown, *History*, 10).[91] Brown points out that in Louisiana, including upper Louisiana, "lands were not to be granted as seigniories," as they were in Canada, "but to individuals in parcels two to four *arpents* wide and forty to sixty *arpents* long" (69), an *arpent* measuring 192 feet. In practice, however, "land concessions seem to have been framed in terms of the seigniorial system" (69), given their large size.[92] One of these large parcels was granted to Boisbriand's nephew, Ste. Thérèse Langloisière, a tract of land on which the village of Prairie du *Rocher* appeared in 1722.[93]

Two early censuses were taken, in 1723 and 1725, revealing that by 1725 the Illinois Country counted "about 600 persons (including slaves[94] and transients)" (Brown, *History*, 13).[95] Over the course of the 18th century, the Cahokia population grew to 3,000 inhabitants.[96] The town was known as a center of the fur trade.[97] It was also famous for its many brothels. Kaskaskia's population also increased, initially with an influx of Canadians, many married to Illinois women:

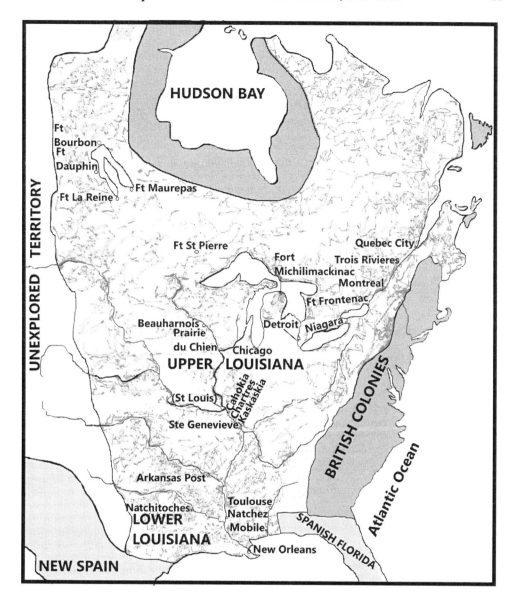

New France in the 1740s (author's map).

The Canadians came to the Illinois country as traders and created a base from which to continue their trading east and west. […] Family ties were important: whenever a person settled, others were likely to follow. As the traders began to make the villages in the Illinois the permanent center of their trade, members of the same extended family—nephews, cousins, relatives by marriage—frequently ended up in the same locales [Brown, *History*, 13].

In exchange for their fur in Canada and their agricultural products in Louisiana, these settlers obtained goods that were not readily available where they lived, and in particular cloth:

There was one task that the women of the Illinois country did not share with their pioneer sisters in the English colonies. Weaving was prohibited by the government, and all cloth had to be purchased either from the king's storehouse or from the merchants who brought it up the river from the sea [Belting, 47].

Of the thousands of emigrants from France who arrived in North America in the second decade of the 18th century, about a hundred moved to the Illinois country, attracted by the availability of land and the promise of a better future. In addition, men who had come as soldiers sometimes married and settled "at the end of their tour of duty, as they were eligible to receive grants of land, [...] an inducement for men who were landless in France" (Brown, *History*, 24).[98] The census left out settlers who did not own farm land, a category that included "traders, voyageurs, several blacksmiths, a gunsmith, a tailor, and a roofer" (Brown, *History*, 12).[99] A few foreigners were found among them, a Spanish miner, a Swiss roofer, etc. (Brown, *History*, 27). It appears that by 1725, the number of settlers born in France was slightly higher than the number of settlers born in Canada, and that the French were slightly more literate than the Canadians (Brown, *History*, 13–14). But the military officers' training was the same since "many Canadians served in the Marine in France" (25). Another census, taken in 1732, showed that the demographic curve was no longer moving up as fast.

On the fertile land between Cahokia and Kaskaskia, farmers grew "[a]ll types of vegetables, fruits, and root crops; the wide prairies provided grazing for horses and livestock [...]. Ducks, geese, and other birds were available along the Mississippi flyway, and fish were abundant in the streams" (Brown, *History*, 6). As long as you had good relations with the Native Americans, pioneer life could be very enjoyable, and the standard of living much higher than in many rural areas of France. Initially, French villages like Kaskaskia, Fort de Chartres, and Cahokia sprung up next to Illinois villages, but it was no longer the case in the 1750s. Initially, French villages were also located on the east bank of the Mississippi River but as land grew rarer, villages sprung up across the river, Ste. Genevieve and St. Louis, for instance.[100]

The settlements in Upper Louisiana were French in appearance, as farmers did not build their houses on their land, but in the villages instead:

> Physically the villages were small pieces of France set down in the wilderness. They offered the inhabitants a secure and social place. Here men could gather and go out to the fields as a group; women could visit, and children could play. The French did not want the isolated, independent farmsteads that the later American pioneers preferred; they desired a gregarious environment [Brown, *History,* 74].

As the name of several villages indicate, the church was the heart of town, the prominent place of the church pointing to the Catholic faith as the "main cultural element that settlers brought with them" (Brown, *History*, 104).[101] The villages were organized around "streets divided into roughly equal blocks" (Brown, *History*, 75). Most houses were solid buildings made out of squared logs fitted into a frame. A house usually had two main rooms, the living and the sleeping area, with a fireplace opening in each room:

> The houses were a story and a half high; they were floored with boards and had a board ceiling that formed the floor of a loft above. The loft could be used for storage or sleeping quarters. The interior walls of the house were plastered and whitewashed. Mullioned casement windows with small panes of glass let light into the interior. Glass was shipped in crates from France. Steep roofs with thatch or wooden shingles overhung the house on each or on all four sides and formed porch or gallery roofs [Brown, *History*, 75–76].

In the country of Illinois, the wealthiest had stone houses built but most of the rich traders lived in New Orleans.[102]

Farmers in the Illinois country also adopted French open-field agriculture, a kind of farming characterized by the existence of a common field, the granting of farmland to individuals, and the obligation for farmers to fence their land to prevent animals from damaging crops.[103] After the harvest, the fences came down and the cattle could graze freely in the common field for a period determined by the village assembly. "The only region in French colonial America where arable land agriculture was dominated by a regime of open-field cultivation was the middle Mississippi watershed, including Prairie du Chien as the northern-most example and Vincennes to the east on the Wabash River" (Eckberg, *French Roots,* 137).

Another French practice involving the community was the maintenance of the roads between the villages. The fact that "communal cooperation was required to make the system work" (Brown, *History,* 73), leads Brown to argue that contrary to popular opinion, "[t]he French actually had about as much experience in managing their civil affairs as did the New England colonists" (Brown, *History,* 35–36).[104] Ekberg, for his part, rejects the notion that life for New England farmers was happier than for the French in their villages of Illinois country.[105] For him, communal life was an expression of the French *joie de vivre.*

Settlers used iron ploughs to cultivate the rich soil and harvest wheat and corn. Farmers grew also hemp, tobacco, flax, and even grapes. Cows, pigs and horses were the most commonly raised farm animals. Barter was the usual means of commercial exchange at the trading posts. The *habitants* bartered among themselves or with the Native Americans, they could also take their products to the royal storehouse to discharge debts or purchase imported items (Brown, 82). In addition to the glass used for windows, and items commonly used to trade with the Native Americans, Upper Louisiana imported "all cloth, […] wine, brandy, prunes, limes, rope, nails, soap, candlestick, cork, long saws, linen, laces, [and] silk stockings" (Brown, 81). Beer was brewed locally, and some tried their hand at wine (Brown, 86). The Amerindians and the *coureurs des bois* sold their meat, pelts or deerskins in Canada, Lower Louisiana, or locally, and, like the farmers, obtained manufactured goods in exchange (Brown, 78). Merchants and *voyageurs* also brought products mined in Illinois country, such as salt and lead, to other parts of the colony.[106] But agricultural products soon took over as the main exports from the Illinois country to Lower Louisiana:

> Food products became Illinois' most important export. Flour, peas, maize, corn, okra, and onions were shipped downriver. Meats were important—buffalo meat (particularly tongues) and venison, and from domestic produce, beef and hams. Bear oil was deemed a good substitute for olive oil and pots of this were traded [Brown, *History,* 79].[107]

The main modes of transportation were the pirogue, in essence a canoe, and the bateau, a ship built out of planks that could carry a much heavier load than the pirogue.[108] "Soldiers and hired voyageurs paddled these boats, slaves were never numerous enough to be the only ones employed in this task" (Brown, 80).[109] For safety reasons, it was customary to travel in groups, as a convoy.[110]

Economically, the colony of Upper Louisiana did not make sense from a mercantilist perspective: it did not have sufficient resources to bring in the revenue the Crown expected. Compared to Lower Louisiana, which exported colonial goods such as "rice, indigo, lumber, tar, cotton, and tobacco," Upper Louisiana had only lead and pelts to send to France. On the other hand, Lower Louisiana would have had a hard time feeding itself without the agricultural goods from the Illinois country (Brown, 83).

Upper Louisiana society allowed for even greater social mobility than Canada and Louisiana, as "day laborers could become land owners and merchants" (Brown, 88). Certain tradesmen managed to build fortunes rather quickly, and apprentices could become masters in their trades since the guild system did not exist in New France. Enterprising soldiers could open trading posts, as did Jean-Baptiste de Girardot in 1733 when stationed in Kaskaskia.[111] The colony was not a classless society but "the segregation that marked social intercourse in France was not carried over into the frontier society" (Brown, *History*, 88). At the top of the social pyramid were the officials of the trading companies and then the representatives of the Crown who replaced them. Next came the habitants, whether they were farmers or voyageurs, then the *engagés*,[112] and finally the black and native slaves (Brown, 89). In terms of gender, it is interesting to note that women seem to have enjoyed a fairly high degree of financial independence in Illinois country.[113]

The most common forms of cross-cultural interaction between the Amerindians and the French were in the areas of language, warfare, marriage,[114] and lifestyle.[115] The Canadians were long used to learning Native American languages and the Native Americans French. The French had adopted the Native American way of waging war.[116] Initially, marriages between the *coureurs des bois* and Native American women were encouraged, particularly if the latter had converted, because it was believed the children of such unions would become French and that, in the long run, all Native Americans would all become "civilized" the French way. Often, however, the reversed occurred, children, and even French husbands, would adopt Native American ways instead.[117] Although the government therefore stopped encouraging such unions, a "significant biological and racial mixing [... still] occurred between the French and the tribes of the forested areas" (*Nos Cousins*, 28).

According to Morgan, even in an area like Cahokia, where relations between the Illinois Indians and the French were not always smooth due to differences in lifestyle, "the Cahokia readily adopted some European practices, especially the raising of hogs and the use of farming implements" (*Land of Big Rivers*, 45). On the frontier, the French learned a great deal from the Native Americans as well: "how to use plants to treat diseases; to eat game bird; to grow corn, sunchoke, pumpkin, maple syrup" (Creagh, 29). Belting mentions persimmon, which grew well in the Kaskaskia area, and that "the habitant learned to use as an astringent, as a cure for dysentery, and to make a bread from its pulp to carry on long trips" (11). The French adopted clothing and shoes (moccasins) that were better suited for the kind of life they led than those made in Europe.[118] They learned to enjoy a sauna bath.[119] As already noted, they used the local mode of transportation, the canoe, and the bateau.[120] Conversely, Native Americans adopted European products such as alcohol, firearms, as well as manmade tools and fabric. Many converted to Christianity. Sometimes Europeans also adopted Old World recipes to cure diseases, the Iroquois' anedda tea against scurvy; pine resin to prevent the infection of wounds; and a paste of plantain leaves for snakebites.

4. Trouble in Acadia, 1744–1748[121]

Near the small fishing port of *Havre à l'Anglois* on Ile Royale (Cape Breton Island), the French had broken ground for the construction of the fortress of Louisbourg in

1719.[122] Once completed in 1740, it was the largest and most expensive fortified complex in North America. But as the French bolstered their presence, Acadia remained a constant theater of Franco-English conflict not only in the 1720s but later as well.[123] As tensions between France and England mounted, naval warfare rose in strategic importance. France therefore tried to compete with the Royal Navy—or at least not fall too far behind. In addition to tonnage, the number of cannons, usually between 60 and 80, became a prime indicator of a warship's value. As New France was sending oak wood for the construction of new ships, French shipyards kept busy from the 1720s onward, producing an average of eight ships a year in the 1740s, most of them frigates designed for speed and easy maneuvering. By 1744, the French Navy had at its command 51 flagships and 27 frigates, still far fewer than the Royal Navy with its 127 vessels.[124]

Under Maurepas, a member of the Academy of Science, navigation had become a serious academic discipline. Modern instruments, like the octant, the marine chronometer, and the sextant, allowed for more and more precise calculation of longitude and latitude.[125] New techniques in cartography helped improve geographical knowledge. In addition to these British inventions, Henri-Louis Duhamel du Monceau (1700–1782) introduced math-based shipbuilding techniques and created the discipline of marine engineering in 1741. Ships of the French Navy and the Merchant Navy were of top quality in the 18th century and their number increased significantly. But given the superior size of Great Britain's fleet, Maurepas usually used the French Navy defensively, mostly to escort merchant ships and to transport troops between France and the colonies, all the while avoiding British vessels as much as possible.[126]

The War of the Austrian Succession was one of the early foreign crises Louis XV

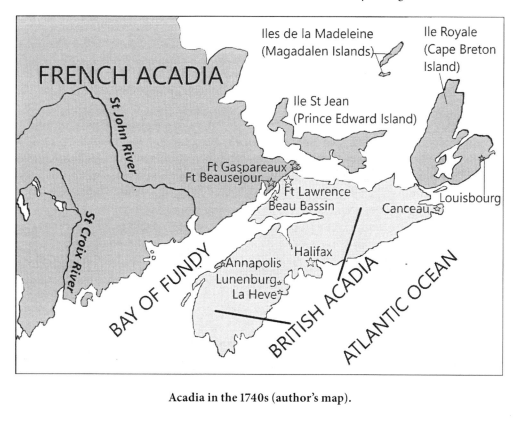

Acadia in the 1740s (author's map).

had to face. It started at Charles VI's death in 1740 when Prussia invoked the Salic law to prevent Maria-Theresa from succeeding her father as Empress of the Holy Roman Empire. Although alliances shifted frequently during the eight-year-long war, the kingdoms involved were Austria, Great Britain, and the Netherlands on one side, Frederic the Great's Prussia, Spain, and Bavaria, on the other. France joined the Prussian camp in 1744 only. The War of the Austrian Succession also played out in North America, mostly in Acadia and Louisiana, where it is known as King George's War.

In Acadia, Saint-Ovide proved a gifted governor. He oversaw the construction of the fortress of Louisbourg that was finally complete and operational in 1740. He also succeeded in retaining the Mi'kmaq's loyalty by generously distributing muskets and ammunition after 1713 when Acadia fell under British command and was renamed Nova Scotia. Saint-Ovide, however, was a corrupt administrator who used his office in the pursuit of his own commercial ventures, including privateering. He was also a smooth talker who managed to keep his job until 1739 in spite of the *commissaires ordonnateurs'* incriminating reports to Maurepas and the Secretary of State of the Navy's repeated admonitions. Saint-Ovide was a close friend of three brothers, sons of Navy officer François du Pont Duvivier (1676–1714) who had organized the Acadian settlement of Ile Royale in 1713. The brothers had entered military service and had moved rapidly through the ranks. They were the wealthiest family on the island. When Maurepas finally recalled Saint Ovide in 1739, Isaac-Louis de Forant (1685–1740) replaced him. A naval officer and knight of the order of Saint-Louis, he arrived accompanied by *commissaire ordonnateur* François Bigot. Neither one of them was impressed by the local troops or their officers. In fact, the new administrators' task was to clean up the colony's finances and to remedy the garrison's problems of lax discipline, absenteeism, and drinking by getting rid of undesirable elements. But following Forant's untimely death in 1740, the old routine returned after the du Pont brothers managed to involve Bigot in their commercial activities, including privateering in wartime.

Against British expectations, France had remained neutral in 1739 during the War of Jenkin's Ear between Spain and England. When France entered King George's War in 1744, Governor Beauharnois felt confident that his alliance with the Huron, Ottawa, Potawatomi, and Ojibwe would hold. Yet trouble was brewing in Ohio, around the Cuyahoga River valley and by Sandusky, where a group of Huron led by Nicholas Orontony had found refuge after fleeing from the Ottawa in the Detroit area. Although La Salle had claimed the Ohio Valley for France in 1682, it had remained the preserve of the Cayuga and Seneca, members of the Iroquois Confederacy, as well as the Shawnee until the 1740s. Now, both the French and the British were interested in doing business with them and were actually already operating in the Ohio and Allegheny valleys.

Upset by Beauharnois' inaction following their complaints about the Ottawa, Orontony and his tribe sided with the British during the war. After five French traders returning to Detroit[127] were killed in the Spring 1747, Beauharnois ordered a few raids against British traders in the Ohio valley and on the New England frontier. Among the Franco-Indian leaders was an Ottawa chief name Pontiac—or Obwandiyag (c. 1714–1769) who later played an important role at the close of the Seven Years' War. Beauharnois also appointed Céloron de Blainville as commander of Fort Saint-Frédéric on Lake Champlain in 1747 to defend the colony's frontier.[128] But he worried about the status of France's alliances with the Amerindians, as the absence of new shipments of goods from France during the war was likely to endanger these alliances. He also had reservations about the French Canadians' willingness to fight. With these perceived weaknesses, he feared an invasion of Quebec City above all and had the city's fortifications reinforced. The Mohawk attacked Montreal in 1746.[129] In the face of these threats and despite scarce resources, Beauharnois decided to declare war for fear of losing face and prestige.

In 1748, Beauharnois's successor, Roland-Michel Barrin de La Galissonière (1693–1756) sent Céloron to Detroit with a convoy of fresh troops and supplies to quell the Native American insurrection in the West (Balvay, *L'Epée*, 36–37).[130] Later that year, he enjoined Céloron to bolster French claims on the Ohio Valley by marking the territory with lead plates nailed on trees at the mouth of Ohio River tributaries. Nearly three hundred men took part in the 1749 expedition that lasted five months. Its purpose was also to halt the British push westward, more specifically to observe and report on British movement in the area (Eccles, *The French*, 199). Wealthy Virginia merchants and plantation owners, including young George Washington, had formed the Ohio Company in 1748 as a land speculation operation of a type that was to become all-too common in years to come.[131] Surveyors came to measure "virgin land," the Company purchased that land in bulk from the Crown, and then resold it at retail price to settlers, making a high profit in the process—or so they hoped. Five years later, the last French and Indian War was to start right there as a dispute over the Ohio Valley.

For now, during King George's War, Acadia was the main stake in the conflict between England and France in North America as well as its main theater of operations. As soon as war had broken out, the French had tried to regain control of the area. François du Pont Duvivier (1705–1776) attacked the British settlements of Canso and Annapolis Royal in the spring of 1744. Ironically, his main opponent was a French Huguenot, Jean-Paul Mascarène (1684–1760), whose family had found refuge in Switzerland, England, and finally New England, and who served as governor of Nova Scotia from 1740 to 1749.[132] The war was fought mostly along the border of Acadia and Maine and further south. The French and the Abenaki raided Saratoga, New York,[133] forcing the British out of their settlements north of Albany and killing nearly 10 percent of the adult male population. The British for their part had their eyes set on Louisbourg, a port harboring feared privateers who captured British ships and disrupted commerce between England and New England. In March 1745, 4,000 soldiers and militiamen left Boston determined to take the fortress and chase "the papists" away. The French were aware of British intentions but Governor Louis du Pont Duchambon (1680–1775), François du Pont Duvivier's uncle, was convinced that the garrison could withhold a long siege. After six weeks, however, in July 1745, the French had to capitulate. British troops were then able to occupy Ile Royale until the end of the war.

After the surrender of Louisbourg, François Bigot sailed to France only to receive orders to organize a formidable expedition to recapture the fortress.[134] For once, Versailles spared no expense for New France: Maurepas sent a fleet of 64 ships and more than 7,000 men led by the Duke of Anville in June 1746 and Beauharnois dispatched troops from Quebec under the command of Jean-Baptiste de Ramezay, the former governor's son. The two armies were to join forces in Nova Scotia, retake the peninsula and Louisbourg, and once they had achieved these objectives, march on to New England and then to Boston. Ramezay was ready in July but d'Anville did not arrive until September. By then, the three-month Atlantic crossing had already cost d'Anville hundreds of soldiers, who had died of various diseases, as well as 20 ships, lost to storms and to British privateering.

To make matters worse, nearly half of the men who made it to Acadia died of scurvy, typhus, and typhoid within weeks of their arrival. As if this was not bad enough, d'Anville himself suffered a stroke and died a few days after finally reaching his destination. To top it all, his replacement, realizing that he was not up to the task, tried to commit suicide and resigned. Command of the expedition then passed to sixty-one-year-old Jacques-Pierre de Taffanel de la Jonquière (1685–1752), a captain on one of the expedition's ships. The fleet finally sailed to reclaim Louisbourg on October 26, but inexplicably, the rear admiral changed his mind: he ordered the squadron back to France and Ramezay back to Quebec.[135] Faced with this debacle, Versailles needed scapegoats. It blamed Governors Beauharnois and Duchambon for the fall of Louisbourg. Maurepas recalled the 76-year-old governor of New France, who, rumor had it, was senile—he was not. Duchambon stood trial and obtained an acquittal. Bigot did not have to go to court, just had to justify his actions at length for the next few years.

The conflicts between the Chickasaw and the Choctaw, and by extension their colonial allies, resumed during King George's War (1744–1748) when Pierre de Rigaud, marquis de Vaudreuil-Cavagnial (1698–1778), served as governor of Louisiana (1743 to 1753).[136] Like Beauharnois, he had to contend with the fragility of Franco-Indian alliances, as tribes switched allegiance according to their best economic interest.[137] He often found himself unable to match British offers of goods and gifts. Once the French trading posts had no more goods to trade or give away, British merchants started spreading the rumor that the French were losing the war. They encouraged the Amerindians to side with them instead, which some did, destroying French settlements located between Michilimackinac in the North and Illinois country in the West. The Chickasaw also raided French settlements along the eastern bank of the Mississippi, forcing settlers to retreat to New Orleans. In 1747, the French garrison of Illinois country abandoned Fort de Chartres and moved to Kaskaskia. (After the war, however, construction began on a new Fort de Chartres, a stone fortress this time.)[138]

The War of the Austrian Succession was costly. Great Britain lost 29 warships and of the 50 that remained, 27 were in bad need of repair. The French fleet also suffered. Aware of its weaknesses, the Secretary of State of the Navy had ancient ships decommissioned and replaced with new ones. Until his recall in 1749, over a court intrigue, Maurepas also pleaded with Louis XV to give the kingdom a fleet worthy of its colonial ambitions. However, the Navy suffered a 20 percent budget cut instead between 1749 and 1754—even if it continued to add new and more powerful warships during the interwar period. The 1748 Treaty of Aix-la-Chapelle that put an end to hostilities returned the North American colonies to the pre-war status quo, which pleased no one. France regained Louisbourg in exchange for Madras in India, a decision that upset New Englanders who had carried the human and financial burden of its capture. They also realized that Nova Scotia was British in name only and set out to do something about it—which led to war again. In North America, in fact, King George's War did not really end with the 1748 Peace Treaty.

As soon as that war was supposedly over, Nova Scotia became once again the stake in an armed struggle that opposed the British and the Mi'kmaq this time. Known as Father Le Loutre's War, the conflict lasted from 1749 to 1755. As the British sought to consolidate their presence in Nova Scotia they met with increased resistance on the part of the Mi'kmaq and the French Acadians. In 1749, Governor Edward Cornwallis (1713–1776) established Halifax as the new capital of Nova Scotia, thus raising fear among the French that the Acadian mainland (New Brunswick) might be occupied next, in which case the road to Quebec would be vulnerable as well. Although this fear did not materialize at that point, the issue of the oath of allegiance to Great Britain lingered. Governor Mascarène had not pressed it but his successors, in particular Charles Lawrence, were not as accommodating.

After 1748, the French government's policy was to encourage Acadians to withdraw to French-controlled territory, a strategy designed in part to deprive the British of farmers and thus of food, and in part to protect the route from Louisbourg to Quebec. Three forts were constructed along this vital artery, Fort Gaspareaux in the north, to protect the access to the Magdalen Islands, Île Saint-Jean (Prince Edward Island) and Île Royale (Cape Breton Island); Fort Beauséjour, at the tip of Chignecto Bay, and Fort Menagoueche on the Saint John River.[139] In 1749, at the urging of Catholic priests, half of the French Acadian population left for Ile Saint-Jean, Ile Royale and Chignecto, the marshy area that connects Nova Scotia to New Brunswick. Father Jean-Louis Le Loutre (1707–1772), who led the exodus, was one of those priests who preached that Acadians risked their eternal soul if they took an oath of British allegiance and became subjects of a heretic king.

The Mi'kmaq, on the other hand, and in particular Mi'kmaq Chief Jean Baptiste Cope (1698–1758), better known as Major Cope, refused to leave their ancestral lands in Acadia. They opposed British colonization of what they regarded as their own territory in accordance with treaties signed at the end of Father Rale's war. During the exodus, the Mi'kmaq assisted the French by attacking British ships while the governor of New France provided supplies and weapons to the Mi'kmaq for their guerrilla warfare.[140] Major Cope, who spoke French and had converted to Christianity, ended up joining Le Loutre at Chignecto and, with other Mi'kmaq leaders, took part in a series of raids meant to prevent British settlements. As these conflicts escalated into a war of scalps, the British tried to chase the Acadians and the Mi'kmaq out of Chignecto. However, after months of inconclusive battles, they decided to make separate peace with the Mi'kmaq. Cope was the only Mi'kmaq chief willing to sign the 1752 treaty and peace did not last anyway. Less than six months later, following an attack on Mi'kmaq forces, Cope denounced the treaty.

Although under constant alert, the British continued to build fortifications in the Acadian communities of Pisiguit, Grand Pré, and Chignecto and to create new Protestant villages in Bedford, Lawrencetown, Lunenburg, and Dartmouth. In 1753, 1,400 French and German Protestants came to Lunenville to settle the village but strangely enough, Le Loutre and army captain John Hoffman succeeded in inciting a rebellion against the British in the community. Some of the new settlers even followed Le Loutre when he left. Life was tough for the 2500 residents of Chignecto, however, as the new dykes built to gain land and grain were repeatedly destroyed by the enemy and storm tides. The rich farmers from the Minas area, the breadbasket of the peninsula, responded to calls for help from fellow Acadians in Chignecto and Louisbourg. But they refused to sell to the British.

The Acadians who decided to stay in Nova Scotia were caught between a rock and a hard place. Signing an oath of allegiance to the British Crown meant two things they were unwilling to comply with: accepting the Anglican faith, and for males, serving in British militia in times of need. Besides, had they been willing to do so, they would have been seen as traitors by the Mi'kmaq who had the real fighting power. They too would have become the target of their attacks. Finally, was not Acadia their homeland? These were the lands they had cleared for cultivation, the villages they had built, the place where they lived in harmony with the Amerindians.

For the British, on the other hand, French Acadia was a dangerous proposition. The fortress of Louisbourg was too big and too close to the thirteen colonies for them to ever be safe from future attacks. To boot, for decades now, French Acadians had proven that the oath of conditional allegiance to Great Britain that supposedly guaranteed their neutrality meant nothing. They continued and would continue to fight British occupation. But legally, the province belonged to Great Britain. The French had ceded the land by signing the treaty of Utrecht. Faced with this conundrum, Charles Lawrence, the British governor of Nova Scotia since 1753—and a known Francophobe and anti-papist—therefore opted for a radical solution. He implemented a plan actually proposed by governor Mascarène earlier on in a letter to London, namely "that the French settlers be removed from the Province of Nova Scotia and be replaced by good Protestant subjects."[141] From Governor Lawrence's vantage point, this plan had the dual advantages of eliminating an undesirable and mostly hostile population and of acquiring rich, developed, productive lands free of charge. Besides, once the French food supply route was cut off, this strategy also paved the way for the takeover of the fortress of Louisbourg.

The French and the Mi'kmaq continued to raid British settlements during the early 1750s but Colonel Robert Monckton struck a decisive victory with the capture, after a two-week siege, of the strategic fort of Beauséjour in 1755. During the Bay of Fundy campaign, British soldiers started rounding up French Acadians and deporting them. Then Fort Gaspareaux fell. More Acadians were captured and removed from their homes and villages, forcefully and permanently. Some families were separated, shipped off to various destinations. Some were sent to the thirteen colonies, where they were not welcome, to Britain, to France, and Louisiana—but via France first. In all, over 80 percent of the 14,000 French Acadians who resided in the province in 1755 were deported between 1755 and 1764.[142] Thousands died during this early episode of ethnic cleansing, of disease and drowning at sea. *Le Grand Dérangement*, the plight of the Acadians forced to leave their lands, inspired Henry Wadsworth Longfellow to write his 1847 epic poem, *Evangeline*.[143]

Louisiana, willed into existence by Louis XIV at the end of the 17th century, transformed from a chain of isolated forts in the middle of the wilderness into a sprawling colony by the first half of the 18th century. Built by African slave labor, New Orleans, the new port-city on the Gulf Coast became the hub of a French intercolonial trade network linking France, Africa, the Caribbean isles, and Upper Louisiana. The Illinois country had by then become the colony's breadbasket and seen numerous villages prosper thanks to agriculture. Contrary to the stereotype according to which "French colonists in America shunned and eschewed even subsistence agriculture" (Ekberg, 250), research has showed that when it comes to colonization, the culture clash was not between French traders on the one hand and British farmers on the other, but rather between different conceptions of land use and farming practices in New England and New France.

The development of Louisiana occurred as Franco-Americans were continuing to explore lands located west of the Mississippi River and despite periods of conflicts with Native American neighbors such as the Natchez and the Chickasaw in the south, the Fox and the Iroquois in the north. When the ongoing struggle between England and France for dominance over the north American fur trade intensified in the 1740s, even Native American nations that had been the French's traditional allies, like the Huron and the Ottawa, started to act in accordance with their best economic interests and to switch sides. In Acadia, by contrast, the Abenaki Confederacy continued to fight with the French, but in vain. When the British realized that they could never buy French or

Abenaki loyalty, they decided to rid Nova Scotia of their presence. They started deporting them far away from farms that had been theirs for over two centuries.

5. Tips for Further Investigations

Interesting People to Look Up

Alphonse de Tonty [or Tonti] (1659–1727)
Charles Rochon (1673–1733)
Pierre Dugué de Boisbriand (1675–1736)
Louis Juchereau de St. Denis (1676–1744)
Adrien de Pauger (?–1726)
Etienne de Bourgmont (1679–1734)
Pierre François-Xavier de Charlevoix (1682–1761)
Jean-Baptiste Bénard de la Harpe (1683–1765)
Jean-Paul Mascarène (1684–1760)
Pierre Gaultier de Varennes de la Vérendrye (1685–1749)
Philippe François Renault (1686–1755)
Pierre-Joseph Céloron de Blainville (1693–1759)
Antoine Le Page du Pratz (1695–1775)
Jean Baptiste Cope (1698–1758)
Jean Baptiste Baudreau, dit Graveline II (1715–1757)

Related Primary Texts

Beauchamps, de. *Journal of De Beauchamps' Journey to the Choctaws, 1746.*
Bonnefoy, Antoine. *Journal of Antoine Bonnefoy's Captivity Among the Cherokees.*
Bourgmont, Etienne de. *Exact Description of Louisiana.*
D'Artaguiette, Bernard Diron. *Journal of Diron d'Artaguiette.*
Deliette, Pierre. "Memoir of De Gannes Concerning the Illinois Country."
Raynal, Abbé. "The founding of Louisiana and John Law's Mississippi Scheme," in *A History of the Two Indies*, ed. P. Jimack, 222–225.
Raynal, Abbé. "The Natchez Indians," in *A History of the Two Indies*, ed. P. Jimack, 225–227.
Recommended Film and Series
Bernard Simiot. *Le Temps des Carbec.* Paris: Albin Michel, 1986.
Frontier, a Canadian Netflix series that deals with colonial life around the Hudson's Bay Company in the 18th century.

CHAPTER VI

North America Won and Lost, 1756–1783

This chapter deals with historical events that were to transform the Franco-Americans' world radically, the Seven Years' War and the American Revolution. Although usually studied separately,[1] these two events deserve to be viewed in relation to each other if only because the second is, to a large extent, a consequence of the first. As we will see in this chapter, Great Britain won the quasi entirety of the North America continent through the 1763 Treaty of Paris that put an end to the Seven Years' War—also known as the "the War of Conquest"[2] and "the French and Indian War." But in 1783, a mere twenty years after the fall of New France, another Treaty of Paris granted over half of Great Britain's territorial conquest to the United States of America following the new nation's victory, thanks to French support, over the British.

The Anglo-Franco conflicts that form the core of this chapter are best understood as part of the genesis of the modern nation-states we know today. As Hodson and Rushforth aptly recall, "the process of Anglicization in eighteenth-century North America owed much of its force to French colonization."[3] But at the same time, it is important to remember that until the American Revolution, people had little say in their own destinies. As wars were won and lost, entire populations could be, and were, traded just like the pieces of land they lived on. Understandably, national allegiances were fragile and in flux for the inhabitants of North America in the late 18th century, foremost for the new British citizens of Canada who remained linguistically and culturally French, but for the linguistically and culturally British subjects who became American citizens as well. In-between, at the multiple points of interaction between colonials, Native Americans, and Africans, all kinds of plurilingual and pluricultural ways of life co-existed, driven by human needs for subsistence, shelter, and companionship.

1. Decline of the Absolute Monarchy in France

When seeking to account for the loss of New France, historians usually turn to the weakening of the French monarchy as the most plausible explanation.[4] For sure, Louis XV's reign was a period of questioning of tradition and authority that undermined the Crown's power and its prestige. The King's infidelities had led to a division within the royal family as early as 1736 and the royal had image suffered its first public blow during the War of the Austrian Succession.[5] The Treaty of Aix-la-Chapelle that concluded it brought neither defeat nor victory for France as it called for the return of all conquered territories, an outcome Voltaire ironically characterized as "working for the King of Prussia" (Haine, 65). With time, the rift at Versailles only grew wider between two camps, on the one hand conservative traditionalists gathered around the Queen and the *dauphin*, the King's eldest son and presumed heir, and on the other hand partisans of the Enlightenment who had as their spokesperson, the King's mistress, the marquise de Pompadour.[6] Torn between the conservatism of the royal family and the progressivism of his lover, Louis XV became inconsistent in his decisions and with time ceased to be "well-beloved" by his people (Nester, 17–20).[7] His growing unpopularity may in fact have led to the 1757 attempt on his life (Gaxotte, 173–174). When the King died unexpectedly in 1774 after contracting small-pox, very few mourned him.

On the international scene, the latter part of Louis XV's reign marks the ebbing of French dominance and the beginning of English supremacy. The Glorious Revolution had produced a constitutional monarchy in Great Britain (1688–89). By the 1740s, French philosophers had already started to look up to the United Kingdom as a better polit-ical and economic model. They criticized France's absolutist government and praised the British parliamentary system. They also took issue with France's mercantilism and praised free enterprise. Montesquieu and Voltaire were both Anglophiles. Montesquieu (1669–1755), a lawyer, political philosopher, author of *Persian Letters* (1721), *The Spirit of Laws* (1748), was an advocate of the theory of separation of power who had spent 18 months in England.[8] Voltaire (1694–1778), a witty and prolific writer, historian, and phi-losopher, who became famous for his struggle for freedom of speech and religion, had spent three years (1726–1728) in exile in England. Montesquieu and Voltaire belonged to the philosophical movement known as the French Enlightenment, a network of schol-ars and scientists who made significant contributions to the advancement of knowledge. Etienne Bonnot de Condillac (1714–1780), in fact, was the author of a book on that very topic, *Essay on the Origin of Human Knowledge* (1746), and Claude Adrien Helvetius (1715–1771), in *De l'esprit*, or *Essays on the Mind* (1758), speculated on the ways in which knowledge is acquired.

Although Enlightenment philosophers' areas of expertise were diverse and their ideas sometimes clashed, for instance on the issue of slavery, they shared a common set of principles: the notion that the advancement of knowledge depends on reason, on ratio-nal thought, and scientific investigation instead of faith and tradition; a mostly optimistic vision of humanity as an aggregate of individuals endowed with natural rights as opposed to subjects burdened by duties[9]; the understanding that these natural rights are freedom of thought, opinion, and religion; as well as the right to seek knowledge and happiness; and a political understanding of good government as based on a social contract between the people and their leaders and the attendant principles or representation and separa-tion of powers.[10] While many of these philosophers were deists, some, like Diderot and D'Holbach, were atheists, an explosive proposition in a kingdom that claimed to owe its legitimacy to God himself.

The publication that best exemplifies the spirit of the Enlightenment in France is *L'Encyclopédie, The Encyclopedia, or Reasoned Dictionary of the Sciences, Arts and Trades*, a gigantic publishing project that yielded 72,000 articles, more than 3,000 illustrations, and took a quarter century to complete (1743–1772). This monumental scientific project was co-edited by Jean Le Rond d'Alembert (1717–1783), a mathematician, physicist, and music theorist who is remembered for his work on the laws of motion (d'Alembert's prin-ciple) and Denis Diderot (1713–1784), a philosopher, essayist, novelist, and playwright

(Chappey). Other famous philosophers of the period include Jean-Jacques Rousseau (1712–1778) who is well-known as the author of *Discourse on the Origin and Foundations of Inequality among Men* (1754) and many other important works, including works of pedagogy and fiction; and Nicolas de Caritat, Marquis of Condorcet (1743–1794), who left many writings on economy and finances as well as essays on women's rights and against slavery.

For most Enlightenment philosophers, the principle of liberty applied not only to people but to goods as well. According to the dominant economic theory of the period, physiocracy, trade had to be free of the obstacles imposed by mercantilist policies. "Laissez faire" was the rallying cry of merchants and physiocrats like du Pont de Nemours, Quesnay, and Turgot, who viewed agriculture as the only source of the wealth of nations and individuals.[11] It was in this context that very large plantations developed in the 18th century and the volume of goods traded during that time increased in a spectacular fashion.[12] Both economic sectors, trade and agriculture, were making a minority of people wealthy: a very small number of French families (550) controlled the French triangular trade and a minority of them, 4 percent, controlled 25 percent of business. Nantes was the only French provincial town to boast ten millionaires by the second half of the 18th century and to have slave traders in the mayor's office well into the 19th century. In Nantes, but also in La Rochelle, Bordeaux, Le Havre, Saint-Malo, Lorient, slave traders formed the social elite and a powerful political lobby that was able to prevent the abolition of slavery in the early days of the French Revolution (Dorigny and Gainot, 24–27). These wealthy commoners formed a (small) social class (*high bourgeoisie*) that competed with the nobility in all areas.[13]

New bourgeois social institutions soon rivaled the court in cultural matters with the creation of coffee houses and salons, the gathering places of the intellectual elite.[14] The wealthy *bourgeoises* who hosted them invited the best and most prestigious philosophers, novelists, artists, musicians, and scientists to present and discuss their work. Although several famous philosophers were themselves clergymen (Condillac, Raynal,[15] Sieyès), the Roman Catholic Church rejected these new philosophical ideas as a threat to its own doctrines. It was hardly surprising since "the pretensions of the absolute monarchy and the divinely inspired Catholic Church were questioned and found wanting" by the *philosophes* (Haine, 66–67). The Church considered these new ideas to be heresies and warned good Catholics to resist their sway. The French Clergy even succeeded in preventing the *Encyclopédie* from being published in France for a while. But it could not stop it: many volumes were published in Switzerland instead and smuggled into France. The Vatican then placed it on its Index of Prohibited Books (Darnton).

As the *Encyclopédie*'s publishing story illustrates, freedom of expression did not exist in 18th-century France and the Catholic Church was still quite a powerful censor at the time. Nonetheless, the grip of the Church on the French population was starting to loosen. Many European rulers, for instance, were interested in these new ideas and simply disregarded the Church's objections. French philosophers took up residence at European courts at a time when French culture dominated everywhere on the continent and French was the lingua franca. Voltaire and Helvetius were invited to live at the court of Frederick the Great of Prussia an invitation they accepted. Later, in 1773–74, Catherine II of Russia invited Diderot to her court in Saint-Petersburg when his financial situation was dire. Even the common folks were showing signs of increased disaffection towards the Catholic Church. As this religious institution was the keeper of vital statistics prior to the French Revolution, the people still depended on it for the recording of all major life events, births and baptisms, marriages, deaths and funerals. But they were starting to disregard the Church's precepts in other area, contraception, for instance, as historian Roger Chartier showed in *The Cultural Origins of the French Revolution*.[16] At the same time, the Church faced competition among the elite from a new "universal" religion that entered France in 1773 and quickly took roots, Free Masonry.[17]

The clash between proponents and opponents of the Enlightenment was felt at court and everywhere in high society. The socio-political tensions that divided the kingdom, the struggle between the old traditionalist elite and the new forward-thinking bourgeoisie, was not only a matter of ideology but also a reflection of the social contradictions of the time. On the one hand, France had a vibrant intellectual life. It could boast great progress in the sciences, philosophy and the arts. It had a lively culture, with great novelists like Lesage, l'Abbé Prévost, Diderot, Rousseau, Sade; playwrights like Marivaux and Beaumarchais; painters like Watteau, Chardin, Boucher, Greuze, Fragonard. The press was starting to develop with new publications like the *Mercure de France* and the *Mercure Galant*. In cultural matters, Louis XV pursued politics of prestige as his predecessors, showcasing his own furniture style and completing new architectural projects in Paris, the Plazza Louis XV (now Place de la Concorde); the church of La Madeleine (1769) and the church Sainte-Geneviève—which later became the Panthéon (1769) (Nester, 41–43). On the other hand, if artists and craftsmen who worked for the monarch benefited from these cultural policies, the common folks did not. While there were no wars on French soil during Louis XV's reign, the gap between rich and poor showed no sign of narrowing. At a time when most of the French lived in the country, agriculture produced hardly enough to feed them. Life expectancy improved slightly, reaching 30 by the end of the 18th century, but the expectation was low to begin with.[18] Political institutions did not change during Louis XV's reign. France still lacked a unified code of law or a justice system valid throughout the kingdom. In terms of rights, the French did not enjoy freedom of expression or religion. The social organization in three estates was an impediment to progress, as was censorship, which could deprive book publishers of the fruits of their investments at a moment's notice. More shockingly perhaps, torture was still in use as the horrific punishment of Damiens, the man convicted of attempted regicide in 1757, illustrates.[19] If part of Louis XV's unpopularity came from the fact that France fought for nothing in the war of the Austrian Succession, France's devastating loss against England in the Seven Years' War was to do the rest.

2. The Seven Years' War, 1756–1763

The Canadians call the war that turned them from French to British subjects "the War of Conquest." The British and Americans designate the same war by the name of their enemies: "the French and Indian War."[20] The French call it the "Seven Years' War" because the war that resulted in the loss of their North American colonial Empire was part of a global military struggle for territorial control that lasted seven years, from 1756 to 1763. Some historians view it as a first world war in light of the great number of Western European powers involved[21] and of its wide geographical scope—Europe, North America, Central America, West Africa, India and the Philippines. A total of 63 battles were fought in Europe alone, 30 in North America, 6 in the Caribbean, 12 in Asia, and 3 in Africa.

Over a million people died during the Seven years' War, more of them civilians than military ("Statistics of Wars..."). By the time war started, new alliances had replaced old ones. France had not forgotten how unreliable an ally Prussia had turned out to be in the War of the Austrian Succession.[22] England, governed by a King from the House of Hanover, felt compelled to side with Prussia but Prussia now threatened Austria, whose interests aligned with those of its former enemy, the Kingdom of France. The core of the conflict was between the two main colonial powers of the mid–18th century, France, and the UK, who were vying for dominance, not only in Europe and North America but also in India and the Indian Ocean. France had the more powerful army of the two, Great Britain, the greatest navy in the world (Dull, *Age of the Ship of the Line*, 89–90).

The French had revived their East India Company as a private company in 1723.[23] The East India Company had the right to sign treaties with foreign powers, to mint coins, and to dispense justice. For these activities, it needed a private fleet of large vessels equipped for combat; a large staff of navy officers, explorers, sailors, and cartographers; as well as private troops on the ground. Turning away from the Atlantic, the Company refocused on East India and trade picked up between Lorient and the Far East. The number of expeditions to the Far East illustrates this trend: only 3 to 4 ships a year traveled the great distance between 1664 and 1719 but that number increased to 10–11 a year between 1720 and 1770. After 1723, the East India Company specialized in the trade of luxury goods: calico, china, tea, sugar, Arabica coffee, and precious metals (Haudrère, 73–85). It was very successful financially, catching up with the Dutch and English East India companies. Shareholder earnings were very high. At a time when the budget of the French Royal Navy was ten million, the Company was able to pay 41 million in dividends in 1731 and 34 million in 1741.[24]

These high profits were due in part to the prosperous colonies the East India Company had established in the Mascarenes islands and India. French trading posts and manufactures existed in Surat since 1668; in Chandannagar (Chandernagor) since 1673 and Puducherry (Pondichéry) since 1674. In 1722, the company added a trading post in Mahé (Malabar) and succeeded in keeping it when the British tried to force them out in 1724 and 1725. In 1725, Puducherry became the French capital of the Indian Ocean. Pierre Benoist Dumas (1696–1745), who was governor from 1735 to 1741, fortified the city, beautified it, and made it prosper thanks to a mint.[25] In 1741, the population included 1,200 French people and 120,000 Indians.

The development of the Mascarene Islands was mostly as the work of Bertrand François Mahé de La Bourdonnais (1699–1753). A native of Saint-Malo, Brittany, Mahé had become famous as a young officer when he secured French victory in the capture of the port that was to bear his name, Mahé, India, in 1724. He served as governor of the French Mascarene Islands in the Indian Ocean, Île de France (Mauritius) and Île de Bourbon (Réunion) from 1735 to 1740. From 1718 onward, slaves were brought from Madagascar, Africa, and India to raise cattle, clear the forests, grow coffee and sugar cane, and produce foodstuff. Mahé turned Port-Louis into a military base for operations in the Indian Ocean. The port had a fleet of five warships and a garrison of 1,700 men. When hostilities with England had broken out in India during the War of the Austrian Succession, Mahé had returned to naval service. From 1740 to 1749, he headed a French fleet that saved Madras and Pondichéry (Haudrère, 207–216) but his disagreement with the policies of Joseph François Dupleix (1697–1763), Dumas' successor as Governor of India, cost him his governorship (Gaxotte, 231–239).

Dupleix was a man with big ideas. Believing that the best way to enrich the Company was to control large territories he broke with his predecessor's policy of non-interference in local affairs, formed alliances with local princes, built an army of native troops, and exported Versailles-style splendor to the courts of his Indian allies (Haudrère, 217–223). From 1742 to 1754, the French colonies and protectorates covered almost all of India, a development that alarmed the British. Although the colonial policies Dupleix put in place were costly, things were going well for the French. But for Jean-Baptiste de Machault d'Arnouville, who served as Secretary of State of the Navy from 1754 to 1757, Dupleix's extravagance poured oil on the fire instead of appeasing the British. Using false allegations against him, the authorities therefore forced his departure in 1754. This was a boon for the British who took advantage of the power vacuum of the interim to make headways in India.

When the Seven Years' War officially broke out in spring 1756, Georges Duval de Leyrit (1716–1764) had been governor of India for two years. The French and their Indian allies lost to England at Plassey, Bengal, in 1757, a British victory that some have seen as the starting point of the British Raj. A Franco-Irish officer, Thomas Arthur de Lally-Tollendal (1702–1766), replaced De Leyrit as the French governor-general of India in 1758. Thanks to the four battalions he brought along, he successfully attacked the British in Madras shortly thereafter. However, he also lost the Battle of Wandiwash in 1760 and the siege of Puducherry that left the city in ruins a year later. The British captured him and sent him to London as a prisoner of war but the French, who wanted a scapegoat for the loss of India, demanded his return to France. They put him on trial and executed him for treason in 1766.

To understand the Seven Years' War in North America, it is important to remember that "[i]n the Americas, the War of the Austrian Succession had changed nothing and settled nothing" (Eccles, *The French*, 198). In North America, the war was also a Nine Years' War since it started in 1754 instead of 1756. Some historians, like J.M. Morgan, have even argued that, in Illinois Country, it actually started in December 1751, when Native Americans conspired to massacre French settlers (*Land of Big Rivers*, 119–132).[26] One could say that from a North American vantage point, it was the last episode in a war that had lasted the entire century. From the French point of view, the stakes in North America were particularly high as they involved control over the huge territory of New France and Louisiana, from the Gulf of Mexico to the Great Lakes and east of the Mississippi to the Appalachian Mountains. The lucrative fur business and the fishing rights off Newfoundland also weighed in the balance.[27] From the British colonials' point of view, French presence in the Ohio Valley was a threat to the Protestant identity of North America as New Englanders feared Catholic influence over this region.[28] Because both Britain and France viewed the Ohio Valley as crucial to the full realization of their colonial ambitions, the armed conflict started there, in 1754, long before the declaration of war.[29]

The French and the British claimed the Ohio Valley as their own, the French by virtue of first occupancy as a colonial power, the British supposedly because the rightful owners of the land, the Iroquois, had become British subjects in 1713. British settlements in the area endangered not only French commerce but also and more importantly perhaps communication between Canada and Louisiana (Eccles, *The French*, 199). The French were aware that the Native Americans in that area would not welcome them with open arms. Céloron de Blainville had observed hostility towards the French on the part of the Mingo, Shawnee, and Miami during his expedition in the Ohio Valley. And yet, most Native Americans were to side with the French during the war. Due to their small numbers, between 60,000 and 70,000 at the time, French settlers were less of a threat to Native Americans than the two million British people spread out in the 13 colonies.

In 1751, Céloron had refused to comply with La Jonquière's plan of destroying the Miamis but Charles de Langlade (1729–1801), a Franco-Ottawa war chief, had agreed to carry it out and had burned down the Miami village of Pickawillany a year later.[30] When the British failed to retaliate for the Miami massacre, however, the Miami started to reconsider their alliance with them. As a better strategy than offensive war, Céloron had recommended self-defense, i.e., strengthening the border with New England by constructing a chain of forts from Lake Erie to the Upper Ohio River valley. Michel-Ange Duquesne de Menneville (1700–1778), who served as Governor General of New France from 1752 to 1755, followed up on Céloron's suggestion. In 1753, he sent 1,500 men set up a line of forts to protect the area: Fort Presque Isle (Erie, Pennsylvania); Fort Le Boeuf (Waterford, Pennsylvania); Fort Machault (Franklin, Pennsylvania) and, after destroying Fort Prince George nearby, Fort Duquesne (Pittsburgh, Pennsylvania).

The Ohio Company sent its surveyor, Christopher Gist, and a twenty-two-year-old lieutenant colonel named George Washington (1732–1799) to Fort Le Boeuf to demand French withdrawal from the Ohio country. The French refused, of course, and responded with their own ultimatum to evacuate "their" land (Eccles, *The French*, 201–202). A similar scenario repeated itself a year later. In May 1754, a militia from Virginia led by Washington and a group of Mingo warriors ambushed a French party and killed Joseph Coulon de Villiers de Jumonville (1718–1754), a military officer stationed at Fort Duquesne, as well as ten of his men.[31] The British claimed Jumonville was spying around Fort Necessity, the French that Jumonville was on a diplomatic mission. In retaliation, French troops from Fort Duquesne caught up with Washington and forced him to surrender. Washington had to sign a statement, in French, admitting that he had ordered Jumonville's murder. Because Britain and France were not officially at war, the affair had international repercussions.[32]

Skirmishes became even more frequent in 1755. That year, the new commander of Fort Duquesne, Daniel Hyacinthe Liénard de Beaujeu (1711–1755) organized a preemptive attack on a British force led by General Edward Braddock (1710–1755).[33] The Battle of the Monongahela deserves mention because the French-Canadian officer who led the small troop made out of French soldiers, Canadian militia men, and Indian warriors fought bare-chested and dressed in the same attire as his native allies, among them Charles de Langlade and perhaps also Pontiac.[34] The French and their allies won the battle but both Beaujeu and Braddock died in combat. A British attack on Fort Niagara was repelled that year as well, but Commander Jean-Armand Dieskau failed to capture Fort Edward and was taken prisoner. In Acadia, Admiral Edward Boscawen organized an effective blockade of the Gulf of Saint Lawrence (Eccles, *The French*, 205–206). In fact, the naval battles that were taking place off the coast of Newfoundland prior to the official start of hostilities contributed to the declaration of war (207–208).[35]

Following a French attack on Saxony in May 1756, Great Britain declared war on France and selected General James Wolfe (1727–1759) as commanding officer in North America. France appointed the marquis Louis Joseph de Montcalm (1712–1759) to replace Dieskau in New France and to lead French operations.[36] Louis Antoine de Bougainville (1729–1811), who later became famous for his exploration of the South Pacific, served as aide to Montcalm during the French and Indian War.[37] At the time, the governor of New

France was Pierre de Rigaud de Vaudreuil-Cavagnial (1698–1778), an officer who had served previously as governor of Trois-Rivières and then of Louisiana for over ten years. Because he was the first governor to be born in Canada, the usual conflicts between metropolitan and colonial authorities over the proper ways to conduct war in North America were exacerbated. Governor Vaudreuil understood guerrilla warfare and General Montcalm, a more traditional officer, made no secret of his disrespect for the "Canadian" governor and even ignored his orders a few times. The same animosity existed between "the French army contingent and the Canadian regulars" (Eccles, 206).

New France also suffered from Versailles' focus on the war in Europe. Compared to Great Britain, the authorities were not particularly supportive of the war effort in New France. Louis XV famously rejected Montcalm's request for more troops and French public opinion ranged from indifferent to openly hostile to the notion of fighting to keep Canada French. For these people, France had nothing to do over there, in "the most detestable northern country in the world." "Why on earth did we have to settle in a country covered by snow and ice eight months in a year and inhabited by barbarians, bears, and beavers?" Voltaire wondered out loud in 1756.[38] French Anglophiles also deplored that New France was a cause of continuous friction with England. Others argued, and rightly so, that it was a drain on the French economy. But to lose the colony was altogether unthinkable. And yet, this is precisely what happened.

At sea, the British had the upper hand from the start of the war. Their strategy was to retake Louisbourg, blockade maritime access, and thereby prevent French soldiers, supplies, and communication from reaching Canada. On land, the French and the Indians initially had the upper hand, with a first victory at Fort William Henry in 1757 and another at the Battle of Carillon a year later.[39] Montcalm defeated a British army of more than 16,000 with fewer than 4,000 men (Eccles, *The French*, 207–209). In the end, though, the British strategy worked out well. Louisbourg surrendered in July 1758 and its fall marked a turning point in favor of Great Britain in the North American war.[40] The French soon lost the other strategic access point to the St. Lawrence valley, Fort Frontenac. The same year, the Forbes expedition led to the capture of Fort Duquesne in November,[41] which was razed and rebuilt as Fort Pitt, the future city of Pittsburgh. A month earlier, in October 1758, representatives of Great Britain and three Amerindian Nations signed the Treaty of Easton that granted the Iroquois, Lenape, and Shawnee exclusive possession of the Ohio country in exchange of the promise not to fight with the French.[42]

In 1759, the British pursued their advance on New France, capturing Fort Carillon, Lake George, and Lake Champlain before laying siege to Quebec City. In September 1759, the French and the British fought the Battle of the Plains of Abraham in the vicinity of Quebec City. It ended in French defeat and in the death of both generals, Montcalm and Wolfe.[43] This British victory led to the fall of Quebec City and to the signing of the Articles of Capitulation of Quebec. The terms of capitulation guaranteed that the French habitants would not be deported—although they were free to go to France if they wanted to. Those who chose to stay were told that they could keep their religion and their possessions. A year later, after a vain attempt to retake Quebec City, Montreal and Detroit fell as well. The marquis de Vaudreuil surrendered the entire colony of Canada in September 1760.[44]

In Acadia, the victors wasted no time and resumed their policy of deportation almost immediately. In fall and winter, they loaded thousands of Acadians who had lived on Ile Saint-Jean (Prince Edward Island) and Ile Royale (Cape Breton Island) on ships

Capture of the ships *Le Prudent* and *Le Bienfaisant* during the siege of Louisbourg in 1758 [*Prise du Vaisseau Le Prudent et du Bienfaisant devant Louisbourg*]. Engraving by Pierre Canot, 1771 (courtesy Bibliothèque nationale de France/Gallica).

bound to France. Several hundred managed to escape to a camp south of *Baie des Chaleurs*, where a French Navy Officer, Charles Deschamps de Boishébert (1727–1797) was organizing their temporary re-settlement on Beaubears Island. The Isle Saint-Jean Campaign was the first in a series of British campaigns meant to eradicate French presence in the territories now under British control. It was followed, also in 1758, by the expulsion of Acadians who lived along the Petitcodiac River and of those who had settled in the current New Brunswick and Gaspé areas along the southern bank of the St. Lawrence River. In the spring of 1759, Acadians who lived along the Saint John River were forcefully removed and some murdered during the Ste. Anne Massacre. Fleeing British advance, Acadians found refuge along the *Baie des Chaleurs* and the Restigouche River, but British troops raided these camps as well, capturing and expelling over 300 refugees from that area in 1761. A third of the deported Acadians died from disease or drownings (Eccles, 207).[45]

Things did not look quite as desperate for the French the following year. In 1762, the French under Chevalier de Ternay and the Count of Haussonville tried to invade Newfoundland and they did in fact capture the island of St. John in May. Emboldened by this victory, hundreds of Acadians near the towns of Halifax and Lunenbourg gathered to celebrate. The authorities arrested 1,300 of them and loaded them on ships bound to Boston only to have Massachusetts send them back to Halifax. Meanwhile, British and Yankee forces were able to make a surprise landing on the island of St. John in September 1762, thus triggering the last battle of the French and Indian Wars, the Battle of Signal Hill, as well as the last defeat for the French.[46]

Spain's entry into war on the side of France delayed peace talks that had started in 1761 and resumed in 1762. Through the secret Treaty of Fontainebleau that year, France ceded Western Louisiana to Spain, in effect all of the territories located on and beyond the western bank of the Mississippi. France and Great Britain signed the Treaty of Paris that put an end to the Seven Years' War in February 1763. It marked the quasi disappearance of the first French colonial empire and closed the era of French dominance in the world. During negotiations, the French strategy was to keep profitable areas, even if they were small, and to give up colonies that required significant investments, even if they were large in size. Of the vast territory of New France, France only retained the tiny islands of Saint Pierre and Miquelon, off the coast of Newfoundland, famous for their fishing grounds and highly profitable. Spain, for its part, exchanged Florida for Cuba and the Philippines (Eccles, *The French*, 235–239). In India, France kept five establishments that were to remain French until 1949[47] and, in the Indian Ocean, the Mascarenes islands. The French East India Company suffered so many losses during the Seven Years' War in terms of settlements, fleet, and income, that it declared bankruptcy in 1764 and was dissolved in 1769. The Crown took over the administration of the Indian Colonies and of the Mascarenes in 1764.[48] With the dissolution of the East India Company, trade opened to private companies.[49]

In the West Indies, France retained the profitable isles of Guadeloupe, Martinique, Saint Lucia, and Saint-Domingue.[50] After the war, the French Caribbean colonies continued to prosper and undergo rapid expansion. Nicknamed "Pearl of the Antilles," Saint-Domingue was the richest of the West Indies islands during the pre-revolutionary period, producing 40 percent of the sugar and 60 percent of the coffee consumed in Europe, while at the same time remaining one of the biggest producers of indigo and cotton.[51] The slave trade went on unabated during the last quarter of the 18th century, with 20,000 new slaves arriving in Saint-Domingue alone each year. In order to secure the steady delivery of slaves from Africa, France also successfully negotiated the retention of its gateway to African slavery, the island of Gorée in Senegal.[52]

If the French gave up so easily on New France, preferring to it the Caribbean islands and fishing grounds in the North Atlantic, it is probably because the colony was far from being as much of an economic asset as the British colonies were. Still, nothing could hide the fact that the loss of New France was such a humiliating defeat that authorities on the ground had to be punished for bringing shame to the country (Eccles, *The French*, 238). Fifty-five officials were accused of dereliction of duty and brought to France to stand trial. Among them were the governors of New France and Acadia, Vaudreuil and Bigot, who each spent time in the Bastille in 1761 and 1762. Vaudreuil was acquitted but Bigot had to pay 1,500,000 livres in restitution.[53] The famous trial known as "L'Affaire du Canada" lasted two years.

The 1763 Treaty of Paris marked the United Kingdom's ascent to the position of uncontested world power.[54] At the time, the population of New England already numbered over 1.5 million while Quebec only had 63,000 inhabitants (Codignola, "American Revolution," 69). The British Crown's decision to take over all France's former North American possessions had initially more to do with the desire to let the thirteen colonies prosper in full security than with the wish to expand westward. The Proclamation of 1763 therefore adhered to the terms of the Treaty of Easton by declaring once again all territory west of the Appalachian Mountains to be Indian lands. In other words, it explicitly prohibited what the Ohio Company so ardently desired: the selling of land and the creation of British settlements in the Ohio and Allegheny Valleys. Herein lies one of the sources of the conflict that arose almost immediately between Great Britain and its North

American colonies at the conclusion of the Seven Years' War. The other source of conflict was the cost of war. Like all nations that took part in the Seven Years' War, Great Britain was crippled by its war debt. As opposed to France, who took out loans to finance it, the British chose to plug the deficit with tax money, or phrased a bit differently, to make the colonies pay for the war. Not surprisingly, the Yankees vehemently objected to this policy.

The Native Americans had their own reasons to resent the British takeover of New France. Although the Royal Proclamation of 1763 established the Appalachian Mountains as the border between the thirteen colonies and Indian lands, the Red Coats did

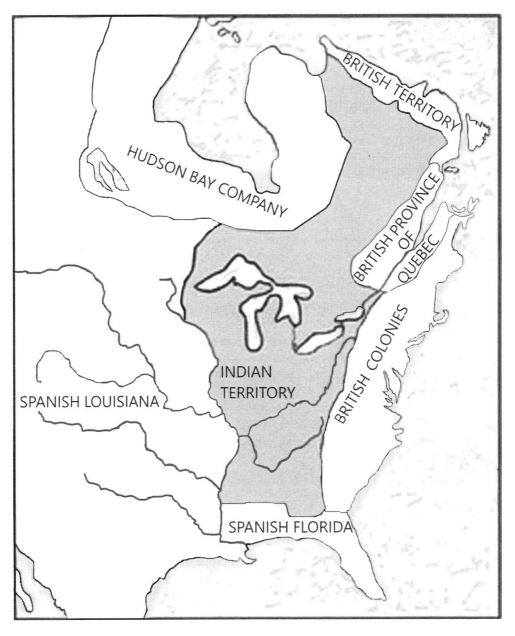

North America after 1763 (author's map).

not withdraw from the Ohio and Allegheny Valleys after the war. Instead, they not only started to treat the Native Americans as conquered nations, they also engaged in biological warfare to permanently remove them from the area.[55] As a result, the Lenape and the Mohicans, the Ottawa and Ojibwe, the Potowatomi and Wyandots, as well as the Shawnee, led by Charlot Kaské, the Miami and even Iroquoian nations such as the Seneca rebelled against British presence in an area that was supposedly theirs, attacking forts and taking prisoners. If Pontiac's Rebellion[56] is often mentioned as a first instance of pan-tribal cooperation against British colonization, it is also remembered as a particularly brutal war, with Native American violence matched by British atrocities.[57]

Although the Pontiac rebellion failed after a year of fighting, and thus missed its initial goal of clearing native lands of British presence, it led to changes in British personnel and policies in North America. Lord Amherst, who was seen in London as responsible for the Pontiac Rebellion, was removed as Commander-in-Chief and replaced by Thomas Gage (1718–1787), who managed to end the war by negotiating with one Native American Nation at a time. Except for Kaské, who crossed the Mississippi River rather than accept British sovereignty, all Native American nations that had engaged in war against England had signed peace treaties by 1765. The atrocity of the war, however, renewed the British government's conviction that it was best to keep British settlers and Native Americans apart, hence its firm stand on the Appalachian Mountains as the line of demarcation between them. This position had as its corollary the notion that Native American nations had rights over the lands they lived on. American settlers, by contrast, saw this proclamation as an infringement on their right to conquest and their resentment, added to other grounds for complaint, fed the armed rebellion against the British government a decade later.

3. North America After 1763

What did the fall of New France mean for Franco-Americans? The French of Louisiana did not accept defeat easily. In 1768, anti–Spanish revolts occurred in New Orleans prior to the Spanish takeover. The French owners of large plantations, the *grands blancs*, did not welcome the first Spanish governor, Antonio de Ulloa (1716–1795), and even forced his recall in 1768 (Creagh, *Nos Cousins*, 200–201). After his departure, the rebels asked France to support the creation of "a semi-independent republic," a proposal the French government was not opposed to. Spain, however, was not interested, and sent a greater military force instead to take control of Louisiana and to punish the rebels (Eccles, *The French*, 242–243). Things calmed down in the 1770s and the arrival of Spanish settlers and Irish refugees contributed to the growth of Lower Louisiana and to its increased cultural diversity.

As for the French and their Native American allies of Illinois country, they greatly outnumbered the British occupants, but like the Canadians and Louisianans, they now lived in a country that was no longer theirs officially.[58] "What was the reaction of the populace when the official notice [of the transfer of their land to Great Britain] was read at the church door after mass? Other than the fact that many habitants voted with their feet and left, we have no record" (Brown, *History*, 151). And yet, the sense of abandonment by France, the feelings of dispossession, and the humiliation of becoming subjects of France's hereditary enemy must have been great, all the more so, Brown suggests, because at the same time in France the Crown outlawed the Jesuit order that had long provided New France with its clergy (Brown, *History*, 152).[59]

French-speaking villages continued to emerge during the last decade of the 18th century in the Illinois country, most of them on the Western bank of the Mississippi. In the 1760s, a man from Brittany, Francis Azor, started a mining settlement in Missouri known as "Mine à Breton," near a creek called "Fourche à Renault."[60] In 1763, "the French company of Maxent, Laclède, and Co. of New Orleans" sent two agents, Pierre Laclède (1729–1778) and his step-son René-Auguste Chouteau (1749–1829) to the Illinois country where they founded the city of St. Louis (Randall, 1027), or so the story goes.[61] In *French Roots of the Illinois Country*, Ekberg defines the Illinois Country "at the end the French regime (1763) and the founding of St. Louis (1764)," as "the settlement area, on both sides of the Mississippi, running from St. Louis in the north to Kaskaskia"[62] in the south, including the communities of Cahokia, St. Philippe, the fort and the village of Chartres, Prairie du Rocher, and Ste. Genevieve (32–33).[63] He also shows that

> the inhabitants of these communities shared not only their way of settling and exploiting the land but also their language and their ethnicity; they were all francophone, and they were virtually all of French, French Canadian, French Indian, and French Creole extraction [239].

Franco-Americans, in other words, who inhabited the Illinois Country and Louisiana at the end of the Seven Years' War, found themselves in a situation similar to that of the Acadians in 1713 but strangely enough "the British failed to introduce any civil government in this area [the Illinois Country] between 1768 and 1778" (Creagh, *Nos Cousins*, 147). As a result, life after annexation initially went on as if nothing had happened: the same communal togetherness that had characterized the villages since their foundation remained, with boat and horse races in the summer, gambling and drinking on weekends, outdoor games, dancing, and banquets in the fall, ice skating and big Mardi Gras celebrations in the winter (Creagh, *Nos Cousins*, 148).

Nonetheless, some of the villages, like Cahokia, saw their population flee and re-settle across the Mississippi. The city of St. Louis, at the confluence of the Missouri and Mississippi Rivers, was founded shortly after the 1762 Treaty of Fontainebleau transferred all French territories located west of Mississippi to Spain:

> St. Louis was founded on *de jure* Spanish territory […] as a fur-trading outpost, because it was a fortified town, and because of it became the capital of Upper Louisiana. Although St. Louis was founded to serve as an outpost for the trading activities of Maxent, Laclède, and Company, the community soon acquired a pattern of settlement and land usage that was of long standing in the Illinois Country [Ekberg, *French Roots*, 96].

Its foundation in effect robbed the British traders of the take-over of the fur trade they had anticipated (Creagh, *Nos Cousins*, 148–149).

André Prévos, in his history of the French in Iowa, recalls several Frenchmen who left their mark in the history of the Upper Mississippi Valley during the Spanish Louisiana period: Cardinal, Giard [Girard], Dubuque, and Tesson. Jean Marie Cardinal[64] fled across the Mississippi in 1763 after allegedly killing two American fur traders in Wisconsin[65] and was "the first white man to settle in Prairie du Chien."[66] Basil Giard was another early settler of Prairie du Chien, who probably left Kaskaskia to settle there in 1779 and engage in the fur trade.[67] Julien Dubuque, from Quebec City, was also among the first white Europeans to settle in Iowa. In 1785 he requested permission from the Spanish Governor to mine for lead near the city that now bears his name, Dubuque, Iowa.

Nicknamed "Little Cloud," or "Little Night," he was well-liked by the Fox and is said to have married the Native American woman who had actually discovered the mine.[68] In 1799, Honoré Tesson was also awarded a land grant in Iowa by the Spanish administration.[69] Well into the 19th century, villages bearing French names appeared in the Mississippi Valley, places like Goudeau, Moreauville, Latanier, Lecompte, and others. Gilbert Din writes that the area of the Arkansas Post similarly remained "a region where the Indian trade and forest products still accounted for the largest activity" during the Spanish Louisiana period (Din, 130).[70]

Whereas the French of Lower and Upper Louisiana formed the white settler majority, the Acadians were truly squeezed out of their lands. Between 1755 and 1785 over 3,500 of them sailed for France. Some settled in their homeland for good but many had a hard time fitting in and chose to leave again. After thirty years of exile for some, these Cajuns, according to the English pronunciation of the word "Acadians," found their way back to North America, to Louisiana this time.[71] The Spanish government gave them small plots of land along the Mississippi and the bayous where they practiced subsistence agriculture (Cook, 375–376). They settled mostly along Bayou Lafourche and in Saint-James and Saint-Gabriel d'Iberville's parishes.

After the 1763 conquest, Canada became a British colony and was renamed the Province of Quebec.[72] As Eccles puts it, "[t]he Canadians now became British subjects with some of the rights and privileges of Englishmen, and the disabilities of Roman Catholics, including the inability to hold any office under the Crown" (Eccles, *The French*, 240). They were given the choice of leaving the colony or becoming British subjects. For many habitants, however, swearing an oath of allegiance to the British Crown was not an option since it meant betraying their Catholic faith. Clearly, with French Canadians forming 99 percent of the population and the majority of them now prevented from participating in local government, the risks of rebellions were great. Recognizing the danger, the first British Governors of the province, James Murray and Guy Carleton, advocated for change. Their efforts would eventually lead to the Quebec Act of 1774. In the meanwhile, the Canadians did not rebel:

> Unlike Louisiana, the Canadian dominant class had been eliminated, replaced by British administrators, backed up by some fifteen hundred regular troops. Moreover, the mass of the Canadians had lost their respect for the seigneurs and ex-officers in the colonial regular troops who had lost the war and delivered the people into servitude, but of whom many were now actively collaborating with the conquerors, in the hopes of regaining their dominant position in society [Eccles, *The French*, 243–244].

Paradoxically, the fall of New France had perhaps its greatest impact in the thirteen colonies. Initially, it was Parliament's decision to make the American colonies pay for their share of the war debt that met with opposition. The Stamp Act of 1765, a law establishing a tax on all print matter used in the colonies, led to the formation of a colonial Congress that met in New York to prepare a response. As a justification for their refusal to comply with the act, the Yankees, who had no representation in London, argued that there could be "no taxation without representation" according to the English Bill of Rights of 1689. Their claim fell on deaf ears, however. Instead, more acts of Parliament followed in 1767–1768. Known as the Townshend Acts, they all re-affirmed the Crown's right to tax the colonies and sought to raise revenue through indirect taxes on all products imported from England.[73] The conflict between England and the colonies escalated with the 1770 Boston Massacre, a confrontation between British soldiers and Bostonians that led to the shooting death of several colonial patriots. Resentment over corrupt officials and their abusive practices led to attacks on British ships that culminated in the Boston Tea Party in 1773. Faced with ongoing resistance and increasingly violent opposition to its rule, the British Parliament issued a series of coercive acts known in America as the Intolerable Acts of 1774. Parliament's goal was to punish the Americans for their resistance to taxation and for their defiance of the government in London. If one of the Acts undid Massachusetts' right to self-governance, four of them were in direct retribution for the Boston Tea Party.

Another act passed during the same legislative session was unrelated but perceived as intolerable as well by the Yankees, the Quebec Act of 1774. Despite promises to Native Americans, the Quebec Act expanded the province of Quebec to include Montreal, Ontario and the Illinois territory—the current states of Illinois, Indiana, Michigan, Ohio, Wisconsin and Minnesota. Given that the Crown had prohibited any western expansion of the American colonies, this enlargement of the province of Quebec was seen as a provocation. The issue of religion, as handled in the Quebec Act, was also a sore point for the Yankees. So as to allow French-Canadians to participate in local government, language linking allegiance to the Crown to the Protestant faith in the oath of allegiance was dropped. In addition, French Canadians were granted the right to remain Catholics and to use French civil law in domestic cases—although in criminal and administrative matters English common law was used.[74]

The Quebec Act of 1774 was inspired by pragmatism and lessons learned by the first British governors of the province. The situation on the ground—in effect a British government imposed on a French population—required mutual adaptation on the part of the governed and their new leaders. In the area of government, this accommodation entailed the adoption of the French top-down model of governance, that is, the abandonment of the principle of representation and the absence of legislative assemblies in the province. As the French past could hardly be erased by fiat, the land organization in parishes was retained and countless buildings adorned with French and Catholic symbols were simply rededicated. In the province, the French-Canadian upper class was usually pleased with the Quebec Act.[75] Unlike their British counterparts, the early Franco-Canadians were not political animals who had moved to Canada to create a better society. They only became interested in politics once the British victors forbade them to move around in their country as they wanted and as they had had done for generations. They were particularly resistant to one of their duties as British subjects, enrollment in the British army, and this, despite best efforts on the part of *seigneurs* and clerics to cooperate with British officials in that area.

The thirteen American colonies, as well was the English-speaking minority in the province of Quebec, viewed the "French" colonial model enforced through the Quebec Act with suspicion, possibly as a first move against their own local elected assemblies. In addition to the irksome issue of the closing of the Western frontier, it also stood as an attack on the Protestant faith given the latitude granted the "Papists." And then there was the issue of taxation without representation. Unlike the French revolutionaries who fought for political (and religious) freedom in 1789, the British had already completed their Glorious Revolution and earned their Bill of Rights a century earlier. Initially, therefore, the American colonists would perhaps have been content if London had treated them as full-fledged, instead of second-class, subjects by allowing them to send their own elected officials to Parliament. It was the government's intransigence that pushed them to break with the mother country and this although they were British at heart. In September 1774, the colonies organized their First Continental Congress to plan their joint response to the Coercive Acts. After drilling their own militia, they fought the King's troops at the battle of Lexington and Concord in April 1775, thus launching the American War of Independence.[76] The rest is history: emboldened by their victory, the United States proclaimed their independence in July 1776.[77]

Many Americans of French Huguenot descent played a prominent role during the American Revolution. To name just a few: Elias Boudinot (1740–1821), a lawyer from New Jersey who served as President of the Continental Congress in 1782–1783, and as a congressman later on; the Boston silversmith Paul Revere [Rivière, or Rivoire] (1734–1818), who famously rode at midnight to alert the Continental Army of the British's approach before the battle of Lexington; Daniel Roberdeau (1727–1795), a Philadelphia merchant who represented Pennsylvania in the Continental Congress in 1776–1777; Ephraim Brevard (17 ??-1781), a physician from North Carolina, who signed the 1775 Mecklenburg Declaration of Independence. Charles Gratiot (1752–1817), a fur trader from St. Louis financed the Illinois Campaign (1778–1779). Francis Marion (1732–1795), a South Carolina planter and military officer fought in the French and Indian War and in the War of Independence. Henry Laurens (1724–1792), a wealthy slaver merchant and plantation owner from South Carolina, was also a revolutionary leader; William Bayard, Jr. (1761–1826), a New York City banker; Antoine Bénézet (Anthony Benezet) (1713–1784), the Philadelphia abolitionist; Gabriel Manigault (1758–1809), an architect who was the scion of the wealthiest family in North America in 1770.[78] James Bowdoin [Baudoin]: 1729–1790, grandson of Pierre Baudoin arrived in 1680. Four of the most influential politicians of the revolutionary era were of French ancestry: John Jay (1745–1829), grandson of Augustus Jay who came after the revocation of the Edict of Nantes; Gouverneur Morris (1752–1816) whose mother, Sarah Gouverneur (1714–1786) was a Huguenot; Alexander Hamilton (1755–1804), the son of Rachel Faucette, also of Huguenot stock. Jones notes that the "French Huguenots were […] so well assimilated by the time of the Revolution that little remained to distinguish them from the rest of the colonial population" (51).

4. France's Role in the War of Independence, 1775–1783

Louis XVI (1754–1793), who was only twenty years old when he became King of France in 1774, was by all accounts a good Christian but not a king who could do much to reverse the progressive course France had embarked on. As the ideals of the Enlightenment continued to gain ground in France, its proponents applauded the American Declaration of Independence as the embodiment of progress and liberty over "English tyranny."[79] As early as 1765, Charles Gravier, Count of Vergennes (1719–1787),[80] had predicted that once the French were out of the picture in North America, it would not take long for the Americans to throw off their shackles. As French Foreign Minister from 1774 to 1787, Vergennes was sympathetic to American efforts to shake the English yoke.[81] When Patriots approached French embassy staff members in London in 1774, he did not immediately respond: King Louis XVI had to be convinced first that it was in France's best interest to support the American cause. From 1775 onward, however, Vergennes encouraged secret efforts to aid the Patriots, sending cash and ammunitions through a shell company created for that purpose—Roderigue Hortalez and Company—that was directed by playwright Pierre Caron de Beaumarchais, author of The *Marriage of Figaro*.[82] At that time, France gave "a million livres to furnish arms to the American rebels" and "[t]he following year, France and Spain provided a further million each" (Eccles, 248).

In 1776, Benjamin Franklin (1706–1790)[83] and Silas Deane (1738–1789)—whom John Adams (1735–1826) replaced in 1778[84]—came to France to ask for assistance in the War of Independence.[85] At a time when France could not openly receive American envoys at court without risking war with England, Jacques-Donatien Le Ray de Chaumont (1726–1803) played a key role as intermediary between the American Delegation and French officials. Chaumont, as Governor of the *Invalides*, the wounded veterans' hospital in Paris, had his entries at court and the King's ear.[86] Born in the city of Nantes, he was a wealthy aristocrat, and like Beaumarchais an early supporter of the United States.[87] His residence in Passy (now Paris) served as headquarters for the American delegation led by Benjamin Franklin. Le Ray de Chaumont also equipped John Paul Jones' naval squadron[88] and put his fortune at the United States' disposal.

Initially, King Louis XVI was reluctant to engage in a new war. France had not entirely recovered financially from the Seven Years' War and the French Navy was still being rebuilt. Some advisors also cautioned that the Americans might not be capable of winning a war against such a formidable enemy as Great Britain, or that, in spite of the Declaration of Independence, they may choose to reconcile with London. Both scenarios would put France in an awkward position should she hasten to respond to American calls for assistance. Between 1776 and 1778, therefore France remained officially neutral. Secretly, however, Beaumarchais continued to purchase and ship guns, gunpowder, and ammunitions to the Continental Army while providing discreet economic assistance.[89] It is estimated that by 1777, France had provided over five million *livres* (French pounds) in aid and 90 percent of the weapons used at the battle of Saratoga. Moreover, French officers were given leave to join the Continental army on their own if they so wished prior to France's official entry in the war. While in France, Deane was introduced to several French officers, among them Baron de Kalb, Baron von Steuben, and Casimir Pulaski who became a major-general in the Continental Army under George Washington. Deane was able to enlist twenty-year-old Gilbert du Motier, marquis de Lafayette (1757–1834). Friedrich Wilhelm von Steuben (1730–1794), a Prussian officer introduced to Benjamin Franklin by his friend the French Minister of War in 1777, Count of Saint-Germain, became George Washington's Chief of Staff.[90]

The Continental Army's victory at Saratoga convinced France that the United States could win the war.[91] In February 1778, France signed two treaties of alliance with the United States that Congress ratified in May.[92] The first was a Treaty of Amity and Commerce that formally recognized the new nation; the second a Treaty of Alliance in the event of a war with Britain (Eccles, *The French*, 250).[93] The latter took effect the following month when Britain declared war on France. From then on, the French openly sent troops and naval forces to North America. As Admiral of the French fleet, Count Charles Hector d'Estaing (1729–1794) brought "12 ships of the line and four frigates" to the Delaware Bay (252) and part of the French forces. These 3,000 men, including 500 free men of color from Saint-Domingue, took part in the battles of Rhode Island and the siege of Savannah in 1779, fighting side by side with 2,000 Americans.[94] However, with both ending in defeat and the British forces greatly outnumbering the Franco-American troops, the prospect of American victory faded:

Only French financial aid and supplies kept the American forces active; loans and subsidies amounted to forty-eight million livres by 1782, plus considerably more for naval support. In 1781, Vergennes noted that the American war had cost France over two hundred million livres a year. At the same time, the American Congress could not bring itself to levy a national tax to finance the war [Eccles, *The French*, 253].

In spring 1780, French ships again bypassed British defenses and successfully delivered 5,500 soldiers to Rhode Island. Their commandant, Jean-Baptiste de Rochambeau (1725–1807), was sent to assist Washington's army, but when he arrived, he sensed that the Americans were just about to give up the fight.[95] Washington and Rochambeau also disagreed on strategy, with the former insisting on re-taking New York,[96] and the latter on attacking in Virginia to prevent a meltdown of the American forces in the south. In the summer of 1781, George Washington's Continental Army and Rochambeau's 7,000 men met in White Plains, New York, to discuss strategy. In the end, the decision was made by Navy Admiral François Joseph Paul de Grasse (1722–1788) who had arrived in the West Indies with 29 ships and 3,200 soldiers, and chose to take on the British at Norfolk in the Chesapeake Bay, instead of New York.[97] At that point, "Washington grudgingly gave way to Rochambeau and agreed that the allied armies would march south to Virginia. From this point on, the French were completely in command of the campaign" (Eccles, *The French*, 257).

The Continental and the French armies entered Philadelphia and marched south to Yorktown where they arrived in September. De Grasse's fleet joined with the squadron from Newport, Rhode Island, led by Jacques-Melchior de Barras (1719–1793)[98] and together, they attacked the British fleet as planned in September 1781, forcing it to retreat to New York. The outcome of the Battle of the Capes was that the French gained control of the Chesapeake Bay, De Grasse was able to deliver the 3,200 soldiers that were then placed under Lafayette's command, and Barras to unload the artillery material that was needed for the siege of Yorktown. Lafayette had already fought and been wounded at the Battle of Brandywine as well as the Battle of Rhode Island in 1778.[99] By late September, General Cornwallis was isolated in Yorktown, with almost as many French soldiers as Americans taking part in the siege of the city. Louis Antoine Jean Le Bègue de Presle Duportail (1743–1802), a lieutenant-colonel in the French Royal Corps of Engineers, served as commander of all engineers in the Continental Army:

> From then on [after the Battle of the Capes], the siege was directed by the French corps of engineers, an elite unit, employing eighteenth century textbook military tactics. Neither Washington nor any other American officer had had any training for, or experience with, this type of set-piece warfare. The only engineers the Americans had were French officers, seconded to it [Eccles, *The French*, 258].

The siege lasted about a month and Cornwallis surrendered on October 19, 1781.[100]

The French from the Illinois country supported the cause of independence, mostly because of their displeasure with the British Regime (Creagh, *Nos Cousins*, 194).[101] As noted earlier, the wealthy fur trader Charles Gratiot Senior (1752–1817), for instance, provided funding for the Illinois campaign. Although initially apprehensive after the bloodless takeover of their town by the Virginians led by Colonel Rogers Clark in January 1778, the inhabitants of Kaskaskia soon celebrated the arrival of American troops and many Frenchmen joined them. However, Franco-American relations deteriorated after the war brought chaos to Illinois Country (Creagh, *Nos Cousins*, 198). Lankford reports that the

French of Illinois already had mixed feelings towards Americans during the War of Independence as "the attempts of several Americans to wield autocratic power in Illinois, were experienced as periods of anarchy punctuated by times of tyranny."[102] Following the invasion of Canada in late 1775, Quebec also contributed around 150 soldiers to the insurgent army. Overall, 1800 Franco-Canadians were to fight along the American Patriots during the War of Independence (A. Chartier, 14).[103]

Washington would have liked to march on to Canada, but Rochambeau's orders were not to assist in a war of conquest. Since the American forces were insufficient on their own, the plan was abandoned (Eccles, *The French* 260). By 1782, as France and Spain were seriously considering an invasion of England, the British government and the public were keen on ending the war in North America. Spain wanted to continue the war until it could reclaim Gibraltar from Great Britain, but France was broke and wanted it to end. Vergennes proposed to create an Indian buffer zone under Spanish control between the United States, that would remain confined to eastern seaboard, and Spanish Louisiana. Given their pressing desire to expand west, this proposal was totally unacceptable to the Americans, who, as a result, decided to exclude France and Spain from the negotiating table and bargained with the UK directly. An American delegation approached the British with a proposal for a separate peace treaty[104] and Lord Shelburne, the British Prime Minister and main negotiator, offered his American counterpart, John Jay, a deal England had so far refused to consider, all of the Indian land east of the Mississippi River, north of Florida and south of Canada. These very generous terms were meant to undermine the Treaty of Amity and Commerce signed by the United States and France in February 1778, or more specifically to replace France as the preferred trading partner of the United States.

Through the 1783 Treaty of Paris, Great Britain recognized the independence of the thirteen colonies and looked forward to the development of the United States where it could and would continue to send people and goods. At the end of the war, France had little to show for.[105] She had lost 2,112 men fighting for American liberty and the nation she had fought had de-facto become the favored commercial partner of the nation she had helped.[106] In addition, she faced a crippling debt of 1.3 billion *livres,* an untenable financial burden that was soon to usher the fall of the monarchy. Moreover, despite the huge support France provided the United States during the War of Independence, her role was a bone of contention in the United States from the start. In the early days of the Republic, the American delegation in Paris did not trust the French. If Franklin knew how to be subtle and diplomatic, John Adams did not understand the French, who were, in his view, too slow to provide assistance. Despite factual evidence that "the United States of America owes its independence, its emergence as a nation, mainly to French support; financial, logistical, and direct military aid" (Eccles, *The French*, 265), there are still two storylines on France's role in the War of Independence. One states, accurately, that France was a true ally of the young American Republic, that Great Britain would have kept its American colonies had the French refused to assist the American Patriots. The other is a narrative of national creation free of foreign intervention, in which the new nation begets itself and France becomes "a revolting ally," and the United States' "oldest enemy."[107]

Contrary to that story, Franco-American friendship was celebrated immediately after the war. American and French officers who had served together during hostilities founded the Society of the Cincinnati in 1783. Named after Lucius Quintus Cincinnatus, its goal was to perpetuate the transatlantic fraternity the war had engendered and to promote understanding and friendship between France and the United States.[108] American founding members included Georges Washington, Henry Knox (1750–1806), and Alexander Hamilton (1755–1804). Among the French founding members were Le Ray de Chaumont, Pierre L'Enfant, who became a U.S. citizen and designed the U.S. capital, Washington, D.C., Lafayette, Louis de Noailles, who moved to abolish feudal rights on August 4, 1789, during the French Revolution,[109] and Charles Armand Tuffin, Marquis de la Rouërie, who became a counter-revolutionary leader during the French Revolution.[110] However, because only officers above a certain rank could be admitted, and because all of the French officers who participated in the war were aristocrats, the Society of the Cincinnati was viewed with suspicion in some quarters. During his stay in France, for instance, Benjamin Franklin helped Mirabeau[111] write his first published work, a critique of the Society of the Cincinnati, which both deemed incompatible with the egalitarian values of a republic.

In this chapter, we saw France lose her North American colonies to Great Britain and Voltaire applaud to France's defeat.[112] Not all French people agreed with him. Several generations later, Alfred de Vigny still bemoaned the loss of France's North American province.[113] American historians have tended to view France's defeat in the French and Indian War as inevitable,

> as evidence that the despotic and inflexible French Empire was always destined to fail. Parkman,[114] in particular, framed the clash between France and Britain in North America as an epic battle "'of the past against the future' [...] of barren absolutism against a liberty, crude, incoherent, and chaotic, yet full of prolific vitality." Obsessed with what French colonies were not, these historians failed to grasp what they were: societies that grew, functioned, adapted, collapsed, and influenced what came later [Hodson and Rushforth, 20].

We also saw Great Britain, two decades later, lose her original North American colonies to separatist Colonials who established a Republic thanks to the assistance of the French monarchy.

But as Rafe Blaufarb points out, "France's contribution to American independence is often neglected in popular accounts of that revolution," because "a nation might want to remember its struggle for independence as the exclusive work of its own citizens" (Blaufarb, *Bonapartists*, xvii). And so it is that, from the birth of the Republic to today, the United States has been a divided nation when it comes to its relationship to France. Some like John Adams, John Jay, or Alexander Hamilton, who were and remained British at heart,[115] viewed France with distrust, as an unreliable partner at best. Others, like George Washington, Thomas Jefferson,[116] and Gouverneur Morris, saw France as an ally and a friend. So did the citizens of Kentucky who called one of their cities Louisville—and later their whiskey "Bourbon"—in honor of King Louis XVI, and those of the 36 U.S. towns who named themselves Lafayette in recognition of France's military assistance in the war of independence.

5. Tips for Further Investigations

Interesting People to Look Up

François de Grasse (1722–1788)
Charles-Henri d'Arsac de Ternay (1723–1780)

Jacques Le Ray de Chaumont (1726–1803)
Jean-Baptiste de Rochambeau (1727–1808)
Charles-Victor d'Estaing (1729–1794)
Charles Michel de Langlade (1729–1801)
Gilbert du Motier de Lafayette (1757–1834)

Related Documents and Texts

"Declaration of Independence, July 4, 1776."
"The Paris Peace Treaty of September 30, 1783."
"The Quebec Act October 7, 1774."
Raynal, Abbé. "The Savages of Canada," in *A History of the Two Indies*, ed. P. Jimack, 209–212.
"The Royal Proclamation–October 7, 1763."
"Treaty of Amity and Commerce Between the United States and France; February 6, 1778."
Related Secondary Texts
Godechot, Jacques. "The Atlantic Revolution. Characteristics and Causes," in *France and the Atlantic Revolution*, 1–26.
Nester, William, R. "Killing Fields, 1757," in *The French and Indian War*, 213–251.

Related Films and Works of Fiction

Battle of the Brave [*Nouvelle France*] (2004).
The Last of the Mohicans, a novel by James Fennimore Cooper (1826).
The Last of the Mohicans, a 1992 film adaptation of Cooper's novel.
Wolfe and Montcalm, directed by Allan Wargon (1957)
Philippe Simiot, *Le Banquier et le Perroquet* (a fictional biography of banker Stephen Girard).
Films on the War of Independence are too numerous to list. Here are just a few:
John Adams, 2008 HBO miniseries (available on Amazon Prime).
Turn, Washington Spies, 2104 AMC series (available on Netflix). Lafayette, Rochambeau, and De Grasse are featured in Episode 8 in Season 4.

CHAPTER VII

Franco-American Relations in the Age of Revolutions, 1784–1800

This chapter focuses on a relatively short period, from 1784, when Congress ratified the Treaty of Paris, to the turn of the century, with the rise of Napoleon Bonaparte to power in France in 1799 and the end of the John Adams administration in 1801. Those two decades are of great significance for the United States and for France as, in each case, they mark the birth of modern Western democracy.[1] In America, the 1783 Treaty of Paris concretized the independence from Britain proclaimed in 1776 and the ratification of the Constitution in 1788 instituted the American Republic. In France, the Revolution of 1789 led to the replacement of an absolute, with a constitutional monarchy before engendering a republic in 1792. Among the many reasons to examine the revolutionary era up close, two of them are particularly relevant for this study. The first one is that the French Revolution divided American public opinion and that this domestic division set the tone for future Franco-American relations. The second is that the many Frenchmen who found refuge in America during those years, particularly those who came from the Caribbean, were to leave a lasting imprint on the young American republic. Section 1 centers on French visitors and immigrants to the United States prior to the Revolution and on Franco-American relations during the first phase French Revolution. In section 2, the focus is on the French republic and in section 3, on the second wave of French immigration to the United States it unleashed. Section 4 deals with the deterioration of Franco-American relations in the 1790s.

1. Friends: Franco-American Relations During the French Revolution of 1789–1792

In spite of anti–French sentiment in part of the American elite, Franco-American friendship was strong following the War of Independence.[2] The war had created personal bonds between military officers of both nations and many Frenchmen returned to the United States once it was over. French culture was popular in the United States at the time, and so was the French language. There were French communities in Boston, the U.S. base of the French fleet until 1787, and in Philadelphia. Although the teaching of Greek and Latin defined a liberal arts education in those days, Harvard already had a French instructor—but not Yale. Most of the French who settled in the United States shortly after U.S. independence were officers who had served in the Revolutionary War and kept in contact with their American friends. Pierre Charles L'Enfant (1754–1826), a graduate of the French Academy of Fine Arts and Architecture (*Académie des Beaux Arts*), had served as a military engineer during the War of Independence under Washington and Lafayette.[3] After the war, he stayed in the United States, changed his name from Pierre to Peter, and opened a civil engineering firm in New York. A friend of Alexander Hamilton (1757–1804), he became the renowned architect President Washington entrusted with the design of the federal capital, Washington, D.C., in 1791.[4] As Roger Kennedy has showed, French architects were often called upon to built or assist in the construction of the new federal buildings (Kennedy).

Paul Joseph Guérard, better known as Joseph Nancrède (1761–1841), came to the United States as a soldier in Rochambeau's army and participated in all his major campaigns. He returned to France in 1783 for two years and by 1787 was gainfully employed teaching French at Harvard. Author of a French textbook, Nancrède was also the publisher of the short-lived French newspaper, *Le Courrier de Boston* (Stern). Pierre Etienne (Peter Steven) du Ponceau (1760–1844), who had a gift for languages, came to America as Baron von Steuben's secretary in 1777. After the war, he worked as a jurist in Philadelphia, but his real passion was the study of Native American languages. His brilliant scholarship in that area opened the doors of the American Philosophical Association to him in 1791. Anne-Louis de Tousard (1745–1817), who had also served under Washington, went back to France after the Continental Army disbanded but returned to the United States in 1795 to oversee the fortifications of West Point and Newport.[5] A few French veterans of the War of independence also sought to make a quick fortune in the Caribbean islands through farming or in the import/export business with the United States. With so many well-educated Frenchmen involved in the genesis of the American Republic, it is hardly surprising that French aesthetics left an imprint on early American architecture and urban design.[6]

Between the American and the French revolutions, a few enterprising French professionals and businessmen not associated with the armed forces also settled in the United States. The most important, if not the best-known of them, is probably Stephen (Étienne) Girard (1750–1831), who arrived in Philadelphia in 1775, became a resident of the city and a U.S. citizen, and made a huge fortune in international shipping through commerce with Bordeaux, where his father's company was located, and Saint-Domingue, where his brother resided and conducted business.[7] Pierre Jacques Brissot (1754–1793), known as Brissot de Warville, came to the United States for a totally different reason: to establish contacts with American abolitionists.[8] A journalist, Brissot had been jailed in France for his political opinions and had spent a few years in exile in England to avoid spending more time in the Bastille. In 1788, he travelled to the United States and wrote a three-volume account of his American experience, *Nouveau Voyage dans les États-Unis de l'Amérique septentrionale* (*New Journey in the United States of North America*), published in 1791. Bissot fell in love with the young republic and was even planning on moving here with his family. But the Revolution broke out in France and it was too exciting for him not to be part of it.[9]

Among the many causes that led the French to topple their absolutist government, the most direct one was the national debt.[10] The unending wars and the politics of prestige favored by Versailles had broken the bank, and the various solutions proposed by a succession of finance ministers had made no real dent in the problem. They had resorted, of course, to the usual panacea of remedies, loans and taxation, but the additional tax burden had only engendered an economic crisis, making the French people hungrier and more miserable. Old Regime French society was divided into three classes, or orders, two that were privileged, i.e., tax-exempt, the nobility and the clergy, and one, the Third Estate, that had to foot the bill, a situation that had become unbearable.[11]

The political crisis that had been brewing for decades in France came to a head once the principles defended by Enlightenment philosophers were enshrined in the American Constitution. It seemed all a sudden more feasible to reach that goal in France as well. The notion that all men are created equal and endowed with natural rights, such as life, liberty, and the pursuit of happiness; that governments exist to guarantee these rights; and that their power emanates from the people, gained more traction in French civil society in the 1780s. The revolutionary leaders were not initially common folks but rather well-off bourgeois and even aristocrats. Many of them, when they spoke of freedom, had in mind the liberty of commerce, free trade, and by justice, they understood the replacement of royal arbitrariness by the rule of law. Reining in the power of the monarch, like the British had done in England a century earlier, getting the King to accept a constitution, was all they initially wanted.

In their struggle, both camps turned to the people for support. In 1789, the King convoked a provincial assembly that had not met since 1614, the Estates General.[12] The bourgeoisie, for its part, opened up political clubs that served as fertile recruitment ground for the Parisian street. A few weeks after their initial meeting, Estate General Representatives in favor of a constitutional monarchy began to meet separately and to draft a Constitution. On July 14, 1789, a crowd of Parisians stormed the infamous prison of the Bastille, the very symbol of arbitrary justice, or more precisely its armory. In the euphoria of victory, the Constituent Assembly approved, on August 4, a motion by Louis-Marie de Noailles (1756–1804)[13] that abolished the feudal system. (Many of them regretted it the next day, but it was too late.) The Old Regime was dead and the principles on which it was founded declared irrelevant. Thus, following a few riots and the King's initial resistance, a constitutional monarchy replaced the absolute monarchy. It was to be short-lived.

Throughout August 1789, the Assembly worked on the Declaration of the Rights of Man and of the Citizen. It proclaims that "men are born and remain free and equal in rights"; these rights being liberty, property, security, and resistance to oppression, and that national sovereignty resides in the nation, not the person of the King. It was adopted in August. In October 1789, the seat of government moved from Versailles to Paris following a women's hunger march that brought the royal family back to the capital. Initially, moderates led by the Count of Mirabeau controlled the most influential political club, the Society of the Friends of the Constitution, where the motions for the Assembly were prepared, and thus also the course of the revolution. But the extravagant festivities that marked the first anniversary of the French Revolution could not hide that, by July 1790 already, divisions were tearing the revolutionary movement apart. Advocates of the constitutional monarchy considered that the revolution was over; advocates of the republic thought that it was just beginning. A year later, in June 1791, the royal family's failed attempt to flee to Austria, the Queen's homeland, reinforced the democrats' suspicion that the King was just paying lip service to the new ideas and would never accept a constitution.[14] On July 17, 1791, proponents of the republic demonstrated against the Assembly's decision to let Louis XVI keep his throne in spite of his treasonous actions. Fifty citizens were killed during the demonstration but peace and quiet returned briefly after the King formally accepted the Constitution. A newly elected Legislative Assembly then replaced the Constituent Assembly in October.

During that early phase, the U.S. government welcomed the French Revolution. The Marquis of Lafayette, then commander of the National Guard, offered a key to the Bastille to George Washington, "the father of liberty," and between 1789 and 1792 "American sympathy for the French Revolution was in the stage of enthusiasm" (Childs, *French Refugees*, 41). The French Revolution confirmed the righteousness of the American Revolution and justified it. The two nations also acted in similar ways, with regard to land distribution, for instance. After the Revolution, the American government confiscated the lands of Loyalist *émigrés* (60,000 people, 24 percent of the population). The Constituent Assembly did the same when it nationalized the estates of the Catholic Church and of noblemen who chose to leave France after July 1789, selling land in small plots to the peasantry.[15]

Beyond these commonalities, however, the American and the French revolutions differed substantially in ways aptly captured by Condorcet at the time:

> It [the French Revolution] was more complete, more entire than that of America, and of consequence was attended with greater convulsions by the interior of the nation, because the Americans, satisfied with the code of civil and criminal legislation which they had derived from England, having no corrupt system of finance to reform, no feudal tyrannies, no hereditary distinctions, no privileges of rich and powerful corporations, no system of religious intolerance to destroy, had only to direct their attention to the establishment of new powers to be substituted in the place of those hitherto exercised by the British government. [...] [W]hereas the French revolution [...] had to embrace the whole economy of society, to change every social relation, to penetrate to the smallest link of the political chain, even to those individuals, who living in peace upon their property, or by their industry, were equally unconnected with public commotions, whether by their opinions and their occupations, or by the interest of fortune, of ambition, or of glory [Condorcet, *Outlines*, 266–266].[16]

Condorcet's analysis makes it plain to see that not everyone in France had welcomed the Revolution. Conservative clergymen and royalists loyal to the absolute monarchy were the first to go into exile or to take arms against the revolutionaries. In 1789, the *émigrés* were members of the royal family, the King's brothers and aunts, or noblemen close to power during the Old Regime. Most of them went to Italy and Austria, thinking they would be back as soon as the rebellion failed. But as François Alexandre Frédéric de Liancourt (1747–1827)[17] aptly replied to Louis XVI when the King inquired about "the rebellion," it was "not a rebellion but a revolution."[18]

2. *The French Republic and Its Enemies*

From the spring of 1792 to the summer of 1794, the French Revolution turned violent. France was at war with practically all European monarchies, zealous revolutionaries started eliminating anyone suspected of treason, which led to a new exodus from France, and slave rebellion in the colonies brought new refugees to the United States.[19] American attitudes toward the French Revolution changed accordingly. The French Revolution was supposed to herald an era of universal peace but in the spring of 1792, the minority party in the Assembly, the *Girondins*, agitated for war with Prussia and the export of the Revolution to the rest of Europe. The situation in France was dire. Parisians were rioting due to food shortages and counter-revolutionary armies led by French and European aristocrats were getting ready to invade the country. France declared war on Austria in April 1792 but the King, who was secretly in contact with the enemy and felt confident Austria would win, made use of his veto right and refused to sign decrees passed by the Legislative Assembly in June. On August 10, 1792, a mob of Parisian *sans-culottes*[20] led by George Danton (1759–1794) sacked the Royal Palace. In late summer, foreign troops defeated the French revolutionary armies and entered France. Parisians exasperated by the course of events massacred hundreds of royalist prisoners in early September.

That month, the French were nonetheless able to elect their representatives for the first time in the history of their country.[21] On September 19, 1792, the Legislative Assembly was dissolved and replaced the next day by a new assembly, the Convention, as the new assembly was called. On September 20, the French revolutionary armies stopped the advance of enemy troops at Valmy. On September 21, the monarchy was abolished, and the republic proclaimed. In Autumn 1792, Year I of the Republic, Louis XVI was accused of treason and arrested. Meanwhile, the French volunteer army continued to win unexpected victories against the European coalition. The Convention was mostly composed of moderate delegates but two factions soon came to dominate the political scene, the Girondins, liberal republicans who governed in 1792–93; and the Montagnards, social democrats, who governed in 1793–94. The Girondins favored war, conquest, and annexation with the goal of creating a "big nation," a monarchy-free Europe. But in the fall of 1792 the most pressing item of business was King Louis XVI's trial. The Girondins were in favor of pardoning the King, the Montagnards, who thought that concessions to the *sans-culottes* were necessary in order to retain popular support for the regime, moved to put the King on trial, and won. The Convention found Louis XVI guilty of treason by a two-third majority and sentenced him to death by a one-vote majority. He was guillotined in January 1793 and Queen Marie-Antoinette followed him on the scaffold a few months later.

The regicide rekindled the civil war in the western provinces. Brittany and Vendée rose up against the new regime in a war that lasted from 1793 to 1796.[22] The French king's death also outraged the monarchies of Great Britain, Spain, and the Netherlands who banded together to fight the War of the first Coalition against France. In addition, Great Britain provided support to royalist rebels not only in Brittany but also in the Caribbean. A few French generals switched sides and went over to the enemy. General Dumouriez, a hero of the first revolutionary battles, defected to Austria. The Viscount of Noailles deserted, crossed enemy lines, and settled in England before coming to Philadelphia. Lafayette, who had U.S. citizenship, tried to immigrate to America as well but was captured by the Austrians and kept in jail for five years.

Public opinion in Paris held the Girondins responsible for the military crisis as they were the ones who had agitated for war in the first place. The Parisian *sans-culottes*, who suffered most from the deteriorating economic situation, played an increasingly important political role in those years. On June 2, 1793, the Montagnards staged a coup: 80,000 angry Parisians led by Jean-Paul Marat (1743–1793) marched on the Convention and demanded the removal from office and arrest of 129 Girondins they viewed as guilty of treason. News of the arrest of elected members of the Convention resulted in new uprisings in Normandy, Bordeaux, and southeastern France.[23] France was now divided politically between, on the one hand an upper bourgeoisie consisting of constitutional royalists frightened by the progress of the revolution they had unleashed, and on the other the middle class ready to fight for the Republic to the bitter end with the help of the *sans-culottes*. In an effort to calm political tensions and to reassure the public, the Convention adopted a new Constitution it had prepared the previous year. Disputes between liberals and social democrats over some provisions had delayed its completion but voters had finally approved it a referendum. One of the representatives who had worked on the Constitution of Year I was Thomas Paine (1737–1809), an honorary citizen of France, and an elected member of the Convention.[24] The Constitution of Year I never went into effect, however. Instead, for reasons of national welfare and security, the Convention instituted a revolutionary government composed of a Committee of Public Safety (*salut public*), a Committee of General Security, and a Revolutionary Tribunal.

The political events unfolding in France since July 1789 had sent shock waves into the island colonies, particularly in Saint-Domingue. On the eve of the Revolution, the "Pearl of the Caribbean" enjoyed unrivaled prosperity as the world's premier producer of coffee, sugar, and cotton.[25] The colony, home to over thirty thousand whites and well over half a million slaves, was organized as a slave society.[26] Its social structure was hierarchical and based on race, with the plantation owners, the *Grand Blancs*, at the top, white administrators and clerks, or *petits blancs*, below them, and then the free "people of color," or mulattos, who, like the *signares* of Senegal, owned plantation property (one third in Saint-Domingue) and slaves (one quarter). At the bottom of the social hierarchy were the maroons, slaves who had fled the plantations and lived in the mountains, and finally, the slaves.[27]

French intellectuals like Brissot, Condorcet, Lafayette, Olympe de Gouges (1748–1793), and the *Société des Amis des Noirs* [*Society of the Friends of Blacks*] had denounced the slave trade and agitated for the abolition of slavery for years.[28] In principle, the Revolution made all the inhabitants of French Caribbean free and equal but the *grands blancs* did not want to lose their free labor force. Although Louis XVI had not invited the colonies to participate in the Estates General, twenty self-appointed deputies from the nobility left Saint-Domingue for Versailles. When the Crown refused to admit them as delegates of the nobility, the election commission, in need of voting members, admitted six of them as representatives of the Third Estate. Martinique then asked for, and obtained two representatives, Count Arthur Dillon (1750–1794) and Elie Moreau de Saint-Méry (1750–1819), and Guadeloupe three more.[29]

Initially, plantation owners welcomed the Revolution as an opportunity to get rid of "*l'exclusif*," the obligation to trade exclusively with France.[30] As the only segment of the colonial population represented in the Constituent Assembly, the deputies from the West Indies used economic arguments successfully to justify the colonies' exclusion from the legislation on the rights of man and the citizen, pointing out that "the Caribbean trade represented more than one third of French commerce" (Munro, 1075).[31] Organized in a wealthy and powerful lobby, the Club Massiac, they fought the abolitionists in the press and in the Assembly.[32] Moreau de Saint-Méry, for instance, a famous colonial jurist and fervent advocate of slavery, opposed the notion of racial equality put forth by abolitionists, proposing instead the alleged "superiority of the white race" as a justification for colonial rule and for the strict division between white and colored—at any of the sixteen shades of black he postulated.[33] For the first two years of the Revolution, the *grands blancs* mostly succeeded in imposing their agenda, which was to prevent abolitionists from getting the floor in the Assembly and to make sure that efforts on the part of *mulâtres* (mulattos) and free blacks to gain representation went nowhere. As a result, the Caribbean colonies continued to be represented by *grands blancs* only in the Constituent

Assembly. The issue of slavery was raised on several occasions between 1789 and 1791, by Brissot and Robespierre among others, but Moreau de Saint-Méry's contention that the abolition of slavery would ring the death knell of the colonies won the day in those years.

Resistance to white power was growing in colonies, however. News of the Revolution had traveled fast, through "sailors, often ex-slaves" (Dubois, 90). As early as August 1789, house slaves were organizing a rebellion in St. Pierre of Martinique (Butel, 209) and the agitation soon spread to the entire French Caribbean. The realization that the Declaration of the Rights of Man and the Citizen was not going to apply to all inhabitants of the colonies led to insurrection, which in turn, prompted the Constituent Assembly to grant civil and political rights to the 28,000 free mulattos of the Caribbean colonies in May 1791. The slaves and maroons of Saint-Domingue, who were excluded from the legislation, burnt plantations, liberated slaves, killed white masters, and gained control of the northern part of the island on August 23, 1791. Over a period of several weeks, 4,000 of the 32,000 whites were slaughtered and over a thousand plantations destroyed. Surviving whites retaliated by killing 15,000 slaves in September (Butel, 224–226). In France meanwhile, the Jacobins were increasingly able to rein in the colonial lobby. In 1792, the Legislative Assembly passed a decree proclaiming the civil and political equality of free blacks.[34] In October 1793, they also found the East India Company, which had its seat in Hôtel Massiac, guilty of counter-revolutionary activities, seized its goods, ships and buildings, and guillotined several of its directors (Haudrère).

French plantation owners opposed to the French Republic joined the ranks of the counter-revolution at that point. Anticipating the imminent abolition of slavery, planters and agents who remained in the colonies tried to place Martinique, Guadeloupe, and

Burning of Le Cap. General Revolt of the Blacks. Massacre of the Whites, 1791–1804 [*Incendie du Cap. Révolte générale des Négres. Massacre des Blancs*]. Folded woodcut vignette in Anon., *Saint-Domingue, ou l'histoire de ses révolutions* […]. Paris: chez Tiger, 1820 (Internet Archive).

Saint-Domingue under British jurisdiction through the Treaty of Whitehall, negotiated in 1793 and adopted in 1794. In exchange for a lucrative export tax, the British were to station troops to protect the white population from slave insurrections. The treaty also stipulated that the islands would return to French control once a king was restored to the throne of France (Butel, 227–229). Among the French signatories to the Whitehall treaty was Pierre Victor Malouet (1740–1814), a royalist colonial administrator and owner of a sugar plantation on Saint-Domingue. Ignace Joseph de Perpignan and Louis de Curt (1722–1804) represented Guadeloupe.[35] Representing Martinique was Louis-François Dubuc (1759–1827), a creole and distant cousin of Joséphine de Beauharnais, who had served as a French army officer before inheriting his father's Martinique plantation (and his debts) in 1786. As a result, the colonial regime, including slave trade and slavery, remained in place in Martinique while the island was under British control, from 1794 to 1802. British forces also occupied Guadeloupe from April to December 1794 when the army of the French Republic chased them.[36]

In September 1793, the French government charged three *représentants en mission* (envoys) with the enforcement on the ground of the decrees granting civil and political rights to mulattos and free people of color. In the island colonies, the envoys, Léger-Félicité Sonthonax, Etienne Polverel, and Jean-Antoine Ailhaux, were assisted in their task by a regiment led by Victor Hughes.[37] In the north of the island of Saint-Domingue, François-Dominique Toussaint-L'Ouverture (1743–1803), who had led the slave rebellion since 1791, joined forces with the armies of the Republic. The abolition of slavery was proclaimed in Saint-Domingue and, once order had returned, elections were held. On September 24, 1793, Saint-Domingue elected its first three representatives to the National Convention: a white man, Louis-Pierre Dufay (1752–1804); a free mulatto, Jean-Baptiste Mills (1749–1806); and a former slave, Jean-Baptiste Belley (1746–1805). In Paris, the three men wasted no time moving for the abolition of slavery, a motion that was approved unanimously by the Convention on February 4, 1794. From then on "the Caribbean became a central theater in the global conflict that raged between France and Britain" as ex-slaves transformed "into citizen-soldiers" (Dubois, 224).[38]

Ironically, the phase of the French Revolution that produced this progressive legislation is remembered by its grim nickname, "the Terror." The regime's adversaries—whose numbers increased as months went by—and, later, historians have used the label as a stigma, as a synonym of "terrorism." But revolutionaries like Maximilien Robespierre (1758–1794) claimed it as a badge of honor,[39] because they were convinced that citizens could be "terrorized" into "virtuous," i.e., revolutionary, behavior. Once the Law of Suspects took effect in September 1793, citizens were encouraged to act "virtuously" and report anyone thought guilty of non-republican activities to the authorities. The revolutionary police arrested nobles, relatives of *émigrés*, former officials and officers suspected of treason, as well as hoarders of goods, as enemies of the Revolution and sent them to revolutionary tribunals to answer for their crimes. Justice was swift and verdicts executed almost immediately. In all, the tribunals sentenced 17,000 suspects to death. Leaving out war casualties, about 35,000 to 40,000 died during the dictatorship. While aristocratic victims were fewer in number, the percentage of victims was higher among them than in any other social class. Priests, nuns, and monks who had refused to take the oath of allegiance to the Republic were a prime target of persecution, particularly during the period of intense de-Christianization (1792–94) (Higonnet, *Goodness*, 54, 56).

Notwithstanding the bloodshed, the Revolutionary government managed to keep the support of the Parisian street for over a year, due largely to its policy of price control on basic goods. The Montagnard Convention accomplished amazing feats within a short span of time.[40] It carried out a complete and durable reform that turned the principles of the Declaration of the Rights of Man into law. It established a separation between the French State and the Roman Catholic Church. It thoroughly reformed secondary and higher education and adopted the metric system. The French Republic was the first democratic regime not only to abolish slavery in 1794, but also to treat black men as full-fledged citizens who could vote and be elected to public office. All this was accomplished while squelching out rebellions in provincial France and pushing back European coalition troops out of France. By the end of 1793, therefore, the rationale for the Jacobin dictatorship no longer existed. But instead of a return to normalcy, there was an upsurge of revolutionary violence. In the end, the French people wearied of the Terror and disagreements among revolutionary leaders did the rest. Georges Danton was guillotined in April 1794 and Robespierre in July. When the Terror ended, in the summer of 1794, the Convention drafted a new constitution that went into effect in July 1795. The executive branch of the new government was composed of five directors, hence its name: the Directory. Like the preceding revolutionary governments, the new regime was to be short-lived, lasting only from 1795 to 1799.

3. Seeking Refuge in America: French Immigration to the United States

The French who came to the United States between 1790 and 1799 were political refugees for the most part, although not all of them of the same political persuasion, far from it. In fact, every phase of the French Revolution brought a new wave of French people to America, Royalists after 1789, former members of the Constituent and Legislative Assembly in 1794, and former members of the Convention in 1795. At each stage of its development, in short, the French Revolution sent scores of exiles from mainland France and from the island colonies to the United States, as many as 10,000 from France, and over 25,000 from the French Caribbean island colonies (Creagh, *Nos Cousins*, 208). As opposed to the Huguenots, "the French men and women who came to America during the 1790s did not establish lasting settlements which could gradually integrate into American society […]. Many French immigrants returned home" (Hebert C., 451).

The first political immigration to the United States during the revolutionary period was the result of the National Assembly's abolition of religious orders in February 1790.[41] Within a few years, one hundred thousand men and women had to leave their abbeys and convents after these buildings became state property. Men and women in religious orders deemed useful to society (those for instance, in the health, teaching, and charity sectors)[42] could continue their work as civilians, provided they swore an oath of hatred to the old monarchy. The situation was more dicey for members of contemplative orders, as they were deemed "useless to society" by the revolutionaries. Many went to North America, thus increasing the ranks of orders already present there, such as the Recollects, Franciscans, and Ursulines. American membership in the order of French Christian Brothers (*Frères des Ecoles Chrétiennes*), also called De La Salle Brothers, grew from 272 members in 1721 to 920 in 1792. Other congregations started anew. Arrived in the United States in 1790, Pierre-Joseph Didier was the first Benedictine to immigrate to the

United States and to live in Ohio and Louisiana. Only twenty-four French priests immigrated between 1791 and 1799 but they played a crucial role in the development of the Roman Catholic Church in the United States, arriving as they did on the heels of the 1789 establishment of the Diocese of Baltimore under John Carroll, the first American bishop. That year, at the Bishop's instigation, the Catholic Georgetown University opened near Washington, D.C.[43]

In his *Voyage to America*, François-René, viscount of Chateaubriand (1768–1848), recalled how he travelled to Baltimore with a group of Sulpician fathers fleeing the French Revolution and seeking refuge in the United States. In 1791, that very group of French Sulpician priests founded St. Mary's Seminary for the training of American priests. "Six of the twenty-four French priests who came between 1791 and 1799 became bishops" (Childs, "A Special Migration," 163). Like those Sulpicians, who were recommended to Bishop Carroll by the Pope, visitors from France and immigrants to the United States carried letters of introduction from friends who were acquainted with Americans. Chateaubriand himself arrived in Philadelphia with outstanding credentials, among them a letter from George Washington's friend "Colonel Armand," the marquis Armand de la Rouërie (1751–1793).[44] The aspiring writer only stayed in America from July 1791 to January 1792, most of the time traveling, taking notes for his future works,[45] and waiting for the revolution to blow over in France. As a royalist, he had little sympathy for the new American Republic and even less for the French Revolution and the institutions it created.[46] Similarly, his adoption of the myth of the "noble savage" in his literary work, had more to do with nostalgia for New France than with an actual acquaintance with Native Americans. In one respect, however, he had a point, namely when he commented on the European habit of appropriating Native American lands: "Sooner or later," he predicted, "the Cree, the Cherokee, the Chickasaw will be squeezed by the white population of Tennessee, Alabama, and Georgia and suffer either exile or extermination" (*Voyage to America*, 385).

From 1793 onward, aristocrats who had been initial supporters of the French Revolution, and who, in some cases, had held office in the Constituent and/or Legislative Assembly, started arriving in the United States. Somewhat paradoxically then, French royalists fleeing the French Republic sought refuge in another republic: "all the blue blood that had managed to escape the French Revolution was showing up in the United States" (Creagh, *Nos Cousins*, 208).[47] Although emigration was punished by the confiscation, nationalization, and sale of one's estate, it was still preferable to death by the guillotine.[48] The largest influx of French refugees arriving from Europe occurred in 1794, and in addition to Philadelphia, virtually "all major ports of the East Coast, New York, Boston, Charleston, as well New Orleans, received their share of French people" (Creagh, *Nos Cousins*, 209). Many prominent French aristocrats had fled France following the Storming of the Tuileries Palace in August 1792 and lived comfortably with relatives and friends across the English Channel. In England, they made friends and cultivated acquaintances with members of prominent Anglo-American families—the Binghams, the Schuylers, the Van Rennselaers—that proved useful after the Pitt government banished foreigners in 1794. Suddenly forced to leave England yet unable to return to France, these refugees sailed to America with stacks of letters of introduction that guaranteed smooth entry into Philadelphia high society.[49] Two of these refugees, Bon Albert Briois de Beaumetz (1755–1801) and Charles-Maurice de Talleyrand-Périgord (1754–1838),[50] who were friends, travelled together from London to Philadelphia. Moreau-Saint Méry and the Viscount of Noailles had arrived earlier in the capital of the United States. The Chevalier de Liancourt, who had been Arthur Young's guest in England, joined them in the fall. The five of them knew each other as they had served together as representatives in the Constituent Assembly.[51]

The best known of these five refugees is undoubtedly Talleyrand, who lived in Philadelphia from 1794 to 1796. Talleyrand belonged to the best circles of the French aristocracy and as a first-born son, should have inherited his parents' estates and titles. Due to his clubfoot, however, his family forced him to renounce his claims and to embrace a religious career instead. Resentment over his destiny may explain why, as representative of the Clergy at the Estates General, the Bishop of Autun, as he was known in those days, supported or even instigated many anti-clerical measures.[52] Nicknamed "the prince of diplomats," Talleyrand served virtually under every government before, during, and after the Revolution. Prior to coming to the United States, he had spent a few years in England after defecting during a diplomatic mission in 1792. Two year later, he was on his way to the United States where he had many social connections.[53]

François Fürstenberg centers his study of the United States in the mid–1790s around the five noblemen mentioned above in his 2014 book *When the United States Spoke French: Five Refugees Who Shaped a Nation* (28–29). Although they had not really chosen to live in America, he argues, these refugees ended up playing a considerable role—economic, cultural, and political—in a U.S. capital that boasted 30,000 souls and was "awash with French people, French goods, and French culture" (17). All of them found an occupation if they stayed a few years, a few started families and became U.S. citizens. Moreau de St. Méry had a bookstore that was a true cultural center in Philadelphia (Rosengarten). Beaumetz married an American. Talleyrand befriended the Dutch banker Théophile Cazenove (1740–1811), an agent of the Holland Land Company, and became involved in banking and finance (Furstenberg).[54]

By the mid–1790s, the French made up 10 percent of the population of Philadelphia. All kinds of clubs and associations allowed these people to meet and hold formal social gatherings. Under the aegis of Peter Stephen du Ponceau and Stephen Girard, the French Benevolent Society of Philadelphia assisted destitute immigrants. The Society for Liberty and Equality allowed convinced republicans to meet among like-minded brothers. The Lodge of "the Perfect Union" welcomed Free Masons (Creagh, *Nos Cousins*, 214–216). Oellers' Hotel hosted banquets for special occasions. French intellectuals like Brissot de Warville or the chevalier de Liancourt, who wrote a book on the American prison systems decades before Tocqueville, sought and often gained admission at the American Philosophical Society. Charles Févret de Saint-Mémin (1770–1852) made a name for himself as an engraver, creating "between 1796 and 1810 [...] more than 900 distinctive portraits of what amounts to a veritable who's who of federal America" (Rolfe, "Saint-Mémin," 1038).

Despite their common language, political, racial, social, and financial factors divided the French-speaking community. In Philadelphia, refugees could run into official representatives of the government they were fleeing. The cozy relations that existed between some French *émigrés* and U.S. government officials was a source of complaints on the part of ambassadors of the French Republic to the United States like Fauchet and earlier Genêt.[55] Not all French speakers were white. French was also the language spoken by free people of color from the island colonies and by slaves. Moreover, there were in Philadelphia, two distinct French neighborhoods. The working-class French lived north of Market Street. The French social elite, even upper-class exiles who had a hard time accessing their funds or had lost everything, resided south of it, in the chic neighborhood, thanks to their connections and the hospitality of American friends. Few of the immigrants had been able to liquidate assets prior to leaving France or the colonies, but those with funds in international or in U.S. banks were in a good position to purchase land.[56]

There was plenty of land available in the United States and settlement along the frontier with Canada was encouraged by the U.S. government. The run for land had begun in 1776, when the State of New York had created the land commission to sell "wild lands" in the buffer zone with Canada. As the area was subject to conflicting claims, however, it could only be properly defended if people moved there.[57] Then, in 1783, Great Britain ceded to the United States huge tracts of wilderness from the Great Lakes to the Mississippi valley. Except for Native Americans and French settlers, these territories were practically empty. Several American speculators bought huge tracts of land in the hope of reselling them for a profit. The Ordinance of 1785 brought some order to the land speculation frenzy because it required that land be surveyed prior to sale, which in turn made titles more secure, and the transfer of property easier (Treat, 179).[58] In 1788, Oliver Phelps and Nathaniel Gorham bought 6 million acres of land in New York State from the Commonwealth of Massachusetts. In 1792–93, the Holland Land Company acquired two-thirds of the Phelps and Gorham Purchase.[59]

During the French Revolution, American land speculators' favorite target purchasers were wealthy actual, or potential, exiles like France's former Prime Minister, Jacques Necker and his daughter, the writer Germaine de Staël.[60] Several French refugees themselves were involved in land speculation following the opening of the vast backcountry stretching beyond the Allegheny Mountains. For those wary of urban revolutionary violence, hiding in the American countryside was a welcome proposition. A few wealthy refugees, responding to "[a]dvertisements in the French gazettes published in Philadelphia," purchased or leased farms (Hebert, C. 453). The most famous of these French aristocrats turned American farmer was Henriette-Lucy Dillon-Gouvernet (1770–1853). The marquise de La Tour du Pin had fled France with her family under trying circumstances in 1794, bought a farm near Albany, New York, and, according to her own account,[61] loved her life as an American farmer. She reported having good relations with Native American women who came by her house to trade. She explained to her readers that she had bought four slaves to work on the farm because it was nearly impossible to find farm hands, and, in guise of apology, let it be known that she had freed them when the farm was sold and she returned to France.

Most upper-class French people who settled in the countryside preferred a kind of communal living to the private setting the Dillon-Gouvernet had chosen. Thus, several French settlements came into existence in the Ohio Valley and the states of New York and Pennsylvania. In 1789, the Scioto Company purchased land in Ohio and sold part of it to a group of French immigrants before actually paying for it.[62] Because the agent, William Playfair was dishonest and kept the company's money for himself, the French found out when they arrived that they had paid for land they did not own.[63] About 500 of them settled in Appalachian Ohio along the Ohio River and founded the town of Gallipolis ("City of the Gauls") instead.[64]

Financiers Robert Morris, John Nicholson, and Stephen Girard provided funds to purchase 1,600 acres of land in northeastern Pennsylvania in the early 1790s. Workers built the village of Azylum (*Asile français*) as a refuge for French people fleeing the turmoil of the Revolution. Located on the Susquehanna River north of Wilkes-Barre, it consisted of thirty log cabins, including a large one, *la grande maison*, intended for Queen

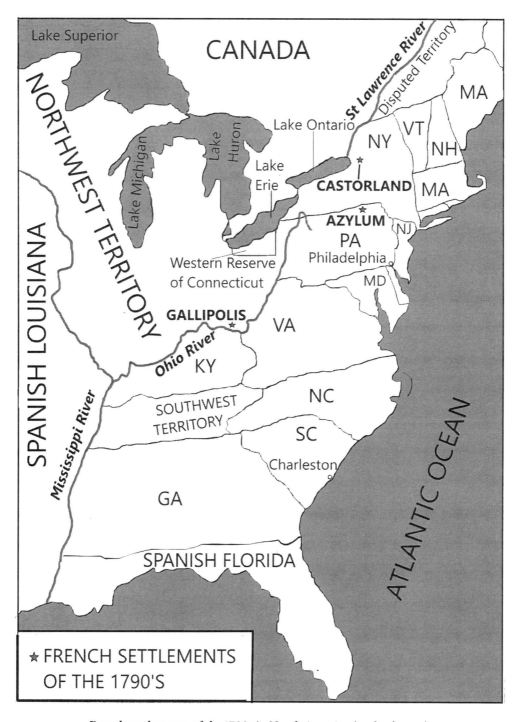

French settlements of the 1790s in North America (author's map).

Marie-Antoinette, who unfortunately was already dead by the time the first exiles arrived in the fall of 1793.[65] Soon the village had a mill, a blacksmith, shops, a schoolhouse, a church, an inn, and even a theater. A small community of noblemen and non-juring clergy lived there, the marquis de Blacons was the innkeeper; the viscount of Noailles was engaged in financial speculation. The chevalier Louis-Narcisse Baudry de Lozières (1761–1841), Moreau's brother-in-law, and, like him, a plantation owner, former member of Club Massiac, and bona fide racist,[66] ran the general store. Occasional visitors like Talleyrand or Louis-Philippe were welcome and feted (Clarke, 76–78).

In 1791, Alexander Macomb, William Constable, and Daniel McCormick had purchased four million acres of land in Upstate New York, one eighth of the state, at a very low price, at a time when the state needed cash (Macomb Purchase). A portion of this land eventually fell into French expatriates' hands. When Macomb went bankrupt, his associate, Constable, set out to sell American land in France through a French Company, *la compagnie de New York*.[67] Several Franco-Americans were involved in the Company: James St. John de Crèvecoeur (1735–1813), author of the *Letters from an American Farmer* (1782)[68] and James Le Ray de Chaumont, Jacques-Donatien's son, who had married an American, Grace Coxe (Clarke, 98–100; 109–122). Also prospecting for French investors in the early 1790s was Chaumont's brother-in-law, the banker Pierre Chassanis. Starting in 1793, the settlement of Castorland (Beaverland) was created out of the Macomb purchase on the Black River in Upstate New York (Clarke, 47–50). Designed and developed by architects Simon Desjardins and Pierre Pharoux, it was to welcome its first settlers in 1796. It too failed in the end, however.[69] T. Wood Clarke passed the following harsh judgment on the settlement: "The Castorland colony, because of geographical inaccessibility, interference from managers in Paris unfamiliar with local conditions, incompetence, extravagance, and misrepresentation, was doomed to failure from the start" (57).

Frontier life took its toll on people who tended to have led pampered lives in France. For members of the French upper-class, whether they stayed in Philadelphia or ventured out into the country settlements, having to accomplish simple tasks like shaving or getting dressed on one's own was not only unaccustomed but also a sign of social demotion. By the late 1790s, most of the inhabitants had left those villages and moved away (Clarke, 79–84). While these French immigrants tended to come from the best circles of French society and returned to France as soon as circumstances allowed, their servants and people from the lower classes tended to remain in the United States permanently. It was the case of hired hands who had worked in Azylum, for instance. When the masters left, several families settled in nearby Pennsylvania towns, soon to blend with the local population. Catherine Hebert writes about other Frenchmen who settled in small towns, one individual at a time, thereby starting the pattern of assimilation into the American social fabric that was to become the hallmark of French immigration, a model that explains why there are no "Little Frances" in the United States:

> Many a Pennsylvania town appears to have had its French character, or characters. For instance, Dr. Seraphim lived and practiced in Pottsgrove, Dr. Charles Julian Ponchon introduced the tomato plant in the New York community, Jean-François Dupuy served as an officer in the masonic lodge in Wilkes-Barre, a miniature painter and a musician settled in Lancaster, three Frenchmen were living at Middletown, and in western Pennsylvania, M. Visinier was running a French school at Washington [C. Hebert, 453].

A larger city like Pittsburgh "attracted some twenty French settlers between 1793 and 1797" (453) in addition to the priests and merchants who visited and left.

Gallipolis, Castorland, and Azylum are the most famous French settlements of the 1790s but a few others deserve to be mentioned. A tract of land purchased by Huguenots from Picardie in the first quarter of the 18th century was sold in 1794 to Paul Henri Mallet-Prevost, another refugee from the French Revolution. As the settlers spoke French, the name stuck, giving birth to "Frenchtown," New Jersey. In Western Pennsylvania, a young immigrant from Geneva, Albert Gallatin (1761–1849), started the Francophone settlement of New Geneva, a village of only a dozen settlers that boasted glassworks and a gun factory in addition to a mill, store, and houses (Hebert, C. 453).[70] Those two settlements also yielded permanent residents of the United States.

Another group of French refugees that was to remain permanently in the United States came from Saint-Domingue. A first wave of refugees arrived in 1791 and a second, larger one, in 1793, in both cases following violent slave insurrections. In the summer of 1793, nearly three hundred ships transported over 4,000 white people and 20,000 refugees of color to the United States. Two thousand of them landed in Philadelphia where a yellow fever epidemic soon broke out.[71] They had few chances of returning to their Saint-Domingue plantations after the Convention abolished slavery in 1794 and all inhabitants, whatever their color, became French citizens.[72] Some planters from Saint-Domingue and Guadeloupe chose to rebuild their plantations in Trinidad and Cuba. Pennsylvania had abolished slavery in 1780, so hundreds of French slaves gained their freedom, much to the aggravation of their masters who tried to go around the legislation or to leave the state as fast as they could. The *grands blancs* tended to settle in the Carolinas, Georgia, and Louisiana, often with their slaves, and to live in southern cities like Charleston, Savannah, and increasingly, New Orleans. Two names stand out among the *grands blancs* who started the cultivation of cotton in Georgia: Denis Cottineau de Kerloguen (1745–1808) and Jean Bérard de Moquet, marquis de Montalet (1762–1814). Born to the wealthy gentry of Nantes, Cottineau was an officer in the French navy and a hero of the Battle of Savannah during the War of Independence. His wife, Luce de Mocquet, was from Saint-Domingue, where Cottineau also owned a plantation. In the aftermath of the 1793 slave insurrection, the family relocated to Philadelphia before starting a new plantation near Savannah, Georgia. Luce's brother, Bérard de Moquet, had also purchased land nearby, on Sapelo Island, where he too had a plantation. But there were others in similar circumstances. Baudry des Lozières, Moreau de Saint-Méry's brother-in-law, and Garesché du Rocher started new plantations in the United States as well. Jacques-André Rodrigue (1759–1844) came to the United States in 1793, married Marie-Jeanne d'Orlic, the sister of another refugee planter from St. Domingue in 1798, and together, they made a new fortune.[73]

Not everyone was as successful. Former plantation owners who had left in a hurry to save their lives and lost everything had to work for a living in the United States and often to change profession. In Philadelphia, many of them were employed as doctors, dentists, lawyers, publishers, or capitalizing on the French reputation for good food, elegant fashion, and refined culture, developed businesses in those areas.[74] There was a vibrant French press in Philadelphia, mostly publications by and for exiles from Saint-Domingue. Claude-Corentin Tanguy de la Boissière, a planter from Saint-Domingue, published the *Journal of Refugees from Saint-Domingue in America* (*Journal des Colons de Saint-Domingue réfugiés en Amérique*), *and L'Etoile Américaine* (*The American Star*). Stephen Girard and Jean-Simon Chaudron, a clockmaker who had managed his father-in-law's plantation, founded *L'Abeille Américaine*[75] and Louis Gateau the *Courrier de la France et des Colonies*. When yellow fever hit Philadelphia in 1793, Jean Devèze, a French doctor who had treated the disease in Saint-Domingue, was put in charge of Bush Hill hospital.[76] A dental surgeon named Le Breton worked with a wealthy Philadelphia clientele. Jean Anthelme Brillat-Savarin, who became the toast of Parisian society following the publication of his *Physiology of Taste* in 1825, earned a living as a teacher of French and violin during the three years he spent in Boston, New York, and Philadelphia (Furstenberg, 102). French immigrants and exiles with little or no financial capital took jobs as clerks, craftsmen, coiffeurs, cooks, skilled workers, and teachers. Others gave dancing lessons, created, and sold fancy clothes, shoes, and hats, made and sold bread, pastry, ice cream, jewelry, watches, and guns. A few women opened schools for young ladies.

Like their American counterparts, the French high society left Philadelphia during the summer months to escape the heat. These journeys on horseback in the backcountry offered an opportunity to gather different insights about American society. Liancourt traveled with his faithful dog,[77] Louis-Philippe, with his two brothers. Both wrote about their travels. Charles H. Sherrill, in *French Memories of Eighteenth-Century America*, states that French immigrants and travelers published no less than 70 memoirs and travel logs between 1775 and the installation of the federal government in Washington in 1800 (2–3).[78] If these writings, as well as diaries and letters, offer evidence of some of the French refugees' excellent integration into American high society, they cannot conceal the desire to return home to France one day expressed by many of them.

Nearly all French visitors who, like Chateaubriand, left a diary or a memoir about their American experience had something to say about slaves and Native Americans. The Duke of Orléans (1773–1850), son of Philippe-Egalité, and future king of the French (Haine, 102),[79] came to the United States after the Directory promised to free his two younger brothers, the Duke of Montpensier, 18, and the Count of Beaujolais, 13, if he agreed to take them far away. After waiting for his brothers for four months in Philadelphia, where they arrived in February 1797, the Duke took them on a discovery trip that lasted many months. Visiting Mount Vernon, Louis-Philippe of Orleans noted that George Washington owned "about 400 negroes," maliciously reported that the general's cook had escaped, and that the cook's six-year-old daughter was delighted about her dad's newly won freedom. "Black people," the Duke added, "are often surprised when we greet them because no one does it here." Like Chateaubriand, he sided with the Native Americans, who were in his view, the victims of the whites' greed in their unending quest for land. Without excusing the massacres of pioneers by Native Americans, he understood "what makes the Indians act with such cruelty; […] they say […] they don't know how to deal with the white people anymore because what the whites kill in them is irremediably lost" (95–96). Reading these texts, one gets the distinct impression that the French better recognized the humanity of Native- and African Americans than Americans of English descent. But the visitors quoted here were from metropolitan France, where slavery did not exist, and, as we saw, the French from the island colonies had a quite different opinion on the matter.

4. Foes: The Genêt Affair, the Jay Treaty, and the Quasi-War

Despite close personal contacts between members of the French and American elites, Franco-American relations deteriorated following the proclamation of the French

Republic. It did not take long, at least among American high society, for the notion to take root that there were two distinct revolutions, the good one being American and the bad one French. Much of the negative publicity originated in letters from France and testimonies from refugees who painted the picture of a revolution gone awry. But it also came from England, a nation that successfully had repressed the anti–Catholic Gordon Riots in 1780 and, in 1794, outlawed a movement closer to the spirit of the French Revolution, the Radical Artisans' Corresponding London Society. Anti-French propaganda found in the British press and political pamphlets, such as Edmund Burke's famous pamphlet, *Reflections on the Revolution in France* (1790), resonated with those Americans who still viewed Britannia as the mother country.

Not all Americans held anti–French Revolution views, however: the Democratic-Republicans and their societies applauded the proclamation of the Republic in France, as did the common folk in general.[80] Popular support took various forms, wearing the tricolor cockade, organizing, and participating in banquets and demonstrations, and singing French revolutionary songs. In other words, the topic of the French Revolution deeply divided the American public, so much so that according to historian John P. Clark, it was, for a long time, the only *foreign* political event to split U.S. public opinion. Interestingly, attitudes towards France and the French Revolution also played a key role in the formation of political parties in the young American Republic. Under the Washington administration, the Federalists led by Alexander Hamilton, secretary of the treasury, and vice-president John Adams (1735–1826), were in favor of strong commercial ties with Great Britain and preferential tariffs.[81] By contrast, the Democratic Republicans, Secretary of State Thomas Jefferson and James Madison (after 1791) favored an alliance with France and free trade.

Disagreements came to a head during the tenure of Edmond-Charles Genêt as French ambassador to the United States.[82] Ambassador Genêt arrived in America in 1793 but instead of going straight to Philadelphia to present his credentials to the President, he traveled to Charleston in an effort to gather support for France's war against the first coalition.[83] Virtually all towns and villages the French ambassador visited feted him and he was able to recruit American sailors. According to Creagh (178–179), the people of Charleston, where a sizeable number of Americans of French Huguenot descent resided, were the first to celebrate the fall of an absolute monarchy that had persecuted them for centuries and forced them to leave their country because of their religion. Nonetheless, their attitude towards France was not as clear-cut as this account implies. As has often been noted, several Federalist founding fathers were also of French Huguenot descent and certainly not on the side of the French Republic: John Jay and James Bowdoin (1726–1790) were the grandsons, respectively, of Auguste Jay and Pierre Baudoin who had arrived in North America after the revocation of the Edict of Nantes (1685). Gouverneur Morris (1752–1816) had a mother of French Huguenot stock, Sarah Gouverneur (1714–1786), and so did Alexander Hamilton: Rachel Faucette (1725–1768).[84]

None of these Federalists shared Ambassador Genêt's assumption—and that of the Girondin government he represented—namely that the United States would honor the 1778 Treaty of Amity and Commerce and provide military assistance to France in time of war. President Georges Washington made it very clear that the United States would remain neutral when, on April 22, 1793, he issued a proclamation warning that any U.S. citizen who aided one of the parties at war would suffer the consequences (Furstenberg,

316–317).[85] The president's proclamation outraged the Democratic Republicans and led to the Pacificus-Helvidius debates, a pamphlet war between Alexander Hamilton, who defended Washington's stand, and James Madison (1751–1836), who accused the Federalists of being secret monarchists and of hating the French Republic. In the end, the Federalists' view on the matter prevailed and Genêt's activities were condemned as the intervention of a foreign power in U.S. affairs. Washington asked France for the ambassador's recall and obtained it. The Genêt Affair also led to Thomas Jefferson's resignation of as Secretary of State.[86]

As American trade suffered from British ship seizures and skirmishes along the Canadian border, the Federalists wished for better relations with England.[87] To that effect, Washington sent Chief Justice John Jay (1745–1829) to England in 1794 in hopes of negotiating a treaty. At the same time, he appointed a Democrat-Republican, James Monroe (1758–1831), as U.S. Ambassador to France. A supporter of the French Revolution, Monroe received a public ovation when he spoke in the convention hall in 1795. From the new Directory government, he obtained the release from prison of both Lafayette's wife and Thomas Paine, who as an ally of the Girondins, had voted against the King's death, and spent the Terror in jail.[88]

John Jay came back to the United States in the spring of 1795 with a treaty that pleased only those Americans favorable to close relations with England. In light of the paucity of British concessions, the treaty angered Democratic-Republicans who viewed it as a betrayal of American commercial interests. By placing the border between the United States and Canada "at the level of the Great Lakes," the Jay Treaty was detrimental to the Franco-Amerindian *métis* communities living along these shores. As their lands opened to colonization, these communities were forced to move west, with some settling by the Red River in Manitoba, and north of the Hudson Bay.[89] The French government for its part took issue with the granting of "most favored nation status" to the U.K., a nation they were at war with at the time and viewed the Jay Treaty as a repudiation of the 1778 Treaty of Alliance (Furstenberg, 330–339). But the Directory had most pressing matters to deal with at the time.

The Royalists, who had hoped to win the elections in the fall of 1795 and re-instate the monarchy, rekindled the war in Brittany and staged a coup in October. The general who crushed this Royalist uprising in Paris was none other than Napoleon Bonaparte (1769–1821) (Haine, 87). War against the European Coalition was going to pave the way for the young general's ascent to power. In 1795, Prussia withdrew from the Coalition and Spain made peace with France, thus becoming an ally of France through the San Ildefonso treaty.[90] But war still raged between France and Great Britain and between France and Austria when George Washington reiterated his plea for neutrality in his 1796 Farewell Address. As his retirement from public life brought the U.S. revolutionary era to a close, the issue of the nature of Franco-American relations was thus left open. The presidential election of 1796 opposed two reluctant candidates who had both served as envoys to France, John Adams for the Federalists,[91] and Thomas Jefferson for the Democratic-Republicans. Adams won the presidency, with 71 electoral votes to 68 for Jefferson. The struggle between the partisans of France and those of Great Britain was far from over.

By the time John Adams took office in 1797, Franco-American relations had soured to such a point that there was talk of war. The new president therefore decided to send a delegation to Paris in a gesture of conciliation.[92] It was composed of seasoned negotiators, Elbridge Gerry (1744–1814) a veteran politician close to Hamilton and Adams,[93] Charles C. Pinckney (1746–1825), who had just successfully negotiated the Treaty of Friendship, Limits and Navigation on the Mississippi River with Spain (1795), and John Marshall (1755–1835), soon to serve as U.S. Chief Justice. However, the three envoys had a hard time obtaining a meeting with Talleyrand, who had become the French Secretary of State by then. Instead, French agents approached the Americans and made several demands as a pre-condition to the requested meeting with the French minister: a huge low interest loan for France (to finance war in Europe), the renunciation of American damage claims for the ships seized by the French, and a big bribe for Talleyrand himself. Talleyrand, who was well aware that the Federalists were no friends of France, was trying to win time. But the envoys were offended and simply refused to comply. In the end, Talleyrand gave in and met with them without, however, promising to stop attacking U.S. ships.

The two Federalist ambassadors, Pinckney and Marshall, then returned to the United States to report to the President Adams, who, together with Congress adopted a belligerent stand and started preparing for war. The Democratic Republicans wondered out loud about the government's true designs and demanded to see the correspondence on the talks in France, a request that Adams granted, hiding the French agents' names under the letters X, Y, and Z, that gave the affair its name. President Adams made the XYZ report public on July 6, 1798, and voided all bilateral treaties with France the next day. French pirates started blocking American access to ports in Saint-Domingue, thus marking the beginning of the Quasi-War. The relation to France had become such a hot button issue in American civil society that Alexander Hamilton did not shy from calling the Jeffersonians more French than American.

In the context of this Quasi-War, it is hardly surprising that the new group of French exiles that made their way to the United States after the fall of the Convention, namely former members of this assembly, was treated with more suspicion than their predecessors by the authorities. Such was the case of Constantin François de Chasseboeuf, Count of Volney (1757–1820), a disciple of Voltaire who had spent time in prison during the Terror but escaped the guillotine. A well-known atheist, Volney arrived in the United States in 1795 and started touring the country, taking notes for a book that was published in France in 1801 (and in 1804 in the United States), *View of the climate and soil of the United States of America*.[94] Wondering which kind of research Volney was truly conducting, the John Adams administration accused him of being a spy for France, or more precisely of being part of French efforts to reclaim New France.[95] But vice-president Jefferson, who greatly admired the French scholar's work, gained him admission to the American Philosophical Society and translated 20 chapters of Volney's *Ruins of Empire*. Another famous exile arrived in 1795 was Antoine Jay (1770–1854), who lived in the United States from 1795 to 1802. Another friend of Thomas Jefferson, he taught French to the famed future jurist Lemuel Shaw, who was a child at the time. After returning to France he became a famed publicist and a sworn enemy of the monarchy during the Restoration (1815–1830).

According to C. Hebert, anti–French sentiment was on the rise in the United States right at the time when "the country was beginning to undergo a moral reawakening in which ministers and other leaders warned against French immorality and depravity" (457). With the XYZ affair pouring oil on the fire, it was not difficult for enemies of France to "reawaken old prejudices against French treachery and infidelity, prejudices based on fears that reached back to the era of the French and Indian War" (458). The French were the target of discrimination in two fields, engineering, and science. "French military engineers appear to have been forced out of the services or to have been denied employment upon application" (463), and the 17 Frenchmen who had been elected to the American Philosophical Society between 1792 and 1797 "stopped participating, perhaps because of general apathy to their efforts" (473). One of them, Volney, wrote in the preface to his book on North America, that "in the Spring of 1798 there broke out so violent an animosity against France, and a war seemed so inevitable, that I was obliged to withdraw from the place" (Volney, *A View....*, vi–vii).

With nationalism on the rise, the Federalist Congress passed the Alien and Sedition Acts in July 1798. Residency requirements for immigrants seeking citizenship went up from five to fourteen years. The government could arrest and deport citizens of enemy nations in times of war and those suspected of anti-government sentiments in time of peace.[96] Finally, the Sedition Act restricted freedom of speech by preventing anyone to speak against the president or the federalist government. As life in the United States became difficult for the French, they started to leave the country *en masse*: "Thirteen vessels departed between mid–July and mid–August, 1798, with special permits by the President of the United States to take French persons and their possessions back to the Continent or the West Indies" (Hebert, C. 466). In the end, these legal measures backfired and served Thomas Jefferson (1743–1836) and his party.

During John Adams' administration (1797–1801), France felt confident in her power. At the conclusion of his Italian campaign in late 1797, Bonaparte returned to Paris a hero after his victory over Austria. Moreover, he had taken it upon himself to conclude a peace treaty extremely favorable to French interests with the defeated enemy, the Treaty of Campo-Formio. Such was the popularity of the dashing young general, still in his late twenties at the time, that it soon became an object of concern for a French government wary of dictators but also self-interested and corrupt. The Directors thus dispatched Bonaparte on a scientific and military mission to Egypt and the Middle East (1798–99) that, despite some scientific advances, turned into a real fiasco.[97] First Admiral Nelson destroyed the French fleet in the Mediterranean, then the remainder of the French army was lost to war and disease. Upon returning empty-handed to France from the disastrous Egyptian campaign, Bonaparte seized his opportunity to regain some of his lost laurels by ending the third and last insurrection in the province of Vendée in October 1799. He also put an end to Directory regime. With the help of his brothers and one the directors, Sieyès, Bonaparte, overthrew the regime on Brumaire 18th of Year IX of the Republic (November 9, 1799). By then, the French were ready for change, having lost confidence in a Directory government that had mismanaged public finances, devaluated the currency, caused economic hardship, committed electoral fraud to stay in power, and tolerated corruption and constant infighting among the political leaders (Godechot, 187–196).

If it did not come to an open war between France and the United States, the years 1798–1800 are nonetheless known as "the Quasi-War" due to the intensity of the conflicts at sea, where the United States, the Batavian Republic (Holland), and Great Britain fought France and Spain. While French pirates continued to prevent American ships from docking in Saint-Domingue, the U.S. navy retaliated by capturing French merchant vessels and later supporting François-Dominique Toussaint-L'Ouverture (1743–1803) in his liberation struggle of Saint-Domingue.[98] The Quasi-War did great damage to France's reputation in the United States, a freeze in Franco-American relations illustrated by the prevailing negative view on the (bad) French Revolution as opposed to the (good) American, and symbolized by the non-renewal of Nancrède's position as Professor of French at Harvard in 1801. Meanwhile, changes in political personnel were in the air in both countries.

French visitors and immigrants who came to the United States in the last two decades of the 18th century could not see the young American Republic for the global power it was to become one day. What they saw instead was a capital of a few thousand inhabitants and huge unoccupied expanses of land, a country in the early stage of its development, a new nation in the orbit of, but clearly at the periphery of Western Europe, as François Furstenberg has showed. The fact that most of the famous visitors mentioned in this chapter returned to France as soon as opportunity availed itself clearly supports that claim. With the Federalists in power, Franco-American relations continued to deteriorate in the aftermath of the Jay Treaty, nearly leading to war between France and the United States in the last two years of the 18th century, an episode known as the "Quasi-War." Moreover, the vital importance of commerce in the disputes between partisans of Great Britain and partisans of France confirms Furstenberg's claim that, at that time already, "the United States was enmeshed in a multi- or perhaps pre-national world centered around the movements of people, goods, and capital" (71). In terms of exports to the United States, however, the fact that France was losing to Great Britain was a cause of such great concern for the French that the idea of "replacing the U.S. as food provisioner [to the French island colonies] with some other nearby source" (88), namely Louisiana, gave birth, according to Peter Hill, "to the diplomacy of 'retrocession.'" Once the next waves of revolutionary violence hit Saint-Domingue at the beginning of the 19th century, many new refugees from the island colonies settled in Louisiana and in the southern states for good. They were to play a key role in 19th-century American history as advocates of slavery.

5. Tips for Further Investigations

Interesting People to Look Up

Julien de Lallande Poydras (1740–1824)
Jean-Baptiste Belley (1746–1805)
Stephen Girard (1750–1831)
Alexander McGillivray (1750–1793)
Janvier Littée (1752–1820)
Jean-Pierre [François] Blanchard (1753–1809)
Pierre L'Enfant (1754–1825)
Louis-Antoine, Viscount of Noailles (1756–1804)
Henriette-Lucy, Marquise de la Tour du Pin Gouvernet (1770–1853)
Joseph Gervais (1777–1861)

Related Primary Texts

Desjardins, Simon, and Pierre Pharoux. "Castorland Journal 1793. Arrival and First Explorations," in *Castorland Journal*, 1–74.
La Tour du Pin, Henriette de. *Recollection of the Revolution and the Empire*, 173–255.
Moreau de Saint-Méry. *Voyage aux Etats-Unis de l'Amérique, 1793–1798*.
Volney, Constantin de. "Gallipolis or the French colony on the Ohio," I, *View of the climate and soil of the United States of America*, 355–406.

Related Secondary Texts

Godechot, Jacques. "The Atlantic Revolution: Characteristics and Causes," in *France and the Atlantic Revolution, 1770–1799*, 1–26.
Furstenberg, François. *When the United States Spoke French*, 1–34.

Related Films and Fiction

Chateaubriand, René de. "Prologue," in *Atala*, 1–4.
Jefferson in Paris, directed by James Ivory, 1995.
John Adams. HBO mini-series, directed by Tom Hooper, 2008.
Simiot, Philippe. *Le Banquier et le Perroquet* (a fictional account of Stephen Girard's life in Philadelphia).

CHAPTER VIII

Franco-Americans in Antebellum America

Over the course of the period covered in this chapter, 1799 to 1861, the United States expanded "from sea to shining sea," to acquire its current geographic shape. By the end of the 18th century already, the north American Republic occupied most of the territory east of the Mississippi River and south and the St. Lawrence and the Great Lakes. Some states, like New York, Massachusetts, Connecticut, North Carolina, Virginia, and Georgia had ceded land they had claimed previously to the federal government, and in the process, new states were created: Vermont was admitted to the Union in 1791, Kentucky in 1792,[1] and Tennessee in 1796. In the following decades, more states were to emerge out of the Northwest Territory Congress established in 1787. Moreover, the young nation was soon to double in size through the purchase of Louisiana. The myth of Manifest Destiny that served as justification for this westward expansion originated in part in the new opportunities afforded by the Louisiana Purchase.[2] It built on an understanding of the "American people" as white, protestant, and English-speaking and on the notion that the new lands were empty. To the extent that it conveniently ignored the very real presence of French, Native American, and *métis* populations, this assumption flew in the face of reality.[3] The third section of this chapter therefore describes how "[i]n the heart of North America, francophone populations—of European, American Indian, and African ancestries—greeted American pioneers as they pushed westward into a presumably empty continent" (Hobson and Rushforth, 20). But first, the reasons that led to Napoleon Bonaparte's decision to sell Louisiana to the United States must be explored, as we will do in section 1, "Napoleon and Slavery: Prelude to the Louisiana Purchase." How the Louisiana Purchase itself unfolded is the topic of section 2. This major coup of the Jefferson administration was to allow the conquest of the West, which was explored, mapped, and surveyed by Americans led by the locals,[4] and also, as we will see in section 4, Franco-Americans who continued to explore and push the frontier of the United States further west.

1. Napoleon and Slavery: Prelude to the Louisiana Purchase

Upon seizing power in a coup in 1799, Napoleon Bonaparte famously declared that the French Revolution was over.[5] His Consulate government pursued three main goals, to preserve the legacy of the Revolution with regard to civil rights, to reconcile the French people, and to make peace with the world. In many regards, the Consulate was successful. The civil war in Vendée finally ended. France signed peace treaties with Austria in

143

1801 and England in 1802, a positive outcome even if peace lasted only a year. The government pardoned *émigrés* and allowed them to return to France provided they pledged allegiance to the new regime. Freedom of religion was the law of the land and *Concordats*, separate agreements with Catholics, Protestants, and Jews, ensured the separation of Church and State. Just as importantly, jurists were hard at work on the Civil Code, the set of democratic laws that were soon to be the law of France.

In the spring of 1799, President Adams had formed a commission tasked with finding ways of putting an end to the 1778 Alliance officially, offer American neutrality in exchange for compensation on shipping losses, and in effect, stopping the Quasi-War. American negotiators arrived in Paris in March 1800 and negotiations between the two nations resumed. The First Consul made his position clear: either the 1778 Treaty remained in place, in which case France would agree to the U.S. compensation demands; or it was void, in which France saw no reason to compensate the United States. The talks led to a treaty that reiterated Franco-American amity but did not resolve the issues at hand. The only solid point in the Convention of 1800, known as the Treaty of Mortefontaine in France, was perhaps Article I, which proclaimed "firm, inviolable, and universal peace" as well as "true and sincere friendship between the French Republic and the United States of America."[6] For the rest, it was simply agreed to postpone discussions on both issues at hand—the cancellation of the 1778 treaty and the compensation for losses. Meanwhile in October 1800, First Consul Bonaparte was recuperating Spanish Louisiana and Thomas Jefferson was rushing to a presidential victory fueled by popular hostility to the Alien and Sedition Acts.

In the 1770s, reclaiming the territory West of the Mississippi for France was just the pipe dream of a few Frenchmen living in Spanish Louisiana.[7] Following France's victory over Spain at the conclusion of the War of the Pyrenees,[8] however, the Directory government took an interest in this idea and even asked Spain to return the Louisiana colony during the negotiations that led to the 1795 Peace of Basel. Spain rejected the proposal at the time and offered the eastern part of Santo Domingo instead, thus giving France control over the entire island. Napoleon Bonaparte, perhaps because he had failed in Egypt, dreamt of a French colony in North America. The opportunity to make that dream come true arose in 1800 when King Charles IV of Spain agreed to return Louisiana to France in exchange for an extension of the Duchy of Parma that the French armies had conquered.[9] The Treaty of Ildefonso of October 1, 1800, was kept secret however, for fear of causing trouble with the United States (Havard, Vidal, *Histoire*, 705–706). During the Confederation and the Federalist periods, the issue of navigation on the Mississippi River had been just as divisive as the alliance with France in U.S. politics. Although the Treaty of Paris seemed advantageous to the United States in that regard, Spain had closed off free navigation in 1784, thus preventing U.S. trade of using the waterway.[10] Following a period of uncertainty, Spain had finally granted the United States free navigation on the river and the right to store goods in New Orleans in 1795. In 1798, however, Spain revoked the use of New Orleans. Had it not remained a secret, the return of Louisiana to France in 1800 would no doubt have been seen as a threat to U.S. interests.

In Bonaparte's vision, Louisiana was to serve as an extension of France's island colonies. Saint-Domingue, "the Pearl of the Caribbean" was to regain the rank of foremost producer of exotic goods it had held prior to the Revolution and the 1794 abolition of slavery.[11] The French government had expected that black citizens of the islands would continue working on plantations after they left the army, but few were interested in an activity that was, for all practical purposes, the same as slavery. The law passed in 1795 to punish vagabonds had backfired and encouraged *marronage*, escape to the hills, more than agriculture (Butel, 241–242). The Ministry of the Colonies, which was staffed with men like Elie Moreau de Saint-Méry, Pierre Victor Malouet, and Barbé-Marbois,[12] felt vindicated and their conviction that the abolition of slavery had been a mistake was shared by the First Consul. Napoleon Bonaparte was in favor of slavery not only because he viewed it as necessary for the economic prosperity of France, but also for personal reasons: his first wife, Josépine Tasher de la Pagerie (1763–1814), was born to a wealthy creole family that owned a sugar plantation and 150 slaves in Martinique.[13]

Napoleon's economic plan hinged on his ability to re-introduce slavery in the Caribbean, in other words, to deprive people of color of the rights they had just earned. As soon as his Consulate government was in place in 1799, he decreed that the colonies were to be ruled by special laws, not by the laws of the French Republic. But when new administrators arrived in Guadeloupe in early 1801 to enforce these decrees, black islanders were outraged, rebelled, and seized power in October. France sent new troops to quell the rebellion and the repression was particularly gruesome. The black general Louis Delgrès (1766–1803), a native of Guadeloupe, was right to claim that Bonaparte had betrayed both the ideals of the Revolution and the interests of black citizens. Instead of surrendering, however, he and 400 of his soldiers committed suicide (Dubois, 400). Following the failure of the Guadeloupean revolution, slavery was reinstated in 1802, blacks and mulattos lost their French citizenship, and mixed marriages were outlawed.

Unlike Saint-Domingue and Guadeloupe, Martinique had not experienced emancipation since French planters had placed the island under British jurisdiction in 1794. In 1802 France regained the island through the Treaty of Amiens after England agreed to recognize the French Republic and to restitute colonial possessions she had occupied during the war. Saint-Domingue, meanwhile, was moving toward independence under the leadership of Jean-Dominique Toussaint-L'Ouverture (1743–1803), a former slave who dreamt of turning the colony into a free, independent nation.[14] After the Directory appointed him military commander of the island, Toussaint made his first moves toward autonomy. In 1798–99, he fought and beat French troops sent to regain control of the island, and with the assistance of the U.S. government, fought French piracy in the Caribbean during the Quasi-War. As soon as French defeat neared in Saint-Domingue, in March 1798, most colonists fled. Jean-Jacques Dessalines (1758-1806), who had served as an officer in the French army, slaughtered those who could not find ways and means to escape, 2,000 at Cap-Français, 900 in Port-au-Prince, and 400 at Jérémie.

In the spring of 1800, the Consulate dispatched a fleet of 4,000 sailors to the island to counter Toussaint's plans. Although warned not to conquer the Spanish part of the island, which Spain had ceded to France in 1795, Toussaint went ahead anyway after forcing the government's emissary, Roume de Saint-Laurent, to give him written authorization to invade.[15] When the government in Paris learned of these developments, a new expeditionary force of 23,000 sailors was sent to Saint-Domingue, landing in January 1802 (Havard and Vidal, *Histoire*, 709). Unfortunately, a yellow fever epidemic ravaged the French troops soon reducing their numbers to 12,000 men, according to General Leclerc, the French commander and Bonaparte's brother-in-law.[16] After a few months of warfare, the French troops captured Toussaint and sent him to France where he died in prison in 1803.

The treachery of his capture outraged mulatto officers like André Rigaud, Alexandre

Pétion, and Jean-Pierre Boyer who had initially fought against Toussaint. Realizing that the real point of the military campaign was to reinstate slavery, Pétion formed a rebel army in October 1802 and the Haitian revolution broke loose. Other generals, Nicolas Geffrard, Henri Christophe, and Dessalines soon joined Pétion. They fought the troops of Rochambeau, son of the hero of the American War of Independence, and Noailles in a ferocious war.[17] However, once Dessalines took command of the insurgent army in May 1803, it proved to be stronger and defeated the French by November. Once it was clear that the French army would not be able to reconquer Saint-Domingue, Bonaparte had to face the futility of his dream of an American empire. There was no more hope of resurrecting New France after the loss of Saint-Domingue. Saint-Domingue became the Republic of Haiti, an independent nation, on January 1, 1804.[18] On December 2, 1804, Bonaparte became Napoleon I, Emperor of the French, and from then on, his focus was exclusively on Europe. But before, he sold Louisiana to the United States.

As William Freehling notes, "[i]rony abounded in one reason for Napoleon's expanded offer [of Louisiana]. Slaveholders' greatest fear for their security, a massive slave revolt, had lately engulfed Haiti, damaging Napoleon's army, and partially dissuading him from further New World risks" (73). Although he dispatched Pierre-Clément de Laussat to North America to reclaim Louisiana formally for France, the First Consul and his representatives, Barbé-Marbois and Talleyrand, were already negotiating the sale of part of this newly re-acquired territory to the United States. The loss of Saint-Domingue had another important repercussion for the United States: it brought more refugees from the French colonies. About 10,000 whites, many with their slaves, fled to Cuba and Louisiana during the third wave of emigration. All in all, 20,000 French people fled the Caribbean islands for Louisiana between 1789 and 1806. They were to play a crucial role in the agricultural development of the South and in events leading up to the Civil War. Among the 1803 refugees, for instance, was Louise Lassy de Moreau (1782–1860) who, in 1805, married Edward Livingston, owner of a rice plantation, Congressman, Secretary of State under Andrew Jackson (1767–1845), and a vocal advocate of the slave trade and slavery.

2. The Louisiana Purchase[19]

After learning of the secret retrocession of Louisiana to France, President Thomas Jefferson worried that a French Louisiana would be a great danger to the nation and irremediably damage Franco-American relations. Therefore, he asked James Monroe, who was ambassador to France, and Robert Livingston, who served as a private supplier to the French troops in the Caribbean, to negotiate the purchase of the city-port of New Orleans. Their efforts led nowhere but Jefferson then asked Pierre Samuel du Pont de Nemours (1739–1817) to come up with a new plan. Du Pont, who had settled in the United . States in 1800, suggested a much larger purchase: all of French Louisiana.[20] Charles A. Cerami characterizes the Louisiana Purchase as "Jefferson's great gamble," the title of his book, and a gamble it was: had that deal also failed, conflict between France and the United States would have become unavoidable. Fortunately, the bargain suited both parties and legal objections were therefore soon set aside.[21]

On April 30, 1802, the United States purchased Louisiana for the sum of 80 million francs, minus 20 million in compensation for losses endured during the Quasi-War.[22] Robert Livingston, James Monroe, and François Barbé-Marbois signed the Treaty in

Paris and Jefferson announced the purchase on July 4, 1803. "The peaceful resolution of the Louisiana crisis was enthusiastically celebrated across the country. Americans had avoided war with the greatest military power on earth, a war they were ill-prepared to fight and might very well have lost" (Onuf, 47). The changing of the flags ceremony, from Spain to France, took place in New Orleans on November 30, 1803, and from France to the United States a month later. A banquet in honor of Franco-American friendship concluded ceremonies. As the U.S. territory doubled in size, the newly added lands were initially organized into an Orleans Territory, with New Orleans as its capital, and a Louisiana territory, with St. Louis as its capital. Over the course of the 19th century, 14 U.S. states were carved out of the 828,000 square miles of French Louisiana: Arkansas, Iowa, Missouri, Kansas, Oklahoma, Nebraska, Minnesota, Louisiana, New Mexico, Texas, South Dakota, Wyoming, Montana, and Colorado. From one day to the next, some 50,000 people of French, African, and Hispanic descent changed nationality (Havard and Vidal, *Histoire*, 717), as stipulated in Article III of the Louisiana Purchase Treaty.[23]

The switch in nationality was problematic in many regards. W.J. Eccles comments that "[t]hey [the French] were not to be treated as citizens, having equal rights in the country that had usurped them," and he quotes Gouverneur Morris in support of his claim: "'I always thought that when we should acquire Canada and Louisiana it would be proper to govern them as provinces and allow them no voice in our councils.'" Eccles also mentions dismissive attitudes towards the Franco-Americans of Louisiana on the part of President Jefferson who is said to have declared that "liberty would be wasted on the Creoles since 'the principles of a popular government are utterly beyond their comprehension,' and that '[n]ot one in fifty understands the English language'" (Quoted in Eccles, 269). Creagh, for his part, mentions a dispute between French and American officers during a ball in New Orleans shortly after the Louisiana Purchase: it was about which dances, English or French, should be played first. The French also resented the American prohibition to celebrate Bastille Day (*Nos Cousins*, 240).[24]

William Freehling has speculated that the Louisiana Purchase did more harm than good to the United States, that without it "the Civil War would have been far less likely" (81).[25] One of the factors that was to exacerbate the conflict between the northern, industrial states and the southern, agricultural states was indeed a difference in attitudes towards slavery. Although slavery was not entirely absent in the north, its obvious incompatibility with the principle of human equality professed in the Declaration of Independence led many northerners to wish for the disappearance of this institution. For them, according to Freehling, the western expansion made possible by the Louisiana Purchase represented a way "to diffuse blacks into specks" (74).[26] By contrast, at a time when the cultivation of cotton was enjoying a great boom in the south, plantation owners viewed the slaves' free labor as vital to the economic life and expansion of their states, particularly in the rich Natchez district.[27] By mechanizing the separation of cotton and seed, the invention of the cotton gin significantly reduced labor cost, and made cotton a very profitable crop (Jones, 167).

The French refugees from the Caribbean islands who settled in Louisiana strengthened slavery's hold on the south because, unlike the Spanish governor of Louisiana Francisco de Carondelet who had outlawed slavery in 1796, they were unabashed advocates of slavery and of the superiority of the white race. As the American governor of the Louisiana territory, Isaac Briggs outlawed the slave trade in 1804 but it continued unabated thanks to pirates like Jean Lafitte who operated from an island south of New Orleans,

Barataria (Ramsay, 30). Many of the French refugees who settled in Cuba instead of Louisiana during the revolutionary era also engaged in piracy against American ships since the United States supported Toussaint L'Ouverture. When Cuba expelled all its 9,000 French residents in 1809, they went to Philadelphia, Missouri,[28] Georgia, Texas, but mostly to Louisiana where the language, culture, and religion were the same, and in particular to New Orleans. With this large influx of people, the city of New Orleans doubled in size. As Cécile Vidal puts it:

> the white Saint-Dominguan refugees who landed in the city [of New Orleans] during the revolutionary period found a place they could easily call home. Not only were these exiles bound to Louisiana's inhabitants by ties of blood or economic interests,[29] but they were also held together by a shared commitment to racial slavery [Vidal, *Caribbean New Orleans*, 498].

Due to the *Code Noir* and the by-then long history of freeing slaves, there were also free people of color (*gens de couleur libres*) among the French refugees, most of them of mixed race, well-educated, and property-owning. New Orleans already had a sizeable population of mulattoes in spite of the prohibition of biracial unions. Together with the Free Blacks they formed an intermediary class between whites and slaves and made New Orleans the U.S. city with the largest free black population after 1812. As Louisiana became more and more Americanized over the course of the century, however, the social status of both groups declined.

French refugees played a key role in the early economic development of Louisiana. Antoine Sorrel des Rivières (1737–1830), a planter and colonel in the French Corps of Engineers who escaped from Saint-Domingue, started a plantation in the *Poste des Attakapas* (St. Martinville, Louisiana). Those who settled in the Natchez district contributed to the cotton boom. Thanks to their plantations, the U.S. cotton production increased from 9 percent of the world supply in 1791 to 70 percent in 1810. French refugees who settled in the Mississippi delta introduced a new variety of sugar cane and built large sugar plantations.[30] Some of these plantations can still be seen today: the Destréhan Plantation in the Lower Mississippi Valley, built in the 1780s; the St. Joseph Plantation in Vacherie, Louisiana; Guillaume Duparc's Laura Plantation, also in Vacherie Louisiana; Valcour Aimé's *Bon Séjour* Plantation (now Oak Alley)[31]; and Pierre Sauvé's Lone Star and Providence Plantation. Overall, 75 plantations were already producing five tons of sugar by 1806.[32] At the end of the first decade of the 19th century, the Louisiana population counted 40,000 souls, with the largest concentrations found in Iberville, Bâton-Rouge, and New Orleans, the main U.S. port for the export of cotton and sugar. By 1840, New Orleans had over 100,000 inhabitants, which made it the fourth largest city in the United States. The Louisiana planters were also the wealthiest Americans at the time.

Since the free labor of slaves, who also constructed the levee system, made this wealth accumulation possible, one of the plantation owners' greatest fear was that the Caribbean slaves who were brought to Louisiana would rebel like their brothers in Saint-Domingue. Such a slave rebellion did in fact occur in 1811 as a protest against awful working conditions on the sugar plantations. Known as the German Coast Uprising, it was led by Charles Deslondes and was the largest slave revolt in U.S. history. Unfortunately, it ended very badly for the slaves and very cruelly for Deslondes.[33]

The part of French Louisiana known as Louisiana today became a U.S. state in 1812. That year, steamboat navigation from Pittsburgh to New Orleans started on the Mississippi River.[34] The British started the War of 1812 (1812–15) in order to stop American expansion, but the 1815 Battle of New Orleans was one of the decisive American victories that put an end to the conflict. Although part of the United States, Louisiana remained largely French until the Civil War. French was an official language and French customs, traditions, and religion were part of daily life. Louisiana had a French press since 1794 when Louis Duclot started publishing *Le Moniteur de la Louisiane*. It was followed by *L'Abeille de La Nouvelle-Orléans*, which François Delaup founded in 1827. Other towns had their own paper: Bâton Rouge had its *Gazette* since 1819, Natchitoches its *Courrier* since 1824, Saint-Martinville its *Gazette des Attakapas*. Moreover, many 19th-century governors were of French origin: Jacques Philippe Villeré, the second governor (1816–20) was born in a family of plantation owners whose roots went back to Iberville's expedition in the late 17th century. Pierre Derbigny, the sixth governor (1828–29) was born in France in a family that fled to United States in 1791. Armand Beauvais of Pointe Coupée, succeeded him as the seventh Louisiana governor (1829–30) and then Jacques Dupré as the eighth (1830–31); André Bienvenue Roman, as the ninth (1831–35); Alexandre Mouton as the eleventh (1843–46); Paul Octave Hébert, as the fourteenth (1853–56).

People of French ancestry also established roots on the East bank of the Mississippi River. Louis LeFleur, for instance, was born Louis LeFlau in Mobile in 1762, the son of a French soldier and of Jeanne Girard. He became a riverboat trader, married two "half-French nieces of the Choctaw Chief Pushmataha" (Yancy), and following the establishment of the Mississippi Territory in 1798, opened a trading post on the Pearl River, probably on the location of LeFleur's Bluff State Park today, where travelers could get food, lodging, horses, and entertainment. The post was in territory linking Mississippi to Tennessee carved out from land the U.S. government pressured the Choctaw to sell in 1801. The Natchez Trace, as it is called, was later used by American pioneers as they moved west. LeFleur continued to run his river-transport operations and even worked for the U.S. authorities in that capacity. In 1812 he opened a second inn known as French camp. We also know that he was a witness to the signing of a treaty, as the Choctaw ancestral lands shrank over the first three decades of the 19th century. His son Greenwood was educated in Nashville, became a major in the U.S. army and served in the War of 1812 and the campaign to Pensacola in 1814–15. He became Chief of the Northwestern Division of the Choctaw just before the Choctaw were forced off their lands in 1830 (Yancy).

According to Edward H. Spicer, the Choctaw were one in a group of "Five Civilized Tribes that also included the Creeks, Cherokees, Chickasaws, and the Seminoles" (Spicer, 69). The "civilized" Native Americans for Spicer were those who had adopted the European way of life, who were farmers, dressed and lived like Europeans (69–70). By contrast, "the Comanches, Osages, Cheyennes, and others who relied on buffalo and other kinds of games for subsistence" were the wild Indians. And yet, although "these features of their way of life were decisive in the American view and encouraged the distinction between 'civilized' and 'wild' tribes" (70), all tribes were forcibly removed from their lands between 1831 and 1848 during the infamous "trail of tears."[35] The Bureau of Indian Affairs was created in March 1824 to hold in trust Native American lands, in yet another sign of these nations' dominated position.[36]

3. French Guides to the Wild West[37]

Following the Louisiana Purchase, the fate of the French was sensibly different in Upper and Lower Louisiana since the latter fared extremely well under the U.S. regime, particularly if they owned plantations. According to André Prévos, the French of the Illinois Country, who were "proud of their past and of their position," initially "exhibited disdain and impatience at the presence of the Americans, although they also hoped to profit from the latter's presence" (366). While they were able to preserve their language and some aspects of their culture until the early 20th century,[38] the open-field agricultural system that had served them so well did not survive for long. It slowly disappeared during the first half of the 19th century "[u]nder the influence of Anglo-American law and practices and the pressure of increased population" (Ekberg, *French Roots*, 241). The same process occurred in the Detroit area, where the French had been farming since the beginning of the 18th century.[39] The fact that two scions of prominent St. Louis families like Auguste Pierre Chouteau (1786–1838) and Charles Gratiot, Jr. (1786–1855) graduated from West Point in 1806 is a sure sign of the early assimilation of the French element into the American mainstream: it shows that it started as soon as the Illinois country became American.[40]

St. Louis's convenient location at the confluence of the Missouri and Mississippi rivers had attracted the fur traders who founded the city in 1763, Pierre Laclède (1729–1778) and his stepson Auguste Chouteau (1749–1829). Laclède and his partner in New Orleans, Gilbert Antoine de St. Maxent (1724–1794), were successful merchants who had obtained a six-year trading-monopoly for the area. Auguste was the son of another trader, René-Auguste Chouteau (1723–1776), a Frenchman who had immigrated to Louisiana, married Marie-Thérèse Bourgeois in New Orleans, fathered a son, and then abandoned

French habitation in the Illinois Country. Engraving for Henri Victor Collot's *A Journey in North America*, showing a French Creole, late 18th-century house formed of upright hewn timbers and sharp pitched roof (courtesy Missouri Historical Museum, Missouri Historical Society).

wife and child. Mrs. Chouteau had then become Pierre Laclède's common-law wife, and since she was still legally married to Chouteau all the children she had with Laclède bore her married name instead of his.[41] By 1803, the Chouteau had been living for decades in St. Louis where they were known as one of the prominent families, families that were still engaged in the fur trade or related activities at the time.[42]

In American history, St. Louis has become famous as the starting point of many American explorations of the West,[43] as the Gateway Arch reminds us today. The most famous of these explorations was undoubtedly the Lewis & Clark expedition (1804–1806). Following the Louisiana Purchase, a changing of the flag ceremony took place not only in New Orleans[44] but also in St. Louis, on March 9, 1804. Havard and Vidal characterize this event as "highly symbolic" (717) because among the attendees were Meriwether Lewis and William Clark, whom President Jefferson had just commissioned to explore the newly acquired U.S. territory.[45] William Clark's December 23 entry in his journal even specifies that the ceremony took place "on the portico of [Charles Gratiot's] home."[46] The Gratiot were certainly among the Frenchmen the explorers quizzed about their knowledge of the West prior to departure. Although billed as an American exploit, the Lewis & Clark expedition "rested in part on cartographic and ethnographic knowledge" gathered by the French[47] over the course of the preceding centuries (Havard and Vidal, 718).

Several Frenchmen were part of the expedition, "two French canoemen, or *voyageurs*, one of whom could speak many Indian languages, while the other was a skilled hunter" (Hitchcock, 108).[48] Havard and Vidal identify the two Frenchmen as the "Franco-Omaha Pierre Cruzatte and François Labiche" (*Histoire*, 718).[49] That the American explorers encountered Franco-Indians everywhere they went is hardly a surprise, as Daniel Royot explains:

> In the years preceding the Louisiana Purchase, greater numbers of the Nor'westers were Métis, emerging from decades of intermarriages between French Canadians and native women. Newcomers to the trade were most likely to throw in their lot with these Métis people and find their own native women mostly in Ojibwa, Cree, Mandan, and Hidatsa villages [131].[50]

Once the Lewis and Clark expedition arrived among the Mandan Indians of North Dakota, "they secured an Indian interpreter named Chaboneau"[51] and "[h]is wife, Sacajawea (Bird Woman)" who went along on the expedition and displayed "patience, courage, and helpfulness" (Hitchcock, 129).[52] Charbonneau knew how to cook and once impressed everyone with *boudin blanc*, a "sausage made from stuffed buffalo intestine,"[53] while Sacajawea "was able to identify edible plants and roots that the men had never seen before, including currants, wild licorice and wild onions" (Avey).[54] Hitchcock also mentions that Captain Clark had "a negro servant" (108).

From Pittsburg, the starting point of the expedition, to St. Louis, its winter quarters, the explorers encountered many French people. They met Guy Briant on the Ohio River in September and George Drouillard,[55] whom they hired as an interpreter at Fort Massac in Illinois on November 11, 1803. They called on Louis Lorimer, a native of Montreal married to a Shawnee woman who was serving as Commandant of Cape Girardeau at the time.[56] The man was well known because of "Laramie Station," a trading post he had "established with his father to trade with the Indians of Ohio" (Lewis, Nov. 23).[57] A Mr. Blean (actually Blouin) informed Clark on December 5 "that no provisions had arrived." In St. Louis, "French hands" or "*engagés*" were hired to accomplish certain tasks (May 11, 18, Nov. 6, 1804), and French traders were encountered throughout the voyage.

Until the American explorers reached the Rockies, the places they visited and stayed at were French or Native Americans. Near Pittsburgh, they stopped at Bruno Island, a place "named for Félix Brunot, a French physician who settled in Pittsburgh about 1797" and "was reportedly a friend of Lewis."[58] They visited St. Charles on May 21, 1804, saw Moreau Creek, went by Lacrush (La Croix) creek and Cape Jeradeau (Girardeau) on November 23.

They arrived in St. Louis on December 8, 1803, and spent the winter there because they couldn't get to La Charette.[59] The prominent St. Louis families provided useful information and invited them to their social gatherings.[60]

The borrowing of French words in the Lewis & Clark Journals testifies to the ongoing presence of the French in parts of a country the American expedition was supposed to be "discovering." The explorers adopted the French way of traveling by "perogue" (*pirogue*) and the French habit of hiding "their goods in *caches*" (Hitchcock, 140).[61] They refer to a particular geographic formation as a byo (*bayou*) (Nov. 18, 1803). When they cross the Mississippi, they land "at the upper *habitation* on the oposite [sic] side." Many geographic features are simply translated from French to English: "*Côtes noires*" becomes "Black Hills"; "*rivière jaune*," "yellow river" (Havard & Vidal, *Histoire*, 718–719) and "la Roche jaune," Yellowstone (Hitchcock, 133). Some words get mistranslated, so when the "rivière à vase" becomes the "Cow River" instead of the Muddy River (Lewis, Nov. 25); "Vide Poche" (Empty Pocket) becomes "Viele Pauchr" (Clark, Dec. 7, 1803), a reference to a small French town close to St. Louis named after the French-born governor of Spanish Louisiana, Carondelet.

Similar observations apply to Zebulon Pike's *Journal of a voyage to the source of the Mississippi in the years 1805 and 1806*. Commissioned at about the same time as Lewis and Clark, Pike set out "to explore the source of the Mississippi making a general survey of the river and its bounderies [sic] and its productions both in the Animal, vegetable and mineral creation: also to include observations on the savage inhabitants of its Banks" (August 10, 1805). An abundance of French words testifies to the adoption by the Americans of a number of local cultural practices with regard to modes of transportation ("peroque" or "pirogue" for *pirogue*; "bateaux" for *bateaux*; *portage*), or labor ("*engagé*" for hired hand). An animal like the "*reynard d'argent*" (silver fox), which is unknown to the Americans but known to the French, is named in that language in the text. Pike also reads the outdoor temperature in "the Mercury of Reamour" [Réaumur]. The name of a great number of locations explored are French: "Buffalo or Beauf riviere" (August 12, 1805); "three Bateaux" (August 17, 1805); "the rapids De Moyen" (Aug. 20, 1805); " the rapids of the Riviere De Roche" (Aug. 28, 05); "the river L'eau Clare" (*l'eau claire*); Lake Pipin [Pépin]; La Rivere De Corbeau (the Raven River); "Fond du Lac" (bottom of the lake); Le Montaign qui Tromp a L'eau (*La montagne qui trempe à l'eau*) correctly translated as "the mountain which soaks in the river" (September 14, 1805).[62]

Like the Lewis and Clark expedition, Zebulon Pike's party encountered many French people on the way. On "August 16, at 3 o'clock P˙ M˙ [they] arrived at the house of a French man situated on the W side of the river." On September 1, 1805, they "were saluted, and received with every mark of attention by Monr. Dubuque the proprietor … we dined with him." On that day, Pike also gratefully acknowledges that a certain "M. Blondeau" has found and brought back to him two of his men who had wandered off and he thought to be lost for good. On September 21, the party "[p]assed the Encampment of a Mr. Ferrebault," probably a fur trader. Without French interpreters, it would be impossible to communicate with the Native Americans, which is why on September 8, 1805, Pike "[e]mbarked two Interpreters—one to perform the whole voyage, by the name of Pierre Roseau; and the other Joseph Rieuville."[63] Their job was not only to translate but also to explain foreign customs. What is the meaning of "a small *red Capot* hung on a Tree"? It's "a sacrifice by some Indians to the *Bon Dieu*," the interpreter explained (Pike's Journal, October 6, 1805). The interpreters were also useful in that they were usually better at assessing danger.[64] In some cases, two interpreters were needed to deliver a message, as was the case with the Puants or the *Folles Avoines* Nation.[65]

But Pike's journal also suggests that relations between the new American conquerors and the Native Americans were not optimal. Based on his description of casual encounters the reader gets a sense that the Indians were out to take advantage of the Americans, "holloring, 'how do you do'" (Aug. 26, 1805) to get favors or gifts,[66] when not overtly mocking them.[67] At one point, Pike gets indignant when he sees an English instead of an American flag flying over a Native American dwelling.[68] The term "conqueror" seems appropriate here considering Pike's attitude and discourse. On September 17, 1805, for instance, he recalls an anecdote that leaves no doubt about his sense of superiority over Native Americans:

> I was Shewn a point of Rocks from which a Sioux woman cast herself and was dashed into a thousand pieces on the rock's below. She had been informed, her friends intended matching her to a man she dispised, they having refused her the man of her choice. She ascended the Hill Singing her death Song and before they could overtake her and stop her purpose, She took the lover's leap! and ended her troubles with her life—a wonderful exhibition of Sentiment for a Savage.

Beyond the blatant denial of basic humanity implied in the exclamation "for a savage," the explorer also asserts his power over Native Americans by making clear that he is not there merely to "observe," but also to warn "the Savages which had fallen under our protection by our late purchase from the Spaniard's" (Sept. 9, 1805) that it was their duty to cooperate. Pike notes approvingly of the U.S. government's efforts to teach the Lac People,[69] a Chippewa (Ojibwe) tribe, the "science of agriculture"[70]—as if they had never grown their own food before. In his council address to the "Gens De Lac," he impresses on them that they are no longer to do business with unlicensed traders, or else.[71] The traders, presumably Frenchmen,[72] he writes, had "taken great pains to impress on the minds of the Savages an idea of our being a very Vindictive, ferocious and warlike people. This impression was given no doubt with an evil intention…" (Sept. 3, 1805).

The problem, however, is that the French and the Native Americans had intermarried for so long that it was very difficult to say who was Native American and who was French.[73] Consider for instance that all Sioux Indians who were asked to sign "the Granting of the Lands at this place, Falls of Saint Anthony & St Croix and the making peace with the Chippeways" on 23 September 1805, had a French name: le Fils de Buichon, Le Petit Corbeaux, L'Orignal levé; Le Fils de Penichon; Le Grand Partisan; Le Demi Douzen; Le Beccasse; Le Boeuf qui Marche. Another Sioux witness is called Outarde Blanche. Some families of French ancestry had long lived in the area. A native of Green Bay, Augustin Grignon (1780–1860), for instance, was a descendant of the "father of Wisconsin," Charles Langlade (Kellogg, 333). He worked as "a fur trader and general entrepreneur," married to the daughter of a *folle avoine* and a French Canadian. They lived in

Kaukana until 1832 when he obtained land near Fort Winnebago. Prévos mentions a relative of his, Charles Gaulthier de Warville (1737–1801), *dit* De Langlade, a resident of Wisconsin, who sired a considerable number on mixed-blood children with *panis* women of various First Nations, Sioux, Winnebago, Ottawa, Sac Fox, Menominee, in addition to those born of his legitimate wife.

In Pike's travel log, the French are either more or less assimilated to the "Savages," forgotten—as when the Louisiana Purchase is presented, above, as a deal between the United States and Spain. They are for him on their way out, like the "welcoming establishment" that was "formerly under the charge of a Mr. Charles Bousky" (January 9, 1806), or an unpleasant, pesky, presence of "polite hypocrites."[74] Nonetheless, the fact that the French were there first, were the real explorers, gives Zebulon Pike sometimes the feeling that his is not a genuine exploration: "Came to large Island and Strong water early in the morning, passed the place where Mr. Rienville and Mons Perlier wintered in 1797." This comment, consigned in the October 10, 1805, entry of the journal, is an acknowledgment that the French were there first, that he is retracing their steps. Even the description of the architecture the beaver dams he would have liked to make, he realizes, "has been already exhausted by various Travellors."

The Mr. Rienville, also Rieuville, mentioned above in Pike's account was actually Joseph Renville (1779–1846), son of a French-Canadian fur trader and a Sioux who lived in Minnesota and had been hired as an interpreter. He would soon fight on the British side in the War of 1812, a war that had the expansion of the United States, particularly in the Great Lakes area, as one of its stakes. Fighting on the other side was Lieutenant Colonel Pike, who after an unsuccessful expedition to New Mexico, was captured by the Spaniards, released and then killed in the war of 1812. Renville was to be part of Stephen H. Long's unsuccessful expedition to the headwaters of the Red River in 1823.[75]

Among the Western explorations that took place during the Era of Good Feelings, a period that brought Americans together at the close of the War (1817–1825), those led by Stephen Harriman Long (1784–1864) stand out. William H. Keating (1799–1840),[76] who accompanied Long on his 1823 expedition to the West, wrote an account in which he commented on the French character of the local population, not in positive ways around Fort Wayne, however:

> The town or village is small; it has grown under the shelter of the fort and contains a mixed and apparently very worthless population. The inhabitants are chiefly of Canadian origin, all more or less imbued with Indian blood. Not being previously aware of the diversity of the character of the inhabitants, the sudden change from an American to a French population has a surprising, and to say the least, an unpleasant effect… [Keating, I, 96].[77]

Keating cannot be seen as someone who disliked the French, however. He was on the contrary, a Francophile, someone who had studied abroad and greatly admired the French education system (*Considerations*, 70). But miscegenation was too much for him. It is interesting to note that the distinction between "French from France" and "French from America" implied in Keatings remarks made its appearance at about the time as the United States officially expressed the desire to be left alone, free of Spanish, British, French, or for that matter Native American interference. In 1823, U.S. President James Monroe proclaimed the Monroe Doctrine: he offered Western nations a guarantee of U.S. non-interference in European affairs in exchange for their promise to stop colonizing the Americas.

4. French Explorers and Settlers of the Wild West

In the first half of the 19th century, the task of exploring the vast territory of the Western United States fell mostly upon officers of the U.S. Corps of Engineers established in 1802 by President Jefferson. While the main goal of these explorations was to map the country and to investigate its natural resources, there was also great interest in deriving economic benefits from the fur trade. Already on the decline by the late 1830s due to the depletion of furry animals by trappers and hunters,[78] the fur trade of the first decades of the century was by then organized by large Companies, such as John Jacob Astor's American Fur Company.[79] Astor had also created the Pacific Fur Company, conceived as a rival to the Hudson's Bay Company and the more recently founded North West Company operating out of Montreal. The purpose of Astor's Pacific Fur Company was not only to conduct business but also to establish U.S. presence in Oregon. Two expeditions had been necessary to start the trading post of Astoria in 1810, one transporting staff and partners by sea from New York around Cape Horn, and another, led by Wilson Price Hunt (1783–1842), bringing 65 Astorians by land across the Rockies (Morris).[80] Like previous endeavors of this kind, the land expedition included several Frenchmen and Franco-Americans: Pierre and Marie Dorion,[81] Joseph Gervais, who later settled in the Willamette Valley,[82] and Etienne Lucier (1786–1853), the first Oregon farmer.[83] But the war of 1812–1815 put an end to Astor's Oregon dream.[84]

At about the same time, the Missouri Fur Company created in 1808 by Manuel Lisa (1772–1820) in St. Louis was expanding west, exploring the Upper Missouri basin. Pierre Ménard (1766–1844), a long-time resident of Illinois Country and a member of the Indiana Territorial Legislature led the Company's first expedition in 1809, together with Andrew Henry (1775–1832). Their goal was to return a Mandan Chief to his tribe, to collect furs, and to establish trading posts along the way. Auguste Pierre Chouteau organized a second expedition in the same area in 1810, before serving as captain in the Territorial Militia in 1812. After the war, the Company continued to explore the Upper Missouri basin until its dissolution in 1824. Andrew Henry (1775–1832), who had been a partner in the Missouri Fur Company, also formed the Rocky Mountain Fur Company with future Congressman William Henry Ashley (1778–1838).[85] From 1822 to 1832, they explored Northern Colorado and discovered the lowest point in the Continental Divide, the South Pass in Wyoming in 1824.[86]

General Andrew Jackson's decisive victory at the Battle of New Orleans in 1815 had made him a national hero, as had his annexation of West Florida in 1821. A wealthy slave-owning plantation owner from Tennessee, Jackson ran and lost against John Quincy Adams in the presidential election of 1824. Following the creation of the Democratic Party, Jackson ran again and this time won. The extension of voting rights to white males over twenty-one but also the removal of Native American tribes from the South stand out as salient characteristics of the Jacksonian Era (1825–1849), as does the expansionism justified by the doctrine of Manifest Destiny. Summarizing advances towards trans-continental expansion made in the 1820s and 1830s, Schubert points in particular to the "great inroads into the Mexican Southwest and Oregon" (II, 3), where excellent agricultural land could be found, and to the opening of the Santa Fe trade to Americans.

Franco-Americans were the first to explore most of the Rocky Mountains.[87] The French-Canadian for whom the city of Provo, Utah, is named, Etienne Provost (1785–1850), for instance, was already running a trading post in Taos, New Mexico, prior to

Mexican Independence. He trapped in the Southwest and in particular the Green River basin in the 1820s already and was probably the first European to see the Great Salt Lake in 1824–25. Another Frenchman from St. Louis, Antoine Robidoux (1794–1837) left his mark in Southern Colorado.[88] A speaker of French, Spanish, and English, Robidoux may have explored the Uinta Basin with Etienne Provost in 1824. By 1828, he had settled in Santa Fe, was living with a Mexican woman, and had taken Mexican citizenship, which enabled him to trade legally. He is best remembered for establishing Fort Uncompahgre near Delta in Colorado, "arguably the first permanent trading operation west of the continental divide."[89] He later built Fort Robidoux at the confluence of the Uinta and Whiterocks Rivers in northeastern Utah and named the main river in this basin "Duchenes River."

A little younger than Provost and Robidoux, Pierre Louis Vasquez (1798–1869) also explored the Plains and the Rocky Mountains while working for the American Fur Company. The son of fur trader Benito Vázquez and of Marie-Julie Papin, a French Canadian, he was born and educated in St. Louis. In the 1820s, he traded with the Pawnee and later with the Crow. In the 1830s he moved further west and operated in the Rocky Mountains, where he was known as "Old Vaskiss." He left colorful letters to his older brother Benito about frontier life and even requested that novels be sent to him. With William Sublette,[90] Vasquez built a fort that bears his name on the South Platte River, on the location of Platteville, Colorado, in 1835, "one of four prominent trading posts that sprang up along the South Platte in the 1830s, along with Fort St Vrain, Fort Jackson, and Fort Lupton" ("Louis Vasquez," *Encyclopedia of Colorado*). He is remembered for helping Jim Bridger, who discovered Bridger's Pass in Wyoming, establish Fort Bridger in 1842.[91]

Another Frenchman, Benjamin Louis Eulalie de Bonneville (1796–1878), made a name for himself as an explorer of the American West. Benjamin, his two brothers, and his mother Marguerite, left France to accompany Thomas Paine when he returned to New Rochelle, New York, in 1803. Marguerite's husband, the publisher Nicolas Bonneville, was in jail at the time for having compared Napoleon Bonaparte to Oliver Cromwell. In the United States, Marguerite served as Paine's housekeeper until his death in 1809. In return, Paine left her his farm to cover the education of her sons.[92] Benjamin entered West Point in 1813, became an officer in the U.S. army, and served in various posts in the West. Following a trip to France in 1824, he was stationed in Missouri where he caught the exploration bug. Consequently, he petitioned for and obtained a leave of absence and in 1832 launched an expedition to Oregon financed by the American Fur Company. That journey, which lasted much longer than anticipated,[93] cost Bonneville his commission. But it also yielded new segments of the Oregon trail and a route to California discovered by a member of the Bonneville expedition, Joe Walker, possibly as the groundwork for a later invasion. In Washington, D.C., Bonneville met the writer Washington Irving at John Jacob Astor's house and sold him his maps and notes. Irving then published *The Adventures of Captain Bonneville* in 1837. A year earlier, Bonneville's commission was reinstated, and he resumed his military career. He served in the Mexican War, "the terrible Indian Wars of the West" (Keenan)[94] and in the Civil War.

The history of Wisconsin, Minnesota, North and South Dakota, Iowa, even, is full of references to the Franco-Canadians who started settlements in those (future) states. Among them we find Michel Brisbois (1759–1837), a fur trader who fought for the British during the 1812 war; Hercule Louis Dousmans (1800–1868), the first millionaire in Wisconsin, who was apprenticed in the fur trade to Jean-Joseph Rolette (1781–1842), a native of Quebec who served as the American Fur Company's agent in Prairie du Chien. Descendants of French Huguenots,[95] like Daniel Trabue (1760–1840) who founded the town of Columbia, Kentucky,[96] and new immigrants from France were also living on the American frontier. Roaming the vast expanses of Kentucky, was 25-year-old John James Audubon (1785–1851), for instance.[97] By 1810, he and his business partner Jean-Ferdinand Rozier (1777–1864) had settled further west by St. Genevieve. In 1824, Rozier then formed a lead mining and smelting partnership with another new French immigrant, his nephew Firmin René Desloge (1803–1856).[98]

The resident employees who staffed the stockades and trading posts created by the various fur companies sometimes received the visit of dignitaries and artists.[99] To give but a famous example, Francis A. Chardon, born in Pennsylvania of French extraction, was hired by the American Fur Company and served as clerk and trader at Fort Union and Fort Clark in the 1830s, and then later at Fort Berthold, in North Dakota.[100] Like the French white Indians of the past, Chardon married several Sioux women, fathered numerous children, and died at Fort Berthold in 1848.[101] His *Journal at Fort Clark, 1834–1839*, offers a descriptive account of "life on the upper Missouri; of a fur trader's experiences among the Mandans, Gros Ventres, and their neighbors, of the ravages of the small-pox epidemic of 1837."[102] One of Chardon's visitors was the artist George Catlin (1796–1872), to whom we owe *Descriptions and Illustrations of the manners, customs & conditions of the North American Indians*, the title of the two volumes he published following his eight years adventures in the West. Crossing the plains with two French guides in 1832, "Ba'tiste et Board," Catlin noted that "the fur traders in these parts are almost exclusively French" (Havard and Vidal, 719).

That same year, in 1832, a war broke out between the Sauk Nation and the United States as Chief Black Hawk crossed the Mississippi River from Iowa, seeking to reclaim ancestral lands in the State of Illinois.[103] During the War of 1812, the Sauk had allied with the British and fought U.S. troops led by future U.S. president Major Zachary Taylor in the area of the quad cities, close to Fort Armstrong, the fort built in 1816 on the Illinois side of the Mississippi River. Colonel George Davenport was stationed there.[104] The Black Hawk War of 1832 was soon over, the "British Band," defeated, and Black Hawk imprisoned. Antoine LeClaire, a Franco-Potawatomi, served as a translator when the peace treaty was signed between Keokuk (1780–1848), a Sauk Chief, and the U.S. government who opposed Black Hawk (Prévos). His wife, a relative of a Sauk chief, received land on that occasion on condition that a house be built on the place where the treaty was signed. Antoine LeClaire (1797–1861) obliged and built the first house in Davenport, Iowa, which is why he is now regarded as the town's founder.[105] These and other Frenchmen who came to Iowa before it was part of the United States territory appear as quasi mythical figures, vaguely contrasted against an even more vaguely defined historical background. Such was the case with Julien Dubuque and his friendship with the Indians who worked for him in his lead mines and his alleged marriage with the Indian woman who is said to have discovered the mines:

> Among the many facts which established Le Claire's fame in Iowa history, was his participation in the elaboration of the autobiography of Black Hawk, the famous Indian chief. This work was recorded after Black Hawk's war of resistance against the U.S. Army in order that, as Le Claire indicated in his introductory notice: "the people of the United States might know the causes that had impelled him to act as he had done, and the principles by which he was governed. In accord with this request, I acted as interpreter and was particularly cautious to understand the

narrative of Black Hawk throughout—and have examined the work carefully since its completion—and have no hesitation in pronouncing it strictly correct in all particulars [Prévos, 94].

A Frenchman and an American of French ancestry distinguished themselves among the group of Western explorers of the 1830s: Joseph Nicollet (1786–1843)[106] and John C. Frémont (1813–1890).[107] Although a successful mathematician, astronomer, and geographer, Nicollet ran into financial difficulties in France following the July Revolution of 1830 and came to the United States in 1832 to seek his fortune. In St. Louis, he offered his services to the Chouteau, proposing to map the Upper Mississippi River hydrographical basin.[108] The Chouteau agreed to finance Nicollet's 1836–37 expedition to Fort Snelling, Minnesota, close to where Pierre Parrant, nicknamed *oeil de cochon*, had opened the first saloon of the (future) state, in a place called Fountain Cave, today's St. Paul.[109] Nicollet launched his exploration and geographical survey of the area, while at the same time making friends with an Ojibwe family. One of the outcomes of his first exploration was to correct Zebulon Pike's map of the area.[110] This accomplishment earned him an appointment in the brand-new Corps of Topographical Engineers, established July 4, 1838, and the mission "to map the land between the Mississippi and Missouri Rivers" (Bray). Accompanying him on that second expedition were Joseph Renville, Joseph LaFromboise, a guide for the American Fur Company, and 25-year-old John Charles Frémont (1813–1890).[111] A year later, Nicollet and Frémont mapped the area from Fort Pierre to Devil's Lake, North Dakota, and back, along the Côteau des Prairies to Sisseton, South Dakota, where the Nicollet Tower stands today.[112] Their guide this time was Louison Frenière. Unfortunately, Nicollet died in 1843 before his report and map reached the Senate.

The most famous of the 19th-century American explorers was John C. Frémont, who led five explorations from St. Louis to California in the 1840s.[113] The son of a French-Canadian immigrant schoolteacher and of the daughter of a prominent Virginia planter with whom he had eloped, Anne Beverley Whiting, Frémont was born in Savannah, Georgia. After his father's death in 1818, his mother moved to Charleston where he was able to receive an excellent education thanks to friends of the family.[114] Following a short stint as mathematical instructor in the Navy, Frémont joined the U.S. Topographical Corps and Nicollet's expedition, where he not only gained valuable experience in the trade, but also made contacts that would prove useful in later years. One of them was Thomas Hart Benton (1782–1858), the first Senator of Missouri—elected for a first time in 1821 and four more times later on—and a champion of Westward expansion. Frémont also met Benton's pretty 16-year-old daughter Jessie with whom he eloped in 1841 (Richards, 44). Once the two young people were married and this regrettable episode forgiven, Senator Benton became a strong supporter of his son-in-law's endeavors in the West.

In 1842, the Corps of Topographical Engineers tasked Frémont with surveying and mapping the Oregon Trail.[115] Frémont prepared for his expedition in St. Louis, where he hired Cyprian Chouteau to deal with logistics, Charles Preuss to make maps,[116] and the unknown Kit Carson (1809–1868) to serve as a scout. They all left Kansas City on June 10, 1842 (Hyde, xi). It is during this expedition that Frémont famously climbed a 13,000 ft. peak in Wyoming[117] and planted the U.S. flag at the top, thereby symbolically claiming the Rocky Mountains and the West for the United States. Upon Frémont's return to Washington, D.C., Jessie co-wrote the report of the expedition and it became an instant success. According to Hyde:

Few books can claim to reshape cultures and nations: Frémont's Report did both. It made Frémont a household name as a dashing explorer, spy, and, eventually, a candidate for president. The text and its detailed maps also convinced thousands of people to move to Oregon and California [xi].

From the spring of 1843 to August 1844, Lt. Frémont led a second expedition that also departed from St. Louis. Its goal it was "'to connect the reconnaissance of 1842 with the surveys of Commander Wilkes on the coast of the Pacific ocean, so as to give a connected survey of the interior of our continent'" (quoted in Hyde, xii). After running into Kit Carson and rehiring him, the explorers surveyed the front range of the Rocky Mountains in Colorado, moving north to South Pass, and crossing into California by early spring. On the way back, they crossed the Mohave Desert, the Great Basin, and the Rockies, and then took the Arkansas River to get back to St. Louis. Once again, John and Jessie collaborated on the expedition's report and because it "combined adventure story, science, and politics with even more skill" than its predecessor, it was also a great success.[118]

Frémont's third expedition occurred in 1845, as the U.S. government was preparing for war against Mexico. Prior to Mexican independence in 1824, Spain had ceded Eastern Florida to the United States through the 1819 Adams-Onis Treaty. Following Mexican independence, Mexico had claimed California, up to the Oregon border, as well as Texas. But in 1836, an independent Republic of Texas was born,[119] lasting only the few years until its incorporation into the Union in 1845. A year earlier, James K. Polk (1795–1849), a Southern Democrat, had been elected on a platform of territorial expansion into Oregon and Texas either by peaceful means, though purchase, or by military force.[120] Following

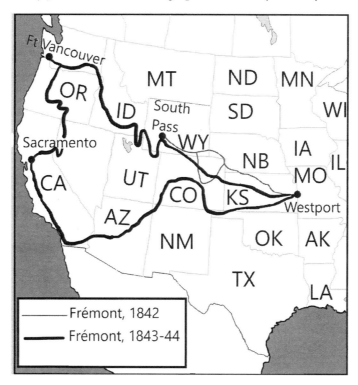

Map of John C. Frémont's Explorations (1842–1844). Based on a map created by Daniel Watkins (Map of Explorations 2013, Georgia Historical Society).

U.S. provocation, the Mexicans attacked, and the United States declared war. Although California was part of Mexico at the time, Anglo settlers had started move in. The arrival of Frémont's party in California coincided with a rebellion of settlers against the Mexican authorities, a revolt known as the Bear Revolt. Perhaps at the instigation of the authorities in Washington, Frémont's men joined the rebels to form the Bear Flag Rebellion that led to the short-lived Republic of California. Around that time, Frémont purchased a huge tract of land in California (Richards, 43–47).

When U.S. forces arrived, however, Frémont was arrested and sent to Washington to be court-martialed, even though "[i]n the eyes of many, [he] was a mistreated hero" (45). Senator Benton, who wished to see St. Louis and San Francisco joined by railroad, urged his son-in-law to resume his work once President Polk pardoned him. Frémont's fourth expedition took place in 1848–1849 but turned into a disaster as the route he chose proved impractical and the journey costly in human lives. He then decided to build a ranch on his California property and to move his family there. His luck was about to turn. Gold was found on his property of Las Mariposas, making him soon a wealthy man. Frémont's political career was about to begin.

In the history of the United States, the antebellum period is characterized by a new focus on the nation itself, a re-centering exemplified by the loosening of ties with other nations. It is the case for France during the Jeffersonian years with the end of the Quasi-War and the Louisiana Purchase and for Great Britain after the War of 1812. It is also the case for Spain, with the retrocession of Florida, and for Mexico, with the incorporation of Texas into the Union in 1845, and the cession of the vast territory of California in 1850. All these events and conflicts had at their core a desire for Western expansion towards the Pacific, a belief that Americans were meant to occupy the land from coast to coast, a creed articulated in an expression coined in 1845: "Manifest Destiny."

We saw that as American pioneers and settlers moved West, they met French people everywhere, that "[v]irtually every account written in English of traveling, trading, pioneering, hunting, settling, or surveying on the early nineteenth century frontier is saturated by men with French names" (Watts, 95). These French people had already settled the land and more often than not inter-married with members of the First Nations. During this period, however, the traces of French North America began to fade, as American settlers moved further and further west and new states emerged, Ohio in 1803, Louisiana in 1812, Indiana in 1816, Mississippi in 1817, Illinois in 1818, Missouri in 1821, Arkansas in 1836, and Texas in 1845. The new territories of Iowa (1846), Wisconsin (1848), California (1850), and Oregon (1859) would soon provide enough land for many other states. Still, "[l]ong after France divested itself of its North American colonies, evidence of this [New France's] rich history saturated the young U.S.," as we will see in the next chapter (Hodson and Rushforth, 20). At the same time, the struggles over the nature of those states as slave or free states exacerbated tensions between North and South.

5. Tips for Further Investigations

Interesting People to Look Up

Gilbert Antoine de St. Maxent (1724–1794)
Jean-Baptiste Pointe du Sable (1750–1818)
Simon Favre (1760–1813)

Don Carlos de Hault de Lassus (1767–1842)
Éleuthère Iréné Dupont de Nemours (1771–1834)
Jacques La Ramée (1784–1821)
John James Audubon (1785–1851)
Pierre Chouteau (1789–1865)
François Chouteau (1797–1838)
Firmin René Desloge (1803–1856)
Joe Rolette (1820–1871)

Related Primary Texts

Chardon, F.A. *Chardon's Journal at Fort Clark,* 3–320.
Frémont, John C. *Frémont' First Impressions. The Original Report of His Exploring Expeditions of 1842–1844.*
Lewis, Meriwether, and William Clark. *Journals of the Lewis and Clark Expeditions.*
Pike, Zebulon. *Journal of a voyage to the source of the Mississippi in the Years 1805 and 1806.*

Related Film and Novels

Houssaye, Sidonie de la. *Les Quarteronnes de la Nouvelle-Orléans.*
Into the West (2005), TV miniseries produced by Steven Spielberg.
The Revenant (2015), a film directed by Iñárritu, Alejandro G.
Simiot, Philippe, *Carbec L'Américain.* (The novel takes place in the New Orleans and on the Mississippi River between 1827 and 1845).

CHAPTER IX

French Idealists, Gold Seekers, and Soldiers in the Young United States

New visitors and immigrants from France continued to arrive in the United States over the course of 19th century, a voyage that required few administrative steps if you could afford passage. The French authorities did require that candidates to exile establish a passport prior to leaving the country but the French people were used to it since they needed identification papers to travel within their own country. Once in the United States, they marveled at the liberty afforded U.S. citizens: they needed no ID to move around, there was no surveillance system similar to the one they had known in France, or any kind of restrictions placed on the people's movements, except if you were a person of color.[1]

Apart from a few celebrity visitors like the Marquis de Lafayette and Alexis de Tocqueville, the increasingly large number of Frenchmen who came to the United States intended to stay. One may distinguish between three types of French immigration to the United States prior to the Civil War. In the first group, we find, once again, refugees fleeing France for political reasons, in other words the usual flow of political exiles who arrived after every change of regime,[2] the people Madeleine Bourset described as forming "the emigration of exclusion." After Napoleon I lost the battle of Waterloo in 1815, the allied powers restored the monarchy in France. Two brothers of the guillotined king Louis XVI succeeded each other on the throne between 1814 and 1830. Although nominally a constitutional monarchy, the regime became more and more authoritarian with time, particularly under Charles X's rule. In 1830, a revolution toppled him and brought another king to power, Louis-Philippe I, who had resided in the United States in the early days of the American Republic. In 1848, following an economic and a financial crisis, his "July Monarchy" was replaced by a second republic that lasted until 1851, at which time President Louis Napoléon Bonaparte decided to follow in his uncle's steps and to crown himself Emperor (1852).[3]

In the second group of French people who came to stay were immigrants attracted by the vast American expanses for idealistic reasons. "[D]uring the entire nineteenth century and up to first World War, the United States became Utopia builders' favorite playground" (Cordillot, *Utopistes*, 21), attracting as many "100,000 men, women and children," spread out in hundreds of colonies, most of them intent on rebuilding society from scratch. There were Moravian communities in Wisconsin, and in Iowa alone, a Swedenborgian and an Amana community as well as a Phalanx. Although not all Utopian communities[4] created in Antebellum America were French, many had "either had several members born in France or they were inspired by French ideologies" (Prévos, 230).

162

Frenchmen seeking economic opportunity formed the third group. Between 1820 and 1828, French immigrants only numbered between 300 and 500 each year, but their numbers increased to several thousand a year in the 1830s, before reaching over 10,000 in 1846 and over 20,000 in 1847 during the Gold Rush, the topic of the third section.[5] According to Cordillot, "between 1851 and 1860, the number of Frenchmen entering the United States was officially 76,357, that is as many as during the preceding decade, when 77,262 had arrived" (142). It is worth noting that the number of French candidates to exile was high despite Napoleon III's[6] efforts to crack down on emigration.

The last section is devoted to several Franco-Americans who played a significant role in the conflict over slavery that led to the Civil War. As Leonard Richards has showed, the discovery of gold in California exacerbated the struggle between advocates and opponents of slavery and these two issues, in turn, played a determining role in shaping the political career of John C. Frémont both in California and during his bid for the U.S. presidency.[7] But there were also Franco-Americans, particularly in the deep South, who believed that in the absence of a viable labor market, slavery remained a necessity. In 1860, on the eve of the Civil War, when 47 percent of the Louisiana population was enslaved, most French planters were determined advocates of the perpetuation of slavery. In that context, the case of a recent immigrant from France, Pierre Soulé, is interesting to consider.

1. French Political Refugees in Antebellum America

The United States welcomed French political refugees at virtually each change of regime and, as mentioned above, there were many of them over the course of the 19th century.[8] Napoleon's 1799 coup, for instance, was protested by a group of Breton noblemen that included Joseph Picot de Limoëlan (1768–1826). Limoëlan, who had fought in the counter-revolutionary armies in Western France, plotted with several co-conspirators to murder Bonaparte on Christmas Eve 1800, using *a machine infernale*, in other words, a bomb. The assassination attempt, known as the *Attentat de la rue Sainte Nicaise*, failed because the bomb went off after Bonaparte's carriage had already gone by. But it killed at least nine people and injured dozens of others. A few conspirators were caught, put on trial, and sentenced to death, but Limoëlan managed to escape and to hide for several years. In 1805, he was able to travel to the United States where he earned a living as a portrait painter. He then entered a seminary and in 1812, became a priest known as Father Clorivière. He died in 1826 and is buried in the crypt below the chapel of the Visitation Monastery in Georgetown (Kelly). Another French immigrant who arrived in the United States in 1803 and made a name for himself was Charles-Honoré Lannuier (1779–1819), a cabinet maker by trade whose Empire-style furniture can now be seen at the Metropolitan Museum of Art.[9]

The next change of regime, from Consulate to Empire, occurred in 1804 when Bonaparte crowned himself Emperor, as he sought not only to bridge political divisions, establish order and the rule of law in France, but also to fit among crowned rulers on the European stage. Key to his political vision were the adoption and implementation of the Civil Code (Napoleonic Code, 1804) and of the Penal Code (1810).[10] The Civil Code reaffirmed the principles of liberty, individual liberties and rights (including divorce), equality before the law; and the separation of Church and State. It also included steps backward: an absence of gender equality, with the Civil Code treating the father as head of the family, a return to primogeniture, that is the privileging of the first-born son in matters of inheritance, and, as we saw already, the reinstatement of slavery in the Caribbean colonies. The Civil Code adopted in 1825 in Louisiana was based on the same principles as the Napoleonic Civil Code.

Within France, Napoleon I created an efficient administrative structure that remained in place for nearly two centuries. His regime was a meritocracy that encouraged social mobility, with emphasis placed on equality of chances and achievements rather than social origin or wealth. Numerous rewards were available for outstanding service to the state, many non-hereditary titles (of prince, duke, etc.), as well as medals, like the Legion of Honor that was created in 1802. With regard to domestic policies, Napoleon's goal was to prevent social unrest and revolutionary chaos. To that effect, he put in place a police state that had individuals under constant police surveillance; he instituted censorship of the press and theaters (as a gathering place, they could lead to riots).[11] He forbade labor unions and strikes. Workers who disobeyed these laws were blacklisted. Another drawback of the First Empire is that France was at war with the rest of Europe during most of Napoleon's reign.[12] Historians have characterized these wars differently based on their national angle, as wars of liberation meant to export the French Revolution to Europe, in French view; as wars of conquest, meant to impose French hegemony all over Europe, in British view. If until 1814, Napoleon was almost always victorious on land, he never managed to beat the UK at sea.[13]

Two French generals who had fought alongside Napoleon earlier on, Moreau and Humbert, later disapproved of him and ended up in the United States. The first one, General Jean Victor Moreau (1763–1813), had assisted Napoleon Bonaparte when he toppled the Directory government in 1799. But in 1805, his public stand against the creation of the First Empire earned him the Emperor's ire and he was sentenced to exile. Moreau arrived in New York City with his wife, traveled around the United States, and settled in Morrisville, Pennsylvania. For several years, French exiles gathered at his home, and foreign dignitaries courted him, eager to enroll him in efforts to overthrow Napoleon. When the War of 1812 broke out, President Madison offered him an officer commission but he declined after hearing of Napoleon's debacle in Russia. Instead, he returned to Europe to fight against Napoleon.[14] He was critically injured at the battle of Dresden in 1813 and died shortly thereafter.[15]

While in the United States, Moreau befriended another French exile, Baron Jean Guillaume Hyde de Neuville (1776–1857), who came from quite a different social and political background as him.[16] Neuville, whose aristocratic British family had accompanied the Stuarts in their French exile in 1745, was a lawyer, physician, and a devoted Royalist who had served as a spy for the exiled French princes in the early phase of the French Revolution. At the start of the Consulate, he tried in vain to convince Napoleon to restore the Bourbon monarchy and then worked as a physician under an assumed identity in Lyons. Initially viewed as a suspect in the 1800 attempt on Napoleon's life, he was allowed to go free. In 1806, he struck a bargain with the Emperor: he accepted to go to the United States in exile in exchange for recovering his confiscated estates. He settled in New Brunswick, New Jersey, a mere thirty miles away from Moreau's residence. "Both Hyde and Moreau taught in the *Ecole Economique* established for the children of 'French emigrants and other strangers,'" a "refugee school [that] was quite avant-garde, coeducational and ecumenical" (Childs, "A Special Migration," 166). Later, Hyde de Neuville helped General Moreau obtain service in the Coalition's army in 1813 through his contacts.[17] During the Bourbon Restoration, he served as French ambassador to the United States,[18] then as Deputy and Minister of the Navy. He remained interested in the issue of Franco-American trade relations all his life and published a book on that topic in 1837.[19]

The second disgruntled general of the *Grande Armée* was Jean Joseph Humbert (1767–1823).[20] He too had fought against the *Chouans* rebels in Western France and in the famous Army of the Rhine alongside Napoleon. He also participated in the campaign against St. Domingue under the command of Bonaparte's brother-in-law, General Leclerc, who lost his life during the campaign. A true believer in the republican regime, Humbert belonged to the group of disillusioned officers who felt that Napoleon's imperial mania was a betrayal of the revolution's ideals. Dismissed from the army in 1803, he immigrated to Louisiana in 1810 and saw service as a private soldier in the War of 1812. After the war, he remained in the United States, working as a schoolteacher until his death in 1823. Also worth mentioning is Maximilien Godefroi, an architect forced to flee France during the Napoleonic era who settled in Baltimore where he designed St. Mary's chapel, "the first Gothic building in the United States" (Childs, "A Special Migration," 161).

Exiles who rejected Napoleon's regime were far fewer than those who came to the United States after the Empire fell.[21] In the Spring of 1814, after the Prussians and Russians invaded France, Napoleon abdicated. But he came back to power for three months in 1815 and was only removed from office for good after the Battle of Waterloo in June 1815. Rumor has it that prior to his exile to the island of St. Helena, Napoleon had contemplated settling in America.[22] Whether he decided against it or never really had that option is unclear but many of his faithful officers did come to the United States where they found moral support and sympathy. Blaufarb reports that numerous manifestations in favor of Napoleon took place in New Orleans, some of them violent, and that in 1815, in a climate of fear and suspicion, Governor William C. Claiborne noticed that a group of Bonapartist officers were meeting at the *Café des exilés* in New Orleans (*Bonapartists*, 36).

As the Restoration authorities banned the Bonaparte family from France in 1815, several of its members immigrated to United States. Napoléon I's older brother Joseph Bonaparte (1768–1844), who, for a few years, had been King of Naples and Sicily and King of Spain and the Indies, traveled to New York City in 1817 under an assumed name, "Count of Survilliers." He lived in Philadelphia for a while, before settling at Breeze Point, a mansion overlooking the Delaware River that he had built in Bordentown, New Jersey.[23] His wife, Julie Clary, did not come with him, settling instead with their daughters first in Frankfurt, Germany, then in Florence, Italy. Joseph therefore took a mistress, Annette Savage, who gave him two American daughters.

During the nearly two decades Joseph Bonaparte lived in the United States, Point Breeze served not only as a refuge for many French exiles but also as a salon for prominent Americans such as Henry Clay, Daniel Webster, and John Quincy Adams. As the Mexican War of Independence (1808–1821) came to a close, Bonaparte was reportedly offered the title of "Emperor of Mexico" in 1820 but declined (Stroud, 40–44).[24] His nephew, Achille Murat (1801–1847), the son of Napoleon's sister Caroline and Admiral Joachim Murat, Marshal of France and King of Naples, joined him in 1821 (Selin). Prince Murat had grown up in Austrian exile with his mother and siblings following his father's execution in 1815. After obtaining permission to immigrate, he purchased land and slaves in Florida, renounced his titles, and took U.S. citizenship. Fluent in French, English, and

Italian, he married Catherine Willis Gray, a great-grand-niece of George Washington, in 1826 and eventually became a lawyer, first in Tallahassee, and then after his return from a four year stay in Europe in the early 1830s, in New Orleans. Lafayette visited him during his 1824–25 U.S. tour, and he became friends with Ralph Waldo Emerson. After losing part of his fortune in 1837, he returned to Florida where he died in 1847.[25]

Blaufarb writes that "[a]lthough no exact figures are available, contemporary estimates suggest that in the three years following Waterloo as many as thirty thousand French came to the United States," including "five thousand Alsatians" alone, most of them economic migrants (*Bonapartists*, 20):

> So popular was the city [of New Orleans] as a destination among French immigrants that at least fifteen hundred out of a total population of twenty-seven thousand in 1820 were actual French citizens fresh from Europe. Thus, added to the native francophone Creole population and the ten to twelve thousand Domingan refugees who arrived in 1809, French speakers in the 1810s constituted at least 75 percent of the city's population [Blaufarb, *Bonapartists*, 21].

The largest group of French refugees who came to the United States in the aftermath of Napoleon's defeat were army officers, "hundreds of Bonapartist faithful" (Blaufarb, "Notes," 104).[26] Some of them, like the generals Charles and Henri Lallemand, had been sentenced to death in absentia for helping Napoleon return to power in 1815.[27] General François Antoine "Charles" Lallemand (1774–1839) had played a key role in ensuring the success of Napoleon's escape from Elba in February 1815 and earned the Emperor's trust.[28] After Waterloo, the British did not allow him to share the Emperor's exile, as he wanted, but they did not turn him over to the French authorities either. Instead, he spent a few months as a prisoner in Malta, and then, following his escape in 1816, joined his brother Henri in Philadelphia. General Henri Dominique Lallemand (1777–1823) had distinguished himself on the battlefield, thus earning the title of Baron, and participated in a failed plot to secure an artillery depot. After Napoleon's second abdication, he had escaped to England and then to the United States.[29] Also sentenced to death by the Restoration authorities for their unwavering support of Napoleon, Generals Bertrand Clauzel (1772–1842) and Charles Lefebvre-Desnouettes (1773–1822) were able to escape and join the group of officer refugees in the United States. Another prominent member of the Napoleonic military establishment was Emmanuel de Grouchy (1766–1847), "the French Marshal whom Napoleon blamed for his defeat at Waterloo" (Selin, "Grouchy"), and who apparently wished for nothing else than to obtain a royal pardon and to go back to France (Blaufarb, *Bonapartists*, 93).[30] Not all exiles from the First Empire were officers, however.

As Blaufarb explains, "so-called *conventionnels*, former deputies of the National Convention who had voted for Louis XVI's death in January 1793," also found it wise to leave France during the Restoration and many found their way to the United States (Blaufard, "Notes," 104).[31] The most famous of them was Joseph Lakanal (1762–1845), a former professor of Rhetoric and Philosophy who had been instrumental in reorganizing the French national education system during the revolutionary era, had served as a member the Council of the Five Hundred during the Directory (1815–1830),[32] and returned to his professorial activities during the Empire. A founding member of the most prestigious French scientific institution, the *Institut de France*, Lakanal had met and corresponded with Jefferson and Madison.[33] In the United States, he first settled near the Swiss winemaking colony of Vevey, on the Ohio River, but soon joined fellow Frenchmen when they moved to Alabama. All these French refugees were welcomed in the United States:

"Wherever they went, the French exiles (at least the prominent ones) were greeted with warm admiration" (Blaufard, *Bonapartists*, 35). But less well-known members of the French contingent of Napoleonic refugees also fared well in the United States. Anthony [Antoine G.] Quervelle (1789–1856), for instance, who arrived in Philadelphia in 1817 and became a U.S. citizen in 1823, made a fortune as a cabinet maker.[34] Several of his American Empire style tables commissioned by President Andrew Jackson can be seen at the White House. Blaufarb argues that the American Francophilia characteristic of the second decade of the 19th century had more to do with Anglophobia following the War of 1812 than with admiration for the fallen emperor. Perhaps. But Congress's generosity towards these French immigrants would seem to indicate that that something else than Anglophobia was the cause of the American support of the French refugees.

On March 3, 1817, Congress divided the Mississippi Territory in two halves, the western portion becoming the state of Mississippi, and the eastern part the Alabama Territory.[35] An episode known as the "Alabama Fever," the opening of the Alabama territory in 1817, brought along the usual intense land speculation as well as an influx of settlers eager to grow cotton and reap the benefits associated with a crop that was in great demand in the early days of the industrial revolution:

> Land sales combined with the formalization of squatter claims swelled the settled portion of the Alabama lands. In 1810, the population of Alabama was estimated as being under 10,000; by 1820 that number had risen to more than 127,000 and by 1830 had topped 300,000. The population continued to increase, so that by 1860 it was just short of one million [Keith, "Alabama Fever"].

As great fortunes were created in the process, the southern states also gained in political clout within the Federal government.

Although disagreements, and even duels,[36] were common among the exiled French officers, most of them belonged to the French Emigrant Association, an organization that petitioned for and obtained a land grant from Congress through the same act that created the state of Mississippi on March 3, 1817.[37] The land in question was located in the Territory of Alabama, on grounds taken away from Native Americans. The area had started attracting settlers in 1814, at the conclusion of the Creek War.[38] Congress granted the group of French immigrants 144 sections of 640 acres each along the Tombigbee River to grow vine and olive, hence the name of the settlement, the Vine and Olive Colony.[39] A French contingent of around 200 people, including a few women,[40] left Philadelphia by ship and arrived in Mobile at the end of May 1817 and by mid–July at their destination, a place on the Tombigbee River named *Ecor Blanc* [White Cliff] by French explorers a century earlier.

Led by General Lefebvre-Desnouettes the colony located in Marengo county[41] included four townships: Demopolis (City of the people), which was actually off the grid and had to be abandoned; Linden, the county seat, named for Napoleon's victory at Hohenlinden; Aigleville (Eagle town), named after Napoleon's emblem; and Arcola, named after Napoleon's victory over the Coalition forces in 1796.[42] The settlers were mostly refugees who had come earlier on from Saint-Domingue, not the *grands blancs* who had bought plantations in Louisiana and Georgia, but *petits blancs,* craftsmen[43] and members of the liberal professions. Unfortunately, the soil and the climate turned out to be wrong for the cultivation of grapes and olives. In 1822, Congress allowed the French immigrants to keep their allotment even if they could not produce grapes or olives and some of them, like André Curcier and Frederick Ravesies, started growing cotton instead. However, most of the original settlers left the colony to go to Louisiana or to return to France.

A group of them had in fact sold their lots right away, and even forced some settlers to sell theirs against their will (Blaufarb, *Bonapartists*, 93–94). They needed cash to finance "an audacious plan to establish a fortified camp in the disputed Texas borderlands, a region claimed by both the United States and Spain," with an eye, perhaps, towards an invasion of Mexico (Blaufarb, *Bonapartists*, 86).[44] The history of the colony they created, the *Champ d'Asile* [Field of Azylum] has been told by many people and in many different ways: a few former settlers, like Louis L'Héritier, L. Hartmann, Jean-Baptiste Millard, and Just Girard, published accounts of their personal experience in Texas. General Charles Lallemand, the leader of the operation, told it mostly to a French audience in the melodramatic mode, as a celebration of persecuted innocence from which emerged "the romantic figure of the farming soldier who, like the Roman emperor Cincinnatus, left a glorious military career to embrace a rustic and peaceful life" (Terrien, 91). In the 1950s, Simone de la Souchère offered a mostly sympathetic account of the adventures of "Napoleon's soldiers in America," not only in Texas but also upon their return to New Orleans. Historian Rafe Blaufarb has sought to demystify the long accredited romantic vision of Bonapartist officers who decided to settle in the borderlands of Spain and the United States. More recently even, Yevan E. Terrien has offered a more positive and astute interpretation of the Texas colony as "a motley collection of nations" (89).

Champ d'Asile: settlers at work establishing their town [Champ d'Asile: travaux des colons pour l'établissement de leur ville]. Engraving by Pomel, 1818 (courtesy Bibliothèque nationale de France/Gallica).

What we know for sure about the colony is that Charles Lallemand's immediate support group included his brother General Henri Lallemand, General Antoine Rigau,[45] and the administrator George Nicolas Jeannet–Oudin, a nephew of George Danton, the revolutionary leader, who was in charge of administration and finance.[46] *Champ d'Asile* was located close to Galveston Island where pirates Jean and Pierre Lafitte were not only providing material support to the colony but also conducting an illegal traffic in slaves between 1817 and 1821.[47] The soldiers who had been recruited to settle at *Champ d'Asile* knew very little about the actual goals of the enterprise, but if Blaufarb is correct, neither did their leaders: was the purpose of the French colony in Texas to invade Mexico? Was it to support the Latin American Independence movement? Was it to free Napoleon from St. Helena so he could rule over a South American Empire? Or was it to create a peaceful bucolic colony of soldiers-farmers?

Blaufarb highlights General C. Lallemand's duplicity because the latter chose to paint a rosy picture of the *Champ d'Asile* for worldwide distribution although the settlement was anything but a success. Lallemand penned a proclamation, titled "Extract of a Letter from a French Settler," a document widely reproduced in the American press, Francophone and Anglophone, but also in the liberal newspapers of Restoration France (Blaufarb, *Bonapartists*, 106). Blaufard notes that Lallemand actually only spent little time in Texas, from March 10 to July 24, 1818, when, under pressure from the Spaniards, the colony was abandoned, and most settlers relocated to New Orleans. Furthermore, he claims, the settlement was an utter failure during its short existence; all it succeeded in doing was to fuel conspiratorial rumors and create diplomatic incidents as the French government, the Spanish Crown, and the U.S. authorities kept wondering what these French officers were up to. Moreover, he adds, the *Champ d'Asile* arose "suspicion and anger [...] from the perceived ingratitude of the French exiles" among the American public (*Bonapartists*, 106)—or should we say among that section of the American public that had felt very little sympathy for revolutionary France since the early days of the Republic.

Yervan Terrien does not dispute that the establishment of this French military camp in Texas pleased neither the United States nor Spain, or that the French officers' goals were difficult to fathom. But by examining "the words, deeds, and ideas of the colonists themselves" (90), he brings a welcome corrective to Blaufard's negative depiction of the *Champ d'Asile* Bonapartists as a band of ruthless opportunists who never achieved anything. For instance, much of the factionalism that sometimes erupted in violent struggles, he argues, can be attributed to the real difficulty the settlers had in obtaining supplies and most importantly food. Not only had prices shot through the roof in New Orleans, the colony's supply center, traders and pirates were also trying to profit from them: "In the heart of cities, in the middle of deserts, in Texas as on the banks of the Seine corrupt beings are found who speculate on the poverty of their fellow men for a bit of gold," Hartman and Millard wrote in the account of their experience at *Champ d'Asile* (quoted in Terrien, 94). Nonetheless, despite the constant hunger they felt, the veterans worked hard to create their settlement:

> Life at Champ d'Asile was, indeed, largely communal and cooperative. Divided into three cohorts for military purposes, the colonists labored on collective tasks for six hours a day, mostly to clear the land, build lodgings and erect fortifications. Along with the four forts, they build two guardrooms, a warehouse, and 14 log cabins, which housed the veterans with similar proximity to what they experienced in the military [Terrien, 93].[48]

Terrien's article also revisits Blaufarb's contention that Bonapartist endeavors in the borderlands easily blurred "[t]he lines between patriot and profiteer, liberator and enslaver" (*Bonapartists*, 67). By teasing out the various strands of principles and aspirations found among the veterans of Napoleon's *Grande Armée*, he is able to distinguish between divergent positions among the settlers on the issues of race and slavery and more concretely to identify different attitudes towards the African Americans and Native Americans the settlers encountered and dealt with. What all these veterans had in common, however, is just as important as what set them apart. Whether they were French or not,[49] they shared a pre-national sense of identity grounded in the principles of the Declaration of the Rights of Man and their echo in Napoleonic law. The Bonapartists of the borderlands were "neither ordinary emigrants nor proscribed individuals, but voluntary expatriates and 'citizens of the world'" (Terrien, 99). This cosmopolitanism, in turn, explains the appeal of their endeavor not only among "French Liberals and British Whigs favorable to an amnesty for Napoleon" but also among "Freemasons of both sides of the Atlantic, merchants favorable to Latin American revolutions, and Anglo-American abolitionists" (Terrien, 101). Thanks to them, the image of the immigrant to America changed in the French imagination: the cosmopolitan soldier fighting for worldwide enlightenment replaced that of the selfish counter-revolutionary nobleman.

To the extent that he shared their republican values, Pierre Soulé (1801–1870) fits that description as well, although he arrived in the United States a decade later than Napoleon's close followers. The son of a Napoleonic lieutenant general, Soulé was only 16 when his participation in a plot against the Bourbon monarchy in 1817 forced him to hide for a year. The young Jacobin then studied law in Paris and graduated in 1822 before returning to oppositional politics. As a member of the board of the liberal publication *Le Nain Jaune*, together with Alexandre Dumas, he published editorials on King Charles X's government that landed him in court. He avoided a one-year prison sentence by escaping to London and apparently found passage from England to Haiti, where he reportedly met with Haitian president Jean-Pierre Boyer. By 1826, he had settled in New Orleans where he made social connections very fast, even meeting President Andrew Jackson at this residence, L'Hermitage, in 1827. Soulé's social trajectory took a decisive turn upward in 1828 when he opened a law practice and married Armandtine Mercier, a "belle of the Vieux Carré" (Green and Kirkwood, 220).[50] We will return to his role as a Southern Democrat Senator in section 4.

A few years earlier, in 1824–1825, the United States had feted the return of the 67-year-old Marquis de Lafayette to its shores.[51] Lafayette's farewell tour in celebration of the first half century of the American Republic lasted over a year, covered the 24 U.S. states, and was paved with honors such as town re-naming, monument dedications, and the institution of "Lafayette Day."[52] Lafayette attended many commemorative events in the Northeast before heading south to visit his old friend Thomas Jefferson at Monticello. He was welcomed at the White House by President James Monroe, addressed Congress and attended a banquet Congress hosted in his honor. In the spring, he travelled to the Carolinas, Georgia, Alabama, first to Demopolis, where he met with members of the Olive and Vine Colony, and Mobile. He then crossed the Mississippi to Louisiana, visiting New Orleans, then taking the steamer to Baton Rouge, Natchez, St. Louis, and Kaskaskia. His journey then took him to Tennessee (Nashville), Kentucky (Louisville, Frankfort, and Lexington), Ohio (Cincinnati and Gallipolis) and Pennsylvania (Washington), before returning to the Northeast.

If Lafayette's tour was geared towards the past, towards the early days of the American Republic, several Frenchmen who visited the United States in the first half of the 19th century were more interested the present, in the modernity of the country. Michel Chevalier (1806–1879) studied the transportation system and banking during his visit in 1834 and 1835. A Saint-Simonian, Chevalier wrote several books on the insights he gained from his trip, among them the Americans' "love of work" and judicious use of time.[53] Alexis de Tocqueville (1805–1859) and Gustave de Beaumont (1802–1866) came to the United States to examine the American prison system. At a time when public opinion in France was moved by Victor Hugo's indictment of the French penal system in *The Last Day of a Condemned Man* (1829) and *Claude Gueux* (1834), the July Monarchy government sent Tocqueville and Beaumont, both lawyers by profession, to study the American prison system with a view towards making improvements in France.[54] During the nine months the young aristocrats from Normandy spent in the United States, they visited prisons in a dozen states both in the north and in the south. When they returned to France, they jointly published their report, *Système pénitentiaire aux États-Unis, et de son application en France* [*On the Penitentiary System in the United States and its Application to France*] in 1833.

But more importantly, Tocqueville and Beaumont made extensive observations about life in the United States in the 1830s. A compendium of Tocqueville's insights on the American economy, society, and political life, *Democracy in America* appeared in 1835 (volume I) and 1840 (volume II). In it, Tocqueville praised the democratic, decentralized system of government, the pragmatism of the American people, and a civil society happily balancing freedom and equality, as evidenced in the associative spirit of the citizens (Åhr, "Tocqueville"). But he also viewed lack of education, in particular among elected officials, the tyranny of the majority (or public opinion), and slavery as major problems.[55] Although the fame *Democracy in America* brought to his friend eclipsed his own by far, Beaumont also published the fruit of his reflections on American society in the form of a novel critical of American slavery, *Jacksonian America: Marie or Slavery in the United States* (1835).

2. Utopian Communities

During much of his American journey, Lafayette was accompanied by Frances Wright, a wealthy friend of his, nearly four decades younger than him, who would become a U.S. citizen in 1825. A feminist freethinker and abolitionist, Wright also had a great interest in the social experiments that were being conducted on American soil at the time.[56] In early spring 1825, for instance, she visited *Harmonie*, the utopian community created by the German religious refugee George Rapp in Pennsylvania. In France, many people were also growing disaffected with their country's failure to live up to the French Revolution's democratic promise. As disenchantment grew over labor's exploitation and the capitalist system during the industrial revolution, workers turned to Utopian movements seeking to achieve economic and political equality. With its vast empty expanses, an absence of rigid class barriers that seemed to "move American society as a whole towards the ideal of universal fraternity and justice" (Cordillot, 22), the United States seemed for many people to be the ideal place for implementing the ideas of proto-communist thinkers like Charles Fourier (1772–1837)[57] and Etienne Cabet (1788–1856).[58]

As a philosopher, Charles Fourier devised a theory—the theory of four movements—that sought to return the world to its initial, God-given harmony. What that meant in practice was to move away from the pre-existing political, economic, and social forms of organization. A critic of a capitalist system based on waged labor, Fourier sought to replace it with a network of shareholder associations. Social harmony, Fourier thought, could be achieved once individuals were given a chance to discover their own talents and to develop them to the fullest because people who love what they do are not only happy but also more productive. As his theory of passional attraction (*attraction passionnelle*) did not only apply to the realm of professional occupations but also to human and social relations, his critique of patriarchy and marriage made him one of the first feminist thinkers. Fourier's plan was to start experimenting on a small scale, by creating communities, called "phalanxes," that would then join together and form a perfect society all over the world. The first phalanx was created near Versailles in France in 1833, while Fourier was still alive, but it failed after a few months for lack of funding (Cordillot, 98).

Two men, one American, one French, played a crucial role in implementing Fourier's ideas in the United States, Albert Brisbane (1809–1890) and Victor Considérant (1808–1893). Brisbane, who had met Fourier (and Considérant) in Paris in 1832, became his most zealous American follower, contributing to the establishment of nearly forty of these communities.[59] Thanks to a vigorous media campaign orchestrated by Brisbane and journalist Horace Greeley, the American public familiarized itself with Fourier's ideas.[60] As a result, phalanxes appeared in a dozen states from the early 1840s onward, from the East Coast (Maine, Massachusetts, New York) to the Mid-west (Ohio, Illinois, Indiana, Kansas, Michigan, Wisconsin).[61] Most of them lasted only a few years, but the North American Phalanx of New Colts, New Jersey, beat the odds and lasted 15 years (1841–56). The better-known *Phalanstères* are the Brook Farm Institute of Agriculture and Education in Massachusetts (1841–1847); the Sodus Bay Phalanx (1844–46); and the Wisconsin Phalanx (1844–50). Ohio alone had five *phalanstères*. According to Cordillot, material difficulties were not the only cause of their disappearance in the late 1840s and early 1850s. Rather, at a time when the conflict between north and south was about to explode over the issue of slavery, Fourier's contention that wage labor was a form of slave labor seemed simply out of touch with the realities of American society (102).

Considérant, who had visited Brisbane and several phalanxes in 1852, chose a place near Dallas in Northern Texas as the most suitable place to establish a Fourierist association. Aware of the difficulties many of the settlements faced in their initial phase, Considérant decided to outsource the development of the *Réunion* phalanx to a settlement agency, whose job it was to prepare the land and the buildings that would house the immigrants. Unfortunately, other difficulties surfaced, and in particular a xenophobic Know Nothing majority in the Texas legislature that was openly hostile to immigrants and particularly immigrants suspected of abolitionist preferences (Cordillot, 107). By the time the French immigrants arrived, the settlement was not ready and infighting among the 128 settlers did the rest. Considérant left the *Réunion* phalanx to live in San Antonio from 1856 to 1869. By 1858, all that was left of the phalanx was a coop store.[62]

Another important French utopist thinker was Etienne Cabet, an advocate of workers cooperatives as an alternative to capitalism.[63] Like Fourier, Cabet envisioned social reform as a bottom-up movement. His Icarian community was a small-scale democratic society that elected officers to manage its various operations, farming, of course, but also industry (flour mills), and a multi-lingual press that served to recruit new members. Like in a sect, members had to forfeit their personal property, unless they just visited. Marriage was mandatory but divorce was allowed. Children were educated together, not with their parents. Apart from Icarian beliefs, there was no religious doctrine or church, so Sunday was a free day devoted to reading or enjoying life, or to group activities such as music and theater.

The first Icarian community appeared in Texas, in the Fort Worth–Dallas area.[64] Cabet had purchased land from the Peters Company in London, in a deal that was far from favorable to the 70 French immigrants who arrived in New Orleans in February 1848. Their timing was off, since the Republic had been proclaimed for the second in France a few days earlier, thus voiding one of their main reasons to immigrate.[65] They were also under considerable time pressure to get to their land, establish their settlement, and start planting, as cultivation of the land prior to July 1, 1848, was a condition of the sale (Cordillot, 35). Despite infighting, the hardships of the journey, and other terrible challenges (malaria, cholera, and malnutrition), the surviving members of the settler group were able to achieve their goal and claim their land. But they were just too exhausted to go on. Instead, they slowly walked back to Shreveport, and then to New Orleans. In sum, "Cabet's followers' first attempt to create the ideal community ended in total chaos" (Cordillot, 42).

In the first months of the Second Republic, Cabet himself lost interest in his immigration pet project as he was busy running for election in Paris. After the bloody repression of the workers' movement in late June 1848, however, new groups of Icarians departed for the United States. According to Cordillot, almost 500 hundred people had already left when Cabet himself decided to immigrate in December 1848. In New Orleans, the Icarians learned that the Mormon settlement in Nauvoo, Illinois, was unoccupied since 1846, and they made their way to Illinois to create the first permanent Icarian Community there.[66] As opposed to the Texas colony that survived less than a year, the Illinois community initially prospered, growing to 500 members by 1855.[67] But as Cabet became power-hungry, dissent brewed and the community split in two. In 1856, Cabet's die-hard supporters followed him to St. Louis where he died shortly after their arrival. It took them two years to restart an Icarian community in Cheltenham, Missouri. After Cabet left for Missouri with almost half of the colonists, the dissidents had a hard time keeping the Illinois community going. By 1860, they had disbanded, with some of the members joining the Iowa Icarians and some remaining, like the families that created the first winery in Illinois, Baxter's Vineyards and Winery.

In 1852, another group of Icarians had established a community in the eastern part of the state of Iowa, close to Queen City, a village also located in Adams County. After a difficult start, this colony was actually relatively successful at raising cattle and selling wool. It obtained a charter of incorporation from the State of Iowa in 1860 and managed to pay off its debts and make a profit by supplying the U.S. army with food during the Civil War (Prévos, 242–245). Young Icarians also contributed to the war effort by enlisting in the Union army. Journalist Charles Nordhoff, who visited the Iowa colony in 1874, reported that the French-speaking community boasted a total of 65 members, most of them French, but not all. He described the village as composed of a main hall, a large two-story building where all members shared meals and children went to school, that was surrounded by a dozen log cabins, one per family. The community published two French newspapers, *La Jeune Icarie*, and *Le Communiste libertaire*. However, the Iowa colony also experienced a split along age lines that was followed by both the disbanding of the "old Icarians" by 1878 and the removal of 8 families of "young Icarians" to a different part of the property. The Iowa colony lasted nearly half a century before melting into the general population by 1898 (Prévos, 247–248).

Another group of French people established an Icarian community in California. Earlier in his life, Jules Leroux (1805–1883) had participated in the French phalanx established by his brother Pierre Leroux (1797–1871) in Boussac, France, in the 1840s. Pierre Leroux was a humanitarian philosopher and a close friend of writer George Sand who funded the phalanx's printing operation and supported its various endeavors, such as the publishing of a newspaper and volumes of workers' poetry. A sincere republican, Jules left France for England following the proclamation of the Second Empire, and then took his family to the United States in 1866. He settled in Kansas, where he founded the colony of New Humanity. A printer by profession, Jules Leroux published a newspaper called "*L'Etoile du Kansas, organe de la République française et universelle*" (*The Kansas Star, publication of the French and Universal Republic*) from 1873 to 1880 before moving with his family to California where he founded the Icarian-Speranza Utopian community north of San Francisco in 1881. The colony attracted around 55 members but lasted only five years. For two years, Leroux published another paper, *L'Etoile des pauvres et des souffrants* [*The Star of the Poor and the Suffering*] but he died in 1883, and with him the Icarian movement in the United States (Prévos, 252–253).

3. The French and the Gold Rush

The discovery of gold in California took place in January 1848 and despite efforts to keep it secret, gold seekers started to arrive by late spring of that year (Rohrbough, 1–2). As news of the discovery spread, it attracted people from all over the world, including France, a country hit by an agricultural and an economic crisis in 1845–1846. The French press reported on the California discovery in October 1848 at the same time as it announced the failure of Cabet's Icarian community in Texas. A few weeks later, confirmation by the U.S. president that the gold discovery was not a hoax still failed to convince everyone. Skeptics thought that it was fake news, a ploy on the part of the Americans to "populate the recently acquired territory of California" (Rohrbough, 18).[68] In the American press, as well as the Francophone *Courrier des Etats-Unis*, which was published in New York, the California gold was front page news.[69] According to journalists, the entire San Francisco population was leaving town in search of gold and everyone wanted to be wealthy real fast.

As *la ruée vers l'or* (the Gold Rush) was attracting people by the thousands, in particular from mid–1848 to mid–1849, a few French people of means saw it as an opportunity, not necessarily to mine gold, but to trade with the miners (Rohrbough, 37–38). The French press, however, also warned about the dangers that awaited potential immigrants in California, a society with a high rate of criminality, full of gamblers, drunks, and murderers. Commenting on the diverging American and French experience of the Gold Rush, Rohrbough writes:

> French images of the miners showed shadowy skeletons with sacks of gold in search of something to eat. For the Americans, these stories told of immense wealth; for the French, they suggested an absence of the basic necessities [49].

Once the first individuals wealthy enough to make their way to America on their own had left France, it was the turn of California Companies to emerge and transport French citizens in larger numbers. During the first half of 1849 alone, 14 such companies were created, with "collective share offerings total[ing] some 28 million francs" (Rohrbough, 56) and by 1850, 83 had come into existence (58). The modern Argonauts[70] had to pay not only the equivalent of a worker's yearly income for passage but also a membership fee to join a company. The New York Mining Company, for instance, charged $350, promising in exchange "provisions for two years, arms, munitions, a library of three thousand volumes, musical instruments, and, finally, everything necessary for the mining operations" (Rohrbough, 55).[71]

At a time when steam was quickly replacing sail on ships, French Forty Niners had two options to reach California, through Panama and via Cape Horn. Most sailed in a small group, like the 12 young men from the village of Bruley in Lorraine examined by Rohrbough, who chose the longest route around Cape Horn, a tedious journey that could last up to 6 months (73–74). Mme de Saint-Amant, whose husband expected to become the French Consul in California, traveled ahead of her husband via the Panama route and reported on her trip in letters that were published in the press (Rohrbough, 100–102). The Americans she encountered, she wrote, although "respectful" of women, were "armed to the teeth like brigands in melodramas" and had "an air of marching off to war" (Quoted in Rohrbough, 197). Upon arriving in San Francisco, most French Forty Niners were disappointed to find out that they were not alone: "We saw, in a country that we supposed to be almost deserted, 500 to 600 ships, 3,000 to 4,000 houses" (Quoted in Rohrbough, 102). In addition, the support promised by the Companies failed to materialize,[72] leading to further disappointments (Rohrbough, 107–109).

Equipped with a compass and a Spanish dictionary, aspiring miners made their way to gold fields on foot, except for those who could afford a boat to Sacramento. Along the way they found out that everything offered for sale (food, clothes, tools) was very expensive. French Consul Patrick Dillon reported in his dispatches to the French ministry that the French established camps "around the Saint Joachim River and the streams that flow into it" (124) in an area where French Canadians were already mining when the French arrived, most of them between fall 1849 and fall 1850 (177). In all, "10,000 Frenchmen were working in the gold fields by June 1850" (quoted in Rohrbough, 177). As most of them observed, wages were much higher than in France but so was the cost of living (178).

In the placers, miners "soon came to recognize that mining for gold in California was not a free-for-all; rather, it was an exercise of hard work conducted according to carefully established rules" (182), such as "staking and holding a claim" (113). French visitors to the camps deplored the miners' low standard of living,[73] especially since the hard work seldom paid off, or at least failed to meet their initial fabulous expectations.[74] On the contrary, as competition intensified with the influx of miners from all over the world, their situation worsened when Americans started to display anti-foreigner feelings. Although Mexicans, the enemy in a recent war, and Hispanics in general, were their primary target,[75] American xenophobia did not spare the French, especially when "they had good claims" (Rohrbough, 200). About the conflicts between American and French miners in the goldfields, Rohrbough writes:

> The French were among the first group of foreign miners in the northern mines, where they established some of the most productive camps. Here as elsewhere, they were intensely loyal to their own mining communities. French language was a defining element here, so the French

in the placers joined in communities of French-language speakers. They were uninterested in learning English and generally indifferent to their neighbors, except in common hostility toward Indian peoples. This French strength was also their vulnerability. For their clannishness marked them as a people apart, alien sojourners who had come to harvest wealth and then immediately return home with their gold. A degree of friction between the Americans and the French was always a characteristic of the early camps, where they lived in proximity to one another. With the growing competition over sites and claims, it was inevitable that this friction would intensify [203–204].

Conflicts intensified after the California Legislature approved a twenty dollar a month tax on all foreign, i.e., non–English speaking, workers on April 13, 1850 (206). In most cases, however, these conflicts were promptly resolved thanks to the intervention of officials who pointed out that violence was bad for business. The exception was the blow out between Americans and French that took place in April 1851 at Mokelumne Hill (212).

At about the same time, the French government was taking charge of an "official emigration [that] moved some 3,300 French citizens to California" (Rohrbough, 3). The first prong of this endeavor consisted in offering one-way tickets to California to members of the *Gardes mobiles* in an effort to get rid of undesirable elements, mostly "insurgents from the rebellious *faubourgs* of Paris" (Rohrbough, 217).[76] The second was the Lottery of the Golden Ingots, a national drawing for tickets to California that provided free passage from Le Havre to San Francisco to 17 ships full of French nationals (Rohrbough, 220). Most of these people were to remain in California for good (242). The educated among them established themselves as professionals, bankers, doctors and lawyers for instance, and others left their mark in the area of entertainment, opening restaurants, theaters, and brothels. Commerce was another source of attraction to California for the French, especially the city of San Francisco, "where the real drama of the search for riches was played out" (Rohrbough, 3–4).[77] They exported and sold French products that were in great demand, and in particular "wines, brandy, and champagne" (Rohrbough, 179) and played an important role in the development of San Francisco and Los Angeles.[78] Rohrbough summarizes the "long echo" of the French presence in the following way:

> The French came to California in surprisingly large numbers. They came to the goldfields; they settled in camps, in towns, and in the city of San Francisco. They were a significant presence in commercial life. They made important contributions in the emerging entertainment industry, especially music, theater, and prostitution [253].

One of those successful businessmen was Joshua Chauvet (1822–1908), born Josué Chauvet in a village of the province of Champagne. Chauvet travelled with the California Company via Cape Horn, arrived in San Francisco in September 1850, and made his way to Mollekumne Hill where many French miners had already established camp. After trying his hand at mining without much success, Chauvet opened a bakery and built a grist mill. Then, together with his father, he bought 500 acres of land in Glen Ellen, settled in the Sonoma valley in 1856, married in 1864, had two sons, built another grist mill, a sawmill, a brickyard, installed a water system for the town, started growing wine and established a winery. He became a U.S. citizen in 1868 and a prominent member of the community, owner of what is now the Jack London Saloon, and of Chauvet Hotel.[79] Annick Foucrier, who has written a history of the French in California, has traced the survival of Francophone communities created those years, due in part to the addition of new immigrants from France, well into the 20th century.

Not all Frenchmen who came to California succeeded, however. Two adventurers who failed overcame their disappointment by trying their luck in Mexico, where gold deposits were supposed to be found as well. After creating a mining company in Sonora, the Count of Raousset-Boulbon and Charles de Pindray convinced several hundred Frenchmen from San Francisco to come and join them in Mexico, where, after defeating Mexican troops, they promptly proclaimed la *République de Sonore*. The Republic of Sonora lasted a month. Pindray killed himself, Raousset-Boulbon embarked on new American adventures, and most of the men returned to San Francisco (Rohrbough, 255–256).[80]

4. Franco-Americans During the Civil War

Under the Mexican regime, California had been a slavery-free state. The early Forty Niners, the small, individual gold diggers were hoping it would stay that way so as to prevent large companies from bringing slaves and taking away their work and their shot at wealth. Therefore, "rumblings against slavery were commonplace" there (Richards, 67). In 1846, President Polk had sent Congress the "Two Million Bill," requesting that amount of money to negotiate the purchase of New Mexico and California with the Mexican government. At that point, a group of Democrats led by David Wilmot had proposed an amendment to the bill that would have outlawed slavery in new states and territories, not for humanitarian reasons, but so that slaves would not compete with white laborers. In the end, Wilmot's proviso was defeated and the Mexican War, fought from 1846 to 1848, ended with the United States' annexation of 55 percent of Mexico's territory, including California, and much of today's Southwestern states.[81]

As new states were being admitted to the union in the 1840s, the battle over slavery heated up. In D.C., "many believed that [President] Polk, a Tennessee slaveholder, was part of a Slave Power Conspiracy to extend slavery" (Richards, 63) and that the war with Mexico had been fought with that purpose in mind. "With the signing of the Treaty of Guadalupe Hidalgo in February 1848 and the simultaneous announcement of gold in California, the expansionist dimension of the American nation was unveiled for all to see" (Rohrbough, 201). By the end of President Polk's term in 1849, however, no action on California had been taken and Polk's successor in the White House, President Zachary Taylor, also a slaveholder, was in favor of respecting the abolition of slavery in places purchased from Mexico and letting the states decide otherwise. In the end, California was admitted to the Union in September 1850 as a non-slavery state so as to protect labor from big corporations.[82] But big business moved in anyway, and by the late 1850s, the lone miner had become a figure of the past:

> As the mines became the workplace of wage workers, mainly Cornish, Irish, and some Chinese, the profits increasingly went to absentee owners. [...] The big mines also had a worldwide impact. Thanks mainly to their production, the world's gold supply shot up by six or seven times. More gold was extracted between 1848 and 1858 [...], than the world had produced in the previous 150 years [Richards, 89].

The fight between North and South over slavery was far from over, however. Among Franco-Americans who endorsed slavery and its extension to new states and territories, Dr. Rodrigue[83] and Judge Lecompte pushed southern claims to the limit in Kansas, while Senator Pierre Soulé of Louisiana was at the forefront of the movement that led southern states to secede from the Union in 1861. Interestingly enough, "Louisiana counted 19,000 free men of color in 1860, more than any other state: in second place, South Carolina, only had half that many" (Creagh, *Nos Cousins*, 254). In Missouri, Senator Benton had been elected on a pro-slavery ticket but by the end of the 1840s, he had reversed his position and was therefore booted out of office in 1850 (Richards, 63–65). His son-in-law, John C. Frémont, who by 1848 "had become the nation's most famous explorer, rated by the popular press far above Lewis and Clark" (Richards, 43), was one of the two first senators elected to represent the new state of California in 1850. As he drew the short term, however, he was up for reelection in 1852 already. He too was a free-soiler and "showed strong signs of opposing the Deep South," which is why he was targeted for removal from office by the Southern Democrats and lost his bid for reelection. At that point, "California was no longer any threat to Southern dominance of the U.S. Senate" (Richards, 117) because the two California senators supported virtually all pro-slavery initiatives in the 1850s.

But this was not enough for the Southerners who felt short-changed by California's admission to the Union as a free-soil state and frustrated by the prospect that the entire West may soon be closed to slavery. Expanding in the Caribbean, where slave plantations were aplenty, seemed like a good idea at the time, as did the acquisition of more land from Mexico in the Southwest. After Spain rejected the U.S. offer to purchase the island of Cuba in 1848, Southern expansionists decided to take it by force. The August 1851 invasion led by Narciso López failed, however, and the next one, planned for the following year, was never executed. Meanwhile Pierre Soulé, the Senator from Louisiana, agitated for military action in Cuba, and once appointed U.S. ambassador to Spain, "made it clear that his mission was to acquire Cuba by hook or by crook" (Richards, 123).[84] Following the rejection by Spain of a new offer to purchase Cuba in 1853, Soulé met in 1854 with the U.S. ambassadors to France and England in Belgium where they issued the "Ostend Manifesto," a document threatening Spain with war in case of a new rejection of the U.S. offer to purchase the island of Cuba. When the Pierce administration disowned this initiative, however, Soulé resigned and there was no more talk of annexing Cuba (Richards, 123–124).[85]

Jennifer Green and Patrick Kirkwood have recently re-assessed Pierre Soulé's reputation as a "radical southern politician," as "a peripheral extremist," arguing that his politics were actually aligned with the "Young America" wing of the Democratic Party.[86] His stand on slavery, they claim, was less ideologically than pragmatically motivated, based on the notion that the southern economy would collapse without it. But more importantly perhaps, they showed that he was far from the only one to agitate for U.S. expansionism in the Caribbean and Central America, or even to advocate the recourse to filibustering as means to that end.[87] In another regard, his joined advocacy of American nationalism and international republicanism, he shared Young America's vision of a transnational republicanism (228–233). Green and Kirkwood therefore raise the following question:

> That Soulé and Buchanan held similar positions and enjoyed the same revolutionary associations while serving in Europe begs the question as to why, other than their divergent career trajectories, one has previously been cast as a peripheral extremist within the historiography and not the other [237].

Is it preposterous to suggest that it may have something to do with Soulé's Frenchness?

Another strategy favored by Southern Democrats to expand the realm of the agricultural South was to divide California in two, get a hold of the southern portion of the state to grow rice, cotton, and sugar, and to purchase more land from Mexico. The plan called for the construction of a railroad linking San Antonio to the Pacific that would provide Southern states with access to the ocean without going through the north. The most vocal advocate of this strategy was James Gadsden (1788–1858), who together with elected officials from the California state assembly, laid the ground for the introduction of pro-slavery legislation in California. A first step in that direction was the passage, in 1853–1854, of the California Fugitive Slave Act, a law that lapsed a year later, however. A second step was the call by state legislators for a second constitutional convention as a preliminary move for the state's division in half but that plan too failed. Then, Henry A. Crabb, after losing his seat in the California Assembly, formed the Arizona Colonization Company in 1856 and invaded Sonora in 1857. The Mexican government stopped the invaders and put the survivors, including Crabb, in front of a firing squad (Lindsay).

But the layout of the transcontinental railroad turned out to be a strong factor of division between North and South as both vied for it to be built in their states. While William Aspinwall and Cornelius Vanderbilt were betting on a Central American railroad to shorten transportation time from California to the East coast, James Gadsden persisted in his idea of a southern transcontinental railroad. He got his way in 1853 when the Secretary of War, Jefferson Davis, approved funding for the survey of possible southern routes and appointed his friend Gadsden ambassador to Mexico to negotiate the sale of the land needed for the construction of a southern railroad along the Gila River in Arizona. Gadsden succeeded and bought 45,000 square miles of land in December 1853.

The Gadsden Purchase infuriated Northerners, and in particular Congressman Benton who wanted the railroad to go from St. Louis to California through the Rockies. But another project was also in the works, a railroad that would go further north through Kansas. In 1854, Senator Stephen A. Douglas introduced the Kansas-Nebraska Act, a bill that called for creating two new territories out of the northern section of the Louisiana Purchase so as to provide land for a northern transcontinental railroad: the Nebraska Territory and the Kansas Territory. The Act turned out to be incredibly divisive as it also called for repealing the ban on slavery in Kansas, or rather, letting voters decide on the issue.[88] It passed in the House in May 1854 but it was a Pyrrhic victory if there ever was one for it provoked an outrage in northern states.

The same year, the Franco-American physician Aristide Rodrigue (1809–1857) established the territory of Kansas with Albert Boone and the town of Aigle chauve ["bald eagle"] as its capital. Rodrigue came from a family of plantation owners from Saint-Domingue who had found refuge in the United States in 1793.[89] A year later, Aigle Chauve was renamed Lecompton, in honor of another Franco-American, Judge Samuel Lecompte (1814–1888) who served as Chief Justice of the Supreme Court of Kansas Territory from 1854 to 1888.[90] As proponents of slavery moved to Lecompton, anti-slavery settlers flocked to the nearby town of Lawrence. In the camp opposing the expansion of slavery to Kansas was Isaac Cody (1811–1857), father of the legendary Buffalo Bill, who recalled this episode in free-state politics in his memoirs.[91] With both groups intent on influencing the outcome of the vote and the future of Kansas as a slavery or a free state, Judge Lecompte, a Democrat partial to slaveholding interests, accused members of the Lawrence anti-slavery camp of treason. This episode contributed to the series of violent "Bleeding Kansas" clashes between the pro-slavery border ruffians and the free-staters that lasted until the Civil War broke out.[92]

These events cost the Democrats dearly in the next electoral cycle. In 1856, the new Republican Party selected John C. Frémont as its first candidate ever to stand for election as U.S. president on an anti-slavery expansion platform. Known nationally as "the

Pathfinder" owing to his explorations, he was still young and had a pretty wife who basked in his aura and was referred to in the press as "our Jessie."[93] Frémont did very well in the north: "For in the free states, a whooping 83% of the eligible voters went to the polls, and the vast majority voted for someone other than the Pennsylvania Democrat," James Buchanan (Richards, 171). Nonetheless, Frémont's run for president was mired by a defamation campaign orchestrated by the Democrats.[94] As James Myall has pointed out, Frémont was the first presidential candidate to be accused of not being born in the United States, although he was born in Savannah, Georgia.[95]

As the Democrats succeeded in carrying the swing states, James Buchanan was elected and Colonel Frémont lost. He did particularly poorly in the state of California where the ranch he had purchased from the Mexican authorities in 1847, Las Mariposas, was located. As the ranch was on a "floating" land grant, its boundaries were hard to determine but Frémont had fought miners and squatters in court and succeeded in gaining legal confirmation that three gold mines he claimed were on his property were indeed his. It was therefore easy for his political opponents to depict him not only as a "nigger lover"[96] but also as an enemy of the little man, of the miners. Still, he might have been a better U.S. president than James Buchanan, who, according to some sources, "brought political disaster to the White House" (Sintes and Sellin). He came close, in fact, to being the last U.S. president.

Since Southerners like Soulé were already calling for the break-up of the Union before the election, James Buchanan's most pressing issue as president was

COL. FREMONT
PLANTING THE AMERICAN STANDARD ON THE ROCKY MOUNTAINS.

Colonel Frémont planting the American standard on the Rocky Mountains. Election Poster, 1856 (Library of Congress).

its preservation. But his flip-flopping on key-issues, like the purchase of Cuba, the Kansas-Nebraska Act, and slavery, created political chaos instead. What the country needed was a president who could reconcile the interests of northern manufacturers, who, at a time when industry was developing rapidly,[97] wanted high tariffs on imports, and southern plantation owners who sold their agricultural products to England. Buchanan's actions exacerbated the conflict instead. Prior to his inauguration he intervened in a case that was before the Supreme Court, the Dred Scott case. The slave Dred Scott (1799–1858) had sued for his freedom on the ground that he had lived in the state of Illinois and the Territory of Wisconsin where slavery was outlawed. The case ended with a denial of freedom for the plaintiff and opened the door to the possibility of extending slavery to all the territories (Khan, 35–38). Then, in 1858, a banking crisis hit the northern states particularly hard, Brigham Young's Mormons went to war against the Federal Government, and the Bloody Kansas skirmishes continued.

Things came to a head between northern and southern states during the 1860 presidential campaign when Abraham Lincoln (1809–1865) proposed to ban slavery from all U.S. territories, a proposal viewed in the south as a preliminary move towards the abolition of slavery. Lincoln's landslide election to the presidency created such an uproar in the south that within weeks seven slave states (South Carolina, Mississippi, Alabama, Florida, Georgia, Louisiana and Texas) had seceded from the Union and formed the Confederate states of America. In early spring, Arkansas, North Carolina, Tennessee, and Virginia joined them. As war broke out in April 1861, President Lincoln put the Department of the West under Major General Frémont's leadership. Frémont retook Springfield, Illinois, and pushed back the Confederate army out of Missouri in 1861. He also gave Ulysses S. Grant his first command at Cairo, Illinois.[98]

Lincoln issued the Emancipation Proclamation in January 1863. With it, the stake of the American Civil War (1861–1865) was no longer just the preservation of the Union but also the abolition of slavery. When the bloody war that claimed the lives of well over half a million soldiers was over, its undisputed outcome was that the North (and with it the West) took off economically and became prosperous while the South, the richest part of the nation up to then, lost both its political clout and its wealth. Due to a large extent to the abolition of slavery, the war left the southern states' agriculture and commerce in ruins while the north was expanding its railroad system and increasing its manufacturing base, thereby also attracting workers.

The Civil War also divided the Franco-American population, mostly concentrated in the South and supportive of the Confederacy. When the Civil War started with the attack on Fort Sumter in April 1861, a Francophone and West Point Graduate, General P.G.T. Beauregard (1818–1893) was in charge.[99] On the other side, French immigrants formed the 55th New York Volunteer Infantry known as the *Gardes de Lafayette* that fought in the Union Army.[100] Led by Colonel Régis de Trobriand, a journalist at the *Courrier des Etats-Unis* since the 1840s, it lost over sixty men to battle and disease during the war.[101] Later on, "from 1848 to 1880, most French refugees chose to settle in New York, and to a lesser extent in other big cities" where many contributed to the workers' movement (Cordillot, 144).[102] Nonetheless, at the time of the Civil War, the French balance sheet was clearly tilted towards the South, even in the case of France since Emperor Napoleon III not only personally favored the Confederate cause[103] but also put additional pressure on the United States government by intervening in Mexico in 1862 (Haine, 112–113). In many ways, the Civil War deserves to be regarded as the end of French influence in the United States. A strong indication of this symbolic and very real decline was the adoption of English as the only official language in Louisiana.

The stories of the Vine and Olive Colony, of the Champ d'Asile settlement, of Fourier and Cabet's followers in the United States, and of important U.S. politicians like senators John C. Frémont and Pierre Soulé all testify to French people's participation in the making of the United States in the 19th century. In that regard this chapter lends support to Edward Watt's contention that the dominant narrative "elaborated by Anglo empire builders" (5) sought to marginalize French contributions but that a divergent narrative, produced at the state level and found in archival records kept in historical societies, tells a different story. That dominated discourse celebrates the French frontier as a place of cultural and linguistic diversity and exchange, and, in the case of the Utopian settlements discussed in section 2, of social experimentation.

Up to the Civil War, the institution of slavery contested the myth of a unified American people, a division that applied to the Franco-American population as well as to the rest of the nation. The Confederate government tried to have Britain and France help break up the Union blockade on the Gulf of Mexico's ports and cities, but these European nations did not intervene in the Civil War, choosing instead to support the establishment of a short-lived Catholic Empire in Mexico. With the defeat of the Confederacy at the end of the Civil War and the abolition of slavery, the French population of the South lost much of its wealth as well as its political influence, as English replaced French and the political and administrative personnel became primarily Anglo. The Acadians, who had been "the backbone of the Democratic party in South Louisiana" (Brasseaux, *French, Cajun*, 70), suffered particularly from their defeat.

5. *Tips for Further Investigations*

Interesting People to Look Up

John Pintard, Jr. (1759–1844)
Peter Grain (1785–1857)
Sarah Grimké (1792–1873)
Baroness Micaela Almonester de Pontalba (1795–1874)
Paul Tulane (1801–1887)
Angelina Grimké (1805–1879)
Ézéchiel Jules Rémy (1826–1893)
Auguste Juilliard (1836–1919)
Mitch Bouvier (1837–1876)

Related Primary Texts

Kinzie, Juliette. *Wau-Bun. The Early Day in the Northwest* (1856).

Related Fiction

Shannon Selin, *Napoleon in America.*
Philippe Simiot, *Carbec mon Empereur.*

Related Films

Désirée (1954) with Marlon Brando as Napoleon, Jean Simmons as Désirée, and Cameron Mitchell as Joseph Bonaparte.
Gone with the Wind (1939) with Vivian Leigh as Scarlett O'Hara and Clark Gable as Rhett Butler.

CHAPTER X

The Western and the Statue

Franco-American Relations in the National Age

Franco-American relations are the focus on this chapter in several ways. Section 1, "Becoming Minority Cultures," deals with domestic relations and shows how the Francophone populations of Quebec, Louisiana, and Illinois lost ground in terms of numbers and influence in the country and became ethnic minorities. Section 2, "Creating the Nation: The Western, Facts and Fiction," defines what is meant by "National Age" in this chapter's title. Focusing on the symbolic dimension of the Conquest of the West, I argue that this foundational myth resonates far beyond national borders and that its worldwide appeal resides in its foregrounding of individualism as a conception of the self that is indispensable and must be acquired in a democracy. The Western as a genre resonated especially in France, a country that became a nation at the same time as the United States, that faced the same "e pluribus unum" challenge of creating national unity out of a patchwork of ethnicities and nationalities (Le Bras and Todd, 77), and that contributed extensively to this literary genre.[1] Section 3, "American Francophilia in the 19th Century," therefore centers on commonalities between the two nations at the end of 19th century, first in terms of close personal relations between French and American individuals, and then in institutional settings. Although restricted to a wealthy elite at the time, these interactions have the merit of highlighting the presence of commonalities between French and American nationals in an era obsessed with national difference. This section also underscores another dimension of nationalism, the institution of "sites of memory" (Nora) devoted to the nation, including the most famous of them, the Statue of Liberty. Finally, section 4, "Franco-American Relations and National Stereotypes in the Age of Mass Culture," reflects on the relationship between actual historical events involving France and the United States in the 20th century and on the creation and use of pre-conceived notions of the other nation, both positive and negative.

1. Becoming Minority Cultures: Quebec, the Old Illinois Country and Louisiana

In the early 19th century, the province of Quebec was divided into Upper Canada (Ontario), where new Anglophone immigrants tended to concentrate, and Lower Canada (Quebec), where the French formed the majority. In 1837 and 1838 conflicts between the Francophone majority of the Legislative Assembly in Lower Canada and the colonial government resulted in insurrections against the Crown of England that were led by Louis-Joseph Papineau of the *Parti Canadien*.[2] These rebellions failed, hundreds were arrested, and several leaders were exiled to Australia, or hanged. Some, like Papineau, crossed the border and settled in the United States (Chartier, 16). A High Commissioner, Lord Durham, was appointed to examine the causes of the rebellions and to suggest remedies. The 1839 Durham Report proposed that the two parts of the province be merged into one. With the creation of the province of Canada in 1840 the Francophone majority of Lower Canada became a Francophone minority in the new entity (Schull). Then, in 1867, the British Parliament created the Federal Dominion of Canada, and East Canada became the Province of Quebec.

Overall, the 19th century was a period of transition that did not benefit Franco-Americans economically, socially, or politically.[3] While still the majority population in Quebec, French-Canadians started to migrate to western Canada[4] or the western United States to find new agricultural lands, and then, starting in the 1850s, to New England, where the industrial revolution created more opportunities than in Canada.[5] According to Pierre Anctil, "emigration appears as one of the most fundamental elements of the history of Quebec in the 19th century" (27). The departure of more than 300,000 French Canadians for the United States in the last two decades of the 19th century, turned Quebec into a rural province and a fertile ground for the development of nationalist ideology (27–28).[6] The stereotype of the large, hard-working, pious, Francophone Canadian family living a simple, autarkic life in the middle of the woods emerged in those years, a cliché transmitted through Louis Hémon's famous novel *Maria Chapdelaine* (1913), for instance.

By the 1880s, the French Canadians had become a minority in the country they had created. "Speak white!" the insult hurled at a Quebecois politician in the House of Commons of Canada on October 12, 1889, offers a snapshot illustration of the unequal power balance between the triumphant Anglophone majority and the stigmatized Francophone minority (Doty). For over half a century the rallying cry of Anglo nationalists, the demeaning order to "Speak white!" given by Anglophones to their Francophone counterparts, encapsulates their monopolizing of social, economic, and political power.[7] Ironically, the Quebecois who had migrated to the United States were almost better off than those who had stayed in Canada.[8]

As economic migrants often do, the Canadians who came to work in factories on the East Coast intended to go back to Canada as soon as they could afford to. For those determined to save and go back to Quebec, the credit union was probably a god-sent invention. A German export, the *Caisse Populaire de Québec* founded in 1901 by Alphonse Desjardins was a parish-based response to predatory lending, and the first institution of its kind in North America (Bergengren, 79–82). In 1908, Desjardins also helped create the first credit union in the United States, St. Mary's Bank of Manchester in New Hampshire, to serve the local French-speaking community. As is usually the case, however, the goal of amassing a fortune became a point on an always receding line on the horizon for the majority of these economic migrants. Instead, they ended up building "Little Canadas" and staying in their new country. But the pride the Franco-Americans felt in their own language and in their cultural heritage was for them a good reason to resist assimilation,[9] as was the presence of Francophone institutions like parochial schools, medical clinics, newspapers, social organizations, and a church with a priest who was one of them.[10] In fact, as Louise Peloquin-Faré points out, the existence of "Little Canadas" itself worked as a disincentive to go back to Canada: why return home when you are already living in a French-Canadian environment?[11]

In the former Illinois Country, little changed initially for the Francophone population of what had been New France after the region became part of the United States: "The French people cared little about the new borders and felt everywhere at home in North America" (Louder and Waddell, 3). Agriculture remained an important activity for them all and over time mining and forestry replaced traditional occupations like the fur trade, hunting, or fishing (2). French Canadians continued to create new towns in the Great Lakes region. Louis Campeau (or Campau) (1791–1871), for instance, founded Grand Rapids, Midland, and Saginaw in Michigan in the first quarter of the century and Léon Tromblé, Bay City, Michigan (McQuillan, 98). French Canadians contributed to the development of forestry in Michigan, with small communities of woodsmen established in "Au Sable, Alpena, and Tawas" (105). In the Upper Peninsula, copper mines that opened in the mid–1840s near Marquette attracted other Franco-Americans. Sizeable Francophone communities also existed in urban centers like Detroit, Chicago, and St. Paul-Minneapolis, in part due to emigration from Alsace.[12] Starting in 1808, Father Gabriel Richard (1767–1832) established eight Catholic schools in the Detroit area, one of which later became the University of Michigan (Childs, "A Special Migration," 162).

In Missouri, south of St. Louis, miners continued to work in the lead mines and Francophone villages survived into the 20th century (Gold, 124). In the state of Illinois, new French towns emerged: Bourbonnais founded in 1830 by Noël Le Vasseur (1798–1879) attracted over 1,000 families from Quebec in the 1840s. French towns continued to grow in the state up to the Civil War, when lack of farmlands pushed the migrants further west (McQuillan, 101–103). Some of these pioneers settled near the railroad in Waterville and in Concordia, Kansas, forming small Francophone island communities that survived until the beginning of the 1920s (103). In the 1870s and 1880s, Pierre Bottineau was instrumental in the creation of new French-Canadian settlements on fertile agricultural lands along the Red River in Minnesota and North Dakota. Although the Anglophone population soon dominated in cities like Crockston and Red Lake Falls, the Francophone community had its own priest and physician as late as the 1880s (104–105).

In Louisiana, as the Francophone population increased, some families started to migrate further west in search of land.[13] French families that had immigrated to Louisiana maintained personal ties with their relatives in France for many years (Rémond, I, 232–233). A famous example is that of painter Edgar Degas (1844–1917) who visited his maternal uncle's family in 1873 and painted a famous picture, "A Cotton Office in New Orleans," during his visit.[14] But the diverse origins of the Francophone population of Louisiana —Acadia,[15] the Caribbean, and France—created additional problems in the face of looming Americanization. There was no unified Francophone community like there was in Quebec or the Northeast, but rather a patchwork of Francophone communities that were divided linguistically, racially, and socially: the white Creoles of New Orleans spoke standard French, but the black Francophones spoke creole, and the Acadians Cajun French (Brasseaux, *French Cajun*). By the 1880s, many Cajuns had become poorly paid agricultural workers who toiled with former slaves on plantations run by white Creoles. Together, poor blacks and whites organized several strikes in the 1880s (Cook, 377).[16] The fluidity that existed among the dominated social groups allowed Cajun to become the dominant Francophone culture and language of the region (Waddell, 198).[17]

The Catholic Church tried to serve as a bridge between the various Francophone communities spread over the United States and Canada (Lalonde, 22) and to provide support in the face of a stigmatization that originated not only in linguistic and cultural but also in religious difference. After U.S. independence, France's support and participation in the American Revolution slightly modified the perception that the "popery" threatened the very identity of the nation (McQuillan, 107–108). Thus, in the last decade of the 18th century, the first six American Catholic dioceses were created. This achievement soon paled compared to the expansion the Church was to enjoy in the 19th century, and this in spite of accusations of allegiance to Rome by movements such as the Nativists and the Know-Nothing.

Under the French regime, the government had devoted about 12 percent of the colony's budget to education,[18] medical care,[19] and social assistance,[20] and outsourced all those services to the Catholic Church. In parishes that were often poor, the priest therefore offered both spiritual and material support. In Quebec, the Church initially suffered after the Conquest due to lack of income and of personnel. In the United States too, it faced numerous other challenges: "Protestant dominance, republicanism, a secularized culture, and expanding religious and ethnic pluralism" (Brett, 90). Nonetheless, the Church experienced a "phenomenal growth and increasing ethnic diversity in the 19th century" (Brett, 91). Madelyn Jones notes, for instance, "an expansion of the Catholic membership reflected in the number of churches built, the creation of new dioceses and the rise of the Catholic press" (148).[21]

Indeed, 60 new dioceses were established between 1800 and 1850 and, interestingly, 31 of the 60 new bishops appointed during those years were French-born.[22] Under the leadership of these bishops, Catholic religious orders resumed their activities as providers of education, healthcare, and social services, gaining a strong presence in the United States. In 1836, for instance, a group of French nuns, the Sisters of St. Joseph, came from Lyon to St. Louis to open a school for the deaf. Within two decades they had established two convents, one in Cahokia, and one in Carondelet—a village near St. Louis named for the former governor of Spanish Louisiana. Over time, the order expanded to Philadelphia, St. Paul, Toronto, San Diego, and Southern Arizona. Similarly, the American branch of the Society of Saint Vincent de Paul was established in St. Louis in 1845 and soon expanded its social services to the newly created dioceses.[23]

Building on its Spanish legacy, Catholicism established itself as the dominant creed in the Southwest. By 1906, 90 percent of the religious membership was Catholic in California, Nevada, New Mexico, and Arizona (Brett, 93). In New Mexico, for instance, a young Breton named Théodore Rouault (1850–1940) came to the United States as a priest in 1876, ministered in Yuma, Arizona, and then in Mesilla, New Mexico. There he fell in love, married, and made a fortune in the canning business in Las Cruces, specializing in chili and tomatoes.[24] In Tucson, Arizona, where construction on Saint Augustine Cathedral started in 1858, the sisters of St. Joseph of Carondelet founded lasting educational institutions, the first elementary and the first secondary schools, in addition to a school for the Tohono O'odham, the local Native Americans, near the Spanish mission of San Xavier del Bac. In 1870, they also established the first hospital in the city and another one for injured miners in Prescott.[25] By the 1880s, over half a million students were enrolled in parochial schools in the United States (Jones, 255).[26] By the beginning of the 20th century, when the National Conference of Catholic Charities was created, the Church had also become a major player in the fight against poverty in the United States. By 1915, there were so many Catholic hospitals in the country that the Catholic Hospital Association of the United States and Canada was established.[27]

At the same time, Catholic institutions of higher learning made their appearance across the country, as liberal arts colleges at first. The oldest university west of the Mississippi, St. Louis University in St. Louis, Missouri, was founded in 1818. Then came Fordham University in the Bronx in 1841; the University of Notre Dame in South Bend, Indiana, and Villanova University, in Villanova, Pennsylvania, in 1842; the College of the Holy Cross in Worcester, Massachusetts, in 1843; Loyola University of Maryland in 1852; Seton Hall in South Orange, New Jersey, and the University of San Francisco in 1855; and Boston College in 1863, among others. After the creation of the first public research university, Johns Hopkins in Baltimore in 1876, many Catholic institutions became research universities as well. Georgetown University, the oldest Catholic and Jesuit University in the country (1789), added a school of medicine in 1850, a law school in 1871, and a graduate curriculum in the arts and sciences in the 1880s. Loyola University was founded in Chicago in 1870 and the Catholic University of America in Washington, D.C., in 1887.[28]

In contrast to the expansion enjoyed by Catholic institutions, the French and the French-Canadian populations represented an increasingly small percentage of the general population of the United States. By the second half of the 19th century, immigration from France had slowed to a trickle.[29] Small groups of very poor, often illiterate immigrants still left disadvantaged areas of France like Aveyron and Brittany to settle in rural areas of the United States. The Basque, who were shepherds, settled in the West, Arizona, California, Colorado, and became famous for a while for their traditional ball game, Basque pelota, or jai alai.[30] It was used for decades as a sport to gamble on in Las Vegas and Florida casinos. Other French immigrants worked in mines or factories (Creagh, *Nos Cousins*, 366–383). As in the past, some of the immigrants from France were political exiles, particularly after the failure of the Paris Commune.[31] Those immigrants tended to settle in big cities (Creagh, 337–351). In New York, for instance, they "took over the 8th Ward" in the 1870s according to a witness account (Quoted in Creagh, 337). Often highly politicized and active in labor unions as well as the socialist and communist movements (Perrier), they were viewed with suspicion by the authorities particularly in the wake of the Hay Market Affair.[32] For several decades, young males who emigrated were exempt from the draft in France, but this dispensation ended in 1905. Many of those who were already in the United States applied for naturalization and stayed for good (Peloquin-Faré, 403) but mandatory military service prevented others from coming.

Compared to large waves of immigrants that came first from northern and western Europe and then from Austria-Hungary, Italy, and Turkey, between 1890 and World War I,[33] immigration from France was not only numerically insignificant but also in decline. French Canadians, for instance, the dominant ethnic group in Michigan in the early 1800s, accounted for only 5 percent of the population by the 1850s (McQuillan, 99). In Louisiana, the number of immigrants from France declined sharply over time: from 11,552 in 1850 to 6,500 in 1900, to 1,521 in 1950 (Brasseaux, 29). "Very few people migrated from France to the United States: no more than 4,200 departed between 1820 and 1850" (Montbrial, 455). By contrast, the immigrant population from other countries increased by leaps and bounds in the 19th century: 151,000 came to the United States in the 1820s, 599,000 in the 1830s; 1,713,000 in the 1840s, and 2,314,000 in the 1850s (M. Jones, 93). By 1860, 13 percent of the U.S. population, 4,136,000 out of 31,500,000, was foreign-born (M. Jones, 117).

The Catholic population grew as well, from 50,000 at the beginning of the century to over 3 million by 1860 (Brett, 90, 91). The mass immigration from Ireland, Germany, and Italy was predominantly Catholic, making up as much as a third to half of all immigrants during those years. Within the Catholic church itself, however, the Francophones lost ground numerically, as indicated by the sharp decline in the number of appointments of French-born bishops during second half of the 19th century: from over 50 percent between 1800 and 1850 to 12 percent of all appointments between 1850 and 1900.[34] Faced with the cultural diversity of its membership, the American Catholic Church increasingly responded by "encouraging Americanization—including English language parochial instruction, attendance at public schools, and acceptance of religious pluralism" (Brett, 93). The Irish were poor and numerous, but they spoke English. For them, like for the French farmers of Restoration France Stendhal described in *The Red and the Black*, the Church offered an avenue of social mobility. Many young Irish immigrants, and to a lesser degree Germans, chose, therefore, to join a religious congregation or the priesthood if opportunity availed itself. Consequently, even in the Church where the French had been heavily represented only recently, they suddenly became a minority.[35] Lacking the numbers to survive as such in the United States, the native Francophone population started to suffer stigmatization. In Louisiana, the trend started when Anglophones arrived in large numbers after the Civil War.[36] According to Brasseaux, even topics related to the French, like the history of Louisiana, of its cultural heritage, and its language became negligible options in academe.[37]

2. Creating the Nation: The Western, Facts and Fiction

The conquest of the North American continent was completed during the second half of 19th century. Thirteen new western states were added to the Union in the last two decades, and once Arizona and New Mexico became states in 1912, the continental United States of America achieved territorial unity. Technological, industrial, and financial revolutions occurred during those years. In late 1858, it still took 21 days to go from St. Francisco to St. Louis by stagecoach and the transport of merchandise by convoys of ox-drawn wagons was slow and inefficient (Portes, 104). The last stagecoach used to transport passengers drove to Deadwood, South Dakota, in 1876. A few years later, by 1884, the stagecoach had already become an artefact of folklore. It was used in shows telling the story of the West and re-enacting its attack by bandits (Portes, 105). Between those dates, advances in communication and transport allowed the two coasts to get closer and the country to start feeling one, geographically speaking. The stagecoach mail service inaugurated by Henry Wells and William G. Fargo, who created the famous bank in California during the Civil War, was soon beaten to the finish by the Pony Express, whose riders covered the distance from St. Louis to San Francisco in 10 days, less than half the time it took a stagecoach to cover the same route (Portes, 106).[38] The telegraph made long distance communication possible in the 1860s and the invention of the telephone in 1872 made it available to the wealthy a few decades later. After the completion of the first transcontinental railroad in 1869, the replacement of the stagecoach by the train, and the expansion of the rail network, commerce became possible on a large scale. New business opportunities linked to the transport revolution emerged: the first mail order catalog in 1872, commercial refrigeration, and soon the automobile and cinema. Steel frame architecture and the elevator made the skyscraper and the Statue of Liberty possible.

These objective milestones in the formation of the nation also feed the reservoir of memories that constitutes the national patrimony. In that regard, the conquest of the American West is undoubtedly the historical event that has generated the most images.

Next to the New York skyline, the West is the most distinct embodiment of the United States today, an icon that does not exist separately from the narrative that recounts the creation of the American nation. As the mythic site of its genesis, the West was the topic of American literature as soon as American literature came into existence, and the subject of American cinema as soon as that technology made its appearance. As early as 1826, James Fenimore Cooper told of the early struggle over the frontier during the Seven Years' War. In a bold pre-emptive move, the *Leatherstocking Tales* eliminated both the French and the Mohicans who stood in the way of territorial expansion. In that regard, *The Last of the Mohicans* anticipates later versions of the western story in which the conquest is described as the take-over of "virgin" lands, lands where there are no Indians and no French. Nearly a century later, one of the first American films, *The Great Train Robbery* (1903), is set during the last phase of a conquest that was still in progress at the time the film was made and would end with the victory of law over lawlessness.[39]

The 1962 Hollywood movie, *How the West Was Won*, famously recounts the five phases of this conquest, the taming of the rivers by intrepid explorers, the crossing of the plains in wagons to reach the California coast and the goldmines by the pioneers, the struggle over the definition of the nation during the Civil War, the highly symbolic connecting of east and west through the completion of the telegraph and the transcontinental railroad, and finally, the triumph of justice and the imposition of the rule of law exemplified by the victory of the sheriff over the bandit. All modern republics have their national myth(s) of creation, but the United States is unique in that it has produced both a literature and a cinema entirely devoted to the making of the American nation, the western. This literary and cinematic genre has been exported not only to France but also all over the world where it has enjoyed the same success. Why is that so?

The period of nation-building occurred in the United States and France at roughly the same time, the first part of the 19th century for the urban masses in both countries, and after the Civil War in the United States, and during the Third Republic (after 1870) in France for the rest of the population. France too produced various national creation stories in the 19th century. There were travel guides assessing and investing the national territory and novels presenting extant local cultures as remnants of a distant past at the beginning of the century. By World War I, nationalist literature had taken an aggressively chauvinist tone and did not shy from advocating the exclusion of "foreigners."[40] The rejection of modernity and the defense of tradition found in that French nationalist literature epitomized one pole of the tension between progress and tradition that structured French society at the time, just like the struggle between the American industrial North, the harbinger of modernity, and the agricultural South, the advocate of tradition, divided American society during the Civil War. Contrary to the stereotype that opposes a conservative France holding on to tradition to a progressive America always open to innovation, tradition and progress are opposite poles on a social continuum found in both societies. It makes no sense, therefore, to nationalize concepts that are universal.

As Craig Calhoun pointed out however, nationalist discourse is not just a national product, it also depends for its genesis "on a more global, indeed international rhetoric" (3). France and the United States, or at least select representatives of their respective countries, also built their nations discursively in narratives that contrasted them. In the previous chapter, several French travel narratives about the United States were mentioned, but this production did not stop then. "Between 1865 and 1914," Emily Burns writes in *Transnational Frontiers*, "the production and reception [in France] of visual representations of American western landscapes, cowboys, and particularly American Indians, reveal that the American West was not a fixed concept, but a transnational discourse" (3). Tangi Villerbu, who devoted a book to the French story of the conquest of the West, has showed how French narratives shaped identity, in part, by presenting the West as the birthplace of the new individual generated by American democracy. With a few exceptions, most of these French narratives of the West tell the same story of conquest and have the same set of male characters as their American counterparts: initially, the explorer, the trapper, and the settler, and later on, the lonesome cowboy, the bandit, and the sheriff.[41] In the American context, these characters make sense because they provide identification models. But why would the French and other foreign nationals find them attractive as well? It is, I believe, because they are all exemplars of male individualism, a key ingredient in the construction of modern national identity.

The term "individualism" has many different meanings and three of them are interesting to consider in discussing the role of the American West in the elaboration of a sense of national identity both in the United States and in France in the 19th century. In its first acceptation, the term "individualism" is associated with the central characters of the story told in this book so far, the Native American and its European counterpart, the white Indian. Because of their freedom, the Indian and *coureur des bois* are often thought of as the epitome of individualism.[42] They were, after all, individuals who left their homes and families to explore and live most of the time as nomads. But because they returned to, and lived, at least part-time, in a village or a tribe, their sense of belonging was presumably anchored in their attachment to these communities of origin. The aristocratic refugee is another individualist character already encountered in these pages as well. Wealthy enough to afford passage to North America, he was well-connected, spent a few years in the new American Republic, but usually returned home. In the pre-national age, aristocrats were individualists because "fidelity to oneself" was their motto. The aristocratic sense of identity rested on a form of individualism that required adequacy between the self and his sense of *noblesse oblige*, the obligation, as a unique link in an aristocratic chain, to live up to a certain set of inherited expectations.[43]

These two forms of individualism are different from the individualism that prevails in contemporary societies. In that third sense, individualism in a key concept of western democracy, indeed a pre-requisite for it since nation-states are entities built on the premise of a social contract, the law of the land, between the state and the individual citizen. One way to illustrate this point is to remember the relative novelty of the concept, to recall, for instance, that under the French monarchy, estates cast votes, not individuals, as they do in a republic. In the democratic age, the nation, "we, the people," is the aggregate of all these individual entities called citizens. National identity also trumps all other forms of belonging because it is the only form of identity recognized by law, as documented by a state ID or a passport.

In its formative stage, when the nation-state is still weak, it is combative and intolerant: it requires that competing forms of belonging and identity be eliminated, if necessary, by brutal force. Historically, those deemed incapable of renouncing their association with pre-national forms of belonging, like tribalism or allegiance to "throne and altar,"[44] those unwilling to adopt the national language, or those identifying with competing forms of religious or national identity on the national territory—in the 19th-century United States, Mormonism, or "foreign potentates"[45]—were fought militarily. The Native

Americans' and the *coureurs des bois*' allegiance was temporary and bound to communities other than the national community. How could they possibly have believed a national story that eliminated them or denied their existence anyway? Besides, familiarity with two old competing creation myths, one Native American, one Catholic, must have inclined them to a certain relativism, a doctrine incompatible with the absolute faith in the nation and the pledge of undivided allegiance it demands of its citizens. Finally, their way of life and particularly their constant crossing of linguistic and cultural boundaries made them less receptive to the "regime of one-ness" characteristic of, and imposed by, the nation-state.[46] Initially therefore, war and segregation on reservations were necessary, as far as the U.S. government was concerned, to eliminate the danger the Native- and the Franco-Americans posed to national cohesion. Once the nation-state grew stronger, more mellow forms of cooptation were used. As a nation-state gains in strength and self-assurance, education, and the promise of improved economic status attached to it, becomes an effective form of cooptation that is commonly used to coax pre-nationals into assimilation. By providing total immersion in the dominant national culture, the boarding school proved to be an effective instrument of cultural homogenization, both for Bretons or Algerians in France, and for Native Americans in the United States.[47] It is no coincidence if laws mandating primary education were passed in most of the continental United States between 1867 (Vermont) and World War I, roughly at the same time as the territorial unity of the nation was achieved, in some cases like Arizona, even before statehood.[48] Similarly, the laws that made primary education secular, mandatory, and free were passed in the early 1880s in France.

The fact that, beyond nationhood, alternate ways of being human exist tells us that feeling, behaving, and acting as individual citizens is not something that is genetically programmed but rather something that must be learned. This education, in turn, has to be ongoing, start anew with every generation in each and every democracy. When there was no mandatory education, the male characters of the American national story provided identification models that, in one respect, were specific to the United States but, in another regard transcended their site of origin to offer universally valid models of masculine individualism. In the first stage of the nation's development, the explorer, the trapper, and the settler struggle alone, and triumph over the forces of nature.[49] Later on, stories of Indians and cowboys, of bandits and sheriffs, instill the notion that law always wins over lawlessness, that civilization wins over savagery in the end. That these prototypes of individualism are all white males is not particularly surprising considering that women and minorities had no citizenship rights in the 19th century.[50]

But what about Belle Star (1848–1889)? Calamity Jane (1852–1903)? Annie Oakley (1860–1936)? Well, the first of them, a horse thief, became famous upon her violent death in 1889, and represents, therefore, a model to avoid rather than emulate. The other two made their appearance as historical figures in Buffalo Bill's Wild West, the most famous of the open-air vaudeville shows that told the story of the conquest visually through real-life scenes.[51] Buffalo Bill's Wild West show became the most famous of these shows because it toured Europe eight times between 1886 and 1906 (Cody), including in France, where it met with great success. By the time women made their entrance into the story of the conquest, the West was no longer a territory to be conquered and appropriated, it had become part of "the rich legacy of memories" Ernest Renan viewed as constitutive of a nation's soul.[52] Like the Native American, the favorite character in the show in Europe, the Western heroines were paid to play their part in what was no longer a living

Buffalo Bill's Wild West Entente Cordiale Col. W. F. Cody, 1905 (courtesy Buffalo Bill Center of the West, Cody, Wyoming; Buffalo Bill Museum, 1.69.2173b).

culture, not even a re-enactment of the past, but a collage of imagined heroic remnants of a bygone era that now belonged to the national patrimony.

A 1905 poster announcing one of Buffalo Bill's Wild West Show's last tours of France celebrates the *entente cordiale* (cordial understanding) between the two nations while at the same time underscoring the transnational dimension of nationalism and the American West's function in its elaboration. The poster depicts a French and an American cavalry officer sitting on horseback, each holding a gigantic flag of their respective country, while Bill Cody, dressed in Western gear, sits on a white horse in central position between them. Taken together, these three characters establish a visual link between the national, represented by the flags and the soldiers, and the West, symbolized by Bill Cody, thus reinforcing the message that male individualism occupies center-stage in the national story. But the choice of anonymous military men to represent France and the United States, rather than real historical figures,[53] adds something important to the tale. A decade before World War I, the soldiers serve as a reminder to the male citizen of his civic duty, of his obligation to die for his country if necessary.

Europe produced a great deal of Western literature, a genre long regarded as "popular" and therefore neglected by scholars. In the French production of Western literature, Gustave Aimard (1818–1883) occupies a special place as the first writer to use the Wild West as his subject matter. Aimard was an adventurer who traveled to South and North America, where he married a Comanche, and worked as a trapper in the 1840s and a gold miner.[54] Between 1857, when he published *The Trappers of Arkansas*, and 1882, when he wrote *The Bandits of Arizona*, Aimard produced nearly 60 novels about the West. Although the titles of his novels[55] would seem to indicate that he made good use of the stock characters of the Western, Villerbu convincingly argues that Aimard actually offered an alternative image of the West as "a place that put into play European national identities, as well as American ones" (106).[56] Starting in 1875, the German writer Karl May (1842–1912) produced over a dozen novels centered around the Apache character of Winnetou, novels that became even more famous than Aimard's. Albert Bonneau (1898–1967) also pursed a literary career in this vein, writing dozens of Western novels, including two series around the character of Catamount.[57] More recently, so did Pierre Pelot (1945–), author of *The Dakota Trail* in 1967 and creator of a series around the character of Dylan Star, a young Confederate. Over the years, all these novels and countless others have been translated, imitated, and disseminated all over the world, re-written for children,[58] and adapted to cinema. The Western has also found a home in the *bande dessinée*, as the Belgian series Lucky Luke illustrates,[59] it has even inspired French hip-hop.[60]

3. American Francophilia in the 19th Century: A High Society Phenomenon

Centered on individualism, the Western can be used in all democracies as a support to civics to teach citizens to conceive of themselves as autonomous, self-sufficient, entities and to accept the rule of law, as opposed to personal justice of the vendetta kind. That the genre, as fiction or film, targets mass audiences, and is associated with popular culture, is thus hardly surprising. Next to it, however, there is a vast body of literature devoted to the description of other nations or more precisely meant to highlight their specificity in relation to the writer's own nation. The same way prominent French visitors produced literature about the United States prior to the Civil War, the same way American travelers wrote about France and Europe. Just for the period of the Restoration and July Monarchy, the number of wealthy and/or prominent American men and women who visited and wrote about France is quantitatively impressive, as the work of historian Guillaume Bertier de Sauvigny illustrates.[61]

James Fenimore Cooper, who had greeted Lafayette when he arrived in New York in 1824, was probably the first non-political American celebrity to consign to paper his impressions on France. Cooper moved to France with his family in 1826 to school his children and to capitalize on the European success of *The Last of the Mohicans*. While living abroad he adopted the British high society practice of the *Grand Tour*,[62] visited several other European countries on which he commented in series of six travel accounts published in the United States between 1836 and 1848: *Gleanings in Europe, Italy*; *Gleanings in Europe: the Rhine, Switzerland, Italy, England, and France*. His second book on France is entitled *A Residence in France*. Cooper also wrote *Notions of the Americans*, a travel narrative addressed to Lafayette and other friends in Europe, as well as a *Letter to General Lafayette*, a comparative analysis of the cost of government in France and the United States. The last example is a reminder that if the 19th century is the age of the nation, it is also the age of comparison. Anthropology, Law, Economics, History, Philology, Sociology: as soon as the humanities and the social science disciplines appeared, they made use of comparative methods (Griffith). Among them, Comparative Literature is specifically dedicated to the identification of national differences. Inaugurated by Germaine de Staël's works *On Literature* (1799) and *On Germany* (1813), it also represents a more sophisticated attempt to theorize national difference than the traveler's subjective observations.[63] Irwin Wall writes that "[t]o some extent the French will always define themselves against an 'other,' and the United States will always loom to fill the role of a foil" (1097). The reverse is also true. The logic of nationalism does to a certain extent explain this special relationship and so do the quasi-simultaneous births of the two republics.

Asynchrony, however, often allows national differences to be cast in a bright light and commonalities to remain in obscurity. In France, "the tyranny of public opinion" identified in the early 19th century by Tocqueville (and Stendhal) as the source of U.S. conformism and the main flaw of American society has been contrasted to the excellence of French culture, used to justify the French "cultural exception," and thus resistance to "Americanization." But the necessity to conform to the rule of law is common to all democracies, which means that all individuals are at the same time individualists, to the extent that they define themselves as unique, and conformists to the extent that they are expected to conform to a myriad of expected forms of social behavior. This double nature alone shows the fragility of a stereotypes that seek to contrast the French and the American on that basis, by opposing, for instance "Gallic individualism" to "American conformism" (Kuisel, 2). It is hardly surprising, therefore, that stereotypes conveying the opposite meaning, exist, like the notion of Gallic conformism conveyed by Rabelais's famous "*moutons de Panurge*," or the American reputation of "rugged individualism."[64] Similarly, when Thierry de Montbrial casts the tendency to export democracy to the world not only as a specificity of U.S. policy but also a source of anti–Americanism in France,[65] he overlooks how closely related France and the United States are in that regard. Just like the United States tends to believe that "what is good for America is good for the rest of the world," so too the first French Republic saw it as its mission to bring its own values of *liberté*, *égalité*, and *fraternité*, to the rest of Europe during the revolutionary era, so too did the Third Republic when it took its *mission civilisatrice* to its African and Asian colonies on the exact same assumption as the United States. As democracies, France and the United States are both what Pierre Bourdieu called "imperialisms of the universal," intent on exporting their value systems, political institutions, and national and cultural products wherever they can.[66]

But they are also republics in competition with each other. Since the birth of American democracy, for instance, it has been customary to point to France's decline on the world stage even though two hundred years later, the game is still on. Sameness of purpose and divergence of national interests under specific historical circumstances explain how the two nations can produce both negative judgments about the other (namely when these interests collide) and positive ones (when they don't). To make sense of value judgments, that repeated time and time again, turn into national clichés, one must inquire, therefore, about their place of origin, the historical context in which they are produced, the social group(s) from which they emanate and/or the social group(s) they purport to define.[67]

With these caveats in mind, Franco-American relations may be characterized as a secondary preoccupation for both nations in the 19th century, with manifestations of friendly sentiment dominating in both countries overall. The most vivid testimony of harmony between the two nations is undoubtedly France's gift of the Statue of Liberty to the United States.[68] It was the idea of Édouard de Laboulaye (1811–1883), a professor of Comparative Law at the *College de France*, who, like many of his fellow citizens, was greatly shaken by the news of President Lincoln's assassination on April 15, 1865 (Khan, 12–14). An abolitionist who believed in democracy and in the special relationship between his country and the United States, Laboulaye thought of the monument as an expression of hope, hope of racial harmony in the United States following the abolition of slavery and the President's assassination, and hope that the republican regime would soon be restored to France (Khan, 10). The Statue of Liberty was to be a Franco-American project in terms of financing, with the French people paying for the statue, and the American people for the pedestal, and in terms of realization, with a French sculptor, Frédéric-Auguste Bartholdi, an American architect, Richard Morris Hunt,[69] and a French engineer, Gustave Eiffel, collaborating to lead the project to completion (16). The statue was unveiled on October 28, 1886, with nearly a million spectators in attendance (176).

If comparative cultural analysis is an attempt to define one's nation in opposition to another, being able, as a citizen, to locate one's place in national history can only contribute to reinforcing the sense of national belonging. National monuments, such as the Statue of Liberty, fulfill that role, as reminders of the nation's values,[70] and for descendants of the 12 million immigrants who disembarked on Ellis Island between 1892 and 1924, of their personal ancestry. Conservation is therefore important when it comes to creating the "rich legacy of memories" (Renan) that constitutes the national culture. In a move that paralleled the creation in the 1830s of a French government agency devoted to the restoration of historical monuments and the preservation of the national patrimony,[71] President Theodore Roosevelt signed the Act for the Preservation of American Antiquities in 1906,[72] shortly after the establishment of the first six national parks, all of them located in the western United States.

At the time when actual contacts between French and U.S. citizens remained the privilege of the happy few, the move towards conservation followed a period of Western tourism for the wealthy during the Gilded Age that was primarily devoted to big game

The Statue of Liberty at the Gaget-Gauthier Foundry in Paris (1884) [*La statue de la Liberté dans les ateliers Gaget-Gauthier, à Paris*] (Wikimedia Commons).

hunting and buffalo safaris. In fact, so much wildlife was killed during those hunting expeditions that several species were brought near extinction (Villerbu).[73] A response to such excesses, the conservation movement that followed invented a new kind of tourism centered this time on the magical beauty of a nature kept in a nearly virgin state by the will of man.[74] Still reserved, prior to World War I, to a tiny minority of Americans and, as Portes has showed, "of leisure," i.e., with time and money, this new Western tourism extolled the restorative virtues of nature to a growing number of wealthy industrialists in need of rest (Portes, 91–96).

Some of these Frenchmen, however, were looking for more than serendipity in a natural environment. Money and love attracted them as well. In the heyday of the industrial revolution, impoverished French aristocrats were seeking business opportunities just as much as their American counterparts. Business associations at times led to Franco-American marriages, as in case of the marquis de Morès mentioned by Portes. The French nobleman came to the United States in 1882, married the daughter of a New York banker, made a fortune in the West, and gave the name of his wife, Medora, to the town he founded in North Dakota.[75] This Franco-American marriage would seem to correspond to the pattern identified as typical for the period by many historians. High society transatlantic marriages that took place during the Gilded Age, they say, were motivated by economic interest on the part of the French man and by the desire for an aristocratic title on the part of the American woman.[76] But, as Nicole Léopoldie argues and demonstrates in her 2017 PhD dissertation, the cliché of the French noble marrying into American wealth does not suffice to account for these alliances. For one thing, "while marriages to British nobility, like that of Consuela Vanderbilt to the Duke of Marlborough, were admired and portrayed as storybook romances, marriages to French nobility were often looked at with suspicion and contempt" (Léopoldie, 41). Some traditional anti–French sentiment may have been at play in this assessment, but it is also true that the French titles meant little in terms of material possessions due the abolition of privileges during the French Revolution. Even in terms of prestige and symbolic power, they may have appeared less valuable than their British equivalents due to their multiplication during the Napoleonic regime. American heiresses married French aristocrats nonetheless for a variety of reasons[77]: (1) cultural difference, the exotic appeal of the national other, is undoubtedly a source of attraction for non-conformists in any culture; (2) love, which had become the accepted social norm as the basis of marriage in Western societies by the end of the 19th century; (3) idealism, the belief that international friendship contributes to peace[78]; (4) opportunity, perhaps the most important factor to account for these unions. In addition to traditional exclusive social settings, such as private dinners and ball, new select socio-cultural spaces, such as the ocean-liner, luxury train, the country club, the horse race, appeared during this period. All provided a confident cosmopolitan elite with opportunities to socialize and, in some cases, to form marital.unions.[79]

The wealth of the American women who married British and French aristocrats came from the industrial revolution, or more specifically, from the immense fortunes created by their relatives, termed either "captains of industry," if their contributions to the economic wealth of the nation are seen positively, or "robber barons" if they are seen as built illegitimately through ruthless business practices and on the back of exploited workers (NEH, "The Industrial Revolution"). However, most of the big business tycoons of the Gilded Age turned philanthropists later in life, and as such they played a crucial role in the creation of urban cultural institutions such as libraries, art museums, and universities, all over the country, in other words the "sites of memory" so crucial for the establishment of a national patrimony and for the sense of self-worth of any civilized nation.[80] Much of the art collected for these museums came from Europe, and from France in particular: "In the years before World War I, articles providing physical descriptions of France and Paris and about French literature and art proliferated in popular American magazines" (Walton, 16). In yet another expression of the ambient Francophilia of the Gilded Age, many collections of contemporary art were started with paintings from France, with some patrons purchasing indiscriminately the works of the *pompier* artists sanctioned by the Académie des Beaux Arts and the rebel impressionists. John D. Rockefeller was the main sponsor of the Cleveland of Art,[81] Andre Carnegie of the museum that bears his name in Pittsburgh. In New York, Henry Clay Frick and William Vanderbilt II both provided mansions to serve as the museums that bear their names and to house art collections they donated. One of these patrons of the world of art, the steel magnate Charles M. Schwab, even had French architect Maurice Hébert build him a 75-room mansion that "combined details from three French chateaux on a full city block" near Central Park in New York.[82]

In addition to the transatlantic marriage and the world of art, higher education is another area where American Francophilia manifested itself in the 19th century. Prior to the last quarter of the 19th century, there were no American institutions of higher education beyond the traditional liberal arts curriculum dispensed in colleges run by churches of various denominations.[83] European universities therefore attracted young American men of independent means, but also women since France allowed them to audit university lectures. The favorite study abroad destinations were the United Kingdom and France at the beginning of the 19th century, when those countries were at the forefront of scientific advances, and "Berlin, Leipzig, Göttingen, and Strasburg"[84] (Walton, 13), by the end of the century when Germany was recognized as the leader in science and technology.[85] The modern, secular American university was created in response to a growing need for higher education in the United States as the population increased. Here again wealthy Americans played a key role: Johns Hopkins University in Baltimore, Maryland, was founded in 1876 with a huge donation from a patron who had made his fortune investing in railroads. Stanford University in California was founded in 1885 by Leland Stanford, another railroad investor; the University of Chicago by oil industry magnate J.D. Rockefeller in 1889 and Rockefeller University in New York in 1901. Carnegie Mellon in Pittsburgh was created by steel magnate Andrew Carnegie in 1900, and the list goes on.

As these new institutions could not immediately satisfy the growing need for higher education, young Americans continued to go to Europe to study. By the end of the 19th century the growing number of luxury liners and competition among the cruise-ship companies brought down the fare, making the transatlantic voyage affordable to the middle class. Young Americans started to view European degrees as an avenue of social mobility in their own country given the large demand for instructors in the new American universities.[86] Walton states that Germany acquired the reputation of being the place to go for "serious studies" in the pre–World War I period. She also provides evidence that the gendered stereotype of France as feminine arose at that time due to its association with "soft" disciplines like architecture,[87] dance, music, painting, sculpture, language, and literature, as well as the perception that American women preferred to travel to France (Walton, 16–21).[88] But there may be more pragmatic reasons for the choice of Germany as the preferred study abroad destination by American male students than its association with "hard," "masculine," sciences.[89] If your family came from Germany, wouldn't it stand to reason that you would rather go to that country, where you may be able to enjoy the support of relatives, than to France? Moreover, as Harry W. Paul showed, the issue of the so-called "decline" of France in the area of science is a more complicated issue than it first appears since it has more to do with differences between France and Germany in terms of pedagogy and educational structures than with science itself. On that score, the cliché of France as soft and unscientific is hard to sustain considering the number of French scientists who rose to prominence during this period, Marcellin-Berthelot, Louis Pasteur, Pierre Curie, Marie Curie, to name but a few.

Facts also challenge the perception of the arts as soft women disciplines. The vast majority famous French artists of the late 19th century were male, painters like Monet, Renoir, Manet, Degas, composers like Gounot, Offenbach, St. Saëns, Bizet. Most of the architects who built American cities had studied and trained in France:

> The emerging nation's pride in its postal service, demonstrated by its post offices, belief in its judicial system, as embodied in its courthouses, commitment to the education of its masses, as illustrated in its libraries, aspirations in the intellectual field as portrayed in its universities, confidence in its political structures, as symbolized in its state capitols—this pride was to find its expression in the monumental buildings it erected throughout the land. It was an era of building hospitals from scratch, and schools and colleges from ground zero. Each large city had to have its grand museum, in addition to its great railroad station. [...] [W]ith remarkable few exceptions, all such structures still standing in this country today [...] were, for the great majority, designed by *Beaux-Arts*-trained architects [Carlhian, 197].[90]

But in male-dominated universes, feminization is a common way of demeaning the other. French *fin de siècle* xenophobes, for instance, depicted "north America as a gynocracy" (Roger, 195), at the very moment when American Francophobes were depicting France as feminine and soft.

This kind of biased perception matters nonetheless because it produces real effects, in this case a drop in the number of Americans enrolled in French universities. Realizing that they were losing the higher education battle with Germany the French fought back. In the private sector, they created the *Alliance française* in 1883 as an organization devoted to the teaching of French all over the world.[91] In the public sector, they reformed their university system in ways that made studies in France more palatable to foreign students (Walton, 25–26). As a result, "in 1900 there were 1,799 foreign students attending French universities, that number rose to 4,818 in 1908 and to 6,188 in 1914" (Walton, 26). In addition, organizations such as "the Franco-American Committee (1895), the American Association of Arts in Paris (1896)," and others were put in place to acclimate American students to life in France (Walton, 26). More importantly, formal links between specific universities were established to enable the exchange of professors with American universities such as "Harvard, Columbia, and Chicago" (27). The result of these efforts was to create "a real cultural exchange between the United States and France" (28), particularly among educators familiar with both educational systems, such as Henry Johnson, Gilbert Chinard, Gustave Lanson, and Maurice Collerey (27–30). Gustave Lanson was also instrumental in developing Literary History as a scientific discipline and in imposing this scientific approach to literature as a discipline worthy of inclusion in the American graduate school curriculum.[92] The establishment in 1883 of the Modern Language Association as the national professional association of scholars of the national literatures, initially English, French, and German, made the advanced study of modern languages a legitimate discipline in the modern university.

4. Franco-American Relations and National Stereotypes in the Age of Mass Culture

Specialists in the field of international relations hold the disenchanted view that feelings are seldom the source of a nation's intervention on another nation's behalf. Rather, they say, national self-interest is. Thus, according to Montbrial, "[t]he French intervention [in the American War of Independence] owed nothing to sentiment, as neither did later American interventions on the Old Continent in 1917 and 1942" (452). For that reason, they further argue, international relations are best envisioned as networks of interdependent relations in the areas of geopolitics, economics, and culture (451). As seen here earlier in the case of the Quasi-War, the good or bad image a nation has of the other is largely dependent on the state of their political and commercial relations. Furthermore, the memory of past events generates contradictory images of the other nation that, like those embedded in the national memory itself,[93] are powerful and can be recalled and mobilized in support of such or such present or future action. From an American vantage point, the Monroe doctrine of non-intervention could be used and was used to justify a position of neutrality at the outbreak of World War I and World War II, and conversely, the memory of French support in the War of Independence was brought back to memory to expect intervention (on the part of France) and intervene (on the part of United States) in the same wars.[94]

What makes international relations such a complex field to investigate is that, under normal circumstances in a republic, there is no such thing as a unified public opinion: on the contrary, the very essence of democracy resides at best in the exchange of opinions, at worst violent clashes over opposite standpoints. In a democracy, public opinion is best described as a field of tension between divergent positions in virtually every domain. To go back to the genesis of national images, one may therefore safely posit that in ordinary life, Francophiles and Francophobes in America, and Atlanticists[95] and anti–Americans in France, co-exist peacefully most of the time, and that they do not even really think along those national lines. It is only when a crisis hits or a given nation intervenes somewhere, somehow, in the world, that the production of clichés and the reproduction of stereotypes kicks into high gear: "Such interventions fundamentally reorient the course of events and thus generate immense collective emotion and become sources of reciprocal images with a structuring impact on the future" (Montbrial, 452). Although these images seldom withstand "the shock of reality" (453),[96] they generate the illusion that there is such a thing as "the French" or "the American," when each people is actually structured by internal divisions similar to those that exist between them.

The tension between pro- and anti-French and pro- and anti-American sentiment spans the entire 19th century in both counties. Thus, on American side, sources of Francophobia included the suspicion that the French rooted for the Confederacy[97] during the Civil War.[98] The War of Mexico increased anti–French sentiment, not only because it took place during the Civil War, but also because it resulted in the establishment, thanks to French military support, of a short-lived Catholic kingdom in the United States' backyard.[99] On French side, two events bred anti–American sentiment in the late 19th century:

the Haymarket Affair, a repression of the workers' movement viewed as expression of the inhumanity of the American capitalist system,[100] and the American invasion of Cuba and the Philippines in 1898, taken by the French as a sign of the United States' imperial ambitions (Montbriand, 456).[101] But more importantly, U.S. hesitation to assist France when World War I[102] broke out re-awakened, in France, the perception created by the American disregard for the 1778 Treaty of Amity, and reinforced during the Napoleonic wars,[103] that the United States was an unreliable ally.[104]

The U.S. army was not particularly strong in pre-war years, but its forces increased tremendously with the reinstatement of the draft. All in all over two million American servicemen ended up fighting in World War I, thereby ending a murderous war that had lasted four years. As it was impossible to transport all these men back to the United States at once when the war ended, France offered them special college courses (Walton 31–32). Thus 5,000 Americans enrolled in Parisian and provincial universities in the first half of 1919, an experience that led many of them to reject the preconceptions they had about France (Kaspi, 17).[105] World War I thus marked an era of "Doughboy and Dollar" tourism (216–233) that Harvey Levenstein has characterized as an "Invasion of the Lower Orders" (214). After the war, the League of Nations was founded at the instigation of President Wilson as a means of preventing future wars. As it happened, the U.S. Senate refused to ratify it, and since it was presented together with the Treaty of Versailles that officially ended World War I, both were rejected. This action "has usually been blamed for the subsequent collapse of the peace settlement of 1919 and the revival of German expansion in Europe" (Keylor, 44). This failure to act after the war did not endear Americans to a French public already puzzled by U.S. hesitation to enter the war.[106]

In France, following a brief period of national unity, a certain political stability was reached as right and left political parties took turns governing. An international crisis occurred when Germany stopped reparation payments agreed upon at the Treaty of Versailles and the French and the Belgian occupied the industrial Ruhr area in 1924. But an American intervention, the Dawes Plan, temporarily solved the crisis and the occupation ended. In 1924, France recognized the Soviet Union. By 1926, a devaluation of the currency stabilized finances and the economy took off. In 1928, the gainfully employed obtained a few social security benefits, and full employment was reached by 1930. But despite an infusion of capital and materials from the United States, the pace of industrialization was slow. France's resistance to the Fordist model made it lose ground in the areas of automobile and movie production, as well as aviation.

As France needed workers to replace men lost during the war (10 percent of the male population), it welcomed refugees from Eastern Europe during reconstruction. Millions of people displaced by the redrawing of European national boundaries, many of them stateless Jews fleeing pogroms, arrived in the country after World War I. Most of them viewed their stay as a stopover on their way to the United States but the 1924 Johnson-Reed Act was to change their plans. From then on, the total number of immigrants admitted to the United States was reduced to 150,000 a year and the number of immigrants from any given country determined as a fraction of the size of the population originally from that country already present in the United States (M. Jones, 276–277).[107] The new "national origin system" openly aimed at maintaining the "'racial preponderance'" of Anglo-Saxons in the United States and practically barred entry to immigrants from Eastern European countries since they had a history of low immigration to the United States. With the borders closed to them, many of these refugees ended up staying in France where their presence re-ignited the xenophobia and anti–Semitism that had already come to full light during the Dreyfus Affair.

In the socio-cultural area, things looked much brighter. The terms used to describe the immediate post-war era, the "Roaring Twenties," *les années folles*, give a pretty good idea of the euphoria that overtook society in the nations celebrating victory at the end of World War I. This was a period of great innovation in the arts, the triumph of cubism, expressionism, surrealism, and modernism, the heydays of music hall and silent film. Women who had played leadership roles while men were at the front were not ready to return to the kitchen. In the United States, they obtained the right to vote and, if they did not in France, they marked their new assertiveness as *garçonnes*, that is by adopting behaviors thought of as masculine such as smoking, driving, and wearing short hair, short skirts and trousers. Paris was a cosmopolitan city that attracted American "expats," the most famous of which are Gertrud Stein, Ernest Hemingway, Waldo Pierce, Ezra Pound, Scott Fitzgerald, Sherwood Anderson, John Dos Passos, and Josephine Baker, a young African-American performing artist from St. Louis, a music hall and movie star who was the toast of town during the interwar period.

The 1930s, by contrast with the 1920s, were seen as terrible, as "*les années noires.*" France's financial and economic situation took a turn for the worse when the Great depression hit between 1932 and 1935 and Germany was no longer able to pay for war reparations. Most of the American expats went home. During the decade that preceded World War II, the struggle between right-wing nationalists and left-wing socialists and communists resumed and became increasingly virulent. The 1930s were marred by violent clashes between the communists, who opposed liberal democracy as exploitation of the little man, and the fascists, who wanted to abolish democracy in France like Mussolini had done in Italy and Hitler in Germany. Across the border, Germany was remilitarizing, the Republic of Weimar fell apart in 1933, and Hitler came to power vowing revenge for World War I's defeat. France and the United Kingdom, who did not want to go to war again, sought to appease him and, hoping he would stop there, let him get away with the annexation of parts of Czechoslovakia. But when Poland was invaded in September 1939, war became unavoidable. All was quiet on the Western Front from September 1939 till May 1940 when the Maginot line failed to hold enemy advances and France was invaded,[108] divided into an occupied and "free" zone between 1940 and 1942, and then totally occupied for the rest of the war. The United States remained neutral for two years until Japan attacked the naval base of Pearl Harbor in December 1941. A few days later, the United States declared war to Japan, Germany, and Italy.

World War II was a catastrophe of unprecedented proportions, killing an estimated 50 to 60 million people in the world, and ravaging Europe once again. Once again, an international organization, the United Nations, was created to prevent future wars, with the victors, the United States, the United Kingdom, France, China, the Soviet Union, sitting as permanent members of its Security Council. Europe's reconstruction was financed by the U.S. Marshall Plan[109] just when the Cold War, a geopolitical conflict between Western democracies and Communist China and the USSR (1947–1991) was starting. Caught in-between, France tried to stake its own course despite American pressures,[110] but ended up "choosing the West" (Wall, *The United States*, 63–77) and joining NATO (127–143). In the face of what they perceived as attempts to turn France into a puppet state of the United States,[111] French intellectuals like Jean-Paul Sartre did not shy from criticizing America in the post-war years, thus reinforcing France's reputation of resistance to all things American.[112]

According to most sources, anti–Americanism was prevalent among opponents of consumer society and advocates of France's cultural specificity in post-war France (1096). Facts, however, contradict the thesis of France's alleged allergy to modernity. For one thing, "the French business classes and technocratic elite were never anti–American" in that sense (Wall, 1095).[113] Concepts typically associated with American enterprise, "'management as rule by persuasion, decentralization, collective decision making, and a new focus on technology to improve productivity' […] were already present among those who planned the new France of the Liberation" (1094). Moreover, France recovered relatively quickly from the war due to the (U.S. sanctioned)[114] nationalization of industrial sectors deemed of primary importance (energy, transportation, banking and insurance). The three decades that followed the war are known in France as *30 glorieuses* because of the material progress, the peace, and prosperity they brought to the country. France caught up with the United States during those years, becoming a modern, industrialized nation, with new high-rise housing, affordable cars, and electric appliances for most,[115] equipped with a solid safety net, and a stronger democracy after women finally got the right to vote. The nation even developed its own force of dissuasion (*force de frappe*) in 1961, thus joining the group of three recognized nuclear-weapon states, the United States, the USSR, and Great Britain.

It is more accurate, therefore, to summarize Franco-American relations in the post-war era as both a rejection of "American interference in their policies" and the simultaneous adoption of business and industrial practices deemed "American" like "productivity, technology, economic methods, academic examples" (Wall, *The United States*, 307). But even the notion that France "Americanized" because it became a consumer society deserves to be challenged. After all, people everywhere in the world prefer to live in comfort than in poverty. Modernization was "American" for reasons of timing only. It occurred in America first because the United States did not suffer on its soil from the wars that destroyed Europe twice in a half century. That is not to say that everyone accepted the efficient productivity model associated with modernization. But then again, the workers' fears of turning into robots, of losing their humanity, were not specifically French. After all, it was Charlie Chaplin, who lived in the United States at the time, who first poked fun at the Fordist system in *Modern Times* (1936). It makes no sense to nationalize a concept like "modernization." People acquire certain products or services because they fulfill a particular need not because of their national provenance.[116] Besides, the post-war critique of modernity often presented as specifically French was far from being the exclusive preserve of French intellectuals in the 20th century. It as the Frankfurt School after all that denounced mass culture as alienating and many American intellectuals applauded. All things considered, Franco-American friendship was strong again in the immediate post-war era. As French brides were joining their husbands in the United States, the very same French intelligentsia reputed for its anti–Americanism imported jazz to Europe and welcomed African American writers and intellectuals.[117]

The Western and the Statue of this chapter's title are emblematic of the relation of reciprocity between the United States and France in the late 19th and 20th century: the United States gave France the Western, France gave the United States the statue. More importantly, both emblems bring to mind the centrality of nationhood as a "factor of vision and division" (Bourdieu) in the modern world. Lacorne and Rupnik (and studies that center on anti–Americanism or on Francophobia only in general) imply that stereotypes are produced in a vacuum when they write that "[w]hether as a model or a bête noire, America has never ceased to fascinate and exasperate the French" (1). But the relation of fascination and exasperation between France and the United is not a one-way street; the fascination and exasperation are mutual, even if they are not always synchronized. Reviewing *The American Enemy*, Philippe Roger's history of French anti–Americanism, Herrick Chapman expressed the hope that the book would be read not as a confirmation of "prejudices about France but as a wise guide for thinking about how xenophobias of all kinds travel from one generation to another" (434). While it is important to understand the historical persistence of national biases, awareness of their longevity does not suffice to combat them. (If it were the case, Chapman would not need to *hope* that Roger's book will have the intended effect instead of its opposite). In order to neutralize them, it is also necessary to understand that they are intellectual constructs, faded snapshots of a past historical moment rather than the manifestation of some kind of imaginary essence.

As we saw in this chapter, stereotypes, including national ones, are always simplifications, mental shortcuts that tell only part of the story. They are usually based on values, opinions, and emotions generated internally, within a specific geographic and historical national environment, geared toward fellow citizens, and projected onto national others in unusual circumstances such as a war. They can be uttered and taken as insults or appropriated and claimed as badges of honor. But in order to account properly for these feelings and opinions and to really combat them, one need to understand not only the context of their emergence, but also the nature of the intranational or international struggles that produced them, in other words to locate the creation of positive or negative images of the other in a narrative that takes into accounts both sides of it, not just one.

5. Tips for Further Investigations

Interesting People to Look Up

Pierre Bottineau (1817–1895)
Jean-Baptiste Salpointe (1825–1898)
Kate Chopin (1850–1904)
Gaston Lachaise (1882–1935)
John Vernou Bouvier III (1891–1957)
Louise Bourgeois (1911–2010)
Pierre Salinger (1925–2004)
Daniel Lanois (1951–)
Brett Favre (1969–)
Beyoncé Giselle Knowles (1981–)

Related Fiction

Gustave Aimard, *The Adventurers*, 1858.
Morris and René Goscinny, *Calamity Jane*.
Yves Berger, *La Pierre et le Saguaro*, Paris: Grasset, 1990.

Related Documentaries and Films

Africa to America to Paris. A 1997 film for the Humanities.
An American in Paris, directed by Vicente Minnelli, 1951.
Cemetery without Crosses [*Une Corde, un Colt…*], directed by Robert Hossein, 1969
Blueberry, directed by Jean Kounen, 2004.
Speak White. 1980 short film based on a poem by Michèle Lalonde (1970).

Epilogue

After World War II, the Little Canadas slowly disappeared in New England.[1] Franco-Americans who had done well moved back to Quebec or to the suburbs as old industrial centers were being abandoned or revitalized. Chartier therefore characterizes the years 1935–1960 as a period of assimilation.[2] A case in point is the beat poet Jack Kerouac (1922–1969): a Franco-Canadian of Breton ancestry, he grew up speaking French at home until age 6 in Lowell, Massachusetts, learned English in school, went to Columbia University on a football scholarship, and wrote most of his work in English.[3] As their communities were disappearing, Franco-Americans grew more self-conscious among their American neighbors and lost the pride their parents had felt in their language and culture.[4] At a time when U.S. elites were enamored with French culture, they became aware that the French they spoke was not the French that was spoken in France, that they mixed English words with it, and that their accent was different from the French spoken abroad (Peloquin-Faré, 306–309).

In Quebec, however, things were changing in the opposite direction by the 1960s. The province was going through a *révolution tranquille* (quiet revolution) that brought about the secularization of government, society, welfare, education, and the modernization of the province. Emboldened by these developments, some Quebecois were calling for Quebec's independence, when the President of France, Charles de Gaulle, concluded a speech with the cry of "*Vive le Québec Libre!*" (Long Live Free Quebec!) during an official visit to Montreal in 1967. This expression of solidarity with Quebecois nationalists may have been a very belated apology for France's abandonment of its North American subjects in 1763. Needless to say, this breach of protocol on de Gaulle's part created a diplomatic incident with the Canadian government. While Quebec did not obtain its independence, the Quebecois gained in self-confidence and assertiveness during those years. Since then, they have affirmed their identity as Franco-Canadians and demonstrated that linguistic and cultural diversity are not only possible but also valuable.[5] In a way, they have reconnected with the multilingualism and multiculturalism that had been part of their history from the start.

De Gaulle's intervention in Canadian affairs also led to a cooling in Franco-U.S. relations.[6] Irwin Wall writes that "[t]he high point of anti–Americanism in France was probably reached during the Vietnam war" (Wall, 1095). As he notes, however, the critique of America by the French student movement "owed practically everything to the works of American intellectuals" (1096). Besides, anti-war protests were far from being unique to France. In Western democracies, the Vietnam War was unpopular everywhere among the post–World War II generation. The movement started in the U.K. and Australia, but more protests took place in the United States between 1963 and 1973 than anywhere else in the world. Most of these protests were staged on the campuses of large U.S. universities and led by students who called for social change. In the United States, this vocal generation of baby boomers scored a significant victory when the Civil Rights Act was passed in 1964.[7]

The tremendous increase in the student population in colleges and universities accounts, in part, for the global scope of the demonstrations so common in the 1960s and 1970s. A sign of the western nations' maturity, this era was a time when it became socially admissible for formerly stigmatized minorities everywhere to show pride in their roots. Once separatist movements fizzled out and the risk of autonomy disappeared, hyphenated identities became acceptable, fashionable even. African Americans and Native Americans, Basques, Bretons, Corsicans, Irish, or Quebecois had no more qualms about their poor, oppressed ancestries (Fishman, 489).[8] In Brittany, where the Breton language had practically disappeared, students started learning it again and it is now one of the languages other than French that students may learn in high school. This ethnic revival movement also found its expression in music and literature. The song "Acadian Driftwood" that was written in 1975 by the Canadian-American group The Band, for instance, recalls Acadian history and testifies to that generations' interest in its Francophone ancestry.[9]

Immigration from the United States to France is low, with American immigrants making out 0.6 percent of the French population as of 2018.[10] Immigration from France to the United States has not increased in any significant manner in the late 20th and early 21st centuries. Patrice Higonnet, quoting figures from official U.S. immigration surveys, puts the total emigration from France since 1820 at 740,000 ("French," 380). Jacqueline Lindelfeld notes that "migration since World War I has most often been an isolated phenomenon propelled by self-motivation,[11] one exception being a wave of (mostly temporary) political refugees during World War II"—by which she probably means anti–Fascists, including Jews, fleeing Nazi-occupied France (Lichtenfeld, 4). She further describes the "flow of French immigration" as "steady but numerically insignificant," with an average of "2,460 people a year for the 1981–1995 period" compared to "14,900 from the United Kingdom."

This "low rate of recent immigration from France accounts for the relatively small size of the current French population in the United States" (3). According to the 1990 census, the total number of French-born people residing in the United States was 119,233, or "0.048 percent of the total population" (10). The interactive MLA language map that aggregates "data from the American Community Survey" based on more recent surveys provides similar figures (up to 0.3 percent). It also shows a minority presence in virtually every state of the Union with the greatest concentration of French speakers in the Northeast, Louisiana, and California.[12] As Prévos notes, "French Americans have few relational or organizational networks. (The *Alliance française* seems to be an exception.) They wield little power in the American political, religious and economic systems" ("French," 280). They also tend to naturalize and assimilate easily.

Despite these low immigration figures and the small percentage of French-born residents in the United States, French remained the most frequently studied foreign language in American colleges and universities for the first half of the 20th century and was only passed by Spanish in the 1960s.[13] Enrollment in college French increased significantly a first time after World War II, when the G.I. Bill enabled veterans to go college, and a second time when baby boomers reached college age in the 1960s and 1970s.[14] Enrollments in French and German have gone down since, in part due to the elimination of foreign language requirements at many secondary and higher education institutions,[15] and also due to the perception that they are not as "useful" in the modern world as Spanish.[16] Still, American students continue to take French in junior and high school, in college, even in some pre-schools and foreign-language elementary magnet schools, and this although the study of a foreign language remains optional at many American schools. Many parents and young adults are aware that the mental gymnastics it takes to learn a foreign language or to live in a different culture is an asset in itself—whether or not the language is ever used later in daily life.

Enrollment Figures	1958	1977	2016
Spanish	126,303	377,131	712,608
French	157,900	246,244	175,666
German	107,870	135,474	80,594
Italian	9,577	33,294	56,743

Evolution of Foreign Language Study in U.S. Colleges. Number of students enrolled in the Fall of these years. Source: MLA Language Data Base

In France, high school foreign language education goes back to the 1830s (Rothmund, 15) but the start of German and English studies as means of communication instead of purely literary studies dates from the 1870s (Ringer). Until the 1960s German was the most frequently taught language in France and "English" meant "British English." It is no longer the case today. France has an ambitious national foreign-language curriculum that is based on the expectation that every student graduating from high school be able to communicate in two foreign languages.[17] Because all French students since 2005 have to take English, the number of French people able to communicate in that language has increased tremendously, to the horror of some traditionalists who deplore the "neo-French" that proximity between the two languages has created (see Borer). Unlike France, Canada has no federal ministry of education but as both English and French are official languages, the advantages of being bilingual are obvious. Thus in 2016, 15 percent of Canadian children age 5 to 17 were already bilingual and that percentage was more than twice as high (33 percent) in Quebec (Turcotte).

Over time, pedagogical methods have changed tremendously as the focus of foreign language education moved from reading and writing skills to speaking and listening comprehension. The many study abroad programs that came into existence in the 20th century reconnected with the belief that immersing oneself in another language and culture is the surest way of becoming bilingual, a belief going as far back as Jacques Cartier. The Junior Year Abroad programs that appeared in the 1920s at the University of Delaware and Smith College allowed American students to study for a year in France while earning American credit for about the same amount of tuition they would have paid had they stayed on campus (Walton, 68). Junior Year Abroad students were not only expected to learn the French language and to absorb French culture they were also thought of as American ambassadors of good will to France (69). By the 1930s, over 5,000 students were already enrolled each year, and after a hiatus during the war, the programs resumed in 1945.

Other exchange programs appeared in the mid–1950s, sending around 2,500 American students to France by the end of the decade, five times more than the number of French students going to the United States in those days (111). Walton argues that "in the Cold War era study abroad as a form of Franco-American cultural relations served both national interests and internationalism simultaneously because the result was not indoctrination, homogenization, or conversion, but rather an appreciation of difference" (112). By the end of the 1970s, over 6,000 Americans were going to France each year and nearly 2,000 French students came to the United States.[18] The Fulbright Program, for instance, aimed at instilling "mutual understanding" between the two countries "through the increase of exchanges of scientific, technical, and professional knowledge" (118). About the same number of French and American students, between 200 and 300 a year, participated in that program in the 1950s (120).

Tourism between France and the United States has been increasing continuously since the 19th century. Harvey Levenstein, who has studied American tourism to France extensively,[19] divides the 20th century into three phases, first a period of "Great Depression Follies" when tourism was still restricted to an elite; then the post World War II of the 1950s and 1960s when air transport between the two continents started to make transatlantic travel affordable for the middle class; and finally, since the 1970s, an era of cheap flights and mass tourism that caters to a wide variety of sociological profiles and tastes. Numbers speak for themselves: in 2018, 4.4 million visitors from the United States arrived in France, generating 6.3 billion euros in revenue.[20] Among non–European countries, the United States came first as supplier of tourists, with twice as many visitors to France as China. The same year, the United States welcomed 1.8 million visitors from France,[21] of which 42 percent stayed in New York City and state; 22 percent visited the South Atlantic (Washington, D.C., and Florida); 16 percent went to Arizona and Nevada, and 28 percent to California.[22] This contemporary tourism to the West has produced a new kind of French literature that is best exemplified by the novels of Philippe Labro (1936-), a former Fulbright student,[23] and the beautiful, poetic prose that the magnificence of the West and the immensity of its skies have inspired Yves Berger (1931–2004).[24]

Although France abandoned its policies of linguistic and cultural protectionism in the 1980s, as well as what some critics viewed as "its pathological anti–Americanism,"[25] a reverse trend occurred in U.S. academe. As French society was warming up to the United States, Francophilia was on the wane in American universities. Writing in 1994, Irwin Wall wondered whether "American intellectuals [were] themselves slipping into the danger of being called, or even becoming, anti–French" (1084).[26] Indeed, in the context of the American culture wars, France soon became the scapegoat for both sides.[27] Seen as the epitome of frivolity by one camp due to the import of "French theory" and "French Feminism" in the humanities, France was denounced in the "French theory" camp as universalist and hostile to multiculturalism. But these debates were petty squabbling compared to the French bashing tsunami that hit America in March 2003. Convinced that Iraq was developing a nuclear program, the Bush administration sought the support of the United Nations for a military intervention, but France refused to play along. In a speech at the U.S. Security Council, the French Foreign Minister announced that his country would make use of her veto. The anti–France campaign that followed was virulent in the media and accompanied by a boycott of French products (Vaisse). One of the outcomes of this Franco-American crisis was a temporary downturn in College French enrollments, study abroad, as well as American tourism to France. But the era of Freedom Fries did not last. Soon Americans were eating French fries and flocking to Paris again.

One may expect that until the world leaves the national age behind, which is not going to happen any time soon, France and the United States will continue their rocky love affair, with great shows of solidarity in the face of disasters like Hurricane Katrina,

9/11, the terrorist attacks on *Charlie Hebdo* and the kosher supermarket, or Notre-Dame de Paris's fire, and less glorious moments in times of geopolitical and commercial disagreements.[28] Nonetheless, certain signs point to the genesis of a common international culture, beginning with the founding, after World War I, of Franco-American sites of memory like the Musée Franco-Américain du Château de Blérancourt or the American cemeteries in France. Tourism has also, in many ways, internationalized national sites of memory, as the establishment, in 2008, of UNESCO's list of Intangible Cultural Heritage illustrates. Nonetheless, although the number of international visitors is impressive, the French who visit the United States and the Americans who visit France still make up only a tiny percentage of the population of their country, respectively 1.34 percent of the U.S. population and 2.6 percent of the French population.

More significant, therefore, is the transformation of everyday life brought along by the neo-liberal economy: the existence of common transnational cultures in the areas of sports, entertainment, music, cinema and television, fashion, and food, the adoption of English as the lingua franca of Western democracies, and the ease of transnational communication provided by social media. If some mobilization movements continue to have a national character (Black Lives Matter and gun control in the United States, or the *Gilets Jaunes* in France), others, like the struggles for women and gay rights and the environment, point in the direction of a transnational culture. Protests against the socio-economic ravages caused by the 2008 economic crisis have also mobilized millions of people around the world, including the United States and France. It is impossible to predict the effects that life, even part-time life, in these transnational spaces, virtual or not, will have on one's sense of national identity but the risks of total cultural homogenization are low. Any French person entering the United States or any American entering France immediately feels—like Dorothy in Oz—that this is not home. At the airport already, everything is similar—the modern equipment, uniforms, and formalities—and yet nothing is the same. France remains France and the United States remains the United States. The differences are subtle but significant and therefore in greater need of analysis.

To conclude, neither France's stature on the world stage today nor the influence of the small French population in the United States can explain the Franco-American love affair exemplified by over two centuries of close relations. While an in-depth investigation of this subject is long overdue, it stands to reason that the persistent American interest in all things French can only have something to do with to the "significant number of individuals [who] claim French ancestry" (Lichtenfeld, 8). The more research I conducted on this topic, the more I became aware of the incomplete nature of this book, which is just an overview of the vast topic of the French roots of North America and of the continued presence of people of French descent in the United States. On a positive note, the historical nature of the discipline of French in American universities, with its research specializations in the 16th, 17th, 18th, 19th, and 20th and 21st centuries, provides quite a suitable institutional setting to advance scholarship in historical Francophone studies. While "[t]he records of such a history are comparatively few and widely scattered" (Belting, 7),[29] this scattering, mostly in state archives, libraries, museums, and historical societies, makes research all the more accessible to a great number of scholars spread out all over the country. Apart from contributing to this scholarship, French departments and French Studies programs could also serve as a clearing house for the compilation and dissemination of a secondary literature in an area that is already extensive and growing all the time.

Chapter Notes

Preface

1. See Le Hir, "Imagining the Discipline…"
2. The original letter can be found in the Archives of the Missouri Historical Society.
3. For a short biography of William Morrison, see Webpages on Institutional Websites, Weyerhaeuser Museum of Morrison County, MN.
4. As my anecdote illustrates, there is a community need for information about the United States' French past. Insofar as *French Immigrants and Pioneers in the Making of America* is a direct response to that need, it is a Public Humanities project.

Introduction

1. This quote came to my attention in Dean R. Louder and Eric Waddel's *Du Continent Perdu à l'Archipel retrouvé*. It comes from Clarke Blaise's *Tribal Justice*, 158. A map in Louder and Waddel's book offers a visual illustration of the accuracy of the claim found in Blaise's novel (xix).
2. See Pinette, "Un 'étonnant mutisme.'"
3. Prévos seems to think that the French immigrants are partially responsible for this oversight: "It is said that, in a sketch of his life, Henry David Thoreau began with 'I am of French extract' yet never alluded to this fact later in the sketch. This fact is illustrative of both the history of the French in America and, also, as a characterization of the attitudes of the descendants of French immigrants toward their ancestry" (*Frenchmen between two Rivers*, I, 1).
4. "En Amérique, terre d'immensité, non d'angoisse, on peut toujours aller voir plus loin, à l'ouest des Appalaches, où il y a de la terre en abondance pour les migrants venus d'Europe, Irlandais, Allemands, Scandinaves," Debray, 108.
5. On the French naming of places and people, see Jacques Portes, 37.
6. Most of the examples quoted here come from Creagh, *Nos Cousins d'Amérique*, 14–15. For an exhaustive overview, see the "List of place names of French origin in the United States" in Wikipedia.
7. Ronald Creagh views Pierre François Xavier de Charlevoix (1682–1761) as "an 'ecologist' before his time" because he bemoaned the senseless carnage of furry animals carried out by the French. See Creagh, *Nos Cousins*, 30.

8. See Joseph Price, "La Jeune Francophonie Américaine."
9. The course syllabus proposed by Pinette in "'Un 'étonnant mutisme,'" illustrates this point (194–203).
10. Havard and Vidal "Making New France New Again…"
11. None of this would have been possible without the assistance of the First Nations the French were to encounter. In spite of idealized representations, this relationship has been a privileged one overall, for the French as well as the Native Americans, no doubt, as Gilles Havard explains, because of the presence of Franco-Indians in a great number of Native American communities. See Havard, *Continent*, 20.
12. For an overview of the history of New France, see Brazeau.
13. Hence the recurrence of "traitors"—from Etienne Brûlé to Médard Chouart des Groseilliers and his brother-in-law, Pierre-Esprit Radisson—in that history.
14. The translation of all French texts quoted in this book, including this one, are mine unless otherwise indicated.
15. "But like the Yankee politicians of Lafayette's day (some of whom derided Louisianans as 'too ignorant to elect suitable men'), American historians have long trivialized the French colonial empire, shunting most of the places and peoples it touches to the margins of their larger narratives" (Hodson and Rushforth, 20).
16. For a brief treatment of my topic, see Higonnet, "French"; Prévos, "French"; and Hillstrom, "French Americans."
17. Naming the various groups of French descent living in the United States can be problematic (Prévos "French," 286). Barkan, for instance, uses the term "French Canadians" to refer to Americans of Franco-Canadian descent although the term "French Canadians" usually refers to Canadians of French descent living in Canada (Lamarre). Louis Péloquin-Faré uses the term "Franco-Americans" to refer to the same people. Louise Laurie C. Hillstrom uses the term "French Americans" to refer to all groups of French descent, not only of French-Canadian, descent. Both that term and "Franco-Americans" are used here to refer to all these groups.

18. Although MacDonald's remark applies to Fort de Chartres only, it is pertinent to New France as a whole.

Chapter I

1. On the concepts of savagery and civilization to characterize Native American and French people in the North American context, see Balvay, *L'Epée et la plume*, 101–111.

2. Balvay distinguishes five main Native American nations that interacted with the French in New France: the Algonquian; the Iroquoian; the Siouan; and Muscogian; and the Natchez (*L'Epée*, 53–55). "Most Algonquian nations practiced some form of exogamy. It was taboo for a man to marry any female—cousin, aunt, niece, and siblings—who belonged to his clan." McDonnell, *Masters of Empire*, 10.

3. "We tend to forget, that the microbial shock that eradicated 90% of the aborigine population was the most important feature of the encounter between Europe and America." Havard and Vidal, *Histoire*, 194–195.

4. On the voyages of discovery, see Creagh, "L'invention de l'Amérique," in *Nos Cousins d'Amérique*, 17–24; Hunt, "The Link between the Renaissance and Overseas Explorations," *The Renaissance*, 63–77; Weber, "The Great Discoveries," in *A Modern History*, 57–63.

5. On the Middle Ages, see George Duby, *Histoire de la Civilisation française*, vol. I, 9–240; Weber, "Europe in the Middle Ages," *A Modern History…*, 3–35.

6. See Haine, chapter 4, 37–43; Labrune and Toutain, 38–39.

7. On the rise of money, see Elias, 206–207; Le Goff, *Money in the Middle Ages*, 14–59.

8. See Elias, "Dynamics of Feudalization," in *The Civilizing Process*, 195–208.

9. See Elias, "On the Sociogenesis of the State," in *The Civilizing Process*, 257–362.

10. For a map of French mints, 1550 to 1620, see Duby and Mandrou, *Histoire de la civilisation française*, vol. I, 303.

11. On the relation between money and the genesis of the state, see Elias, 206–208, 253–254; 359–361; and Le Goff, 50–60.

12. On the Renaissance, see Haine, 43–47; Labrune and Toutain, 42–43; Weber, 37–106.

13. Elias's description of the last stage of state formation centers on France. See "The Power Balance within the Unit of Rule…" in *The Civilizing Process*, 312–344.

14. See Elias, "On the Sociogenesis of Taxation," 344–362.

15. Elias describes this process in "On the Sociogenesis of *Minnesang* and Courtly Forms of Conduct" (236–256). He calls it "The Courtization of Warriors" (387–397) when applied to 17th-century France and in particular to Louis XIV's court.

16. On the Renaissance, see Hunt, *The Renaissance*, 1–32; Mandrou, *Histoire de la Civilisation française*, vol. I, 243–345; Labrune and Toutain, *L'Histoire de France*, 46–47; Weber, *History of Modern Europe*, 37–105.

17. See Hunt, "The Influence of the Renaissance on Monarchies and Government," in *The Renaissance*, 33–48; Weber, "Principalities and Powers," in *A Modern History*, 113–146.

18. See Hunt, "The Link Between the Renaissance and the Reformation," *The Renaissance*, 49–62; Weber, *A Modern History of Europe*: "The Crisis of Christianity and Christendom," 147–181; "The Reformed Religions," 242–254, and "Counter-Reformation and Catholic Reform," 252–264.

19. For a discussion of early Franco-Spanish rivalries in the North American colonial context, see McGrath, 2–32; and Weber, "Chapter 6. Struggles for Empire," 265–312 and 331–339.

20. As we will see in the next chapter, the wars of religion continued to ravage Europe during the Thirty Years' (1618–1648).

21. See Abreu de Galindo, 3. Favier gives Jean de Béthancourt and Gafider de La Salle as the first settlers of the Canary Islands in 1402 (410).

22. On the Voyages of Discovery, see Havard and Vidal, "Les explorations sous patronage royal," *Histoire*, 33–34; "The Link between the Renaissance and Overseas Explorations," *The Renaissance*, 63–77; Weber, "The Great Discoveries," in *A Modern History*, 57–63.

23. In "Slavery," Martin Munro points out that "the Atlantic slave trade did not begin in the New World but has its roots in mid–15th-century Portuguese-controlled plantations on the island of Madeira" (1075).

24. On the Portuguese voyages of discovery, see Nowell, 25–45; Favier, 414–419 and 537–567.

25. On the Spanish voyages of discovery, see Nowell, 46–80; Favier, 439–536.

26. "The royal missions entrusted to great explorers aim less at expanding a kingdom's territory than at obtaining a monopoly over new commercial routes." Creagh, *Nos Cousins*, 23.

27. On the Vikings in North America, see Weinmann, 47–65.

28. On Cabot, see Weinmann, 43–45, who calls him "the under-gifted explorer who succeeded" (43) by contrast to Cartier, "the gifted explorer who failed" (40).

29. Pickett underscores the importance of fishing grounds for a Catholic country like France that demanded that the faithful abstain from meat on fasting days (47). See also, Bouchard, 36–37; Michallat, "Fishing," and "Whaling"; Hiller, "Newfoundland." Prévos mentions the mysterious appeal these "wonderful regions" had on the French imagination: "Early legends told by Breton fishermen mention boats which had been pushed westward for weeks and landed on mysterious and unchartered shores […] peopled by remarkable individuals" (Prévos, 14).

30. On the early development of trade and commerce, including whaling, see Biggar, 18–37; Eccles, 2–3, and O'Leary.

31. On Jean Ango, see Gaffarel; Creagh, *Nos Cousins*, 21; Nowell, 83.

32. Opinions differ as to who footed the bill for the first voyage. John Dickinson believes it was strictly a private venture -although the King expressed interest (15); Havard and Vidal think that the King provided support as well (*Histoire*, 35).

33. Verrazano was long believed to have been born in Florence. In his article on Verrazano, Jo Edwards, for instance, gives "near Florence" as his birthplace and so does Creagh in *Nos Cousins*, 23. Verrazano is now thought to have been born in Lyon, France.

34. On Verrazano's voyage, see: Brebner, 88–97; Brevoort; Dickinson, 15–16; Creagh, *Nos Cousins*, 21–22; Dickinson, 14–30; Havard and Vidal, *Histoire*, 34–35; Hoffmann, 105–115; Kellogg, 12–14; Pickett and Pickett, 47–48; Soyez, 12–14; Trudel, *Histoire*, 33–63; and Weinman, 40–43.

35. On French cartographs of North America, 1520–1763, see John Nothnagle, who writes that "French contributions to the exploration and the cartography of North America are not very well known" (24).

36. On Cartier's voyages, see Biggar, H.P., 6–17; Brebner, 98–113; Dickinson, 17–25; Eccles, 4–8; Havard and Vidal, *Histoire*, 35–45; Hoffmann, 115–121; Kellogg, 15–24; Nowell, 83–84; Pickett, 47–48; Soyez, 15–45; Trudel, *Histoire*, 65–175; and Weinmann, 67–99.

37. A bishop introduced Cartier to the King.

38. Cartier's ships were called *La Grande Hermine*, *La Petite Hermine*, and *L'Emerillon*. *L'hermine*, an animal that is similar to a white weasel, or stoat, is a symbol of Brittany.

39. Cartier discovered the river on August 10, the day Catholics honor Saint Lawrence. For an interactive map of his voyages, see the webpage "Cartier, Jacques, 1534–1542." On the river itself, see Labrecque.

40. Havard and Vidal's figures are similar: 110,000 Iroquoian and Algonquian (*Histoire*, 196).

41. Data from Laval University quoted in Soyez, Jean-Marc, *Quand l'Amérique s'appelait Nouvelle France*, 49. On the First Nations, see Soyez's chapter 3, "Indien: 'qui ne peut se domestiquer,'" 47–77. See also Spicer, 11–13; Traisnel, "Quebec," 960.

42. See *Jacques Cartier and his Four Voyages to Canada* (1540).

43. For other retelling of Cartier's voyages to the New World, see Pickett, 48–61; Trudel, *Histoire*, 65–175.

44. On Roberval, see Kenny.

45. Quotes from French texts, such as this one, are my own translation.

46. On the Wars of Religion in France, see Weber, "The Crisis of Christianity and Christendom," in *Modern History of Europe,* 147–180, 294–299; Labrune and Toutain, *L'Histoire*, 50–53.

47. On the Reformation in France, see Creagh, *Nos Cousins d'Amérique*, 153–155.

48. On the topic of "Protestant New France" (Trudel's expression), see Eccles, 8–10; Havard and

Vidal, 45–55; Hoffman, 125–143; McGrath, 33–49 and 57–72; Pickett and Pickett, 62–83; Trudel, *Histoire*, 177–212. Hoffman states that by 1556, "Spain had almost lost control [to the French] of the waters of the Caribbean and of the port [Havana] that was the assembly point for Spanish ships returning to Europe with the treasures of the Americas" (129).

49. On the Wars of Italy, see Weber, 142–145; Labrune and Toutain, 48–49.

50. "The French explorer Villegagnon, who traveled to Brazil in 1555–1558, though favorable to reformed ideas, never thought this implied a breach with Rome" (Weber, 174).

51. On the 1555 expedition to Brazil, see Creagh, *Nos Cousins*, 155, Nowell, 84.

52. The island is now known as Villegaignon [or Villegagnon] Island.

53. See Thévet, *Les singularitéz de la France Antarctique*.

54. Montaigne was the first to formulate the theory of the *bon sauvage* [good native], which rests on two notions, "first that no custom can be rejected offhand because it differs from our own, and second that, in light of the force of tradition, innovation should always be introduced at a slow pace" (Creagh, *Nos Cousins*, 26).

55. Jean Nicot (ca. 1525–1600) popularized the use of tobacco in France. On Nicot, who gave his name to the word "nicotine," see Rosenstein. Gilbert states that "by around 1630, it [tobacco] was clearly also a European product" (1135).

56. On the early slave trade, see Munro, 1075.

57. On the significance of de Léry's *History of a Voyage Made to the Land of Brazil*, see Jeanneret's entry in Hollier's *New History of French Literature*. See also Charles Forsdick, "Travel Writing."

58. On the Franco-Spanish rivalries over Florida and Carolina, see Eccles, 10–11; Havard and Vidal, *Histoire*, 45–55; Hoffmann, 205–290.

59. On "The First Voyage to Florida," see Creagh, *Nos Cousins*, 155–161. According to McGrath, Jean Ribault had served the British admiralty for at least ten years prior to this appointment and may have been a spy. See McGrath, 50–57.

60. For a detail account of the Charlesfort settlement, see McGrath, 73–95.

61. Chapter 6 of McGrath's *Early French Florida* (96–115) is devoted to Fort Caroline. For Théodore de Brye's iconographic depiction of the fort, see the webpage "Fort Caroline, Représentation du. *Arcis Carolinae Delineatio*, 1591."

62. On Menéndez's biography prior to his intervention in Florida, see McGrath, 110–115. On his intervention in Florida, see McGrath, 117–155.

63. On the artist Le Moyne de Morgues, see Rolfe.

64. Le Challeux wrote that the 50 women and children of the colony were slaughtered as well, a claim disputed in Spanish sources.

65. The inlet still bears the name of this event, Matanzas, *"slaughter"* in Spanish.

66. See Nowell, 85. Havard and Vidal mention this episode, as based on a witness account, and de Gourgues' subsequent reply (*Histoire*, 54). Creagh

does as well (*Nos Cousins*, 159). McGrath, who quotes contemporary French and Spanish sources, and the account of the retaking of San Mateo in Suzanne Lussagnet's *Les Français en Floride*, do not mention these signs or these words.

67. On Le Moyne's iconographic series on North America, see Havard and Vidal, 51.

68. On the St. Bartholomew's Massacre, see Weber, 296; Labrune and Toutain, 50–53.

69. See Haine, 51; Labrune and Toutain, 54–55; and Weber, 298.

70. Russell describes initial British efforts and concludes: "While the settlers were valiant in their efforts to colonize, the colony ultimately disappeared for unknown reasons" (3).

71. Soyez (13) presents Gonneville's story as factual. So do Butel, *Histoire*, 24, and Claude Levi-Strauss in *Tristes Tropiques* (86).

Chapter II

1. On the Portuguese exploration of Newfoundland, see Hiller, "The Portuguese Explorers."

2. See Servant, *Les Compagnie de Saint-Christophe*; Eccles, 29–31; Heuman, 8.

3. For an overview of early British colonization efforts, see Howell, "The First English Colonial Empire," 113–134.

4. On the early Spanish North American colony of St. Augustine and Florida, see Pickett and Pickett, "Chapter 4, St. Augustine," 84–97, and McGrath.

5. Such is the topic of Pickett's and Pickett's *The European Struggle to Settle North America*.

6. See Russell, "Origins of the Southern colonies," 4–5.

7. On Henri IV and the Edict of Nantes, see Labrune and Toutain, 54–55; Weber, 298.

8. See Pickett and Pickett, "Chapter 5, English Colonization Efforts," (100–128) and "Chapter 6, Jamestown" (129–148). In a chapter on the French "first comers" to the British colonies, Forsdick mentions a pilgrim family named Mullins (originally "Molines" in French) onboard the *Mayflower*. He adds that Huguenots "had the tendency to corrupt names […] to conceal the fact" (125). William (Guillaume) Molines, his wife and son did not survive very long in America, but their daughter Priscilla did. Through her marriage to John Alden, she became "the ancestress of that celebrated New England family, the Aldens" and of the second president of the U.S., John Adams (125). Nathan Gillette, a French Huguenot who had immigrated to England at the end of the Wars of Religion, settled in New England in 1630. He is the ancestor of King C. Gillette (1855–1932), the inventor of the Gillette safety razor. See Adams, *King C. Gillette*. On French immigration to New England prior to 1785, see also M. Jones, 16–17.

9. Creagh calls the companies of Rouen, Saint-Malo, La Rochelle, and St. Jean de Luz "the first capitalist ventures" (*Nos Cousins*, 22–23). See Julien, chapter I, *Les Français en Amérique* on the colonial legacy of the 16th century.

10. On Henri IV's role in the colonization of New France, see Barbiche.

11. Havard and Vidal write that Henri III voided La Roche's monopoly after a coalition of Saint-Malo merchants sued for unfair competition (61–62).

12. On La Roche's colonization attempt, see Biggar, 38–41; Eccles, 13; Dickinson, 28–29; Havard and Vidal, *Histoire*, 62–63.

13. On the early fur trade, see Biggar, 29–33; Brebner, 114–122; Havard and Vidal, *Histoire*, 59–61; Jacquin, 13–34; Trudel, *Histoire*, 213–244.

14. On Tadoussac, see Bouchard, 33–90; Lebel. A visual representation of the first fair at Tadoussac can be found in Allaire, 54.

15. See Bernard, "Montagnais."

16. Chauvin did not keep his promise to establish a Catholic colony, perhaps because being a Calvinist, he did not intend to. He died in 1603 however, which left him little time to do so. On Chauvin, see Biggar, 41–46; Morley; Eccles, 13–14; Dickinson, 29–30.

17. Jacquin devotes a chapter of his book on the "White Indians" to the *truchements*, the interpreters, and to the lives they led (35–61).

18. On the wars of religion in France, see Weber, 294–298.

19. On Aymar de Chaste, see Biggar, 46; Dickinson, 29–30; Trudel, *Histoire* I, 252–254. According to Trudel, Cap-Chat is the only reminder of de Chaste in Canada.

20. On the 1603 voyage, see Biggar, 46–50; Eccles, 15–17; Julien, chapter II; Kellogg, 46–49; Nowell, 86; Trudel, *Histoire* I, 254–269. For interactive maps of Champlains's voyages, see the webpage "Champlain, Samuel de, 1604–1616."

21. On Champlain, see Trudel, "Champlain"; Julien, chapter III; Kellogg, 45–64; Soyez, 79–102; Weinmann, 105–176, and the Virtual Museum of New France at the Canadian Museum of History.

22. See Fiquet, "Brouage in the Time of Champlain: A New Town Open to the World."

23. For an analysis of Champlain's writings about his voyages, see Berthiaume.

24. On the *tabagie*, see Havard and Vidal, 72–75. See also Beaulieu, "The Birth of the Franco-American Alliance."

25. Kellogg notes that "[t]he Indian trade was the chief resource of the colony of New France. Agriculture developed slowly, but the fur trade grew by leaps and bounds" (101).

26. For a newer, critical edition of *Des Sauvages*, see Heidenreich and Ritch.

27. On the terms used to designate members of the First Nations, see Havard, "Introduction," 9–10.

28. For a biography of Pierre Du Gua de Mons, see Waters. His last name is spelled different ways, "Du Gua or Dugua; "de Monts" or "de Mons." See also Kellogg, 49–50.

29. See "Charter of Acadia Granted by Henri IV of France...."

30. On the first Acadian colony, see Arsenault; Biggar, 51–65; Carpain, 166–169; Dickinson, 33–36;

Eccles, 15–19; Gannon, 49–50; Havard and Vidal, *Histoire*, 75–80.

31.   See Ader-Martin, "Présence protestante en Nouvelle France."

32.   "By a strange coincidence, Champlain walked twice on the very lands the 'Pilgrims' would later select for their colony: Plymouth Bay. The French, before the English, came close to choosing it as New France's foundational site. 'It would be a very suitable place to build on and lay the foundations of a republic' [Champlain wrote]" (Weinman, *Du Canada au Québec*, 108).

33.   Pauline Arsenault states that "Acadia" was originally thought of as "Arcadia," the ideal, utopian place of perfect harmony found in Greek mythology (115).

34.   See Havard and Vidal, "Les communautés de pêche de l'Ile Royale," *Histoire*, 444–448.

35.   On the *rang canadien*, the characteristic French way of dividing the land into rectilinear longlots, see Soyez, 125–127. For maps and explanations about longlots in the St. Lawrence River valley, around Detroit, Green Bay, the Illinois Country, Louisiana, the Arkansas Post and even Texas, see Ekbert, "French Longlots in North America," *French roots of Illinois Country*, 1–30. The practice of dividing land in that manner dates back to medieval Europe.

36.   See William B. Munro, *The seigneurs of old Canada: a chronicle of New-World Feudalism.*

37.   On Hébert, see Bennett. Hébert was the first officer of justice and the first farmer of New France.

38.   On Lescarbot, see Baudry. On the relations between Champlain and Lescarbot, see Thierry. On Acadia in Lescarbot's days, Havard and Vidal, *Histoire*, 75–80.

39.   On Champlain's cartography, see Heidenreich and Dahl.

40.   On the Order of Good Cheer, see Thierry.

41.   Acadia at the time was home to the Wabanaki Confederacy composed of the First Nations of the Abenaki, Mi'kmaq, Passamaquoddy, and Penobscot.

42.   On the first years of the colony, see Biggar, "The Two Monopolies of de Monts," 51–68; "The Freedom of Trade," 69–93; and "Champlain's Company, 1614–1620," 94–114; "The Caëns Company and its Union with Champlain's, 1621–1627." See also Eccles, 15–31; Dickenson, 38–42; Havard and Vidal, 80–86.

43.   See Eccles, 19–28. For an overview of the early history of New France, see also Brown, *History*, 2–4.

44.   See Weinmann, *Du Canada au Québec*, 155.

45.   Havard and Vidal (80) de-emphasize the role played by Champlain in the foundation of Quebec City, as does Jean-Yves Grenon, calling it a *comptoir* (a trading post) and underscoring the more crucial role played by businessmen like de Monts, who was after all Champlain's boss. The fact that de Monts was a Protestant, they suggest, may explain the preference for Champlain, as does the fact that all accounts concerning the voyages and settlements of the period are from him. The pages devoted to de Monts here are also based on *Voyages of Sieur de Champlain to New France.*

46.   See Maureen Waters, "Hurons"; on the Franco-Huron alliance, Gervais, 181–182; and Labelle, "'Faire la chaudière,' The Wendat Feast of Souls, 1636."

47.   Underscoring the "distinctiveness of European-Native contact in northeastern North America in the seventeenth and eighteenth centuries," Havard notes, in *The Great Peace of Montreal of 1701*, that these alliances were to be "long-standing" (15) and "influenced both by inter-colonial rivalries and by the existence of antagonisms among Native peoples" (16).

48.   Joseph Chailley-Bert examines reasons behind the creation of such companies, the different types of companies (trade, colonization, and both), and their goals, means, and charters in the first chapter of his book.

49.   Balvay states that a trade alliance necessarily led to a military alliance and that Champlain had no choice but to go to war with his Huron allies. See *L'Epée et la plume*, 136.

50.   Nicolas Marsolet (1587–1667) became an important interpreter for the colony, a friend of Etienne Brûlé, and a fur trader, who remained a *coureur des bois* well into his 70s. His prosperity earned him the nickname of "Petit roi de Tadoussac" (little king of Tadoussac). He lived to be 90. See Soyez, 112–114.

51.   The couple never had children on their own, but they adopted three little Montagnais girls.

52.   Champlain's description of the Huron way of life can be found in *Voyages of Sieur de Champlain to New France, Made in the Year 1615.*

53.   Royot provides other examples of Frenchmen who lost their ways in nature well into the 18th century, thereby underscoring "the influence of the environment on colonial minds" (100).

54.   On Marie of Medici's Regency, see also Labrune and Toutain, 56–57; Weber, 129.

55.   On the "Régime seigneurial in New France," see Havard and Vidal, *Histoire*, 415–424.

56.   On Richelieu, see Bercé, 118–133; Dickinson, 42–46; Weber, 233–239; on his role in making New France a Catholic colony, see MacKinnon.

57.   It stopped being the institution that introduced bills for consideration.

58.   See Stoudt's biography of Nicolas Martiau.

59.   See Kadlec on "Code Michau." Louis XIV signed on to a similar edict in 1669.

60.   Due to opposition of the Parliament of Paris, and then of the regional parliaments, Marilly's legislative reform, with the exception of a few articles, never became law (Kadlec, 40–51).

61.   On the *Compagnie des Cent Associés*, see Creagh, *Nos Cousins d'Amérique*, 32–33; Havard and Vidal, *Histoire*, 86–92.

62.   In his entry on the Jesuits, Thomas Lappas provides a brief history of the order as well as an overview of their activities in New France. Weber comments: "catholic governments usually ignored the subversive possibilities of the Jesuits and sought their aid. They knew them as the best-organized, most effective, and probably the most intelligent of regular orders, and wanted them on their side. Even

the converted Huguenot Henri IV relied on their support" (*A Modern History*, 258).

63. On the capture of Quebec by the Kirk brothers, see Havard and Vidal, 88–89. On David Kirk, see Moir. David Kirke (c. 1597–1654), who grew up in the port city of Dieppe, Normandy, was the son of a rich London merchant and a French woman. He had four brothers.

64. On the Thirty Years' War, see Weber, *A Modern History*, 271–276.

65. On "The Extraordinary Fiscal Increase" under Richelieu and Louis XIII, see Bercé, 135–139.

66. In England, by contrast, the British Parliament refused to approve tax increases requested by King Charles I for the conduct of the Thirty Years' War. Instead, Parliament passed the 1628 Petition of Right, a series of provisions meant to limit royal authority: a) no taxes without Parliament approval; b) no billeting of soldiers without consent; c) no arbitrary or illegal imprisonment, a measure further defined by the Habeas Corpus Act of 1679; d) no arbitrary use of martial law. See Weber, *A Modern History*, 307–309.

67. On the militarization of France during Louis XIII's reign, see Bercé, 139–145; Weber, *A Modern History*, 332–333.

68. But this tried-and-true economic system would fall apart in 1649–50 following the destruction of the Huron confederacy. See Havard et Vidal, "La Chute de la Huronie," in *Histoire*, 92–99.

69. On the Chevalier Isaac de Razilly and the formation of the Company of New France, 1627–1629, see Biggar, 132–149.

70. On Razilly and the colonization of Acadia, see Havard and Vidal, *Histoire*, 89–90.

71. On Charles Menou d'Aulnay, see Havard and Vidal, *Histoire*, 90.

72. Leslie Choquette offers a fine, detailed analysis of immigration from France to Canada in *Frenchmen into Peasants*.

73. For a short biography of Etienne Brûlé, see Jo Edwards. See also Havard and Vidal, 322, and Kellogg, 51–52. For a map of his routes, see the website, "Brûlé, Etienne,1615–1621."

74. Guillaume Aubert offers interesting insights on the "Coureurs de bois."

75. On Nicollet's life, see Hamelin; also "The Voyage of Jean Nicolet, 1634–1635," in Kellogg, 65–83. For a map of his routes, see the website "Nicollet, Jean, 1634."

76. The Chippewa include both the Ojibwa, around Lake Superior, and the Saulteaux, west of Lake Superior. For an overview of contemporary scholarship on Franco-Native American relations, see Englebert and Teasdale, "Introduction," in *French and Indians*.

77. *Masters of Empire* underscores the central role these nations played as the French expanded westward: "We often lumped them under the more general category of Algonquian speakers, and not recognized that they all spoke Anishinaabemowin—a distinct subset of Algonquian. And we have failed to appreciate their significance in the history of the continent. Despite their central location in what the French called the *pays d'en haut* [...], they have remained largely invisible to Euro-American observers" (Mc Donnell, 5–6). On the Pays d'en haut, see St-Onge, Gilbert, and Frenette.

78. According to some accounts, Nicollet came across the Menominee, a Native American nation that lived on wild rice and sturgeon, by Green Bay in 1634. Thinking he had reached Asia, he wore a Chinese ceremonial dress to impress them at their first encounter. Charlevoix, who visited the Menominee in the 1720s, called them *folles avoines* because of their partiality to wild rice and described them as "the finest and handsomest men in all Canada." See Hamelin; Anon, "Menominee History."

79. On Father de Quen, see Tremblay's entry in the *Dictionary of Canadian Biography*. De Quen was the author of the *Relations of the Jesuits* for the Year 1655–1666. For a map of De Quen's routes, see the website "Quen, Jean de, 1647."

80. "Public piety was revived by missionary propaganda and by stronger emotional appeals" (Weber, 258). Art played an important part in eliciting these religious emotions. Weber adds that "along with ostentation went formalism" (259). On the "Counter-Reformation and Catholic Reform," see Weber, *A Modern History*, 252–259.

81. On the missions to the New World, see Creagh, "L'arme religieuse: les Jésuites," *Nos cousins*, 34–45. Havard and Vidal, "L'église Missionnaire," *Histoire*, 171–183.

82. "A partir de 1632 et pour un demi-siècle, une partie importante des hommes et des femmes qui fondent les institutions religieuses de la Nouvelle-France (missions, éducation, hôpitaux, diocèse) ont connu une expérience mystique. On dit que le tiers des catholiques français du XVIIe siècle déclarés saints depuis ont vécu un temps au Canada" (Rousseau, Louis, 132).

83. Havard and Vidal, *Histoire*, 91.

84. See Maureen Waters' article, "Ursulines."

85. On Paul de Chomedey de Maisonneuve, see Béland.

86. By the middle of the 17th century, "[t]the division of North America had stabilized, it seems: the British French, Dutch, and Spaniards had each cut out their own preserve, with the Indians claiming the in-between, in particular the Iroquois who still sought complete independence" (Creagh, *Nos Cousins*, 46).

87. See Choquette, "From Sea Monsters and Savages to Sorcerers and Satan."

88. "The conversion strategy was elaborated by the Society of Jesus. In 1632, Father Le Jeune was the first to propose stabilizing nomadic tribes, turning them into farmers, and teaching their children in minor seminaries" (Creagh, *Nos Cousins*, 35).

89. On Brébeuf's life, see Latourelle.

90. On Du Tertre's *History of the French West Indies*, see Loiselle. See also Blackburn, "The Testimony of Du Tertre," (on the treatment of slaves in the French Caribbean), 287–289.

91. On the history of French Guiana, and Daniel

de la Touche de La Ravardière's first voyage to Cayenne, see Arthur Henry, "Premier Voyage de La Ravardière," in *La Guyane française, son histoire, 1604-1946*, 10-15. Devèze writes that there is no documentation on that voyage other than the book written by Jean Mocquet (118), *Voyages en Afrique, Asie, Indes orientales et occidentale*s, published in Paris in 1617. See also Julien, "La colonization des Antilles et de la Guyane avant Colbert" (chapter III).

92. A second exploratory journey took place in 1609, this time with the goal of finding a suitable location for a colony. De la Touche had to postpone his colonization project when he lost royal support following the King's murder in 1610. After finding two wealthy associates to sponsor his efforts, Nicolas de Harlay and François de Razilly, de la Touche left with the two men from Cancale, Brittany, onboard three ships and with a group of 500 settlers in 1612. Hostility on the part of the Portuguese led to the colony's abandonment in 1615 after several battles. About 400 men returned to France but some chose to stay and live among the Tupinambas.

93. On the colonization of Saint Christophe, see Abénon, 115-116; 122-124; Blackburn, 280-281; Butel, *Histoire des Antilles*, 25-27; Devèze, 140-146.

94. See Sims, "The Establishment of the French in the West Indies and the Commencement of Trade, 1626-1660," 14-51.

95. On the early French settlements in the Caribbean islands, see Blackburn, 280-281; Butel, *Histoire des Antilles*, 27-35; Devèze, 147-151; Servant, and Roulet.

96. "Boucaner" meant to smoke meat and the verb itself is based on a word used by the Tupi of Brazil.

97. See Butel, Chapter III, "Vivre en flibustier." *Les Caraïbes au temps des flibustiers*, 73-109. Butel defines "amatelotage" as a business, not a sexual, association between two men (211).

98. On Jacques Dyel du Parquet, see Boucher, 72-102.

99. On the Spanish Caribbean, see Devèze, 13-111.

100. The French Caribbean islands are called different names: Iles du Vent (Windward Islands) West Indies, Lesser Antilles.

101. See Haigh, "Guadeloupe."

102. Devèze writes that Guadeloupe already had 700 French settlers by 1639 (149).

103. Robin Blackburn observes that "[i]n a familiar pattern, the Company of the Isles did not thrive, though its governors prospered as owners of large plantations" (282).

104. Charles Huault de Montmagny (ca. 1583-1657) served as governor of New France after Champlain's death.

105. "The case for a French colonial strategy was made by the Huguenot Antoine de Montchétien in his *Traité de l'Economie politique* (1615), a work which influenced Richelieu" (Blackburn, 280). See also Eccles, "Merchants and Missionaries," 32-6; Nowell, 88-89.

106. On the "Age of Tobacco and indentured servants" in the French Caribbean, see Butel, *Histoire des Antilles*, 35-39.

107. See Butel, "Les Premières formes de Colonisation," in *Les Caraïbes au temps des flibustiers*, 159-200.

108. Ronald Creagh states that "the slave trade existed in Southern France as late as the 15th century" and that "French consuls stationed in the Middle East would purchase slaves for the Mediterranean galleys as late as the Revocation of the Edict of Nantes" [1685] (*Nos Cousins*, 129). Comparing African with American slavery, Heuman writes: "In Africa, slavery was a long-standing institution. Unlike the new World, slavery was not tied to producing agricultural commodities on a grand scale; instead, slavery in Africa was generally organized on a more domestic and small-scale basis" (14).

109. According to Hodson and Rushforth, the French were already "prospecting" in Senegal by the end of the 16th century: "The French presence was important enough to rankle other Europeans: in 1594, a Portuguese missionary anchored in the Senegal River remarked that many of the region's inhabitants 'speak French well and have even been to France.'" Quoted in Hodson and Rushforth, 21.

110. Molière's 1685 comedy *Don Juan* opens with a monologue in which Sganarelle praises tobacco as "the passion of respectable men" for its ability to "replenish and relax the human brain" and "instruct souls in virtue."

111. The capture of Algiers by the French in 1830 is usually seen as the start of the second French colonial empire. It rose over the course of the 19th century in Africa and Asia and fell in the 1950s and 1960s.

112. "From 1600 to 1760, the very existence of New France rested on the politics of alliance with the aborigines. […] The Hurons, Odawa, Illinois, Chactas, Alibamons, although demographically weakened by epidemics, played a central role on the North-American geopolitical chessboard" (Havard and Vidal, *Histoire*, 255).

113. Blackburn writes that "[t]h colonization [of the Lesser Antilles islands] was financed partly by the French *marine de guerre* and partly by merchants from Dieppe and Le Havre" and that "the dispatch of a French naval squadron also gave evidence of official interest in the colonization effort" (282).

114. These two rebellions are known as *la fronde parlementaire* (1648-1651) and *la fronde de*s *princes* (1651-1653). See Bercé, "11. France, the Fronde and the Ministry of Mazarin," 157-182; Haine, 56; Labrune et Toutain, 58.

115. The Netflix series *Versailles* rightly presents this marriage as an unhappy one. The King was an unfaithful husband, who had at least 15 "royal mistresses"—an official title—and many illegitimate children. Moreover, non-payment of Maria Teresa's dowry led to the war of Devolution (1667-1668).

Chapter III

1. "The royal authority was able […] to impose a more uncompromising absolutism [in New France than in France]," due to the weakness of the local authorities, and "to prevent the formation of the established organizations it sought to get rid of in the kingdom," i.e., assemblies of the "nobility, provinces, municipalities, etc." Havard and Vidal, *Histoire*, 162.

2. Scott Haine suggests a tripartite division of Louis XIV's reign: "The first (1661–1672) was a time of peace, prosperity, and cultural creativity. During the next two periods, Louis tried to satisfy his virtually inexhaustible thirst for glory and power by waging war. The period between 1673 and 1688 saw a measure of success as French power expanded. But then, from 1688 until his death in 1715, his ambition far exceeded his power, and his reign ended on a note of frustration" (Haine, 61).

3. "Louis died deplored by all, but the memory of men who build great monuments or who kill many people endures when the details wear away. 'Every crime is permitted when it makes us great,' declaimed the hero of a seventeenth tragedy. Louis XIV is still remembered as Louis the Great" (Weber, 301).

4. Le Tellier, who helped nationalize the army and pushed the King to revoke the Edict of Nantes, trained his own son, the marquis de Louvois (1641–1691) so he would be able to replace him when he died.

5. The archives of this administrative branch of government provide a wealth of information on New France and on the ways the French government viewed and dealt with the First Nations.

6. On *lettres de cachet*, see Weber, 237. Nicolas Fouquet, for instance, who had expected to become prime minister at Mazarin's death, fell into disgrace instead, was arrested, put on trial, and died in prison.

7. McCullough argues that the royal authorities did not send "armed tax collectors" to subjects who did not pay their taxes but used the following "coercive measures" instead: "1) the seizure of livestock and property belonging to the individual debtor; 2) the physical imprisonment of the individual debtor; 3) the establishment of a *contrainte solidaire* in which the tax burdens allotted to a certain parish were borne entirely by five or six of its wealthiest members, and 4) the sending of *garnisaires*, or garrisons, into debtors' households with orders to remain there until the taxes were paid" (McCullough, 12).

8. "By 1700 some 200 hospitals participated in what historian Michel Foucault has called 'the great confinement'; within their walls resided 100,000 people considered outcasts: Gypsies, Protestants, beggars, the unemployed, the transient, the insane, and those deemed to be witches, prostitutes, and juvenile delinquents. Under Louis, obviously, public order and religious conformity were two sides of a single coin" (Haine, 60).

9. As opposed to the former Provost, who was appointed by the Paris Parliament, the Chief of Police was appointed by the King and answered directly to him. See Haine, 57.

10. On the new civil administration, see Haine, 57; Weber, 247. Just for the fiscal administration, McCullough mentions the following jobs: *receveur des tailles, collecteurs* in the towns and parishes; *receveurs particuliers* at the seat of the election; and *receveurs généraux* at the seat of the *généralité* (12).

11. On Louis XIV's wars, see Haine, 62–63; Weber 276–280.

12. "The line between succor and social control was often very fine. *Les Invalides* not only sheltered infirm soldiers and the aged, but also incarcerated those who could be belligerent and rowdy" (Haine, 60).

13. "The Versailles of Louis XV has inherited from Louis XIV a tradition of diplomatic intelligence unrivaled in Europe to the point where [by the 18th century] it is diplomats of French origin […] who are chosen to represent foreign courts, and this in France itself" (Fumaroli, xxiii).

14. Louis XIV "expanded Richelieu's idea of the academy by creating academies of dance (1661), inscriptions (1662), science (1666), architecture (1671), and music (1672). These expert bodies codified standards for the arts—such as the 'three unities' of time, place, and action for drama—and helped popularize science among the nobility and upper classes of the cities" (Haine, 59).

15. According to Weber (311), the 1679 Edict of Saint Germain reformed the teaching of law in an effort to make French law (as opposed to Roman law) the standard in the kingdom. On "The fiscal system under Louis XIV," see Mccollim, 14–49.

16. "To mobilize resources, the 17th-century state had created a staff of public servants who sought efficiency and, in its service more and better information […]: statistics, population census, registration of births, deaths, and marriages, tables that showed the movement of prices. Ideally, they were supposed to direct and control everything. In practice, there was no general plan, no efficiency, a great deal of interference, and much local control" (Weber, 233). See also "The Rise of the Administrative Monarchy," in Mccollim, 50–88.

17. "Mercantilism was not favored by merchants who could make more profits when they were free to trade with the highest bidder. Some sought to go around Colbert's policies by having boats built in the Caribbean and Canada and selling their goods in foreign ports. Colbert responded with a July 18, 1671, royal ordinance that explicitly forbade such practices" (Mims, 208).

18. "L'identité antillaise était claire pour le pouvoir: provinces de l'outre-mer, les Iles devaient servir l'économie du royaume, fournir à la métropole, et à elle seule, du sucre, du café, du coton, de l'indigo, des produits à consommer ou à 'verser' dans l'étranger, et en échange, recevoir d'elle seule également les vivres, les vêtements et autres marchandises nécessaires à la vie quotidienne" (Butel,

Histoire des Antilles, 117). See also Julien, chapter IV, "Les Antilles et la Guyane au temps de Colbert."

19. The *Canal Royal en Languedoc*, renamed *Canal du midi* during the French Revolution, is a showcase example of a new waterway: it links the Mediterranean to the Atlantic Ocean.

20. See Eccles, "War and Trade," 100–130.

21. The famous popular folk song "Auprès de ma blonde" dates back to that war.

22. On the founding of the East and West Indies Companies in 1664, see Régent.

23. On the East India Company, see Raynal, "Voyages, settlements, wars and commerce of the French in the East Indies," 47–61.

24. See Blackburn, "The Construction of the French Colonial System," 282–285. For a fictional account of the development of colonial trade during Louis XIV's reign, the creation of the West and East Indies Companies, including the port of Lorient, see the first volume of Simiot's historical saga, *Ces Messieurs de Saint-Malo*.

25. On "The New Colonial Age under Louis XIV," see Butel, *Histoire des Antilles*, 51–69; on "Colbertism and the Caribbean colonies," see Devèze, 209–214; Julien, "Le Canada au temps de Colbert," (chapter VI and VII). See also Pritchard, "Trade and Exchange," 189–229.

26. On the Franco-Dutch War, see Pritchard, 267–300.

27. See Abénon, 124–127.

28. See Mims, "The Establishment of the West India Company. Its Concessions, Privileges, and Composition," 68–81. See also Trudel, *La Seigneurie de la Compagnie des Indes Occidentales*.

29. See Butel, "La révolution sucrière," *Histoire*, 69–83; Mims, "Colonia Exports: Sugar," 260–280; and Timothy Roberts, "Sugar."

30. On the "Administration of the French isles from 1674 to the Seven Years' War," see Devèze, 224–233.

31. Starting in 1674, the royal authority also created a stamped-paper farm.

32. On tax farming, see Mccollim, 15–29.

33. On Western Domain tax farmers, see Pritchard, 248–249.

34. Little is known about Oudiette. Mims mentions Oudiette in the context of the liquidation of the West Indies Company as the "farmer general of the Domaine d'Occident" (290).

35. Aubert de la Chesnaye is the author of a 1697 pamphlet on Canada reproduced, in part, in Margry's *Mémoires et Documents,* Vol. VI. It deals with the *coureurs des bois* (3) and the First Nations of the *Pays d'en haut* (6–7).

36. On Bertrand d'Ogeron, see Butel, "De la flibuste à l'habitation sucrière," *Histoire des Antilles*, 83; Pritchard, 274–283.

37. See Butel, " Le temps des pionniers, *Histoire des Antilles*," 25–50.

38. On the population of Saint Domingue in the late 17th century, see tables 2 and 3 in Hroděj.

39. On the buccaneers, see Pritchard, 78–79, 105–106, Butel, "La Fin de la Flibuste," and Coupeau.

40. See Mims, "Colonial Exports, Tobacco," 249–259.

41. See Butel, "Les Antilles à la fin du XVIIème et au début du XVIIIème siècle," in *Les Caraïbes au temps des flibustiers*, 251–276.

42. On the slave trade, see Devèze, "Chapitre VIII, La Traite des noirs vers les Antilles aux XVIIe et XVIIIe siècles," 153–171.

43. See Mims, "The Fight against the Dutch," 195–224.

44. In fact, a trading post established in Senegal in 1626 was renamed Fort Saint-Louis in the Kings' honor in 1659.

45. The sons of the Princess Henrietta Maria—daughter of Henri IV and Marie of Medici—and King Charles I of England, James and Charles lived in exile in France following the beheading of their father in 1649. They returned to their country when Charles became king in 1660. James, the Duke of York, was granted vast territories in North America and New York was named in his honor in 1664. He succeeded his brother as King James II but lost his throne in 1688 and returned to France where he died in exile in 1701.

46. See Dickinson, "Une colonie à la mesure d'un continent" in *Les Français en Amérique*, 51–70.

47. On colonial French society, see Creagh, *Nos Cousins d'Amérique*, 46–40; Eccles, "Colbert's colonies," 66–99.

48. Havard and Vidal (*Histoire*, 393) point out that all cities in New France were at some point of other of their history surrounded by a stockade.

49. On medieval society and the division between the men who prayed, the men who fought, the men who worked, and those who ruled, see Weber, *A Modern History*, 4–12.

50. On French society in the 16th and 17th centuries, see Weber, *A Modern History*, 242–245.

51. In *Nos Cousins d'Amérique*, Ronald Creagh explicitly refers to New France as a country of *Bourgeois-gentilhommes* because there, unlike metropolitan France, "you could be a seigneur without being a noble" (48).

52. Butel (85) writes that in the Caribbean islands, similarly, former pirates could become plantation owners.

53. For a list of the governors prior to 1663, see "Governor of New France" in Wikipedia.

54. For a list of governors from 1663 to 1763, see "Governor General of New France" in Wikipedia.

55. For further details, see Havard and Vidal, "3. Pouvoirs et institutions," in *Histoire*, 147–191. See also Pritchard, "Government and Politics," 230–264.

56. Book publishing was also by royal privilege only in 17th century France.

57. When an African slave burned down her master's house in 1734, for instance, her initial sentence was to burn alive, but the Sovereign Council changed it to death by hanging.

58. According to Louis Rousseau (138), the Catholic Church made real inroads in Quebec much later only, from 1840 to World War II. See also Havard and Vidal, "Le Canada du Roi-Soleil," in *Histoire*, 99–102.

59. On the *coureurs des bois*, see Havard et Vidal, "Le Pérou des coureurs des bois," in *Histoire*, 102–108. See also Creagh, *Nos Cousins*, 50–59, Royot, 30–33. M. Brown distinguishes between the *voyageurs*, who had "a congé from the governor of New France" and were authorized to explore and trade and the "runners of the wood" (*coureurs des bois*), who were "traders without permits" (3). Creagh identifies a more complex hierarchy (51–52).

60. See "Une nouvelle sexualité," in *Histoire de la Nouvelle France*, 373–384.

61. See Havard and Vidal, "'Ne faire qu'un seul peuple,' De l'optimisme à la 'mixophobie,'" *Histoire*, 367–384.

62. Creagh adds that the French authorities viewed the Native Americans as an asset: "Although they were better hunters and trappers than the French, they were paid less. There was no need to transport this labor force, or to pay to bring them wives the King had to raise and endow […]. The Indian was a resource" (*Nos Cousins*, 27).

63. On the cultural clash between the noble representatives of royal power and the locals, in particular the white Indians, see Jacquin, 117–155.

64. See Choquette, "From Sea Monsters…," 55–56.

65. "The Indians had no moral or social taboo against brandy, and they drank to enjoy visions, to get women (which the French did too), to get rid of inhibitions, and to be able to satisfy their desire for revenge. Alcohol consumption often led to quarrels and murders" (Creagh, *Nos Cousins*, 28).

66. On the conflicts between Bishop and Governor, see Havard and Vidal, *Histoire*, 99–100.

67. See Eccles, *Frontenac, the Courtier Governor*; Brazeau, "Frontenac, Louis de Buade, Comte de (1622–1698)."

68. On the struggle between Frontenac and the Jesuits, see Creagh, *Nos Cousins*, 39. On Frontenac's conflict with Mgr. Laval, see Creagh, *Nos Cousins*, 55–56.

69. On Jean Talon, whose "chief goal was attend to the interests of France and to increase her prestige on the world scene," see Longo, "Talon," 1109. Havard and Vidal view Talon's arrival in New France as the real impetus for the implementation of the "royal centralization project" (*Histoire*, 101).

70. Richard C. Harris starts his study of the "Seigneurial system in early Canada" at that time, probably for that reason.

71. "Some 10,000 pioneers are at the origin of today's 6 million French Canadians." Havard and Vidal, *Histoire*, 204.

72. "Historians know much more about emigration from France to Canada than from France to Acadia or Louisiana. The most recent research by Mario Bolena, a demographer, sets the number of immigrants to the St. Lawrence Valley at 35,000. The American historian Leslie Choquette, for her part, sets the total number of departures to Canada at 70,000 and to Acadia at 7,000, seasonal migrants included. This is little, compared to the 300,000 immigrants to the French Caribbean or the 700,000

welcomed by the thirteen North American colonies; it is nonetheless a lot, compared to the 7,000 immigrants to Louisiana" (Havard and Vidal, *Histoire*, 204–205).

73. On longlots and their later export to the Illinois country and as far as Louisiana and Texas, see Ekberg, *French Roots*, 5–30.

74. Royot, in a section entitled "Feudal New France" (24–27) argues that the colony was a replica of the mainland. The examples he gives (*coureurs des bois*, farmers) show that there was much more freedom in New France.

75. "'Il ne seroit pas de la prudence de dépeupler son Royaume comme il faudroit faire pour peupler le Canada,' Colbert wrote to intendant Talon in 1666" (Balvay, *L'Epée et la plume*, 28.) Balvay notes that the authors of the article on the colonies in the 18th-century *Encyclopédie* made the exact same point nearly a century later.

76. Rosemary Chapman has devoted an article to the "Filles du Roy." See also Julie Roy on Jeanne Mance, one of the founders of the Hôtel-Dieu in Montreal, and the organizer of the King's Daughters' reception in New France.

77. On the birth of the province of New France, see Kellogg, "Annexation," 179–190; Nowell, 89–90.

78. Interestingly enough, a few Amerindians were also granted seigneuries in Sillery close to Quebec City in 1651. See Michel Lavoie, "Des Indiens Seigneurs au temps de Louis XIV "; Havard and Vidal, *Histoire*, 278.

79. See Havard and Vidal, Des élites canadiennes dominées par la noblesse," *Histoire*, 538–548.

80. Havard and Vidal believe that the urban business bourgeoisie was wealthier than the nobility in Canada. See *Histoire*, 548–550.

81. L.P. Rousseau notes that "the political and religious authorities in New France abandoned their encouragement of mixed marriages because they were no longer perceived as necessary to the development of the colony" (798).

82. See Kellogg, "Tribal Wars and Dispersion, 1635–1654," 84–100; Creagh, "La guerre des Iroquois," *Nos Cousins*, 31–32.

83. For a good, concise introduction to this topic, see Podruchny, "Fur Trade."

84. Firearms were more readily available in the 17th century after the invention of the flintlock that made the use of muskets much safer.

85. On the Fall of Huronia, see Havard and Vidal, *Histoire*, 92–99; Jacquin, 63–87. Creagh notes that the destruction of Huron lands led to a rethinking of the Jesuits' conversion strategy: from then on, missionaries followed the Native Americans in their migrations. See Creagh, 37.

86. War with the Iroquois would resume between 1660 and 1667 but tensions let up when "in December 1665, with nary a French shot fired, Seneca, Cayuga, Onondaga, and Oneida leaders came to Quebec and agreed to a comprehensive treaty with the French. The following year, after two largely unsuccessful French expeditions, even the more

belligerent Mohawk Iroquois recognized the need for peace" (McDonnell, *Masters of Empire*, 39–40).

87. Balvay argues that the relative equality that existed between Hurons and French as long as they saw each other as "brothers" was replaced by a relation of subordination following the demise of Huron power which is best exemplified by the recourse to the metaphor of the "father," Onontio. See Balvay, *L'Epée et la plume,* 132. See also Havard and Vidal, "Les mamelles d'Onontio," *Histoire,* 261–265.

88. "Even as the troops of the Carignan-Salières Regiment landed at Trois-Rivières in 1665, they were greeted by more than four hundred Anishinaabe warriors from the Lakes. If the Natives could or did communicate with the French soldiers, they would have certainly put the Iroquois-French conflict in a broader context. While the French may have suffered heavily from the Iroquois attacks, they were only at the edges of this conflict. Indeed, from the perspective of the Anishinaabeg, the French were only minor players in an Indian conflict that stretched over generations" (McDonnell, *Masters of Empire*, 34).

89. In 1664, the British invaded New Amsterdam. "The disappearance [of the Dutch] reduced the number of players in North America to three, the British, Iroquois, and the French" (Creagh, *Nos Cousins*, 46).

90. "While the French were afraid of losing their alliance with these nations, the reverse was also true: the Great Lakes nations wanted at all costs that a separate peace between the Iroquois League and New France be avoided" (Havard, *The Great Peace...*, 41).

91. On the *Troupes de la Marine*, see Balvay, *L'Epée et la plume* 38–51.

92. On the military forces present in New France at the time, see Havard and Vidal, *Histoire,* 183–191.

93. The pattern of Franco-native marriages emphasized by McDonnell can be observed again later in the Illinois country. Practically all the early French settlers of Kaskaskia mentioned by Natalia Belting had Indian wives (13–15).

94. "Huron and Ottawa Indians reached Trois-Rivières in a roundabout way in the spring of 1653 and explained their predicament. They said that they were now hiding from the Iroquois in a region beyond Huronia and had a big accumulation of furs and that they hoped to come down the following year in sufficient numbers to defy the Iroquois" (Nute, "Chouart des Groseillers").

95. For detailed information on Médard Chouart, sieur des Groseillers and Pierre Esprit Radisson, see Nute's *Caesars of the Wilderness*. See also, Creagh, "'We were Caesars,'" in *Nos Cousins,* 57–58; Ibson, "Minnesota," 810; Jacquin, 108; Lappas, "Radisson." McDonnell deflates Groseilliers' and Radisson's claim to being "Caesars of the Wilderness": "The 'poor miserable' Indians they encountered and described would have reminded them that they survived only with their help" (44). For a map of of his explorations, see the website, "Groseillers, Médard Chouart des, 1654–1660."

96. Louise P. Kellogg notes that "[t]he discovery and publication of Radisson's journals awakened much interest among western historians. After Nicolet he was the first Frenchman whose account of voyages to the Northwest had been preserved. According to the various interpretations of his journals, he may have been the first white man in Iowa, in Minnesota and in the Dakotas, or in Manitoba, and possibly the first white man to visit the Mississippi River. The dates of his voyages have never been satisfactorily determined. His four voyages must have occurred sometime between 1652 and 1663" (104). See also Kellogg, 108–115. For a map of his voyages, see the website "Radisson, Pierre-Esprit, 1659–1660."

97. The Canadian Netflix series *Frontier* deals with colonial life around the Hudson's Bay Company but later, in the 18th century.

98. On Albanel, see Bouchard, 101–107. Lake Albanel in Jamésie, Quebec, is named in his honor. For a map of his explorations, see the website "Albanel, Charles, 1672."

99. Taking off for months and sometimes years and covering thousands of miles on foot served at the same time as "a rite of passage" (Creagh, *Nos Cousins*, 53) for young men, which may partly explain their rowdiness when they arrived in villages, particularly when they traveled in "bands of one to three hundred" men (54).

100. See Royot's chapter, "New France Goes West," 34–48, and Belvay, *L'Epée*, 30–31.

101. The French called the Ottawa, or Odawa, the "Ouatouais" (McDonnell, 10).

102. In letter 46 on North America, Antoine-Denis Raudot recalled that although the mission at Sault-Sainte-Marie was the first one to be established in the *Pays d'en haut*, it no longer existed by 1710, when he was writing, due to the Saulteurs' propensity "to mock our mysteries." In Margry, *Mémoires et Documents*, Vol. VI, 8.

103. Nicolas Perrot wrote a memoir on his experiences among the First Nations. On Perrot, see Hele; Havard, *The Great Peace,* 206–207; Kellogg, 122–131; 135–138, McDonnell, 38–39. For a map of his explorations, see the website "Perrot, Nicolas, 1665–1689."

104. See Havard and Vidal, *Histoire,* 110. The same paternalistic discourse can be found as late as 1746 in De Beauchamps's address to the Choctaw. See Beauchamps, *Journal of De Beauchamps' Journey to the Choctaws, 1746,* 265–266.

105. See Nancy O' Brien Wagner, "Duluth," 397.

106. His name is spelled many ways: Jolliette, Joliet, Jolliet. See Maureen Waters, "Joliet (Jolliett), Louis (1645–1700)." See also Kellogg, 131–134 and chapter X, "Exploration of the Mississippi Valley, 1671–1682." For a map, see the website "Jolliet, Louis 1673–1694."

107. See Nowell, 90; Waters, "Marquette, Jacques (1637–1675)" and "Michigan," 805. For a map of Marquette's journeys, see the website "Marquette, Jacques, 1673."

108. See Margry, *Mémoires et Documents*, Vol.

VI, Chapitre II, Entreprises de Daniel Greysolon-Dulhut, 19–54. For a map of his explorations, see the website "Greysolon Dulhut, Daniel, 1678–1679."

109. On Daniel Greysolon Duluth, see Creagh, "L'ouverture du Nord-Ouest," *Nos Cousins*, 62–63; McDonnell, *Masters of Empire*, 56–57.

110. On the Mississippi River's importance, see Charron. On the exploration of the Mississippi by Marquette and Joliet, see Creagh, "L'accès au Mississippi," *Nos Cousins*, 61–62; Nowell, 90–91.

111. Morgan (45) also mentions the French name for the Missouri river: the Ozage.

112. On the spread of missions in the *pays d'en haut*, see Kellogg, "The missions, 1660–1675," 139–178. For an overview of the missions in Illinois country in the 17th century, see the table in Creagh, *Nos Cousins*, 39. On the Missions to New France, see Havard and Vidal, *Histoire*, 171–183.

113. Rollings explains that the large Native American population the Spaniards had encountered over a century earlier was gone: "The Casqui, Pacaha, Colingua, Utiangue, Quigualtam, Tula, and Lacane pople of de Soto's time had disappeared" (40–41). This population decline may have been "the result of a long-term drought that struck the region from 1549 to 1577" or it may have been caused by "epidemic diseases" (41).

114. On La Salle's expedition, see Havard et Vidal, *Histoire*, 105–108. Creagh writes: "In Frontenac's days, it was the lure of profit that made Cavelier turn to exploration" and that "like Etienne Brûlé, Jean Nicolet, Louis Joliet, Le Sueur, La Vérendrye, Perrot, de Tonti or Iberville he started out as a *coureur des bois* and was later promoted to 'explorer' by historians" (Creagh, *Nos Cousins*, 58). See also Creagh, "Les Mésaventures du Sieur Cavelier de La Salle," *Nos Cousins*, 66–75. Pierre Le Sueur visited the Sioux in the last decade of the 17th century. See Margry, *Mémoires et Documents*, vol. VI, Part I, Chapter III, 55–93.

115. The second and third volumes of Margry's *Mémoires et Documents* are entirely devoted to La Salle's assignments and explorations in North America, as well as to related correspondence. For a map, see the website "La Salle, Robert-René, Cavelier de, 1670–1687."

116. For a map of Father Hennepin's travels in North America, see the website "Hennepin, Louis, 1678–1680."

117. "When Frenchmen first arrived [in the Illinois country], they established outposts in association with client Indian tribes. Starved Rock, Pimiteoui (Peoria), Cahokia, Kaskaskia and Fort de Chartres were all settlements at which various tribes of Illinois Indians (Kaskaskia, Tamaroa, Peoria, and Mihigamea) lived in close proximity with Frenchmen" (Ekberg, *Colonial Ste. Genevieve*, 86). See also MacDonald, "French Illinois," 1–15; and White, 23–142 (Illinois Country) and 145–208 (New Orleans).

118. André Prévos (I, 27) writes that "by 1681, French voyageurs and explorers had seen all of the eastern shores of today's Iowa."

119. George Sabo III (76) underscores another aspect of the significance of La Salle's exploration, its anthropological dimension: "We are fortunate that late seventeenth-century Frenchmen participating in La Salle's famous exploration and settlement venture left detailed descriptions of greeting ceremonies they participated in when they encountered two native Arkansas tribes—Quapaws and Caddos."

120. Creagh explains that La Barre was "the creature of the merchants" who had suffered after La Salle became the beneficiary of the fur trade instead of them—thanks to the existence of new forts, Fort Frontenac and Fort Saint-Louis. Both were seized by the new governor. Creagh, *Nos Cousins*, 70–71.

121. We find the following statement on the online exhibit "*La Belle*, the Ship that Changed History:" "In 1686, *La Belle*, the one remaining expedition ship, wrecked in a storm and sank to the muddy bottom of Matagorda Bay where it rested undisturbed for over 300 years. In 1995, archaeologists located the 17th century ship and began a decades-long and often unprecedented process of excavating, recovering, and conserving the ship's hull, along with more than 1.6 million artifacts."

122. Although today's name "Des Moines" means "Monks" or "Of Monks," the name we find on the first 1703 map of the area is "Le Moinegona," probably the French transcription of a Native American term. On the early French presence in Iowa, see Prévos and Ibson, "Iowa."

Chapter IV

1. Prior to Versailles, the Tuileries Palace in Paris had been the royal residence since Henri IV. The Tuileries became the seat of government again from the 1789 Revolution to the end of the Second Empire. It burned down during the Commune.

2. On Louis XIV, see Hatton.

3. The "Sun King" nickname originates in the young king's participation in the role of Apollo in the *Ballet de la nuit* in 1658 at what was then the hunting lodge of Versailles.

4. Louis XIV was short, 5 feet 4, hence the high heels and the tall wigs that made him look much taller.

5. The oldest surviving buildings are Maison Jacquet on rue Saint-Louis, built in 1675, and the Porte Saint-Louis, rebuilt in 1697.

6. It was named after Claude de Ramezay (1659–1724) who became governor of Montreal in 1704 and served as acting governor of New France from 1714 to 1716. Three of Ramezay's four sons died in tragic circumstances, including a hurricane off the coast of Acadia that destroyed the ship carrying the governor's third son in August 1725. See Zoltvany, "Ramezay, Claude de." See also the webpage on "Navigation."

7. On the importance of diplomacy and rituals in Franco-Amerindian relations, see Balvay, *L'Epée et la plume*, 140–149.

8. A document examined by Doreen Walker

provides evidence that a school that was training young men in the trades of masonry, roofing, carpentry, key-cutting, tailoring but also in the arts of sculpting, guilding, woodcarving already existed in the parish of saint-Joachim near Montreal during Laval's tenure as a bishop.

9. Michel Le Tellier's son, the marquis de Louvois took over the ministry of war at his father's death in 1685. "After Colbert's death in 1683, the Marquis of Louvois became the most trusted advisor to Louis XIV. The Sun King embraced Louvois's doctrine of military strength as the foundation of French power" (Haine, 62–63).

10. On the Glorious Revolution, see Weber, *A Modern History*, 30–312; on the War of the Grand Alliance, or "Nine Years' War in America," see Pritchard, 301–357.

11. William of Orange had married James II's daughter Mary in 1677. She had been raised as an Anglican.

12. "The civilian population was then less than eleven thousand, only a quarter of which, about 2,750, would have been males between the ages of sixteen and sixty. The military thus dominated society by sheer weight of numbers, being by far the largest single cohesive group in the colony" (Eccles, *The French*, 123).

13. A common form of a persecution was *the dragonnade*, the quartering in Protestant households of soldiers who were at liberty to vandalize, rape, and torture because their crimes went unpunished. See Creagh, *Nos Cousins*, 163–164.

14. On the Revocation of the Edict of Nantes (Edict of Fontainebleau), see Fosdick, 38–73; Haine, 60–61; Joutard; Weber, 300, and 405–406 (for the rationale behind it), and Butler, 13–40. Butler argues that Louis XIV meant "to keep rebellion minimal and ex-Protestants working in France" and that "the plan worked. At least 650 of the roughly 800 ministers left the country, and most of the rest abjured, while at least 80% of the laity remained in France, most of whom also abjured" (20).

15. Crocketagne settled in Ireland, his son changed the family name to "Crockett" when they moved to North America. Winders, 9.

16. Isaac Lenoir was the ancestor of the American Revolutionary War General William Lenoir (1751–1839) who later served as speaker of the North Carolina Senate. See Shrader, "William Lenoir."

17. Pierre Dieppe was one of actor Johnny Depp's ancestors. See Meikle, 21.

18. On Huguenot immigration following the Revocation of the Edict of Nantes and on the experience of fleeing France, see Chappell; on the "considerable cultural influence" exerted by these French immigrants, particularly in South Carolina, see Jones 19–20; on Huguenot settlements in the British colonies, see Butler, 41–67; Creagh, *Nos Cousins*, 168–189; Fosdick, 125–375; Havard et Vidal, *Histoire*, 204–237 and Watson.

19. See also Creagh, "Rhode Island," *Nos Cousins*, 174–175. Creagh writes that the French Huguenots were sold bogus land claims and that, although they

had cleared the land, they had to leave because their claims were not valid. *Nos Cousins*, 175. A similar dispossession occurred in New Oxford.

20. On Meyzonnat, see Lagarrigue.

21. On Jansenism, see Weber, *A Modern History of Europe*, 260–262.

22. The 60 articles of the *Code Noir* are reproduced in Dorigny and Gainot's *Atlas de l'Esclavage*, 76–79. On the *Code Noir*, see Blackburn, 290–292; Pritchard, 88–92.

23. See Eccles, "The Slave Colonies, 1683–1748," 165–197.

24. See *Edict du roy, portant que les nobles pourront faire le commerce de mer, sans déroger à la noblesse*. Vérifié en parlement le 13 aoust 1669.

25. In 1902 a volcanic eruption wiped the city off the map.

26. On d'Angennes, see Pritchard, 166–167, 202–204.

27. Heuman puts that figure at 1,275,000 for the years 1700 to 1760 and 1,980,000 for the years 1761 to 1810. The estimates on the import of slaves to the Caribbean include Spanish, British, French, Dutch and Danish transports. They go down significantly after the British abolition of the slave trade in 1807 (23). Heuman's book contains maps of the slave trade (24).

28. See Jo Edwards. "Huguenots."

29. On Jean-Baptiste Ducasse [Du Casse], see Blackburn, 293–29, Butel, *Histoire des Antilles*, 84–87, and Vidal, "Compagnie du Sénégal."

30. See also Butel, "La fin de la flibuste," in *Les Caraïbes au temps des flibustiers*, 201–230.

31. Peter Faneuil's godfather was another French Huguenot from Boston, Pierre Baudouin (1640–1706), patriarch of the prominent Bowdoin family and of father of James Bowdoin (1726–1790), revolutionary hero and governor of Massachusetts for whom Bowdoin College is named. See Brown and Fosdick, 83–92.

32. W.J. Eccles therefore aptly calls his chapter on New France between 1683 and 1713 in *The French in North America* "War and Trade."

33. See Royot, "The Wilderness at Stake: The Colony at the Crossroads," 49–64.

34. On Chevalier de Troyes's campaign see the website, "Troyes, Pierre de, 1686."

35. The Lachine massacre represented the culmination of attacks on French positions by Iroquois warriors. See Kellogg, "Iroquois War and the West, 1682–1689," 221–242, and Julien, "La guerre iroquoise et anglaise" (chapter VIII).

36. On the military organization of New France during Frontenac's second term as Governor, see Eccles, *Frontenac*, 212–222.

37. The village of Chedabucto, for instance, was pillaged several times between 1688 and 1690.

38. On Saint-Castin, see Sauvageau, "Saint-Castin et la Défense vctorieuse de l'Acadie, 1670–1701," in *Acadie*, 11–98. See also Pritchard, 336–346; Havard and Vidal, *Histoire*, 378–379.

39. "The troupes de la Marine proved to be of little use, except to garrison forts in exposed areas,

and as a labour force. Most of the fighting was done by the Canadian militia in small war parties led by regular officers, many of them Canadian" (Eccles, *The French*, 108).

40. See Waters, "Cadillac"; Creagh, 63–64; Weyhing; and Zoltvany. The latter explains that Cadillac left Acadia after his habitation near Port Royal was destroyed in British attacks during the War of the Grand Alliance, a reversal of fortune that led to his move to Quebec.

41. Lake Pontchartrain in Louisiana is named after this Secretary of the Navy.

42. On Pontchartrain's colonial policies, see Balvay, *L'Epée et la plume*, 32–35.

43. See Macpherson, "Iberville, Pierre Le Moyne d'," (1661–1706)." For a map of his voyages, see the website "Iberbille, Pierre Le Moyne, d,' 1686–1702."

44. See Eccles, *The French in North America*, 111–112; Pannekoek and Scott.

45. "They had beaten back the direct attacks by the English colonies, carried the fighting to their frontier settlements, and forced the Iroquois to terms." Eccles also points out that the French realized that it would be smarter to swear the Iroquois to neutrality, so as to keep them as a buffer between the two colonies, than to continue to fight them (*The French*, 112).

46. In *The French in North America*, Eccles mentions that a 1685 decree, similar to the 1669 edict concerning trade in the West Indies, allowed "nobles resident in Canada [… to] engage in commerce and industry without sacrificing their noble status" (Eccles, 126).

47. In 1701, Mrs Cadillac and Mrs de Tonty, wife of Alphonse de Tonty, an officer serving under Cadillac, successfully petitioned the authorities for the right to join their husbands in the *pays d'en haut*, which made them the first European women to live in the area. See Margry, "M'" de Lamothe et de Tonty veulent rejoindre leurs maris" (25 Août 1701). *Mémoires et Documents*, Vol. V, 209.

48. See Weber, 278. The Rhine became the border with Germany. France gained the province of Alsace and regained Pondichéry in India.

49. "After many months of cross-Atlantic bickering and bargaining, the Canadian fur trade community took over the marketing of beaver and formed a company for the purpose; but the terms of the agreement, and the huge glut of fur, virtually guaranteed failure" (Eccles, *The French*, 111). Eccles informs the reader a few pages later that "moths and vermin […] effectively disposed of it [the glut problem]" (132).

50. De Callière had requested the position of Governor General in 1688 but Frontenac was chosen instead. See Eccles, *Frontenac*, 199.

51. See Appendix 3 for the text of the Treaty of Montreal (1701) in Havard, *The Great Peace*, 210–211. The paternalistic discourse that characterizes the governor's address is echoed decades later in De Beauchamps's address to the Choctaw. See Beauchamps, *Journal of De Beauchamps' Journey to the Choctaws*, 1746, 265–266.

52. Kellogg devotes a chapter to this topic,

"The West Evacuated, 1689–1701," 243–267. Gilles Havard provides a more up-to-date and thorough account of the events leading to it in *The Great Peace of Montreal of 1701: French-Native Diplomacy in the Seventeenth Century*. The book features four maps of Native and Euro-American settlements around that time (xii–xv), as well as a copy of the treaty (111–118). His research is particularly valuable in that it is based on French diplomatic sources that contain accounts of "speeches of the Native people that have been recorded in diplomatic minutes" as found either "in the colonial correspondence or in the *Histoire de l'Amérique septentrionale* by Bacqueville de la Potherie" (9).

53. On Cadillac and the foundation of Detroit, see Weyhing. For official documents related to the "Foundation of the city of Détroit-Pontchartrain," see Margry, *Mémoires et Documents*, Vol. V, 204–347. See also Ronald Creagh, *Nos Cousins*, 63–64; Guillaume Teasdale, "Chapter I, Early Land Occupation," in *Fruits of Perseverance*, 9–24; and Waters, "Detroit." According to Zoltvany's article, Cadillac's efforts to settle Detroit were both self-interested and counter-productive, as most of the fur business profited New York places instead of New France. Instead of dismissing Cadillac and admitting he had been wrong to support him, Pontchartrain made him Governor of Louisiana, "the most dismal colony of the French empire" in 1710. For a map of his voyages, see the website "Cadillac, Antoine Laumet, dit de Lamothe, 1694–1701."

54. Vauban, *Moyen de rétablir nos colonies de l'Amérique et de les accroître en peu de temps*. See "La vision de Vauban pour le Canada" on the CEFAN website.

55. On Maurepas's colonial policies, see Balvay, *L'Epée et la plume*, 35–36.

56. The Canadian leaders thought that the nations of the Great Lakes, whom Cadillac had volunteered to entice to move to Detroit, would sell their furs to the Iroquois, now that they were no longer at war, and bypass Montreal since the fur prices offered in Albany were higher. See Eccles, *The French*, 115.

57. "Première formation d'une chaine de postes entre le fleuve St Laurent et le Golfe du Mexique," in Margry's *Mémoires and Documents*, Volume V. The book contains official correspondence related to the establishment of these "posthouses."

58. Volume IV of Margry's *Mémories et Documents* is devoted to d'Iberville's achievements in North America, including his correspondence with the authorities in the Ministry of Marine, and even exchanges with Ducasse. See also Butel, "De la flibuste à l'habitation sucrière," *Histoire des Antilles*, 83–85.

59. For official documents related to Juchereau's appointment, see Margry, *Mémoires et Documents*, Vol. V, 349–350 and 363–367.

60. On Sauvole's government, see Margry, *Mémoires et Documents*, Vol. IV, Chapter 4.

61. Bienville remained in office until 1713, when Cadillac arrived from France, and later served two more terms as governor.

62. For an overview of French presence in the

Illinois Country, see Belting, "Chapter II Kaskaskia Beginnings, Mission, 1703–1718," 10–22; Nasatir, "The Exploration of the Missouri. I. Under the French Regime," 1–57. On the first French settlements in that area, see also Creagh, *Nos Cousins*, "Le Pays des Illinois," 76–82. The area is also referred to as "the American bottom" (MacDonald, 1).

63. According to Creagh, one of La Salle's clerks, François de La Forest, stayed with Tonty at Fort St. Louis des Illinois.

64. On Tonty's activities in Illinois Country, see Margry, *Mémoires et Documents*, Vol. V, Part II, chapters 1 and 9; Creagh, *Nos Cousins*, 78–80. Like Creagh, Belvay describes life in and around the Illinois forts as centered primarily on the fur trade (211–230) but also as a cohesive society in terms of Franco-Amerindian relations (*L'Epée et la plume*, 263–278).

65. Centering on Arkansas, Arnold discusses the following governing entrepreneurs: Pierre de Coulange, Paul Augustin de la Houssaye, and Pierre-Joseph Favrot. Cadillac fits Arnold's description perfectly for both Canada and Louisiana.

66. Ekberg points out that "no civil records exist [...] for the earliest history of the Illinois Country (1699–1722)" and that "the habitants in the region were merely squatters on the land that they were cultivating" (*French Roots*, 35). On the Arkansas Post and its significance as a trading post and a stopover between Illinois and Louisiana, see Lankford. *La Poste des Arkansas* moved three times due to floods and served as a military fort during the Seven Years' War.

67. "Although in popular opinion the French always had good relations with and were sympathetic to the Indians, this was not the actuality. The extermination of the Fox and the revolt of the Natchez in 1729 bring this out clearly" (Brown, *History*, 59).

68. According to Creagh (77), the Native American population of the Illinois in 1665 was composed of 3,000 Kaskaskia, as well as Cahokia, Tamaroa, and Peoria, for a total of 8,000 souls. On Franco-Indian interaction in the Illinois Country, and in particular the role of language in framing the "terms of encounter" between Indians and missionaries, see Morrissey.

69. Brown tells the edifying legend that surrounds the foundation of the second Kaskaskia: Chief Rouensa had a daughter, Marie, an early convert who refused to marry Michel Accault (or Ako), a *coureur des bois* because of his debauchery, and this despite her father's insistence. Upon reflection, however, it dawned on her that as a wife, she could use her influence to convert husband, father, and mother, and with the support of Fr. Gravier, she succeeded (Brown, *History*, 3–4). See also Belting, 13–15; MacDonald, 125–130.

70. According to Creagh, the foundation of these villages in Illinois took place in the context of the rivalries between Jesuits and the newcomers, the Fathers of the Foreign Missions. The latter were part of Tonti's expedition when they created Cahokia. On

Cahokia and Kaskaskia in the early 18th century, see Creagh, *Nos Cousins*, 40–45; and after annexation, 145–149.

71. By the end of the 19th century, the peninsula of Kaskaskia "became an island, the town, not entirely destroyed, each spring lost a few more buildings as they toppled into the ever-widening Mississippi. The village site today is entirely gone" (Belting, 8).

72. See Margry, *Mémoires et Documents*, Vol. V, Part III, chapter XIII. "MM. d'Artaguiette et de Bienville envoient aux Illinois pour châtier des Canadiens qui y causaient des désordres. Description des moeurs des Illinois Kaskaskias, de leur religion, de leurs mariages et de leurs chasses (1711)."

73. According to Pénicaut's own statement, he was employed as a master carpenter by the French authorities to build boats and to repair them during campaigns. The account of the twenty-two years he spent in Louisiana, entitled "Relation de Pénicaut," can be found in Margry, *Mémoires et Documents*, Vol. V, 375–586.

74. Balvay devotes chapter 2 of *L'Epée et la plume* to "The Construction of Forts," 63–97. See also Havard et Vidal, "Le double réseau de forts," *Histoire*, 435–444. The authors underscore the symbiotic relation between fur and fort.

75. "At a grand council of the friendly tribes, Frontenac took up a hatchet, brandished it in the air, and sang the war song, his officers following his example. The Christian Indians of the neighboring missions rose and joined them, and so also did the Hurons and the Algonquins of Lake Nipissing, while Frontenac led the dance, whooping like the rest. His allies, roused to martial frenzy, promised war to the death, and several years of conflict followed." *Appleton's Cyclopaedia of American Biography*, vol. III, 554.

76. In his *Short History of the Indians of the United States*, Edward Spicer estimated that Native Americans numbered around 300,000 in 1700 and Europeans "no more than 200,000" (14).

77. On the significance of tobacco in interactions between the French and the Native Americans, see Parsons, who suggests that smoking tobacco with the Native Americans may have represented "ongoing attempts to incorporate the French into an aboriginal world" (35).

78. On the adoption of white Indians into Native American tribes, and Franco-Indian relations, see Jacquin, 157–189; Balvay, *L'Epée et la plume*, 111–122 and 169–186.

79. For Creagh, religion explains this conception of the frontier: "The American protestants practiced segregation: they saw themselves like the New Israel facing the Beast of the Apocalypse" (*Nos Cousins*, 27).

80. Brown, Creagh, Ekberg, Havard, among many others, underscore this difference.

81. The Iroquois remained neutral, but the governor's decision had unintended consequences: "[T]he understanding with New York led to a thriving clandestine business economic alliance between the

merchants of Montreal and Albany […]. The merchants of Albany paid higher prices for beaver than did the Canadian monopoly company; moreover they paid cash" and the goods they sold "in particular the English woolen cloth, duffel, and stroud" were cheaper and more popular than the equivalent French products (Eccles, *The French*, 116–117).

82. Chrestien LeClerq, who served as a Recollet missionary with the Mi'kmaq of the Gaspé area, wrote a bilingual dictionary. He also translated and recorded a 1677 speech by a Mi'kmaq elder comparing benefits and drawbacks of Mi'kmaq and French ways of life that can be found in Calloway, "A Micmac questions French 'civilization,'" 49–52. On the Recollet Missions, see Margry, "Missions des Recollets," in *Mémoires et Documents*, Vol. I, 3–34.

83. On the War of the Spanish Succession, see Pritchard, 358–401. Pontchartrain's son Jérôme was Secretary of State for the Navy from 1699 to 1715.

84. For a short history of the relations between the French and the Houma, see Brasseaux, *French, Cajun*, 117–130.

85. If Havard and Vidal are correct, Spicer's estimate of 300,000 Native Americans in 1700 (14) would seem too low.

86. In subsequent years, numerous hostile encounters between the French and the First Nations occurred in Lower Louisiana. By the time a peace treaty was signed in 1718 the Chitimacha tribe had significantly fewer members than the 4,000 who lived in the area in 1700.

87. On Crozat, see Brown, *History as They Lived It*, 7; Creagh, *Nos Cousins d'Amérique*, 108–109; and Vidal's article in *France in the Americas*.

88. Brown's *History as They Lived It* is mostly devoted to the early French presence in these states. See also: Thomas J. Lappas, "Indiana," "Missouri," and Cécile Vidal, "Illinois Country."

89. "In 1712, under Crozat's regime, when civil government was established, a Superior Council was created for the administration of civil and criminal justice" (Brown, *History*, 8).

90. In "Laumet," Zoltvany suggests three reasons for the Cadillac legend: 1) He is the founder of a major U.S. city, Detroit; 2) He left an abundant correspondence that puts him in a very favorable light; 3) He hated the Jesuits, which "endeared him to English Protestant historians as one of the few persons in the history of New France who dared assert his independence of priestly control and defend the prerogatives of the state against the church."

91. On Franco-Indian relations in the Illinois country, see Ekberg, "Red Man-White Man," in *Colonial Ste. Geneviève*, 86–124.

92. On this topic, see Ekberg, *Stealing Indian Women. Native Slavery in the Illinois Country*.

93. On "The First Fox War, 1701–1716," see Brown; Kellogg, 268–289; Havard and Vidal, 294–297.

94. The Confederacy included the Mi'kmaq, Maliseet-Passamaquoddy, Abenaki, and Penobscot.

95. See Susan Castillo, "Lahontan, Louis-Armand de Lom d'Arce, Baron de (1666–1715)." A lake in

Northern Nevada bears Lahontan's name. For a map of his explorations, see the website "Lahontan, Louis-Armand de Lom d'Arce, baron, 1684–1689."

96. The myth is based on "distortions" such as the one identified by Gilles Havard in the representation of "Huron leader Kondiaronk (also known as 'Le rat,' or 'The Muskrat')," who "was no imaginary Indian with an *au courant* flair for social criticism" but rather one of the architects of the treaty, "a flesh-and-blood person who lived on the shores of Lake Huron" (*The Great Peace*, 3).

Chapter V

1. In his description of the area of Kaskaskia Charles du Tisné highlighted the Illinois country's excellent soil, big rivers, and beautiful trees, an area he deemed most appropriate for settlement. He also mentioned the presence of a lead mine, and perhaps of a silver mine. See "Voyage fait par M. du Tisné en 1719," in Margry, *Mémoires et Documents*, Vol. VI, Part II, Chapter 8, 307–313.

2. Among these historians are Natalia M. Belting, Carl J. Ekberg, Margaret K. Brown, and more recently M.J. Morgan. See also Vidal, "Illinois Country."

3. Although tensions increased following the French settlement in Louisiana and the capture of Pensacola in 1719, conflicts between Spain and France were rare in North America.

4. See Haine, 6, and Labrune et Toutain, "L'absolutisme hésitant," 62–63.

5. In 1719, all French trading companies merged into one, the Indies Company (*Compagnie perpétuelle des Indes*). When the Royal Bank and the Indies Company merged in January 1720 John Law became Finance Minister (*Contrôleur Général des Finances*), a position he held less than a year. On John Law, see Belting, 17; Blackburn, 296–297; Creagh, *Nos Cousins*, 109–110; Havard and Vidal, *Histoire*, 130–133.

6. On Louisiana's beginnings, see Creagh, *Nos Cousins*, 100–106; Havard and Vidal, *Histoire*, 120–146; on the first French immigrants to Louisiana, see Creagh, "Volunteers and Deported," *Nos Cousins*, 107–114, and "Cherchez la femme," *Nos Cousins*, 115–122.

7. On John Law and the Company of the West, see Cécile Vidal "Compagnie d'Occident"; see also Creagh, *Nos Cousins*, 109–110; Brown, *History*, 7–8; and "Introduction," in D'Artiguiette, *Journal of Diron d'Artiguiette*, in Mereness, 18–19.

8. Port-au-Prince was established on the West Coast of Saint Domingue later, in 1749, and an earthquake destroyed it two years later.

9. These criteria are spelled out in the Company's instructions to Louisiana's Chief Engineer, Mr. Perrier : "*Il s'agit principalement de se mettre dans l'endroit le plus commode pour la communication avec la Mobile, soit par mer, soit par le lac Pontchartrain, le moins en danger d'estre inondé dans les débordemens et, autant qu'il sera possible, près des meilleures terres à cultiver.*" "Instruction pour M.

Perrier, ingénieur en chef de la Louisiane," in Margry, *Mémoires et Documents*, vol. V, 604. A sentence on the next page (605) makes clear that these "best lands" were intended for the cultivation of *froment*, wheat, which unfortunately did not grow well in that area. See also Taylor, "New Orleans."

10. The April 14, 1718, instructions from the Company seat in Paris to M. Perrier were clear in that regard: "*Il faut, par toutes sortes de moyens, ouvrir l'entrée du fleuve*" ("*The River's entrance has to be opened up, by whatever means necessary*"). The sentence is highlighted. "Instruction pour M. Perrier, ingénieur en chef de la Louisiane." Margry, *Mémoires et Documents*, vol. V, 602.

11. In the Company of the Indies' "Instructions," Biloxi is presented as "*le premier comptoir de la Compagnie et le centre de ses affaires*," "the company's main trading post and its business center." Margry, *Mémoires et Documents*, vol. V, 619. See also Isabelle Gournay, "Architecture," 82.

12. Le Blond de la Tour was a Chief Engineer and head of a team that included Pauger, Boispinel, and Franquet de Chaville. Margry, *Mémoires et Documents*, Vol. 5, "Instructions pour M. Le Blond de la Tour, Nov. 8, 1719," 610–614.

13. On Juchereau de Saint-Denis's explorations of New Mexico and his travels to Mexico, see Margry, *Mémoires et Documents*, Vol. VI, Part II, Chapter 6, 193–202.

14. On Bénard de la Harpe's explorations of Arkansas, see Margry, *Mémoires et Documents*, Vol. VI, Part II, Chapter 7, "*Voyages de Bénard de la Harpe sur la Rivière Rouge et sur l'Arkansas*," 241–306 ; and chapter 10, "*Bénard de la Harpe avance dans l'Arkansas au-dessus d'un lieu qu'il nomme le Rocher Français*," near today's *La Petite Roche*, in other words Little Rock, AR. "Arkansas," pronounced without the final 's' in French, means "Quapaw" in Algonquin.The inhabitants of Saint-Malo, Brittany, are called *Malouins*, hence the name La Harpe, a native of Saint-Malo, gave to the fort.

15. See George H. Odell, "La Harpe, Jean-Baptiste Bénard, Sieur (1683–1765)," and Rollings, 50–52.

16. On Charles du Tisné's explorations, see Margry, *Mémoires et Documents*, Vol. VI, Part II, Chapter 8, "Du Tisné, Le Missouri, et l'Arkansas," 307–315. See also MacDonald, 39, 41–35.

17. MacDonald states that Cadillac "was a thoroughly dislikable person, and most of the inhabitants of Kaskaskia [...] harbored ill feelings" toward him. He therefore suggests that Du Tisné may have played a trick on him, producing "an ore sample apparently rich in silver when the Illinois-Missouri region contained no such deposit" (43) to send him on a wild goose chase. Cadillac returned to France in 1717, sold his possessions in and around Detroit, and never came back to North America.

18. In 1714, an epidemic killed two to three hundred people in Illinois Country (Belting, 13).

19. On De Liette (or Desliettes), see Russ. A cousin and associate of Tonty, De Liette left a long memoir on the Illinois Indians with whom he lived for an extended period of time. See also MacDonald,

"Fort Commandant, Pierre Charles Desliette (1725–29)," 49–53.

20. "In 1718, after the founding of the *Compagnie d'Occident* (Company of the West), which had been granted a commercial monopoly in Louisiana, the Illinois Country became an administrative part of the colony of Mississippi, although it had previously belonged to Canada." Vidal, "Illinois Country," 594–595.

21. See Ekberg, *French Roots of Illinois Country*, 32; Brown, *History*, 8. Creagh writes: "Five years later, on May 12, 1722, the Company of the Indies would come to a decision: the Illinois Country would become a province with a Provincial Council placed under the authority of the Superior Council of Louisiana." *Nos Cousins*, 84. "[The council], composed of the commandant, the chief clerk, the keeper of the storehouse or *garde magazin*, and underclerk, the engineer, the captain of the troops garrisoning the post, the lieutenant, and two second lieutenants, was to be the principal administrative and judicial body" (Belting, 16).

22. "Regulations for governing the colony, submitted by the Company for the king's approval September 5, 1721, provided for the division of the country into military districts—New Orleans, New Biloxi, Mobile, Alibamous, Natchez, Yazou, Natchitoches, and Illinois." Belting, 16.

23. Brown (*History*, 9) who spells his name "Pierre Degué de Boisbriant," discusses his activities. Ekberg spells his name "Pierre Dugué de Boisbriant" in *Colonial Ste. Genevieve*. Reid mentions that he was one of Frontenac's "*protégés*."

24. On Fort de Chartres, see MacDonald, "The Four forts de Chartres," 22–27; Morgan, "Chartres: French and Indian Successes," in *Land of Big Rivers*, 69–89; Ekberg, *French Roots*, 42–44; Brown, *History*, 61, and 137–145.

25. Bernard Diron d'Artaguiette published his *Journal* as inspector general of Louisiana for the year 1722–1723. A translation is available in Mereness.

26. Boisbriand was governor of Louisiana from 1724 to 1727 when Etienne de Périer replaced him.

27. See the website "Otoe and Missouria: 500 years of History."

28. On de Bourgmont's explorations, see Margry, *Mémoires et Documents*, Vol. VI, Part II, Chapter XXI, "Etienne Veynard de Bourgmont établit le fort d'Orléans sur le Missouri et va faire faire la paix aux diverses nations de ce fleuve avec les Padoucas," 385–452. See also MacDonald, "Etienne de Véniard de Bourgmont and Ignon Ouaconisen (Françoise Missori): An Explorer and an Indian in Paris," 130–138.

29. The Quadruple Alliance included France, Britain, Austria, and the Netherlands. The reason for the war was that Philip V of Spain, Louis XIV's grandson who had become King of Spain under the condition he would not claim the French throne, was seeking to have the Treaty of Utrecht overturned.

30. A letter from the Directors of the Indies Company dated October 25, 1720, deals with Native

American slaves. The Company has learned that *voyageurs* in the Illinois country incite Native American tribes to fight each other and then purchase the slaves they have captured. The directors order the Louisiana authorities to stop this illegal practice as it is not only contrary to royal ordinances but also prejudicial to the Company's business interests. Margry, *Mémoires et Documents*, Vol. VI, Part II, Chapter IV, "Les Voyageurs français achètent des esclaves aux nations qui se font la guerre du côté des Illinois, du Missouri, et de l'Arkansas," 316.

31. According to Pamela Gay-White, however, Louis Juchereau de Saint-Denis played a greater role in inspiring "the loyalty of tribes," and thereby "facilitating the establishment of trade routes to East Texas" (1032) than his "would-be rival," Le Moyne de Bienville. See also Amber Wingfield, "Bienville, Jean-Baptiste Le Moyne, Sieur de (1680–1767)."

32. The population of Canada increased significantly in the 18th century. See Dickinson, 71–76.

33. The Atlantic crossing was hardly a better experience for those convicts than it was for slaves transported from Africa: "Chained on board, they had the worst conditions of passage on the ships, and many did not live to arrive in Louisiana" (Brown, *History*, 28). On the same page, Brown adds that "thousands of criminals arrested in France were sentenced to be deported, but only about 900 ever reached Louisiana."

34. "[T]he company was obligated to recognize the *coutume de Paris* as the law of Louisiana, and to send to the country 6,000 white habitants and 3,000 negroes" (Belting, 16).

35. Albert Girard states that "from May 1719 onward, the Company of the West was the most formidable business venture ever seen up to then. It ruled Louisiana and Senegal, as well as Canada through the fur trade. To this domain, it added the Far East, that is the Isles of Madagascar, Bourbon, and France, the Soffala Coast in Africa, the Red Sea, Persia, Mongolia, Siam, China, and Japan" (22). See also Romain Bertrand.

36. On the casket girls, see Creagh, *Nos Cousins*, 117–118.

37. One of the "*baleine* brides" was the inspiration for Antoine François Prévost's 1731 *Manon Lescaut*, the novel on which Giacomo Puccini based his famous opera. See Creagh, *Nos Cousins*, 117; Havard and Vidal, *Histoire,* 223.

38. According to Augeron, some Frenchmen even took Amerindian women slaves to France where their condition was similar to the status of other servants. Aee "Des esclaves…".

39. Those were not the first African slaves on North American soil: Virginia had slaves a century earlier and South Carolina since 1670.

40. On Louisiana as a slave colony, see Havard and Vidal, *Histoire*, 237–247.

41. Clearly, the Regent, who had handed the financial reins of France to a gambler, was not beyond reproach. Besides, the Mississippi Bubble was just one of the many scandals that rocked France during the Regency. Infamous for its immorality, the period witnessed several other serious diplomatic and political crises: the Cellamare conspiracy, an attempt to replace Philip of Orleans with Philip V of Spain in 1718; and the 1720 Pontcallec conspiracy that had the same goal.

42. According to instructions signed at the seat of the Company of the Indies in Paris and sent to Louisiana, the directors were Veu, Law, Rigby, Castanier, d'Artaguiette-Diron, Mouchard, Savalette, Dupleix, and De July.

43. However, after giving birth to ten children in twelve years, the queen began to sleep alone and the King to search for intimacy elsewhere.

44. "Under Fleury's wise and pacific counsel, France enjoyed a sustained period of peace, from 1726 to 1741, with economic expansion continuing into the 1770s. European commerce jumped 400 percent and colonial trade by the even more amazing figure of 1000 percent. Indeed, France' s growth rates in many sectors of the economy were higher than those of England, which was already starting into the Industrial Revolution" (Haine, 64).

45. Beauharnois was Governor General of New France for two decades, from 1726 to 1747. A town south of Montreal and a fort on Lake Pépin in Minnesota bear his name. Margry, *Mémoires et Documents*, Vol. VI, Part III, Chapter XV, "Formation d'un établissement chez les Sioux au bord du Lac Pépin," 541–582.

46. The fort was located on Lake Pépin, at today's border between Wisconsin and Minnesota.

47. On La Perrière, see Russ. The fort was abandoned during the Fox war. Also Eccles, "The Long Peace, 1713–1744," 131–164.

48. On the Fox wars, see Creagh, *Nos Cousins*, 88–99; Havard et Vidal, "La Guerre des Renards," *Histoire*, 294–297. On "The second Fox War, 1727–1738," see Kellogg, 314–340.

49. Kellogg labels the peace period with the Fox, 1714–1727, a period of "Reoccupation of the Posts" (290–313).

50. On La Vérendrye, see Zoltvany. On Saskatchewan, an area first explored by Gaultier de la Vérendrye, see Durnin.

51. On La Vérendrye's explorations, see Margry, *Mémoires et Documents*, Vol. VI, Part III, Chapter XVI, "Pierre Gautier de la Vérendrye découvre à l'ouest du Lac Supérieur …," 583–634. See also Havard, "L'héritage français," 563–566, and Nowell, 91. For an interactive map, see "Vérendrye, Pierre Gaultier de Varennes et de la, 1632–1639."

52. Kellogg examines the "[c]hanges in the Fur Trade Methods, 1738–1759" (364–385) that led to increased French presence in the Northwest, particularly in Wisconsin (386–405).

53. Bourgmont stayed in France after his Indian guests returned to America. See Balvay, "Cinq 'Sauvages'…".

54. On the Mallet brothers' expeditions, see Margry, *Mémories et Documents*, Vol. VI, Part II, Chapter XII, "Les Frères Mallet […] découvrent la rivière Platte," 453–472.

55. See Augeron, "Une sourde conquête," 132–136.

56. On the history of Baton Rouge, see Martin.

57. On the Natchez Rebellion, see Havard and Vidal, *Histoire*, 297–305 and P. Woods.

58. See Le Page du Pratz, *The History of Louisiana*.

59. See Le Page du Pratz, "The Alienation of the Natchez. Reply of the Stung Serpent." Havard and Vidal view him as an advocate of the *"vivre ensemble,"* a communal way of life for aborigines and French alike. See *Histoire*, 309.

60. Balvay, who calls him d'Etcheparre, argues that if he "likely tyrannized the Natchez, it can hardly be said that his predecessors were more humane in their treatment of the local natives" ("The French and the Natchez," 152).

61. Underscoring the rapid increase in the number of expeditions and the number of slaves transported from Africa to the Caribbean and North America, Dorigny and Gainot provide the following total figures for the Atlantic slave trade: 1563 to 1600: 31,698 slaves; 1601 to 1700: 469,803 slaves; 1701–1800: 4,808,607 slaves. Following the end of the slave trade in 1815, those figures declined but were still high: 2,633,278 slaves between 1801 and 1866 (20). For the number of expeditions, see "Les chiffres de la traite," 20–21.

62. Saint-Domingue "had 130,000 inhabitants in 1726, including 100,000 slaves" (Devèze, 160). Between 10,000 and 15,000 African slaved arrived yearly in Saint-Domingue during the last quarter of the 18th century.

63. Figures on "L'Europe négrière : les ports," are from Dorigny and Gallinot's *Atlas des Esclavages*, 24–25.

64. Margaret Brown provides biographical sketches for a few of those emigrants from France. See *History*, 17–23.

65. See also Creagh, *Nos Cousins,* 133–134.

66. "The Ursulines had slaves and took part in the slave trade [...]. The Jesuits had one hundred and thirty slaves working on their very productive plantation" (Creagh, *Nos Cousins*, 131).

67. See Havard and Vidal, "Les Noirs libres," *Histoire*, 529–534.

68. See Havard and Vidal, "La violence des maîtres et des autres blancs à l'encontre des esclaves," *Histoire*, 500–511; "Les résistances à l'esclavage," 511–529 ; Creagh, "L'Esclavage en Louisiane," *Nos Cousins*, 129–137. Creagh writes that by the time Blacks and Indians started to unite and stir in Lower Louisiana, around 1748, slaves in general came to be regarded "as a class" by the authorities. *Nos Cousins*, 135.

69. Most French slaves transited through Saint-Louis of Senegal: "By the eighteenth century, a vibrant French-Senegalese community had developed around the settlement at Saint-Louis, giving rise to a class of wealthy, property-owning *signares* (mixed-race women, from the Portuguese *senhoras*): in 1767, for example, the *signare* Caty Louette possessed nearly seventy slaves, marking her as the settlement's richest inhabitant" (Hodson and Rushforth, 21).

70. The word "creole," however, initially designated white people, or descendants of a white person, who were born in the colony of Louisiana, the Caribbean, or the Mascarenes, as opposed to people born in France. For instance, Napoleon's first wife, Empress Josephine, was a creole from Martinique. See Havard and Vidal, "La créolisation de la communauté servile," *Histoire*, 493–496. See also Louis-Pascal Rousseau, "Métis."

71. On the large Louisiana plantations, see Havard and Vidal, *Histoire,* 551–555.

72. Creagh titles his chapter on 18th-century French Louisiana "The Birth of an Aristocracy" (*Nos Cousins*, 123–128). On the royal administration of Louisiana, see Havard and Vidal, *Histoire*, 148–162.

73. On piety in Canada and Louisiana, see Havard and Vidal, "Dévotion des Canadiens, impiété des Louisianais?" The authors answer their own question by saying that despite their attendance at church, the people of New France did not let the Church control them as much as it did their counterparts in France (*Histoire*, 575–580). See also Brasseaux, "The moral Climate in French Colonial Louisiana."

74. Belting states that "French-Indian marriages [...] were not at all to the liking of either the Company of the Indies or later to the royal ministers" (74), a bias that may have had to do with the nobility's understanding of society as a hierarchical class structure. In any case, from 1728 onward, Native American widows of Frenchmen could not legally keep their husbands' possessions, a position Louisiana's Superior Council justified by making a distinction between "régnicoles" (real subjects of the king) and people worthy of the king's protection (i.e. Native Americans). On the topic, see Havard, "'Protection' and 'Unequal Alliance.'" The authors note, however, that the decree was never enforced because it was contrary to the best interests of the Frenchmen the widows could remarry (Havard and Vidal, *Histoire*, 277).

75. On war with the Chickasaw, see Havard and Vidal, *Histoire*, 305–307; Phelps, "The Chickasaw, the English, and the French, 1699–1744."

76. According to Mereness, the Choctaw's alliance with the French rested on their animosity towards South Carolinians who had sold many of them into slavery prior to the arrival of the French. *Travels in the American Colonies*, 259.

77. Antoine Bonnefoy's *Journal of Captivity among the Cherokees* provides a first-hand account of the dangers involved in navigating the Mississippi, even in large convoys. For one thing, it took a long time to travel. Bonnefoy's party, for instance, left New Orleans on August 22 and did not make it to the mouth of the Ohio River until November 14, nearly three months later. Bonnefoy also witnessed how, in the Cherokee village where he was held captive, "three English traders were daily instigating the savages to continue to make war upon us [the French]" (250). Later on, after his escape, when

Chickasaw men asked Bonnefoy "why the French won't give them peace," he replied, "not to expect peace until they had driven the English from their villages" (254).

78. The British had a clear demographic advantage: "Around 1725, New France counted 20,000 inhabitants, and New England 350,000" (Creagh, *Nos Cousins*, 86).

79. See Balvay, "The French and the Natchez: A failed Encounter."

80. For a discussion of "The politics of Gifts," see Balvay, *L'Epée et la plume*, 133–136.

81. Forty soldiers were killed, Diron d'Artiguiette and his officers were burnt at stake (Brown, *History*, 132).

82. See Codignola, "Céloron de Blainville, Pierre-Joseph (1693–1759)."

83. A French Canadian, the ancestor of business magnate and former presidential candidate Ross Perot (1930–2019) moved to Louisiana around that time, in the 1740s.

84. This policy of war by proxy was common practice, as documented by official correspondence between local authorities and the Secretary of State of the Navy.

85. On Cahokia and the nearby village of Prairie du Pont, see Ekberg, *French Roots*, 54–64; Morgan, "Cahokia: French and Indian Struggles," in *Land of Big Rivers*, 43–68.

86. On Kaskaskia, see Eckberg, *French Roots*, 64–79; Brown, *History*, 10–11.

87. On "Philippe Renault and St. Philippe," see MacDonald, 38–39. On the topic of "Early mining in the Northwest," see Kellogg, 341–363.

88. Renault introduced black slavery in Illinois. There is disagreement on how many African slaves were sent to the Illinois Country. Creagh writes that Renault "brought five hundred slaves from Saint-Domingue" (*Nos Cousins*, 83). Brown questions that number: "Many authors state that Renault brought 500 slaves; the mining company might have agreed to import 500, but the census data shows there were never that many in the Illinois" (Brown, *History*, 11). The census figures quoted by Brown indicate that there were around 200, not 500 slaves in the area at that time. The figures quoted by Ekberg in his demographic table for the Illinois Country refer to a later period. By 1752, there were 446 Black slaves and 149 Indian slaves there (*French Roots...*, 152). In 1791 by contrast, slaves numbered 631 just for St. Louis and Ste. Genevieve.

89. For detailed information on agricultural practices in Illinois Country, see Ekberg, "Tilling the Land in Colonial Illinois" (*French Roots...*, 171–212), and "Appendix: Gristmills and River Vessels" (265–282). See also Havard and Vidal, "Le Pays des Illinois, grenier à blé de la Louisiane, " *Histoire*, 457–460.

90. On "Town government," see Ekberg, *Colonial Ste. Genevieve*, 335–375.

91. On land grants in Illinois Country, see Havard and Vidal, "L'agriculture de type européen au Canada et au Pays des Illinois," *Histoire*, 424–432.

92. Belting devotes chapter III of her book to "The village of Kaskaskia," and particularly to the description of streets, houses, and population (23–40). Chapter IV, "Life in the Village" provides a good indication of the villagers' way of life based on their possessions, as inventoried at time of death (41–51). Chapter V, "Making a Living," centers on the tools used by the villagers, which serves as a source of information on their professional activities (52–67). Finally, chapter VI, "Social Life and Customs" describes weekend and holiday celebrations as well as life events such as baptisms and marriages (68–77). Ekberg provides similar information for Ste. Genevieve in *Colonial Ste. Genevieve*.

93. Brown devotes her book to what remains the village of Prairie du Rocher up to this day. See *History as They Lived it. A Social History of Prairie du Rocher, IL*. See chapters 4–7.

94. "The slaves of the company and for Renault's mining business were the majority of the slaves listed in the census; only seventeen black slaves were distributed among the various inhabitants of the Fort de Chartres region" (Brown, *History*, 12). The high price of slaves, "equivalent to the amount for purchase of a house and lot" explains why most habitants could not afford to have any (Brown, *History*, 51). Ekberg provides the following figures for the number of Indian slaves in the Illinois Country in 1752: 60 males and 89 females (*French Roots*, 152). The numbers include the Indian slave population for the villages of Kaskaskia, Chartres, St. Philippe, Prairie du Rocher, Cahokia, and Ste. Genevieve. See also Ekberg, "Slave values," *French Roots...*, 157–161.

95. Brown offers detailed information on the number of habitants and the composition of the population in Illinois Country under the French Regime in *History as They Lived It*, 10–31. See also Ekberg, "Daily Life in the Colonial Community," in *Colonial Ste. Genevieve*, 284–333.

96. Ekberg provides a demographic chart for the year 1752 by gender and race (white, black, or Indian slave) for the following Illinois Country villages: Kaskaskia, Chartres, St. Philippe, Prairie du Rocher, Cahokia, and Ste. Genevieve, a tiny hamlet at that time. The total population, including missionaries and soldiers, was 1,380. Ekberg, *French Roots...*, 152.

97. Creagh highlights the corruption that developed along with the fur trade in Illinois Country: "In this colonial setting, where corruption comes from the top, traders and merchants do not hesitate to compromise the interests of the King of France and to sell their pelts to the British in Orange or New York. They thereby avoid paying taxes and make greater profits. They also get paid faster" (*Nos Cousins*, 78).

98. Brown provides biographical sketches for a few soldiers and officers who remained in the Illinois country after their service ended. See *History as They Lived It*, 23–26.

99. On trades in New France, see Havard and Vidal, "Les artisans urbains," *Histoire*, 555–557.

100. Initially, historians thought that Ste. Genevieve was founded in the 1730s, but Ekberg dates its foundation to two decades later, when land pressure intensified on the east bank of the Mississippi (*Colonial Ste. Genevieve*, 2–25). He adds: "Ste Genevieve was founded during a brief respite in the almost continual warfare of the eighteenth century" (50).

101. Brown states that despite the official prohibition of immigrants with other religious affiliations than the Roman Catholic Church, "a few Swiss and German settlers in the Louisiana colony were Lutherans and Calvinists. There were even one or two Jews" (Brown, *History*, 104).

102. Creagh writes that stone houses became more common in Illinois country after annexation. *Nos Cousins*, 147.

103. See Ekberg, "Open-Field agriculture," in *French Roots…*, 111–137, and Brown, *History*, 72–73.

104. "All adult men (twenty-five and over) seem to have been able to participate, and free blacks and widows may have, too. The franchise may have been less restrictive in the Illinois than in New England" (Brown, *History*, 56).

105. Ekberg picks up on an observation Thomas Jefferson made during a 1787 trip through the province of Champagne, France, namely that the French were "certainly less happy and less virtuous in villages than they would be insulated with their families on the grounds they cultivate" (Quoted in Ekberg, *French Roots*, 263).

106. Brown provides detailed information on the voyageurs' activities and contracts based on manuscript sources in *The Voyageur in the Illinois Country*. See also Ekberg, *French Roots*, 33, 46–54; and Royot, "Life in the Pays des Illinois at Mid-Eighteenth Century," 65–77.

107. For an indication on the price such products fetched, see Brown, *History*, 79.

108. For an illustration of the *bateau*, or "American-style flatboat of the type used on the Ohio and Mississippi Rivers" see Ekberg, *French Roots*, 281.

109. In his *Journal*, Antoine Bonnefoy mentions the presence of "a negro" in his *pirogue*. The Cherokees also had a black prisoner who served as a drummer.

110. For a description of such a convoy, see the first pages of Antoine Bonnefoy's *Journal*. See also Ekberg, "Agricultural Commerce in the Mississippi Valley," *French Roots*, 212–238; and MacDonald, "Convoys," 27–31.

111. On the colonial society of Upper Louisiana, see Brown, *History*, 88–93.

112. On "Hired Agricultural Labor," i.e., *journaliers* (day workers) and *engagés*, see Ekberg, *French Roots…*, 161–170. Creagh mentions that the Company of the Indies did not contract only with indentured men, but also with women who worked most of the time as seamstresses, tailors, knitters, but mostly as laundry- or washerwomen" (*Nos Cousins*, 118).

113. Based on her research of marriage contracts, a common practice, Brown concludes that "[w]omen enjoyed a fairly high status" in Illinois country." *History*, 91.

114. Balvay devotes a chapter to Franco-Amerindian marriages in *L'Epée et la plume*, 193–203. See also Creagh, *Nos Cousins*, 29–31.

115. Ronald Creagh maintains that the "[t]he Indians were not bent on preserving their cultural integrity" (*Nos Cousins*, 28).

116. On military tactics in New France, and in particular *la petite guerre*, guerilla warfare, see Balvay, *L'Epée et la plume*, 150–154; and on the commissioning of Native Americans in the French armies, 239–256.

117. "Some observers reported that, regretfully, certain settlers lived a life 'in the imitation of the Indians,' whose mores and customs they completely adopted and without which they could no longer survive" (Creagh, *Nos Cousins*, 28).

118. On the adoption of Indian food and dress, see Havard and Vidal, *Histoire*, 347–349. On the farmers' clothes, see Havard and Vidal, *Histoire*, 557–561. For a visual representation of kind of clothes habitants wore around 1780, see the illustration in Brown *History*, 96.

119. See Creagh, "The Joys of the Sauna," in *Nos Cousins d'Amérique*, 28–29.

120. In the *Pays d'en haut*, voyageurs also ate the local food, *sagamité*, made of hominy, bacon, and grease, corn, wild rice, as well as deer, bear, and smaller furry animals.

121. For a detailed analysis of conflicts in Acadia between 1740 and 1757, including resistance to deportation, see Sauvageau, 191–288.

122. See A.J.B. (John) Johnston, "Louisbourg."

123. For a brief history of Acadia, see Brasseaux, "Four Hundred Years of Acadian Life in North America," in *French, Cajun…*, 37–61. On early Franco-Anglo conflicts in Acadia during the first half of the 18th century, see Sauvageau, 99–190.

124. See Acerra and Meyer, *Histoire de la marine des origines à nos jours*, chapters 2–7.

125. Acerra and Meyer mention the following milestones: Isaac Newton invented the reflecting quadrant, or octant, in 1699 and others perfected it in the 1730s. In 1748, Pierre Le Roy refined the marine chronometer, invented by Jeremy Thacker in 1714 and improved on by John Harrisson in the 1730s. Finally, John Hadley and Thomas Godfrey designed a useable sextant in the 1730s and John Campbell its modern version in 1757 (Acerra and Meyer).

126. A British map from 1720 suggests that the United Kingdom may already have had an eye on New France at that time. See the website "Map of the north parts of America claimed by France…."

127. On Detroit under the French Regime in the 18th century prior to the French and Indian Wars, see Teasdale, Chapter 2 "Seigneurial Tenure and Landholders," in *Fruits of Perseverance*, 25–39.

128. Official documents contain a self-critique of French colonization practices that were geared

primarily towards the crossing of the Rockies and the discovery of the Western Sea. See Margry, *Mémoires et Documents*, Vol. VI, Part IV, Chapter XV, "*Pendant que les Français explorent les terres arrosées par les affluents du Mississippi à l'Ouest, les rives des principaux affluents de ce fleuve à l'est sont abandonnées, malgré les avertissements de ne pas se laisser devancer dans leur occupation. Au moment où les Anglais y pénètrent, le marquis de la Galissonière fait prendre de nouveau par M. de Céloron possession de l'Ohio, que le gouverneur de la Viriginie réclame,*" ["While the French explore lands watered by tributaries of the Mississippi in the West, the shores of this river's main tributaries in the east are being neglected, and this in spite of being warned not to be outpaced in land occupancy. At the very moment the British start filtering in, Marquis de la Galissonière orders M. de Céloron to take possession of Ohio, which the Governor of Virginia is claiming"] (657–732). This chapter also contains correspondence between the French and the British at the onset of the French and Indian Wars.

129. Thanks to Father François Piquet, the other four nations remained neutral or even helped the French as scouts. After the war, Father Piquet dedicated himself to the task of strengthening the Franco-Illinois alliance.

130. See Codignola, "Barrin de la Galissonière, Roland Michel, Marquis (1693–1756)."

131. The Walking Purchase established a precedent for this kind of transaction when in 1737 members of the Penn family began selling land which, according to them, their ancestor had bought from the Delaware (or Lenape) as part of a 1,200,000 acres estate.

132. M. Jones accounts for the ease with which francophone Huguenots assimilated in colonial British society to "the fact that between leaving France and going to American, many of them had spent a generation or more in England, Germany, or Holland." "In them," she adds, "'the process of denationalization' was already far advanced before they even crossed the ocean. It may be, too, that the refugees made a deliberate attempt to throw off the characteristics of a country from which they felt they had been unjustly driven" (51–52).

133. Paul-André Dubois argues that a common Catholic religiosity bound the French and the Abenaki together.

134. Jean-Baptiste de La Rochefoucauld, duc d'Anville (1707–1746,) was the of son Marthe Du Casse and the grandson of Jean-Baptiste Du Casse, the Huguenot convert turnèd pirate then governor.

135. Despite this puzzling decision, the Secretary of State of the Navy appointed de la Jonquière Governor General of New France in March 1749. He served for three years in that capacity until his death.

136. The second marquis de Vaudreuil was the first governor of Louisiana to be born in America and the last Governor General of New France (1755–1763). Creagh writes that during his tenure as Governor of Louisiana, he "stunned the settlers with his sumptuous meals, his extravagant balls, and the quaint etiquette he imposed in a colony still in its frontier days" (*Nos Cousins*, 120).

137. In *Travels in the American Colonies*, Meremess describes such an incident in his introduction to Beauchamps' account of the punitive action the latter led against the Choctaw: "In March 1746, while the French party were gone to Mobile to receive their presents, Red Shoe [a Choctaw chief allied with the British] was busy attempting to bring about peace between the Choctaw and the Chickasaw who were adherents of the English. The chief of the French party returning in time to defeat his efforts, Red Shoe, in a fit of anger, ordered the assassination of Chevalier de Verbois and two other Frenchmen and it was for the purpose of exacting satisfaction for this act that De Beauchamps undertook the mission of which the journal […] is an account" (259–260). His journal provides a prime example of the kind of negotiations that went on between the French and the Native American chiefs they were trying to win over or bring back to their side.

138. On the impact of King George's War and the War of the Austrian Succession on the French North American colonies, see Creagh, "Guerres d'Europe et Colonies Américaines," *Nos Cousins*, 138–139; Dickinson, 95–98.

139. Creagh points out that the construction of these forts was part of the prevailingly defensive politics of France during the 1712–1764 period: "France spent ten times more money on the construction of forts that it did on maintaining its alliances with Indian nations, masters of these territories" (*Nos Cousins*, 86). On the other hand, New France was so huge and the population so scarce that it was "practically impossible to defend" (Creagh, *Nos Cousins*, 78). See also Pritchard, "Elusive Empire," 402–422.

140. On guerilla warfare, and "the cultural gap between French and Canadian officers" during the Seven Year War, see Balvay, *L'Epée et la plume*, 154–159.

141. Quoted in "8.5 Les préliminaires au 'Grand Dérangement.'"

142. See Leblanc, "Les Migrations acadiennes."

143. See Johnston, "Evangeline."

Chapter VI

1. In *The French in North America*, for instance, Eccles devotes chapter 7 to the Franco-Indian Wars, "The Pre-emptive Conquest, 1749–1763," and chapter 8, "Aftermath, 1760–1783" to the War of Independence.

2. See for instance, Dickinson, 99–103

3. As Hodson and Rushforth further explain: "Imperial competition inspired all sorts of developments in the English colonies—including fierce anti-Catholicism, growing royalism, and greater intercolonial alliances—that strengthened colonists' attachment to England and to one another" (23).

4. Nester, for instance, questions the notion that

the French monarchy was still "absolute" in chapter 1 of *The French and Indian War*, 11–44. Labrune and Toutain label their pages on Louis XV's reign *l'absolutisme hésitant*, wavering absolutism (62–63). See also Harris, *Absolutism and Enlightenment*, Manuel, *The Age of Reason*.

5. Louis XV, who had brought his mistress, Marie Anne de Mailly-Nesle, Duchess of Châteauroux, to the front, fell so gravely ill in Metz in 1744 that one feared for his life. The priest who was called to administer the last rites, however, refused to do so unless the dying king sent away his lover. If this cleric's act of defiance was a humiliating episode for the King, it did not have the intended effect. As soon as Louis recovered, he sent once again for his mistress—who unfortunately died upon her return to Versailles, perhaps the victim of poisoning. See Gaxotte, 157–160.

6. Gaxotte writes that Madame de Pompadour was Louis XV's mistress for five years only (1745–1750) but remained his friend until her death. On the relations between Louis XV and Pompadour, see Gaxotte, 160–168; on factionism at court, Gaxotte, 184–189; Nester, 21–37.

7. "After Fleury's death, however, Louis XV was unable to find a singular focus or purpose as king. Reluctantly—for he much preferred hunting and court life, especially entertainments and beautiful women—he returned to the crown's field of battle" (Haine, 64).

8. Donald S. Lutz (193) showed that Montesquieu was more frequently invoked than any other Enlightenment philosopher by colonial pre-revolutionary Americans.

9. The most famous work by François Quesnay (1694–1774) is entitled *On Natural Rights* (1765).

10. On the Enlightenment, see Darnton, 1–40; Nester, 39–43. Gaxotte, who does not hide his dislike for the "philosophical sect," writes that Voltaire and Rousseau loved Native Americans and criticized France's colonization of North America (227–231).

11. Vincent de Gournay was the first to advocate that trade be set free. One ought to "*laisser faire, laisser passer*" (let [goods] go, let them pass), he thought. The Physiocrats used the expression he had coined as a command: "Laissez faire, laissez passer."

12. "Economic expansion led to a dramatic jump in the urban middle classes, the bourgeoisie, and to increased entrepreneurial activity. From around 700,000 in 1700, this diverse class—ranging from large merchants, manufacturers, and bankers to small shopkeepers, craftspeople, and wealthy peasants—grew to approximately 2.3 million by 1789. Nobles also profited from the expansion of colonial and wholesale commerce as well as from mining and metallurgical enterprises. Nobles introduced to their estates the new methods of animal husbandry, fertilization, and crop rotation that were hallmarks of scientific agriculture. The French population expanded from a high of 21.5 million around 1720 to 28.6 million on the eve of the French Revolution" (Haine, 64).

13. On the risks and "benefits" associated with the slave trade in the 18th century, see Devèze, 168–171. The historian names a few slave traders from Nantes who became wealthy (169).

14. On the 18th-century salons, see Kale, "Chapter 1, between the Republic of Letters and the Grand Monde," 20–21; on the salons and the philosophers, 27–28. See also Duby and Mandrou, *Histoire de la Civilisation française*, Vol. II, 116–129.

15. Raynal published his masterpiece, *A History of the Two Indies*, a critique of the French colonial system in New France and the Far East, in 1771. On Raynal, see Sean C. Goodlett.

16. Chartier provides the following additional indices of social secularization: fewer religious vocations, fewer priests and nuns; fewer wills listing the Church as beneficiary; as well as a reduction in the number of services for the dead, hence less money, and less power for the Church.

17. "Generally speaking, Freemasonry grew more, and found greater acceptance, in Protestant rather than Catholic Europe. Yet its popularity in upper bourgeois and aristocratic French society must not be forgotten [...]. It has been estimated that by the 1770s there were 10,000 freemasons in Paris, a city with a population between 500,000 and 600,000. Daniel Roche has further estimated that 10 percent of all eighteenth-century French authors were masonic" (Jacob, 82–83).

18. See Duby and Mandrou, "La Révolution économique et démographique," in *Histoire de la Civilisation française*, Vol II, 71–101.

19. Michel Foucault described Damiens' torture in detail in the opening pages of *Surveiller et Punir*, 9–13.

20. On the French and Indian Wars, see Creagh, *Nos Cousins*, 142–145; Eccles, *The French in North America*, 198–234; Havard and Vidal, "La guerre de Sept Ans en Amérique de Nord," *Histoire*, 621–669; Nester, *The French and Indian War and the Conquest of New France*; Royot, "Shifting Identities," 78–99.

21. Great Britain, Prussia, Portugal, and other allies fought against France, Spain, Austria, Russia, Sweden, and other allies.

22. Prussia had signed a peace treaty with England three years before the war's end.

23. See Haudrère. The shareholder profile was the same, however: members of the court nobility, the aristocracy, merchants, bankers, even philosophers—Voltaire, for instance.

24. See Raynal, "Book 4, "Voyages, settlements, wars, and commerce of the French in the East Indies," in *The History of the Two Indies*, 47–61.

25. See Haudrère, "La monnaie de Pondichéry au XVIIIe siècle," in *Les Français dans l'Océan Indien*, 197–205.

26. On the Seven Years' War in the Illinois Country, see Brown, *History as They Lived It*, 145–146; Morgan, "A Ragged Resource War: British in the Illinois," *Land of Big Rivers*, 135–160, and "Predations and Survivals: French, British, and Indian Illinois," 161–190. Ekberg, by contrast, argued that "[a]lthough the French built the mighty Fort de Chartres in preparation for the French and Indian War

[in 1751], the Illinois Country remained beyond the range of the fighting. Ste Genevieve was a passive pawn in the Anglo-French rivalry upon the chessboard of North America" (*Colonial Ste. Genevieve*, 51).

27. See Dickinson, "Il ne reste que la morue," *Les Français en Amérique*, 103–108.

28. Eccles argues that the English drive to grab Indian lands had much to do with the Protestant ethics. The English Land Companies, he writes, "coveted the land, and the Indian peoples who had failed to cultivate them by husbandry, European fashion, had thereby forfeited their title. They had to be dispossessed by one means or another to make way for those who could make proper use of the land according to Gods's precepts" (Eccles, *The French*, 198–199).

29. On the preparations for war on French and British sides, see Eccles, *The French*, 200–201.

30. Charles de Langlade, Jr., was the son of a Canadian fur trader, Augustin Mouet, Sieur de Langlade, and Domitilde, sister and daughter of Ottawa chiefs. Langlade was bilingual and bicultural, having been raised by his mother but having also received an education in French from the missionaries of Fort Michilimackinac. With his father he established a trading post in Green Bay in 1745. On the Langlade, see McDonnell, *Masters of Empire*, 3–6, 15–16, 112–116, 195–197; 308, 318–319. See also McBride, "Wisconsin."

31. See Creagh, "Une Défaite de George Washington," *Nos Cousins*, 139–140; Eccles, *The French*, 202–203; Furstenberg, "Washington, George (1732–1799)."

32. Eccles writes that Washington "signed the capitulation terms without taking the trouble to inquire too closely into their meaning and subsequently dishonoured them." He links the Native Americans' switch of allegiance to Washington's "ignominious defeat," as it "brought the last of the wavering Indian nations to the French cause. From that point on, the English had not as single Indian ally in the West, while the strength of the French was enhanced immeasurably" (*The French*, 203).

33. Braddock became commander-in-chief for the Thirteen Colonies in February 1755. See Eccles, *The French*, 204–205.

34. On Pontiac, see Waters, "Pontiac (ca. 1720–1769)"; Brown, *History*, 152.

35. On the naval battles during the Seven Years' War, see Dull, "Sea Power and the Outcome of the Seven Years' War," 63–90. Eccles writes: "More than three hundred French ships and eight thousand sailors were seized in English ports or on high seas. This was a serious blow to French maritime strength" (205). For an examination of the Seven Year War in Acadia, see also Sauvageau, 289–357, and Bujol, "L'Acadie vers 1750."

36. On Montcalm, see Béland. On Montcalm and the Oswego Campaign, see Nester, 200–202.

37. On Bougainville, who gave his name to the flower he brought back from the South Pacific, the bougainvillea, see Castillo, "Bougainville, Louis Antoine de (1729–1811)." Bougainville's account of his sojourn in New France was published in English under the title *Adventure in the Wilderness: The American Journals of Louis Antoine de Bougainville, 1756–1760.*

38. About Voltaire's quote, see the webpage on "Snow, A Few Acres of." In the 19th century, the Romantic poet Alfred de Vigny viewed the fall of New France differently than Voltaire: "Like a ship that abandons an entire family on a desert island, France has cast away into Canada an unhappy population speaking the same language I write...." Quoted in McLeman-Carnie, 1193.

39. Fort Carillon is now Fort Ticonderoga. See Crego.

40. The British tried to capture Martinique in 1758 but failed. They did capture Guadeloupe in May 1759.

41. A vital strategic point in this campaign was Fort Ligonier, named after Field Marshal John (Jean Louis de) Ligonier (1680–1770), a French Huguenot whose family had immigrated to England following the revocation of the Edict of Nantes. Ligonier served as Commander-in-Chief of the British forces from 1758 to 1763 (Cubbison).

42. The Lenape also agreed to sell their claims to all the remaining lands they owned in New Jersey.

43. On the conquest, see Eccles, 210–233. Eccles attributes much of the blame for the defeat to Montcalm, who refused to obey the Governor General's orders on several occasions, had a "defeatist" attitude, and handled the battle of Quebec ineptly (234).

44. Kellogg therefore characterizes the 1750s as "the end of the French regime in the Northwest" (423).

45. See Tarrade, "Destinées d'Acadiens: 1755–1785."

46. For an overview of the Indian Wars, "the collective term for the various colonial struggles between Britain and France," see Aubuchon, "Indian Wars," 597; and Jim Fisher, "French and Indian War."

47. They were Pondichéry, Chandernagor, Yanaon, Karikal, and Mahé.

48. The islands continued to prosper under the new governor, Pierre Poivre, who introduced the cultivation of spices, cloves, nutmeg, etc.—fittingly so given his last name, "pepper" in French.

49. In 1785, however, a new *Compagnie des Indes orientales et de la Chine* created new establishments along the coasts of India and in Canton, China. With its fleet of 15 vessels, the company prospered rapidly, bringing 16–18 percent returns on investments to shareholders by 1789.

50. On the French government's preference for the Caribbean islands over Canada, see Butel 118–124; and Dubois, *A Colony*, 30–40.

51. See Devèze, "Le triomphe économique des Antilles françaises à la fin du XVIIIe siècle," 266–279. According to Devèze, there were 32,000 white settlers and 500,000 slaves in Saint-Domingue on the eve of the French Revolution.

52. France purchased Corsica, where Napoleon was born, in 1768.

53. Eccles rejects the notion that Bigot was corrupt: "Much, indeed far too much, has been made of the alleged malversation of the Intendant François Bigot and *munitionnaire du Roi* Joseph Michel Cadet. Recent research has revealed that, far from being the villains previously portrayed, they actually performed prodigies to keep the French armies in the field. Without their efforts the French war effort in New France would have collapsed long before it did. Bigot and Cadet were, in fact, the victims of a pernicious system and used as scapegoats by inadequate ministers and the King to cover up their own incompetence" (Eccles, *The French*, 211–212).

54. See Codignola, "Treaty of Paris (1763)," and Lignereux, "1763, Un royaume pour un empire."

55. Correspondence between Colonel Henry Bouquet and his superior, Lord Amherst, provide evidence that smallpox was willingly spread through contaminated blankets and handkerchiefs.

56. On Pontiac's War, see Havard and Vidal, "La guerre 'de Pontiac,'" *Histoire*, 674–680. Although Ottawa Chief Pontiac, also known as Obwandiyag (c. 1720–1769), gave the rebellion its name his actual role as a leader is disputed by historians. On Pontiac, see also McDonnell, *Masters of Empire*, 18–19, 120–137, and Waters.

57. For instance, a vigilante group from Pennsylvania known as the Paxton Boys murdered Indians who lived in their midst.

58. George Lankford offers concrete examples of French people who remained by the Arkansas Post after the war, the families of Joseph Francoeur and Antoine Janis.

59. According to Brown (*History*, 152), the Jesuits' estates were confiscated to pay for the Seven Years War. The Jesuits had lost their monopoly on missionary work earlier on, "in 1698 when the Fathers of the Foreign Missions were authorized to enter the territory [of New France]" (Creagh, *Nos Cousins*, 40).

60. On Missouri mines, see Gerald Gold, "Les Gens qui ont pioché le tuf …."

61. On St. Louis, see Randall who accredits the commonly accepted attribution of the founding of St. Louis to Laclède and Chouteau. More importantly, Ekberg and Person showed that "St. Ange de Bellerive […] [a]lthough consistently obscured by the long shadows of Laclède and Chouteau, […] was demonstrably more important than they to St. Louis during the critical period of 1765–70. As military commandant, he provided law and order and stability to a frontier settlement that was French, roots and branches, although technically situated in Spanish territory" (*St. Louis Rising*, 4). See also Ekberg, *French Roots*, 96–101. On St. Ange de Bellerive's activities as commandant at Fort de Chartres, 1764–1765, see MacDonald, 115–123. As Belting recalls, "St. Ange de Bellerive was called from his post at Vincennes and left in command of the almost empty fort [de Chartres] until October 10, 1765, when it was surrendered to Captain Thomas Sterling" (8).

62. Creagh describes Kaskaskia as "a prosperous mission." He states that the village became a parish in 1719. *Nos Cousins*, 43.

63. On Ste. Genevieve, see also Ekberg, *French Roots*, 88–96.

64. On Jean Marie Cardinal, see Petersen.

65. Apparently, the French were not always happy to serve as guides to English travelers. Prévos recalls this incident in the following way: "Abraham Lansing and his son doubtless irked the Frenchman. Were these prosperous traders planning to secure a monopoly of the fur trade and drive the French out before their country had actually taken formal possession? Grudgingly, perhaps, Jean Marie and a companion consented to act as guides and servants for Lansing on a trading excursion into the northern wilds. A quarrel ensued, hot words were exchanged, and Lansing and his son were killed. Fearful of English justice, Cardinal hastened southward, stole into Prairie du Chien to get his wife and family, and then fled into Spanish territory" (Prévos, 41).

66. On Prairie du Chien, see Ekberg, *French Roots*, 102–108.

67. On Giard, see Prévos, 55–60.

68. On Julien Dubuque, see Prévos, 42–54. He was the thirteenth child in a family that had moved from St. Louis to the Upper Mississippi basin.

69. On Tesson, see Prévos, 55–60.

70. For a description of the Illinois Country at the end of the 18th century, see Callot, "Chapter XVIII, Pays des Illinois," in *Voyage en Amérique septentrionale*, 287–316, and "Chapter XIX, Missouri," 362–370.

71. See Brasseaux, "A new Acadia," in *French, Cajun…*, 61–68. See also Havard et Vidal, "L'immigration Canadienne, aux origines du pays cajun," *Histoire*, 698–700.

72. See Eccles, "Aftermath, 1763–1783," 235–265; Brown, "Under Three Flags," in *History as They Lived it*, 151–195; Havard and Vidal, "Mourir avec les Français?" *Histoire*, 681–682.

73. One of them also punished the province of New York for refusing to pay for a standing army, that is to provision and quarter British soldiers, in peace time.

74. The Catholic Church even obtained the right to impose tithes.

75. On the Quebec Act, see Traisnel's article on this topic.

76. On "America and the Enlightenment," see Royot, 135–138.

77. For an overview of the American Revolution, see Codignola's article on that topic and Creagh chapter on "La Guerre d'Indépendance" in *Nos Cousins*, 193–199.

78. Elizabeth H. Avery goes even further when she writes: "I am thoroughly convinced that, for the 'advocacy of a more perfect union,' for efforts to obtain a convention and with that in view, for able and influential services during its sessions, and for vigorous and successful efforts to secure the ratification of the Constitution, we are more indebted to four men of Huguenot ancestry, James Bowdoin,

Alexander Hamilton, Gouverneur Morris, and John Jay, than to any other four statesmen of the time" (32).

79. "The Declaration of Independence of July 4, 1776, was well received among liberal intellectuals of the Enlightenment in spite of their very approximate understanding of events." Montbrial, 452.

80. The Republic of Vermont (1777–1790) named a town in his honor, Vergennes, Vermont.

81. On Vergennes's reasons for supporting the American Revolution, and what Dull sees as the "three chief fallacies in Vergennes' British policy," see "France...," 11.

82. See Eccles, The French in North America, 248–249. Beaumarchais, who had already been employed by the French government as an occasional spy, is said to have told the King: "Sire, such a nation must be invincible."

83. See Lessard, "Franklin, Benjamin (1706–1790)."

84. For a short biography of John Adams, see Rofe, 57–58.

85. In America and in France, the Masonic lodge was a breeding ground for revolution. Several founding fathers were free masons: George Washington, Benjamin Franklin, about half of the generals in the Continental Army. So where French revolutionary leaders: Danton, Robespierre, Napoleon Bonaparte.

86. On Jacques Le Ray de Chaumont, see T. Wood Clarke, Emigrés in the Wilderness, 3–20.

87. Chaumont had made a fortune in shipping and manufacturing. His specialty was the production of terra-cotta portrait medallions of, and for the wealthy (Clark).

88. See Mays, "Jones, John Paul (1747–1792)."

89. Spain adopted similar policies, refusing to antagonize Great Britain directly until the 1779 declaration of war but providing aid to the American cause through the Gardoqui trading company via Louisiana and Cuba.

90. There were only a few French officers who had fought in the Seven Years' War and fought again in the War of Independence: François Tilly, Count de Grasse (1722–1788), and Charles-Henri-Louis d'Arsac, chevalier de Ternay (1723–1780). Ternay led the fleet transporting Rochambeau's troops to America and died of typhus in Newport, RI during the war. Godechot writes that the Gazette Françoise, first published in 1780 on presses brought from France to Newport by the French fleet, was "the first Army Newspapers published in the world and the first French-language newspaper published in the United States." Godechot, "La Gazette," 78.

91. This is the commonly accepted interpretation of the French reaction to the U.S. victory at Saratoga but Eccles offers a slightly different interpretation: "Following the spurious American victory at Saratoga, Vergennes became extremely fearful that Britain would offer the Americans terms that they would be glad to accept; namely de facto independence with merely nominal sovereignty resting with the British Crown—ironically the status that

Canada enjoys today—on condition that the Americans join with the British in a war against France and Spain to strip them of their American colonies. He became convinced that war with Britain was now inevitable, hence it would be far better to have it with the Americans as allies rather than foes" (Eccles, The French, 250).

92. "The Alliance of 1778 was, in a manner of speaking, at the beginning of everything. A not necessarily acknowledged premise of nearly all the essays under the diplomatic, military, and economic rubrics is that the very substantial aid France gave our infant republic should have forged a special relationship. They also attest that such a relationship did not materialize in any measurable or objective sense" (Roelker and Warner, xvi–xvii).

93. Brett (55) writes that one of the side-effects of the Franco-American alliance was to "improve Catholicism's public image," and that "independence stimulated its organizational life. In Baltimore, America's first diocese was established in 1789, Mount St. Mary's seminary opened in 1791, and a Cathedral was constructed in 1804."

94. On Admiral d'Estaing's contributions to the War of Independence, see DeLong and Russell, 112–125. According to Boutwell and Gill, several of Jacqueline Bouvier Kennedy's ancestors fought in the war.

95. Eccles writes that "Rochambeau's troops received a frosty welcome from the Americans, as always suspicious and hostile towards Papists and subjects of a crowned monarch" and that "relations between the officers deteriorated rapidly" (Eccles, The French, 254-255). Rochambeau was so fearful that the Americans were about to surrender that he sent his son back to France to warn Vergennes. His fears were confirmed when mutinies broke out in the Patriot's armies of New Jersey and Pennsylvania in January 1781.

96. In the Netflix series, Turn, Washington's Spies, French participation in the war of independence is seriously minimized. Although episode 8, "Belly of the Beast," features Lafayette, it is an American, not a French, officer who speaks up against Washington's plan to attack New York, and in the next episode, "Reckoning," which centers on the Battle of Chesapeake and the siege of Yorktown, Rochambeau and De Grasse are presented as playing minor, supporting roles. Of course, a television series is fiction, but it is this amnesia, the forgetting that there would have been no United States without the French, that allows the American myth of self-liberation. On the other hand, this oversight is understandable. Which country wants to remember owing its independence to another?

97. On Rear Admiral de Grasse's role in the War of Independence, see Russell, 265–286 and Balch, The French in America during the War of Independence.

98. The Count of Barras (1719–1793) was another French naval officer who fought during the Yorktown campaign. See Russell, 261, 265, 267, 272, 274, 278–279, 283, 289.

99. For more information on Lafayette's military contribution to the American War of Independence, see Russell, 254–268, 281–286, 289–290, and 293–294.

100. After Yorktown, De Grasse's fleet was vanquished by Admiral Rodney in the Caribbean.

101. On the War of Independence in Illinois Country, see Ekberg, *Colonial Ste. Genevieve*, 37–68.

102. Commenting on the French migration to Spanish Louisiana between 1787 and 1790, Lankford (98) adds that the French feared "that the Northwest Ordinance of 1787 would require them to release their slaves, which they conceived to mean economic ruin."

103. These Franco-Canadian volunteers, some of whom had fought the British in the French and Indian War, were given land in northeastern New York along Lake Champlain. According to A. B. Chartier (14), around 250 families founded the village of Corbeau, which later became Coopersville.

104. "In addition to Britain's recognition of the independence of the United States of America, they demanded that they be granted the access to the Newfoundland fisheries that they had previously enjoyed as British subjects; similarly, they expected to be granted access to the British West Indies markets. It was their territorial demands that were startling; they demanded that Britain cede Canada to them, that is, the Provinces of Quebec and Nova Scotia as constituted, plus the territory south of the Ohio between the Appalachians and the Mississippi, with the right of free navigation on that river. […]. Coming from delegates of a divided people, who could never have hoped to achieve independence by their own unaided military efforts and were to receive it only as the result of a brilliant French military victory, to make such demands was, to say the least, startling" (Eccles, *The French*, 262–263).

105. France regained her settlement of Saint-Louis in Senegal and the Caribbean Island of Tobago.

106. "The war over, independence gained, the Americans displayed a singular lack of gratitude to the French. The Treaty of Alliance had served its purpose hence it could now be tossed into discard. Thus, when the treaty was put to the test in 1793, the Americans, without a qualm, abrogated it" (Eccles, *The French*, 265).

107. In a period of Franco-American disagreements, John J. Miller and Mark Molesky have carried John Adams's position to extremes and reduced French assistance in the War of Independence to that of the "Revolting Ally." Published in 2004, their book, *Our Oldest Enemy, A History of America's Disastrous Relationship with France,* stands, together with the "Freedom fries," as a major "contribution" to the wave of French bashing that followed France's rejection of the pretexts concocted by the Bush administration to justify its invasion of Iraq in 2003.

108. Arthur St. Clair (1737–1818), who served as President of the Continental Congress and later as governor of the Northwest Territory in 1790, named the city of Cincinnati, OH, in honor of the Society.

109. See Waters, "Lafayette…."

110. Russell mentions the role played by "Colonel Armand" in the American War of Independence, as the commander of "sixty cavalry and as many infantry men" at Deep River in July 1780; and as the commander of "Armand's legion," the troops that "opened the march" on Camden on August 16 (165, 168).

111. Honoré Gabriel Riqueti, Count of Mirabeau (1749–1791) was an early leader of the French Revolution and one of its first victims. His father, a physiocrat, wrote a critique of colonization. An excerpt can be found in Hébert, *L'Amérique française*, 45–51.

112. See Havard and Vidal, "Arpents de neige ou îles à sucre?" *Histoire*, 663–669.

113. See MacLeman-Carnie, particularly page 1194.

114. On Parkman, see Brandao (917), who writes: "His history of New France read 'as a morality tale.' It was the story of a colony doomed to failure because of its ties to the Catholic, absolutist, and feudal values of Old Europe."

115. This is still the case in 2020 according to a commentator like Maureen Dowd: "At some visceral level, […] America must regret being torn away from the royal family. How else can we explain our enduring fascination with dynasties?" (9).

116. See Garrett W. Sheldon, "Jefferson, Thomas (1743–1826)."

Chapter VII

1. On the establishment of the republic in both countries, see Hammersley, "Republicanism."

2. Frances S. Childs' claim, in *French Refugees*, that the Francophobia born of the Seven Years' War was replaced by a Francophilia born of the War of the Independence, seems a bit too simplistic.

3. See Wolosin, "L'Enfant, Pierre-Charles (1755–1825)."

4. James Greenleaf (1765–1843) was involved in the genesis of the federal capital as a land speculator. Born in Boston, he was the scion of a prominent French Huguenot family that had fled to England and changed its name from "Feuillevert" to "Greenleaf."

5. Tousard played an important role in establishing the U.S. Military Academy at West Point in 1802, with a curriculum borrowed from the *Ecole Polytechnique*. He also wrote the first artillery manual used at West Point.

6. For a detailed analysis on this topic, see Kennedy's *Orders from France.*

7. So huge was Girard's fortune that he personally saved the U.S. government from financial collapse during the War of 1812. See Wilson, 257–270.

8. On Brissot's relations to American Quakers, see Anon. "The French Revolution: Quakers and Cockades."

9. As a founding member of the Society of the Friends of Blacks, the French abolitionist society,

and as a representative to the Legislative Assembly, Brissot fought ceaselessly against slavery and for equal rights for Blacks. He became the leader of a party that initially took his name, the Brissotins, before becoming the Girondins.

10. On the French Revolution, see Haine, 71–88. "After 1750 the symbiotic relationship between the Catholic Church and the absolute monarchy lost the allegiance of much of the elite, who turned to the secular, rationalistic, and emerging republican philosophy of the Enlightenment. The result would be the birth of modern political thought as well as the modern nation-state" (Haine, 55).

11. The first order was made out by those who prayed ("oratores"), the Church; the second order of those who fought and went to war ("bellatores"), the nobility; the third order, or *tiers-état*, by those who worked ("laboratores").

12. For an overview of the Revolution, see Loiselle "French Revolution." See also Labrune and Toutain, 64–655, and Caiani, *Louis XVI and the French Revolution*.

13. The Viscount of Noailles was "the most exquisite dancer in the gay court of Louis XVI and Marie Antoinette" (Clarke, 51), a veteran of the War of Independence, and Lafayette's brother-in-law. A few years later, he returned to America as an *émigré*. See Clarke, 51–65.

14. The Parisians blamed Lafayette, who as commander of the National Guard was the royal family's custodian, for their escape. His popularity in France declined from then on.

15. In both cases, these lands were offered for sale in small parcels with the intent of increasing the number of small landowners. Figures are from Godechot, *France*, 40.

16. Based on Jefferson's correspondence with French philosopher Destutt de Tracy, Peter Onuf (48) adds another crucial difference between the two sister republics: "France faced an array of powerful enemies in Europe, determined to reverse the outcome of its revolution; by contrast, the United States would face no serious obstacle to its peaceful expansion across the continent now that the French threat had disappeared."

17. See Journoud, "La Rochefoucauld-Liancourt."

18. The Chevalier de Liancourt became Duke of La Rochefoucault following his cousin's murder during the September massacres of 1792. He himself went in exile to the U.S.

19. On this phase of the Revolution, see the overview in Labrune and Toutain, 66–69; Weber, "The French Wars," 524–533. For a detailed account, see Higonnet, *Goodness*, 32–33.

20. *Sans-culottes* means "men without silk-knee breeches." Silk stockings were a sign of aristocratic, or high-class status.

21. Only tax-paying male citizens over 21 years of age could vote and only 10% of those eligible to vote did, however. In the U.S., "universal" (male) suffrage did not determine the outcome of presidential elections, the Electoral College did.

22. The counter-revolutionary rebels were known as "*Chouans.*"

23. A young woman from Normandy, Charlotte Corday, murdered Marat in July.

24. On Paine, see Thomas Walker.

25. For the history of Haiti during the French Revolution, see Dubois, "Prophecy, Revolt, and Emancipation," in *A Colony of Citizens*, 23–168.

26. For the distinction between a slave society and a society with slaves, see Cécile Vidal, *Caribbean New Orleans*, 498–500.

27. See Heuman, "The World the Planters Made," *The Caribbean*, 45–52.

28. On the Society of the Friends of Blacks, see Dubois, 62–65.

29. Binoche shows that the admission of these representatives of Saint-Domingue was irregular and that their number fluctuated. Among the six admitted in the summer of 1789 he lists the marquis of Gouy d'Arcy and the marquis of Périgny; the chevalier de Cocherel, Gérard, Viau de Thébaudières, and Larchevêque-Thibaut.

30. Although the East India Company had lost its trade monopoly in 1790 it continued to operate and prosper.

31. Munro (1075) adds that in 1776, "the Atlantic slave trade provided French colonies with 20,000 slaves annually and employed 1,000 ships. Out of the total population of 514,849 in the French islands in 1776, 437,738 were slaves."

32. On the colonial lobby, see Butel, 215–224; Dubois, 100–104.

33. Moreau self-published his *Description topographique, physique, civile, politique et historique de la partie française de Saint-Domingue* while in exile in Philadelphia in 1797. His work contains a racial taxonomy that "stands as a precious record of the attitudes of the white elite in pre-revolutionary Saint-Domingue at a time when that minority was holding on to power through racially discriminatory legislation and unprecedented brutality towards slaves" (Garraway, 229). See also Heuman, "The Haitian Revolution," 67–77.

34. Heuman provides the following figures for the population of two French Caribbean islands at the time of the French Revolution. For Martinique in 1789: 5,235 freed people; 10,636 whites; and 83,414 slaves. For Saint-Domingue the same year, the figures are: 24,848 freed people; 30,831 whites; and 434,424 slaves (35).

35. Louis de Curt was a career officer and served as representative of Guadeloupe in the Constituent Assembly before immigrating to London in 1792.

36. See Butel, *Histoire*, 118–124. On the Revolution in Guadeloupe, see Dubois, 124–168.

37. On Victor Hugues and the liberation of Guadeloupe in June 1794, see Dubois, 189–200. On the Haitian Revolution in Cap Français, see Popkin.

38. On the "Maritime War and the foreign invasion," see Butel, *Histoire*, 227–241.

39. As strange as this moral political philosophy may seem today, it would be wrong to view it as the prerogative of a few French loonies—although

Robespierre may have pushed this reasoning to the extreme. In *Goodness Beyond Virtue,* Higonnet rejects "the idea that the essence of Jacobin politics culminated in the immoral and useless Terror of 1793–94," arguing instead that "Jacobinism can still be a model for modern democrats" (1). One may also point out that the founding fathers of the United States used similar rhetoric as the French Jacobins. George Washington and Thomas Jefferson both thought that happiness could not exist without virtue and John Adams believed that virtue and liberty were connected.

40. Between 1834 and 1838, Philippe Buchez and Prosper Roux published a transcript of the minutes of the National Assemblies between 1789 and 1815. Their *Histoire Parlementaire de la Révolution française* takes up 40 volumes. Victor Hugo praised specifically the legislative legacy of the Convention in *Ninety-three,* one of the few French novels on the French Revolution.

41. One of them was the Order of the Most Holy Trinity and of the Captives, an ancient order that served as intermediary between Muslim pirates and Christian governments in negotiations for the release of prisoners.

42. The convents often served as refuge for single or widowed women in Old Regime France.

43. On the topic, see Schuler and Creagh, *Nos Cousins,* 212–213.

44. La Rouërie was not thinking of leaving France himself. He had fought for the cause of liberty in America but "liberty" for him meant the rights of the nobility against infringement by a central state, not those of the Declaration of the Rights of Man. The abolition of privileges, therefore, had put him squarely in the camp of opponents to the Revolution. As the founder of the counter-revolutionary *Association Bretonne,* he was one of the first to take arms against the revolutionaries and to organize the Civil War in Western France.

45. In the U.S., Chateaubriand found inspiration for his famous pre-Romantic works, *Atala* and *René,* both part of *The Genius of Christianity,* as well as for his *Voyage to America.*

46. Chateaubriand's *Essay on Revolutions* (1797) contains a scathing review of the American and the French revolutions. See Le Hir, *National Habitus,* 87–99.

47. Creagh, who uses the term "émigré" in the French sense, as belonging either to the nobility or the clergy, devotes a chapter to "Les Emigrés" in *Nos Cousins,* 208–221. M. Jones uses it in the more common sense and provides an overview of immigration from France and its Caribbean colonies in *American immigration,* 71–73. Harsanyi's book centers on the liberal noblemen.

48. Starting in 1793, each French municipality was required by law to establish a list of the local people who had left the country. Having one's name of the *Liste des Emigrés* was equal to a death sentence.

49. Potofsky (2) writes that "10% of the white population were émigrés or refugees taking flight from the French *métropole* or colonies" in Philadelphia.

50. See Hemmerle, "Talleyrand-Périgord"; also Brace, "Talleyrand in New England"; and Poniatowski.

51. See Furstenberg, "Franco-American Networks and Polite Atlantic Spaces," *When the Unites States Spoke French,* 137–210.

52. A bishop in 1789, Talleyrand was instrumental in drafting and passing the decree nationalizing the Church's estates. He resigned his bishopric after the Pope excommunicated him in 1791 (Hemmerle). He is such a fascinating character that nearly 20 movies have been made about him.

53. Talleyrand was a guest at Aaron Burr's residence on Market Street during his stay in Philadelphia. He was also friends with Alexander Hamilton who was killed by Burr in a duel in 1804. Furstenberg, *When the United States…,* 141.

54. According to Brace, Talleyrand noted in a letter to his friend Germaine de Staël that the U.S. was a great place to make money, provided you already had some.

55. Creagh describes the "popular triumph" the citizens of Philadelphia offered Citizen Genêt on July 4, 1794. By contrast, they booed Talleyrand, Beaumetz, Cazenove, and Moreau, who were watching the festivities from the balcony of a house on Broadway ("La Révolution," 179). On this topic, see also Peter Hill, *French Perception of the early American Republic, 1783–1793.*

56. See Royot, "The Aristocrat and the Backwoodsman," 138–142.

57. On the land issue, see Clarke, *Emigrés in the Wilderness,* 21–27.

58. Treat devotes a chapter of *The National Land System, 1785–1820* to "The System of Surveys."

59. On "Transatlantic Land Speculation," see Furstenberg, *When the United States Spoke French,* 227–286.

60. Balayé (199–200) writes that Germaine de Staël owned land in the United States and still hoped, in 1811, to move there one day. But she never made it.

61. Her Memoirs was published under the title *Journal d'une femme de cinquante ans* [*Diary of a Fifty-year old Woman*].

62. On the Scioto Settlement and the fate of the *émigrés,* see Belote, for a detailed account, and Clarke, 102–108; Oliver, chapter 3 in *Surviving the French Revolution,* 35–49; and Winsor, *The Westward Movement,* 402–404.

63. On the complexities brought along by land claims made by foreigners, see chapter IX in Treat, "The Confirmation of Foreign Titles."

64. On Gallipolis, see Volney, *A View…,* 322–330; Creagh, *Nos Cousins,* 225–227; and Winsor, *The Westward Movement,* 498.

65. On Azylum, see Clarke, 51–84; Creagh, *Nos Cousins,* 222–224; Hebert, C. 458–459; and Wilkinson.

66. Baudry de Lozières was a proponent of slavery and a detractor of "the negrophile aberration," the title of his 1801 book (*Les égarements du négrophilisme*).

67. On the *Compagnie de New York*, see Clarke, 28–32.

68. On Crèvecoeur's *Letters from an American Farmer*, see Osborne.

69. Despite well-documented hard work and diligent preparations, the Castorland settlement failed in the end. See Clarke for a brief overview, 33–50; and Galluci's edition and translation of Desjardins and Pharoux's *Castorland Journal*. It contains a detailed account of their work on the settlement.

70. On New Geneva, see Hebert, C., 459–460. She notes that "Gallatin went on to achieve state and national fame as a Republican representative in the Pennsylvania Legislature, in the United States Congress, and later as Secretary of the Treasury" (460).

71. See George Wilson, "Catastrophe in the Capital of the United States," in *Stephen Girard*, 113–114.

72. "The National Convention declares the abolition of Negro slavery in all the colonies; in consequence it decrees that all men, without distinction of color, residing in the colonies are French citizens and will enjoy all the rights assured by the constitution" (Quoted in Dubois, "The meaning of Citizenship, 1794–1798" in *A Colony of Citizens*, 169–314).

73. The couple was acquainted with Bishop John Carroll and businessman Stephen Girard. As we will see in chapter IX, their two sons later made a name for themselves, Aristide as a physician and politician, William, as an architect. Childs, 94, 104, 204, 210, 226.

74. See Furstenberg, *When The United States Spoke French*, 35–136.

75. On Chaudron, see Creagh, *Nos Cousins*, 216.

76. Devèze and the famed Dr. Benjamin Rush disagreed on the cure, the latter advocating laxatives and bleeding, the former, stimulants and quinine, as recommended today.

77. Furstenberg's book includes a drawing of a Grand Barbet, the kind of dog that accompanied Liancourt on his American journey. *When the United States...*, 230.

78. Monaghan published a bibliography on French travelers to the United States that covers the 1765–1932 period.

79. The Duke of Orleans became Louis-Philippe I, King of the French from 1830 to 1848—not King of France, as Marc Journaud states in "Louis-Philippe (1773–1850)."

80. See John P. Clark, "La Révolution française et la démocratie radicale américaine."

81. "By July of 1780, [...] Adams had revealed the inherent, pro-British attitude of American, free-trade patriots, while Vergennes had exposed France's determination to keep its ally under control—in war and in peace" (Bauer, 667).

82. See Alderson, "Genêt...," and Winsor, *The Westward Movement*, 453, 532, 536–538.

83. Havard and Vidal state that Genêt was also plotting with Georges Rogers Clark to obtain the restitution of Louisiana to France (*Histoire*, 702). See also Furstenberg, 44–53.

84. This observation led Avery to conclude,

perhaps a little hastily, that the U.S. was "more indebted to [these] four men of Huguenot ancestry [...] than to any other four statesmen of the time" (32). Other prominent Americans of French Huguenot descent of the period she mentions include William Bayard, Jr. (1761–1826), a New York City banker and Antoine Bénézet (Anthony Benezet) (1713–1784), the Philadelphia abolitionist; and Gabriel Manigault (1758–1809), an architect who was the scion of the wealthiest family in North America.

85. At the beginning of the war, the British Navy seized all ships that were trading with the French colonies, but the policy changed in early 1794 when ships from neutral nations, i.e., the United States, were excluded. Butel writes that American trade was the beneficiary of this new policy as "colonial goods transited through American ports and the Caribbean turned into one of their best markets" (Butel, 227).

86. See Creagh, "La Révolution et les Français des Etats-Unis."

87. For example, Stephen Girard who "in the early months of 1794 owned five ships" saw them all "seized by Britain or France (two by the British, three by the French) and the cargoes of all five ships [...] confiscated" (Wilson, 136).

88. Paine was re-admitted to the Convention in 1795 but was among the representatives who voted against the 1795 constitution as it did away with universal suffrage. The Convention was dissolved in October. He returned to the U.S. in 1802 at Jefferson's invitation.

89. On the Franco-Indian metis of the Red River, see Rousseau, "Métis," 798; Havard and Vidal, 384.

90. The first San Ildefonso treaty concerned Spain and Portugal. The alliance treaty signed by France and Spain in 1796 is the second Ildefonso Treaty. The most important for our purpose is the third. Signed in 1800, it restored to France the North American Colonies France had ceded to Spain through the secret treaty of Fontainebleau. In exchange, Spain received territory in Tuscany.

91. On John Adams, see Rofe.

92. On the XYZ Affair and Quasi-War, see Nester, *The Hamiltonian Vision, 1789–1800*, 112–158; Furstenberg, *When the United States Spoke French*, 368, 373.

93. Gerry later gave his name to the unfair practice of "gerrymandering," which consists of moving electoral boundaries to gain political advantage.

94. On Volney's relation to the U.S., see Chinard, *Volney et l'Amérique*.

95. These were not baseless accusations on the part of the U.S. government. Acting on instructions from Paris, the French ambassador Pierre Auguste Adet dispatched General George Henri Victor Collot (1750–1805) on a mission meant to assess the feasibility of retaking Louisiana from the Spaniards (Vidal and Havard, *Histoire*, 704). In 1796, Collot left Philadelphia, with one man, Lieutenant Warin, crossing the Alleghenies and then following the Monongahela River. The two men then purchased a bateau, or flatboat, and hired "two Canadians and

three Americans" for a boat trip all the way down to New Orleans (Collot, *Voyage dans l'Amérique*, I, 65). The American officer who shadowed Collot's expedition was Zebulon Pike. Collot wrote an account of his journey, *Voyage dans l'Amérique Septentrionale*, which was published in 1826, in French in two volumes, and in English in one. The book offers thorough descriptions of the main rivers in the Mississippi Basin and of their banks. It also includes an overview of the Native American Warrior forces, which Collot estimates at 30,000, with assessment of their abilities as warriors and of their friendliness towards the French (II, Appendix). Prior to traveling through the United States, Collot was governor when Guadeloupe capitulated to the British in April 1794. See Dubois, 22–26.

96. M. Jones argues that "each of these antiforeign measures failed in its object and recoiled upon its authors" (88–89). The French Republic had adopted similar measures in 1793.

97. A team of over 150 scientists in all disciplines was part of the expedition to Egypt. Some of them transcribed hieroglyphs that were later deciphered by Jean-François Champolion.

98. See Munro, "Toussaint L'Ouverture, François (1742–1803)."

Chapter VIII

1. See Morton, "Kentucky."

2. John O' Sullivan, a contributor to the *Democratic Review*, coined the term "Manifest Destiny" in 1845. See Green and Kirkwood, 230.

3. Royot devotes a chapter of his book, *Divided Loyalties*, to "The Métis" (116–132).

4. On the Louisiana Purchase, see Vidal; Royot, 142–146.

5. On the Napoleonic Era, see Haine, 88–96; Weber, 536–546.

6. For a transcript, see the webpage "Treaty of Morefontaine (Convention of 1800)."

7. See Havard and Vidal, *Histoire*, 701–719.

8. The War of the Pyrenees was the Franco-Spanish front of the War of the First Coalition. It ended in French victory in 1795.

9. Havard and Vidal, "Bonaparte, ou trois semaines de souveraineté française," *Histoire*, 701–719.

10. On rights of navigation on the Mississippi River during the Confederation period, see Kaminski. On "Agricultural Commerce in the Mississippi Valley" in the 18th century, see Ekberg, *French Roots*, 213–238.

11. See Lentz, "La Politique consulaire aux Antilles."

12. Cerami (27) calls Barbé-Marbois "France's impeccably honest finance minister," a man "who had served in Philadelphia as secretary of the French Legation when he was just over thirty years old, loved America as much almost as he loved France, and retained a great many devoted American friends."

13. In 1779, Joséphine had married another creole, Alexandre de Beauharnais, who had served as president of the Constituent Assembly and whose family also owned plantations in Saint-Domingue and Martinique. After he died on the guillotine in 1794, Joséphine was able to recover his fortune and was thus a wealthy widow when Bonaparte met her in 1795.

14. On the Haitian Revolution, see Dubois, "The Boundaries of the Republic, 1798–1804," in *A Colony of Citizens*, 317–422.

15. Toussaint threatened to massacre white people if Roume did not sign. Roume signed and Toussaint invaded.

16. The passage from Leclerc's letter to the Secretary of the Navy containing that information is quoted in Marr and Cathey's article on the Haitian yellow fever epidemic of 1802.

17. The French used wild dogs trained to attack and eat Black insurgents and resurrected Old-Regime tortures.

18. France refused to recognize the independence of Haiti until Haiti paid the sum of 90 million gold francs in compensation for lost property (1838). Haiti paid this debt until 1947.

19. According to Hitchcock, Jefferson was keenly interested in the West and "[i]n 1792, he proposed to the American Philosophical Society to raise money for an exploration of the West" (100). Ripley goes on to say that a Frenchman, André Michaux, was offered the job and went as far as Kentucky before being called back by "the French minister" (101). On the Louisiana Purchase, see Cerami, *Jefferson's Great Gamble*.

20. Jefferson had known du Pont since his tenure as U.S. ambassador to France (1785–1789) and greatly admired him. Du Pont had initially supported the French Revolution but was caught in the revolutionary turmoil. When he was sentenced to death, only the fall of Robespierre saved him. After his house was sacked in 1797, he made plans to leave, and left for the U.S. in 1799. His son, Éleuthère Iréné Dupont de Nemours (1771–1834), was the founder of what became the multinational corporation DuPont. The family has remained influential up to this day, with Pierre S. du Pont IV (1935–) serving as Governor of Delaware and U.S. Representative. On the du Pont family, see Sankey.

21. The Treaty of Ildefonso specified that the French would not sell Louisiana to a third party; the purchase was deemed unconstitutional and exceeding the powers of the U.S. president but the argument that the purchase was necessary to protect U.S. citizens won the day. On the Constitutionality of the Treaty, see Lawson and Seidman, "The First Incorporation Debate."

22. For information on the negotiations that preceded the Louisiana Purchase, see Havard and Vidal, *Histoire*, 711–713.

23. "The inhabitants of the ceded territory shall be incorporated in the Union of the United States and admitted as soon as possible according to the principles of the Federal Constitution, to the

enjoyment of the rights, advantages and immunities of citizens of the United States; and in the meantime they shall be maintained and protected in the free enjoyment of their liberty, property, and the religion which they profess" (Quoted in Lawson and Seidman, 25).

24. For more information on Louisiana under the U.S. regime in Antebellum America, see Creagh, *Nos Cousins*, 237–255.

25. Freehling (81) adds: "So too an imagined American history without the diffusion/colonization mentality, a worldview itself rooted in America's racist mentality, would have been utterly different—and might not have required a Civil War to abolish slavery. Just about the entire spectrum of mainstream American leaders, from Jefferson's time to Lincoln's, conceived that the white men's republic could rid itself of slaves only by turning blacks into barely visible, deportable specks. The Purchase showed that the specks would instead become ever more visible and unremovable, as in Louisiana, and even more productive of political disruption when the specks were diluted, as in Missouri."

26. "The President had hoped that diffusion inside the Louisiana Purchase, as had happened in Missouri, would so dilute slavery that enlightened reformers could unconvulsively finish off the institution, as had happened in northern states before Jefferson's presidency" (Freehling, 78).

27. On the importance of cotton, see Sweeney.

28. Alexander J. P. Garesché settled in Missouri.

29. One might want to add language, culture, and religion to the list of commonalities shared by the French of Saint-Domingue and those of Louisiana.

30. See Havard and Vidal, "Les plantations de Basse-Louisiane," *Histoire*, 432–435.

31. "On May 19, 1836, Valcour Aimé sold Jacques T. Roman the plantation which riverboat captains later dubbed 'Oak Alley'" (Chaillot, "Roman Jacques Telesphore").

32. According to Terry Jones, those sugar cane planters voted against secession in 1861 (189).

33. Deslondes was hunted first by vicious dogs and then by militiamen who chopped off his hands, "broke his thighs, shot him dead and then roasted his remains on a pile of straw" as a warning against further revolts (Rasmussen, 142).

34. On the introduction of steamboats to the U.S. waterways, see Mark Hall.

35. On the trail of tears, see Portes, 73–80. Ironically, they too practiced slavery and "took more than a thousand slaves with them to Indian Territory" (Spicer, 70).

36. According to their website, "The Bureau of Indian Affairs is an agency of the federal government of the United States within the U.S. Department of the Interior. It is responsible for the administration and management of 55,700,000 acres of land held in trust by the United States for American Indians, Indian Tribes and Alaska Natives."

37. This section deals with explorers and guides to the American West, which does not mean that French and Franco-American guides were not found in the East. A good example would be Louis Annance, Thoreau's guide in 1854. See Myall on that topic.

38. "At least until the early decades of the twentieth century, French folklore still survived along with French language and dialects in the Ste Genevieve and Old Mines district" (Prévos, 367).

39. Most of Teasdale's book on the French presence in the Detroit area, *Fruits of Perseverance*, is devoted to the farmers' struggles to gain recognition for their land titles after the War of Conquest and the War of Independence. While in the 1840s, "Detroit's population was essentially French" (138), large migrations to the mid-West following the construction of the Erie Canal led to "marginalizing the French population on the American side of the Detroit River" (138). See also Waters, "Detroit."

40. Victoire, a daughter of Laclède and Marie-Thérèse Chouteau, married a Swiss from Lausanne, Charles Gratiot (1752–1817) in 1781. Gratiot had immigrated to Canada, got involved in the fur trade, and then moved to Cahokia, where he opened a store and provided supplies to the "Conqueror of the Old Northwest," George Rogers Clark, during the American Revolution. He then moved to St. Louis. Their son, Charles Gratiot, Jr. (1786–1855), a West Point graduate, served as a Chief Engineer in the War of 1812 and later in the Michigan Territory.

41. Mrs Chouteau and Pierre Laclède had another son, Pierre, and four daughters, who all had "Chouteau" as their last name since Marie-Thérèse was still married and could not get a divorce. On Pierre Chouteau and Pierre Ménard, see John Reda (173) who credits the two men with easing the transition from French to U.S. territory.

42. On the relations between the French of St. Louis and the Americans at the time of the Louisiana Purchase, see Reda, 163–175.

43. Lappas, in his article on Missouri, notes that, in 1803, "Missouri was the starting point for the Lewis and Clark expedition." "Missouri," 819.

44. The Louisiana Purchase marks the end of Spanish Louisiana, 1763–1803. On Spanish Louisiana, see Creagh, *Nos Cousins*, 200–207. For a detailed account of the transition from Spanish to U.S. control, and in particular French resistance to the new governance, see Vernet.

45. Portes writes that President Jefferson was "a true intellectual who had read all books written by explorers and sent for the most precious maps" (42). Jefferson had decided on the expedition prior to the Louisiana Purchase. On the preparation of the expedition, see Portes, 42–44; on the expedition itself, 46–53.

46. Clark states that it took place on "March 10, 1804" not March 9.

47. As Royot points out, however, "[i]n the journals of the Lewis and Clark expeditions, the terms, 'French' and 'Frenchmen' refer to French Canadians, French Spaniards, and French Americans, never to French citizens" (11). See also chapter 9 in *Divided Loyalties*, "The French Background of the Lewis and Clark Expedition," 147–158; chapter 10,

"Across the Great Ethnic Divide: the French in the Lewis and Clark Expedition," 159–188; and chapter 11, "The French Around and Against the Expedition," 189–213.

48. "[F]ourteen soldiers selected from a large number who had volunteered from the regular army," and "nine young frontiersmen from Kentucky" were also part of the expedition (Hitchcock, 108).

49. The adoption of French names by Native American Chiefs is a practice already documented a century earlier by signatories of the 1701 Peace Treaty of Montreal, namely the representatives of Sable Odawas, Jean Le Blanc and Le Brochet. See Havard, *The Great Peace of Montreal*, 121.

50. For a useful overview of Franco-Indian relations, see Vazeilles.

51. The interpreter's name was actually "Toussaint Charbonneau."

52. Jacques Portes (33) notes that a statue of Sacagawea was erected in the small town of Three Forks, MT during the Bicentennial celebrations of the Lewis and Clark expedition.

53. Frémont later recalled a similar "boudin" feast in *First Impressions* (19).

54. The American author of Western novels, Winfred Blévins is the author of a book on Charbonneau, *Charbonneau, man of two* dreams (1975).

55. According to Havard and Vidal, Georges Drouillard was a *coureur des bois*. His named is variously misspelled in the expedition log as "Drewyer" or "Drewyear."

56. On Lorimer, see Sankey.

57. A native of Quebec, his full name was Pierre-Louis de Lorimier (1748–1812).

58. See note 4 in the *Journal of Lewis and Clark*. This entry mentions another Frenchman, Blaze Cenas, as a resident of New Orleans related by marriage to Félix Brunot.

59. The reason for their change of plan deserves to be mentioned: they could not cross into Louisiana because "the Spanish commandant had not yet been officially notified" (Hitchcock, 106) that Spain had ceded Louisiana to France and France to the U.S.at the end of April 1803.

60. A May 18, 1804, entry in Whitehouse's journal mentions that they danced with the "French ladies, who are remarkably fond of dancing."

61. North of Greeley, CO, a "Wild and Scenic" river bears the beautiful name of "Cache La Poudre River," often shortened to "Poudre River."

62. For an excellent overview of the explorations of the North American continent in the 19th century, see the webpage "After Lewis & Clark."

63. "It appears from Zebulon Pike's journal that [Honoré] Tesson had planned to work as Indian interpreter with the Americans. On August 20, 1805, Pike was at the head of the Des Moines rapids where he met William Ewing who had been sent by the U.S. Government to 'teach the savages agriculture.' […]. Ewing was accompanied by a 'Monsieur Loys Tesson Houire' who informed Pike that he wished to go with him as an interpreter. Tesson

was 'much disappointed' when Pike told him he had no instruction to that effect. Tesson then promised to discover mines which 'no person knew but himself.' Pike left with a rather low opinion of Tesson and wrote that he 'conceived him much of a hypocrite and possessing great gasconism.' After this failure little mention of Tesson or of his actions has ever been found" (Prévos, 58).

64. "My Interpreter was much alarmed, assuring me at our first encounter with the Chippeways, it would be extremely probable they would fire on us, taking us for the Sioux traders, before we could come to an explanation—That they had killed three Frenchmen, whom they caught on Shore about the place last Spring; but notwithstanding his information, I was on Shore in pursuit of a Flock of Elk all the afternoon" (Pike, *Journal*, October 4, 1805).

65. "In my council I spoke to a Frenchman—he to a Sioux, who interprets to some of the *Puants*" (Pike, *Journal*, Sept. 6, 1805).

66. "Indians passed on the opposite shore—they cry'd 'How do you do' wishing us to give them an invitation to come over but receiving no answer they passed on." Pike, *Journal*, Aug. 19, 1805.

67. "Met four Indians and two sqawz with them, give one Quart of made Whisky, a few biscuits and wine & all—I requested some Venison of them, they pretended that they could not understand us but after we had embarked and got put off; they held up two hamz and hollard and laughed at us in derision" (Pike, *Journal*, Aug. 23, 1805).

68. "My party marched early, but I returned with Mr˙ Grant to his Establishment on Red Cedar Lake (having one Corpl with me). When we came in Sight of his House, discovered the Flag of Great Britain flying. I felt indignant and cannot say what my feelings would have excited me to, but he informed me it belongs to the Indians. This was not much more agreeable to me" (Pike, *Journal*, January 4, 1806).

69. Still today, the Chippawa counts several bands of Lac people with a French name: the "Lac du Flambeau Band of Lake Superior Chippewa Indians"; "Lac Courtes Oreilles"; and "Lac Vieux désert."

70. "We had passed the 1st and most difficult shoal when we were met by a Mr. William Ewing who I understand is an Agent appointed to reside with the Lac's to teach them the Science of Agriculture with a French Interpreter, 4 chiefs and 15 men of the Lac nation in their canoes; bearing a Flag of the U States" (Pike, *Journal*, Aug. 20, 1805).

71. Pike told them "[t]hat in their Treaty they had engaged to apprehend all traders who came amongst them without licence that for that time [he] would not examine their traders on that subject but that on my return [he] would make a particular examination" (*Journal*, Aug. 20, 1805).

72. "Met two frenchmen of the N˙W˙ with about 200 pounds on each of their backs with Rackets" (Pike, *Journal*, January 6, 1806).

73. André Prévos (76) writes: "While British and Americans maintained contacts with the Indians-for purely commercial, political, or exploitative reasons and avoided further relations with

members of these tribes, French explorers and traders did not fear intimacy and, more often than not, married Indians in order to strengthen relations between the two groups. The frequency of these marriages between traders and Indian women led many observers to think that Franco-Indian relations were always harmonious and romantic. This contributed greatly to the myth of easygoing and respectful relationships between French and Indians. More detailed observations have revealed, however, that French traders, compared to their British and American counterparts, were only slightly less greedy and condescending."

74. "I must not omit here, to bear Testimony to the politeness of all the principal inhabitants of the Village. But there is a material distinction to be made in the nature of those attentions. That of Messrs Fisher, Frazer & Woods (all Americans) appeared to be the spontaneous effusions of good will, and exultations in their countenance, for it even attended to the accommodation, convenience, pastimes, exercises etc˙ of my men; and wherever they proved superior to the French, openly shewed their pleasure. But the French Canadians were polite through their hypocrisy; and at the same time (to do them justice) natural good manners; but fear in them worked the same effect, that the natural good will did in the others" (Pike, *Journal*, Sept. 8, 1805).

75. On Long and his expedition, see Nichols, "Long, Stephen H. (1784–1864)"; Schubert, "Chapter 1, Across the Father of Waters" 1–27. Havard and Vidal point out that Manitoba was home in the 19th century to "the Métis nation of the Red River," a Franco-Native people. *Histoire*, 384.

76. Keating, who studied mining in France and Switzerland, was a geologist and professor of Mineralogy and Chemistry at the University of Pennsylvania. His book on mining, *Considerations upon the art of mining: to which are added, reflections on its actual state in Europe, and the advantages which would result from an introduction of this art into the United States* appeared shortly before the Long expedition in 1821. See Pierce, 31.

77. Keating published his account under the title *Narrative of an expedition to the source of St. Peter's River, Lake Winnepeek, Lake of the Woods.*

78. With increased American competition, "[t]he French of Green Bay and Prairie du Chien […] stayed in the fur trade long after it ceased to be profitable and lost their lands for the most part by mortgages to John Jacob Astor and the other magnates of the great fur companies" (Kellogg, 404).

79. On the economics of the fur trade in the 18th and 19th centuries, see Carlos and Lewis.

80. See St-Onge, "'Blue beads, Vermillion, and Scalpers'"; Giesecke, "Wilson Price Hunt"; Larry Morris, "Astor Expedition, 1810–1813."

81. See Barman, "Marie Dorion" *The Oregon Encyclopedia.*

82. See Jette, "Joseph Gervais." *The Oregon Encyclopedia.*

83. See Jette, "Etienne Lucier." *The Oregon Encyclopedia.*

84. The area fell under U.S. control in 1818 when Great Britain and the U.S. agreed to use the 49th parallel as a border between the USA and Canada. In the following years, Oregon returned to Canadian control until 1843 when settlers established their own Provisional Government of Oregon. Then, in 1848, the U.S. annexed the Oregon Territory and split it in two in 1853 to create the Washington territory.

85. On Ashley, see Berry, "Ashley and his men," in *A Majority of Scoundrels*, 3–122. Ashley's men are featured in the 2015 film *The Revenant.*

86. On the Rocky Mountain Fur Company, see Don Berry, 237–367.

87. I base this claim on the definition of "Frenchman" in Blévins's *Dictionary of the West* (153): "Frenchman: In the West, usually not a Gaul but a French-Canadian of mixed blood. The term was common among mountain men and probably did not reflect the scorn for other cultures characteristic of many later Westerners. The French-Canadians (sometimes called Franco-Canadians) preceded the Americans in the Western beaver trade, explored much of the country, learned the Native peoples, and developed many of the ways. They brought many words to the mountain man's vocabulary, including *appola, bois d'arc, boudins, carcajou, coulee, engagé, hivernant, mangeur de lard, parfleche, plew.*"

88. Originally from Spain, the Franco-American Robidoux family starts with André (1643–1678) who married in France and came to Canada as an *engagé* in 1664. Antoine belongs to the third North American generation of Robidoux. A historical marker near the railway station in Durango, CO, credits him with building "the first western Colorado trading post (near present-day Delta)." His brother Louis is the founder of Riverside, CA.

89. See Anon., "Fort Uncompahgre." For a detailed account of the Robidoux brothers' activities, see Willoughby. Prévos (53) writes that Robidoux' "ruthlessness with debtors was well-known."

90. On William Sublette, see Berry, "Smith Jackson & Sublette," *A Majority of Rascals*, 123–236.

91. On Louis Vasquez, see the entry based on William Wilson's article on the Colorado Encyclopedia website. French traders could still be found decades later in the Southwest. Keenan (455) mentions "a passing trader named Charles Tribolet" who, in 1886, sold whiskey to Apaches at the most inconvenient time for their ongoing negotiations with their American counterparts.

92. Nicolas Bonneville visited his family for four years (1814–1818) but then returned to France where he gained some fame as publisher of German Romantic literature.

93. Bonneville had requested an extension of his leave of absence, but the letter was never delivered.

94. On Colonel Bonneville's participation in the wars against Native American Indians in New Mexico in 1857–1858, see Keenan, 111–121. On the American Indian wars, see Hook and Hughes.

95. John Faucheraud Grimké (1752–1819),

another American of Huguenot descent, was a noted justice in South Carolina during those years. His daughters, Sarah and Angelina, were abolitionists and women's rights advocates.

96. On Daniel Trabue, see Sioli.

97. See Fowlie and Lucy Audubon's *Life of John James Audubon, the naturalist.* Audubon was the son of Jean Audubon, a French naval officer from Brittany who had fought in the American Revolution, sold a St. Domingue plantation, and purchased a new estate at Mill Grove, near Philadelphia, in 1789—now a national historic landmark of Pennsylvania. John Audubon returned to France and raised two of his natural children at his estate near Nantes. His son, Jean-Jacques Rabin (1785–1851), born in Les Cayes, St. Domingue, took "Jean-Jacques Fougère Audubon" as his legal name. In 1803, Jean Audubon and his friend Claude Rozier decided to send their sons, Jean-Jacques and Jean-Ferdinand, to America to avoid conscription in Napoleon's armies. At the time he immigrated to the United States, Jean-Jacques anglicized his name to John James, moved to Kentucky married in 1808, started his business partnership with Rozier near Ste. Genevieve in 1810, and became a U.S. citizen in 1812. But John James' real passion was drawing birds. The ornithologist is famous for his *Birds of America* and recognized as the great naturalist who gave his name to the National Audubon Society.

98. His son, Firmin Vincent Desloge, became one of the richest men in the world (Huger).

99. For maps of French and Indian forts see McDonnell, viii–ix.

100. Gilles Havard, visiting the graveyard at Fort Berthold, notes that dozens of graves bear French names, although the Arikara, Hidatsa, Mandan reservation is entirely Anglophone today. "L'héritage français des Arikaras," 560.

101. Havard argues that the French influence among the Arikara does not date back to New France but rather to the late 18th and early 19th century as the result of encounters with fur traders from Montreal and St. Louis ("L'héritage…," 566–569). He also devotes part of his article to the topic of miscegenation (569–572).

102. See *Chardon's Journal at Fort Clark* (listed under "primary texts").

103. See Patterson, *Autobiography of Ma-ka-tai-me-she-kia-kiak or Black Hawk.*

104. On the Black Hawk War, see Hall and Hall.

105. See "Davenport's First Citizen" on the website of Scott County Iowa Genealogy.

106. On Joseph Nicollet, see Bray.

107. On the Wikipedia "List of French Americans," Frémont is presented as an "explorer with Kit Carson," a characterization that reduces his stature while enhancing Carson's.

108. See Bray; Schubert, "Chapter I, Across the Father of Waters," 27–36.

109. A fur trapper for the Chouteau, Parrant started distilling liquor when the fur trade dried out. He sold his liquor to soldiers stationed at Fort Snelling. Today's "Pig's Eye Beer" is named after him. See

Fletcher, *A History of the City of Saint Paul,* chapter VI.

110. Bray writes that "Zebulon Pike in 1805 […] placed the mouth of the Crow Wing River too far to the west, making all western maps inaccurate."

111. See "Nicollet Expeditions, 1838, 1839" on the Smithonian's website.

112. The côteau des Missouri, also in North Dakota, where the Battle of the Big Mound took place in June 1863 (Keenan, 270), is another reminder that the French first named many of the places in that area. In that case as well, the guide was the Franco-Indian named Joseph La Framboise (271). Keenan also names Frank Grouard and Baptiste "Big Bat" Pourier as "*non-pareil* scouts" for the American army in the war against the Cheyennes (325).

113. On Frémont's activities as a scientist, see Schubert, "Chapter II, Frémont and the Screaming Eagle."

114. John's mother, who was married to an old man at the time, run away from home with Frémont's father and had her son out of wedlock. On Frémont's youth, see Hyde, viii–ix; Richards, 41.

115. "John C. Frémont," Georgia Historical Society Website.

116. His full name was George Karl Ludwig Preuss (1803–1854).

117. The Peak in Wyoming is known as Fremont Peak today. There are three more Fremont peaks in California, and one each in Arizona, Colorado, and Maine.

118. "The Report's fame, according to the Southern Literary Messenger, would 'survive as long as the Sierra Nevada,' and according to the equally effusive *Democratic Review,* the Report far surpassed Lewis and Clark's for its 'breadth and variety.' Preuss's map, published in 1846 as a separate document, was designed as a trail map about ten feet long, to be mounted on a roller and carried by overland travelers and consulted easily. Its ten-miles-to-the-inch scale offered explicit detail about routes, and it provided hints about camping sites, vegetation, salt licks, and Native people" (Hyde, xvii).

119. Two Franco-American of Huguenot descent on their mother's side, Benjamin (1811–1862) and Henry Eustice (1816–1895) played an important role in the Texas Revolution and the Republic of Texas.

120. John Tyler (1790–1863), the 10th president of the United States (1841–1845), had prepared the ground for annexing Texas. Tyler was of French Huguenot descent.

Chapter IX

1. See Rémond, *Les Etats-Unis,* vol. I, chapter 2, 31–33.

2. Michel Cordillot (141) points out that political exile affected the left disproportionately and that between 1850 and 1880 "most of the main figures of the francophone socialist movement […] belonged to the social-democrat cohorts defeated during the

Second Republic."

3. Creagh examines the profile of French immigrants by regional origin (*Nos Cousins*, 269–277) and by profession (278–291).

4. On Utopias, see Wagstaff.

5. For the number of French passengers entering the United States, see Rémond.

6. Louis Napoléon Bonaparte (1808–1873) was Napoleon Bonaparte's nephew. He was elected President of France during the Second Republic (1848–1851), staged a coup in December 1851, and crowned himself Emperor in 1852.

7. See Richards, *The California God Rush and the Coming of the Civil War*; see also Creagh, "En Californie!" *Nos Cousins*, 257–268.

8. In 1804, Napoleon created the First Empire. In 1815, the French Monarchy was restored. In 1830, a different constitutional monarchy replaced it. In 1848, a revolution restored the republic for a few years. In 1852, Louis Napoleon Bonaparte restored the Empire. In 1870, French defeat in the Franco-Prussian led to the fall of the imperial regime and the restoration of the Republic. A Fascist Vichy Regime ruled France for the duration of World War II. A fourth republic was established at the end of the war in 1946 and lasted until 1958 when General Charles de Gaulle established the 5th Republic which is still France's regime today.

9. On Lannuier, see Peter M. Kenny.

10. The Civil Code was adopted in all conquered nations of Europe until the fall of the Empire in 1814 and in 1825 in Louisiana.

11. See Le Hir, *Le Romantisme*, 7–11.

12. The German campaign of 1805 was followed by the Campaign of Italy (1805–06); the Campaign against Prussia and Poland (1806–07); the Campaign against Austria (1809); the Campaign against Spain and Portugal (1807–14); the Campaign of Russia (1812); and the Campaign of Saxony (1813).

13. The British occupied Martinique and Guadeloupe once again in 1809–18 and the Mascarene Islands in the Indian Ocean in 1810–15.

14. It is worth noting that pirate Jean Lafitte helped Andrew Jackson win the Battle of New Orleans in 1815 in exchange for an amnesty for his men, captured the previous year for smuggling. Ramsay, 62.

15. "Jean Victor Marie Moreau," in *Appleton's Cyclopaedia of American biography*, vol. IV, 389–390.

16. See "Neuville Jean Guillaume, Baron Hyde de," in *Appleton's Cyclopedia*, vol. I V, 497.

17. He wrote a flattering pamphlet about his friend, *Eloge Historique du Général Moreau* (1814).

18. Commenting on the two groups of refugees in the U.S., the "Domingans" and the "Napoleonians," Neuville reportedly said that they "gravitated toward one another, forming […] the 'New Atlantic France.'" Blaufarb, Rafe. *Bonapartists in the Borderlands*, 2.

19. Neuville's book is entitled *Observations sur le commerce de la France avec les États-Unis* (*Observations on trade between France and the United States*).

20. On Jean Joseph Amable Humbert, see Heili.

21. Not all Frenchmen who came to the United States after the first French Empire collapsed were political exiles. In his article on Charles Mame's failed attempt to open a French bookstore in New York, Villerbu mentions a group of businessmen associated with the Le Ray de Chaumont and the exiles from Saint-Domingue who has settled in the south. See Villerbu, "Entre Monde atlantique et jeune république."

22. See Clarke, 125–153, Creagh, *Nos Cousins*, 228–236, Blaufarb, *Bonapartists…*, 1. In *Napoleon in America*, Shannon Selin offers a fictional account of the plot hatched by officers loyal to Napoleon to kidnap the former emperor and bring him to the United States. See also Havard and Vidal, *Histoire*, 701.

23. See Blaufarb, *Bonapartists*, 2; Stroud, Chapter 5, "Point Breeze."

24. See Blaufarb, *Bonapartists*, 81, 86. Joseph Bonaparte returned to Europe in 1840, joining his wife in Florence. Both died within months of each other in 1844–1845. Stroud, 200–220.

25. The actor René Murat Auberjonois (1940–2019) was one of his descendants.

26. Blaufarb argues that most of these officers did not chose exile for political reasons, but rather for economic reasons: "Although some of these men were committed to the ideals of the French Revolution and all of them had certainly benefited from the opening of careers to talent, none had been forced to leave France. Rather, they had voluntarily chosen exile in anticipation of reduced professional prospects in the downsized Bourbon army." "Notes," 107. The victorious powers imposed the downsizing of the French army at the Congress of Vienna in 1815—where Talleyrand proved a formidable negotiator one last time. Blaufarb adds that "some solicited commissions in the United States army, but most of these requests were politely turned down" ("Notes," 107).

27. "Some of the émigrés […] were fleeing arrest warrants issued because they had plotted for Napoleon's return from exile on Elba and had placed their troops at his disposition. Condemned by the royal ordinance of July 24, 1815, they risked execution if apprehended" (Blaufarb, "Notes," 106). Blaufarb adds: "With few exceptions, they were insiders whose proximity to the regime and efforts to reestablish it after Napoleon's first abdication in 1814 marked them for retribution. Of the fifty-seven on the list, eleven would take part in the Vine and Olive venture. They included one marshal (Emmanuel de Grouchy), six generals (the Lallemand brothers, Lefebvre-Desnouettes, Bertrand Clausel, Dominique-Joseph-René Vandamme, and Antoine Rigau), two government officials (Pierre-François Réal and Jacques Garnier des Saintes), and two minor Bonapartists (the journalist Louis-Marie Dirat and Col. J. Jerome Cluis). After the passage of the law of 12 January 1816, they were joined by several former deputies to the National Convention, including two who would take part in Vine and Olive: Joseph Lakanal and Jean-Augustin

Pénières-Delors" (*Bonapartists*, 6).

28. According to Selin, Lallemand was the one who suggested that Napoleon escape to the United States instead of surrendering to the British after Waterloo ("General Charles Lallemand"). Blaufarb adds that Napoleon could have escaped when he was in Rochefort but decided against it. On Charles Lallemand, see Blaufarb, *Bonapartists,* 87–88.

29. Henri Lallemand married one of Stephen Girard's nieces, Henriette, and in 1820 published a *Treatise on Artillery* "that became a standard manual." Selin, "Henri Lallemand."

30. General Vandamme urged Grouchy to join Napoleon at the Battle of Waterloo instead of pursuing the Prussians but Grouchy refused (Selin's webpage on Waterloo). Vandamme was opposed to Lallemand's Texas plans. See Blaufarb, *Bonapartists*, 92.

31. See also Blaufarb, *Bonapartists*, 11–13.

32. He also played a major role in the creation of several prestigious scientific institutions such as Inalco (*L'institut des langues et civilisations orientales*) and the National Museum of Natural History.

33. For a sample of their correspondence, see the webpage "Lakanal and Jefferson letters, 1816."

34. For samples of his art, see the two webpages "Quervelle, Antony."

35. Thanks to the population influx, Alabama was to become a state as well two years later. A minimum of 60,000 inhabitants were required for a territory to become a state. About Alabama prior to the Civil War, see Atkins.

36. On the eve of his marriage to Harriet [Henriette] Girard, Henri Lallemand had a duel with another French officer, François-Louis Taillade who opposed the Texas adventure advocated by the Lallemand brothers. See Selin on Henri Lallemand.

37. "On arrival in America, this diverse collection of refugees found an established community of their compatriots" (Blaufard, "Notes," 108).

38. Chapter 5 in Blaufarb's *Bonapartists in the Borderlands* is devoted to the Vine and Olive Company. The land grant to French exiles, some of whom were wealthy, created resentment on the part of some Americans who questioned the fairness of the act and the fitness of the French people to act as true settlers. Blaufarb offers an account of the September 1817 meeting of the Society for the Cultivation of Vine and Olive. See *Bonapartists*, 49–50.

39. "The cession of Congress by the Act of 3 March last consists of 92,160 acres. [...] These 92,160 acres were divided and measured by the American government in 144 sections of 640 acres each" (Blaufarb, "Notes," 117). For a list of the 347 French immigrant shareholders, see *Bonapartists*, 175–182; for biographical sketches of the immigrants, see Blaufarb, 188–228.

40. Blaufard, in his biographical sketches of the Vine and Olive Colony settlers, mentions Léontine Desportes, Louise Emilie de Mazières, the wife of Jean-Jérome Cluis, Joséphine Verrier Delaunays, Julie Delpit, and several others.

41. The county was named after Napoleon's victory over the Austrians at the battle of Marengo in 1800.

42. For a "Map of the four townships in Marengo County granted to French immigrants by Act of Congress," see Blaufarb, *Bonapartists*, 183–187.

43. "At least five Domingan watchmakers, jewelers, and goldsmiths held allotments in the Alabama settlement: Jean-Simon Chaudron and his son Pierre Edouard, Alexandre Fournier, Pierre Gallard, and Théodore Guesnard" (Blaufarb, *Bonapartists*, 25).

44. About Charles Lallemand's strategy to take control of the Society for the Cultivation of Vine and Olive and his role in the distribution and sale of land, see Blaufarb, *Bonapartists*, 93–94. The French intervened in Mexico in 1838–1839 in an episode known as the Pastry wars caused, in French eyes, by unfair taxation of French products.

45. On Rigau, see Blaufarb, *Bonapartists*, 88.

46. On Jeannet, see Blaufarb, *Bonapartists*, 88–89.

47. The Lafitte brothers had replaced another French pirate, Louis-Michel Aury, while he was plotting for Mexican independence against the Spanish Crown. See Ramsay, 90–97.

48. For a layout of the camp, see Figure 2 in Terrien, 94.

49. "The colony's roster demonstrates that this international recruitment reproduced the cosmopolitanism of Napoleon's army itself: Belgian, German, Irish, Italian, Polish, and Spanish veterans represented as much as one quarter of the officers who settled on the Trinity. Their career in the armies of the empire's satellite states made them quasi-French but also renegades in their home countries, which was motive enough for them to join the expedition" (Terrien, 99).

50. Soulé's biography is based on Green and Kirkwood, 218–219.

51. Although Bonaparte had obtained the general's release from Austrian jail, Lafayette had refused to serve Napoleon's regime.

52. On Lafayette's 1824–25 tour of the U.S., see Delâge and Levasseur.

53. See Kindleberger, 127. The author mentions the following books written by Chevalier: *Lettres sur l'Amérique du Nord, Histoire et description des voies de communication aux Etats-Unis, La liberté aux Etats-Unis, Examen du système commercial…, L'isthme de Panama* (122).

54. For a short introduction to Tocqueville, see Åhr, Johan, "Tocqueville, Alexis de."

55. "Slavery … dishonors labor. It introduces idleness into society, and with idleness, ignorance and pride, luxury, and distress. It enervates the powers of the mind and benumbs the activity of man" (Tocqueville, *Democracy in America*, I, 52).

56. On Frances Wright at *Harmonie*, see Eckhart, *Fanny Wright*, 89–92.

57. On Fourier, see Portes, 82–83.

58. On Cabet, see Johan Åhr, "Cabet, Etienne (1788–1856)"; Cordillot, 25–86; Portes, 83–86.

59. On Brisbane, see Cordillot, 100–101.

60. Brisbane published two books expounding

Fourier's ideas, *Social Destiny of Man* (1840) and *Association: Or A Concise Exposition of the Practical Part of Fourier's Social Science* (1843). From 1843 to 1845 he was also the editor of *The Phalanx, or Journal of Social Science*. Greeley worked for the *New York Tribune*.

61. For the list of Fourierist Phalanxes, see Hinds, *American Communities and Co-opperative Colonies*, 250. On the "Fourieristic Associations and Phalanxes," Hinds, 247–251.

62. For an account of the life of several members of the Réunion phalanx after its collapse, see Cordillot, 127–134.

63. On Cabet, see also "A New French vision of a just world" in Rohrbough, *Rush to Gold*, 15–16.

64. On the Icarian community of Texas, see Cordillot, 25–52.

65. According to Cordillot (39), upon hearing about the fall of the July Monarchy, five of the Frenchmen decided to return to France immediately.

66. On the Icarian colony of the Mississippi valley, see Prévos, "L'exportation des idéaux révolutionnaires."

67. On the Icarian colony of Nauvoo, see Cordillot, 53–86.

68. Rohrbough draws from official correspondence between the French consuls in California and their superiors in Paris, as well as the private correspondence of French Forty Niners. He also examines the Parisian press from November 1848 onward, and in particular the *Journal des Débats* (26–33) as well as the regional press (33–36).

69. On the *Courrier des Etats-Unis*, see Beal.

70. The gold diggers were often referred to as "Argonauts" after the followers of Jason, the Greek mythological figure who went on a quest for the Golden Fleece.

71. On the structure and reputation of those companies, see Rohrbough, 56–72.

72. Many of these companies were sued for false advertising later. See Rohrbough, 249.

73. "An official report from the Ministry of Agriculture and Commerce agreed that the condition of 'our emigrants, if not miserable, is one to be pitied.' Still, the report concluded, with the return of a minimum of F 20–25 a day, French miners have generally accustomed themselves well to their new kind of life" (Rohrbough, 184).

74. "Derbec [the French consul] recounted the story of a Frenchman from the Stanislaus who had harvested a fortune of F 200,000, but his dramatic success was the exception" (Rohrbough, 184).

75. Rohrbough (199) summarizes American xenophobia this way: "They [the Americans] looked down on other peoples, especially non-English-speaking ones. Foremost among these groups were American Indians and Mexicans. These were inferior peoples who did not know how to use the natural gifts given to them. The first targets of the Americans in the goldfields were the Spanish speakers—namely, the Mexicans, Peruvians, and Chileans."

76. "A letter from San Francisco published in the *Constitutionnel*" thus described "the arrival of 150 veterans of the *Garde Mobile* on the *Sérieuse*": "It is a fine corps of men, armed and in uniform. Fifty of them have been conveyed to Stockton at the expense of the French government [and] have gone to the southern mines. Their manner is in every respect inoffensive and their excellent conduct has made a favorable impression, and, like all French immigrants, they have been well received. On arrival, their baggage was lost. A subscription was immediately opened for their benefit. The French consul has done excellent work. He has given them money. This is an assistance which greatly smoothes their way" (Rohrbough, 219).

77. Several Los Angeles institutions, including the Consulate General of France in Los Angeles organized an exhibition on "Pioneers and Entrepreneurs, French Immigrants in the Making of Los Angeles, 1827–1927," from December 3, 2007, to January 13, 2008. The prospectus explained that the French played a role in the development of Los Angeles, with two of them serving as mayor of the city, the French-Canadian Damien Marchessault in 1859–1860; and Joseph Mascarel, who spoke French and Spanish but whose English was shaky, in 1865. Another, Jean-Louis Sainsevain, "engineered the first underground pipes for efficient, clean water distribution."

78. See Chalmers, *French San Francisco*; Demeestere, *Pioneers and Entrepreneurs in Los Angeles 1827–1927*; and Thiery.

79. See Chalmers, "Gold Rush Argonauts," 21–50.

80. See also Chalmers, 43.

81. This territory included parts of Arizona, Colorado, Nevada, New Mexico, and Utah. See "The Treaty of Guadelupe Hidalgo" on the National Archives website.

82. Rohrbough writes that the French "did not understand" why Congress had not "conferred immediate statehood on California in response to the incoming rush of population. With a central government three thousand miles away, statehood seemed a minimal gift to Californians. [...] The news that Congress had adjourned without voting statehood was regarded as a severe blow in California's ongoing struggle for order and led to demonstrations of unhappiness in San Francisco. In French eyes, such neglect was both incomprehensible and dangerous" (Rohrbough, 47).

83. See Andreas, *History of the State of Kansas*, 114, 126, 143.

84. Born in France, Soulé had immigrated after getting in trouble during the Restoration (1815–1830) for participating in liberal secret societies.

85. Richards (141) speculates that "Soulé also probably had a hand in getting Walker to reinstate slavery in Nicaragua."

86. Brasseaux states that the Democratic Party started to spread the "Jacksonian ideology" among Cajuns during Alexandre Mouton's run for governor of Louisiana in the 1840s. He notes that a surprising

thing occurred during the campaign for the 1860s election: the poor Acadians were so impressed by Mouton's speeches that they voted for a secessionist while most of the planters were voting for moderates ("Naissance et Renaissance," 371). On the Cajuns, see also Rushton.

87. In that regard, it is tempting to see a direct line from the "Bonapartists of the Borderlands" to Soulé.

88. See Richards, 155–168.

89. His brother, William Rodrigue, was an architect based in Philadelphia. He also worked on St. Patrick's cathedral in New York. See the entry "William Rodrigue" on the "Philadelphia Buildings" website.

90. See Spurgeon. Judge Lecompte was probably a descendant of another Samuel Lecompte who left Normandy for New France at the turn of the 18th century.

91. See William Cody, "Boys Days in Kansas," in *The Life of the Honorable William Cody*, 38–52.

92. On the Civil War, see Avila.

93. See Richards, 169–174.

94. The Republican Party was not the only political formation to oppose the western expansion of slavery, however, there was a "free-soil" wing within the Democratic Party as well (Richards, 180–182).

95. "The man is not fit to be president. He wasn't born in this country. We can't be sure of his religion—or even see his birth certificate! The man's a dangerous radical. These allegations were hurled at a presidential candidate—not Barack Obama in 2008 nor Ted Cruz in 2016—but the first Republican Candidate for president in 1856 [John C. Frémont]." Myall, "Birtherism is nothing New."

96. The same insult was hurled toward Edward Stanly, a candidate for the California governorship in 1857, even though he owned slaves. Richards, 174–175.

97. Important inventions from those years include the sewing machine, the elevator, and the telegraph. Edwin Drake also drilled the first commercial oil well in Pennsylvania in 1859.

98. Frémont nonetheless ran into trouble when he issued an emancipation proclamation without consulting with the President of the U.S. He was relieved of his functions as a result. His last political appointment was as the 6th Governor of the Territory of Arizona (1878–1881).

99. On P.G.T. Beauregard, see Cocker, Atkins, 193, 203.

100. Creagh notes that "18,000 people born in France were residents of the State of New York in 1855" (*Nos Cousins*, 265). French immigration increased after the failure of the Second Republic, with the French settling primarily around New York, St. Louis, Ste. Geneviève, and California, in particular San Francisco (263–266).

101. Trobriand became a U.S. citizen in 1865 and served for the next thirteen years as a major general in the U.S. army on the Western frontier. He wrote about his experience at Fort Stevenson and Fort Berthold in North Dakota. See Havard, "L'héritage français," 572–577.

102. The bulk of Cordillot's book (135–334) is devoted to French contributions to the American left and the American Labor movement.

103. On French anti-Yankee positions during the Civil War, see Roger, "The Divided States of America," in *The American Enemy*, 65–95.

Chapter X

1. In cinema, the French western was a later product and it tends to be a satire of the initial genre. This development points to national maturity (the Western is no longer needed as a crutch).

2. On the Rebellions of 1837 and 1838, see Buckner; Dagenais; Dickinson and Young.

3. See Dickinson and Young who organize their short history of Quebec around those areas.

4. See Martel, "Quand une majorité devient une minorité."

5. For an excellent overview of French-Canadian immigration to the U.S., see Barkan.

6. Creagh (*Nos Cousins*, 385) writes that 500,000 people left Quebec for the States between 1861 and 1901. Chartier, who lists their exact numbers by place of settlement, comes up with a figure of 573,000 (89). Péloquin-Faré's figure is twice as high: between 900,000 and 1,000,000 (301). For a detailed analysis of the Franco-Canadian migration to Canada between 1860 and 1900, see Chartier, 13–90. See also Anctil's study of "Franco-Americania," the French population in industrial centers of Rhode Islands, Massachussetts, New Hampshire, and Maine, particularly in the textile industry. See also Yolande Lavoie, *L'Emigration des Québecois aux Etats-Unis de 1840 à 1930*.

7. See the "Speak White!" entry in Wikipedia.

8. Armand Chartier describes the period from 1900 to 1930 as a period of "growth and conflicts," anti-immigrant sentiment, and the rejection of hyphenated identities around World War I (139–169).

9. "A link with ethnic history, a means of affirming one's collective identity and a bearer of culture, these three perceptions of French show the high esteem that the 'builders of Little Canadas' accorded the dominated language" (A. Chartier, 306–307).

10. "[L'] appui aux minorités venait uniquement du Québec—en termes de ressources et d'idéologie—et l'unique cadre institutionnel qui véhiculait cet appui était celui de l'Eglise catholique" (Louder, Morisseau, and Waddell, 5).

11. A. Chartier calls the interwar period a "golden Age" for the Franco-Canadians (172–252).

12. See Fouché, *Emigration alsacienne*, 176. Apart from the Midwest, destinations for Alsatian emigrants included California and Texas.

13. Brasseaux, in "Naissance and renaissance" (371), writes that many Acadians had to sell their lands prior to the Civil War and that those who did were the first to Americanize because of the new jobs they found. Louder and Leblanc write about a group of Cajuns who had migrated from Louisiana

to southeastern Texas and still numbered over 80,000 in the 1970s. See "Les Cadjins de l'est du Texas," 259–271.

14. See "A Cotton Office in New Orleans" on Wikipedia. The painting is part of the collection of the *Musée des Beaux Arts de Pau.* The Degas House is now a museum in New Orleans.

15. For an overview of Acadian history and life in contemporary Louisiana, see Heimlich.

16. On Cajun unions, see Cook, 377–381.

17. Stivale, in *Disenchanting Les bons temps,* presents contemporary Cajun culture as the contradictory product of a traditional *joie de vivre* and a sadness associated with a painful history. Harry Oster writes about an interesting cultural phenomenon, the Afro-French spiritual.

18. According to Duguas (34), there were 27 primary schools for boys in the colony by the end of the French regime. Then came the arts and trade schools where boys learned crafts often related to the construction of churches. Some of them, like the Ursuline Academy of New Orleans founded in 1727 accepted female students of all races. Secondary and higher education were limited to a few institutions.

19. The first hospital was founded in 1639 in Quebec. See the webpage "Vie quotidienne, médecine et santé" at the Virtual Museum of New France.

20. See Butler et al., "The Backwoods frontiers," in *The Frontiers and Catholic Identities.*

21. Brett notes (93) that the Vatican considered the United States a "mission field" until 1905.

22. French-born bishops who were the first bishop of the diocese: Cheverus, Boston, 1810; Flaget, Louisville, 1810; Portier, Mobile, 1826 ; Chabrat, Bardstown, KY, 1834; Bruté de Rémur, Vincennes, IN; Loras, Dubuque, IA, 1837; Chanche, Natchez, LA 1841; Lefevere, Detroit, MI, 1841; Odin, Galveston, TX, 1842; Blanchet, F., Oregon City (Portland), OR, 1845; Blanchet, A., Nesqually (Seattle), WA, 1846; Rappe, Cleveland, 1847; Maigret, Honolulu, 1847; Lamy, first Archbishop of Santa Fe, 1850. See Wikipedia, "Historical List of the Catholic Bishops of the United States." See also McGreevey, "Education and the Nineteenth Century Revival," in *Catholicism and American Freedom,* 19–42.

23. Later, in 1910, the Society of Saint Vincent the Paul was instrumental in establishing the network of American Catholic Charities devoted to assistance to the poor, the National Conference of Catholic Charities. See Brown et al., *"The Poor Belong to Us."*

24. See "Théodore Rouault, Biographical Sketch." New Mexico Historical Society.

25. The Carondelet Health network is still a major healthcare provider in Southern Arizona, operating three hospitals and several primary care facilities in the Tucson area today.

26. Willa Cather's famous novel *Death Comes for the Archbishop* (1927) recounts the founding of the Diocese of New Mexico and the building of Saint Francis Cathedral in Santa Fe during the tenure of French Archbishop Jean-Baptiste Lamy in the 1870s and 1880s.

27. The website of the Catholic Health Association of the United States states that today the association runs "600 hospitals and 1,600 long-term care and other health facilities in all 50 states, the Catholic health ministry is the largest group of nonprofit health care providers in the nation."

28. According to Wikipedia, there are nearly 200 Catholic institutions of higher education in the U.S. today. See "List of Catholic Universities and Colleges in the United States."

29. Creagh writes in *Nos Cousins* (391) that in Iowa, for instance, only between 1,000 and 3,000 arrived every ten years during the second half of the 19th century.

30. On Basque presence in California and the Southwest, see Douglass William, *Amerikanuak,* particularly chapters 5 and 6.

31. See Cordillot, "La proscription communaliste."

32. On May 8, 1886, a demonstration in favor of the eight-hour workday degenerated when German anarchists threw a bomb at the police, killing at least eight people.

33. M. Jones quotes a figure of 15 million immigrants from Austria-Hungary, Italy, Russia, Romania, and Turkey between 1890 and 1910.

34. Figures are based on the "Historical List of the Catholic Bishops of the United States" in Wikipedia. Interestingly, many French-born church leaders (and increasingly Belgium-born) were still being appointed as first bishops of new dioceses as the overall percentage of their appointments declined: Crétin, St. Paul, MN, in 1851; Miège, Kansas City, 1851; Goesbraind, Burlington, VT, 1853, Martin, Natchitoches, 1853; Verot, St. Augustine, FL, 1858; Macheboeuf, Denver, 1868; Brondel, Vancouver and Helena, 1879; Glorieux, Boise, ID, 1885; Bourgade, Tucson, 1885. During WWI, Crimont became the first bishop of Alaska (1917) and Jeanmarch, the first bishop of Lafayette, LA (1918).

35. See Gold, McQuillan, Martel, and Louder, Morrissonneau, and Waddell.

36. "In Louisiana, the Cajuns, who had been deported during the 1755 *grand dérangement,* shared the common misfortunes of black slaves and 'free people of color,' Blacks were called 'Frenchmen of color'" (Borer, 16).

37. "Scholarly interest in Louisiana's French experience flagged noticeably in the late nineteenth and twentieth centuries, after a torrent of Anglo-American immigration reduced the state's once dominant Francophone population to minority status. Like other contemporary American minorities, Louisiana's French speakers were reviled in the popular media and ignored by the halls of academe" (Brasseaux, *French, Cajun, Creole, Houma,* 131).

38. Despite its speed, the Pony Express experiment lasted less than two years, 1860–1861, as cost exceeded revenue.

39. The city of Tombstone, Arizona, epitomized the lawlessness of the West, as the famous 1881 gunfight at the O.K. Corral, re-enacted daily, reminds tourists today.

40. On the nationalist discourse on the province,

see Le Hir, *The National Habitus*, 226–265. Maurice Barrès's novel *The Uprooted* is good example of this nationalist-chauvinist discourse (1897).

41. On those myths, see, chapter 1- 3 in Deverell and Hyde.

42. See the entry on "free trapper" in Blévins' *Dictionary of the American West*.

43. See Le Hir, *The National Habitus*, chapter II on Chateaubriand.

44. The civil war fought in Western France during the French Revolutionary era had a competing allegiance, an allegiance to the French absolute monarchy and the Catholic Church, as its stake. Parisian revolutionaries also targeted minorities who spoke other languages or dialects than French, that is, the majority of the rural population before mandatory schooling at the end of the century. See Weber, *Peasants into Frenchmen*.

45. The following words are those of the oath of allegiance to the United States pledged by new U.S. citizens: "I hereby declare, on oath, that I absolutely and entirely renounce and abjure all allegiance and fidelity to any foreign prince, potentate, state or sovereignty of whom or which I have heretofore been a subject or citizen" (Hennessey, 7).

46. What I mean by "regime of one-ness" is best described by Calhoun in *Nationalism*: "Put another way, it has been the tacit assumption of modern social and cultural thought that people are normally members of one and only one nation, that they are members of one and only one race, one gender, and one sexual orientation, and that each these memberships describes neatly and concretely some aspects of their being. It has been assumed that people naturally live in one world at a time, that they inhabit one way of life, that they speak one language, and that they themselves, as individual, are singular, integral beings. [...] Two further guiding assumptions in much modern thinking on matters of identity are that individuals ideally ought to achieve maximally integrated identities, and that to do so they need to inhabit self-consistent, unitary cultures or life worlds. [...] It is thought normal for people to live in one culture at a time, for example, to speak one language; to espouse one set of values; to adhere to one polity" (Calhoun, 18–19).

47. The boarding school can be viewed as a "mellow" form of violence compared to war. Balzac's analogy between the Native American and the Bretons can be pursued here too: first the Vendée wars, then the boarding school to effect assimilation.

48. See the webpage "State Compulsory School Attendance Laws."

49. Written in 1935 and set in the last decades of the 19th century, William Faulkner's short story "The Bear" is a coming-of-age story in which the young man must learn, on his own, to appropriate the knowledge of an old Native American and track and kill a bear by himself.

50. In a chapter of *Democracy without Women* titled "Liberal Individualism, Natural Right, and Sexual Equality in the Political Philosophy of Montesquieu, Rousseau, and Condorcet," Christine

Fauré shows how both Montesquieu and Rousseau, as opposed to Condorcet, denied women individual agency, and hence the rights of "man and the citizen."

51. William Cody (1846–1917) earned his nickname when he was a buffalo hunter who provided meat to the U.S. army. See Cody, "Champion Buffalo Killer," 170–177.

52. "A nation is a soul, a spiritual principle. Two things, which in truth are but one, constitute this soul or spiritual principle. One lies in the past, one in the present. One is the possession in common of a rich legacy of memories; the other is present-day consent, to desire to live together, the will to perpetuate the value of the heritage that one has received in an undivided form" (Renan, 26).

53. By contrast, the tone of the celebration is considerably lighter in a 2005 French poster celebrating the centennial of Buffalo Bill's West Show's visit to Bergerac, France, Cyrano's hometown: it features two riders on horseback, Cyrano, holding a wine bottle, and Buffalo Bill, holding a glass! A copy can be found on the the website of the Buffalo Bill Museum.

54. One of Aimard's novels gives credence to the notion that he may have taken part in the expedition that created the short-lived Republic of Sonora in the fall of 1852.

55. Some of Aimard's titles include *The Frontiersmen, The Pirates of the Prairie, The Indian Scout, Jim the Indian, The Red River Half-Breed*. On Aimard, see also Rohrbough, 277–278.

56. Rohrbough mentions two other early French producers of Western fiction, Eustache, and Henri Mathet, who participated in the Gold Rush and wrote fictional accounts on the Wild West after their return to France, "bring[ing] forth a wide range of exotic characters—trappers, gold miners, Indians in fantastic dress, buffalo, cowboys, sheriffs, and Mormon polygamists..." (266).

57. There is a need for a critical evaluation of the vast corpus of Western literature in French. In Bonneau's case, it is even difficult to find a website listing all his works.

58. Rohrbough mentions two authors of juvenile literature who published novels on the Gold Rush featuring teenagers (258).

59. There are nearly 100 *Lucky Luke bandes dessinées*.

60. M.C. Solaar, "Nouveau Western," for instance (1994).

61. *La France et les Français vus par les voyageurs américains* (1814–1848). See also Levenstein, *Seductive Journeys*, and in particular, "In Search of Taste and Distinction,1786–1848" (2–81); "Paris and Tourism Transformed, 1848–1870" (83–131); and "Gender, Class, and the Rise of Leisure Tourism, 1870–1914" (123–213).

62. On the Grand Tour, see Buzard, 109–132.

63. See the chapter on Germaine de Stael in Le Hir, *The National Habitus*.

64. "Panurge's sheep" is an interesting example as it conveys both the notion of conformism

characteristic of the mass according to Rabelais, and the individualist exception, Panurge. The purpose of the tale is to discourage conformism and to encourage individualism.

65. Montbrial, quoting Duroselle, states that "the Jefferson years were marked by the emergence of the notion of 'moral superiority,' of the 'mission' of U.S. foreign policy, and the sort of subconscious nationalism which makes Americans sincerely believe that 'what is good for America is good for the rest of the world.' This feature of American culture, which has steadily grown over time, is among the most annoying to the French." Montbrial's quotes are from Duroselle's book, *La France et les Etats-Unis*.

66. Khan writes that Lincoln, for instance, "consistently emphasized the important role of the United States in assisting aspiring republics" (9). See also Stovall. *Transnational France*.

67. "Hence to speak of 'the' French vision of the U.S. requires specifying the time period and which group of French people are being considered." Montbrial, 452. "French anti-Americanism, like American anti-French feeling, has always been specific to time, place, and social class" (Wall, "From Anti-Americanism to Francophobia," 1100).

68. It was announced on June 9, 2021, that France was sending a second Statue of Liberty to the U.S., a smaller replica, as a gift for the fourth of July.

69. "In 1846, Richard Morris Hunt from New York was the first American admitted to the then prestigious Paris Ecole des Beaux Arts. He was to be followed by Arthur Dexter and Francis Peabody, both from Boston, in 1852, and then by H. H. Richardson from New Orleans in 1860" (Carlhian, 185).

70. The existence, in various cities of France, of 35 much smaller replica of the Statue of Liberty can be taken as a good indication of the two nations shared values.

71. See Le Hir, *The National Habitus*, 221–238.

72. See "Theodore Roosevelt and Conservation" on the webpage of the National Park Service.

73. Jacques Portes (92) mentions two other wealthy French visitors who tried to settle in the West during the Gilden Age, the Comte de Doré, who created a ranch in a place that became Yellowstone National Park, and Pierre Wibeaux who built a ranch in Montana .

74. See "Yosemite as Art," and "Yellowstone and the Wild West," in Sears, *Sacred Places*.

75. The Marquis de Mores engaged in cattle farming and had a meat packing business. He built a house named the Chateau de Mores, which is now a museum. See the page for "Chateau de Mores State Historic Site" on the State Historical Society of North Dakota website.

76. "According to contemporary American commentator Gustavus Meyers, by 1909, five hundred American heiresses had entered into transnational marriages with titled nobility and had taken nearly $220 million out of the United States to Europe. While these women entered into matrimonial contracts with nobility from all over Europe,

an overwhelming majority of these marriage contracts were established with men from Great Britain and France" (Léopoldie, *The Franco-American love affair*, 32).

77. "Yet, in 1892 the *Social Register of New York* listed thirty-one titled American women, and of those, twenty-one of them were married to Frenchmen" (Léopoldie, 43).

78. "John W. Burgess, political scientist and founder of the School of Political Science at Columbia University, wrote in his memoirs that in 1863 he pledged himself to a career in education with the intention of helping to avoid future wars and destruction" (Walton, 12).

79. "Mixing industrial and commercial wealth with old privilege, the extravagant character of transnational Society began to first take form in the court of Napoleon III, who eagerly welcomed cosmopolitan elites from places like New York and Boston" (Léopoldie, 50). As Marcel Proust's *Remembrance of Things Past* illustrates, this high society did not disappear during the Third Republic.

80. The presence of these institutions contributed to the development of urban tourism, a privilege for the wealthy as illustrated by the practice of "slumming" included in city tours. On that topic see Cocks, *Doing the Town*, 174–203.

81. See Le Hir, "Imagining the Discipline," 34–42.

82. On the mansions built by Maurice Hébert in New York and Fresno, CA, see Powell and Kershaw. The Charles M. Schwab House was razed shortly after World War II. Photos are widely available on the internet.

83. See Graff, *Professing Literature*, and Walton, *Internationalism*, 12–37.

84. France lost the city of Strasburg and the provinces of Alsace and Lorraine as the result of the Franco-Prussian war (1870–1871). "Entire groups of people made a collective decision to emigrate […] when these provinces became part of Germany. Some of them, especially Alsacian Jews, made their way to places such as Los Angeles" (Lichtenfelf, 3). France regained the two provinces after World War I.

85. It was therefore the German university model that was adopted for higher education in the United States, starting with the creation of John Hopkins, as a graduate school only, in 1876.

86. "By the end of the nineteenth century, middle-class Americans could enjoy a safe, pleasant, and short voyage at an affordable price. For about $63.00 an American could purchase a second-class round-trip ticket to Europe, berth with one to three other passengers, and eat quite well in the ship's dining hall" (Walton, 15). "Career enhancement was the primary motive for young Americans to study in Europe before World War I" (Walton, 22).

87. See Carlhian's article on the *Ecole des Beaux Arts*'s influence on American architecture. See also Alexander, "L'impact français sur l'architecture américaine," and Kennedy, *Orders from France*, for the first decades of the 19th century.

88. For comments on the gendering of Italy as

"female," see Buzard, 132–139.

89. The matter was soon closed because within a generation, American universities were able to train their own students.

90. Carlhian (188) explains that "French-trained returning American architects" created school of architectures in the U.S. and that French architects were often brought in "to teach, head departments or become deans at these American schools."

91. Founded in 1902, the Federation of *Alliances françaises USA* unites 100 chapters spread all over the U.S. as of 2021, according to their website.

92. On Lanson, see Compagnon, *La Troisième république des lettres.*

93. The national memory "data bank" must be large enough and contain sufficient national heroes to allow people of different political and/or ethnic persuasion to relate personally to it. Thus, the French right may identify as French because Joan of Arc, a symbol of faith and tradition, is part of their patrimony and the left because French Enlightenment philosophers, as early representatives of progress and democracy, are also included.

94. "When general Pershing arrived in Paris in June 1917 and was received with wild adulation, he stated—at least, so the story goes--'Lafayette, here we are'" (Quoted in Montbrial, 453).

95. "The French *Atlantiste* carries a negative connotation that the American term 'Atlanticist' does not have" (Montbrial, note 3, 458).

96. Montbrial (453) offers as an example the French discontent at the United States' inability to repay their war debt after the euphoria of victory at the end of the War of Independence.

97. Khan reports that "an international antislavery conference was held in Paris in 1867" (40), which goes to show that not all the French of France sided with the Confederates of French heritage.

98. Montbrial writes that "the blockade of the South by the north resulted in a quasi–interruption of cotton export and thus a major crisis of the French cotton industry starting in 1862" (455).

99. "Louis Napoleon and France paid for favoring the losing side in the American Civil War when the reunited government threatened the French-backed regime in Mexico and later stood by [...] while France suffered a disastrous defeat in the Franco-Prussian War of 1870–1871" (Zahniser, xvi).

100. See Roger, "The Empire of Trusts: Socialism or Feudalism," in *The American Enemy*, 219–253.

101. For a list of French publications expressing anti-American sentiment during this period, see Montbrial, 456. On French anti-Americanism related to the invasion of Cuba and the Philippines, see Roger, "From Havana to Manila," in *The American Enemy*, 129–156.

102. World War I started in 1914 but according to Kaspi (26), the United States had sent only 30,000 troops to France by June 1917. The U.S. viewed its relationship to France as an "association," not an as "alliance" (35). The legacy of this association was "a certain amity and a great disillusionment" for the French" (37).

103. "Though lukewarm to American co-belligerency, Napoleon did open French ports to American prizemasters allowing them to sell off vessels captured from the British [during the War of 1812]—a privilege which [...] Washington did not reciprocate. [...] If Americans looking back believed that he had treated them with unwarranted severity, the evidence suggests that although he managed them harshly and to his own advantage, his conduct was not altogether unjustified" (Hill, *Napoleon's Troublesome Americans*, 236).

104. "Before 1917, French academics, like French government leaders, pressed the case of a Franco-American shared history of liberal republicanism, in contrast to German authoritarianism, militarism, and aggression, hoping to engage the United States in the war on the side of the allies" (Walton, 31).

105. "According to Célestin Bouglé, the experience of seeing the French overcome great odds in the war led American soldiers to realize that 'France of the risqué novels [*des romans demi-mondains*] is not the real France,' and they hungered to learn about the 'real' France" (Quoted in Walton, 33).

106. Kaspi puts the blame for the collapse of the treaty on the Senate: "In repudiating the plans of President Wilson, they [Americans] weakened the League of Nations and the principle of collective security. They had a responsibility in organizing the postwar world; yet they did not know how to make peace" (37). Keylor puts some of the blame on President Wilson who "had adamantly insisted on inextricably linking the Treaty of Versailles to the Covenant of the League of Nations" (47).

107. As a result of these restrictive immigration laws, France took over the position of the United States as the world-wide leader on immigration between the two world wars.

108. "France's rapid, humiliating, and unexpected defeat [...] occurred at a moment when the Roosevelt administration could do little but promise increased war materials and supplies if the French agreed to prolong their agony and somehow continue the conflict. From French shores, the only hope rested in an immediate American declaration of War" (Zahniser, xvii).

109. See Wall, *The United States and the Making of Postwar France*, 158–187.

110. "For it was Washington that held the purse strings in postwar France, Washington that tried to establish the contours of French postwar economic growth, financed the military buildup and futile French colonial wars, flooded France and French North Africa with American bases and troops and interfered regularly in ministerial crises and the making and breaking of the cascade of postwar cabinets. American pressure maneuvered the French into Dien-Bien-Phu, and American spy services played a hidden role in the *Affaire des Fuites* (cabinet leaks) that threatened to undermine Pierre Mendès-France in 1954" (Wall, 1089).

111. See Wall, *The United States and the Making of Postwar France*, 135–162.

112. Wall writes that "it is hardly surprising that

French critics focused on the power that was imminently present and influential in France rather than the remote and distant threat, if any perceived it as such, from the East" (Wall, 1089).

113. "Yet it was paradoxically de Gaulle who opened the way for the full coming of the consumer society to France and who opened the floodgates of American investment. He did this by stabilizing at once the political system and French finances, thus providing the security of a presidential regime with the Communist threat reduced and a convertible franc. He also surprised his critics when he went ahead with the Treaty of Rome creating the European market" (Wall, 1095).

114. "Thus, although Congress may have believed the Marshall Plan was market-oriented and interventionist, as Kuisel says, and the French may also have perceived it in that way, in fact it was pretty much neither in its practical effect. And the productivity missions were only a small part of it; they received millions of dollars, while over the four years of the plan French nationalized enterprises received several billions" (Wall, 1094).

115. See Kristin Ross, *Fast Cars, Clean Bodies* and Richard Kuisel *Seducing the French: The Dilemma of Americanization*. Both critics equate "modernization" with "Americanization."

116. Unless prompted to do so, as in the case of an international trade boycott, most people select what they can afford, as the dominance of cheaper Chinese products in the United States and Europe nowadays indicates.

117. See for instance Stovall, *Paris Noir*; and Anderson, Christiann, *Paris Reflections*.

Epilogue

1. For "dramatic, first person accounts" of Franco-American lives in New England, see Hendrickson.

2. A. Chartier's chapter IV, "Towards Assimilation," centers of the Franco-Canadians during the years 1935–1960.

3. On the Franco-American novel, see Péloquin, "Le Roman…."

4. Weil states that Franco-Canadian elites had mixed feelings about France in part because the France of the kings their ancestors had left no longer existed.

5. See A. Chartier, "L'Ethnicité retrouvée, 1960–1990," 323–382.

6. The U.S. government was upset as well about France's interference in its neighbor's affairs and annoyed with De Gaulle in general: "De Gaulle lost no opportunity to tweak the nose of the Americans by demanding payment in gold for excess dollars, challenging the status of the dollar as a reserve currency, and condemning American policy in Vietnam. The more bombastic aspects of his foreign policy-the shout *Vive le Québec libre* […]—and his siding with the Arabs during the six-day war in the Middle East—made him all the more unpopular in Washington" (Wall, 1095).

7. The Civil Rights Act marked the end of the Jim Crow era and put an end to the "separate but equal" doctrine. It prohibits discrimination based on race, color, religion, sex, or national origin.

8. "There is a vast amount of evidence pointing to the conclusion that an 'ethnic revival' of sorts occurred in the U.S.A. between the mid-sixties and the mid-seventies and that it had significantly declined by the late seventies" (Fishman, 489).

9. The last lines of the song are in French. The Wikipedia article on the song contains a link to the lyrics. Written in 1969, "The Night They Drove Old Dixie Down" (1969) by the same band also fits the "back to your roots" category, or at least it did so long as the poverty of the Southern farmer whose story it tells was taken to be the song's focus. More recently, however, interpretative emphasis has switched to the song's historical context, the Civil War, as white supremacist groups started using the song as an anthem. In 1989 Canadian artist Daniel Lanois also wrote an album entitled *Acadie*.

10. Figures are from the website "Immigrés vivant en France en 2019 selon leur pays de naissance."

11. According to Lichtenfeld (43–56), marriage is the most frequent cause of immigration from France, work, usually in professional capacities, comes second.

12. See the webpage "MLA Language Map."

13. The increase in Spanish learners is related to the increase in the Hispanic population in the U.S. and the notion that it is a useful language for that reason. Based on personal experience in Southern Arizona, I know that many Hispanic students, bilingual or not, choose to study French.

14. See the webpage "MLA Language Data Base."

15. In addition, the elimination of the German requirement for PhD studies in scientific disciplines like Chemistry, which had been justified in the past by the predominance of scientific literature written in that language, disappeared once English became the norm.

16. The correlation between the perception of a given language as "useful" and student interest in studying it can be observed in the case of Japanese: enrollments went up significantly since the mid–20th century when very studied the language: 1958: 944; 1977: 10,721; 2016: 68,810. The same remark applies to a lesser extent Chinese: 1958: 615; 1977: 9.798; 2016: 53,069.

17. See the webpage "Les langues vivantes étrangères et régionales" on the site of the French Ministère de l'Education nationale.

18. As many German students as French students studied in the U.S. during those years, while the UK sent only half that many (144–145).

19. Levenstein's *Seductive Journeys* covers the early phase of American tourism to France, from the Revolution to World War I. The book's sequel, *We'll Always Have Paris* starts in the 1930s.

20. See the website "Chiffres clés de l'économie," 5.

21. According to official statistics, 70 percent of

those visitors were tourists, 22 percent were associated with business, 5 percent with education. The other percent named "health," "relatives," and "religion" as reasons for their trip. See "Market Profile France," on the page of the National Travel and Tourism Office.

22. The California numbers may be a bit inflated as many visitors who come to visit the National Parks in the Southwest land in Los Angeles and rent a car.

23. Labro is the author of *L'étudiant étranger* (1986) and *Un été dans l'Ouest*.

24. Yves Berger's literary works include *Le Fou d'Amérique* (1976); *Les Matins du Nouveau Monde* (1987); *La Pierre et la Saguaro* (1990); *L'Attrapeur d'ombres* (1992); *Immobile dans le courant du fleuve* (1994); *Le Monde après la pluie* (1997) and *Santa Fé* (2000).

25. In *We'll Always Have Paris*, Levenstein notes: "In 1984 a surprising poll showed that France, which had been the most anti-American country in Western Europe in the postwar years, was now the most pro-American" (241). Wall writes similarly that "[i]t is generally admitted that since the 1980s France has outgrown its once pathological anti-Americanism" (1083).

26. He noted that ironically, "there exist[ed] a peculiar tendency even among purported admirers of the French to undermine whatever esteem they may still hold in American academic circles" (1098).

27. On this topic, see Mathy, *French Resistance*, and in particular "1. French theory in the U.S.," (27–56); "4. Cultural Studies, Postcolonialism and the French National Idea" (108–133); and "5. Multiculturalism and its Discontents" (134–160).

28. For a recent episode in the trade wars, see Tankersley.

29. "In the *Archives Nationales* at Paris, in the archives of Quebec, in the Cabildo archives of New Orleans, and in the Randolph County courthouse at Chester, Illinois, lie the documents which are the chief few pieces that one must consult before he can draw an accurate picture of the period [late 17th–18th centuries]. Probably the most valuable of these are the Vaudreuil manuscripts included in the Loudoun papers, owned by the Huntington Library" (Belting, 7).

Bibliography

Primary Sources

Beauchamps, De. "Journal of De Beauchamps' Journey to the Choctaws, 1746," in *Travels in the American Colonies*, Mereness, 261–301. https://www.loc.gov/resource/lhbtn.09410/?sp=265.

Bonnefoy, Antoine. "Journal of Antoine Bonnefoy's Captivity among the Cherokees," in *Travels in the American Colonies*, Mereness, 241–259. https://www.loc.gov/resource/lhbtn.09410/?sp=241.

Bourgmont, Etienne de. *Exact Description of Louisiana, of Its Harbors, Lands and Rivers, and Names of the Indian Tribes That Occupy It, and the Commerce and Advantages to Be Derived Therefrom for the Establishment of a Colony* (1713), in Martin, D., 62–70.

Calloway, Colin G., editor. *World Turned Upside Down: Indian Voices from Early America*. Boston: St. Martin's Press, 1994.

Cartier, Jacques. *Jacques Cartier and his Four Voyages to Canada* (1540). An essay, with historical, explanatory and philological notes by Hiram B. Stephens. Montreal: Drysdale, 1890. https://archive.org/details/cu31924103985341/page/n12.

Champlain, Samuel. *Voyages of Sieur de Champlain to New France, Made in the Year 1615*. Translated from the French by Charles Pomerot Otis, in *Voyages of Samuel de Champlain*, vol. III. http://www.gutenberg.org/cache/epub/6825/pg6825-images.html.

Chardon, Francis A. *Chardon's Journal at Fort Clark, 1834–1839*. Edited by Annie Heloise Abel, with an introduction by William R. Swagerty. Lincoln: University of Nebraska Press, 1997.

"Charter of Acadia Granted by Henry IV of France to Pierre du Gast, Sieur de Monts, December 18, 1603." Yale Law School. The Avalon Project. Documents in Law, History and Diplomacy. https://avalon.law.yale.edu/17th_century/charter_001.asp.

Chastellux, Francois Jean. *Travels in North America in the years 1780, 1781, 1782*. New York, 1828. https://archive.org/details/marquistravels00chasrich/page/n6.

Cody, William F. *The life of Hon. William F. Cody, known as Buffalo Bill, the famous hunter, scout and guide: An autobiography*. Hartford, CT: F.E. Bliss, 1879. https://babel.hathitrust.org/cgi/pt?id=uc2.ark:/13960/t4vh5g339&view=1up&seq=7.

Collot, Victor George Henri. *A Journey in North America: containing a survey of the countries watered by the Mississippi, Ohio, Missouri, and other affluing rivers* (1796). Paris: A. Bertrand, 1826. https://www.loc.gov/resource/gdclccn.2004622181/?sp=3&r=-0.306,0.614,1.549,0.668,0.

Collot, Victor George Henri. *Voyage dans l'Amérique Septentrionale ou Description des Pays arrosés par le Mississipi, l'Ohio, le Missouri et autres rivières affluentes* (1796). 2 vols. Paris: A. Bertrand, 1826. https://gallica.bnf.fr/ark:/12148/bpt6k1098776.r=Collot%20Victor?rk=42918;4.

D'Artaguiette, Bernard Diron. "Journal of Diron d'Artaguiette, inspector general of Louisiana, 1722–1723," in *Travels in the American colonies*, Mereness, 17–96. https://www.loc.gov/resource/lhbtn.09410/?sp=17.

"Declaration of Independence, July 4, 1776." Yale Law School. The Avalon Project. Documents in Law, History and Diplomacy. https://avalon.law.yale.edu/18th_century/declare.asp.

Deliette, Pierre. "Memoir of De Gannes Concerning the Illinois Country," in *The French Foundations, 1680–1693*, Pease and Werner, 302–395. https://www.loc.gov/resource/gdclccn.35027786/?sp=324.

Denys, Nicolas. *Description and Natural History of the Coasts of North America* (1632–1670). Translated by William F. Ganong. Toronto: Champlain Society, 1908. https://archive.org/details/descriptionandn00paltgoog/page/n9/mode/2up.

Desjardins, Simon, and Pierre Pharoux. *Castorland Journal: An Account of the Explorations and Settlement of Norther New York State by French Emigrés in the Years 1793–1797*. Edited and translated by John Gallucci. Ithaca: Cornell University Press, 2010.

Durand, du Dauphiné. *Un Français en Virginie* (1686). Edited by Gilbert Chinard. New York: Arno Press, 1979. https://eena-alexanderstreet-com.ezproxy4.library.arizona.edu/cgi-bin/EENA/hub.py?type=getvolume&docid=S2613.

Durand, du Dauphiné. *A Frenchman in Virginia: Being the Memoirs of a Huguenot Refugee in 1686*. Translated by a Virginian. Richmond, 1923. https://searchalexanderstreetcom.ezproxyl.library.arizona.edu/view/work/bibliographic_entity%7Cbibliographic_details%7C4576993#

page/1/mode/1/chapter/bibliographic_entity%7Cdocument%7C4576994.

Edict du roy, portant que les nobles pourront faire le commerce de mer, sans déroger à la noblesse. Vérifié en parlement le 13 August 1669. https://gallica.bnf.fr/ark:/12148/bpt6k97392032.texteImage.

Frémont, John C. *Frémont's First Impressions: The Original Report of His Exploring Expeditions of 1842–1844.* Edited by Ann Hyde. Lincoln: University of Nebraska Press, 2012.

Gourgues, Dominique de. *Histoire mémorable de la reprinse de l'isle de la Floride faicte par les François sous la conduite du capitaine Gorgues, gentilhomme Borderlais le 24 et 27 d'avril de cette annéee 1568*, in *Les Français en Floride*, edited by Lussagnet, vol. 2. Paris: PUF, 1958, 241–256.

Keating, William H. *Considerations upon the art of mining: to which are added, reflections on its actual state in Europe, and the advantages which would result from an introduction of this art into the United States.* Philadelphia: Carey and Sons, 1821. https://archive.org/details/considerationsup00keatrich.

Keating, William H. *Narrative of an expedition to the source of St. Peter's River, Lake Winnepeek, Lake of the Woods, &c.* London: Geo. B. Whittaker, 1825. https://archive.org/details/narrativeofexped00keat_0/page/n9/mode/2up.

Lahontan, Louis Armand de. *Mémoires de l'Amérique Septentrionale.* La Haye: Honoré Brothers, 1709. https://archive.org/details/nouveauxvoyagesd04laho/mode/2up.

Lahontan, Louis Armand de. *Nouveaux Voyages dans l'Amérique Septentrionale.* La Haye: Honoré Brothers, 1701. https://archive.org/details/nouveauxvoyagesd03laho.

Lahontan, Louis Armand de. *Supplément aux Voyages ou Dialogues avec le sauvage Adario.* Amsterdam, 1704. https://gallica.bnf.fr/ark:/12148/bpt6k82269m.image.

La Salle, Nicholas de. *Relation of the discovery of the Mississippi, written from the narrative of Nicholas de La Salle [...].* Translated by Melville B. Anderson. Chicago: The Caxton Club, 1898.

La Salle, René Cavalier de. "On Taking Possession of Louisiana, at the Mouth of the Mississippi, on the 9th of April, 1682." *Collections of the Illinois State Historical Library*, vol. 1. Springfield, IL, 1903, 106–114. https://archive.org/details/collectionsspring01illiuoft/page/106/mode/2up.

La Salle, René Cavelier de. "On the Illinois Country" (1680), in *The French Foundations, 1680–1693*, edited by Pease and Werner, 1–16. https://loc.gov/resource/gdclccn.35027786/?sp=23.

La Tour du Pin, Henriette, Marquise de. *Recollections of the Revolution and the Empire. (Journal d'une Femme de cinquante ans).* Translated and edited by Walter Geer. New York, 1920. https://archive.org/details/recollectionsofr00latouoft.

Laudonnière, René Goulaine de. *Three Voyages* 1565, edited by Charles Bennett. Tuscaloosa: University of Alabama Press, 2001. https://muse.jhu.edu/book/22574.

Leclerq, Chrestien. "A Micmac Responds to the French, ca 1677," in Calloway, 50–52.

Le Page du Pratz, Antoine Simon. "The Alienation of the Natchez: Reply of the Stung Serpent," in Calloway, 90–91.

Le Page du Pratz, Antoine Simon. *The History of Louisiana, or of the Western Parts of Virginia and Carolina [...].* London: T. Becket, 1774. Eighteenth Century Collections Online.

Léry, Jean de. *History of a Voyage to the Land of Brazil, otherwise called America [...]* (1578). Translated by Janet Whatley. Berkeley: University of California Press, 1992. https://www.fulcrum.org/concern/monographs/0r9673976.

Lewis, Meriwether, William Clark, et al. *Journals of the Lewis and Clark Expedition.* Edited by Gary E. Moulton. Lincoln: University of Nebraska Center for Digital Research in the Humanities. https://lewisandclarkjournals.unl.edu/journals/contents.

Lussagnet, Suzanne, editor. *Les Français en Floride: Textes de Jean Ribault [et al.].* Vol. 2. Paris: PUF, 1958.

Margry, Pierre, editor. *Découvertes et établissement des Français dans l'ouest et dans le sud de l'Amérique Septentrionale (1614–1754).* 6 vols. Paris: D. Jouaust, 1876–1886. https://www.loc.gov/resource/gdclccn.01023956v1/?st=text.

Martin, Daisy, editor. *Exploration and Colonial America, 1492–1755.* Ipswich, MA: Salem Press, 2013.

Mereness, Newton D., editor. *Travels in the American Colonies.* New York: Macmillan, 1916.

Montaigne, Michel de. "Of Cannibals," in *Michel de Montaigne: Four Essays* [ca. 1588]. Translated by M.A. Screech. London: Penguin Books, 1995, 1–26. https://archive.org/details/fouressays00mich/page/n5/mode/2up.

Moreau de Saint-Méry, Médéric Louis Elie. *Voyage aux Etats-Unis de l'Amérique, 1793–1798.* New Haven: Yale University Press, 1913. https://archive.org/details/voyageauxtatsu00morerich/page/n7.

"The Paris Peace Treaty of September 30, 1783." Yale Law School. The Avalon Project. Documents in Law, History and Diplomacy. https://avalon.law.yale.edu/18th_century/paris.asp.

Pease, T.C., and Raymond Werner, editors. *The French foundations, 1680–1693.* Springfield: Trustees of the Illinois State Historical Library, 1934.

Pénicault. "Relation de Pénicaut," in Margry, vol. V, 375–586. https://www.loc.gov/resource/gdclccn.01023956v5/?sp=381&st=text.

Perrot, Nicolas. *Mémoire sur les mœurs, coustumes et relligion des sauvages de l'Amérique septentrionale.* Edited by Jules Tailhan. Leipzig et Paris, 1864. Toronto: Canadiana avant 1867, 1968.

Pike, Zebulon. *Journal of a voyage to the source of the Mississippi in the years 1805 and 1806.* Alexandria, VA: Alexander Street Press, 2003. https://eena-alexanderstreet-com.ezproxy4.library.arizona.edu/cgi-bin/EENA/hub.py?type=getdoc&docid=S10208-D001.

"The Quebec Act October 7, 1774: An Act for making more effectual Provision for the Government of the Province of Quebec in North America." Yale Law School. The Avalon Project. Documents in Law, History and Diplomacy. https://avalon.law.yale.edu/18th_century/quebec_act_1774.asp.

Radisson, Pierre-Esprit. *Voyages of Peter Esprit Radisson being an account of his travels and experiences among the North American Indians, from 1652 to 1684*. Edited by G.D. Scull. Boston: Prince Society, 1885. https://babel.hathitrust.org/cgi/pt?id=mdp.39015027068595&view=1up&seq=7.

Raynal, Guillaume. *History of the two Indies: A Translated Selection of Writings from Raynal's Histoire Philosophique et Politique et établissements des Européens dans les Deux Indes*. Edited by Peter Jimack. Burlington, VT: Ashgate, 2006.

Ribault, Jean. *Voyage to Florida* (1562). Excerpt from his *Narrative of the First Voyage, Made in the Reign of Charles IX, King of France, Under the Orders and Instructions of Gaspard de Coligny, Grand Admiral of France, to Make Discoveries and Found a Colony of French Protestants (Huguenots) in Florida*. New York, 1875. https://www.loc.gov/item/02027317/.

"The Royal Proclamation—October 7, 1763." Yale Law School. The Avalon Project. Documents in Law, History and Diplomacy. https://avalon.law.yale.edu/18th_century/proc1763.asp.

Thévet, André. *Les singularitéz de la France Antarctique* (1557). Edited by Paul Gaffarel. Paris: Maisonneuve, 1878. https://archive.org/details/lessingularitez01thevgoog/page/n10.or https://gallica.bnf.fr/ark:/12148/bpt6k99356lt.

Tocqueville, Alexis de. *Democracy in America, vol. I*. Edited by Eduardo Nolla and translated by James T. Schleifer. Indianapolis: Liberty Fund, 2012.

Tocqueville, Alexis de, and Gustave de Beaumont. *On the Penitentiary System in the United States and its Application to France*. Springer Nature Switzerland, 2020. https://link.springer.com/book/10.1007/978-3-319-70799-0.

Tonty, Henri de. "Chapitre XXI. De 1678 à 1684.— Voyages et établissements des Français sur les lacs et le Mississipi sous les ordres de MM. de La Salle et de Tonty," in Margry, I, 573–612. https://www.loc.gov/resource/gdclccn.01023956v1/?sp=581&st=text.

Tonty, Henri de, and Cavelier de La Salle. *On the discovery of the Mississippi, and on the south-western, Oregon, and north-western boundary of the United States*. Edited and translated by Thomas Falconer. London: Samuel Clarke, 1844. https://archive.org/details/ondiscoverymiss00tontgoog/page/n6/mode/2up.

"Treaty of Amity and Commerce Between the United States and France; February 6, 1778." Yale Law School. The Avalon Project. Documents in Law, History and Diplomacy. https://avalon.law.yale.edu/18th_century/fr1788-1.asp.

Volney, Constantin François Chasseboeuf, Comte de. *A view of the soil and climate of the United States of America, with supplementary remarks upon Florida; on the French colonies on the Mississippi and Ohio, and in Canada; and on the aboriginal tribes of America*. Philadelphia: Conrad and Co., 1804. https://babel.hathitrust.org/cgi/pt?id=loc.ark:/13960/t6543c08x&view=1up&seq=38.

Secondary Sources

Abénon, Lucien-René. "La Colonisation Française en Amérique Intertropicale," in Abénon and Dickinson, 109–198.

Abénon, Lucien-René, and John A. Dickinson. *Les Français en Amérique: Histoire d'une Colonisation*. Lyon: Presses Universitaires de Lyon, 1993.

Abreu de Galindo, Juan. *The History of the Discovery and Conquest of the Canary Islands*. London, 1764. Gale/Cengage, 18th Century Collections Online.

Acerra, Martine, and Jean Meyer. *Histoire de la marine française: des origines à nos jours*. Rennes: Ouest France, 1994. https://gallica.bnf.fr/ark:/12148/bpt6k33297358/f9.item.

Adams, Russell. *King C. Gillette, the Man and his Wonderful Shaving Device*. Boston: Little, Brown, 1978.

Ader-Martin, Claude. "Présence protestante en Nouvelle-France," in *Aquitaine, Québec, et Amérique du Nord Francophone*. https://www.aqaf.eu/2017/10/presence-protestante-en-nouvelle-france/.

Åhr, Johan. "Cabet, Etienne (1788–1856)," in Marshall vol. 1, 203–204.

Åhr, Johan. "Tocqueville, Alexis de (1805–1859)," in Marshall vol. 3, 1137–1140.

Aimard, Gustave. *The Adventurers* (1858). https://www.gutenberg.org/ebooks/43716.

Alderson, Robert J. "Genêt, Edmond-Charles (1763–1834)," in Marshall vol. 2, 514–515.

Alexander, Robert L. "L'impact français sur l'architecture américaine (1790–1830)," in Creagh and Clark, 213–228.

Allaire, Bernard. "The European Fur Trade in the Context of Champlain's Arrival," in Litalien, Roth, and Vaugeois, 50–58.

Anctil, Pierre. "La Franco-Américanie ou le Québec d'en bas," in Louder, Morissoneau and Waddell, 25–39.

Anderson, Christiann. *Paris Reflections: Walks through African-American Paris*. Blacksburg: McDonald and Woodward, 2002.

Andreas, A.T. *History of the State of Kansas containing a full account of its growth from an uninhabited territory to a wealthy and important state*. Chicago: A.T. Andreas, 1883.

Anon. "The French Revolution: Quakers and Cockades." *Quaker Strongrooms: A Blog from the Library of the Society of Friends*. https://quakerstrongrooms.org/2015/06/15/the-french-revolution-quakers-and-cockades/.

Arnold, Morris S. "The Significance of Arkansas's Colonial Experience," in Whayne, 131–141.

Arsenault, Pauline. "Acadia in Champlain's New France: From Arcadia to China," in Litalien, Roth, and Vaugeois, 115–120.

Atkins, Leah Rawls. "From Early Times to the End of the Civil War," in *Alabama: The History of a Deep South State*, edited by Rogers, William, Warren, Ward, et al. Tuscaloosa: University of Alabama Press, 2018, 3–333.

Aubert, Guillaume. "Coureurs de bois," in Marshall vol. 1, 310–312.

Aubert, Guillaume. "Louisiana," in Marshall vol. 2, 738–743.

Aubuchon, Jeffrey W. "Indian Wars," in Marshall vol. 2, 597–598.

Audubon, Lucy, editor. *The Life of John James Audubon, the Naturalist*. New York: Putnam, 1870. https://archive.org/details/lifeofjohnjamesa00audub.

Augeron, Michaël. "Des esclaves et des domestiques amérindiens à La Rochelle au XVIIIe siècle," in Augeron and Havard, 83–95.

Augeron, Michaël. "'Une 'sourde conquête': les Indiens du Texas au coeur des rivalités franco-espagnoles au XVIIIe siècle," in Augeron and Havard, 125–152.

Augeron, Michaël, and Gilles Havard. *Un Continent en partage: Cinq siècles de rencontres entre Amérindiens et Français*. Paris: Les Indes Savantes, 2013.

Avery, Elizabeth H. *The Influence of French Immigration on the Political History of the United States*. Redfield, S.D., Journal Observer print, 1890 [reprint E. Research Associates 1972]. https://conservancy.umn.edu/bitstream/handle/11299/177993/una-dissertation-0024.pdf?sequence=1&isAllowed=y.

Avey, Torey. "What Lewis and Clark Ate." *The History Kitchen*, May 31, 2013. https://www.pbs.org/food/the-history-kitchen/what-lewis-and-clark-ate/.

Avila, Orlando. "American Civil War," in Marshall vol. 1, 64–69.

Balayé, Simone. *Madame de Staël: Lumières et liberté*. Paris: Klincksieck, 1979.

Balch, Thomas. *The French in America during the War of Independence of the United States, 1777–1783*. Boston: Gregg Press, 1972.

Balvay, Arnaud. "Cinq 'Sauvages' américains à la cour de Louis XV en 1725," in Augeron and Havard, 75–81.

Balvay, Arnaud. "The French and the Natchez: a failed encounter," in Englebert and Teasdale, 139–158.

Balvay, Arnaud. *L'Épée et la plume: Amérindiens et soldats des troupes de la marine en Louisiane et au Pays d'en Haut (1683–1763)*. Montréal: Presses de l'Univ. Laval, 2006.

Bangor Daily News, March 7, 2016. http://myall.bangordailynews.com/2016/03/07/missouri/birtherism-is-nothing-new-what-we-can-learn-from-the-election-of-1856/.

Barbiche, Bernard. "Henri IV and the World Overseas," in Litalien et Vaugeois, 24–32.

Barkan, Elliot Robert. "French-Canadians," in *Havard Encyclopedia of Ethnic Groups*, edited by Sternstrom et al., 389–401.

Barman, Jean, "Marie Dorion." *The Oregon Encyclopedia*. https://oregonencyclopedia.org/articles/dorion-marie/#.XvE6E-pKjIU.

Baudry, René. "Lescarbot, Marc." *Dictionary of Canadian Biography*. http://www.biographi.ca/en/bio/lescarbot_marc_1E.html.

Bauer, Jean. "With Friends Like These: John Adams and the Comte de Vergennes on Franco-American Relations." *Diplomatic History* 37: 4 (September 2013): 664–692.

Beal, Shelley. "Courrier des Etats-Unis, Le (1828–1939)," in Marshall vol. 1, 314–315.

Beaulieu, Alain. "The Birth of the Franco-American Alliance," in Litalien, Roth, and Vaugeois, 153–162.

Béland, Jean-François. "Maisonneuve, Paul de Chomedey de (1612–1676)," in Marshall vol. 2, 755.

Béland, Jean-François. "Montcalm, Louis-Joseph de Montcalm-Grozon, Marquis de (1712–1759)," in Marshall vol. 2, 834–835.

Belote, Theodore Thomas. *The Scioto Speculation and the French Settlement at Gallipolis: A Study in Ohio Valley History*. Cincinnati: University of Cincinnati Press, 1907. https://archive.org/details/sciotospeculatio01belo/page/n3/mode/2up.

Belting, Natalia Maree. *Kaskaskia under the French Regime (1948)*. Carbondale: Southern Illinois University Press, 1976.

Bennett, Ethel. "Hébert, Louis." *Dictionary of Canadian Biography*. http://www.biographi.ca/en/bio/hebert_louis_1E.html.

Bercé, Yves-Marie. *The Birth of Absolutism: A History of France, 1598–1661*. London: Palgrave Macmillan, 1995.

Bergengren, Roy F. *Credit Union North America*. Kingsport, TN: Southern Publishers, 1940.

Berger, Yves. *La Pierre et le Saguaro*. Paris: Grasset, 1990.

Bernard, Marion. "Montagnais," in Marshall vol. 2, 830–831.

Berry, Don. *A Majority of Scoundrels: An Informal History of the Rocky Mountain Fur Company*. Corvallis: Oregon State University Press, 2006.

Berthiaume, Pierre. "From Champlain's Voyage Accounts to his 1632 Report," in Litalien, Roth, and Vaugeois, 284–301.

Bertier de Sauvigny, Guillaume de. *La France et les Français vus par les voyageurs Américains, 1814–1848*. 2 vols. Paris: Flammarion, 1985.

Bertrand, Romain. "1686. Rendez-vous manqué avec le Siam," in Boucheron, 341–345.

Biggar, H.P. *The Early Trading Companies of New France: A Contribution to the History of Commerce and Discovery in North America*. New York: Argonaut Press, 1965.

Binoche, Jacques. "Les Députés d'Outre-Mer pendant la Révolution française (1789–1799)." *Annales Historiques de la Révolution française* 50: 231 (January-March 1978): 45–80.

Blackburn, Robin. *The Making of New World Slavery: From the Baroque to the Modern, 1492–1800.* London: Verso, 2010. https://hdl-handle-net.ezproxy2.library.arizona.edu/2027/heb.01674.

Blaufarb, Rafe. *Bonapartists in the Borderlands: French Exiles and Refugees on the Gulf Coast, 1815–1835.* Tuscaloosa: University of Alabama Press, 2006.

Blaufarb, Rafe. "Notes and Documents: French Consular Reports on the Association of French Emigrant: The Organization of the Vine and Olive Colony." *Alabama Review* 56:2 (April 2003): 104–124.

Blaufarb, Rafe. "Vine and Olive Colony." *Encyclopedia of Alabama.* http://www.encyclopediaofalabama.org/article/h-1539.

Blévins, Winfred. *Dictionary of the American West: Over 5,000 Terms and Expressions from Aarigaa! to Zopilote.* Fort Worth: Texas Christian University Press, 2008.

Borer, Alain. *De quel amour blessée: Réflexions sur la langue française.* Paris: Gallimard, 2014.

Bouchard, Russel Aurore. *Le Saguenay des fourrures.* 1534–1950. Chicoutimi-Nord: Russel Bouchard, à compte d'auteur, 1989. http://classiques.uqac.ca/collection_histoire_SLSJ/bouchard_russel/saguenay_des_fourrures/saguenay_des_fourrures.pdf.

Boucher, Philip P. *France and the American Tropics to 1700: Tropics of Discontent?* Baltimore: Johns Hopkins University Press, 2008.

Boucheron, Patrick, editor. *Histoire Mondiale de la France.* Paris: Seuil, 2017.

Bourdieu, Pierre. "Deux impérialismes de l'universel," in Fauré and Bishop, 149–155.

Bourset, Madeleine. "L'émigration de l'exclusion (1848–1873)," in Creagh and Clark, 255–270.

Boutwell, Jane, and Brendan Gill. "Origins: The Bouviers." *The New Yorker,* June 1963, 25.

Brace, Richard Munthe. "Talleyrand in New England: Reality and Legend." *The New England Quarterly* 16:3 (September 1943): 397–406.

Brandao, José Antonio. "Parkman, Francis (1823–1893)," in Marshall vol. 3, 916–917.

Brasseaux, Carl A. *French, Cajun, Creole, Houma: A Primer on Francophone Louisiana.* Baton Rouge: Louisiana State University Press, 2005.

Brasseaux, Carl A. "The Moral Climate of French Colonial Louisiana, 1699–1763." *Louisiana History: The Journal of the Louisiana Historical Association* 27:1 (Winter 1986): 27–41.

Brasseaux Carl A. "Naissance et renaissance de la société acadienne louisianaise," in Creagh and Clark, 361–373.

Bray, Martha Coleman. "Joseph N. Nicollet: Biographical Summary." Heritage Museum of the Côteau des Prairies, Sisseton, SD. http://www.sissetonmuseums.org/tower_history.asp.

Brazeau, Brian. "New France," in Marshall vol. 3, 863–866.

Brebner, John Bartlet. *The Explorers of North America, 1492–1806.* Garden City, NJ: Doubleday, 1955.

Brett, Carroll. *The Routledge Historical Atlas of Religion in America.* Hoboken: Taylor and Francis, 2013.

Brevoort, J.C. *Verrazano the Navigator.* New York: American Geographical Society, 1874. https://archive.org/details/verrazanonavigator00brevrich/page/n5/mode/2up.

Brown, Abram E. *Faneuil Hall and Faneuil Hall Market.* Boston: Lee and Shepard, 1900.

Brown, Dorothy M., and Elizabeth McKeown. *The Poor Belong to Us: Catholic Charities and American Welfare.* Cambridge: Harvard University Press, 1998.

Brown, Margaret Kimball. *History as They Lived It: A Social History of Prairie du Rocher, Illinois.* Carbondale: Southern Illinois University Press, 2005.

Brown, Margaret Kimball. *The Voyageur in the Illinois Country: The Fur Trade's Professional Boatman in Mid America.* Saint Louis: Center for French Colonial Studies, 2002.

Buckner, P. "The Canadian Civil Wars of 1837–1838." *London Journal of Canadian Studies* 35:1 (2020): 96–118.

Bujol, Stéphan. "L'Acadie vers 1750. Essai de chronologie des paroisses acadiennes du bassin des Mines (Minas Basin, NS) avant le Grand dérangement." *Études d'histoire religieuse* 70, 2004: 57–77. https://www.erudit.org/fr/revues/ehr/2004-v70-ehr1825729/1006673ar.pdf.

Burns, Emily C. *Transnational Frontiers: The American West in France.* Norman: University of Oklahoma Press, 2018.

Burt, A.L. "The Frontier in the History of New France." *Rapports annuels de la Société historique du Canada/Report of the Annual Meeting of the Canadian Historical Association* 19:1 (1940): 93:99.

Butel, Paul. *Histoire des Antilles françaises, XVIIe-XXe siècle.* Paris: Perrin, 2002.

Butel, Paul. *Les Caraïbes au temps des flibustiers.* Paris: Aubier Montaigne, 1987. https://archive.org/details/lescaraibesautem0000bute?q=Les+caraibes+au+temps+des+flibustiers.

Butler, Ann, Michael E. Engh, and Thomas W. Spalding. *The Frontiers and Catholic Identities.* Maryknoll, NY: Orbis Books, 1999.

Butler, Jon. *The Huguenots in America: A Refugee People in New World Society.* Cambridge: Harvard University Press, 1983.

Buzard, James. *The Beaten Track: European Tourism, Literature, and the Ways to Culture, 1800–1918.* Oxford: Oxford University Press, 1993.

Caiani, Ambrogio A. *Louis XVI and the French Revolution, 1789–1792.* Cambridge: Cambridge University Press, 2012.

Calhoun, Craig. *Nationalism.* Minneapolis: University of Minnesota Press, 1997.

Carlhian Jean-Paul. "L'Ecole des Beaux-Arts and its Influence on American Architects and American Architecture," in Roelker and Warner, 185–206.

Carlos, Ann M., and Frank D. Lewis. "The Economic History of the Fur Trade: 1670–1870." *E-H net,* website of the Economic History Association. https://eh.net/encyclopedia/the-economic-history-of-the-fur-trade-1670-to-1870/.

Carpain, Gervais. "Migration to New France in Champlain's Time," in Litalien, Roth, and Vaugeois, 163–179.

Castillo, Susan. "Bougainville, Louis Antoine de (1729–1811)," in Marshall vol. 1, 175–176.

Castillo, Susan. "Lahontan, Louis-Armand de Lom d'Arce, Baron de (1666–1715)," in Marshall vol. 2, 670–671.

Cerami, Charles A. *Jefferson's Great Gamble: The Remarkable Story of Jefferson, Napoleon, and the Men behind the Louisiana Purchase*. Naperville, IL: Sourcebook, 2003.

Chailley-Bert, Joseph. *Les compagnies de colonisation sous l'ancien régime*. Paris: Armand Colin, 1898.

Chaillot, Jane B. "Chouteau, Auguste." *Dictionary of Louisiana Biography*. https://www.lahistory.org/resources/dictionary-louisiana-biography/dictionary-louisiana-biography-c/.

Chaillot, Jane B. "Laclède, Pierre Ligueste." *Dictionary of Louisiana Biography*. https://www.lahistory.org/resources/dictionary-louisiana-biography/dictionary-louisiana-biography-l/.

Chaillot, Jane B. "Roman, Jacques Telesphore." *Dictionary of Louisiana Biography*. https://www.lahistory.org/resources/dictionary-louisiana-biography/dictionary-louisiana-biography-r/.

Chalmers, Claudine. *French San Francisco*. Charleston, SC: Arcadia, 2007.

Chapman, Herrick. "Review of *The American Enemy: A Story of French Anti-Americanism*." *The Journal of Modern History* 80:2 (2008–2006): 432–434.

Chapman, Rosemary. "*Filles du Roi*," in Marshall vol. 2, 439–440.

Chapman, Rosemary. "Manitoba," in Marshall vol. 2, 763–767.

Chappell, Carolyn Lougee. ""The pains I took to save my/his family': Escape accounts by a Huguenot mother and daughter after the revocation of the Edict of Nantes." *French Historical Studies* 22:1 (Winter 1999): 1–47.

Chappey, Jean-Luc. "1751. Tous les savoirs du monde," in Boucheron, 365–369.

Charron, Donna Card. "Mississippi River," in Marshall vol. 2, 817–818.

Chartier, Armand B. *Histoire des Franco-Américains de la Nouvelle Angleterre, 1775–1900*. Silléry, Québec: Septentrion, 1991.

Chartier, Roger. *The Cultural Origins of the French Revolution*. Durham: Duke University Press, 1991.

Chateaubriand, François René de. *Atala*. New York: Kennedy, 1889. https://archive.org/details/atalachateaubria00chat/page/4/mode/2up.

Childs, Frances Sergeant. *French Refugee Life in the United States 1790–1800. An American Chapter of the French Revolution*. Baltimore: The Johns Hopkins Press, 1940.

Childs, Frances Sergeant. "A Special Migration: Refugees, Adventurers, and Commentators," in Roelker and Warner, 151–183.

Chinard, Gilbert. *Volney et l'Amérique d'après des documents inédits et sa correspondance avec Jefferson*. New York: Johnson Reprints, 1973.

Choquette, Leslie. *Frenchmen into Peasants: Modernity and Tradition in the Peopling of French Canada*. Cambridge: Harvard University Press, 1997.

Choquette, Leslie. "From Sea Monsters and Savages to Sorcerers and Satan: A History of Fear in New France," in Henneton and Roper, 38–59.

Clark, John P. "La Révolution française et la démocratie radicale américaine," in Creagh and Clark, 135–163.

Clarke, T. Wood. *Émigrés in the Wilderness*. New York: Macmillan, 1941.

Cocker, William S. "Pierre G. T Beauregard." *Dictionary of Louisiana Biography*. https://www.lahistory.org/resources/dictionary-louisiana-biography/dictionary-louisiana-biography-b/.

Cocks, Catherine. *Doing the Town: The Rise of Urban Tourism in the United States, 1850–1915*, Berkeley: University of California Press, 2001.

Codignola, Luca. "American Revolution," in Marshall vol. 1, 69–73.

Codignola, Luca. "Barrin de la Galissonière, Roland Michel, Marquis (1693–1756)," in Marshall vol. 1, 122–123.

Codignola, Luca. "Céloron de Blainville, Pierre-Joseph (1693–1759)," in Marshall vol. 1, 231–232.

Codignola, Luca. "Treaty of Paris (1763)," in Marshall vol. 3, 1154–1155.

Compagnon, Antoine. *La Troisième république des lettres: de Flaubert à Proust*. Paris: Seuil, 1983.

Condorcet. *Outlines of an Historical View of the Progress of the Human Mind*. Translated from French. London: J. Johnson, 1795. https://archive.org/details/outlinesofhistor00cond/page/266/mode/2up/search/more+complete.

Cook, Bernard. "Les ouvriers cajuns," in Creagh and Clark, 375–383.

Cordillot, Michel. "La proscription communaliste aux Etats-Unis (1871–1880)," in Creagh and Clark, 333–352.

Cordillot, Michel. *Utopistes et exilés du Nouveau Monde: Des Français aux États-Unis de 1848 à la Commune*. Paris: Vendémiaire, 2013.

Coupeau, Steeve. "Early Haiti, 1492–1804," in *History of Haiti* [online]. Greenwood Publishing (2007): 15–36.

Creagh, Ronald. "La Révolution et les Français des Etats-Unis," in Creagh and Clark, 165–188.

Creagh, Ronald. *Nos Cousins d'Amérique: Histoire des Français aux Etats-Unis*. Paris: Payot, 1988.

Creagh, Ronald, and John P. Clark, editors. *Lès Français des Etats-Unis d'hier à aujourd'hui*. Montpellier: Presses de l'Université Paul Valéry, 1994.

Crego, Carl R. *Fort Ticonderoga*. Charleston, SC: Arcadia Publishing, 2004.

Cubbison, Douglas R. *The British Defeat of the French in Pennsylvania 1758: A Military History of the Forbes Campaign against Fort Duquesne*. Jefferson, NC: McFarland, 2010.

Dagenais, Maxime. ""Those Who Had Money

Were Opposed to Us, and Those Who Were Our Friends Were Not the Moneyed Class': Philadelphia and the 1837–1838 Canadian Rebellions." *American Review of Canadian Studies* 49: 4 (2019): 563–572.

Darnton, Robert. *The Literary Underground of the Old Regime*. Cambridge: Harvard University Press, 1982.

Dash, Michael. "France and the Caribbean," in Marshall vol. 1, 17–26.

Debray, Régis. *Civilisation: Comment nous sommes devenus américains*. Paris: Gallimard, 2018.

Delâge, Denis. "Lafayette en Amérique, ou le retour du 'père français,'" in Augeron and Havard, 295–325.

DeLong, Marlena. "Rochambeau, Jean-Baptiste-Donatien de Vimeur, Comte de (1725–1807)," in Marshall vol. 3, 1003–1004.

Demeestere, Hélène. "Essay." *Pioneers and Entrepreneurs: French Immigrants in the Making of Los Angeles, 1827-1927*. Exhibition Catalogue. (France-Los Angeles Exchange, 2007): 8–11.

Deverell, William, and Anne Hyde. *A History of North America from 1850: Shaped by the West*, vol. 2. Berkeley: University of California Press, 2018.

Devèze, Michel. *Antilles, Guyanes, La Mer des Caraïbes de 1491 à 1789*. Paris: Sedes, 1977.

Dickinson, John A. "La Colonisation Française en Amérique du Nord," in Abénon and Dickinson, 7–108.

Dickinson, John A., and Brian Young. *A Short History of Quebec*, 4th edition. Montreal: McGill-Queen's University Press, 2008.

Din, Gilbert C. "Between a Rock and a Hard Place. The Indian Trade in Spanish Arkansas," in Whayne, 112–130.

Dorigny, Marcel, and Bernard Gainot. *Atlas des Esclavages: Traites, sociétés coloniales abolitions de l'Antiquité à nos jours*. Paris: Autrement, 2006.

Doty, C. Stewart. "'How many Frenchmen does it take to…' One hundred years of discrimination against Franco-Americans." *Thought and Action: The NEA Higher Education Journal* 11 (2): 85–104.

Dowd, Maureen. "Gone with the Windsors." *The New York Times Sunday*, January 12, 2020, 9.

Dubois, Laurent. *A Colony of Citizens: Revolution and Slave Emancipation in the French Caribbean, 1787–1804*. Chapel Hill: University of North Carolina Press, 2004.

Dubois, Paul-André. "La religiosité catholique, ciment de l'alliance franco-indienne au XVIIIe siècle," in Augeron and Havard,107–124.

Duby, Georges, and Robert Mandrou. *Histoire de la Civilisation française*. 2 vols. Paris: Armand Colin, 1958.

Dugas, Louis. "L'Alphabétisation des Acadiens,1700–1850." MA Thesis, University of Ottawa, 1993.

Dull, Jonathan R. *The Age of the Ship of the Line: the British and French Navies, 1650–1815*. Lincoln: University of Nebraska Press, 2009.

Dull, Jonathan R. "France and the American Revolution seen as a Tragedy," in Roelker and Warner, 1–22.

Dupré, Céline. "Cavelier de La Salle, René Robert." *Dictionary of Canadian Biography*. http://www.biographi.ca/en/bio/cavelier_de_la_salle_rene_robert_1E.html.

Durnin, Kathy. "Saskatchewan," in Marshall vol. 3, 1050–1051.

Duroselle, J.B. *La France et les Etats-Unis: des origines à nos jours*. Paris: Seuil, 1976.

Eccles, W.J. *Frontenac, the Courtier Governor*. Toronto: McLelland & Stewart, 1959. https://archive.org/details/frontenaccourtie0000unse/page/n3/mode/2up.

Eccles, W.J. *The French in North America, 1500-1783*. Markham, Ontario: Fitzhenry and Whiteside, 1998.

Eckhart, Celia Morris. *Fanny Wright: Rebel in America*. Cambridge: Harvard University Press, 1984.

Edwards, Jo. "Brûlé, Etienne (c. 1592–1633)," in Marshall vol. 1, 195–196.

Edwards, Jo. "Huguenots," in Marshall vol. 2, 582.

Edwards, Jo. "Ribault, Jean (ca. 1520–1565)," in Marshall vol. 3, 995–996.

Edwards, Jo. "Verrazzano, Giovanni da (ca. 1485–death unknown)," in Marshall vol. 3, 1186–1187.

Ekberg, Carl J. *Stealing Indian Women: Native Slavery in the Illinois Country*. Urbana: Illinois University Press, 2007.

Ekberg, Carl J. *Colonial Ste Genevieve: An Adventure on the Mississippi Frontier*. Tucson: The Patrice Press, 1996.

Ekberg, Carl J. *French Roots in the Illinois Country: The Mississippi Frontier in Colonial Times*. Urbana: University of Illinois Press, 1998.

Ekberg, Carl J., and Sharon K. Person. *St. Louis Rising: The French Regime of Louis St. Ange de Bellerive*. University of Illinois Press, 2015.

Elias, Norbert. *The Civilizing Process: Sociogenetic and Psychogenetic Investigations*, edited by Eric Dunning, Johan Goudsblom and Stephen Mennel and translated by Edmund Jephcott. Malden, MA: Blackwell, 2006.

Englebert, Robert, and Teasdale, Guillaume. "Introduction," in Englebert and Teasdale, xi-xxxiii.

Englebert, Robert, and Teasdale, Guillaume, editors. *French and Indians in the Heart of America, 1630–1815*. East Lansing: Michigan State University Press, 2013.

Faulkner, William. *The Bear* (1942). Carlisle, MA: Applewood Books, 2016.

Fauré, Christine. *Democracy Without Women: Feminism and the Rise of Liberal Individualism in France*, translated by Claudia Gorbman and John Berks. Bloomington: Indiana University Press, 1991.

Fauré, Christine, and Tom Bishop, editors. *L'Amérique des Français*. Paris: François Bourrin, 1992.

Favier, Jean. *Les Grandes Découvertes, d'Alexandre à Magellan*. Paris: Fayard, 1991.

Fiquet, Nathalie. "Brouage in the Time of Champlain: a New Town Open to the World," in Litalien, Roth, and Vaugeois, 33–42.

Fisher, Jim. "Chicago," in Marshall vol. 1, 252–253.

Fisher, Jim. "French and Indian War," in Marshall vol. 2, 477–482.

Fishman, Joshua. "Epilogue: The Rise and Fall of Ethnic Revival in the USA," in Fishman and Gertner, 489–526.

Fishman, Joshua A., Michael H. Gertner, et al. *The Rise and Fall of the Ethnic Revival: Perspectives on Language and Ethnicity.* Berlin: De Gruyter, 2013.

Fletcher, William J. *A History of the City of Saint Paul, and of the County of Ramsey.* Saint Paul: The Society, 1876.

Forsdick, Charles. "Travel Writing," in Marshall vol. 3, 1151–1154.

Fosdick, Lucian. *The French Blood in America.* New York: Baker & Taylor, 1911. https://archive.org/details/frenchblood00fosdrich/page/n11/mode/2up.

Foucault, Michel. *Surveiller et Punir: Naissance de la Prison.* Paris: NRF Gallimard, 1975.

Fouché, Nicole. *Emigation alsacienne aux Etats-Unis.* Paris: Presses de la Sorbonne, 1992.

Foucrier, Annick. *Le rêve californien: Migrants français sur la côte Pacifique (XVIII–XXe siècles).* Paris: Belin, 1999.

Fowlie, Martin. "Audubon, John James," in Marshall vol. 1, 98–99.

Freehling, William. "The Louisiana Purchase and the Coming of the Civil War," in Levinson and Sparrow, 72–83.

Fumaroli, Marc. *When Europe Spoke French.* Translated by Richard Howard. New York: New York Review of Books, 2010.

Furstenberg, François. "Washington, George (1732–1799)," in Marshall vol. 3, 1202–1205.

Furstenberg, François. *When the United States Spoke French.* New York: Penguin, 2014.

Gaffarel, Paul. "Jean Ango." *Bulletin de l'Année 1889 de la Société Normande de Géographie.* Rouen: Société Normande de Géographie, 297–315.

Gannon, Kathryn. "Acadia," in Marshall vol. 1, 49–55.

Gaxotte, Pierre. *Le Siècle de Louis XV.* Paris: Fayard, 1974.

Gay-White, Pamela. "Saint-Denis, Louis Juchereau de (1684–1744)," in Marshall vol. 3, 1032–1033.

Gervais, Gaétain. "Champlain and Ontario (1603–1635)," in Litalien, Roth, and Vaugeois, 180–191.

Giesecke, E.W. "Wilson Price Hunt," in *The Oregon Encyclopedia,* A Project of the Oregon Historical Society. https://oregonencyclopedia.org/articles/hunt_wilson_price_1783_1842_/#.XvE39OpKjIX.

Gilbert, Geoff. "Tobacco," in Marshall vol. 3, 1134–1136.

Girard, Albert. "La réorganisation de la Compagnie des Indes (1719–1723)." *Revue d'Histoire Moderne & Contemporaine* 9:1 (1908): 5–34.

Godechot, Jacques. *France and the Atlantic Revolution of the Eighteenth Century, 1770–1799.* Translated by Herbert H. Rowen. New York: Collier-MacMillan, 1965.

Godechot, Jacques. "La Gazette Française," in Roelker and Warner, 78–92.

Gold, Gerald L. "Les Gens qui ont pioché le tuf: les Français de la Vieille Mine, Missouri," in Louder, Morissoneau and Waddell, 117–127.

Goodlett, Sean C. "Raynal, Guillaume-Thomas-François (1713–1796)," in Marshall vol. 3, 978–979.

Gournay, Isabelle. "Architecture," in Marshall vol. 1, 82–86.

Graff, Gerald. *Professing Literature: An Institutional History.* Chicago: University of Chicago Press, 1987.

Green, Jennifer R., and Patrick M. Kirkwood. "Reframing the Antebellum Democratic Mainstream: Transatlantic Diplomacy and the Career of Pierre Soulé." *Civil War History* 61: 3 (September 2015): 212–251.

Grenon, Jean-Yves. "Pierre Dugua de Mons, Lieutnant General of New France," in Litalien, Roth, and Vaugeois, 143–149.

Griffith, Devin. "The Comparative Method and the History of the Humanities." *History of the Humanities* 2: 2 (Fall 2017): 473–505. https://www.journals.uchicago.edu/doi/full/10.1086/693325.

Grossman, Mark, editor. "Elias Boudinot, 1740–1821." *Encyclopedia of the Continental Congresses.* Amenia: Grey House Publishing, 2014, 119–124.

Haigh, Samantha. "Guadeloupe," in Marshall vol. 2, 535–539.

Haine, Scott W. *History of France.* Westport, CT: Greenwood Publishing Group, 2000.

Hall, John W., and Hall, John W., Jr. *Uncommon Defense: Indian Allies in the Black Hawk War.* Cambridge: Harvard University Press, 2009.

Hall, Mark F. "Steamboats," in Marshall vol. 3, 1092–1093.

Hamelin, Jean. "Nicollet de Belleborne, Jean," in: *Dictionary of Canadian Biography.* vol. I. University of Toronto/Université de Laval, 1966. http://www.biographi.ca/en/bio/nicollet_de_belleborne_jean_1E.html.

Hammersley, Rachel. "Republicanism," in Marshall vol. 3, 986–993.

Harris, Richard Colebrook. *Seigneurial System in Early Canada: A Geographical Study.* Montreal: McGill-Queen's University Press, 1984.

Harris, Ronald Walter. *Absolutism and Enlightenment, 1660–1789.* New York: Harper & Row, 1964.

Harsanyi, Doina Pasca. *Lessons from America: Liberal French Nobles in Exile, 1793–1798.* University Park: Pennsylvania State University Press, 2010.

Hatton, Ragnhild. *Europe in the Age of Louis XIV.* New York: Harcourt, Brace and World, 1969.

Haudrère, Philippe. *Les Français dans l'Océan Indien (XVIIe-XIXe).* Rennes: Presses Universitaires de Rennes, 2014.

Havard, Gilles. *The Great Peace of Montreal of 1701: French-Native Diplomacy in the Seventeeth Century.* Translated by Phyllis Aronoff and Howard Scott. Montreal: McGill-Queen's University Press, 2001.

Havard, Gilles. "Introduction. Singularités franco-amérindiennes," in Augeron and Havard, 7–25.

Havard, Gilles. "L'héritage français des Arikaras," in Augeron and Havard, 559–588.

Havard, Gilles. "'Protection and Unequal Alliance': The French conception of Sovereignty over the Indians of New France," in Englebert and Teasdale, 113–137.

Havard, Gilles, and Cécile Vidal. *Histoire de l'Amérique française*. France: Flammarion, 2014.

Havard, Gilles, and Cécile Vidal. "Making New France New Again. French Historians rediscover their American Past." *Common-place* 7: 4 (July 2007). http://www.common-place-archives.org/vol-07/no-04/harvard/.

Hawke, David Freeman. *Everyday Life in Early America*. New York: Harper and Row, 1988.

Hebert, Catherine A. "The French Element in Pennsylvania in the 1790s: The Francophone Immigrants' Impact." *The Pennsylvania Magazine of History and Biography* 108: 4 (October 1984): 451–469.

Hébert, Robert. *L'Amérique française devant l'opinion étrangère, 1756–1960: anthologie*. Montreal: L'Hexagone, 1989.

Heidenreich, Conrad, and Edward H. Dahl. "Samuel de Champlain's Cartography," in Litalien, Roth, and Vaugeois, 312–332.

Heidenreich, Conrad, and Janet K. Ritch. *Samuel de Champlain Before 1604: Des Sauvages and Other Documents Related to the Period*. Toronto: McGill-Queen's University Press, 2011.

Heili, Pierre. "Jean-Joseph Amable Humbert." *Les Vosgiens célèbres: Dictionnaire biographique*. http://www.ecrivosges.com/vosgiens/bio.php?id=2229&id_bio=2132&operateur=one&recherche=Saint-Nabord&fit=7&whichlieu=Afficher.

Heimlich, Evan. "Acadians," in Lehman, 1–15.

Hele, Karl. "Perrot, Nicolas (ca. 1644–1717)," in Marshall vol. 3, 926–927.

Hemmerle, Oliver. "Talleyrand-Périgord, Charles Maurice de (1754–1838)," in Marshall vol. 3, 1108–1109.

Hémon, Louis. *Maria Chapdelaine: Récits du Canada Français* (1913). Paris: Le Livre de Poche, 1961.

Hendrickson, Dyke. *Quiet Presence: Dramatic, first-person accounts; the true stories of Framco-Americans in New England*. Portland, ME: Guy Gannett Publishing, 1980.

Hennessey, D.L. *Twenty-Five Lessons in Citizenship: With Complete Text of the Constitution of the United States*. 97th edition. Berkeley, 1993.

Henneton, Lauric, and Roper, L.H. *Fear and the Shaping of Early American Societies*. Leiden: Brill, 2016.

Henry, D. Arthur. *La Guyane française, son histoire, 1604–1946*. Cayenne, 1974. https://gallica.bnf.fr/ark:/12148/bpt6k3345844w/f26.item.

Heuman, Gad. *The Caribbean*. London: Bloomsbury Academic, 2006. https://archive.org/stream/caribbean0000heum#page/n7/mode/2up.

Higonnet, Patrice. *Goodness Beyond Virtue: Jacobins During the French Revolution*. Cambridge: Harvard University Press, 1998.

Higonnet, Patrice. "French," in Sternstrom et al., 379–388.

Hill, Peter. *French Perceptions of the Early American Republic 1783–1793*. Philadelphia: American Philosophical Society, Volume 180, 1988.

Hill, Peter. *Napoleon's Troublesome Americans: Franco-American Relations, 1804–1815*. Dulles: Potomac Books, 2005.

Hiller, James K. "Newfoundland," in Marshall vol. 3, 872–874.

Hiller, James K. "The Portuguese Explorers." Heritage Newfoundland and Labrador Website. https://www.heritage.nf.ca/articles/exploration/portuguese.php.

Hiller, James K. "Treaty of Utrecht (1713)," in Marshall vol. 3, 1155–1156.

Hillstrom, Laurie Collier. "French Americans," in Lehman, 655–667.

Hinds, William Alfred. *American Communities and Co-operative Colonies* (1908). Honolulu: University Press of the Pacific: 2005.

Hitchcock, Ripley. *Louisiana Purchase & the Exploration, Early History and Building of the West*. Boston: Ginn and Company, 1903.

Hodson, Christopher, and Brett Rushforth. "Bridging the Continental Divide: Colonial America's 'French Quarter.'" *OAH Magazine of History* 25: 1 (January 2011): 19–24.

Hoffman, Paule. *A New Andalucia and a Way to the Orient: the American Southeast during the 16th Century*. Baton Rouge: Louisiana State University Press, 1990.

Hollier, Denis, editor. *A New History of French Literature*. Cambridge: Harvard University Press, 1989.

Hook, Jason, and Martin Pegler. *To Live and Die in the West: The American Indian Wars*. New York: Routledge, 2002.

Houssaye, Sidonie de la. *Les Quarteronnes de la Nouvelle-Orléans*, 2 vols. Shreveport: Éditions Tintamarre, 2014.

Hroděj, Philippe. "Les premiers colons de l'ancienne Haïti et leurs attaches en métropole, à l'aube des premiers établissements (1650–1700)." *Les Cahiers de Framespa* 9 (2012). http://journals.openedition.org/framespa/1050.

Huger, Lucie Furstenberg. *The Desloge Family in America*. St. Louis: Nordman Printing Co., 1959.

Hughes, Howard. *American Indian Wars*. Harpenden, UK: Pocket Essentials, 2001.

Hunt, Jocelyn. *The Renaissance*. Abingdon-on-Thames, UK: Francis & Taylor, 1999.

Hyde, Anne F. "Introduction," *Frémont's First Impressions*, vii–xxvi.

Ibson, John. "Iowa," in Marshall vol. 2, 601–602.

Ibson, John. "Minnesota," in Marshall vol. 2, 810–812.

Jacob, Margaret C. *Living the Enlightenment: Freemasonry and Politics in Eighteenth-Century Europe*. Oxford: Oxford University Press, 1991.

Jacquin, Philippe. *Les Indiens blancs: Français et Indiens en Amérique du Nord, XVIe-XVIIIe siècles*. Montréal: Libre Expression, 1996.

Jeanneret, Michel. "1578: Twenty Years after His Return, Jean de Léry Publishes His Account of the Villegagnon Expedition to the Bay of Rio de Janeiro. Antarctic France," in Hollier, 240–243.

Jette, Melinda. "Etienne Lucier (1793–1853)." *The Oregon Encyclopedia*. https://oregonencyclopedia.org/articles/lucier_etienne_1793_1853_/#.XvE8f-pKjIU.

Jette, Melinda. "Joseph Gervais, 1777–1861." *The Oregon Encyclopedia*. https://oregonencyclopedia.org/articles/gervais_joseph_1777_1861_/#.XvE68OpKjIU.

Johnston, A.J.B. (John). "Evangeline," in Marshall vol. 2, 421–422

Johnston, A.J.B. (John). "Louisbourg," in Marshall vol. 2, 734–738.

Jones, Maldwyn Allen. *American Immigration*. Chicago: Chicago University Press, 1960. https://archive.org/details/americanimmigrat00jone/page/n5/mode/2up?q=religious+affiliation+with+Protestantism.

Jones, Terry D. *The Louisiana Journey*. Salt Lake City: Gibbs Smith, 2007.

Journoud, Marc H. "La Rochefoucauld-Liancourt, François-Alexandre-Frédéric de, duc (1747–1827)," in Marshall vol. 2, 656–657.

Journoud, Marc H. "Louis-Philippe (1773–1850)," in Marshall vol. 2, 745–746.

Joutard, Philippe. "1685. La révocation de l'édit de Nantes: un événement européen," in Boucheron, 336–340.

Julien, Charles André. *Les Français en Amérique au XVIIe siècle*. Paris: Centre de documentation universitaire et Société d'édition d'enseignement supérieur, 1976.

Jurgens, Olga. "Brûlé, Etienne." *Dictionary of Canadian Biography*. http://www.biographi.ca/en/bio/brule_etienne_1E.html.

Kadlec, Lauriane. "'Le Code Michau': la réformation selon le garde des Sceaux Michel de Marillac," in *Les Dossiers du Grihl* [Online]. *La Vie de Michel de Marillac et les expériences politiques du garde des sceaux*. http://journals.openedition.org/dossiersgrihl/5317.

Kale, Steven D. *French Salons: High Society and Political Sociability: From the Old Regime to the Revolution of 1848*. Baltimore: Johns Hopkins University Press, 2006.

Kaminski, John P., et al., editors. "The United States, Spain, and the Navigation of the Mississippi River." *The Documentary History of the Ratification of the Constitution*, vol. XIII. Madison: Wisconsin Historical Society Press, 1981, 149–52.

Kaspi, André. "Le Concours américain à la France, 1917–1919," in Roelker and Warner, 23–43.

Keenan, Jerry. *The Terrible Indian Wars of the West: A History from the Whitman Massacre to Wounded Knee, 1846–1890*. Jefferson, NC: McFarland, 2016.

Keith, LeeAnna. "Alabama Fever." *Encyclopedia of Alabama*. http://www.encyclopediaofalabama.org/article/h-3155.

Kellogg, Louise Phelps. *The French régime in Wisconsin and the Northwest*. New York: Cooper Square, 1925.

Kelly, John. "Why is a French nobleman who tried to blow up Napoleon buried in Georgetown?" *The Washington Post*, July 20, 2019.

Kennedy, Gregory. "Marshland Colonization in Acadia and Poitou during the 17th Century." *Acadiensis* 42: 1 (Winter-Spring 2013): 37–66.

Kennedy, Roger. *Orders from France: The Americans and the French in a Revolutionary World, 1780–1820*. New York: Knopf, 1989.

Kenny, Neil. "Brazil," in Marshall vol. 1, 185–188.

Kenny, Neil. "Cartier, Jacques (1491–1557)," in Marshall vol. 1, 219–222.

Kenny, Neil. "Roberval, Jean-François de la Roque, Seigneur de (1500–1561)," in Marshall vol. 3, 1001–1002.

Kenny, Peter M. *Honoré Lannuier, Cabinetmaker from Paris: The Life and Work of a French Ébéniste in Federal New York*. The Metropolitan Museum of Art, 1998.

Kershaw, Rosalyn. "Kearney Mansion (1903)." *National Register of Historic Places*. http://historicfresno.org/nrhp/kearney.htm.

Keylor, William R. "'La Fayette, we have Quit!' Wilsonian Policy and French Security after Versailles," in Roelker and Warner, 44–75.

Khan, Yasmin Sabina. *Enlightening the World: The Creation of the Statue of Liberty*. Ithaca: Cornell University Press, 2011.

Kindleberger, Charles P. "Michel Chevalier (1806–1879): The Economic Tocqueville," in Roelker and Warner, 121–150.

Kinzie, Juliette. *Wau-Bun, The Early Day in the Northwest* (1856). Edited by Louise Phelps Kellogg. Old Indian Agency House Portage, 1989.

Kuisel, Richard. *Seducing the French: The Dilemma of Americanization*. Berkeley: University of California Press, 1993.

Labelle, Kathryn M. "'Faire la chaudière': the Wendat Feast of Souls," in French and Indians in the Heart of America, in Englebert and Teasdale, 1–20.

Labrecque, George. "Saint Lawrence River," in Marshall vol. 3, 1023–1026.

Labrune, Gérard, and Philippe Toutain. *L'Histoire de France*. Paris: Nathan, 2008.

Lacorne, Denis, and Jacques Rupnik. "Introduction. France Bewitched by America," in Lacorne and Rupnik, 1–31.

Lacorne, Denis, and Jacques Rupnik, editors. *The Rise and Fall of Anti-Americanism: A Century of French Perception*. Translated by Gerard Turner. London: Macmillan, 1990.

Lagarrigue, Christine. *Mer et Liberté: Pierre Meyzonnat, de Bergerac... à l'Acadie*. Mon Petit Editeur, 2014.

Lamarre, Jean. "French Canadian," in Levinson and Ember, 291–297.

Lankford, George E. "Almost Illinark: The French Presence in Northeast Arkansas," in Whayne, 88–112.

Lappas, Thomas J. "Indiana," in Marshall vol. 2, 598–599.

Lappas, Thomas J. "Jesuits," in Marshall vol. 2, 620–623.

Lappas, Thomas J. "Mississippi," in Marshall vol. 2, 816–817.

Lappas, Thomas J. "Missouri," in Marshall vol. 2, 819.

Lappas, Thomas J. "Radisson, Pierre-Esprit, ca1636–1710," in Marshall vol. 3, 975–976.

La Roque de Roquebrune. "La Rocque de Roberval, François de." *Dictionary of Canadian Biography.* http://www.biographi.ca/en/bio/la_rocque_de_roberval_jean_francois_de_1E.html.

Latourelle, René. "Brébeuf, Jean de." *Dictionary of Canadian Biography.* http://www.biographi.ca/en/bio/brebeuf_jean_de_1E.html.

Lavoie, Michel. "Des Indiens Seigneurs au temps de Louis XIV," in Augeron and Havard, 97–106.

Lavoie, Yolande. *L'émigration des Québécois aux Etats-Unis de 1840 à 1930.* Québec: Conseil de la langue française, 1981.

Lawson, Gary, and Guy Seidman. "The First Incorporation Debate," in *The Louisiana Purchase and American Expansion, 1803–1898*, edited by Levinson and Sparrow, 25–45.

Lebel, Sonia. "Tadoussac," in Marshall vol. 3, 1107–1108.

Leblanc, Robert A. "Les Migrations acadiennes," in Louder, Morissoneau and Waddell, 137–162.

Le Bras, Hervé, and Emmanuel Todd. *L'invention de la France: Atlas anthropologique et Politique.* Paris: Livre de Poche, 1981.

Le Goff, Jacques. *Money and the Middle Ages: An Essay in Historical Anthropology.* Cambridge: Polity, 2012.

Le Hir, Marie-Pierre. "Imagining the Discipline: beyond Frenchness and Francophilia." *Contemporary French Civilization* 21: 2 (Summer-Fall 1997): 32–50.

Le Hir, Marie-Pierre. *Le Romantisme aux enchères: Ducange, Pixerécourt, Hugo.* Purdue University Monographs in Romance Languages. Amsterdam: John Benjamins, 1992.

Le Hir, Marie-Pierre. *The National Habitus, Ways of Feeling French, 1789–1870.* Berlin: De Gruyter, 2014.

Lehman, Jeffrey, editor. *Gale Encyclopedia of Multicultural America.* 2nd edition, vol. I. New York: Gale Research, 2000.

Lentz, Thierry. "La Politique consulaire aux Antilles." Site d'Histoire de la Fondation Napoléon. https://www.napoleon.org/histoire-des-2-empires/articles/la-politique-consulaire-aux-antilles/#ancrel.

Léopoldie, Nicole. *The Franco-American love affair: transnational courtship and marriage patterns during the 19th and 20th centuries.* PhD Dissertation, Paris 7 Diderot & the University of Texas at Arlington, 2017.

Levasseur, A. *Lafayette in America in 1824 and 1825, or Journal of a Voyage to the United States.* Translated by John D. Godman M.D., 2 vols. Philadelphia: Carey and Lea, 1829. http://www.gutenberg.org/ebooks/61518.

Levenstein, Harvey. *Seductive Journeys: American Tourists in France from Jefferson to the Jazz Age.* Chicago: University of Chicago Press, 1998.

Levenstein, Harvey. *We'll Always Have Paris: American Tourists in France since 1930.* Chicago: University of Chicago Press, 2004.

Lévi-Strauss, Claude. *Tristes Tropiques.* Translated by John Russell. New York: Criterion, 1961. https://archive.org/details/tristestropiques000177mbp/page/n7/mode/2up.

Levinson, David, and Melvin Ember, editors. *American Immigrant Cultures: Builders of a Nation* New York: Schuster & Schuster, Macmillan Reference USA, 1997.

Levinson, Sanford, and Bartholomew Sparrow, editors. *The Louisiana Purchase and American Expansion, 1803–1898.* Lanham, MD: Rowman & Littlefield, 2005.

Lignereux, Yann. "1550. Les Normands jouent aux Indiens," in Boucheron, 277–281.

Lignereux, Yann. "1534. Jacques Cartier et les terres neuves," in Boucheron, 262–265.

Lignereux, Yann. "1763. Un royaume pour un empire," in Boucheron, 370–374.

Lindsay, Diane, editor. "Henry A. Crabb, Filibuster, and the San Diego Herald." *San Diego Historical Society Quarterly* 19: 1 (Winter 1973). https://sandiegohistory.org/journal/1973/january/crabb/.

Litalien, Raymonde, Käthe Roth and Denis Vaugeois, editors. *Champlain: The Birth of French America.* Montreal: McGill University Press, 2004.

Loiselle, Kenneth. "French Revolution," in Marshall vol. 2, 482–488.

Loiselle, Kenneth. "Tertre, Jean-Baptiste du (1610–1687)," in Marshall vol. 3, 1118–1119.

Longo, Stephanie. "Talon, Jean (1625–1694)," in Marshall vol. 3, 1109–1110.

Louder, Dean R., and Eric Waddell, editors. *Du Continent perdu à l'archipel retrouvé: Le Québec et l'Amérique française.* Québec: Presses de l'Université Laval, 1983.

Louder, Dean R., Christian Morissonneau and Eric Waddell. "Introduction," in Louder, Morissoneau and Waddell, 1–10.

Lussagnet, Suzanne, editor. *Les Français en Floride: Textes de Jean Ribault [et al.].* vol. 2. Paris: PUF, 1958.

Lutz, Donald S. "The Relative Influence of European Writers on Late Eighteenth-Century American Political Thought." *The American Political Science Review* 78: 1 (1984): 189–97.

Lyons, Chuck. "Frances' Fateful Strike Against the Iroquois." *HistoryNet.* 2007 https://www.historynet.com/frances-fateful-strike-iroquois.htm.

MacDonald, David. *Lives of Fort de Chartres: Commandants, Soldiers, and Civilians in French Illinois, 1720–1770.* Carbondale: Southern Illinois University Press, 2016.

MacKinnon, Greg. "Richelieu, Cardinal Armand Jean du Plessis (1585–1642)," in Marshall vol. 3, 997–998.

Macpherson, Alan. "Iberville, Pierre Le Moyne d' (1661–1706)," in Marshall vol. 2, 593–594.

Manuel, Frank. *The Age of Reason*. Ithaca: Cornell University Press, 1968.

Marr, John S., and John T. Cathey. "The 1802 Saint-Domingue Yellow Fever Epidemic and the Louisiana Purchase." *Journal of Public Health Management and Practice* 19:1 (January-February 2013): 77–82.

Marshall, Bill, editor. *France and the Americas, Culture, Politics, and History*. 3 vols. Santa Barbara: ABC Clio, 2005.

Martel, Gilles. "Quand une majorité devient une minorité: les Métis francophones de l'Ouest canadien," in Louder, Morissoneau and Waddell, 55–79.

Martin, Benjamin F. "Baton Rouge," in Marshall vol. 1, 128–130.

Martin, Daisy, editor. *Exploration and Colonial America (1492–1755)*. 2 vols. Ipswich, MA: Salem Press, 2013.

Mathy, Jean-Philippe. *French Resistance: The French-American Culture Wars*. Minneapolis: University of Minnesota Press, 2000.

Mays, Thomas D. "Jones, John Paul (1747–1792)," in Marshall vol. 2, 628–629.

McBride, Genevieve. "Wisconsin," in Marshall vol. 3, 1224–1225.

McCullough, Roy L. *Coercion, Conversion and Counterinsurgency in Louis XIV's France*. Leiden: Brill, 2007.

McDonnell, Michael A. *Masters of Empire: Great Lakes Indians and the Making of America*. New York: Farrar, Strauss, and Giroux, 2015.

McGrath, John T. *The French in Early Florida: In the Eye of the Hurricane*. Gainesville: University Press of Florida, 2000.

McGreevy, John T. *Catholicism and American Freedom: A History*. New York: Norton, 2003. https://archive.org/details/catholi_mcg_2003_00_6713/page/2/mode/2up.

McLeman-Carnie. "Vigny, Alfred de (1797–1863)," Marshall vol. 3, 1193–1195.

McQuillan, D. Aidan. "Les Communautés canadiennes-françaises du Midwest américain au dix-neuvième siècle," in Louder, Morissoneau and Waddell, 98–115.

Meikle, Denis. *Johnny Depp: A Kind of Illusion*. Richmond: Reynolds and Hearn, 2005.

Mereness, Newton D., editor. *Travels in the American colonies*. 6 vols. New York: Macmillan, 1916. https://archive.org/details/travelsinameric00mere.

Michallat, Wendy. "Fishing," in Marshall vol. 2, 444–447.

Michallat, Wendy. "Whaling," in Marshall vol. 3, 1208–1209.

Miller, John J., and Mark Molesky. *Our Oldest Enemy: A History of America's Disastrous Relationship with France*, New York: Doubleday, 2004.

Mims, Stewart L. *Colbert's West India Policy*. New Haven: Yale University Press, 1912. https://catalog.hathitrust.org/Record/001123188.

Monaghan, Frank. *French Travelers to the United States, 1765–1932. A Bibliography*. New York: New York University Press, 1933.

Montbrial, Thierry de. "Franco-American Relations: A Historical-Structural Analysis." *Cambridge Review of International Affairs* 17: 3 (October 2004): 451–466.

Morgan, M.J. *Land of Big Rivers, French & Indian Illinois, 1699–1778*. Carbondale: Southern Illinois University Press, 2010.

Morris (artist), and René Goscinny. *Calamity Jane* (Lucky Luke series). Dupuis, 1967.

Morris, Larry. "Astor Expedition, 1810–1813." *The Oregon Encyclopedia, A Project of the Oregon Historical Society*. https://oregonencyclopedia.org/articles/astor_expedition_1810_1812/#.XvE4_epKjIU.

Morrissey, Robert Michael. "The Terms of Encounter: Language and Contested Visions of French Colonization—In the Illinois Country, 1673–1702," in Englebert and Teasdale, 43–75.

Morton, Anna. "Kentucky," in Marshall vol. 2, 645–647.

Munro, Martin. "Slavery," in Marshall vol. 3, 1075–1079.

Munro, Martin. "'Toussaint L'Ouverture, François (1742–1803)," in Marshall vol. 3, 1148–1151.

Munro, William Bennett. *The seigneurs of old Canada: a chronicle of New-World Feudalism*. Toronto: Glasgow, Brooke, and Co., 1922. https://archive.org/stream/seigneursofoldca00munruoft#page/n1/mode/2up.

Myall, James. "Birtherism is Nothing New: What We Can Learn from the Election of 1856." *Bangor Daily News*, March 7, 2016. https://myall.bdnblogs.com/2016/03/07/missouri/birtherism-is-nothing-new-what-we-can-learn-from-the-election-of-1856/.

Myall, James. "Louis Annance, a Man of Two Worlds." *Bangor Daily News*, May 26, 2018. http://myall.bangordailynews.com/2018/05/26/maine/louis-annance-a-man-of-two-worlds/#at_pco=smlwn-1.0&at_si=5eebcec4b25b7f56&at_ab=per-2&at_pos=0&at_tot=1.

Nasatir, Abraham P. *Before Lewis and Clark: Documents illustrating the History of the Missouri, 1785–1804*. 2 vols. St. Louis: St. Louis Historical Documents Foundation, 1952. https://babel.hathitrust.org/cgi/pt?id=uva.x000482438&view=1up&seq=5.

Nester, William R. *The French and Indian War and the Conquest of New France*. Norman: University of Oklahoma Press, 2014.

Nester, William R. *The Hamiltonian Vision, 1789–1800. The Art of American Power during the Early Republic*. Washington, D.C.: Potomac Books, 2012.

Nichols, Roger L. "Long, Stephen H. (1784–1864)," in *Encyclopedia of the Great Plains*, edited by Wishart. http://plainshumanities.unl.edu/encyclopedia/doc/egp.war.026.

Nothnagle, John. "Les cartographes de l'Amérique du Nord (1520–1763)," in Creagh and Clark, 25–42.

Nowell, Charles E. *The Great Discoveries and the First Colonial Empires*. Ithaca: Cornell University Press, 1954.

Nute, Grace Lee. *Caesars of the Wilderness. Médard Chouart, sieur des Groseilliers, and Pierre Esprit Radisson, 1618–1710.* New York: Arno Press, 1977.

Nute, Grace Lee. "Médard des Groseilliers." *Dictionary of Canadian biography.* http://www.biographi.ca/en/bio/chouart_des_groseilliers_medard_1E.html.

Odell, George H. "La Harpe, Jean-Baptiste Bénard, Sieur (1683–1765)," in Marshall vol. 2, 654–655.

O'Leary, James. "Basque Whaling in Red Bay, Labrador." Heritage Newfoundland and Labrador. https://www.heritage.nf.ca/articles/exploration/basque-whaling-red-bay.php.

Oliver, Bette W. *Surviving the French Revolution: A Bridge Across Time.* Lanham, MD: Lexington Books, 2013.

Onuf, Peter S. "'The Strongest Government on Earth': Jefferson's Republicanism, the Expansion of the Union, and the New Nation's Destiny," in Levinson and Sparrow, 46–71.

Osborne, Jeff. "American Antipathy and the Cruelties of Citizenship in Crèvecoeur's: Letters from an American Farmer." *Early American Literature* 42: 3 (2007): 529–553.

Oster, Harry. "Les *Spirituals* afro-français des Etats-Unis," in Creagh and Clark, 126–134.

Pannekoek, Frits, and James Scott. "York Factory and the Battle of Hudson Bay." *The Canadian Encyclopedia.* https://www.thecanadianencyclopedia.ca/en/article/york-factory.

Parsons, Christopher M. "Natives, Newcomers and Nicotiania in the History of the Great Lakes," in Englebert and Teasdale, 21–41.

Patterson, John Barton, editor. *Autobiography of Ma-ka-tai-me-she-kia-kiak or Black Hawk,* interpreted by Antoine LeClair. Oquawka, IL, 1882. https://archive.org/details/GR_313

Paul, Harry W. "The Issue of Decline in Nineteenth-Century French Science." *French Historical Studies* 7: 3 (1972): 416–50.

Péloquin, Louise. "Le roman franco-américain," in Creagh and Clark, 401–407.

Péloquin-Faré, Louise. "Les attitudes des Franco-Américains envers la langue française." *French Review* 57: 5 (April 1984): 657–668.

Perrier, Hubert. "L'union républicaine de langue française et les sections française de l'Association Internationale des Travailleurs aux Etats-Unis," in Creagh and Clark, 297–332.

Petersen, William J. "Jean Marie Cardinal." *The Palimpsest* 12 (1931): 414–420. https://ir.uiowa.edu/palimpsest/vol12/iss11/3.

Phelps, Dawson A. "The Chickasaw, the English, and the French, 1699–1744." *Tennessee Historical Quarterly* 16: 2 (June 1957): 117–133.

Pickett, Margaret F., and Dwayne W. Pickett. *The European Struggle to Settle North America: Colonizing Attempts by England, France and Spain, 1521–1608.* Jefferson, NC: McFarland, 2010.

Pierce, Bessie Louise, and Joe Lester Norris. *As Others See Chicago: Impressions of Visitors, 1673–1933.* Chicago: University of Chicago Press, 1933.

Pinette, Susan. "Un 'étonnant mutisme': l'invisibilité des Franco-Américains aux Etats-Unis," in Price, 177–203.

Plouviez, Daniel. *Défenses et Colonies dans le Monde Atlantique.* Rennes: Presses Universitaires de Rennes, 2014.

Podruchny, Carolyn. "Fur Trade," in Marshall vol. 2, 492–495.

Poniatowski, Michel. *Talleyrand aux Etats-Unis.* Paris: Presses de la Cité, 1976.

Popkin, Jeremy D. *You Are All Free: The Haitian Revolution and the Abolition of Slavery.* Cambridge: Cambridge University Press, 2010.

Portes, Jacques. *La véritable Histoire de l'Ouest américain.* Paris: Armand Colin, 2016.

Potofski, Allan. "The 'Non-Aligned Status' of French *Emigrés* and Refugees in Philadelphia, 1793–1798." *Transatlantica* 2 (2006): 2–8.

Powell, John Edwards. "Maurice Hébert." Biographies of Architects, Designers, and Builders. http://historicfresno.org/bio/hebert.htm.

Prévos, André J.M. "French," in Levinson and Ember, 286–291.

Prévos, André J.M. *Frenchmen Between Two Rivers: A History of the French in Iowa.* PhD Dissertation, 2 vols. University of Iowa, 1981.

Prévos, André J.M. "L'exportation des idéaux révolutionnaires français aux Etats-Unis: une entreprise hasardeuse. Le cas des Icariens dans la vallée du Mississippi (1848–1898)," in Creagh and Clark, 135–163.

Price, Joseph Edward. "La Jeune Francophonie Américaine: le contexte historique et social," in Price, 11–42.

Price, Joseph Edward, editor. *La Jeune Francophonie Américaine: Langue et Culture chez les Jeunes d'héritage francophone aux Etats-Unis d'Amérique.* Paris: L'Harmattan, 2018.

Pritchard, James. *In Search of Empire: The French in the Americas, 1670–1730.* Cambridge: Cambridge University Press, 2004.

Ramsay, Jack C. *Jean Lafitte: Prince of Pirates.* Austin: Eakin Press, 1996.

Randall, Hugh. "Saint Louis," in Marshall vol. 3, 102.

Rasmussen, Dan. *American Uprising: The Untold Story of America's Largest Slave Revolt.* New York, Harper, 2011.

Reda, John. "From Subjects to Citizens: Two Pierres and the French influence on the transformation of Illinois Country," in Englebert and Teasdale, 159–181.

Régent, Frédéric. "1664: Colbert et Compagnies," in Boucheron, 321–325.

Reid, Stanford W. "Pierre Dugué de Boisbriand." *Dictionary of Canadian Biography.* http://www.biographi.ca/en/bio/dugue_de_boisbriand_pierre_2E.html.

Rémond, René. *Les Etats-Unis devant l'Opinion française, 1815–1852.* 2 vols. Paris: Armand Colin, 1962.

Renan, Ernest. "*What Is a Nation?*" chapter 9 in *What Is a Nation? and Other Political Writings,* edited by M.F.N Giglioli. New York: Columbia

University Press, 2018.

Renan, Ernest. *Qu'est-ce qu'une nation?* Paris: Calmann-Lévy, 1882.

Richards, Leonard L. *The California Gold Rush and the Coming of the Civil War.* New York: Vintage Books, 2008.

Ringer, Fritz. *Fields of Knowledge: French Academic Culture in Comparative Perspective, 1890–1920.* Cambridge: Cambridge University Press, 1992.

Roberts, Timothy. "Sugar," in Marshall vol. 3, 1098–1100.

Roelker, Nancy, and Warner, Charles K. "Introduction," in Roelker and Warner, xv–xxiv.

Roelker, Nancy, and Warner, Charles K., editors. *Two Hundred Years of Franco-American Relations: Papers of* the *Bicentennial Colloquium.* Newport, RI: Society for French Historical Studies, 1978.

Rofe, Simon J. "Adams, John (1735–1826)," Marshall vol. 1, 57–58.

Roger, Philippe. *The American Enemy: A Story of French Anti-Americanism.* Translated by Sharon Bowman. Chicago: University of Chicago Press, 2005.

Rohrbough, Malcolm J. *Rush to Gold: France, the French, and the California Gold Rush, 1848–1854.* New Haven: Yale University Press, 2013.

Rolfe, Christopher. "Le Moyne de Morgues, Jacques (ca. 1533–1588)," in Marshall vol. 2, 701–703.

Rolfe, Christopher. "Saint-Mémin, Charles Balthazaar Julien Févret de (1770–1852)," in Marshall vol. 3, 1038–1039.

Rollings, Willard H. "Living in a Graveyard: Naïve Americans in Colonial Arkansas," in Whayne, 38–60.

Rosenstein, Roy. "Nicot, Jean (ca.1525–1600)," in Marshall vol. 3, 876–877.

Ross, Kristen. *Fast Cars, Clean Bodies: Decolonization and the Reordering of French Culture.* Cambridge: Massachusetts Institute of Technology Press, 1996.

Rothmund, Elisabeth. "Manuels, auteurs et éditeurs dans les premières décennies de l'enseignement scolaire de l'allemand." *Histoire de l'éducation,* 106 (May 2005): 15–40.

Roulet, Eric. "'Mousquets, piques et canons...' La défense des Antilles française au temps de la Compagnie des îles (1626–1648)," in Plouviez, 301–217. https://books.openedition.org/pur/61934.

Rousseau, Louis. "Grandeur et déclin des églises au Québec." *Cités* 3: 23 (2005) 129–141.

Rousseau, Louis-Pascal. "Métis," in Marshall vol. 2, 797–800.

Roy, Julie. "Jeanne Mance (1606–1673)," in Marshall vol. 2, 761–762.

Royot, Daniel. *Divided Loyalties in a Doomed Empire: The French in the West from New France to the Lewis and Clark Expedition.* Newark: University of Delaware Press, 2007.

Rushton, William Faulkner. *The Cajuns: From Acadia to Louisiana.* New York: Farrar Strauss and Giroux, 1979.

Russ, C.J. "René Boucher de La Perrière." *Dictionary of Canadian Biography.* http://www.biographi.ca/

en/bio/boucher_de_la_perriere_rene_3E.html.

Russ, C.J. "Liette, Pierre-Charles de (di Lietto, Deliette, Desliettes)." *Dictionary of Canadian Biography.* http://www.biographi.ca/en/bio/liette_pierre_charles_de_2E.html.

Russell, David Lee. *The American Revolution in the Southern Colonies.* Jefferson, NC: McFarland, 2007.

Sabo, George III. "Rituals of Encounter: Interpreting Native American Views of European Explorers," in Whayne, 76–87.

St. John de Crèvecoeur, Hector. *Letters from an American Farmer and Sketches of eighteenth-century American,* edited by Albert Stone. Penguin Classics, 1981.

St-Onge, Nicole. "Blue Beads, Vermilion, and Scalpers: The Social Economy of the 1810–1812 Astorian Overland Expedition's French Canadians Voyageurs," in Englebert and Teasdale, 183–216.

St-Onge, Nicole, Anne Gilbert and Yves Frenette, editors. *Francophonies d'Amérique: Les Pays d'En Haut: Lieux, Cultures, Imaginaires.* Ontario: University of Ottawa Press, 2018.

Sankey, Margaret. "The Abbé Paulmier's Mémoires and Early French Voyages in Search of Terra Australis," in West-Sooby, 41–68. https://www.jstor.org/stable/10.20851/j.ctt1sq5wxf.9.

Sankey, Margaret. "DuPont Family," in Marshall vol. 1, 400–402.

Sankey, Margaret. "Lorimer, Louis (1748–1812)," in Marshall vol. 2, 732–733.

Sauvageau, Robert. *Acadie: La guerre de Cent Ans des Français d'Amérique aux Maritimes et en Louisiane, 1670–1769.* Paris: Berger-Levrault, 1987.

Schubert, Frank N. *Vanguard of Expansion: Army Engineers in the Trans-Mississippi West, 1819–1879.* Washington, D.C.: Office of the Chief of Engineers, History Division, 1980. https://www.nps.gov/parkhistory/online_books/shubert/index.htm.

Schuler, Marilyn V. "Le clergé non assermenté et les origines du catholicisme américain," in Creagh and Clark, 204–211.

Schull, Joseph. *Rebellion: The Rising in French Canada, 1837, 1971.* Toronto: Macmillan of Canada, 1996.

Sears, John F. *Sacred Places: American Tourist Attractions in the Nineteenth Century.* New York: Oxford University Press, 1989.

Selin, Shannon. *Napoleon in America.* Dry Wall Publishing, 2014.

Servant, George. *Les Compagnie de Saint-Christophe et des îles de l'Amérique, 1626–1653.* Paris: Champion & Larose, 1914. https://gallica.bnf.fr/ark:/12148/bpt6k3339802h/f17.image.texteImage.

Sheldon, Garrett Ward. "Jefferson, Thomas (1743–1826)," in Marshall vol. 2, 617–620.

Shrader, Richard A. "Lenoir, William." In *NC Pedia,* State Library of North Carolina, 1991. https://www.ncpedia.org/biography/lenoir-william.

Simiot, Bernard. *Ces Messieurs de Saint-Malo.* Paris: Albin Michel, 1983.

Simiot, Bernard. *Le Temps des Carbec.* Paris: Albin

Michel, 1986.

Simiot, Philippe. *Carbec l'Américain.* Paris: Albin Michel, 2002.

Simiot, Philippe *Carbec mon Empereur.* Paris: Albin Michel, 1999.

Simiot, Philippe. *Le Banquier et le Perroquet.* Paris: Albin Michel, 2006.

Sintes, Fabienne et Corentin Sellin. "James Buchanan, un désastre politique à la Maison Blanche." *France Inter,* samedi 11 juillet 2020. https://www.franceinter.fr/emissions/presidents/presidents-11-juillet-2020.

Sioli, Marco. "Huguenot Traditions in the Mountains of Kentucky: Daniel Trabue's Memories." *The Journal of American History* 84: 4 (March 1998): 1313–1333.

Souchère Deléry, Simone de la. *Napoleon's Soldiers in America.* New Orleans: Pelican, 1998.

Soyez, Jean-Marc. *Quand L'Amérique s'appelait Nouvelle-France (1608–1760).* Paris: Fayard, 1981.

Spicer, Edward H. *A Short History of the Indians of the United States.* New York: Van Nostrand Reinhold, 1969.

Spurgeon, Ian. "Lecompte, Samuel Dexter." *Civil War on the Western Border: the Missouri-Kansas Conflict, 1854–1865.* Kansas City Public Library. https://civilwaronthewesternborder.org/encyclopedia/lecompte-samuel-dexter.

Stern, Madeleine B. "Joseph Nancrède, Franco-American Bookseller-Publisher, 1761–1841." *The Papers of the Bibliographical Society of America* 70:1 (1976): 1–88.

Sternstrom, Stephan, Ann Orlov, and Oscar Handling, editors. *Havard Encyclopedia of Ethnic Groups.* Cambridge: Belknap, 1980.

Stivale, Charles J. *Disenchanting Les Bons Temps: Identity and Authenticity in Cajun Music and Dance.* Durham: Duke University Press, 2003.

Stoudt, Joan Baer. *Nicolas Martiau: the adventurous Huguenot, the military engineer, and the earliest American ancestor of George Washington.* Norriston, PA: Norristown Press, 1932.

Stovall, Tyler. *Paris Noir: African-Americans in the City of Light.* Boston: Houghton Mifflin, 1996.

Stovall, Tyler. *Transnational France: The Modern History of a Universal Nation.* Taylor & Francis, 2015.

Stroud, Patricia Tyson. *The Man Who Had Been King: The American Exile of Napoleon's Brother Joseph.* Philadelphia: University of Pennsylvania Press, 2005.

Sweeny, Robert C.H. "Cotton," in Marshall vol. 1, 305–308.

Tankersley, Jim. "U.S. Will Impose Tariffs on French Goods in Response to Tech Tax." *New York Times,* June 10, 2020.

Tarrade, Jean. "Destinées d'Acadiens: 1755–1785. Trente Ans d'épreuves et d'errance pour de futurs citoyens des Etats-Unis," in Creagh and Clark, 107–123.

Taylor, Helen. "New Orleans," in Marshall vol. 3, 866–872.

Teasdale, Guillaume. *Fruits of Perseverance: The French Presence in the Detroit River Region, 1701–1815.* Montreal: McGill-Queen's University Press, 2018.

Terrien, Yevan Erwan. "'A motley collection of all nations': The Napoleonic soldiers of *Champ d'Asile* as citizens of the world." *Atlantic Studies* 10:1 (2013): 89–108.

Thierry, Eric. "Champlain and Lescarbot: An Impossible Friendship," in Litalien, Roth, and Vaugeois, 121–133.

Thierry, Eric. "A Creation of Champlain's: The Order of Good Cheer," in Litalien, Roth, and Vaugeois, 135–142.

Thiery, Clément. "Frenchtown: The Forgotten History of Los Angeles' French Community." *France-Amérique,* March 5, 2020. https://france-amerique.com/en/frenchtown-the-forgotten-history-of-los-angeles-french-community/

Tocqueville, Alexis de. *Democracy in America* (1835), edited by Eduardo Nolla and translated by James T. Schleifer. 2 vols. Indianapolis: Liberty Fund, 2012.

Traisnel, Christophe. "Quebec," in Marshall vol. 3, 959–963.

Traisnel, Christophe. "Quebec Act," in Marshall vol. 3, 964–966.

Treat, Payson J. *The National Land System, 1785–1820.* New York, E.B. Treat & Company, 1910. https://archive.org/details/nationallandsys00treagoog/page/n5/mode/2up.

Tremblay, Victor. "Jean de Quen." *Dictionary of Canadian Biography.* http://www.biographi.ca/en/bio/quen_jean_de_1E.html.

Trudel, Marcel. "Champlain, Samuel de." *Dictionary of Canadian Biography.* http://www.biographi.ca/en/bio/champlain_samuel_de_1E.html.

Trudel, Marcel. *Histoire de la Nouvelle France,* vol. 1. Montréal: Fides, 1963.

Trudel, Marcel. *La Seigneurie de la Compagnie des Indes occidentales, 1663–1674.* Saint-Laurent: Fides, 1997.

Turcotte, Martin. "Results from the 2016 Census: English–French bilingualism among Canadian children and youth." *Insights on Canadian Society,* Statistics Canada, October 3, 2019. https://www150.statcan.gc.ca/n1/en/pub/75-006-x/2019001/article/00014-eng.pdf?st=9aU-fs8T.

Vaisse, Julien. "Anonymous Sources: The Media Campaign Against France." Brookings, July 1, 2003. https://www.brookings.edu/articles/anonymous-sources-the-media-campaign-against-france/.

Vazeilles, Danièle. "Des Français et des Indiens en Amérique du Nord," Creagh and Clark, 76–93.

Vernet, Julien. *Strangers on their Own Land: Opposition to United States Governance in Louisiana's Orleans Territory, 1803–1809.* Jackson: University of Mississippi Press, 2013.

Vidal, Cécile. "Compagnie d'Occident," Marshall vol. 1, 289–290.

Vidal, Cécile. "Compagnie du Sénégal," in Marshall

vol. 1, 290–291.

Vidal, Cécile. "Crozat, Antoine (1655–1738)," in Marshall vol. 1, 322–323.

Vidal, Cécile. "Illinois Country," in Marshall vol. 2, 594–597.

Vidal, Cécile. "Louisiana Purchase," in Marshall vol. 2, 743–745.

Vidal, Cécile, editor. *Caribbean New Orleans: Empire, Race, and the Making of a Slave Society.* Chapel Hill: Omohundro Institute and University of North Carolina Press, 2019.

Villerbu, Tangi. "Entre Monde atlantique et jeune république: Charles Mame et la librairie française à New York au début du 19eme siècle." *Canadian Journal of History* 4: 1 (Spring-Summer 2012): 59–96.

Villerbu, Tangi. *La Conquête de l'Ouest: le Récit français de la nation américaine au XIXe siècle.* Rennes: Presses Universitaires de Rennes, 2007.

Waddell, Eric. "La Louisiane: un poste outre-frontière de l'Amérique française ou un autre pays et une autre culture," in Louder, Morissoneau and Waddell, 195–211.

Wagner, Nancy O'Brien. "Duluth," in Marshall vol. 1, 397–398.

Wagstaff, Peter. "Utopias," in Marshall vol. 3, 1170–1172.

Walker, Doreen E. "*Instruction pour Establir les Manufactures*: A Key Document in the Art History of New France." *Journal of Canadian Art History / Annales d' Histoire de l'Art Canadien* 2: 1 (1975): 1–18.

Walker, Thomas C. "Paine, Thomas (1737–1809)," in Marshall vol. 3, 903–905.

Wall, Irwin M. "From Anti-Americanism to Francophobia: The Saga of French and American Intellectuals." *French Historical Studies* 18: 4 (Fall 1994): 1083–1100.

Wall, Irwin M. *The United States and the Making of Postwar France, 1945–1954.* Cambridge: Cambridge University Press, 1991.

Walton, Whitney. *Internationalism, National Identities, and Study Abroad: France and the United States, 1890–1970.* Stanford: Stanford University Press, 2009.

Waters, Maureen. "Cadillac, Antoine Laumet de la Mothe (1658–1730)," in Marshall vol. 1, 204–205.

Waters, Maureen. "Detroit," in Marshall vol. 1, 371–372.

Waters, Maureen. "Hurons," in Marshall vol. 2, 586–588.

Waters, Maureen. "Joliet (Jolliet), Louis (1645–1700)," in Marshall vol. 2, 627–628.

Waters, Maureen. "La Fayette, Marie-Joseph-Paul-Yves-Roch-Gilbert du Motier, Marquis de (1757–1834)," in Marshall vol. 2, 666–668.

Waters, Maureen. "Marquette, Jacques (1637–1675)," in Marshall vol. 2, 773–774.

Waters, Maureen. "Michigan," in Marshall vol. 2, 805–807.

Waters, Maureen. "Mons, Pierre Dugua de (1560–1628)," in Marshall vol. 2, 829.

Waters, Maureen. "Pontiac (ca. 1720–1769)," in Marshall vol. 3, 961–963.

Waters, Maureen. "Ursulines," in Marshall vol. 3, 1169.

Watson, James Thompkins, Colonel. "Experiences of the French Huguenots in America: The King's Refugees." *Journal of American History* (1908): 122–130. http://www.kuhmann.com/poetry/History/Experiences%20of%20the%20French%20Huguenots%20in%20America%20-%20The%20King's%20Refugees.pdf.

Watts, Edward. *In This Remote Country: French Colonial Culture in the Anglo-American Imagination, 1780–1860.* Chapel Hill: University of North Carolina Press, 2006.

Weber, Eugen J. *A Modern History of Europe: Men, Cultures, and Societies from the Renaissance to the Present.* New York: Norton, 1971.

Weber, Eugen J. *Peasants into Frenchmen: The Modernization of Rural France (1870–1914).* Stanford: Stanford University Press, 1976.

Weil, François. "Les élites franco-américaines et la France," in Creagh and Clark, 385–389.

Weinmann, Heinz. *Du Canada au Québec: Généalogie d'une histoire.* Montréal: L'hexagone, 1987.

West-Sooby, John. *Discovery and Empire: the French in the South Seas.* Adelaide: University of Adelaide Press, 2013.

Weyhing, Richard. "'Gascon Exaggerations': The Rise of Antoine Laumet dit Le Lamothe, Sieur de Cadillac, the Foundation of Colonial Detroit, and the Origin of the Fox Wars," in Englebert and Teasdale, 77–112.

Whayne, Jeannie, editor. *Cultural Encounters in the Early South: Indians and Europeans in Arkansas.* Fayetteville: University of Arkansas Press, 1995.

White, Sophie. *Wild Frenchmen and Frenchified Indians. Material Culture in Colonial Louisiana.* Philadelphia: University of Pennsylvania Press, 2016.

Wilkinson, Norman B. "A French Asylum on the Susquehanna River." *Historic Pennsylvania Leaflet No. 11.* Harrisburg: Pennsylvania Historical and Museum Commission, 1991.

William. A. Douglass. *Amerikanuak: Basques in the New World.* Reno: University of Nevada Press, 2005.

Willoughby, Robert J. *The Brothers Robidoux and the Opening of the American West.* Columbia: University of Missouri Press, 2012.

Wilson, George. *Stephen Girard: The Life and Times of America's First Tycoon.* Conshohocken, PA: Combined Books, 1995.

Wilson, James Grant, and John Fiske, editors. *Appleton's Cyclopaedia of American biography,* Volumes II, III, IV. New York: Appleton, 1900.

Wilson, William A. "Louis Vasquez in Colorado and the Uncertain Histories of Fort Convenience and a Hunter's Cabin," *Colorado Heritage Magazine* 23: 1, 2003.

Winders, Richard Bruce. *Davy Crockett: The Legend of the Wild Frontier.* New York: Rosen Publishing Group, 2001.

Wingfield, Amber. "Bienville, Jean-Baptiste Le

Moyne, Sieur de (1680–1767)," in Marshall vol. 1, 151–152.

Winsor, Justin. *The Westward Movement: The Colonies and the Republic West of the Alleghanies, 1763–1798* (1897). New York: Burt Franklin, 1968.

Wishart, David J., editor. *Encyclopedia of the Great Plains*. Lincoln: University of Nebraska, 2011. http://plainshumanities.unl.edu/encyclopedia/.

Wolosin, Claudia. "L'Enfant, Pierre-Charles (1755–1825)," in Marshall vol. 2, 711–712.

Wood, Clarke. *Emigrés in the Wilderness*. New York: Macmillan, 1941.

Woods, Patricia. "The French and the Natchez Indians in Louisiana: 1700–1731." *Louisiana History: The Journal of the Louisiana Historical Association* 19:4 (Autumn 1978): 413–435.

Yancy, Jesse. "Louis LeFleur, Frontiersman." *Mississippi Sideboard, A Southern Gallimaufry*, March 18, 2017.

Zahniser, Marvin R. *Then Came Disaster: France and the United States, 1918–1940*. Westport, CT: Praeger, 2002.

Zoltvany, Yves F. "Gaultier de Varennes et de la Vérendrye." *Dictionary of Canadian Biography*. http://www.biographi.ca/en/bio/gaultier_de_varennes_et_de_la_verendrye_pierre_3E.html.

Zoltvany, Yves, F. "Ramezay, Claude de." *Dictionary of Canadian Biography*. http://www.biographi.ca/en/bio/ramezay_claude_de_2E.html.

Zoltvany, Yves F., "Laumet, Antoine, dit de Lamothe Cadillac." *Dictionary of Canadian Biography*. http://www.biographi.ca/en/bio/laumet_antoine_2E.html.

Webpages Consulted on Institutional and Private Websites

"Acadian Driftwood." [Song by *The Band*]. Wikipedia. https://en.wikipedia.org/wiki/Acadian_Driftwood.

"Acadian Heartland: Records of the Deportation and *Le Grand Dérangement, 1714–1768*." Nova Scotia Archives. https://novascotia.ca/archives/deportation/exhibit.asp?ID=16&Language=

"Achille Murat, Prince of Tallahassee." Shannon Selin. https://shannonselin.com/2016/06/achille-murat-prince-tallahassee/

"Administration." *New France, New Horizons: On French soil in America*. Library and Archive Canada. https://www.bac-lac.gc.ca/eng/discover/exploration-settlement/new-france-new-horizons/Pages/administration.aspx.

Africa to America to Paris. New York: Films for the Humanities & Science, 1997. https://www.films.com/ecTitleDetail.aspx?TitleID=10291&r=SR.

"After Lewis & Clark." *Rivers, Edens, Empires: Lewis & Clark and the Revealing of America*: An Exhibit. Library of Congress https://www.loc.gov/exhibits/lewisandclark/lewis-after.html.

"American Journeys: Eyewitness Accounts of Early American Exploration and Settlements."

Wisconsin Historical Society. https://www.americanjourneys.org/index.asp.

"Anthony Quervelle, Center Table, 1830." Metropolitan Museum of Art. https://www.metmuseum.org/art/collection/search/1530.

"Antony Quervelle, Wardrobe." Museum of Arts and Sciences in Daytona Beach, FL. https://www.moas.org/Anthony-Quervelle-Wardrobe-1-6727.html.

"Antoine Laumet dit de Lamothe Cadillac, 1694–1701." The Explorers: Virtual Museum of New France. Canadian Museum of History. https://www.historymuseum.ca/virtual-museum-of-new-france/the-explorers/antoine-laumet-dit-de-lamothe-cadillac-1694-1701/.

"*Arcis Carolinae Delineatio*, 1591 Représentation du Fort Caroline." Musée Franco-Americain de Blérancourt. https://museefrancoamericain.fr/objet/arcis-carolinae-delineatio-1591-representation-du-fort-caroline.

"Beyoncé." [American artist]. Wikipedia. https://en.wikipedia.org/wiki/Beyonc%C3%A9.

"Bilinguisme chez les enfants et les jeunes au Canada." Statistique Canada. https://www150.statcan.gc.ca/n1/pub/11-627-m/11-627-m2019090-fra.htm.

"Carignan-Salières Regiment." French Canadian Heritage of Michigan. https://habitantheritage.org/cpage.php?pt=12.

"Carondelet Health Network: Our History." Carondelet Health Network. https://www.carondelet.org/about/our-history.

"Charles Albanel, 1672." The Explorers: Virtual Museum of New France. Canadian Museum of History. https://www.historymuseum.ca/virtual-museum-of-new-france/the-explorers/charles-albanel-1672/.

"Charles Lallemand, Invader of Texas." Shannon Selin. https://shannonselin.com/2014/05/general-charles-lallemand-invader-texas/

"Chateau de Mores State Historic Site." State Historical Society of North Dakota. https://www.history.nd.gov/historicsites/chateau/chateauhistory.html.

"Chiffres Clés du Tourisme: Edition 2018." Ministère de l'économie et des finances, France. https://www.entreprises.gouv.fr/files/files/directions_services/etudes-et-statistiques/Chiffres_cles/Tourisme/2018-Chiffres-cles-du-tourisme.pdf.

"Chouteau Brothers." State Historical Society of Missouri. https://historicmissourians.shsmo.org/historicmissourians/name/c/chouteau/

"Chronology of New France." http://international.loc.gov/intldl/fiahtml/fiachronology.html.

"Collection France in America." Library of Congress. https://www.loc.gov/collections/france-in-america/about-this-collection/.

"Cotton Office in New Orleans" (Degas' painting). Wikipedia. https://en.wikipedia.org/wiki/A_Cotton_Office_in_New_Orleans.

"Daniel Greysolon Dulhut, 1678–1679." The Explorers: Virtual Museum of New France. Canadian Museum of History. https://www.

historymuseum.ca/virtual-museum-of-new-france/the-explorers/daniel-greysolon-dulhut-1678-1679/.

"Davenport's First Citizen (Antoine LeClaire)." Scott County Genealogy. http://www.celticcousins.net/scott/chapter11.html.

"Etienne Brûlé, 1615–1621." The Explorers: Virtual Museum of New France. Canadian Museum of History. https://www.historymuseum.ca/virtual-museum-of-new-france/the-explorers/etienne-brule-1615-1621/

"Explorateurs—Le Canada et la Nouvelle-France Explorations françaises en Amérique du Nord." *Echos d'un Peuple*. Collection virtuelle. http://echo.franco.ca/explorateurs/index.Repertoire_No=2137985650&Voir=journal_revue.cfm.html

"Facts and Statistics." Catholic Health Association of the United States. https://www.chausa.org/about/about.

"Fast Facts: United States Travel and Tourism Industry, 2018." International Trade Administration, U.S. Department of Commerce. https://travel.trade.gov/outreachpages/download_data_table/Fast_Facts_2018.pdf.

"A Few Acres of Snow." [Voltaire's characterization of Canada]. *Wikipedia, the free Encyclopedia*. https://en.wikipedia.org/wiki/A_few_acres_of_snow.

"Fort Ticonderoga." Wikipedia. https://en.wikipedia.org/wiki/Fort_Ticonderoga.

"Fort Uncompahgre." Old Spanish Trail Association. https://fortuncompahgre.org/.

"Governor General of New France." [After 1663]. *Wikipedia, the free Encyclopedia*. https://en.wikipedia.org/wiki/Governor_General_of_New_France.

"Governor of New France." [Before 1663]. *Wikipedia, the free Encyclopedia*. https://en.wikipedia.org/wiki/Governor_of_New_France.

"Henri Lallemand, Napoleonic General: Improving the US Artillery." Shannon Selin. https://shannonselin.com/2014/10/general-henri-lallemand/

"Historical List of Catholic Bishops of the United States." Wikipedia. https://en.wikipedia.org/wiki/Historical_list_of_the_Catholic_bishops_of_the_United_States.

"History of French-speaking people in Wisconsin." University of Wisconsin at Green Bay. https://www.uwgb.edu/wisfrench/library/.

"History of the Choctaw Nation." Mississippi Board of Choctaw Indians. https://www.choctaw.org/aboutMBCI/history/index.html.

"Immigrés vivant en France en 2019 selon leur pays de naissance." Institut National de la Statistique et des Etudes Economiques (INSEE). https://www.insee.fr/fr/statistiques/3633212#:~:text=En%202019%2C%206%2C7%20millions,4%20%25%20de%20la%20population%20totale.

"Industrial Revolution: Robber Barons and Captains of Industry." National Endowment for the Humanities. https://edsitement.neh.gov/lesson-plans/industrial-age-america-robber-barons-and-captains-industry#sect-preparation.

"Jacques Cartier, 1534–1542." The Explorers: Virtual Museum of New France. Canadian Museum of History. https://www.historymuseum.ca/virtual-museum-of-new-france/the-explorers/jacques-cartier-1534-1542/.

"Jacques Marquette, 1673." The Explorers: Virtual Museum of New France. Canadian Museum of History. https://www.historymuseum.ca/virtual-museum-of-new-france/the-explorers/jacques-marquette-1673-1694/.

"Jean de Quen, 1647." The Explorers: Virtual Museum of New France. Canadian Museum of History. https://www.historymuseum.ca/virtual-museum-of-new-france/the-explorers/jean-de-quen-1647/.

"Jean Nicollet, 1634." The Explorers: Virtual Museum of New France. Canadian Museum of History. https://www.historymuseum.ca/virtual-museum-of-new-france/the-explorers/jean-nicollet-1634/

"John C. Frémont." Georgia Historical Society. https://georgiahistory.com/education-outreach/online-exhibits/featured-historical-figures/john-charles-fremont/first-and-second-expeditions/.

"*La Belle*, the Ship that Changed History." Bullock Texas State History Museum, Austin, TX https://www.thestoryoftexas.com/la-belle/the-exhibit.

"Lakanal and Jefferson letters, 1816." Founders Online, National Archives. https://founders.archives.gov/documents/Jefferson/03-10-02-0062.

"Langues vivantes étrangères et régionales." Ministère de l'Education nationale, de la jeunesse et des sports. https://www.education.gouv.fr/les-langues-vivantes-etrangeres-et-regionales-11249.

"List of Catholic Universities and Colleges in the United States." Wikipedia. https://en.wikipedia.org/wiki/List_of_Catholic_universities_and_colleges_in_the_United_States.

"List of Place Names of French Origin in the United States." Wikipedia. https://en.wikipedia.org/wiki/List_of_place_names_of_French_origin_in_the_United_States.

"Liste des Commissaires Ordonnateurs de Louisiane." CEFAN. http://www.axl.cefan.ulaval.ca/francophonie/Louisiane-comm_ordonnateurs.htm.

"Louis Hennepin, 1678–1680." The Explorers: Virtual Museum of New France. Canadian Museum of History. https://www.historymuseum.ca/virtual-museum-of-new-france/the-explorers/louis-hennepin-1678-1680/.

"Louis Jolliet, 1663–1694." The Explorers: Virtual Museum of New France. Canadian Museum of History. https://www.historymuseum.ca/virtual-museum-of-new-france/the-explorers/louis-jolliet-1673-1694/

"Louis-Armand de Lom d'Arce, baron Lahontan, 1684–1689." The Explorers: Virtual Museum of New France. Canadian Museum of History. https://www.historymuseum.ca/virtual-museum-of-new-france/the-explorers/

louis-armand-de-lom-darce-baron-lahontan-1684-1689/.

"Map of the north parts of America claimed by France under ye names of Louisiana, Mississipi. Canada, and New France with ye adjoining territories of England and Spain." Library of Congress. https://www.loc.gov/item/2001624907/.

"Market Profile France, 2018." National Travel and Tourism Office. U.S. Department of Commerce. https://travel.trade.gov/outreachpages/inbound. general_information.inbound_overview.asp.

"Médard Chouart des Groseillers, 1654–1660." The Explorers: Virtual Museum of New France. Canadian Museum of History. https://www. historymuseum.ca/virtual-museum-of-new-france/the-explorers/medard-chouart-des-groseilliers-1654-1660/.

"Menominee History. Early Life in Wisconsin." Milwaukee Public Museum. https://www.mpm.edu/content/wirp/ICW-153.

"MLA Language Database." Modern Language Association. https://apps.mla.org/flsurvey_search.

"MLA Language Map [of the United States]." Modern Language Association. https://www.mla.org/Resources/Research/MLA-Language-Map.

"Navigation. [French Regime]" Library and Archives Canada. https://www.bac-lac.gc.ca/eng/discover/exploration-settlement/new-france-new-horizons/Pages/navigation.aspx#1.

"Nicolas Perrot, 1665–1689." Virtual Museum of New France. Canadian Museum of History https://www.historymuseum.ca/virtual-museum-of-new-france/the-explorers/nicolas-perrot-1665-1689/.

"Nicollet Expeditions, 1838, 1839." Smithonian. https://www.si.edu/object/auth_exp_fbr_EACE0027.

"Otoe and Missouria: 500 years of History." The Otoe and Missouria Tribe. https://www.omtribe.org/who-we-are/history/.

"Pierre de Troyes, 1686." The Explorers: Virtual Museum of New France. Canadian Museum of History. https://www.historymuseum.ca/virtual-museum-of-new-france/the-explorers/pierre-de-troyes-1686/

"Pierre Gaultier de Varennes et de la Vérendrye, 1632–1639." Virtual Museum of New France. Canadian Museum of History https://www.museedelhistoire.ca/musee-virtuel-de-la-nouvelle-france/les-explorateurs/pierre-gaultier-de-varennes-et-de-la-verendrye-1732-1739/.

"Pierre Le Moyne d'Iberbille, 1686–1702." The Explorers: Virtual Museum of New France. Canadian Museum of History. https://www. historymuseum.ca/virtual-museum-of-new-france/the-explorers/pierre-le-moyne-diberville-1686-1702/.

"Pierre-Esprit Radisson, 1659–1660." The Explorers: Virtual Museum of New France. Canadian Museum of History. https://www.historymuseum. ca/virtual-museum-of-new-france/the-explorers/pierre-esprit-radisson-1659-1660/

"Point Breeze Historic District, Bordentown City." Delaware River Heritage Trail. https://delawareriverheritagetrail.org/Point-Breeze-Historic-District.html.

"René-Robert Cavelier de La Salle, 1670–1687." The Explorers: Virtual Museum of New France. Canadian Museum of History. https://www. historymuseum.ca/virtual-museum-of-new-france/the-explorers/rene-robert-cavelier-de-la-salle-1670-1687/.

"Samuel de Champlain, 1604–1616." The Explorers: Virtual Museum of New France. Canadian Museum of History. https://www.historymuseum. ca/virtual-museum-of-new-france/the-explorers/samuel-de-champlain-1604-1616/.

"Sisters of Carondelet: Our History." Sisters of St. Joseph of Carondelet. https://csjcarondelet.org/our-history/.

Speak White. 1980 short film based on a poem by Michèle Lalonde (1970). National Film Board of Canada. https://www.nfb.ca/film/speak_white/.

"Speak White." Wikipedia. https://fr.wikipedia.org/wiki/Speak_white.

"State Compulsory School Attendance Laws," National Center for Educational Statistics, *Digest of Education Statistics,* 2004. https://www.infoplease.com/us/education/state-compulsory-school-attendance-laws.

"Statistics of Wars, Oppressions, and Atrocities in the 18th Century." http://necrometrics.com/wars18c.htm.

"Stephen Girard: America's Napoleon of Commerce." Shannon Selin. https://shannonselin.com/2014/10/stephen-girard/.

"The Treaty of Guadalupe-Hidalgo, 1848." National Archives. https://www.archives.gov/education/lessons/guadalupe-hidalgo.

"The United States and the Haitian Revolution, 1791–1804." Department of State, Office of the Historian. https://history.state.gov/milestones/1784-1800/haitian-rev.

"Theodore Roosevelt and Conservation." Theodore Roosevelt North Dakota. National Park Service. https://www.nps.gov/thro/learn/historyculture/theodore-roosevelt-and-conservation.htm.

"Théodore Rouault, Biographical Sketch." New Mexico Historical Society. https://newmexicohistory.org/2016/10/05/theodore-rouault-bio/

"Treaty of Mortefontaine (Convention of 1800)." Yale Law School's Avalon project. https://avalon.law.yale.edu/19th_century/fr1800.asp.

"Vie quotidienne. Médecine et Santé." [New France] Musée Virtuel de la Nouvelle France. Musée Canadien de l'Histoire. https://www.museedelhistoire.ca/musee-virtuel-de-la-nouvelle-france/vie-quotidienne/sante-et-medecine/.

"La Vision de Vauban pour le Canada." La Nouvelle-France (1534–1760). L'implantation du français au Canada. CEFAN. http://www.axl.cefan.ulaval.ca/francophonie/HISTfrQC_s1_NlleFrance.htm#7.4_La_vision_de_Vauban_pour_le_Canada_

"William Morrison, Fur Trader." Morrison County

Historical Society, Charles A. Weyerhaeuser Memorial Museum, Little Falls, MN. https://morrisoncountyhistory.org/?page_id=404.

"William Rodrigue." Philadelphia Architects and Buildings. https://www.philadelphiabuildings.org/pab/app/ar_display.cfm/110006.

"Yorktown Campaign." George Washington's Mount Vernon. https://www.mountvernon.org/george-washington/the-revolutionary-war/the-yorktown-campaign/

Resources

CEFAN (Chaire pour le développement de la recherche sur la culture d'expression française en Amérique du Nord). http://www.axl.cefan.ulaval.ca/

Echo d'un Peuple. Collection Virtuelle. https://www.echo.franco.ca/index-Repertoire_No=2137985646&Voir=membre.cfm.html.

"France in America/La France en Amérique." A bilingual digital library. *The Library of Congress and the Bibliothèque Nationale de France.* http://international.loc.gov/intldl/fiahtml/fiahome.html.

Francophonies d'Amérique, 1991. "An international learned journal [that] publishes articles produced by academics working on North America's francophone minority populations throughout the continent."

French Colonial History. Journal of the French Colonial Historical Society.

French Review. Journal of the American Association of Teachers of French.

Gallica, the digital library of the *Bibliothèque nationale de France.* https://gallica.bnf.fr/accueil/en/content/accueil-en?mode=desktop.

George Washington's Mount Vernon. Mount Vernon Ladies' Association of the Union. https://www.mountvernon.org/george-washington/the-revolutionary-war/the-yorktown-campaign/

Georgian Historical Society. https://georgiahistory.com/.

Internet Archive. Digital Library of Free and Downloadable books. https://archive.org/

Library and Archive Canada. https://www.bac-lac.gc.ca/eng/discover/exploration-settlement/new-france-new-horizons/Pages/administration.aspx.

Library of Congress E-books. https://www.loc.gov/rr/program/bib/ebooks/lcresources.html.

Milwaukee Public Museum. http://www.mpm.edu/.

Musée Franco-Américain du Château de Blérancourt. https://museefrancoamericain.fr/

Museum of the American Revolution: https://www.amrevmuseum.org/collection/enlisting-foreign-officershttps://www.amrevmuseum.org/collection/portrait-comte-du-perron;

Nova Scotia Archives. https://archives.novascotia.ca/.

Office of the Historian. https://history.state.gov/.

Revue d'Histoire de l'Amérique française, Revue de l'Institut d'Histoire de l'Amérique française.

State Historical Society of Missouri. https://shsmo.org/.

University of Wisconsin at Green Bay. https://www.uwgb.edu/wisfrench/library/

Virtual Museum of New France. Canadian Museum of History/Musée Canadien de l'histoire. https://www.historymuseum.ca/virtual-museum-of-new-france/

"What did Napoleon say about the battle of Waterloo?" Shannon Selin. https://shannonselin.com/2015/06/what-did-napoleon-say-about-the-battle-of-waterloo/

Wisconsin's French. History of French speaking people in Wisconsin. Library of the University of Wisconsin at Green Bay. https://www.uwgb.edu/wisfrench/library/

Index